A-Z SUFF[OLK]

CONTENT[S]

Key to Map Pages	2-3
Large Scale Ipswich Town Centre	4-5
Map Pages	6-156
Large Scale Bury St. Edmunds Town Centre	157
Road	7
Inde	7
Index to Hospitals etc.	08

REFERENCE

Primary Route	A143
A Road	A144
B Road	B1113
Dual Carriageway	
One-way Street Traffic flow on A Roads is also indicated by a heavy line on the driver's left.	
Road Under Construction Opening dates are correct at the time of publication	
Proposed Road	
Junction Names	COPDOCK MILL INTERCHANGE
Restricted Access	
Pedestrianized Road	
Track / Footpath	
Residential Walkway	
Railway	Station, Level Crossing, Tunnel
Local Authority Boundary	
The Broads Authority Boundary	
Posttown Boundary	
Postcode Boundary (within Posttown)	
Built-up Area	NENE DR.
Map Continuation 54	Large Scale Town Centre 157 / Road Map Pages 160

Car Park (selected)	P
Church or Chapel	†
Cycleway (selected)	
Fire Station	■
Hospital	H
House Numbers (A & B Roads only)	13 8
Information Centre	i
National Grid Reference	595
Park & Ride	London Rd. P+R
Police Station	▲
Post Office	★
Safety Camera with Speed Limit Fixed cameras and long term road works cameras. Symbols do not indicate camera direction.	30
Toilet: without facilities for the Disabled with facilities for the Disabled Disabled facilities only	
Educational Establishment	
Hospital or Healthcare Building	
Industrial Building	
Leisure or Recreational Facility	
Place of Interest	
Public Building	
Shopping Centre or Market	
Other Selected Buildings	

SCALE

Map Pages 6-156
1:16,896 3¾ inches (9.52 cm) to 1 mile 5.9cm to 1km
0 ¼ ½ Mile
0 250 500 750 1 km

Map Page 4-5 & 157
1:8,448 7½ inches (19.04 cm) to 1 mile 11.8cm to 1km
0 ⅛ ¼ Mile
0 125 250 375 500m

Fairfield Road, Borough Green, Sevenoaks, Kent TN15 8PP
Telephone: 01732 781000 (Enquiries & Trade Sales)
01732 783422 (Retail Sales)
www.az.co.uk

EDITION 2 2013

KEY TO MAP PAGES

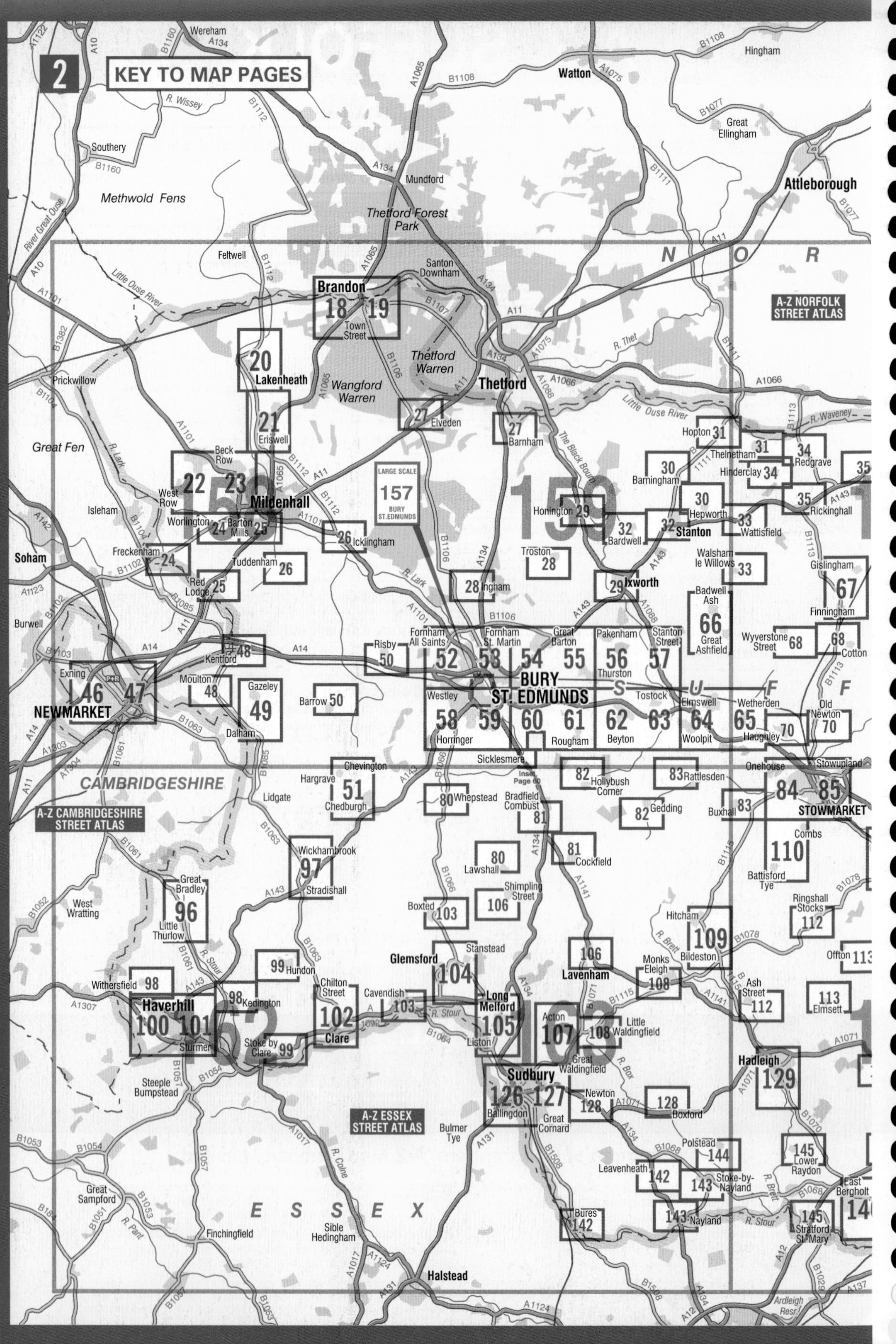

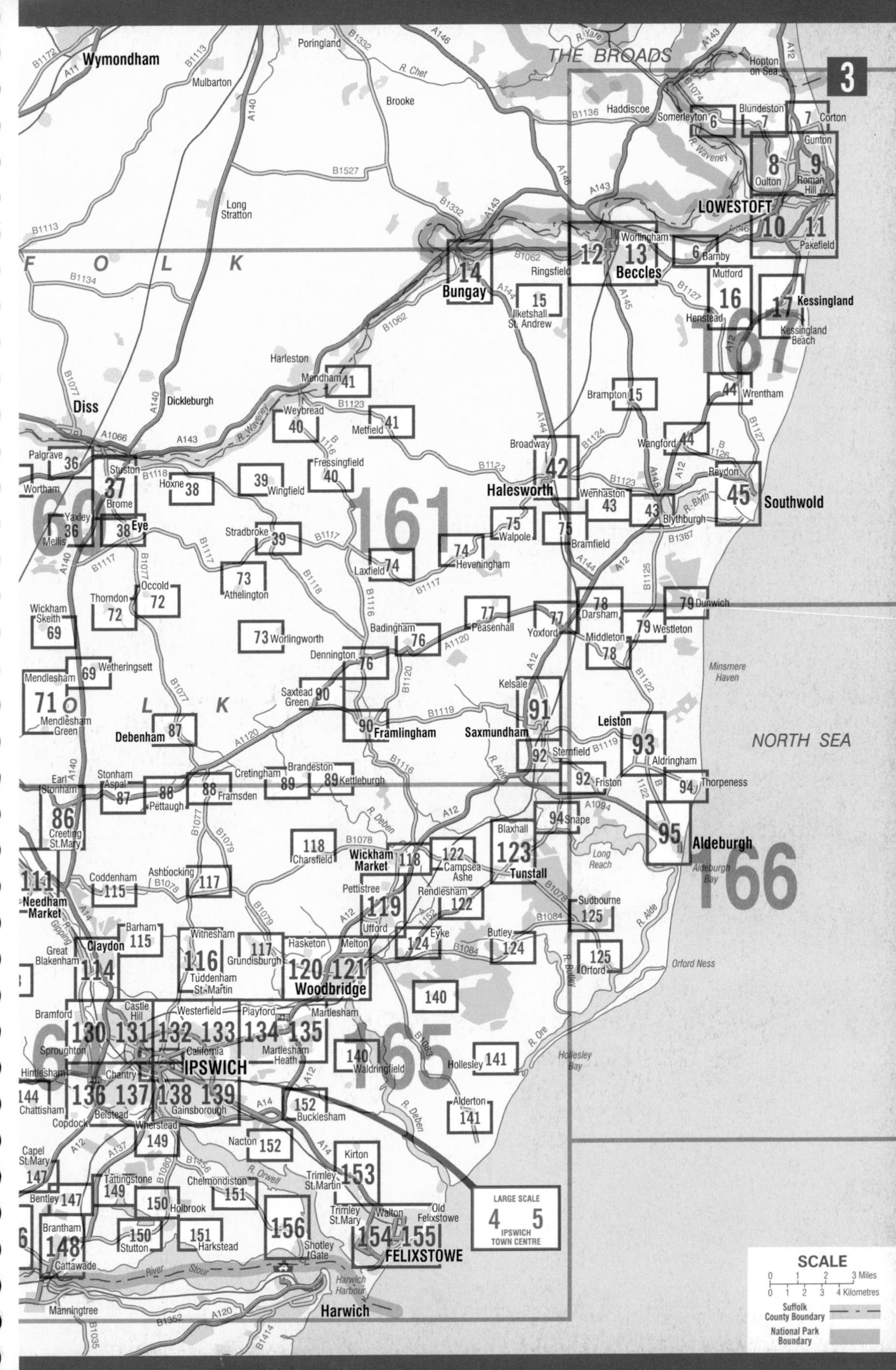
THE BROADS
Wymondham
Poringland
Mulbarton
Brooke
Haddiscoe
Somerleyton
Blundeston
Corton
Hopton on Sea
Gunton
Oulton
Roman Hill
LOWESTOFT
Pakefield
Long Stratton
Worlingham
Barnby
Ringsfield
Beccles
Bungay
Ilketshall St. Andrew
Mutford
Henstead
Kessingland
Kessingland Beach
Harleston
Mendham
Brampton
Wrentham
Diss
Dickleburgh
Weybread
Metfield
Wangford
Palgrave
Stuston
Hoxne
Wingfield
Fressingfield
Broadway
Halesworth
Wenhaston
Blythburgh
Reydon
Southwold
Wortham
Brome
Yaxley
Mellis
Eye
Stradbroke
Laxfield
Heveningham
Walpole
Bramfield
Thorndon
Occold
Athelington
Wickham Skeith
Worlingworth
Badingham
Peasenhall
Yoxford
Darsham
Middleton
Westleton
Dunwich
Mendlesham
Wetheringsett
Mendlesham Green
Dennington
Saxtead Green
Framlingham
Kelsale
Saxmundham
Leiston
Minsmere Haven
NORTH SEA
Debenham
Sternfield
Friston
Aldringham
Thorpeness
Earl Stonham
Stonham Aspal
Pettaugh
Framsden
Cretingham
Brandeston
Kettleburgh
Snape
Aldeburgh
Creeting St.Mary
Charsfield
Wickham Market
Campsea Ashe
Blaxhall
Tunstall
Long Reach
Aldeburgh Bay
Needham Market
Coddenham
Ashbocking
Pettistree
Rendlesham
Sudbourne
Ufford
Eyke
Butley
Barham
Claydon
Great Blakenham
Witnesham
Tuddenham St.Martin
Grundisburgh
Hasketon
Melton
Woodbridge
Orford
Orford Ness
Bramford
Castle Hill
Westerfield
Playford
Martlesham
Sproughton
California
IPSWICH
Martlesham Heath
Waldringfield
Hollesley
Hollesley Bay
Hintlesham
Chantry
Chattisham
Belstead
Gainsborough
Bucklesham
Alderton
Copdock
Wherstead
Nacton
Kirton
Capel St.Mary
Tattingstone
Chelmondiston
Trimley St.Martin
Trimley St.Mary
Walton
Old Felixstowe
Bentley
Holbrook
Brantham
Stutton
Harkstead
Shotley Gate
FELIXSTOWE
Cattawade
Harwich Harbour
Manningtree
Harwich
R. Yare
R. Chet
R. Waveney
R. Blyth
R. Alde
R. Deben
R. Gipping
R. Butley
R. Ore
R. Orwell
River Stour
LARGE SCALE 4 5 IPSWICH TOWN CENTRE
SCALE
0 1 2 3 Miles
0 1 2 3 4 Kilometres
Suffolk County Boundary
National Park Boundary

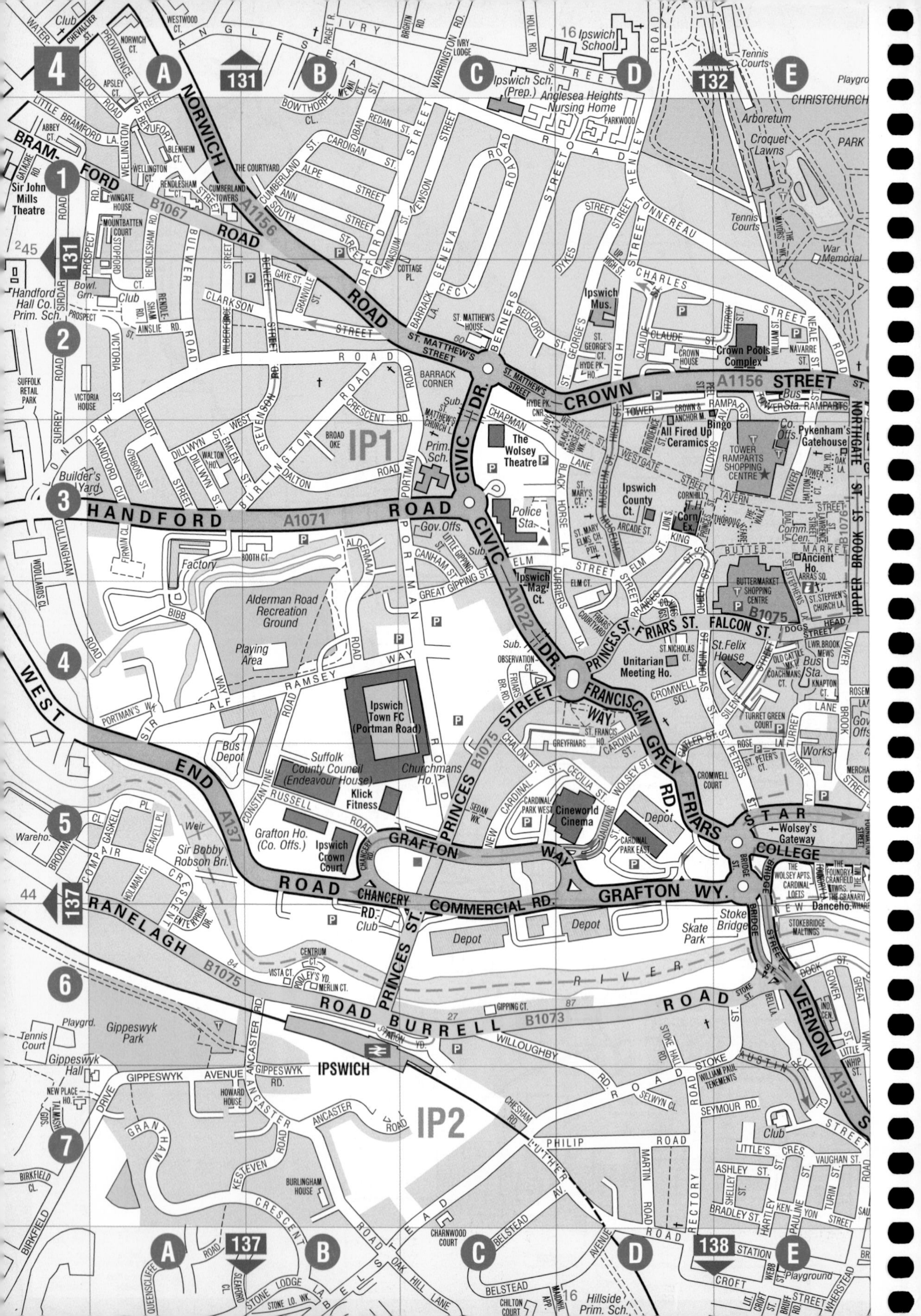

A
B
C
D
E
131
132
137
138
1
2
3
4
5
6
7
44
45
IP1
IP2
IPSWICH
NORWICH ROAD
A1156
B1067
BRAMFORD ROAD
HANDFORD ROAD
A1071
CIVIC DR.
A1022
CROWN STREET
ST. MATTHEW'S STREET
WEST END ROAD
A137
RANELAGH ROAD
B1075
BURRELL ROAD
B1073
GRAFTON WAY
COMMERCIAL RD.
PRINCES STREET
FRANCISCAN WAY
GREY FRIARS RD.
STAR LANE
COLLEGE STREET
VERNON STREET
RIVER
Sir John Mills Theatre
Handford Hall Co. Prim. Sch.
Suffolk Retail Park
Alderman Road Recreation Ground
Playing Area
Ipswich Town FC (Portman Road)
Suffolk County Council (Endeavour House)
Klick Fitness
Ipswich Crown Court
Grafton Ho. (Co. Offs.)
Bus Depot
Sir Bobby Robson Bri.
Weir
Gippeswyk Park
Gippeswyk Hall
Tennis Court
Playgrd.
Ipswich School
Ipswich Sch. (Prep.)
Anglesea Heights Nursing Home
Arboretum
Croquet Lawns
Tennis Courts
War Memorial
CHRISTCHURCH PARK
Ipswich Mus.
Crown Pools Complex
Bus Sta.
The Wolsey Theatre
Police Sta.
Ipswich Mag. Ct.
Ipswich County Ct.
Corn Ex.
All Fired Up Ceramics
Bingo
Tower Ramparts Shopping Centre
Co. Offs.
Pykenham's Gatehouse
Ancient Ho.
Buttermarket Shopping Centre
Unitarian Meeting Ho.
St. Felix House
Cineworld Cinema
Wolsey's Gateway
Stoke Bridge
Skate Park
Depot
Club
Danceho.
Hillside Prim. Sch.
Playground
Factory
Prim. Sch.
Gov. Offs.
Builder's Yard

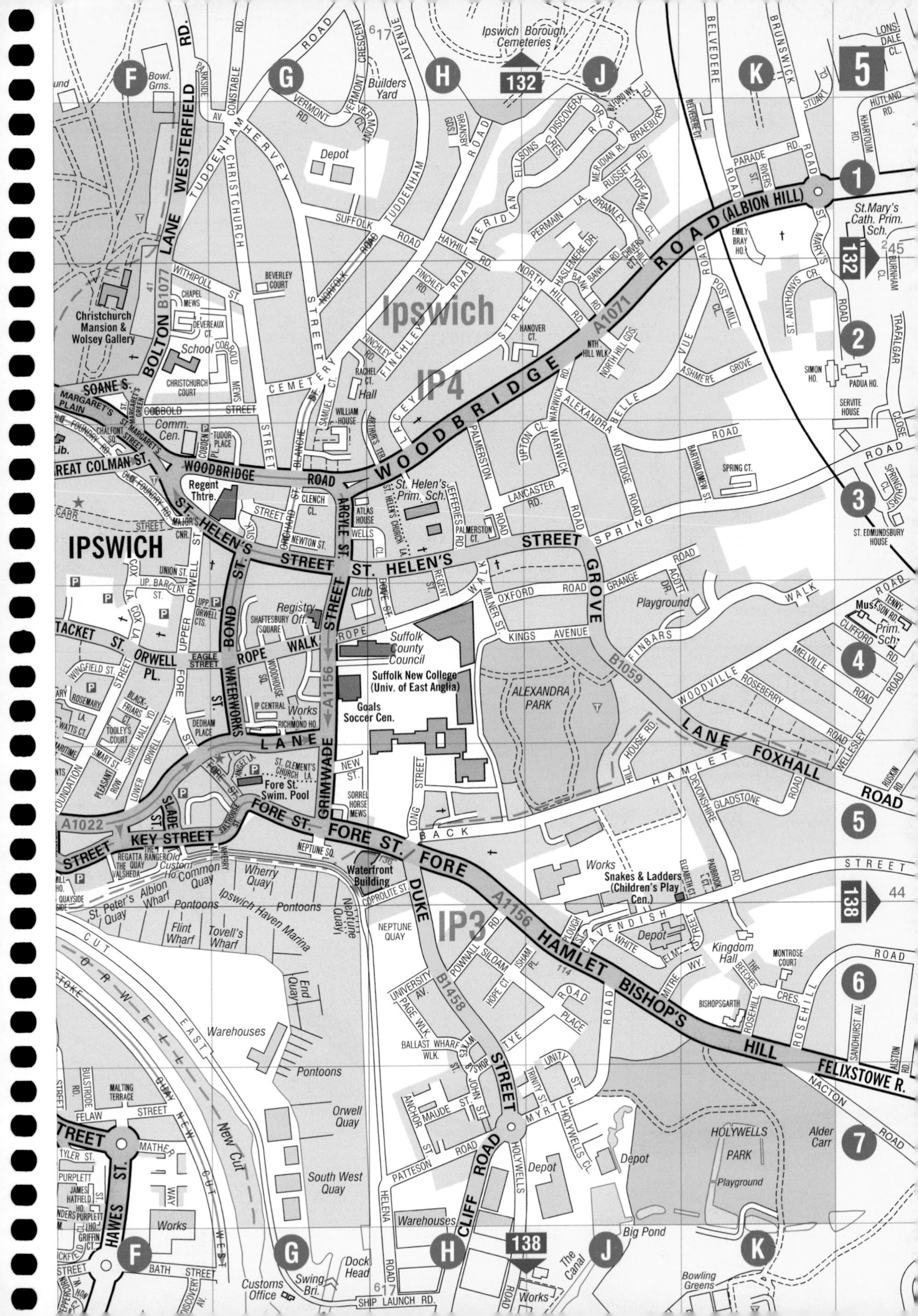

5
F
G
H
J
K
132
138
1
2
3
4
5
6
7
617
245
44
Ipswich Borough Cemeteries
Builders Yard
Bowl. Grns.
Depot
Ipswich
IP4
IP3
IPSWICH
WESTERFIELD RD.
BOLTON LANE
B1077
PARKSIDE
CONSTABLE RD.
TUDDENHAM AV.
CHRISTCHURCH ST.
HERVEY ST.
VERMONT RD.
VERMONT CRESCENT
VERMONT CL.
AVENUE
BRANSBY GDS.
ROAD
TUDDENHAM ROAD
SUFFOLK ROAD
HAYHILL RD.
MERIDIAN
MERIDIAN RI.
FINCHLEY RD.
NORFOLK ROAD
STREET
CEMETERY RD.
ELLISONS CRES.
DISCOVERY DR.
RISE
BRAEBURN
RUSSET RD.
TYDEMAN CL.
BRAMLEY CL.
CHIVERS
HILL
PERMAIN LA.
HASLEMERE DR.
BANK RD.
NORTH HILL RD.
NORTH HILL GDS.
NTH. HILL WLK.
HANOVER CT.
BELVEDERE RD.
BELVEDERE CT.
BRUNSWICK RD.
STUART CL.
LONSDALE CL.
HUTLAND RD.
KHARTOUM RD.
PARADE RD.
RIVERS ST.
ROAD (ALBION HILL)
WOODBRIDGE ROAD
A1071
EMILY BRAY HO.
ST. MARY'S ROAD
St. Mary's Cath. Prim. Sch.
BURNHAM CL.
ST. ANTHONYS CR.
POST MILL CL.
VUE
ASHMERE GROVE
SIMON HO.
PADUA HO.
SERVITE HOUSE
TRAFALGAR CLOSE
ROAD
SPRINGHURST CL.
ST. EDMUNDSBURY HOUSE
BELLE VUE ROAD
ALEXANDRA ROAD
WARWICK RD.
WARWICK ROAD
UPTON CL.
NOTTIDGE ROAD
BARTHOLOMEW ST.
SPRING CT.
SPRING ROAD
LANCASTER RD.
PALMERSTON ROAD
PALMERSTON CT.
JEFFERIES RD.
LACEY ST.
WITHIPOLL ST.
BEVERLEY COURT
CHAPEL MEWS
Christchurch Mansion & Wolsey Gallery
DEVEREAUX CT.
School
COBBOLD MEWS
CHRISTCHURCH COURT
COBBOLD STREET
RACHEL CT.
Hall
SAMUEL CT.
WILLIAM HOUSE
ARTHUR'S TER.
BLANCHE ST.
SOANE S.
ST. MARGARET'S PLAIN
ST. MARGARET'S GREEN
ST. MARGARET'S STREET
CHALFONT SQ.
OLD FOUNDRY RD.
Lib.
Comm. Cen.
COBDEN PL.
TUDOR PLACE
GREAT COLMAN ST.
Regent Thtre.
CARR STREET
MAJOR'S CNR.
ST. HELEN'S STREET
SILENT ST.
ORCHARD ST.
CLENCH CL.
NEWTON ST.
ARGYLE ST.
ATLAS HOUSE
WELLS CL.
St. Helen's Prim. Sch.
ST. HELEN'S CHURCH LA.
REGENT ST.
WALK
MILNER ST.
GROVE
GRANGE ROAD
ACOTT DR.
OXFORD ROAD
KINGS AVENUE
Playground
FINBARS
TENNYSON RD.
Mus.
CLIFFORD RD.
Prim. Sch.
MELVILLE RD.
ROSEBERRY RD.
WOODVILLE RD.
WELLESLEY RD.
B1059
ALEXANDRA PARK
LANE
FOXHALL ROAD
RUSKIN RD.
HILL HOUSE RD.
HAMLET RD.
DEVONSHIRE RD.
GLADSTONE RD.
UNION ST.
COX LA.
UP. BARCLAY ST.
UPPER ORWELL ST.
UPP. ORWELL CTS.
BOND ST.
TACKET ST.
ORWELL PL.
EAGLE STREET
ROPE WALK
Registry Off.
SHAFTESBURY SQUARE
Club
DOVE ST.
Suffolk County Council
Suffolk New College (Univ. of East Anglia)
Goals Soccer Cen.
WOODHOUSE SQ.
IP CENTRAL
Works
RICHMOND HO.
A1156
GRIMWADE STREET
WINGFIELD ST.
ROSEMARY LA.
BLACKFRIARS CT.
TOOLEY'S COURT
SHIRE HALL YD.
WATTS CT.
MARITIME
SMART ST.
FOUNDATION ST.
PLEASANT ROW
LOWER ORWELL ST.
FORE ST.
DEDHAM PLACE
WATERWORKS ST.
ANGEL LA.
ST. CLEMENT'S CHURCH LA.
Fore St. Swim. Pool
NEW ST.
LONG STREET
SORREL HORSE MEWS
A1022
SLADE ST.
KEY STREET
SALTHOUSE ST.
STREET
REGATTA QUAY
RANGER
THE VALSHEDA
Old Custom Ho.
WHERRY LA.
Common Quay
Wherry Quay
NEPTUNE SQ.
Waterfront Building
COPROLITE ST.
Neptune Quay
DUKE STREET
B1458
FORE ST.
A1156
FORE HAMLET
BISHOP'S HILL
FELIXSTOWE R.
BACK HAMLET
QUAYSIDE
MILL HO.
St. Peter's Quay
Albion Wharf
Pontoons
Ipswich Haven Marina
Flint Wharf
Tovell's Wharf
NEPTUNE QUAY
Works
Snakes & Ladders (Children's Play Cen.)
ELIZABETH CT.
PADBROOK CT.
CAVENDISH ST.
PLOUGH ST.
WHITE ELM ST.
Depot
Kingdom Hall
THE BEECHES
MONTROSE COURT
ROSEHILL CRES.
ROSEHILL RD.
BISHOPSGARTH
SANDHURST AV.
ASTON RD.
ROAD
MITRE WY.
POWNALL RD.
SILOAM PL.
ISHAM PL.
HOPE CT.
ROAD PLACE
UNIVERSITY AV.
PAGE WLK.
BALLAST WHARF WLK.
WYKES BISHOP ST.
JOHN ST.
STREET
TYE
UNITY ST.
TRINITY ST.
HOLYWELLS RD.
MYRTLE
NACTON ROAD
Alder Carr
HOLYWELLS PARK
Playground
CUT
ORWELL
EAST
WEST
Warehouses
Pontoons
End Quay
Orwell Quay
South West Quay
New Cut
NEW CUT WEST
STOKE
BULSTRODE RD.
MALTING TERRACE
FELAW STREET
STREET
TYLER ST.
MATHER WAY
PURPLETT ST.
JAMES HATFIELD HO.
PURPLETT HO.
GRIFFIN CT.
HAWES ST.
Works
ANCHOR ST.
MAUDE ST.
PATTESON ROAD
CLIFF ROAD
HOLYWELLS CL.
Depot
HELENA ROAD
Warehouses
Big Pond
The Canal
Dock Head
Swing Bri.
Customs Office
SHIP LAUNCH RD.
BATH STREET
DISCOVERY
Bowling Greens
Works

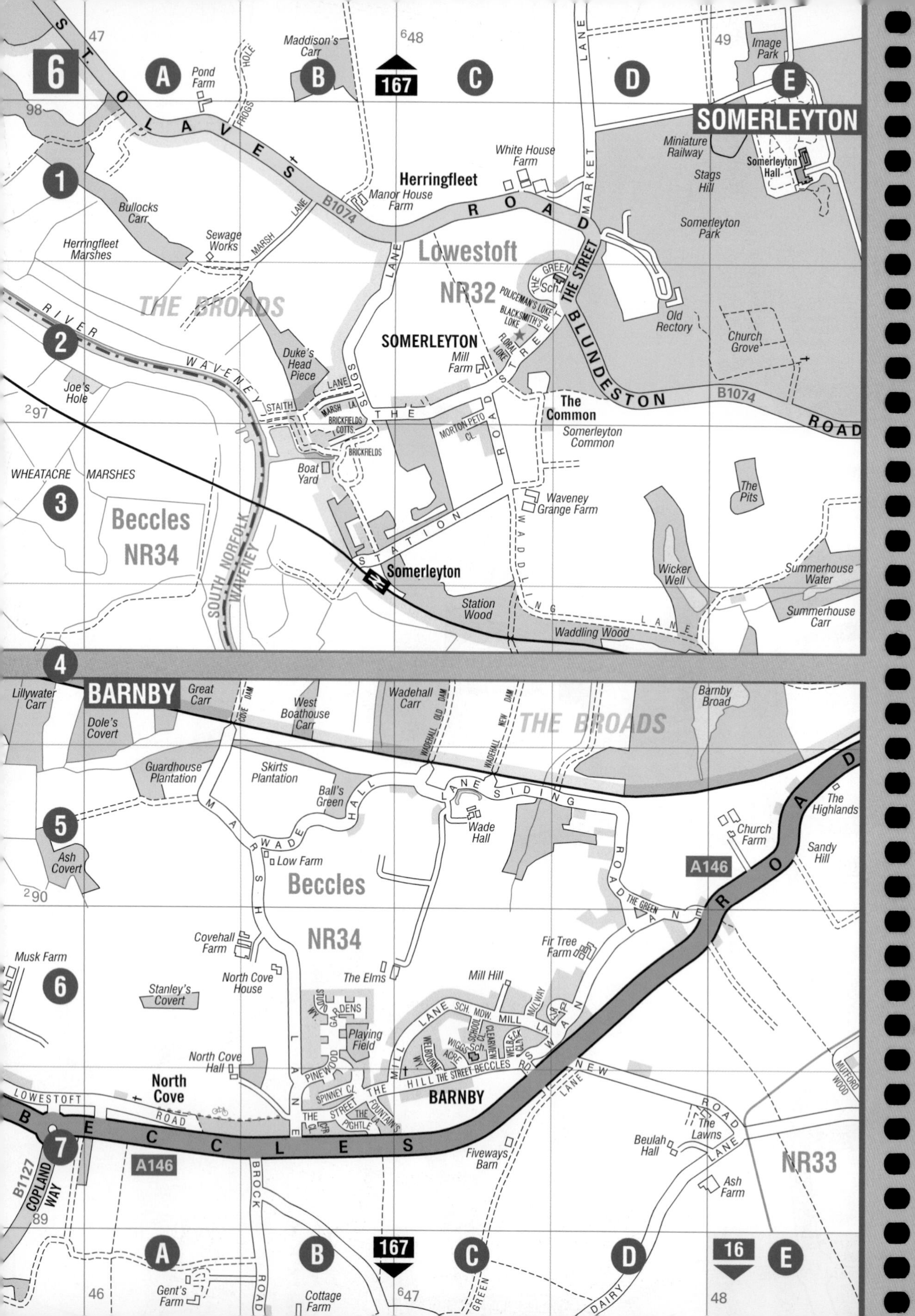

6
SOMERLEYTON
Herringfleet
Lowestoft
NR32
SOMERLEYTON
ST. OLAVES ROAD
B1074
BLUNDESTON ROAD
THE STREET
Pond Farm
Maddison's Carr
Image Park
Miniature Railway
Somerleyton Hall
Stags Hill
Somerleyton Park
White House Farm
Manor House Farm
Bullocks Carr
Herringfleet Marshes
Sewage Works
THE BROADS
RIVER WAVENEY
Duke's Head Piece
Joe's Hole
Mill Farm
Old Rectory
Church Grove
The Common
Somerleyton Common
WHEATACRE MARSHES
Beccles
NR34
Boat Yard
Waveney Grange Farm
The Pits
Somerleyton
Station Wood
Wicker Well
Summerhouse Water
Summerhouse Carr
Waddling Wood
WADDLING LANE
STATION ROAD
SOUTH NORFOLK
WAVENEY
BARNBY
Lillywater Carr
Great Carr
Dole's Covert
West Boathouse Carr
Wadehall Carr
Barnby Broad
Guardhouse Plantation
Skirts Plantation
Ball's Green
Wade Hall
The Highlands
Church Farm
Sandy Hill
A146
Ash Covert
Low Farm
Beccles
NR34
Covehall Farm
Fir Tree Farm
Musk Farm
Mill Hill
The Elms
North Cove House
Stanley's Covert
Playing Field
North Cove Hall
North Cove
BARNBY
LOWESTOFT ROAD
BECCLES ROAD
The Lawns
Beulah Hall
Fiveways Barn
Ash Farm
NR33
B1127
COPLAND WAY
Gent's Farm
Cottage Farm
167
16

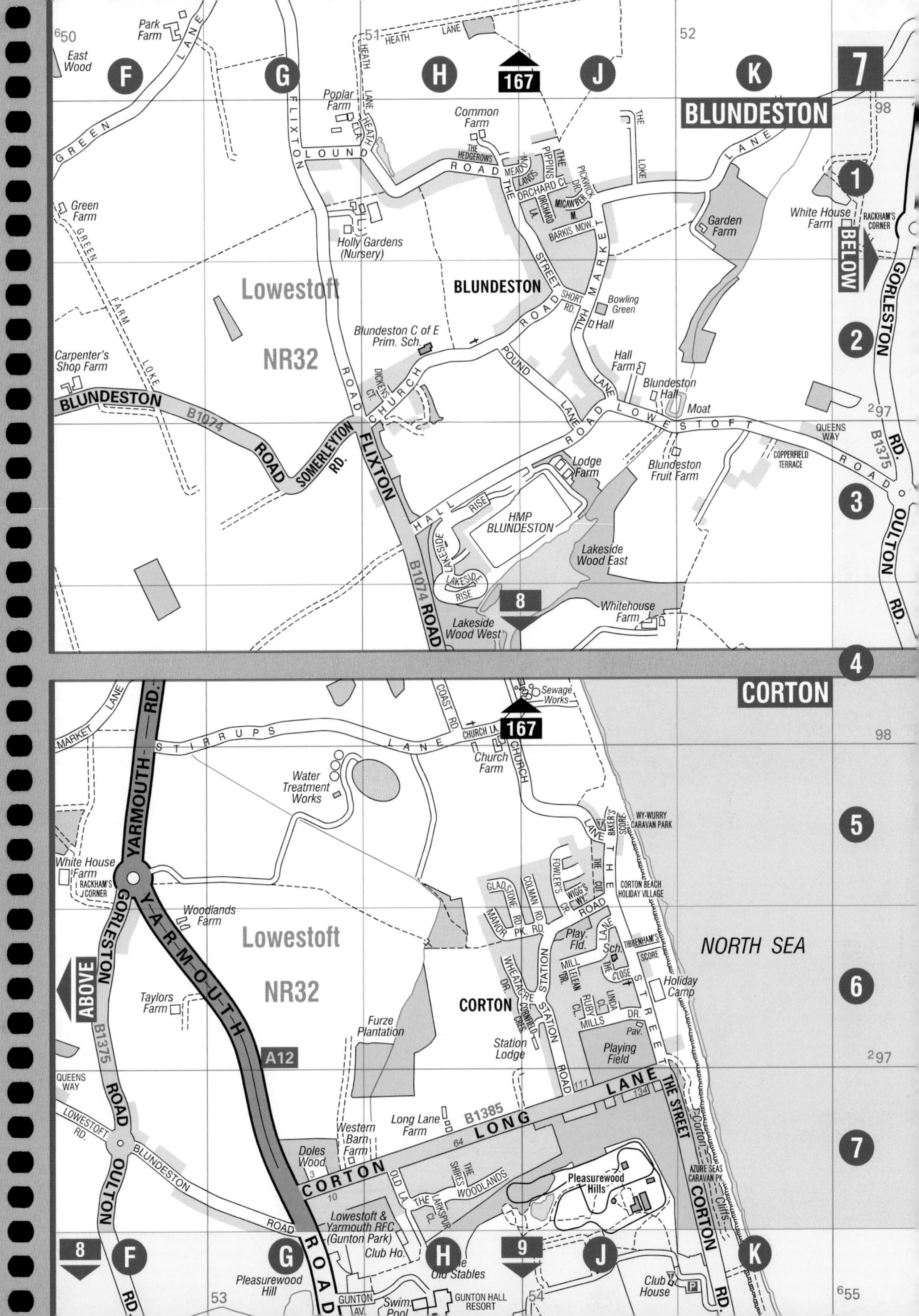
BLUNDESTON
7
167
8
CORTON
167
9
8
BELOW
ABOVE
Lowestoft
NR32
BLUNDESTON
CORTON
NORTH SEA
Park Farm
East Wood
Poplar Farm
Common Farm
Green Farm
Holly Gardens (Nursery)
Garden Farm
White House Farm
RACKHAM'S CORNER
Carpenter's Shop Farm
Blundeston C of E Prim. Sch.
Bowling Green
Hall
Hall Farm
Blundeston Hall
Moat
Lodge Farm
Blundeston Fruit Farm
HMP BLUNDESTON
Lakeside Wood East
Whitehouse Farm
Lakeside Wood West
Sewage Works
Church Farm
Water Treatment Works
WY-WURRY CARAVAN PARK
CORTON BEACH HOLIDAY VILLAGE
Woodlands Farm
Taylors Farm
Furze Plantation
Station Lodge
Holiday Camp
Playing Field
Long Lane Farm
Western Barn Farm
Doles Wood
Lowestoft & Yarmouth RFC (Gunton Park)
Club Ho.
Pleasurewood Hills
AZURE SEAS CARAVAN PK.
Pleasurewood Hill
Old Stables
Club House
GUNTON HALL RESORT
Swim. Pool
Corton Cliffs
BLUNDESTON ROAD
B1074
SOMERLEYTON RD.
FLIXTON ROAD
LOUND ROAD
CHURCH ROAD
GORLESTON RD.
OULTON RD.
LOWESTOFT ROAD
B1375
YARMOUTH RD.
A12
CORTON LONG LANE
B1385
THE STREET
CORTON RD.
STIRRUPS LANE
CHURCH LA.
COAST RD.
MARKET LANE
STATION ROAD
BLUNDESTON ROAD
QUEENS WAY
COPPERFIELD TERRACE

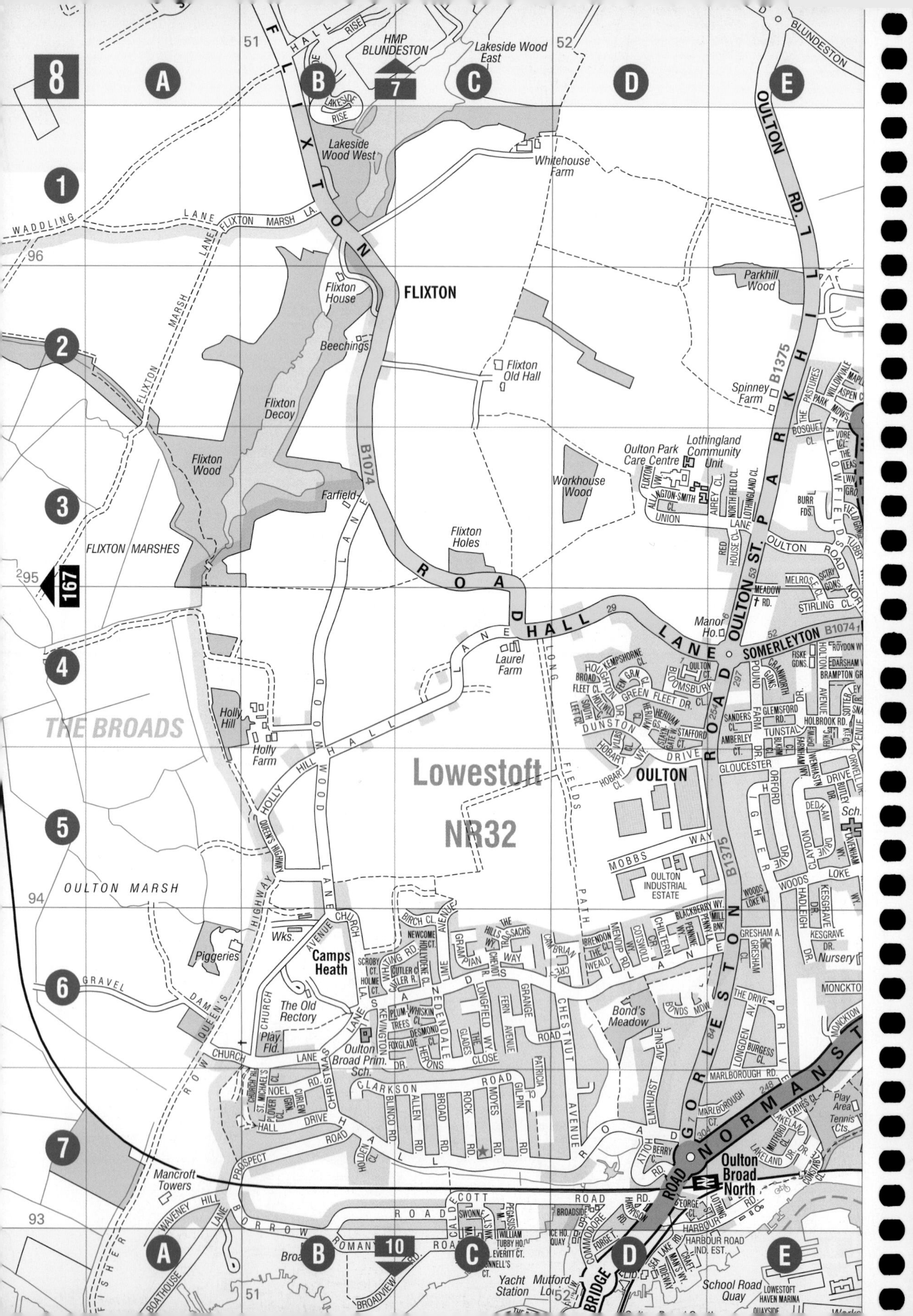
HMP BLUNDESTON
7
Lakeside Wood East
Lakeside Wood West
FLIXTON ROAD
WADDLING LANE
FLIXTON MARSH LA.
Whitehouse Farm
FLIXTON
Flixton House
Beechings
Flixton Decoy
Flixton Wood
Farfield
B1074
Flixton Old Hall
Workhouse Wood
Flixton Holes
FLIXTON MARSHES
167
HALL LANE
Laurel Farm
Holly Hill
Holly Farm
THE BROADS
Lowestoft
NR32
OULTON
OULTON MARSH
Parkhill Wood
Spinney Farm
OULTON RD.
PARK HILL
B1375
Oulton Park Care Centre
Lothingland Community Unit
UNION LANE
OULTON ROAD NORTH
Manor Ho.
SOMERLEYTON
GORLESTON ROAD
OULTON INDUSTRIAL ESTATE
MOBBS WAY
Camps Heath
The Old Rectory
Oulton Broad Prim. Sch.
Wks.
Piggeries
GRAVEL DAM
Bond's Meadow
CHURCH LANE
CLARKSON ROAD
PROSPECT ROAD
Mancroft Towers
WAVENEY HILL
BORROW ROAD
COTT ROAD
NORMANSTON DRIVE
Oulton Broad North
HARBOUR ROAD IND. EST.
Yacht Station
Mutford Lock
School Road Quay
LOWESTOFT HAVEN MARINA
BRIDGE
Play Area
Tennis Cts.
Nursery
Sch.
10
51
52
93
94
95
96

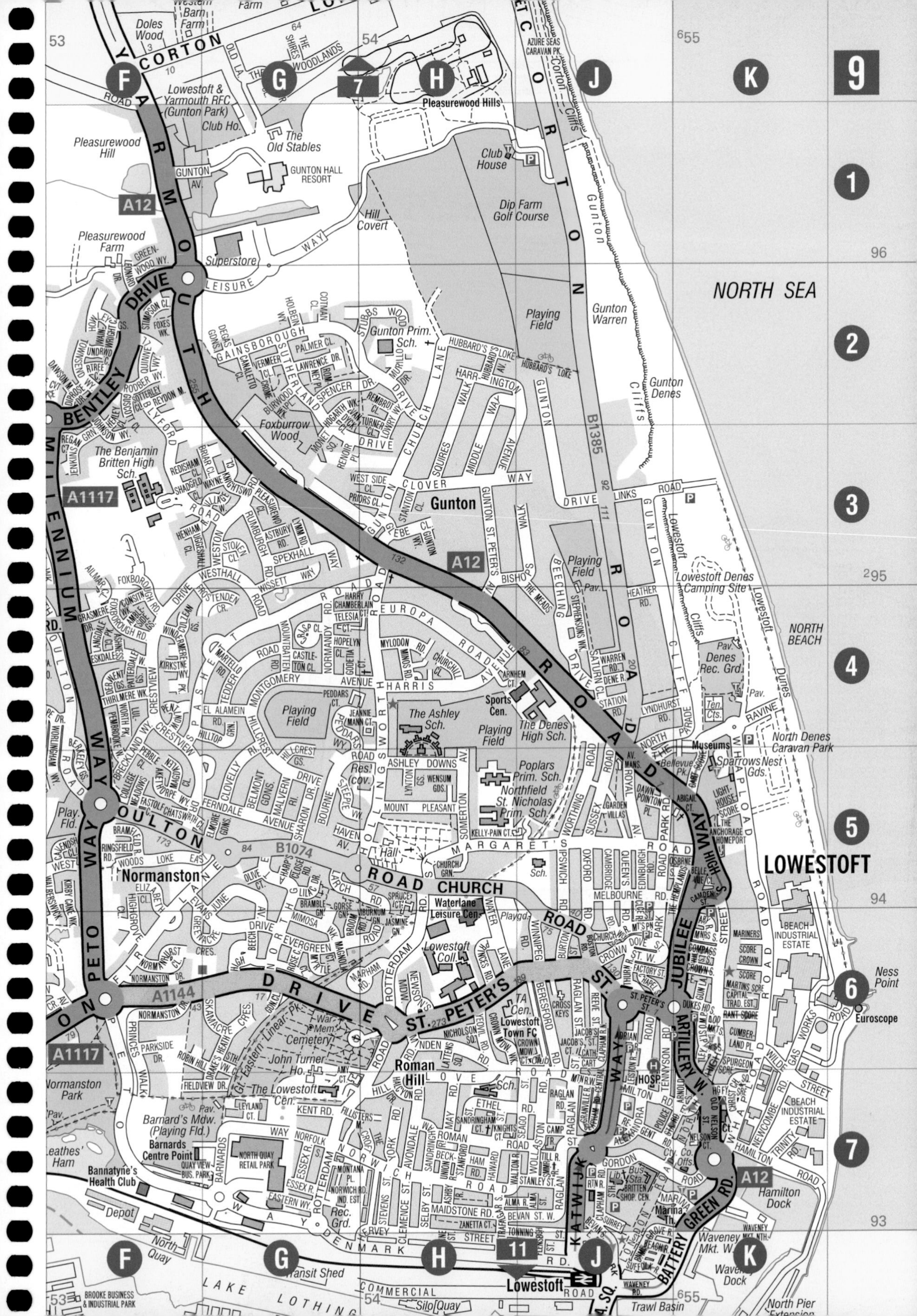
9
NORTH SEA
LOWESTOFT
Gunton
Normanston
Roman Hill
Pleasurewood Hills
Dip Farm Golf Course
Gunton Warren
Gunton Denes
North Beach
Lowestoft Denes Camping Site
North Denes Caravan Park
Ness Point
Euroscope
Hamilton Dock
Waveney Dock
Trawl Basin
Lake Lothing
North Quay
Lowestoft
A12
A1117
A1144
B1074
B1385
YARMOUTH ROAD
CORTON ROAD
GUNTON CHURCH LANE
CHURCH ROAD
ST. PETER'S ST.
JUBILEE WAY
KATWIJK WAY
BATTERY GREEN RD.
DENMARK RD.
OULTON RD.
PETO WAY
MILLENNIUM WAY
BENTLEY DRIVE
NORMANSTON DR.
The Denes High Sch.
The Ashley Sch.
The Benjamin Britten High Sch.
Lowestoft Coll.
Waterlane Leisure Cen.
North Quay Retail Park
Britten Shop. Cen.
Marina Th.
Sparrows Nest Gds.
Lowestoft Town FC

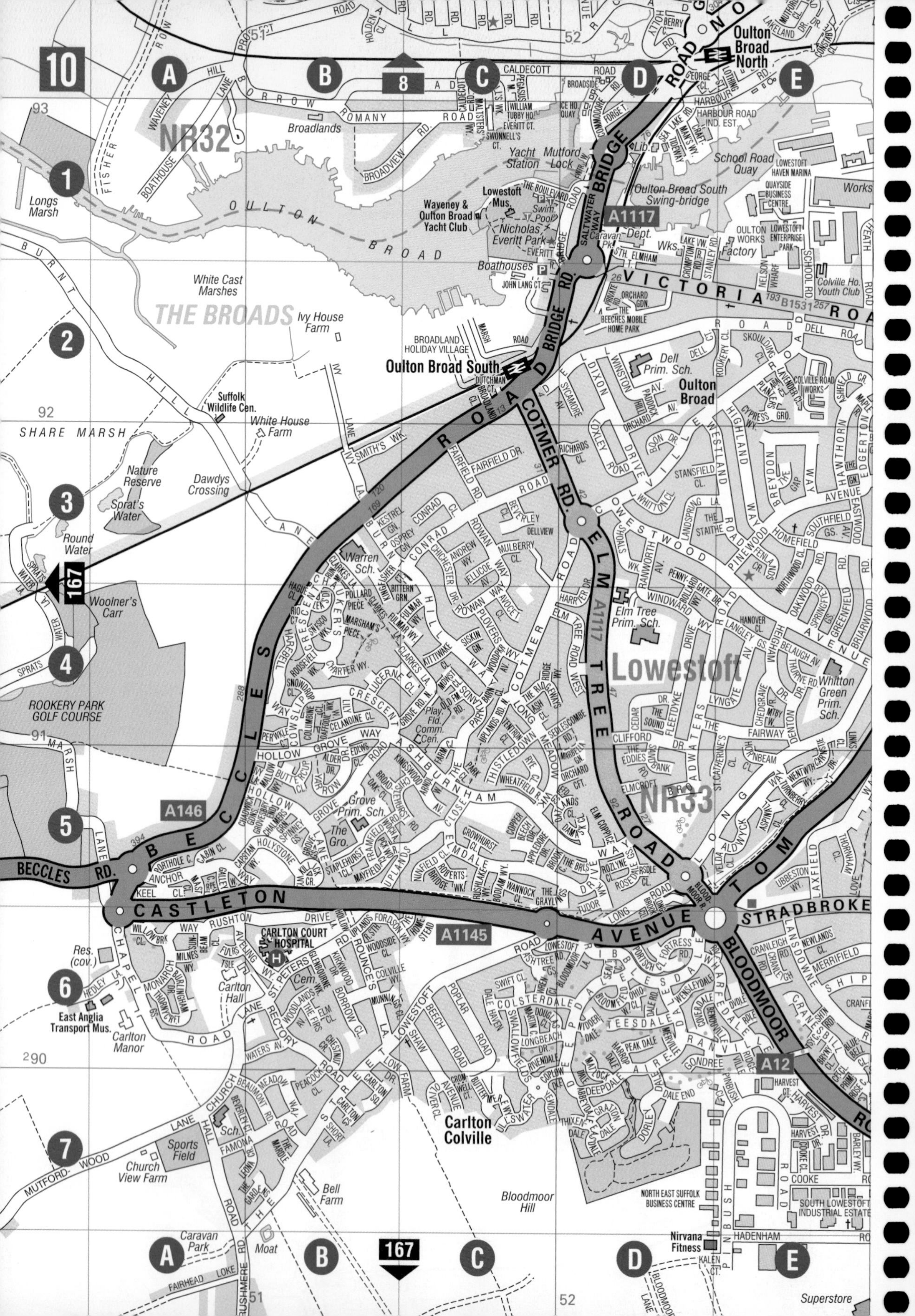
10
8
167
NR32
NR33
Oulton Broad North
Oulton Broad South
Oulton Broad
Lowestoft
Carlton Colville
OULTON BROAD
THE BROADS
Longs Marsh
White Cast Marshes
SHARE MARSH
Ivy House Farm
Broadlands
Yacht Station
Mutford Lock
Lowestoft Mus.
Waveney & Oulton Broad Yacht Club
Nicholas Everitt Park
Boathouses
Oulton Broad South Swing-bridge
School Road Quay
LOWESTOFT HAVEN MARINA
Works
HARBOUR ROAD IND. EST.
BROADLAND HOLIDAY VILLAGE
Suffolk Wildlife Cen.
White House Farm
Nature Reserve
Dawdys Crossing
Sprat's Water
Round Water
Woolner's Carr
ROOKERY PARK GOLF COURSE
Warren Sch.
Dell Prim. Sch.
Elm Tree Prim. Sch.
Whitton Green Prim. Sch.
Grove Prim. Sch.
The Gro.
Play. Fld.
Comm. Cen.
CARLTON COURT HOSPITAL
Res. (cov.)
East Anglia Transport Mus.
Carlton Hall
Carlton Manor
Sports Field
Church View Farm
Bell Farm
Bloodmoor Hill
Caravan Park
Moat
NORTH EAST SUFFOLK BUSINESS CENTRE
SOUTH LOWESTOFT INDUSTRIAL ESTATE
Nirvana Fitness
Superstore
Colville Ho. Youth Club
BEECHES MOBILE HOME PARK
A1117
A146
A1145
A12
B1531
VICTORIA ROAD
BRIDGE ROAD
SALTWATER WAY
BECCLES ROAD
CASTLETON AVENUE
COTMER RD.
ELM TREE ROAD
BLOODMOOR ROAD
STRADBROKE
TOM CRESCENT
CALDECOTT ROAD
ROMANY ROAD
BORROW ROAD
BURNT HILL LANE
MUTFORD WOOD LANE
CHURCH LANE
RUSHMERE RD.
FAIRHEAD LOKE
HADENHAM RD.
PINBUSH ROAD
COOKE ROAD
WESTWOOD AVENUE
COLVILLE ROAD
LONG ROAD
UPLANDS RD.
ASHBURNHAM WAY
HOLLOW GROVE WAY
CHAPEL ROAD
RECTORY ROAD

11
LOWESTOFT SOUTH ROADS
NORTH SEA
Lowestoft
NR32
Lake Lothing
North Quay
Transit Shed
Silo Quay
Town Quay
Inner Harbour
Trawl Basin
Waveney Dock
Hamilton Dock
North Pier Extension
Yacht Club
Marina
Lifeboat Station
South Pier
East Point Pav.
South Beach
Wellington Gdns.
Claremont Pier
Kirkley
Kirkley Cemetery
Kirkley Fen Park
Fen Park Prim. Sch.
East Point Academy
Sports Cen.
Waveney Gymnastics Club
Pakefield
Pakefield Park
Pakefield Prim. Sch.
Sixteen Acre
Caravan Park
Hammonds Farm
Rifle Range
Superstore
Bowls Club
St. Mary's RC Prim. Sch.
Kensington Gdns.
Gov. Offs.
Barnards Centre Point
Bannatyne's Health Club
North Quay Retail Park
Brooke Business & Industrial Park
Riverside Business Park
Waveney Drive
Belvedere Rd.
Horn Hill
Crisp Way
London Road
Kirkley Cliff Rd.
Marine Pde.
Battery Green Rd.
Denmark Road
Commercial Road
Pakefield Road
Beach Farm Residential & Holiday Park
A12
B1532
B1384
F
G
H
J
K
1
2
3
4
5
6
7
93
92
91
90
53
54
55
9
167

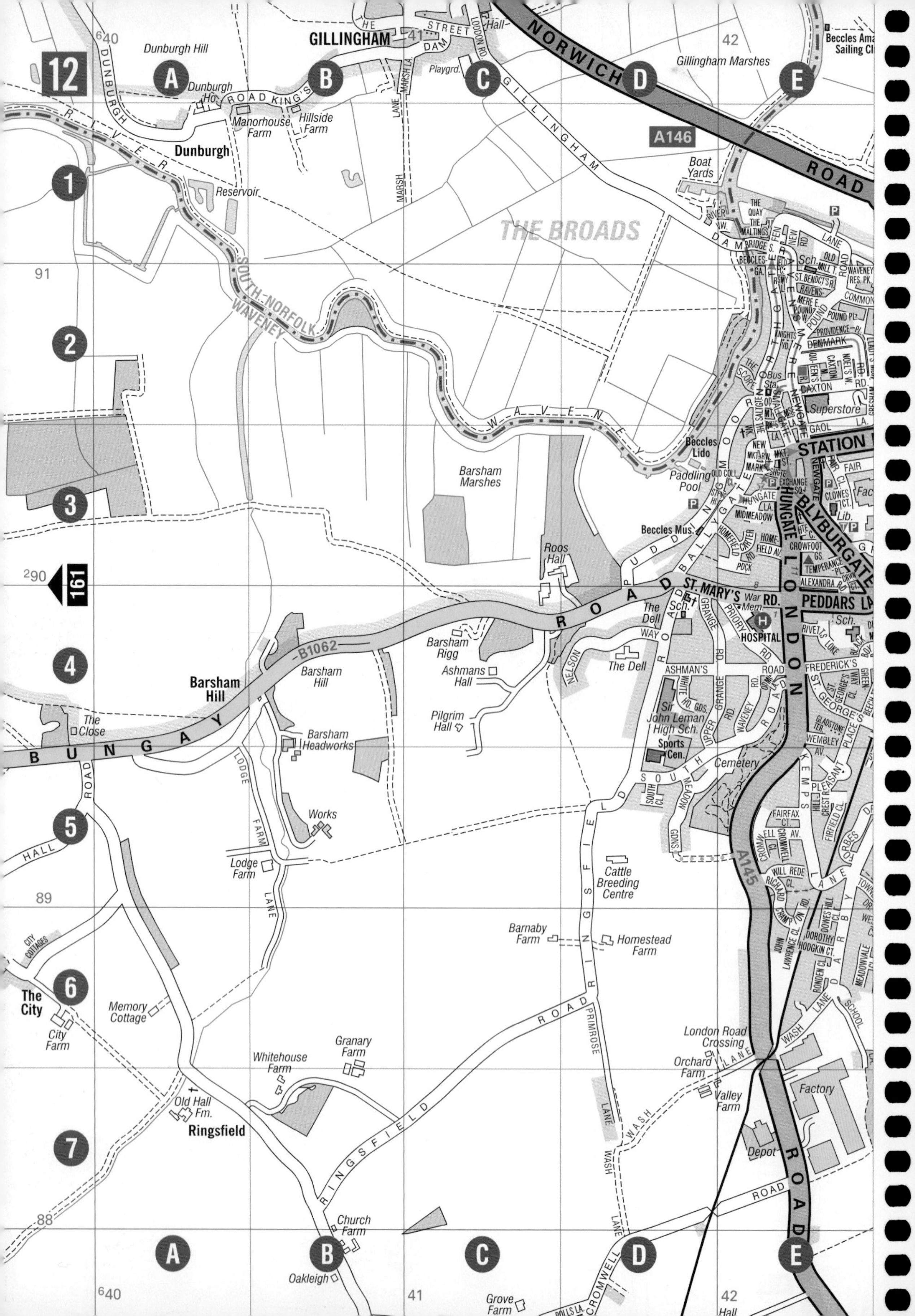

GILLINGHAM
THE STREET
DAM
LONDON RD.
Hall
Dunburgh Hill
DUNBURGH
Dunburgh Ho.
ROAD
KING'S
Manorhouse Farm
Hillside Farm
MARSH LA.
LANE
MARSH
Playgrd.
GILLINGHAM
NORWICH
ROAD
A146
Gillingham Marshes
Beccles Amateur Sailing Cl
Dunburgh
RIVER
Reservoir
Boat Yards
THE BROADS
DAM
THE QUAY
THE MALTINGS
BRIDGE S.
BECCLES
Sch.
OLD MILL T.
WAVENEY RES. PK.
ST. BENEDICT'S R.
RAVENS
COMMON
POUND
PROVIDENCE PL.
DENMARK
SOUTH NORFOLK
WAVENEY
91
KNIGHTS YD.
QUEEN'S
CAXTON
NOEL'S W.
THE SCORE
Bus Sta.
CAXTON
RD.
Superstore
GAOL LA.
STATION
Beccles Lido
NEW MARKET
SALTGATE
NEWGATE
FAIR CL.
Paddling Pool
OLD COLL. CL.
EXCHANGE SQ.
CLOWES CT.
Fac
Lib.
HUNGATE
BLYBURGATE
HUNGATE LA.
MIDMEADOW
Barsham Marshes
Beccles Mus.
HOMEFIELD
CARTER RD.
HOME-FIELD AV.
CROWFOOT GS.
TEMPERANCE
ALEXANDRA
PEDDARS LA.
Roos Hall
PUDDINGMOOR
BALLYGATE
ST. MARY'S RD.
War Mem.
LONDON
290
161
The Dell
Sch.
HOSPITAL
GRANGE RD.
PRIORY RD.
RIVETTS LOKE
BLACK BOY
Barsham Rigg
Ashmans Hall
WAY
NELSON
The Dell
ASHMAN'S ROAD
FREDERICK'S
ST. GEORGE'S
GREEN
B1062
Barsham Hill
Barsham Hill
WHITE HO. GDS.
Sir John Leman High Sch.
UPPER GRANGE RD.
WAVENEY RD.
GLADSTONE TER.
WEMBLEY AV.
Pilgrim Hall
The Close
Barsham Headworks
Sports Cen.
Cemetery
KEMPS
PLEASANT PLACE
BUNGAY ROAD
ROAD
LODGE FARM
SOUTH
SOUTH CL.
MEADOW
GDNS.
Works
FAIRFAX CT.
CROMWELL AV.
CREST R.
FIRFIELD CL.
HALL
Lodge Farm
LANE
Cattle Breeding Centre
A145
WILL REDE CL.
RICHARD CL.
CRAMPTON RD.
89
RINGSFIELD
Barnaby Farm
Homestead Farm
DOWES HILL CL.
DOROTHY
HODGKIN CT.
JOHN LAWRENCE CL.
RONDEN CL.
MEADOWALE
CITY COTTAGES
The City
Memory Cottage
City Farm
ROAD
PRIMROSE
LANE
SCHOOL
WASH LANE
London Road Crossing
Orchard Farm
LANE
Whitehouse Farm
Granary Farm
Factory
Valley Farm
Old Hall Fm.
Ringsfield
RINGSFIELD
WASH
Depot
ROAD
ROAD
88
Church Farm
LANE
Oaklegh
CROMWELL
640
41
42
Grove Farm
Hall
A B C D E
1 2 3 4 5 6 7

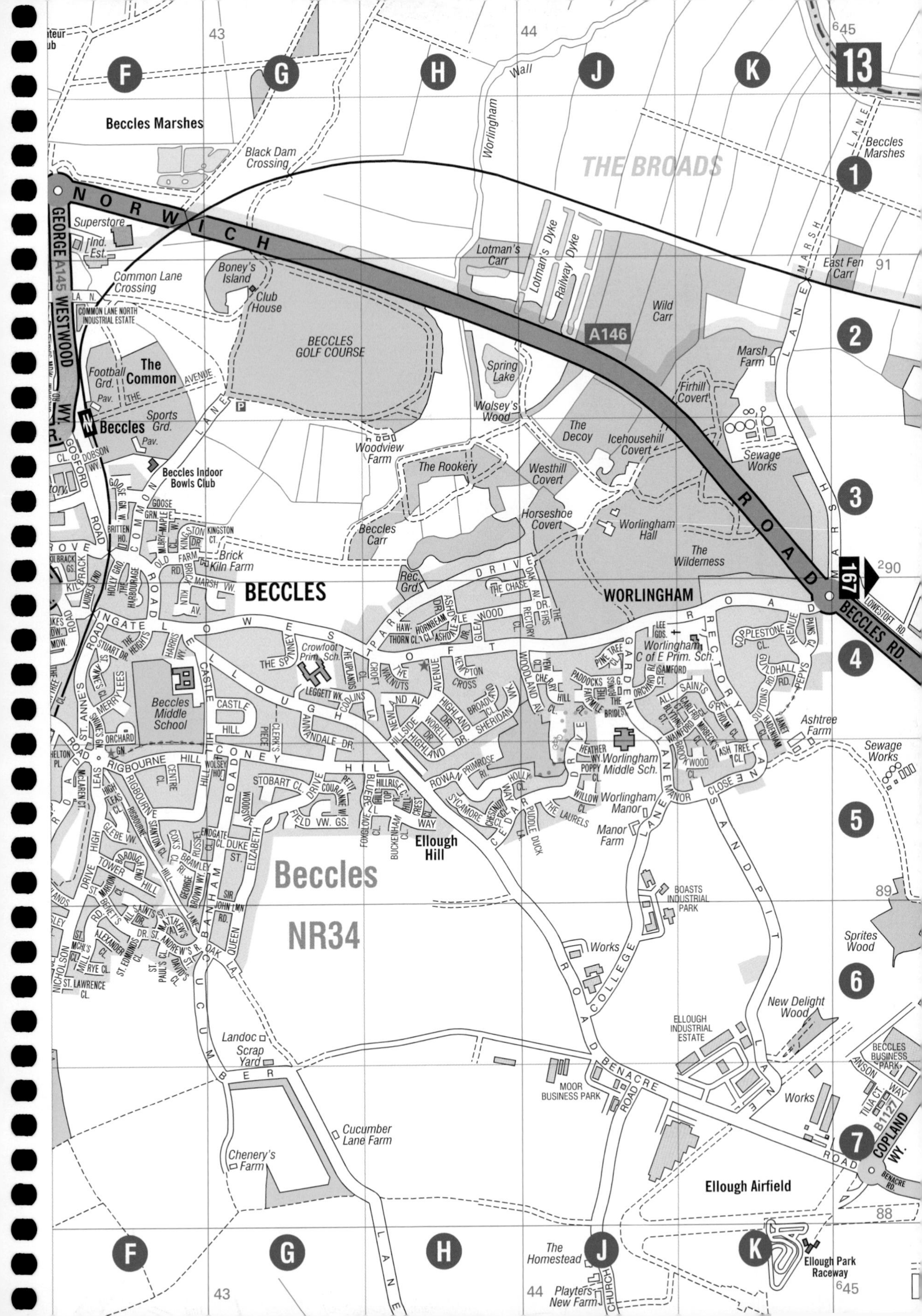
Beccles Marshes
Black Dam Crossing
NORWICH ROAD
THE BROADS
Worlingham Wall
Lotman's Carr
Lotman's Dyke
Railway Dyke
Boney's Island
Club House
BECCLES GOLF COURSE
Common Lane Crossing
COMMON LANE NORTH INDUSTRIAL ESTATE
Superstore
Ind. Est.
GEORGE WESTWOOD WY.
A145
A146
Wild Carr
East Fen Carr
Marsh Farm
Firhill Covert
Spring Lake
Wolsey's Wood
The Decoy
Icehousehill Covert
Sewage Works
Football Grd.
The Common
Sports Grd.
Pav.
Beccles
Beccles Indoor Bowls Club
Woodview Farm
The Rookery
Westhill Covert
Horseshoe Covert
Worlingham Hall
The Wilderness
Beccles Carr
Brick Kiln Farm
Rec. Grd.
BECCLES
WORLINGHAM
167
BECCLES RD.
Crowfoot Prim. Sch.
Worlingham C of E Prim. Sch.
Beccles Middle School
Ashtree Farm
Sewage Works
Worlingham Middle Sch.
Worlingham Manor
Manor Farm
Ellough Hill
Beccles
NR34
BOASTS INDUSTRIAL PARK
Works
Sprites Wood
New Delight Wood
ELLOUGH INDUSTRIAL ESTATE
BECCLES BUSINESS PARK
Landoc Scrap Yard
MOOR BUSINESS PARK
BENACRE ROAD
COLLEGE LANE
SANDPIT LANE
CUCUMBER LANE
Cucumber Lane Farm
Chenery's Farm
Ellough Airfield
COPLAND WY.
B1127
The Homestead
Playters New Farm
CHURCH
Ellough Park Raceway
F
G
H
J
K
1
2
3
4
5
6
7
43
44
645
88
89
90
91

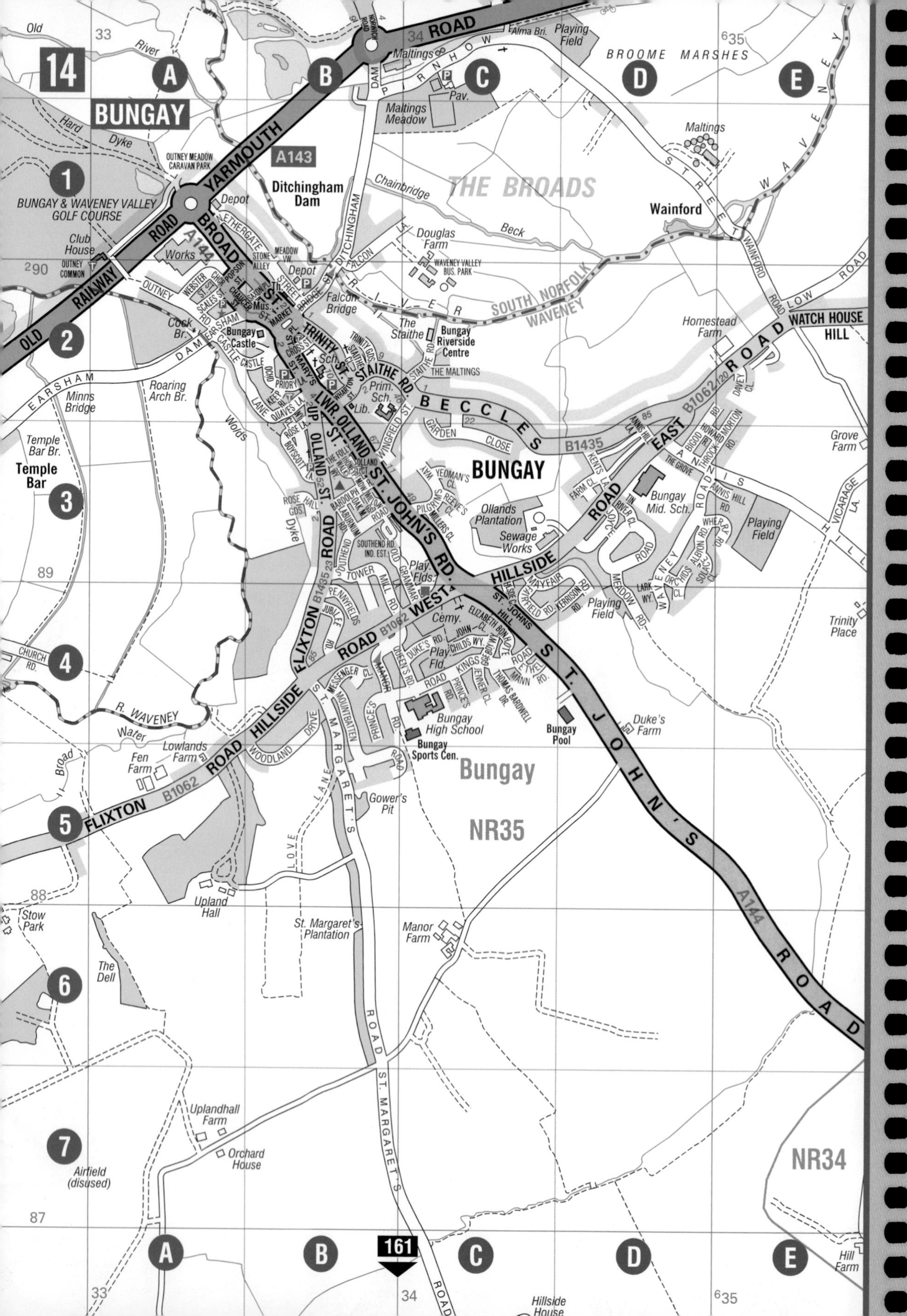

14
BUNGAY
A
B
C
D
E
1
2
3
4
5
6
7
YARMOUTH ROAD
A143
A144
BROAD ST.
Ditchingham Dam
BUNGAY & WAVENEY VALLEY GOLF COURSE
OUTNEY MEADOW CARAVAN PARK
Maltings
Maltings Meadow
Pav.
Playing Field
Alma Bri.
BROOME MARSHES
THE BROADS
Chainbridge
Beck
Douglas Farm
WAVENEY VALLEY BUS. PARK
Wainford
SOUTH NORFOLK
WAVENEY
Falcon Bridge
The Staithe
Bungay Riverside Centre
Bungay Castle
Mus.
Depot
Works
Club House
OUTNEY COMMON
OLD RAILWAY ROAD
OUTNEY
EARSHAM
Cock Br.
Minns Bridge
Roaring Arch Br.
Temple Bar Br.
Temple Bar
TRINITY ST.
STAITHE RD.
THE MALTINGS
Prim. Sch.
Lib.
BECCLES ROAD
B1435
B1062
BUNGAY
LWR. OLLAND ST.
UP OLLAND ST.
ST. JOHN'S RD.
Ollands Plantation
Sewage Works
Bungay Mid. Sch.
Playing Field
Homestead Farm
WATCH HOUSE HILL
LOW ROAD
WAINFORD ROAD
Grove Farm
VICARAGE LA.
Trinity Place
HILLSIDE ROAD EAST
HILLSIDE ROAD WEST
FLIXTON ROAD
Play. Flds.
Cemy.
Play. Fld.
Bungay High School
Bungay Sports Cen.
Bungay Pool
Duke's Farm
Bungay
NR35
ST. JOHN'S ROAD
A144
R. WAVENEY
Water
Broad
Fen Farm
Lowlands Farm
WOODLAND DRIVE
ST. MARGARET'S ROAD
LOVE LANE
Gower's Pit
Upland Hall
Stow Park
St. Margaret's Plantation
Manor Farm
The Dell
Uplandhall Farm
Orchard House
Airfield (disused)
NR34
Hill Farm
Hillside House
CHURCH RD.
161
33
34
635
290
89
88
87

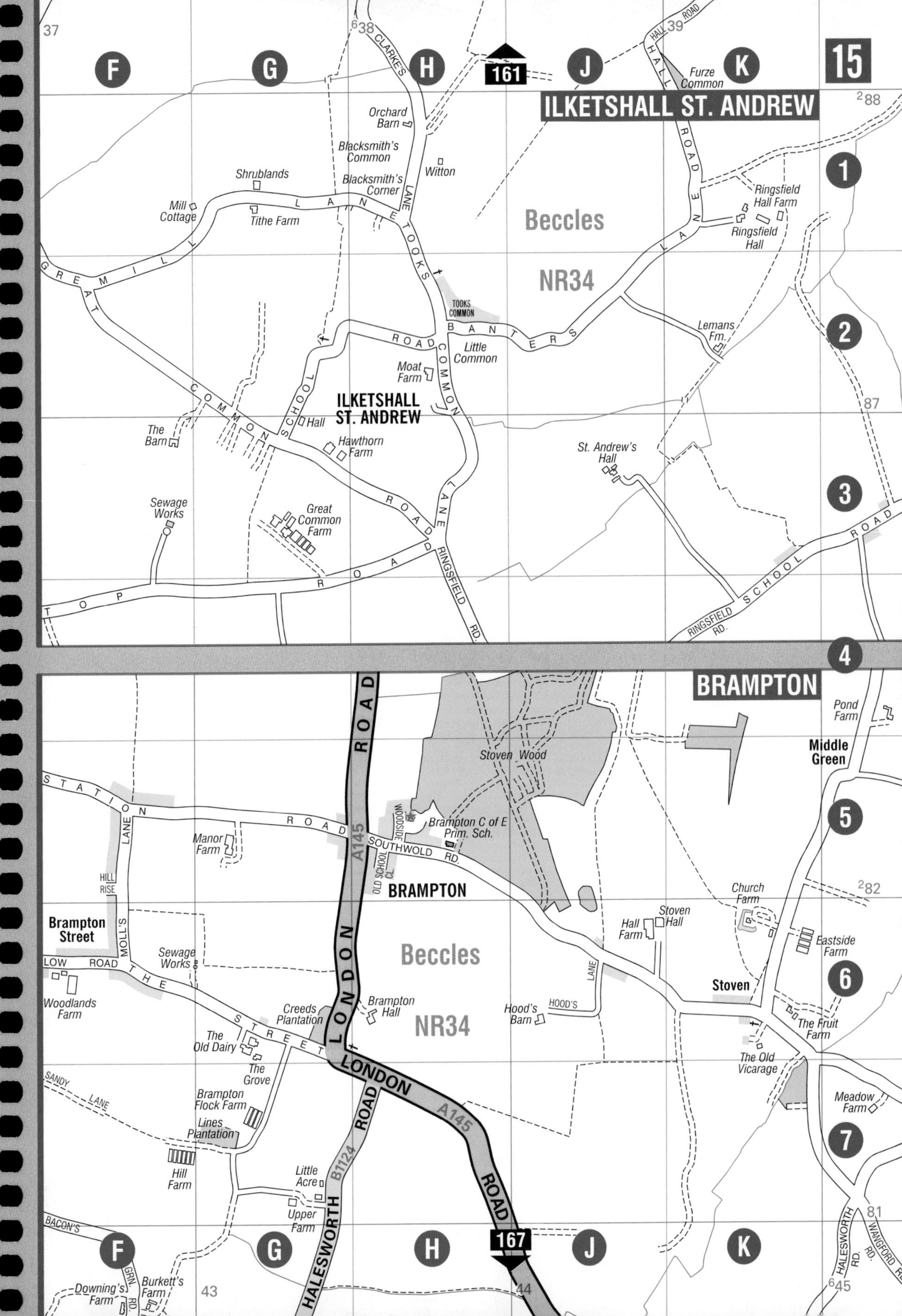
15
ILKETSHALL ST. ANDREW
161
Furze Common
Orchard Barn
Blacksmith's Common
Witton
Shrublands
Blacksmith's Corner
Mill Cottage
Tithe Farm
Ringsfield Hall Farm
Ringsfield Hall
Beccles
NR34
TOOKS COMMON
Lemans Fm.
Little Common
Moat Farm
ILKETSHALL ST. ANDREW
The Barn
Hall
Hawthorn Farm
St. Andrew's Hall
Sewage Works
Great Common Farm
GREAT COMMON ROAD
MILL LANE
TOOKS LANE
BANTERS ROAD
COMMON LANE
SCHOOL ROAD
TOP ROAD
RINGSFIELD RD.
RINGSFIELD SCHOOL ROAD
RINGSFIELD RD.
HALL ROAD
CLARKE'S LANE
BRAMPTON
Pond Farm
Middle Green
Stoven Wood
STATION ROAD
LONDON ROAD
A145
WOODSIDE
Brampton C of E Prim. Sch.
Manor Farm
SOUTHWOLD RD.
HILL RISE
OLD SCHOOL CL.
BRAMPTON
Church Farm
Brampton Street
MOLL'S LANE
Stoven Hall
Hall Farm
Eastside Farm
Beccles
LOW ROAD
Sewage Works
THE STREET
LANE
Stoven
Woodlands Farm
Brampton Hall
Hood's Barn
HOOD'S
Creeds Plantation
NR34
The Fruit Farm
The Old Dairy
The Old Vicarage
The Grove
SANDY LANE
Brampton Flock Farm
Meadow Farm
Lines Plantation
Hill Farm
Little Acre
Upper Farm
B1124
HALESWORTH ROAD
BACON'S
167
Downing's Farm
GRN. RD.
Burkett's Farm
HALESWORTH RD.
WANGFORD RD.
F G H J K
1 2 3 4 5 6 7
37 38 39 43 44 45
288 87 282 81

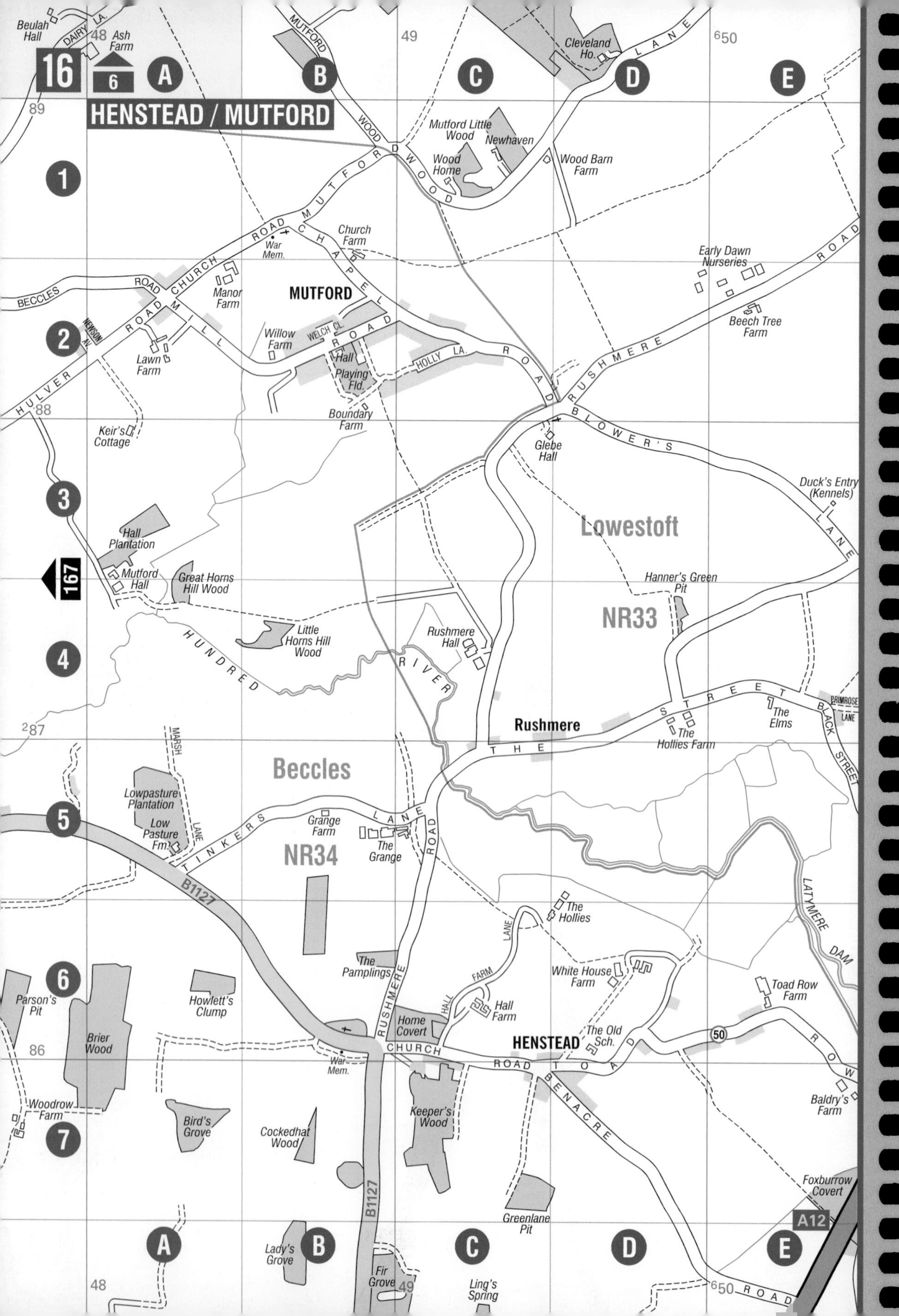
Beulah Hall
DAIRY LA.
Ash Farm
6
MUTFORD
Cleveland Ho.
LANE
MUTFORD WOOD
Mutford Little Wood
Newhaven
Wood Home
WOOD
Wood Barn Farm
MUTFORD ROAD
CHURCH
CHAPEL
Church Farm
War Mem.
Early Dawn Nurseries
ROAD
BECCLES ROAD
Manor Farm
MUTFORD
Beech Tree Farm
NEWSON AV.
MILL ROAD
Willow Farm
WELCH CL.
ROAD
Hall
HOLLY LA.
Lawn Farm
Playing Fld.
RUSHMERE
HULVER
Boundary Farm
BLOWER'S
Keir's Cottage
Glebe Hall
Duck's Entry (Kennels)
Lowestoft
LANE
Hall Plantation
Mutford Hall
Great Horns Hill Wood
Hanner's Green Pit
NR33
Little Horns Hill Wood
Rushmere Hall
HUNDRED
RIVER
THE STREET
Rushmere
The Hollies Farm
The Elms
PRIMROSE LANE
BLACK STREET
MARSH LANE
Beccles
Lowpasture Plantation
Low Pasture Fm.
TINKERS LANE
Grange Farm
The Grange
NR34
ROAD
B1127
The Hollies
LATYMERE DAM
LANE
The Pamplings
RUSHMERE
FARM
White House Farm
Toad Row Farm
Parson's Pit
Howlett's Clump
HALL
Hall Farm
Brier Wood
Home Covert
HENSTEAD
The Old Sch.
50
CHURCH ROAD
ROAD
ROW
War Mem.
BENACRE
Woodrow Farm
Baldry's Farm
Bird's Grove
Keeper's Wood
Cockedhat Wood
Foxburrow Covert
A12
Greenlane Pit
B1127
Lady's Grove
Fir Grove
Ling's Spring
ROAD
A B C D E
1 2 3 4 5 6 7
48 49 650
89 88 287 86

167

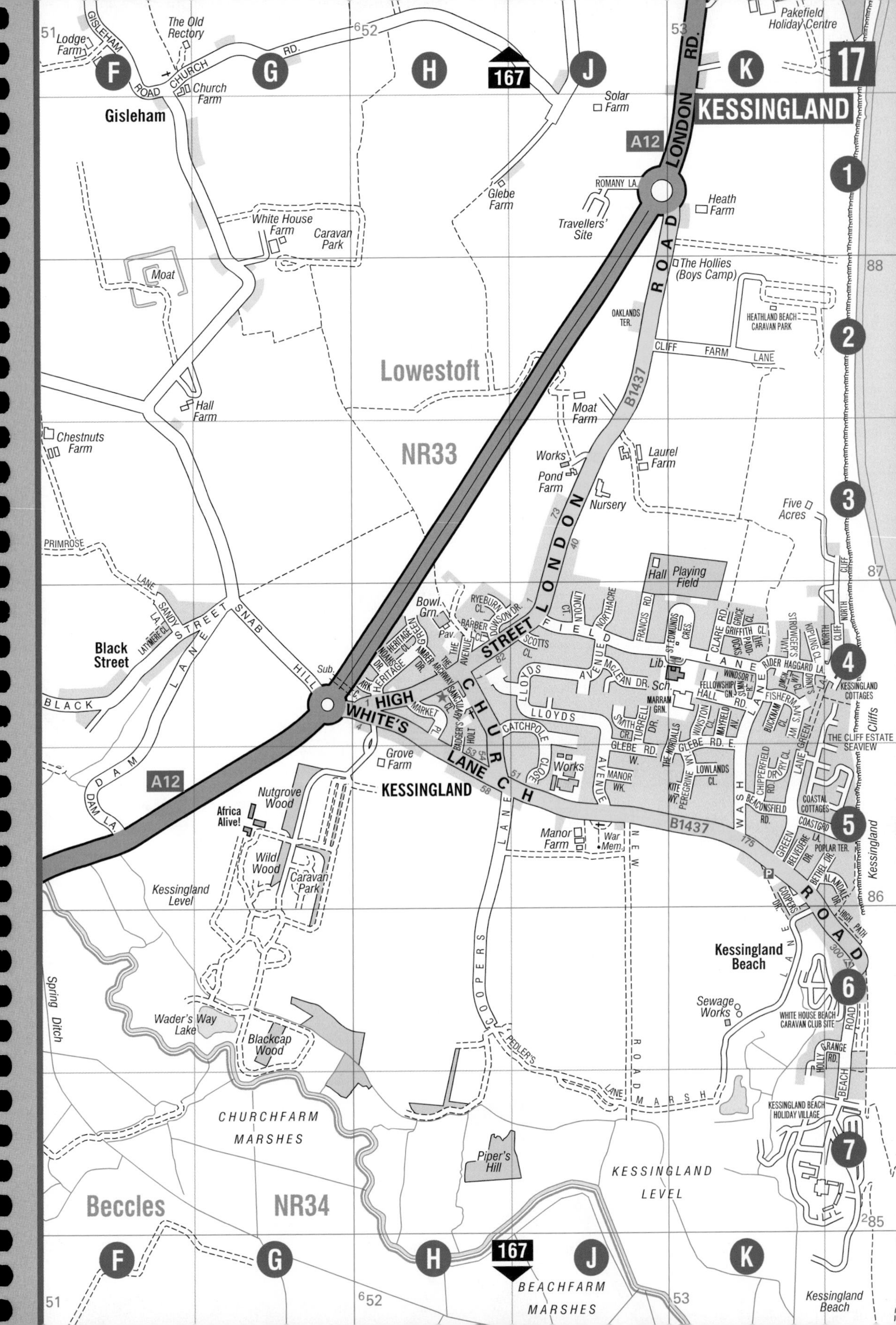

17
KESSINGLAND
Gisleham
Lodge Farm
The Old Rectory
Church Farm
White House Farm
Caravan Park
Moat
Hall Farm
Chestnuts Farm
Lowestoft
NR33
Glebe Farm
Solar Farm
Travellers' Site
Heath Farm
The Hollies (Boys Camp)
HEATHLAND BEACH CARAVAN PARK
Moat Farm
Laurel Farm
Works
Pond Farm
Nursery
Five Acres
Hall
Playing Field
Black Street
Bowl. Grn.
Pav.
Lib.
Sch.
Grove Farm
KESSINGLAND
Nutgrove Wood
Africa Alive!
Wild Wood
Caravan Park
Kessingland Level
Manor Farm
War Mem.
KESSINGLAND COTTAGES
THE CLIFF ESTATE SEAVIEW
COASTAL COTTAGES
Cliffs
Kessingland
Kessingland Beach
Sewage Works
WHITE HOUSE BEACH CARAVAN CLUB SITE
KESSINGLAND BEACH HOLIDAY VILLAGE
Spring Ditch
Wader's Way Lake
Blackcap Wood
CHURCHFARM MARSHES
Piper's Hill
KESSINGLAND LEVEL
Beccles
NR34
BEACHFARM MARSHES
Kessingland Beach
Pakefield Holiday Centre
A12
B1437
LONDON RD.
LONDON ROAD
ROMANY LA.
CLIFF FARM LANE
OAKLANDS TER.
HIGH STREET
WHITE'S LANE
CHURCH LANE
FIELD LANE
LLOYDS AVENUE
CATCHPOLE CLOSE
GLEBE RD. E.
WASH LANE
COOPERS LANE
PEDLER'S LANE
MARSH ROAD
NEW ROAD
BEACH ROAD
SNAB HILL
BLACK STREET
DAM LANE
SANDY LA.
PRIMROSE LANE
GISLEHAM ROAD
CHURCH RD.
167
F G H J K
1 2 3 4 5 6 7
51 52 53 85 86 87 88

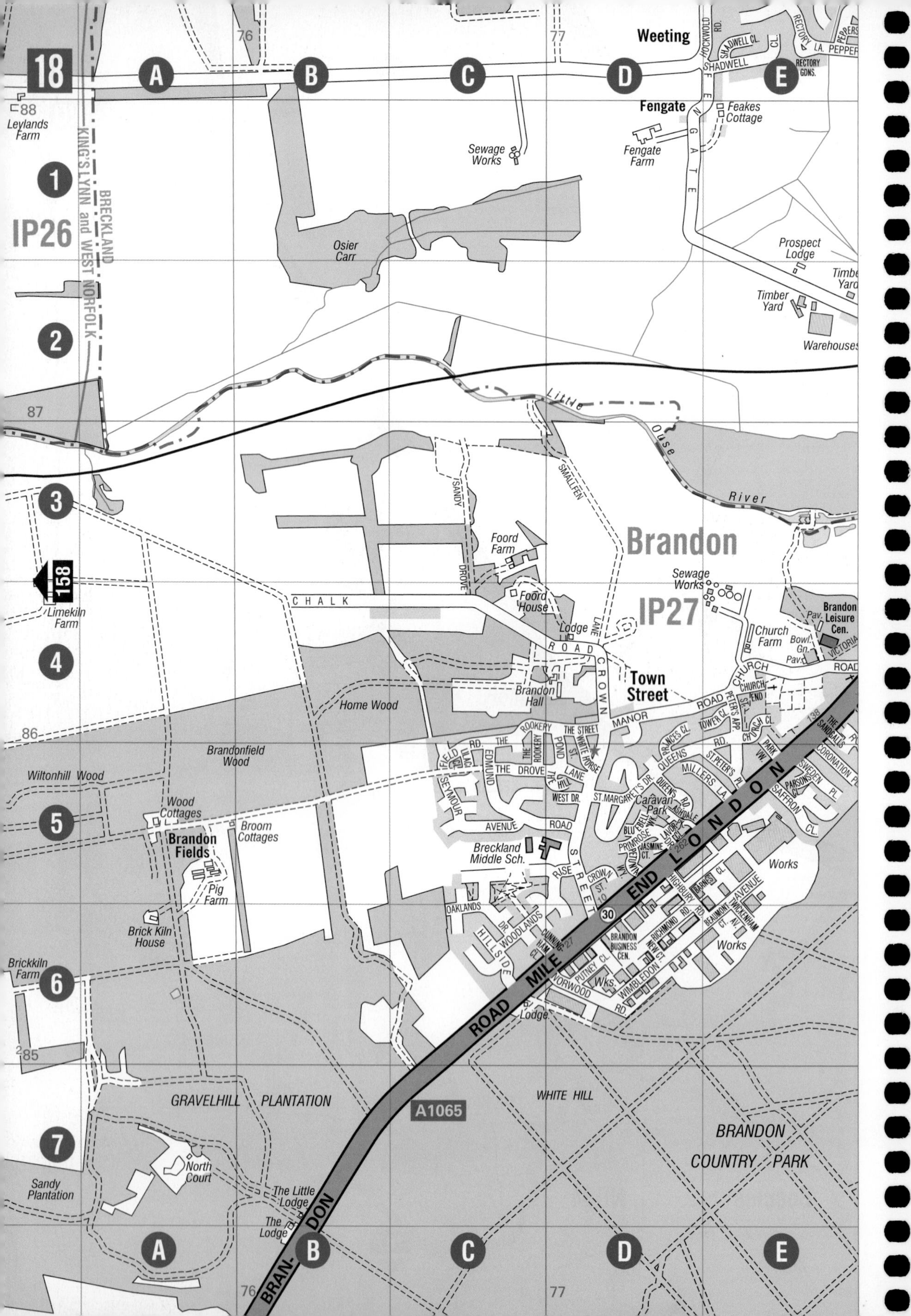

Weeting
Fengate
Feakes Cottage
Fengate Farm
Sewage Works
Osier Carr
IP26
Leylands Farm
KING'S LYNN and WEST NORFOLK
BRECKLAND
Prospect Lodge
Timber Yard
Warehouses
Little Ouse River
Brandon
IP27
Foord Farm
Foord House
CHALK ROAD
CROWN LANE
Town Street
Brandon Hall
Home Wood
Brandonfield Wood
Wiltonhill Wood
Wood Cottages
Brandon Fields
Broom Cottages
Pig Farm
Brick Kiln House
Brickkiln Farm
Limekiln Farm
Church Farm
Brandon Leisure Cen.
Caravan Park
Breckland Middle Sch.
Works
LONDON ROAD
MILE END ROAD
Brandon Business Cen.
Lodge
A1065
WHITE HILL
GRAVELHILL PLANTATION
BRANDON COUNTRY PARK
North Court
Sandy Plantation
The Little Lodge
The Lodge

158

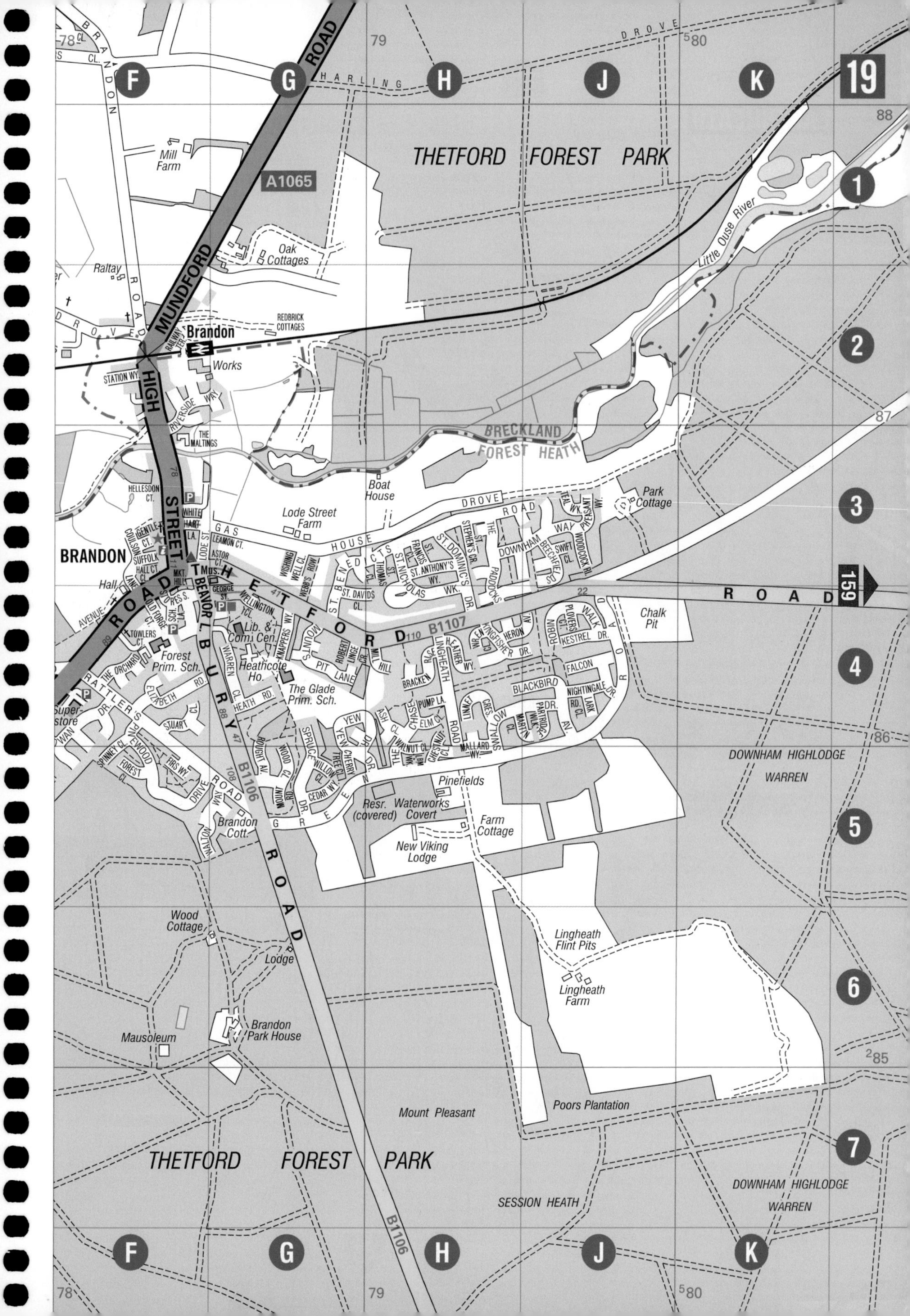

19
THETFORD FOREST PARK
A1065
MUNDFORD ROAD
HARLING DROVE
Mill Farm
Oak Cottages
Raltay
Brandon
REDBRICK COTTAGES
Works
STATION WY.
HIGH STREET
RIVERSIDE WAY
THE MALTINGS
Little Ouse River
BRECKLAND
FOREST HEATH
Boat House
Lode Street Farm
GAS HOUSE DROVE
Park Cottage
BRANDON
Hall
THETFORD ROAD
B1107
159
Chalk Pit
Lib. & Com. Cen.
Forest Prim. Sch.
Heathcote Ho.
The Glade Prim. Sch.
Super-store
BURY ROAD
B1106
GREEN DR.
Pinefields
Resr. (covered)
Waterworks Covert
Farm Cottage
New Viking Lodge
Brandon Cott.
DOWNHAM HIGHLODGE WARREN
Wood Cottage
Lodge
Lingheath Flint Pits
Lingheath Farm
Brandon Park House
Mausoleum
Poors Plantation
Mount Pleasant
THETFORD FOREST PARK
SESSION HEATH
DOWNHAM HIGHLODGE WARREN
F
G
H
J
K
1
2
3
4
5
6
7

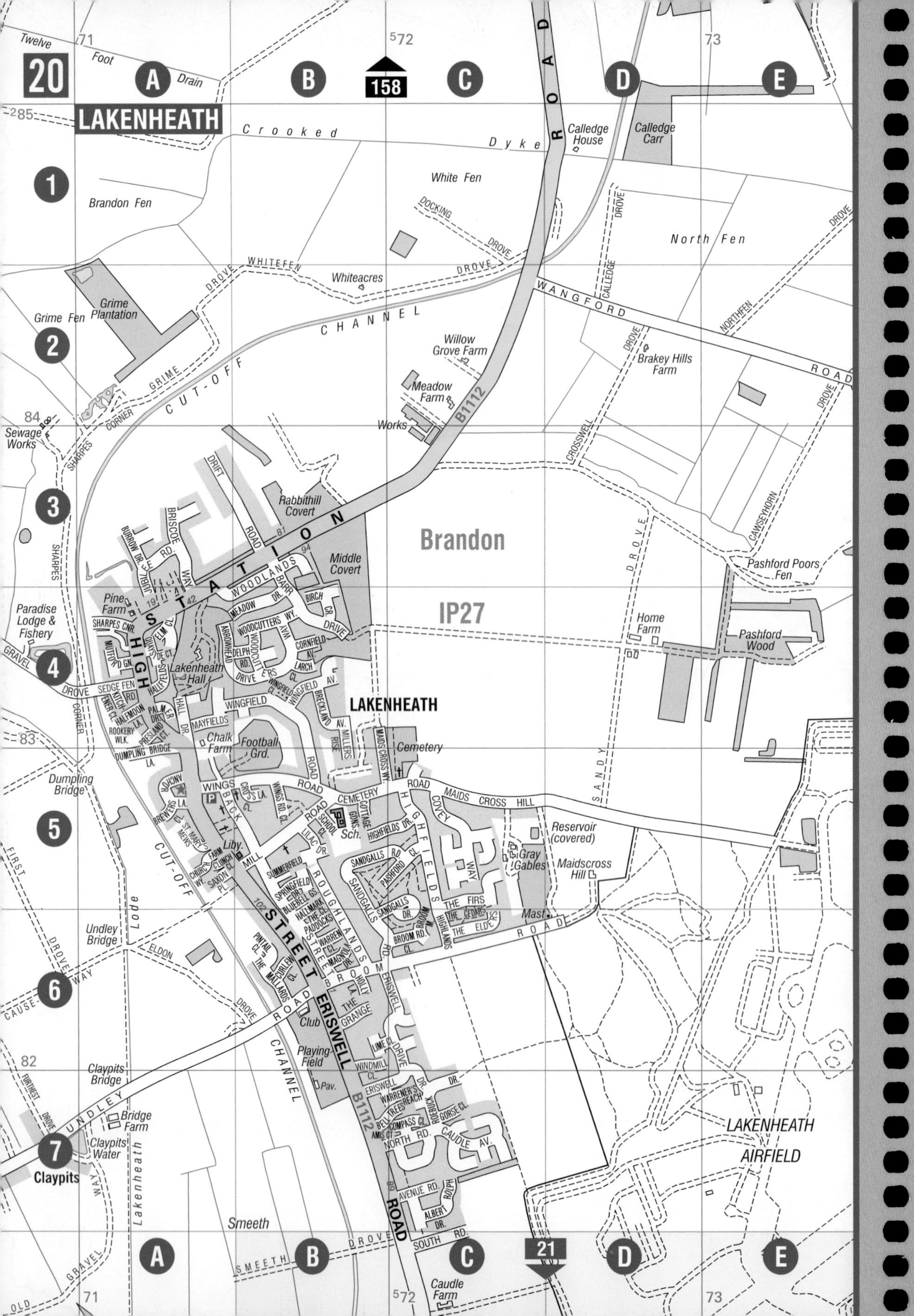
LAKENHEATH
158
21
Brandon
IP27
LAKENHEATH
Twelve Foot Drain
Crooked Dyke
Calledge House
Calledge Carr
White Fen
Brandon Fen
North Fen
Whiteacres
Grime Plantation
Grime Fen
CUT-OFF CHANNEL
Willow Grove Farm
Brakey Hills Farm
WANGFORD ROAD
Meadow Farm
Works
Sewage Works
Rabbithill Covert
Middle Covert
STATION ROAD
Pashford Poors Fen
Pine Farm
Paradise Lodge & Fishery
Home Farm
Pashford Wood
Lakenheath Hall
HIGH STREET
Chalk Farm
Football Grd.
Cemetery
MAIDS CROSS HILL
Dumpling Bridge
Reservoir (covered)
Gray Gables
Maidscross Hill
Sch.
Liby.
Mast.
Undley Bridge
Lode
ELDON
CAUSEWAY
BROOM ROAD
Club
Playing Field
Pav.
ERISWELL ROAD
B1112
Claypits Bridge
Bridge Farm
Claypits Water
Claypits
Lakenheath
LAKENHEATH AIRFIELD
Smeeth
SMEETH DROVE
SOUTH RD.
Caudle Farm
OLD GRAVEL WAY

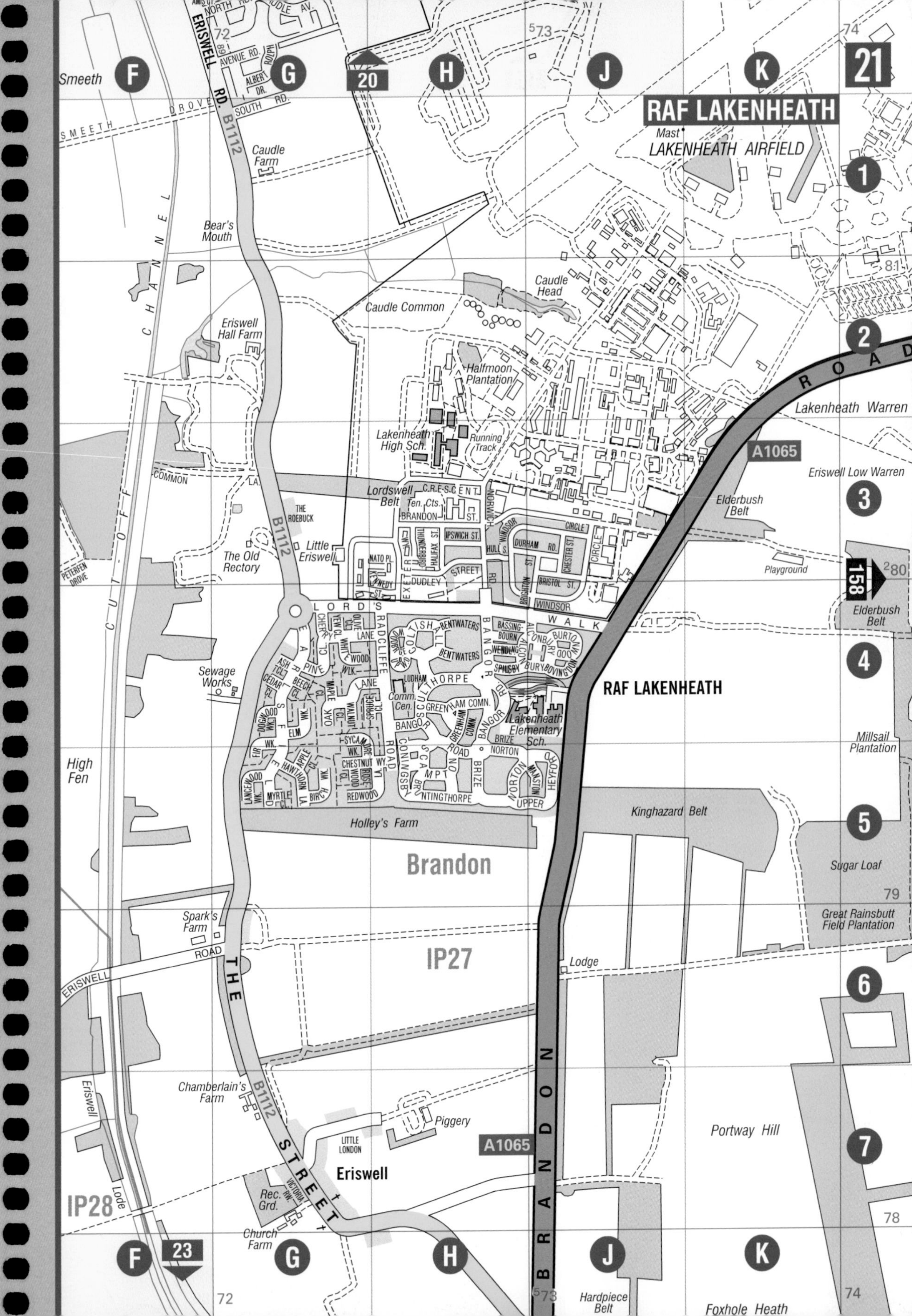
RAF LAKENHEATH
Mast
LAKENHEATH AIRFIELD
Smeeth
SMEETH DROVE
ERISWELL RD.
B1112
NORTH RD.
AVENUE RD.
ALBERT DR.
SOUTH RD.
20
Caudle Farm
Bear's Mouth
CUT-OFF CHANNEL
Caudle Head
Caudle Common
Eriswell Hall Farm
Halfmoon Plantation
Lakenheath High Sch.
Running Track
COMMON LA.
Lordswell Belt
Ten. Cts.
CRESCENT
BRANDON ST.
NORWICH
THE ROEBUCK
Little Eriswell
The Old Rectory
PETERFEN DROVE
IPSWICH ST.
WINDSOR CIRCLE
DURHAM RD.
CHESTER ST.
HULL S.
NATO PL.
HALIFAX ST.
THUNDERBIRD
EXETER
DUDLEY STREET
BRISTOL ST.
BRIGHTON ST.
WINDSOR
LORD'S WALK
A1065
ROAD
Lakenheath Warren
Eriswell Low Warren
Elderbush Belt
Playground
158
Elderbush Belt
CHERRY TR.
YEW CL.
OLIVE CL.
LANE
PINE
WHITE WOOD WLK.
RADCLIFFE
BENTWATERS
COTTISHALL
BANGOR
BASSINGBOURN
WENDLING
SPILSBY
ALCONBURY
BURTONWOOD
BOVINGDON
LUDHAM
CULTHORPE
ASH CL.
CEDAR CL.
BEECH CL.
MAPLE CL.
OAK
WALNUT CL.
SPRUCE CL.
Comm. Cen.
GREENHAM COMN.
Sewage Works
RAF LAKENHEATH
Lakenheath Elementary Sch.
DOGWOOD WK.
ELM
SYCAMORE WK.
CHESTNUT CL.
ROSEWOOD CL.
FIR
HAWTHORN
APPLE CL.
BIRCH WK.
LANCEWOOD WK.
MYRTLE CL.
REDWOOD
CONINGSBY
SCAMPTON
BRUNTINGTHORPE
NORTON
BRIZE
UPPER HEYFORD
MANSTON
Millsail Plantation
High Fen
Holley's Farm
Kinghazard Belt
Brandon
Sugar Loaf
Great Rainsbutt Field Plantation
Spark's Farm
ROAD
ERISWELL
THE STREET
IP27
Lodge
Chamberlain's Farm
Piggery
LITTLE LONDON
A1065
BRANDON ROAD
Portway Hill
Eriswell
Eriswell Lode
Rec. Grd.
VICTORIA WK.
IP28
Church Farm
23
Hardpiece Belt
Foxhole Heath
F G H J K
1 2 3 4 5 6 7
72 73 74 78 79 80 81

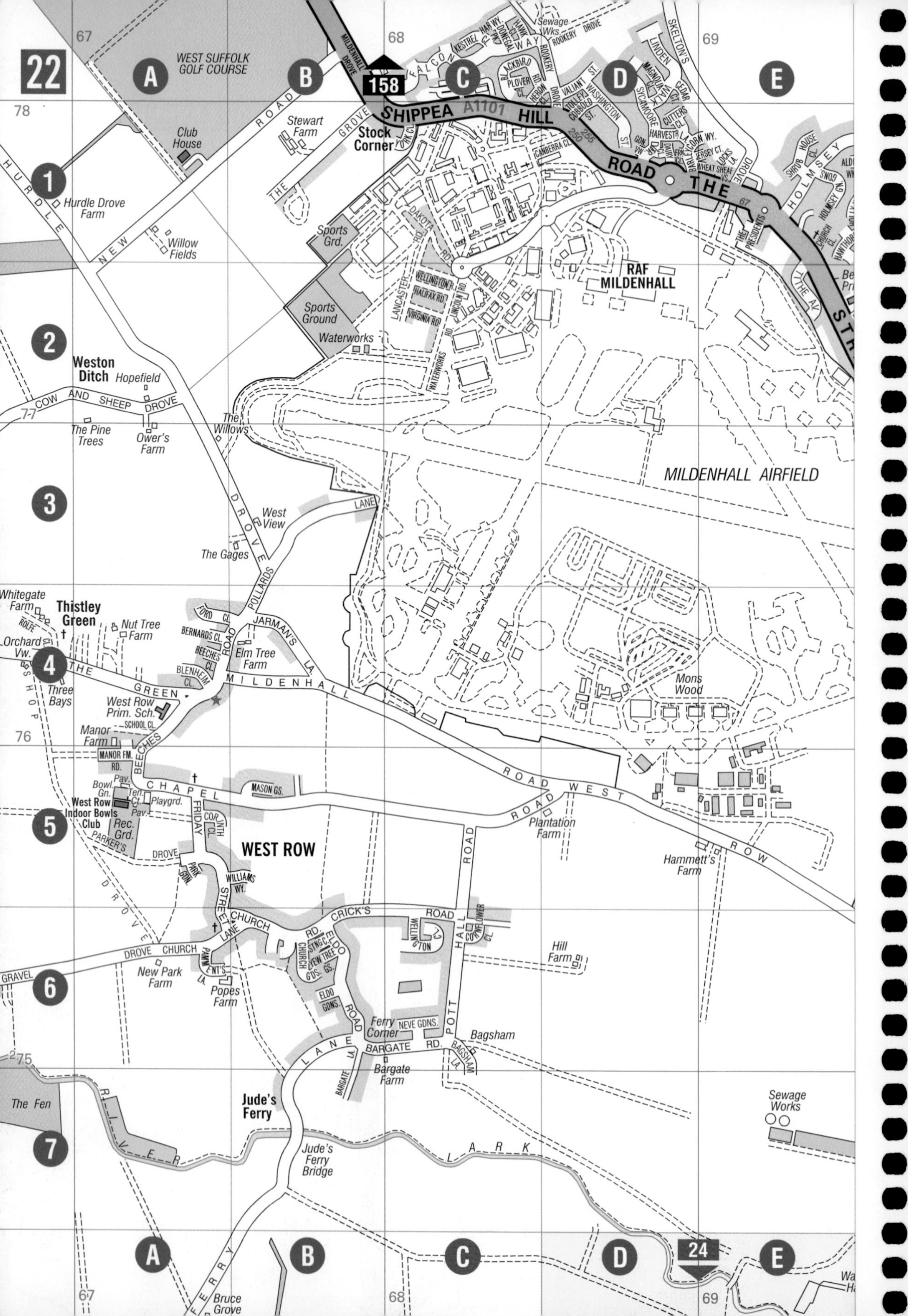
WEST SUFFOLK GOLF COURSE
Club House
Hurdle Drove Farm
Willow Fields
Stewart Farm
Stock Corner
158
SHIPPEA HILL ROAD
A1101
THE STREET
RAF MILDENHALL
MILDENHALL AIRFIELD
Sports Grd.
Sports Ground
Waterworks
Weston Ditch
Hopefield
COW AND SHEEP DROVE
The Pine Trees
Ower's Farm
The Willows
West View
The Gages
Whitegate Farm
Thistley Green
Nut Tree Farm
Orchard Vw.
Three Bays
Elm Tree Farm
MILDENHALL ROAD
West Row Prim. Sch.
Manor Farm
West Row Indoor Bowls Club
Rec. Grd.
Playgrd.
WEST ROW
Plantation Farm
Hammett's Farm
Mons Wood
Hill Farm
New Park Farm
Popes Farm
Ferry Corner
Bargate Farm
Bagsham
Jude's Ferry
Jude's Ferry Bridge
The Fen
RIVER LARK
Sewage Works
Bruce Grove
24

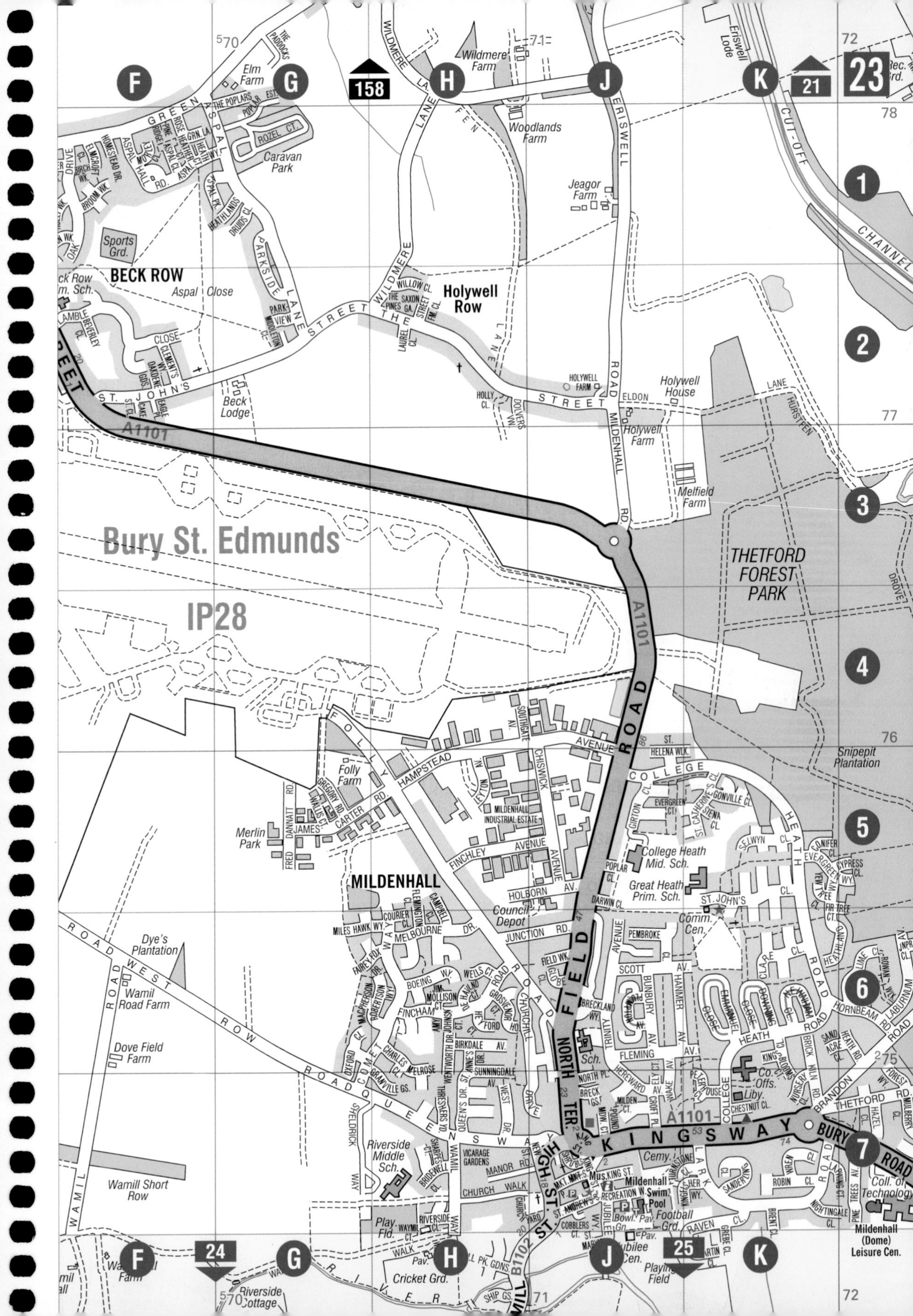

23
158
21
24
25
F
G
H
J
K
1
2
3
4
5
6
7
BECK ROW
Holywell Row
MILDENHALL
Bury St. Edmunds
IP28
THETFORD FOREST PARK
A1101
Elm Farm
Wildmere Farm
Woodlands Farm
Caravan Park
Jeagor Farm
Sports Grd.
Aspal Close
Beck Lodge
Holywell House
Holywell Farm
Melfield Farm
Folly Farm
Merlin Park
Snipepit Plantation
Dye's Plantation
Wamil Road Farm
Dove Field Farm
Wamill Short Row
Riverside Middle Sch.
College Heath Mid. Sch.
Great Heath Prim. Sch.
Council Depot
MILDENHALL INDUSTRIAL ESTATE
Comm. Cen.
Co. Offs.
Liby.
Mildenhall Swim. Pool
Football Grd.
Cricket Grd.
Playing Field
Jubilee Cen.
Coll. of Technology
Mildenhall (Dome) Leisure Cen.
Riverside Cottage
KINGSWAY
NORTH TER.
FIELD ROAD
MILDENHALL RD.
ERISWELL ROAD
WILDMERE LANE
QUEENSWAY
WEST ROW ROAD
HIGH ST.
B1102

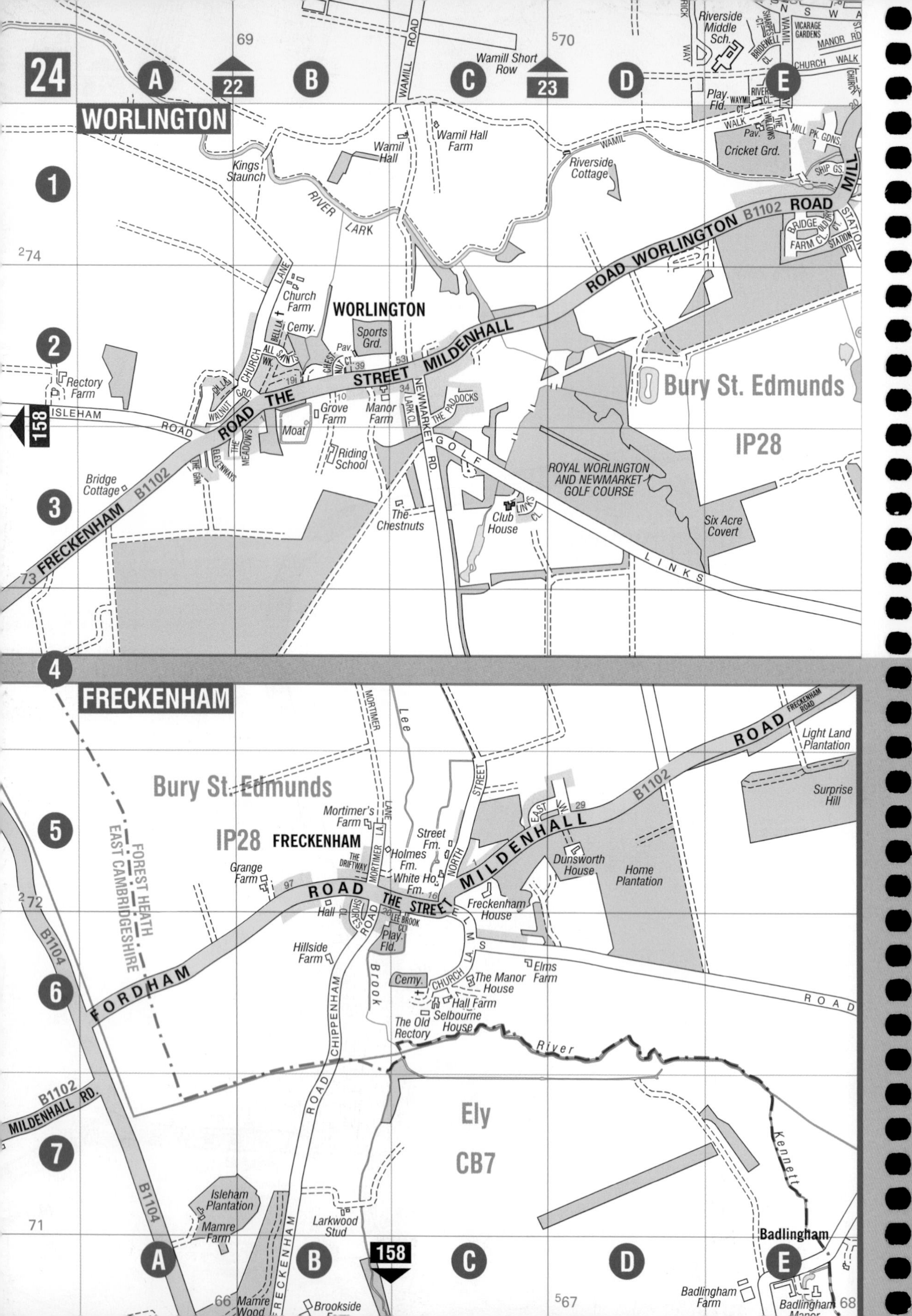
WORLINGTON
FRECKENHAM
Wamill Short Row
Riverside Middle Sch.
Wamil Hall
Wamil Hall Farm
Kings Staunch
River Lark
Riverside Cottage
Cricket Grd.
Play. Fld.
MILDENHALL ROAD
WORLINGTON ROAD
B1102
Church Farm
Cemy.
WORLINGTON
Sports Grd.
Pav.
THE STREET
Rectory Farm
ISLEHAM ROAD
Grove Farm
Manor Farm
Moat
Riding School
NEWMARKET RD.
GOLF LINKS
ROYAL WORLINGTON AND NEWMARKET GOLF COURSE
Club House
The Chestnuts
Bridge Cottage
FRECKENHAM ROAD
Bury St. Edmunds
IP28
Six Acre Covert
Mortimer's Farm
MORTIMER LANE
Lee Brook
STREET
NORTH STREET
Street Fm.
Holmes Fm.
White Ho. Fm.
Grange Farm
Hall
FORDHAM ROAD
FOREST HEATH
EAST CAMBRIDGESHIRE
Dunsworth House
Home Plantation
Freckenham House
Light Land Plantation
Surprise Hill
Hillside Farm
Play. Fld.
ELMS ROAD
Elms Farm
The Manor House
Hall Farm
The Old Rectory
Selbourne House
River Kennett
CHIPPENHAM ROAD
B1104
MILDENHALL RD.
Ely
CB7
Isleham Plantation
Mamre Farm
Larkwood Stud
Badlingham
Badlingham Farm
Badlingham Manor
Mamre Wood
Brookside

22
23
158
158

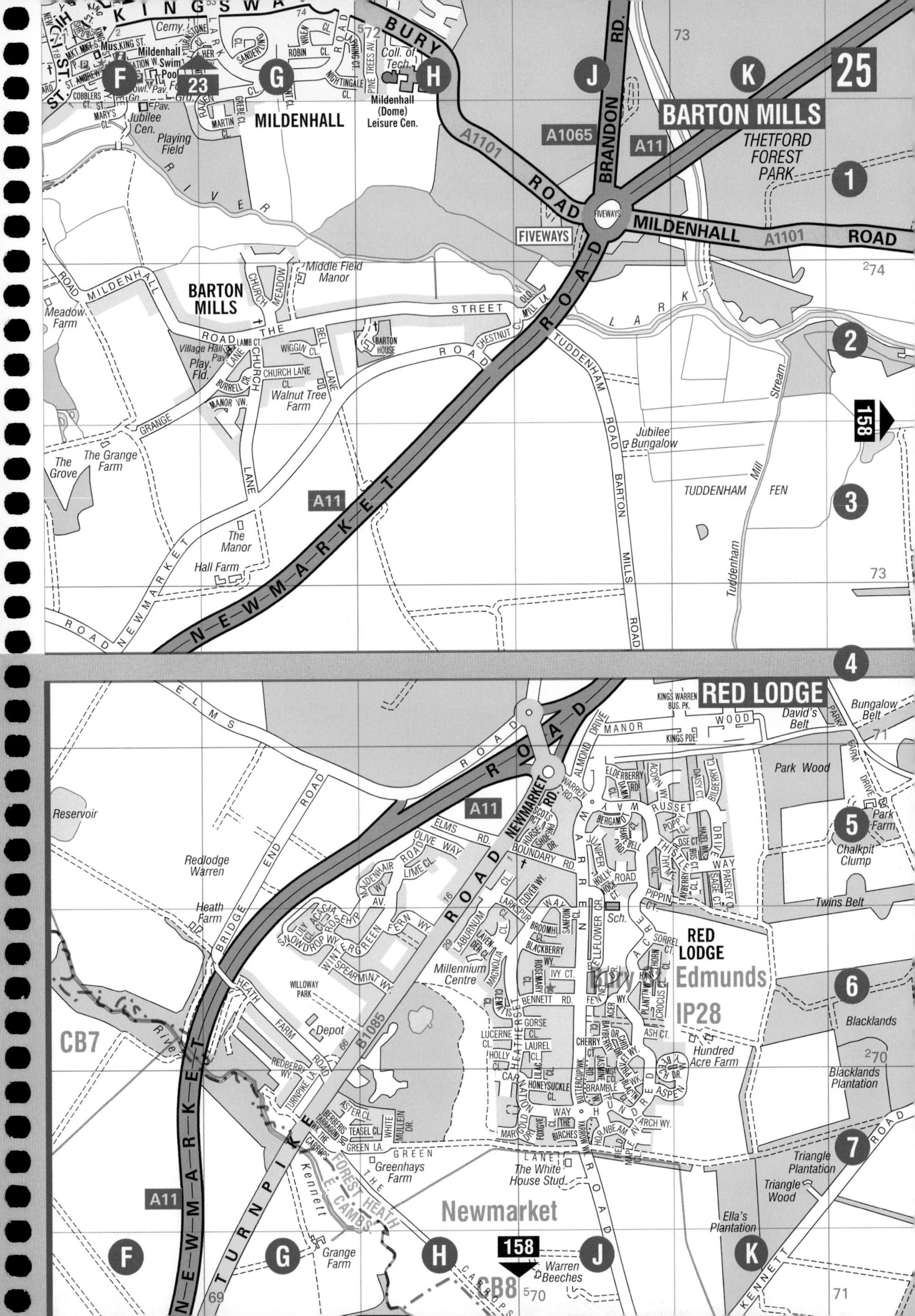

25
BARTON MILLS
THETFORD FOREST PARK
MILDENHALL
Mildenhall (Dome) Leisure Cen.
Coll. of Tech.
Jubilee Cen.
Playing Field
RIVER LARK
A1101
A1065
A11
BRANDON RD.
BURY ROAD
MILDENHALL ROAD
FIVEWAYS
Middle Field Manor
Meadow Farm
Village Hall
Play. Fld.
BARTON HOUSE
Walnut Tree Farm
The Grange Farm
The Grove
The Manor
Hall Farm
TUDDENHAM ROAD
BARTON MILLS ROAD
Jubilee Bungalow
TUDDENHAM FEN
Tuddenham Mill Stream
NEWMARKET ROAD
158
RED LODGE
KINGS WARREN BUS. PK.
Bungalow Belt
David's Belt
Park Wood
Park Farm
Chalkpit Clump
Twins Belt
Reservoir
Redlodge Warren
Heath Farm
ELMS ROAD
BRIDGE END ROAD
WARREN ROAD
Millennium Centre
WILLOWAY PARK
Depot
Sch.
Bury St. Edmunds
IP28
Hundred Acre Farm
Blacklands
Blacklands Plantation
Triangle Plantation
Triangle Wood
Ella's Plantation
CB7
CB8
TURNPIKE ROAD
B1085
Greenhays Farm
The White House Stud
Newmarket
FOREST HEATH
E. CAMBS.
Kennett
Grange Farm
Warren Beeches
KENNETT ROAD
F
G
H
J
K
1
2
3
4
5
6
7

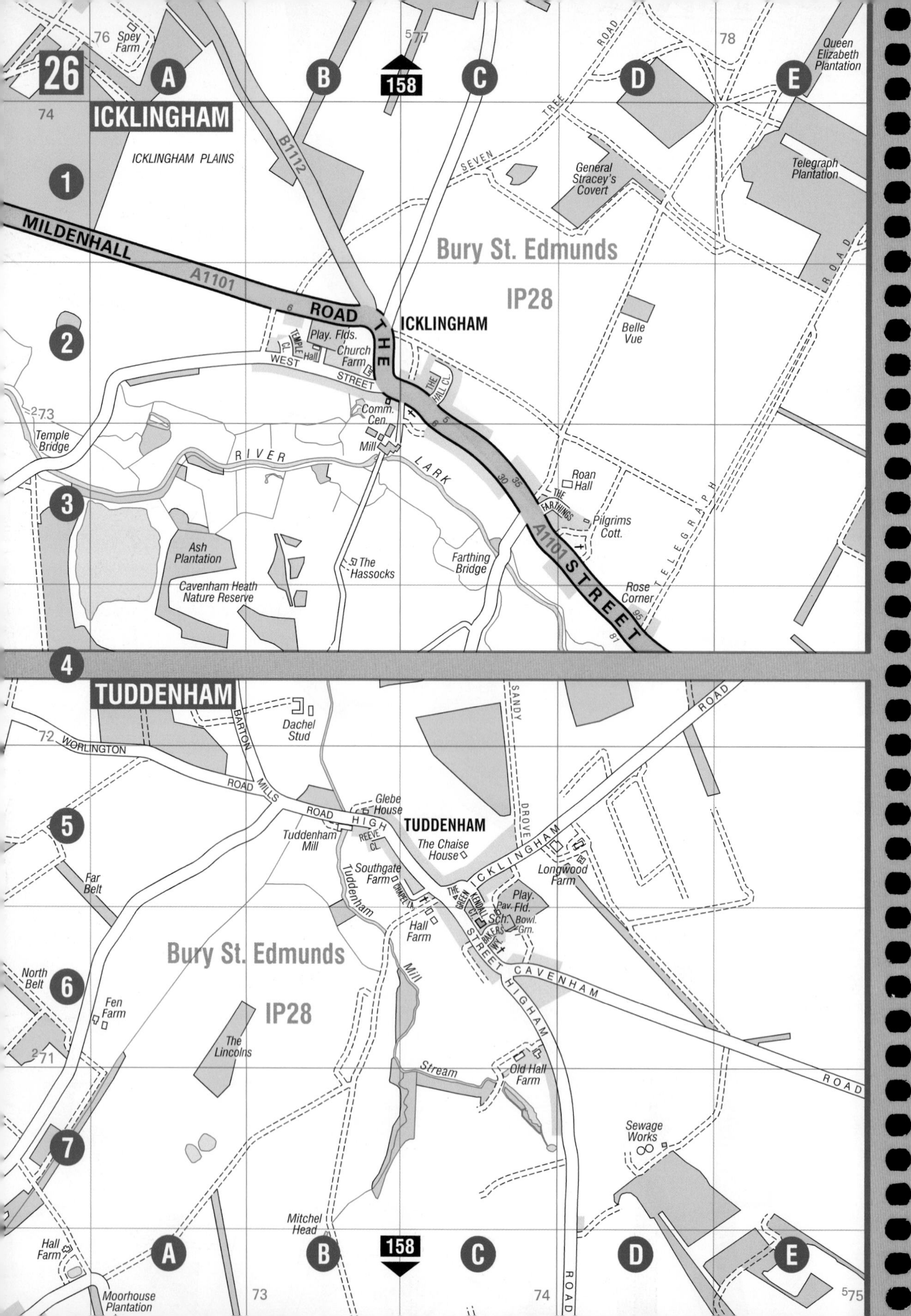

ICKLINGHAM
TUDDENHAM
A
B
C
D
E
158
1
2
3
4
5
6
7
Spey Farm
ICKLINGHAM PLAINS
B1112
MILDENHALL ROAD
A1101
THE STREET
ICKLINGHAM
Bury St. Edmunds
IP28
Play. Flds.
Church Farm
WEST STREET
TEMPLE CL.
Hall
THE HALL CL.
Comm. Cen.
Mill
Temple Bridge
RIVER LARK
Ash Plantation
Cavenham Heath Nature Reserve
The Hassocks
Farthing Bridge
Roan Hall
THE FARTHINGS
Pilgrims Cott.
Rose Corner
TELEGRAPH
SEVEN TREE ROAD
General Stracey's Covert
Belle Vue
Queen Elizabeth Plantation
Telegraph Plantation
ROAD
Dachel Stud
BARTON MILLS
WORLINGTON ROAD
SANDY DROVE
Glebe House
HIGH ROAD
TUDDENHAM
Tuddenham Mill
REEVE CL.
The Chaise House
ICKLINGHAM ROAD
Longwood Farm
Far Belt
Southgate Farm
CHAPEL LA.
THE GREEN
KENDALL CT.
Play. Fld.
Pav.
Sch.
Bowl. Grn.
BAKERS MT.
Hall Farm
STREET
CAVENHAM ROAD
HIGHAM ROAD
Tuddenham Mill Stream
Bury St. Edmunds
IP28
North Belt
Fen Farm
The Lincolns
Old Hall Farm
Sewage Works
Mitchel Head
Hall Farm
Moorhouse Plantation

158
158

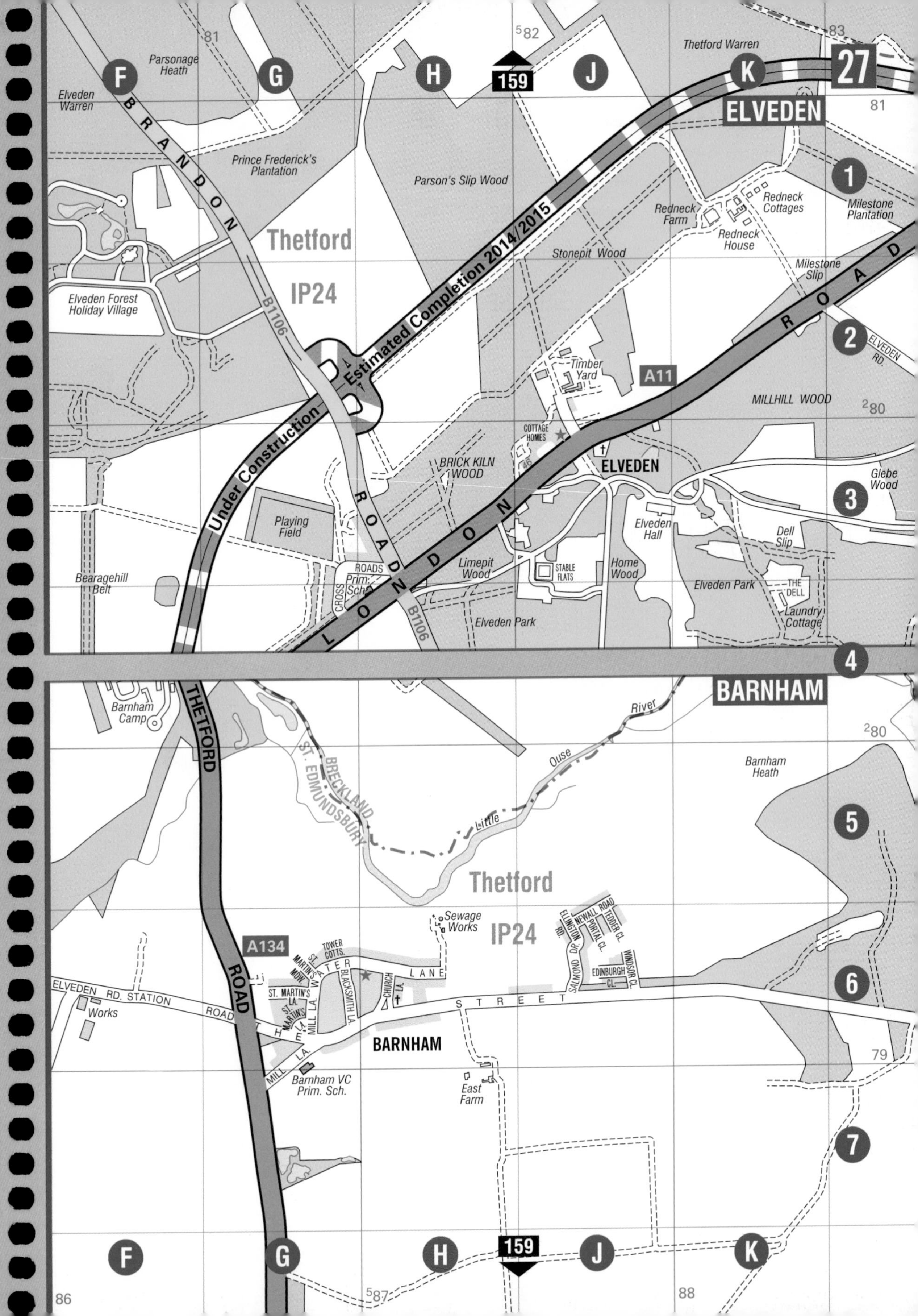
ELVEDEN
BARNHAM
Thetford
IP24
Parsonage Heath
Elveden Warren
Thetford Warren
Prince Frederick's Plantation
Parson's Slip Wood
Elveden Forest Holiday Village
BRANDON
B1106
Under Construction Estimated Completion 2014/2015
Redneck Farm
Redneck Cottages
Redneck House
Milestone Plantation
Stonepit Wood
Milestone Slip
LONDON ROAD
A11
ELVEDEN RD.
Timber Yard
MILLHILL WOOD
COTTAGE HOMES
BRICK KILN WOOD
Glebe Wood
Playing Field
Elveden Hall
Dell Slip
Bearagehill Belt
CROSS ROADS Prim. Sch.
Limepit Wood
STABLE FLATS
Home Wood
Elveden Park
THE DELL
Laundry Cottage
Barnham Camp
THETFORD ROAD
River Little Ouse
BRECKLAND
ST. EDMUNDSBURY
Barnham Heath
Sewage Works
A134
TOWER COTTS.
ST. MARTIN'S MDW.
WATER LANE
BLACKSMITH LA.
CHURCH LA.
ELLINGTON RD.
NEWALL ROAD
PORTAL CL.
TEDDER CL.
SALMOND DR.
WINDSOR CL.
EDINBURGH CL.
ELVEDEN RD.
STATION ROAD
STREET
ST. MARTIN'S LA.
MILL LA.
Works
BARNHAM
Barnham VC Prim. Sch.
East Farm
159
F G H J K
1 2 3 4 5 6 7
81 582 83 81 280 79 86 587 88

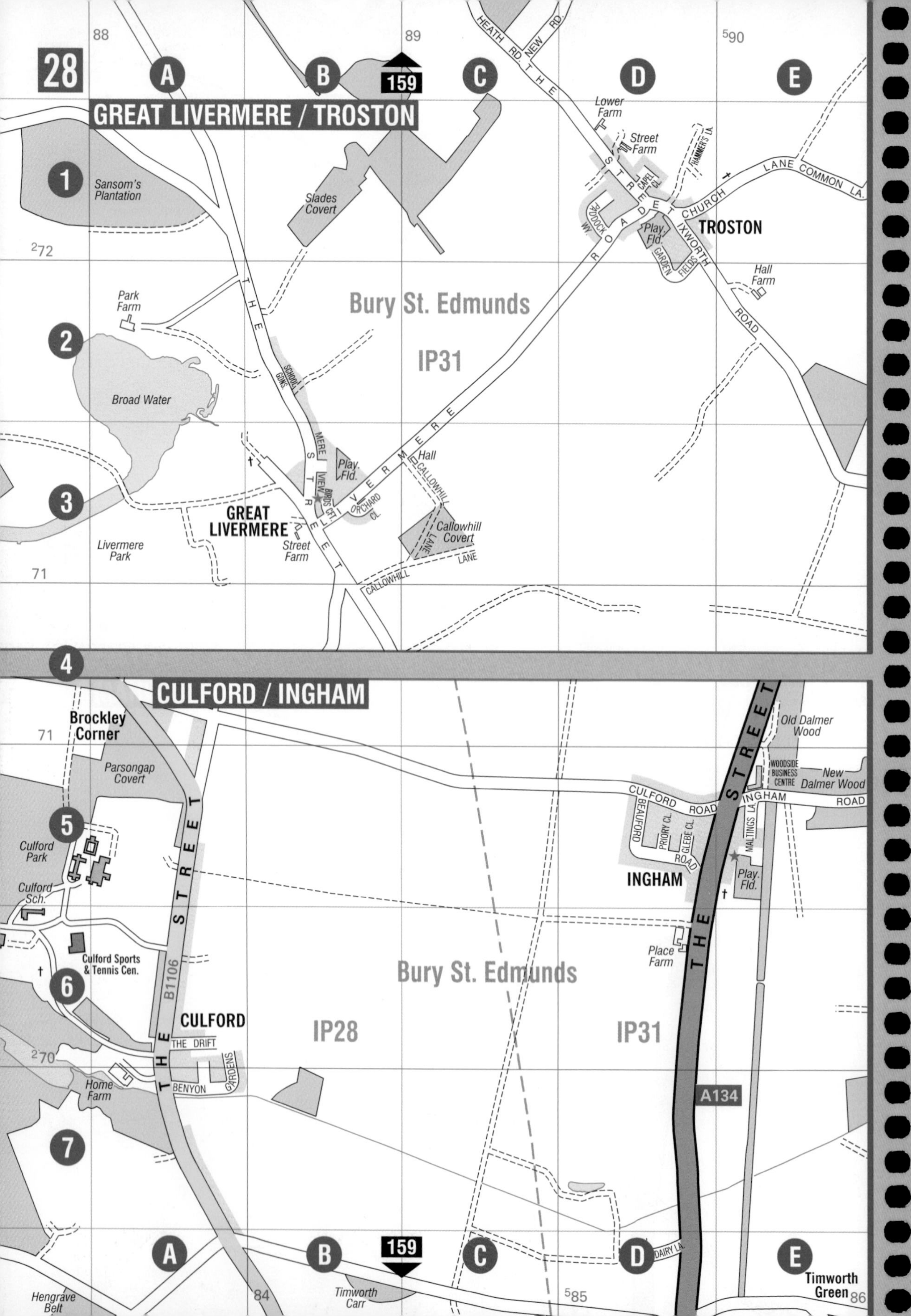

GREAT LIVERMERE / TROSTON
159
Sansom's Plantation
Slades Covert
Lower Farm
Street Farm
HEATH RD
NEW RD.
THE STREET
CAPEL CL.
HAMMER'S LA.
CHURCH LANE
COMMON LA.
PADDOCK WY.
ROAD
Play. Fld.
GARDEN FIELDS
IXWORTH ROAD
TROSTON
Hall Farm
Park Farm
Bury St. Edmunds
IP31
Broad Water
SCHOOL GDNS.
MERE VIEW
BIRDS CFT.
LIVERMERE
ORCHARD CL.
Hall
CALLOWHILL LANE
GREAT LIVERMERE
Street Farm
Callowhill Covert
Livermere Park
CALLOWHILL LANE
CULFORD / INGHAM
Brockley Corner
Parsongap Covert
Culford Park
Culford Sch.
Culford Sports & Tennis Cen.
B1106
THE STREET
CULFORD
THE DRIFT
BENYON GARDENS
Home Farm
Old Dalmer Wood
WOODSIDE BUSINESS CENTRE
New Dalmer Wood
CULFORD ROAD
BEAUFORD ROAD
PRIORY CL.
GLEBE CL.
INGHAM ROAD
MALTINGS LA.
INGHAM
Play. Fld.
Place Farm
Bury St. Edmunds
IP28
IP31
A134
DAIRY LA.
Hengrave Belt
Timworth Carr
Timworth Green

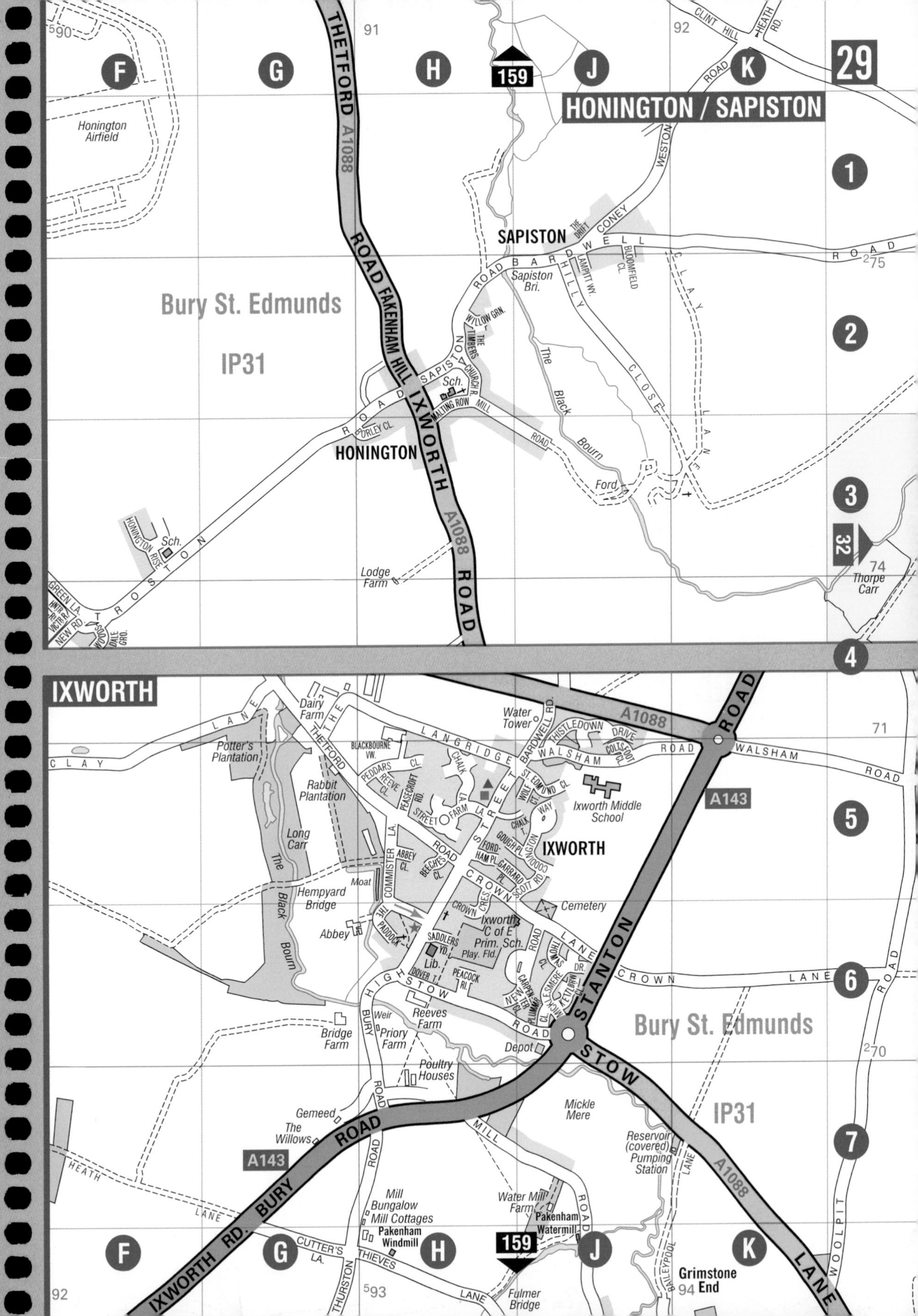
HONINGTON / SAPISTON
IXWORTH
Honington Airfield
Bury St. Edmunds
IP31
SAPISTON
HONINGTON
Sapiston Bri.
The Black Bourn
Ford
Lodge Farm
Thorpe Carr
THETFORD ROAD A1088
FAKENHAM HILL
IXWORTH ROAD
BARDWELL ROAD
CONEY WESTON ROAD
CLINT HILL
HEATH RD.
SAPISTON ROAD
TROSTON ROAD
MILL ROAD
HILLY CLOSE
CLAY LANE
Potter's Plantation
Rabbit Plantation
Long Carr
Dairy Farm
Water Tower
Ixworth Middle School
IXWORTH
Hempyard Bridge
Moat
Abbey
Cemetery
Ixworth C of E Prim. Sch.
Play. Fld.
Lib.
Reeves Farm
Priory Farm
Weir
Bridge Farm
Depot
Poultry Houses
Gemeed
The Willows
Mickle Mere
Reservoir (covered) Pumping Station
Water Mill Farm
Pakenham Watermill
Mill Bungalow
Mill Cottages
Pakenham Windmill
Grimstone End
Fulmer Bridge
LANGRIDGE
WALSHAM ROAD
STANTON ROAD
STOW ROAD
CROWN LANE
BURY ROAD
IXWORTH RD.
HIGH STREET
WOOLPIT ROAD
LANE
A143
A1088
159
32

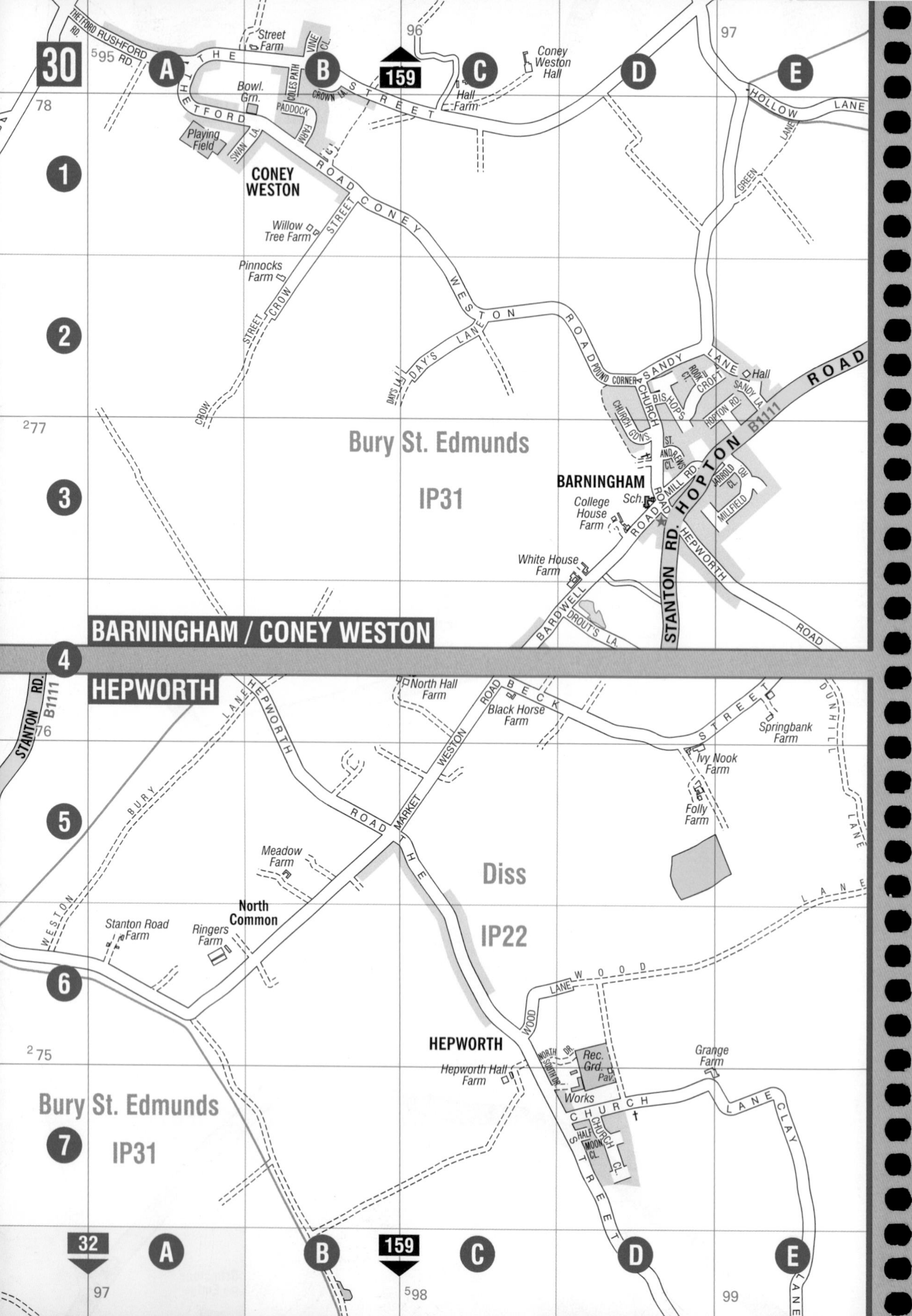

BARNINGHAM / CONEY WESTON
HEPWORTH
CONEY WESTON
BARNINGHAM
HEPWORTH
North Common
Bury St. Edmunds
IP31
Diss
IP22
Bury St. Edmunds
IP31
THE STREET
THETFORD ROAD
RUSHFORD RD.
THETFORD RD.
Street Farm
Coney Weston Hall
Hall Farm
Bowl. Grn.
Playing Field
SWAN LA.
COLES PATH
VINE CL.
PADDOCK
FARM
CROWN LA.
HOLLOW LANE
GREEN LANE
CONEY WESTON ROAD
CROW STREET
Willow Tree Farm
Pinnocks Farm
DAY'S LANE
DAY'S LA.
POUND CORNER
SANDY LANE
SANDY LA.
Hall
ROOK CT.
CROFT
BISHOPS
CHURCH GDNS.
CHURCH ROAD
ST. ANDREWS CL.
HOPTON RD.
MILL RD.
JARROLD CL.
MILLFIELD
HOPTON ROAD
B1111
Sch.
College House Farm
White House Farm
STANTON RD.
HEPWORTH ROAD
BARDWELL ROAD
DROUT'S LA.
STANTON RD. B1111
HEPWORTH LANE
HEPWORTH ROAD
North Hall Farm
BECK STREET
Black Horse Farm
Springbank Farm
Ivy Nook Farm
Folly Farm
DUNHILL LANE
WESTON ROAD
MARKET WESTON ROAD
THE STREET
BURY ROAD
WESTON
Meadow Farm
Stanton Road Farm
Ringers Farm
LANE
WOOD LANE
WOOD
NORTH DR.
SOUTH DR.
Rec. Grd.
Pav.
Works
Hepworth Hall Farm
Grange Farm
CHURCH LANE
CLAY LANE
CHURCH CL.
HALF MOON CL.
CHURCH STREET
159
32
96
97
78
595
277
276
275
97
598
99
A B C D E
1 2 3 4 5 6 7

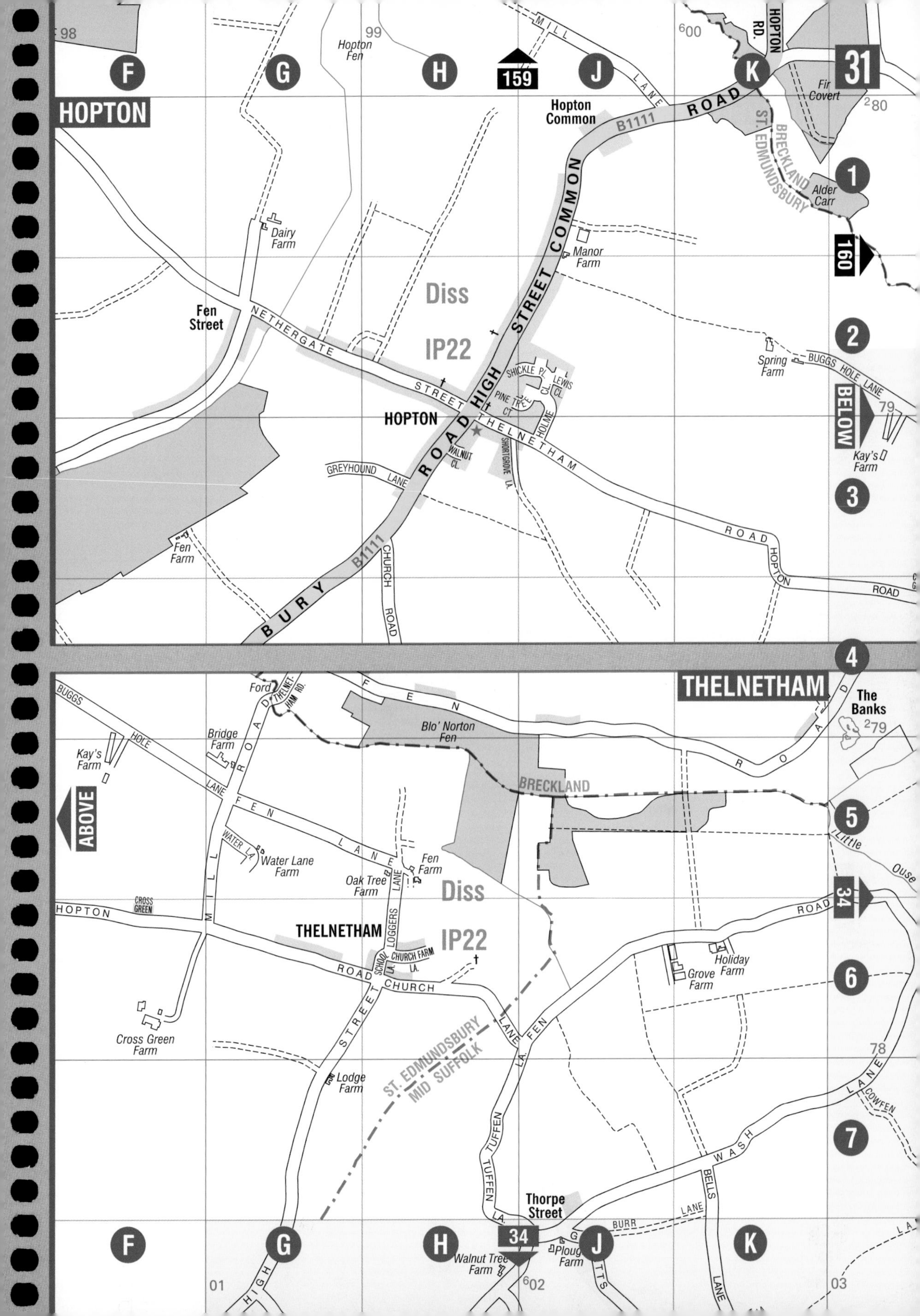

31
HOPTON
THELNETHAM
F
G
H
J
K
159
160
34
BELOW
ABOVE
1
2
3
4
5
6
7
98
99
600
01
602
03
280
79
279
78
Hopton Fen
Hopton Common
MILL LANE
HOPTON RD.
B1111 ROAD
ST. EDMUNDSBURY
BRECKLAND
Fir Covert
Alder Carr
Dairy Farm
Manor Farm
Diss
IP22
Fen Street
NETHERGATE STREET
HIGH STREET COMMON
SHICKLE PL.
LEWIS CL.
PINE TREE CT.
HOLME
Spring Farm
BUGGS HOLE LANE
Kay's Farm
HOPTON
THELNETHAM ROAD
WALNUT CL.
SHORTGROVE LA.
GREYHOUND LANE
Fen Farm
BURY ROAD B1111
CHURCH ROAD
HOPTON ROAD
Ford
THELNETHAM RD.
FEN ROAD
The Banks
BUGGS HOLE LANE
Bridge Farm
Blo' Norton Fen
BRECKLAND
FEN LANE
WATER LA.
Water Lane Farm
Little Ouse
MILL ROAD
Fen Farm
Oak Tree Farm
LOGGERS LANE
HOPTON
CROSS GREEN
ROAD
THELNETHAM
SCHOOL LA.
CHURCH FARM LA.
Grove Farm
Holiday Farm
CHURCH LANE
FEN LA.
Cross Green Farm
STREET
ST. EDMUNDSBURY
MID SUFFOLK
Lodge Farm
COWFEN LANE
TUFFEN LA.
WASH LANE
BELLS LANE
Thorpe Street
BURR LANE
Walnut Tree Farm
Plough Farm
HIGH

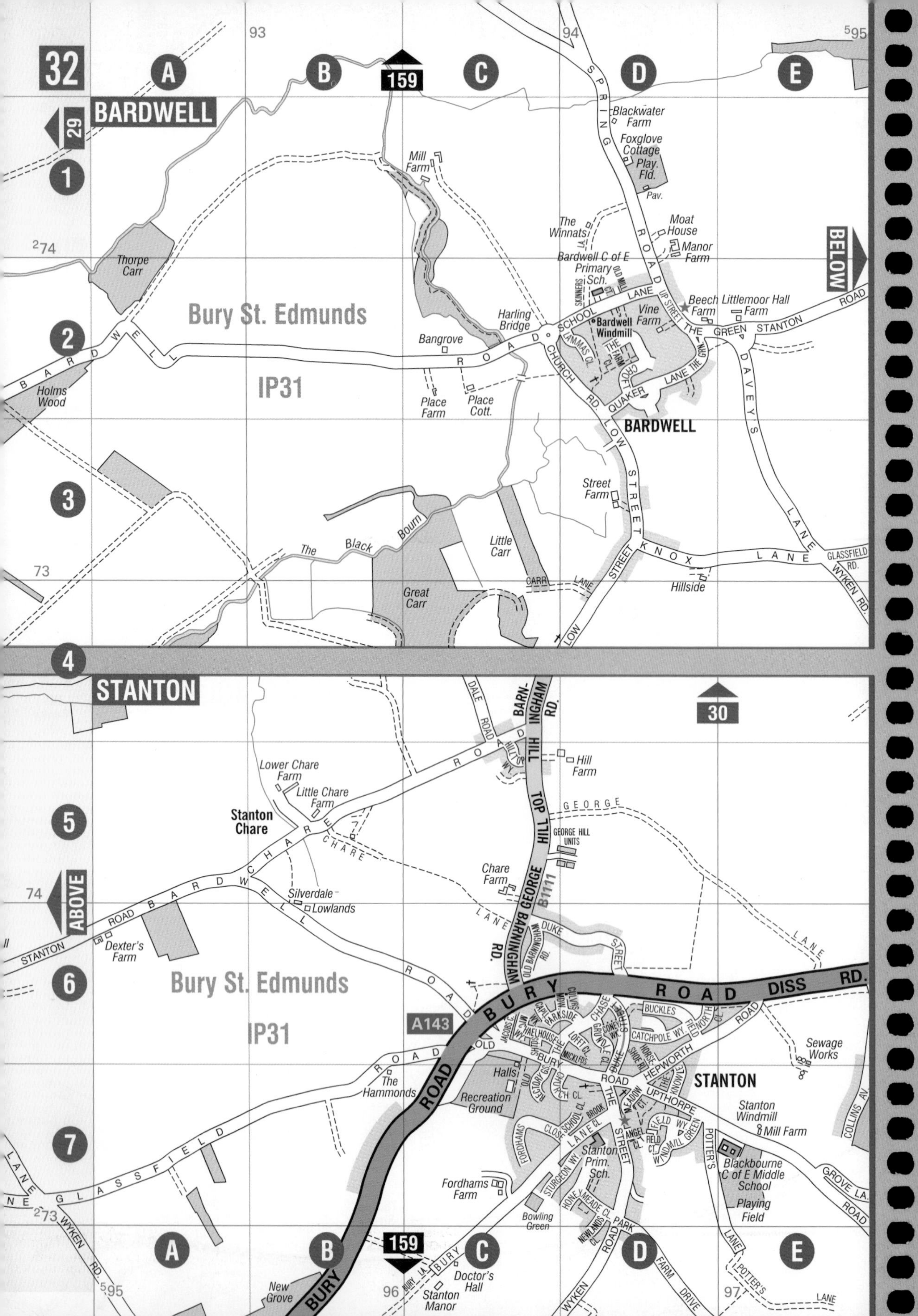
BARDWELL
29
159
BELOW
Blackwater Farm
Foxglove Cottage
Play. Fld.
Pav.
Mill Farm
The Winnats
Moat House
Manor Farm
Thorpe Carr
Bardwell C of E Primary Sch.
Beech Farm
Littlemoor Hall Farm
Bury St. Edmunds
Harling Bridge
Bardwell Windmill
Vine Farm
Bangrove
SCHOOL LANE
THE GREEN
STANTON ROAD
BARDWELL ROAD
CHURCH RD.
QUAKER LANE
DAVEYS LANE
Holms Wood
IP31
Place Farm
Place Cott.
BARDWELL
LOW STREET
Street Farm
The Black Bourn
Little Carr
Great Carr
KNOX LANE
GLASSFIELD RD.
WYKEN RD.
CARR LANE
Hillside
STANTON
30
DALE ROAD
BARNINGHAM RD.
HILL TOP
Hill Farm
Lower Chare Farm
Little Chare Farm
Stanton Chare
CHARE ROAD
GEORGE HILL
GEORGE HILL UNITS
Chare Farm
B1111
ABOVE
Silverdale
Lowlands
BARDWELL ROAD
STANTON ROAD
Dexter's Farm
DUKE STREET
Bury St. Edmunds
BURY ROAD
DISS RD.
IP31
A143
Sewage Works
The Hammonds
Halls
Recreation Ground
CATCHPOLE WY.
HEPWORTH ROAD
UPTHORPE
STANTON
THE STREET
Stanton Windmill
Mill Farm
GLASSFIELD
Stanton Prim. Sch.
Blackbourne C of E Middle School
Playing Field
Fordhams Farm
Bowling Green
GROVE LA.
GROVE ROAD
POTTER'S LANE
PARK ROAD
159
Doctor's Hall
Stanton Manor
New Grove
WYKEN ROAD
FARM DRIVE
BURY LA.
93
94
95
96
97
74
73
A
B
C
D
E
1
2
3
4
5
6
7

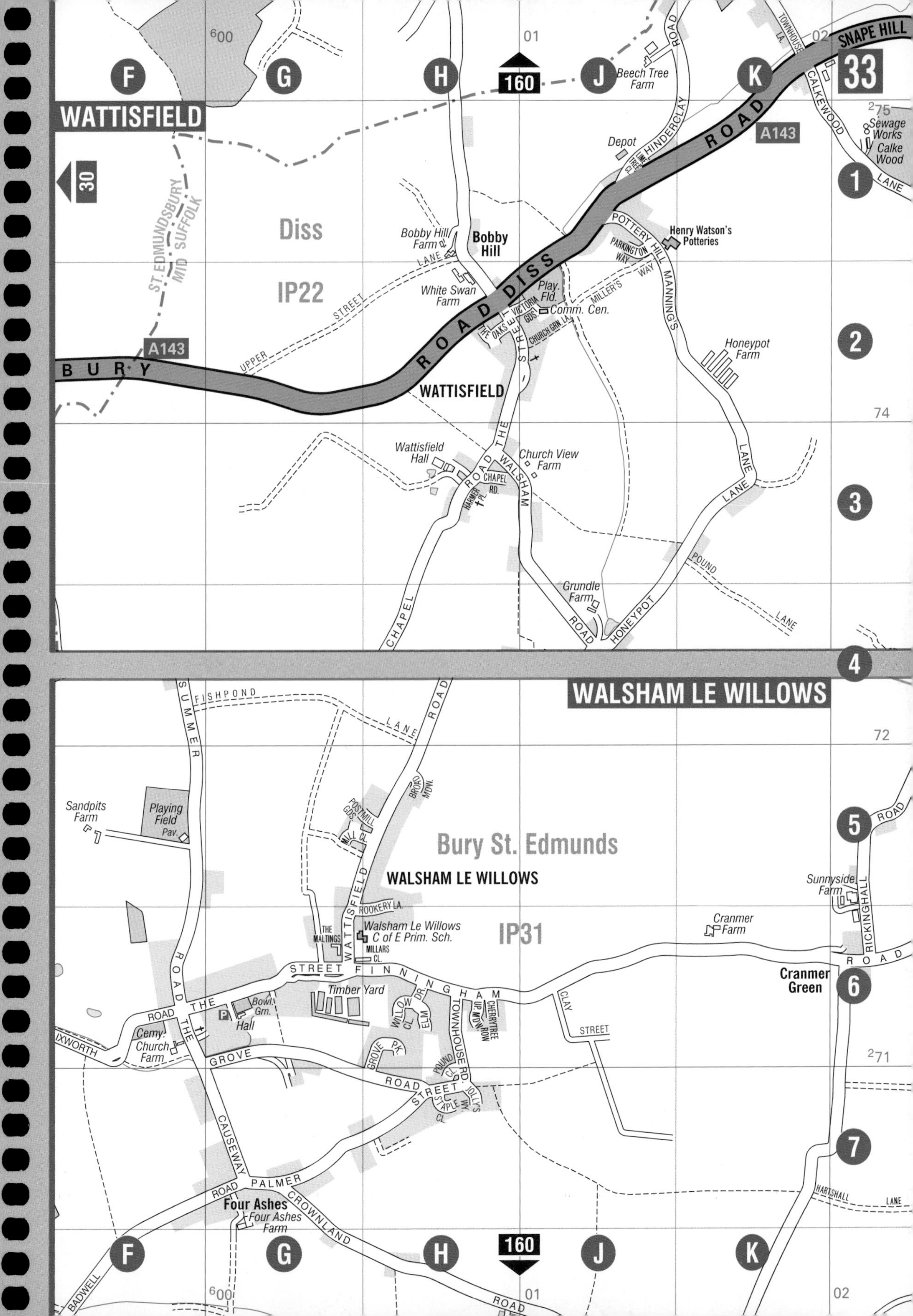

WATTISFIELD
WALSHAM LE WILLOWS
Diss
IP22
Bury St. Edmunds
IP31
Bobby Hill
Bobby Hill Farm
White Swan Farm
Beech Tree Farm
Depot
Henry Watson's Potteries
Honeypot Farm
Wattisfield Hall
Church View Farm
Grundle Farm
Play. Fld.
Comm. Cen.
Sewage Works
Calke Wood
Sandpits Farm
Playing Field
Pav.
Walsham Le Willows C of E Prim. Sch.
Timber Yard
Bowl. Grn.
Hall
Cemy.
Church Farm
Cranmer Farm
Cranmer Green
Sunnyside Farm
Four Ashes
Four Ashes Farm
BURY ROAD DISS ROAD
SNAPE HILL
A143
ST. EDMUNDSBURY
MID SUFFOLK
UPPER STREET LANE
HINDERCLAY ROAD
LIME TREE CL.
TOWNHOUSE LA.
CALKEWOOD LANE
POTTERY HILL
PARKINGTON WAY
MILLER'S WAY
MANNING'S LANE
THE STREET
THE OAKS
VICTORIA GDS.
CHURCH GRN. LA.
THE WALSHAM ROAD
CHAPEL RD.
HARMER PL.
CHAPEL ROAD
GRUNDLE ROAD
HONEYPOT LANE
POUND LANE
FISHPOND LANE
SUMMER ROAD
WATTISFIELD ROAD
BROAD MDW.
POSTMILL GDS.
MILL CL.
ROOKERY LA.
THE MALTINGS
MILLARS CL.
THE STREET
FINNINGHAM ROAD
WILLOW CL.
ELM DR.
TOWNHOUSE RD.
UP. MDW. ROW
CHERRYTREE ROW
CLAY STREET
IXWORTH ROAD
THE CAUSEWAY
GROVE ROAD
GROVE PK.
POUND CL.
STREET
STAPLE CL.
JOLLY'S WY.
PALMER ROAD
CROWNLAND ROAD
BADWELL ROAD
RICKINGHALL ROAD
HARTSHALL LANE
160
30
F G H J K
1 2 3 4 5 6 7
600 01 02
275 74 72 271

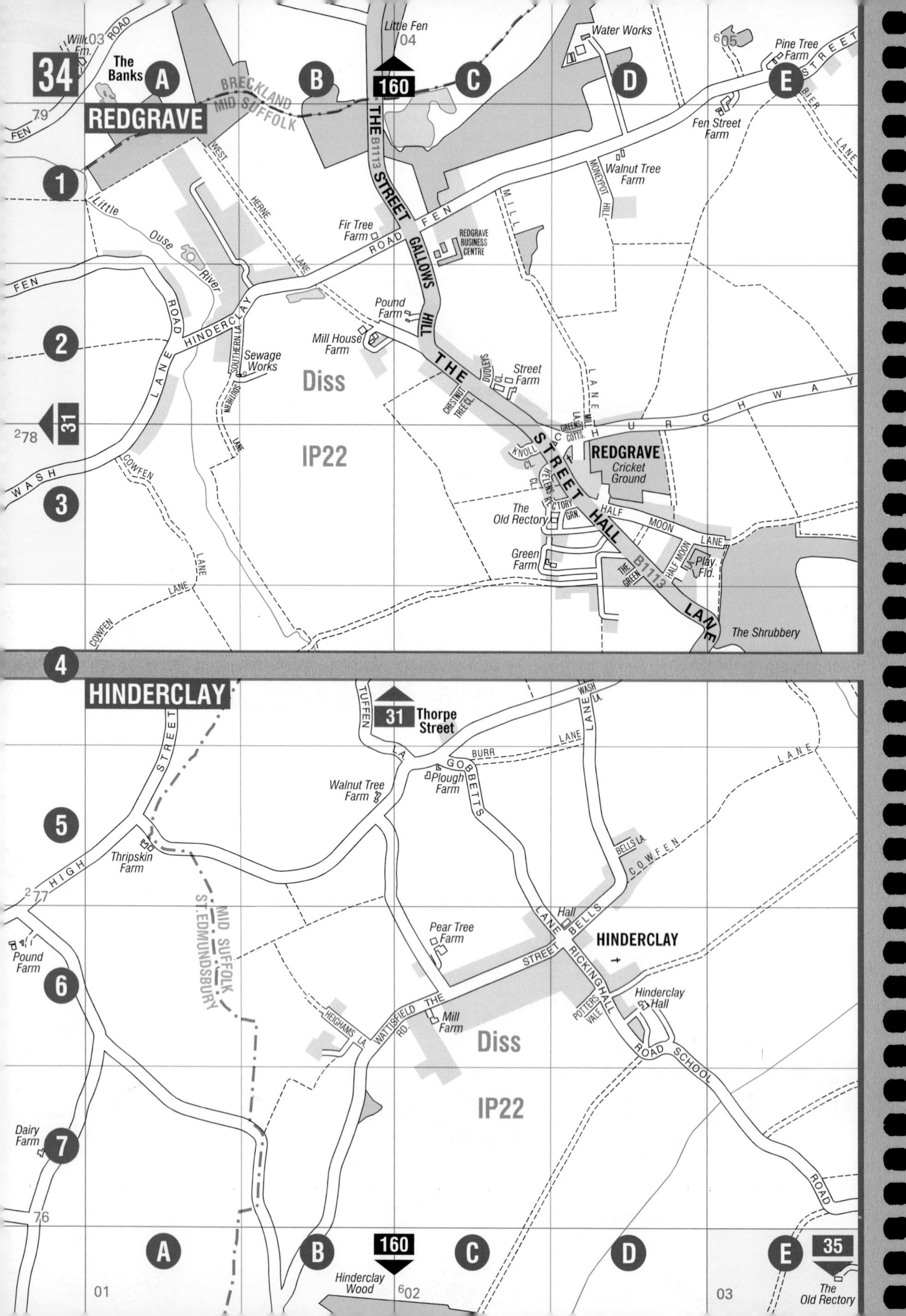

160
31
31 Thorpe Street
160
35

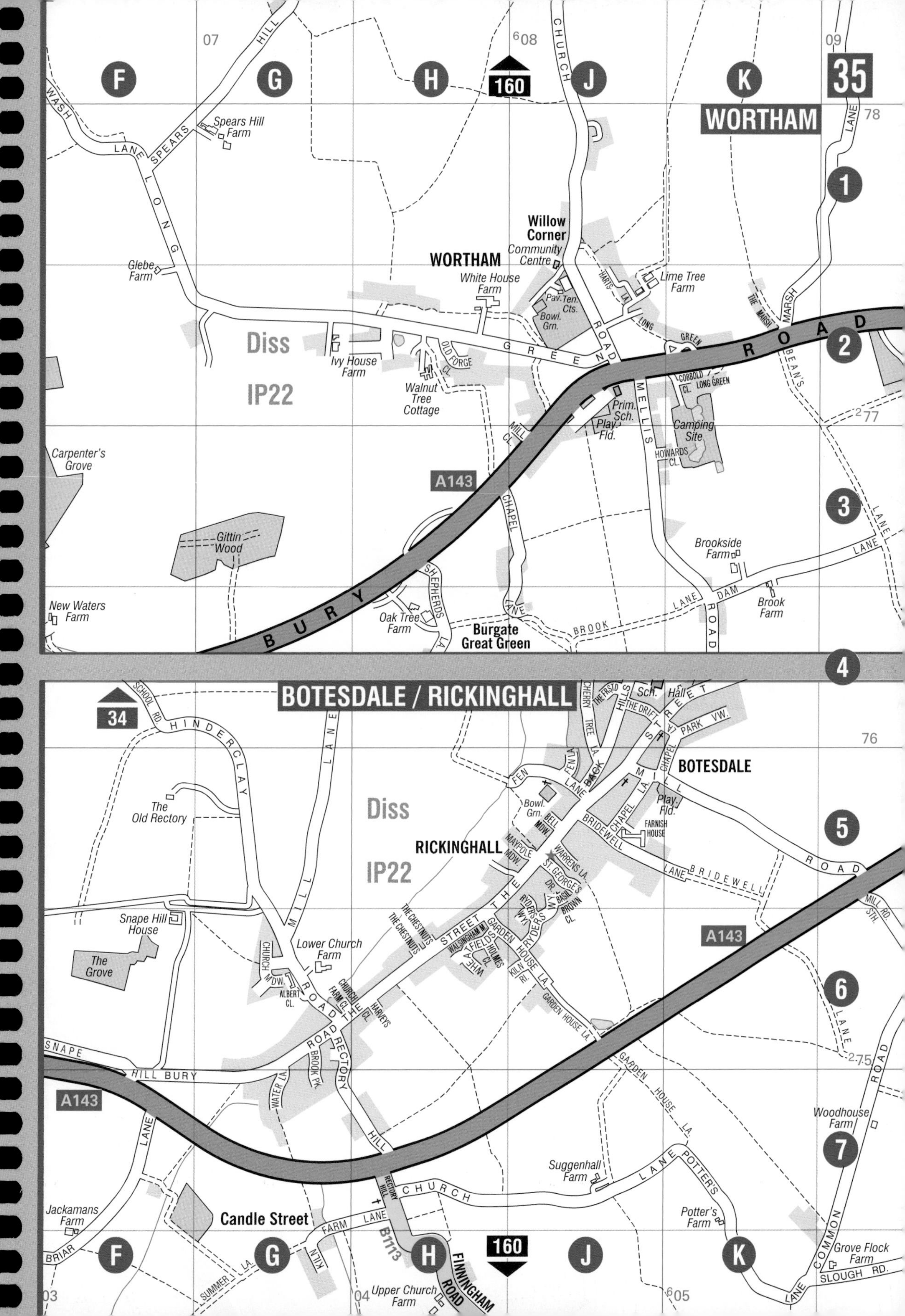
WORTHAM
BOTESDALE / RICKINGHALL
160
34
Spears Hill Farm
Glebe Farm
Willow Corner
Community Centre
WORTHAM
White House Farm
Lime Tree Farm
Pav. Ten. Cts.
Bowl. Grn.
Diss
IP22
Ivy House Farm
Walnut Tree Cottage
Prim. Sch.
Play. Fld.
Camping Site
Carpenter's Grove
A143
Gittin Wood
Brookside Farm
New Waters Farm
Oak Tree Farm
Burgate Great Green
Brook Farm
BURY ROAD
GREEN
LONG GREEN
MELLIS ROAD
CHURCH ROAD
LONG LANE
SPEARS HILL
WASH LANE
MARSH LANE
THE MARSH
BEAN'S LANE
OLD FORGE CL.
MILL CL.
CHAPEL LANE
SHEPHERDS LA.
HOWARDS CL.
COBBOLD CL.
HARTS LA.
DAM LANE
BROOK
The Old Rectory
Snape Hill House
The Grove
Lower Church Farm
RICKINGHALL
BOTESDALE
Bowl. Grn.
Play. Fld.
FARNISH HOUSE
Sch.
Hall
HINDERCLAY
SCHOOL RD.
MILL LANE
FEN LANE
BACK
CHERRY TREE LA.
THE FRSTD
HILLS
THE DRIFT
PARK VW.
STREET
CHAPEL LA.
BRIDEWELL LANE
BRIDEWELL ROAD
MAYPOLE MDW.
BELL MDW.
WARRENS LA.
ST. GEORGE'S DR.
BASIL WY.
BROWN CL.
RYDERS WY.
THE STREET
THE CHESTNUTS
WALSINGHAM M.
WHEATFIELDS
HOLMES CL.
GARDEN HOUSE LA.
KILN RI.
CHURCH MDW.
ALBERT CL.
CHURCH FARM CL.
THE HARVEYS CL.
CHURCH ROAD
RECTORY HILL
SNAPE HILL
BURY ROAD
WATER LA.
BROOK PK.
MILL RD. STH.
Woodhouse Farm
Suggenhall Farm
Jackamans Farm
Candle Street
Potter's Farm
Grove Flock Farm
Upper Church Farm
BRIAR LANE
FARM LANE
KILN
SUMMER LA.
B1113
FINNINGHAM ROAD
CHURCH LANE
POTTER'S LANE
COMMON LANE
SLOUGH RD.
F
G
H
J
K
1
2
3
4
5
6
7
03
04
05
07
08
09
75
76
77
78

PALGRAVE
MELLIS / YAXLEY
LING ROAD
Depot
Oak Farm
Elm Vale Cottage
Elm Vale Farm
Sewage Works
160
DENMARK HILL
DENMARK CT.
LOW'S LA.
GOULDS CL.
Community Centre
Play. Flds.
FORGE BUSINESS CEN.
FORGE CL.
COMMON HILL
UPPER ROSE LANE
LWR. ROSE LA.
ROSE LA.
ROSE LANE CL.
MILLWAY LANE
Millway Farm
PALGRAVE
GEORGE CL.
CHURCH FARM CL.
THE GREEN
ROSE CROSSING
COLEMAN CL.
LIMES CL.
BURLINGTON CL.
BLAND'S FARM CL.
ROAD
CLARKE CL.
SYCAMORE CL.
PRIORY CL.
PRIORY RD.
DRAYCOTT RI.
IP22
Diss
JOB'S LANE
ROAD
37
OLD BURY RD.
IP21
A143
OLD BURY ROAD
NEW ROAD
LION
St. John's House
Goodrich Park
Valley Farm
Dairy Farm
Pond Farm
OLD BURY RD.
THRANDESTON ROAD
LEYS
JUDAS LANE
IP21
Elm Tree Farm
THE MELLIS COMMON
ROBINSONS MILL
ROBINSONS CL.
EARLSFORD RD.
BROWNS ACRE
AGGAS ACRE
Yaxley Manor House
Chapel Farm
Vine Farm
Play. Fld.
Whitegates Farm
MELLIS
Mellis C of E Primary School
ROAD
LANE
NORWICH ROAD
White Ho.Fm.
OLD THE STREET
Bungalow Farm
CHERRY TREE CL.
ST. BREADES CL.
BURNS CL.
MAPLE CL.
Eye
EYE RD.
ROAD
IP23
A140
EARLSFORD
RECTORY RD.
YAXLEY
CHURCH LA.
LYON CL.
MILLSIDE
IPSWICH
Valley Farm Barn
ROAD
Beacon Hill
The Hall
YAXLEY HALL LA.
HALL LA.
Storehouse Farm
IPSWICH ROAD
OLD
A B C D E
1 2 3 4 5 6 7
610 11 12
79 278 275 74

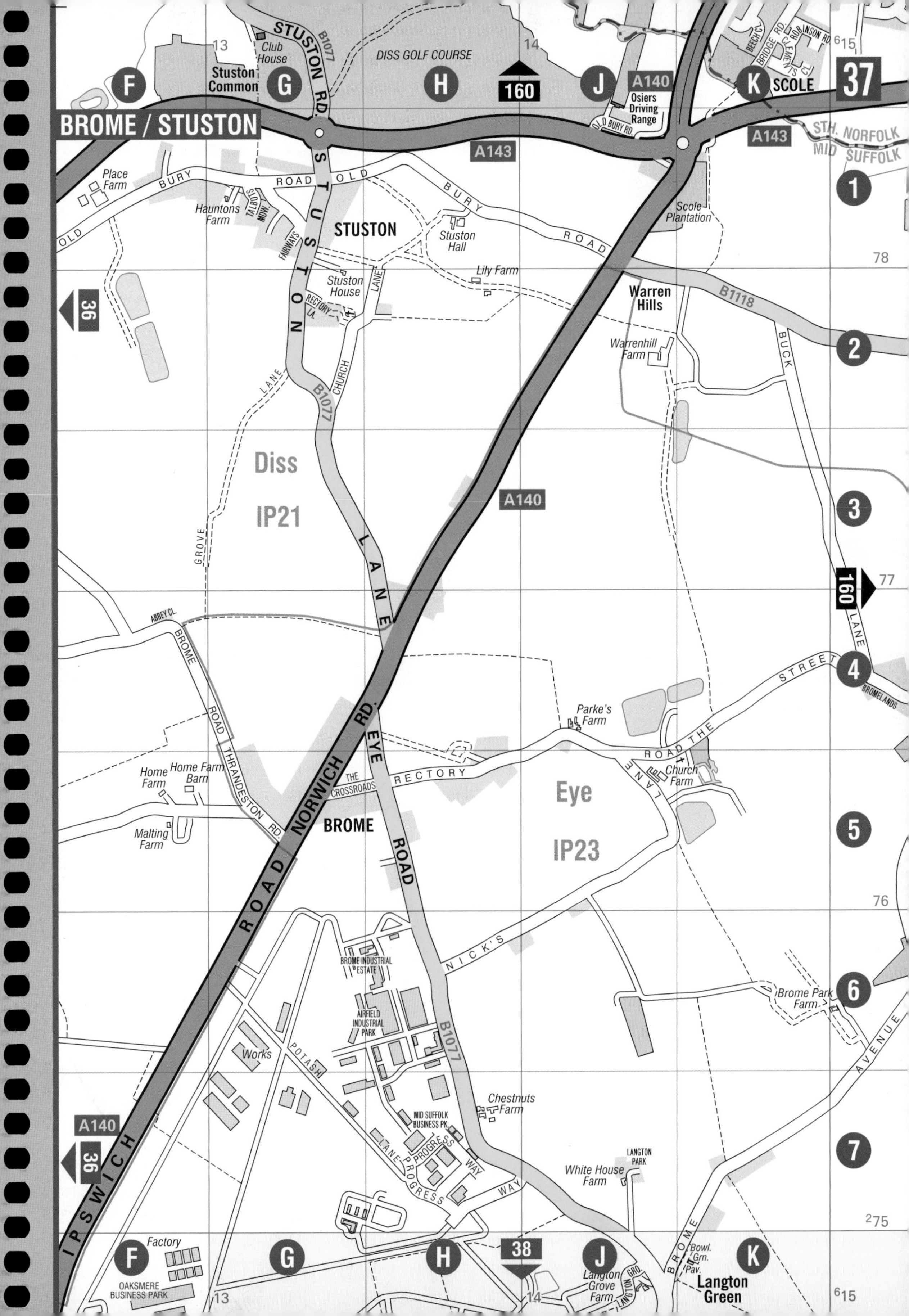
BROME / STUSTON
SCOLE
Stuston Common
Club House
DISS GOLF COURSE
160
Osiers Driving Range
A140
A143
STH. NORFOLK
MID SUFFOLK
STUSTON RD.
B1077
Place Farm
OLD BURY ROAD
Hauntons Farm
STUSTON
Stuston Hall
Scole Plantation
Stuston House
Lily Farm
Warren Hills
B1118
Warrenhill Farm
STUSTON LANE
RECTORY LA.
CHURCH LANE
BUCK LANE
36
Diss
IP21
GROVE LANE
ABBEY CL.
BROME ROAD
THE STREET
BROMELANDS
Parke's Farm
Church Farm
Home Farm
Home Farm Barn
THRANDESTON RD.
THE CROSSROADS
RECTORY ROAD
Eye
IP23
Malting Farm
BROME
NORWICH RD.
EYE ROAD
IPSWICH ROAD
NICK'S LANE
BROME INDUSTRIAL ESTATE
AIRFIELD INDUSTRIAL PARK
Works
POTASH LANE
Chestnuts Farm
Brome Park Farm
AVENUE
MID SUFFOLK BUSINESS PK.
PROGRESS WAY
LANGTON PARK
White House Farm
Factory
OAKSMERE BUSINESS PARK
38
Langton Grove Farm
LANGTON GRO.
BROME
Bowl. Grn.
Pav.
Langton Green
F
G
H
J
K
1
2
3
4
5
6
7
13
14
615
78
77
76
275

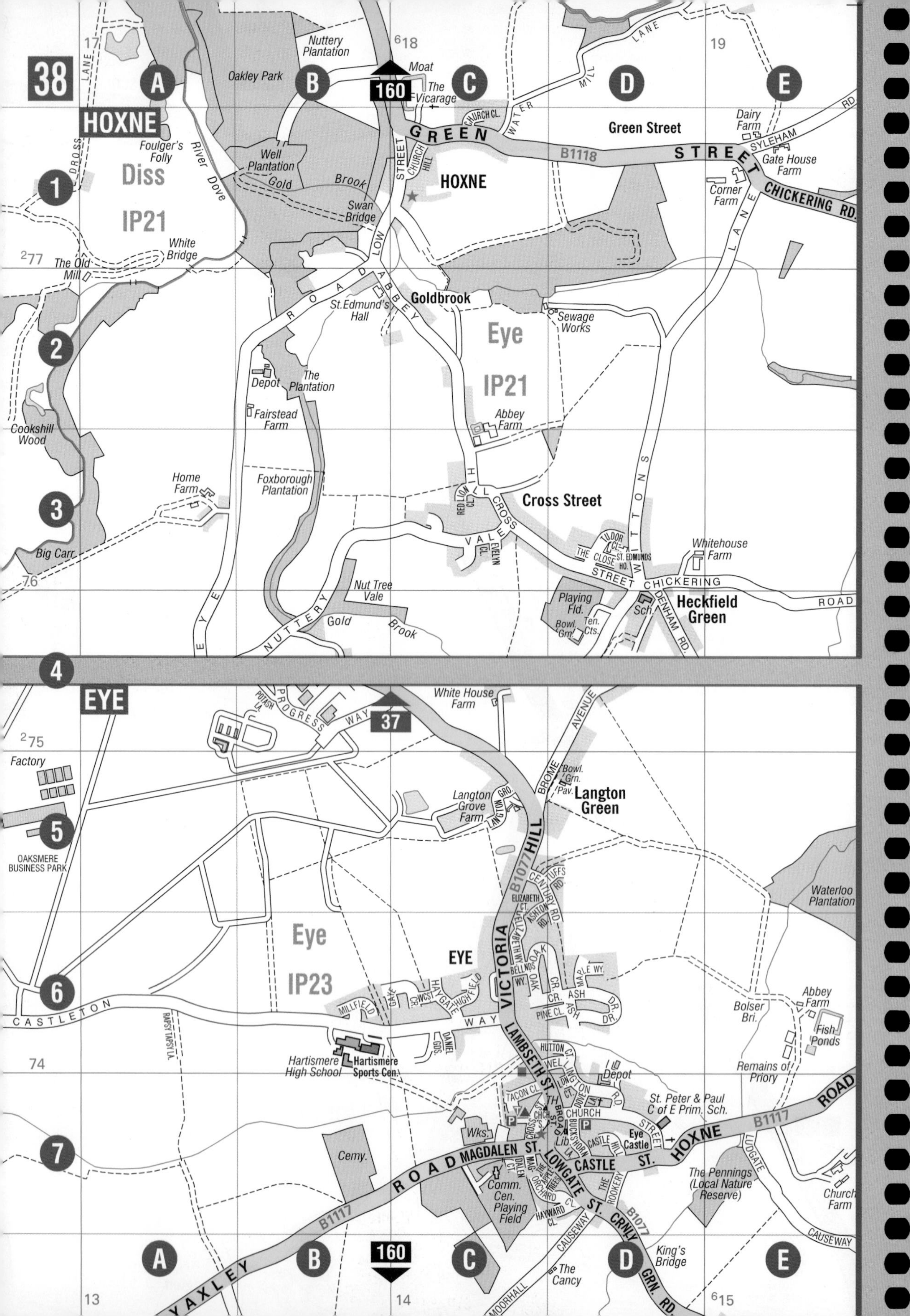
HOXNE
EYE
Diss
IP21
Eye
IP21
Eye
IP23
Green Street
HOXNE
Goldbrook
Cross Street
Heckfield
Green
Langton
Green
EYE
Nuttery
Plantation
Oakley Park
Moat
The
Vicarage
160
37
Foulger's
Folly
River
Dove
Well
Plantation
Gold
Brook
Swan
Bridge
White
Bridge
The Old
Mill
Cookshill
Wood
Big Carr
Home
Farm
Depot
The
Plantation
Fairstead
Farm
Foxborough
Plantation
St.Edmund's
Hall
Sewage
Works
Abbey
Farm
Nut Tree
Vale
Playing
Fld.
Bowl.
Grn.
Ten.
Cts.
Sch.
Dairy
Farm
Gate House
Farm
Corner
Farm
Whitehouse
Farm
GREEN
STREET
B1118
CHICKERING RD.
SYLEHAM
RD.
CHURCH CL.
CHURCH HILL
LOW
ROAD
ABBEY
HILL
CROSS
VALE
EVELYN CL.
RED LION CL.
TUDOR CL.
THE CLOSE
ST. EDMUNDS HO.
STREET
CHICKERING
ROAD
DENHAM RD.
WITTONS LANE
LANE
WATER MILL LANE
DROSS LANE
EYE
NUTTERY
White House
Farm
PROGRESS WAY
POTASH LA.
Factory
OAKSMERE
BUSINESS PARK
Langton
Grove
Farm
LANGTON GRO.
BROME AVENUE
Bowl.
Grn.
Pav.
VICTORIA
HILL
B1077
CENTURY RD.
TUFFS RD.
ELIZABETH CT.
ELIZABETH WAY
ASHTON RD.
OAK CR.
BELLANDS WY.
MAPLE WY.
ASH CR.
ASH DR.
PINE CL.
MILLFIELD
GATE
HAYGATE
HIGHFIELD
CASTLETON WAY
RAPSY TAPSY LA.
DANIEL GDS.
Hartismere
High School
Hartismere
Sports Cen.
LAMBSETH ST.
HUTTON CT.
WELLINGTON RD.
Depot
TACON CL.
CHURCH
BROAD ST.
BUCKSHORN LA.
CASTLE HILL
Eye
Castle
Lib.
Wks.
Cemy.
MAGDALEN ST.
LOWGATE
CASTLE ST.
HOXNE ROAD
B1117
YAXLEY ROAD
Comm.
Cen.
Playing
Field
HAYWARD CL.
THE ROOKERY
CRNLY GRN. RD.
CAUSEWAY
MOORHALL CAUSEWAY
The
Cancy
King's
Bridge
St. Peter & Paul
C of E Prim. Sch.
The Pennings
(Local Nature
Reserve)
LUDGATE
CAUSEWAY
Church
Farm
Bolser
Bri.
Abbey
Farm
Fish
Ponds
Remains of
Priory
Waterloo
Plantation
A
B
C
D
E
1
2
3
4
5
6
7
17
618
19
277
76
275
74
13
14
615

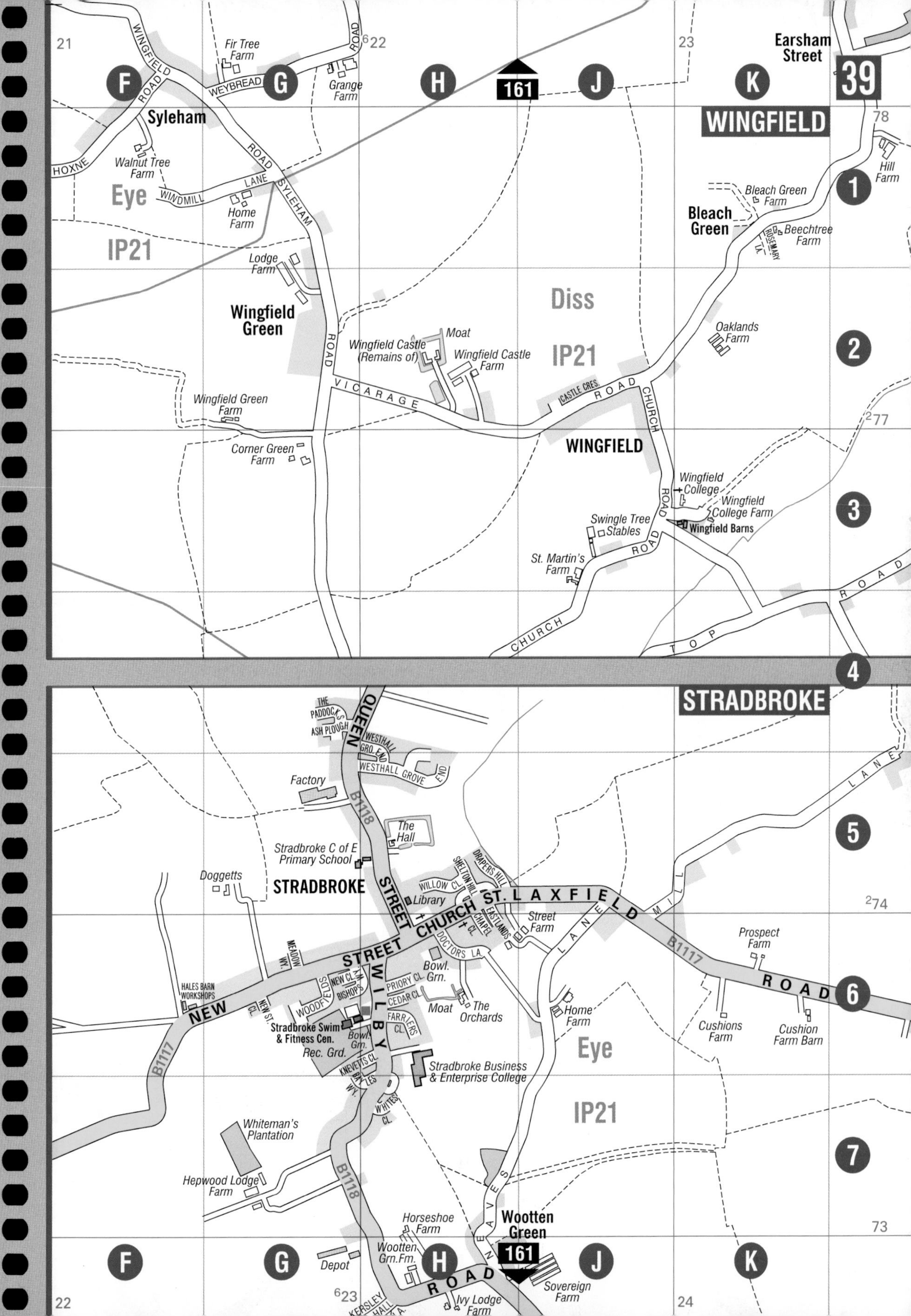
39
WINGFIELD
STRADBROKE
Earsham Street
161
Syleham
Eye
IP21
Diss
WINGFIELD
Wingfield Green
Bleach Green
Fir Tree Farm
Grange Farm
Walnut Tree Farm
Home Farm
Lodge Farm
Moat
Wingfield Castle (Remains of)
Wingfield Castle Farm
Wingfield Green Farm
Corner Green Farm
Hill Farm
Bleach Green Farm
Beechtree Farm
Oaklands Farm
Wingfield College
Wingfield College Farm
Wingfield Barns
Swingle Tree Stables
St. Martin's Farm
WEYBREAD
WINGFIELD ROAD
HOXNE
WINDMILL LANE
SYLEHAM ROAD
VICARAGE ROAD
CASTLE CRES.
CHURCH ROAD
TOP ROAD
ROSEMARY LA.
STRADBROKE
Factory
The Hall
Stradbroke C of E Primary School
Doggetts
Library
Street Farm
Prospect Farm
Bowl. Grn.
Moat
The Orchards
Home Farm
Cushions Farm
Cushion Farm Barn
Stradbroke Swim & Fitness Cen.
Rec. Grd.
Stradbroke Business & Enterprise College
Whiteman's Plantation
Hepwood Lodge Farm
Horseshoe Farm
Wootten Green
Wootten Grn.Fm.
Depot
Sovereign Farm
Ivy Lodge Farm
HALES BARN WORKSHOPS
QUEEN STREET
THE PADDOCKS
ASH PLOUGH
WESTHALL GRO.
WESTHALL GROVE END
B1118
B1117
WILLOW CL.
SHELTON HILL
DRAPERS HILL
CHURCH ST.
LAXFIELD ROAD
CHAPEL
EASTLANDS
DOCTORS LA.
MILL LANE
NEW STREET
MEADOW WY.
NEW CL.
BISHOPS
WOODFIELDS
PRIORY CL.
CEDAR CL.
FARRIERS CL.
WILBY ROAD
KNEVETTS CL.
BAYLES WY.
WHITES CL.
NEAVES LANE
KERSLEY HALL LA.
F G H J K
1 2 3 4 5 6 7
21 22 23 24
78 77 74 73

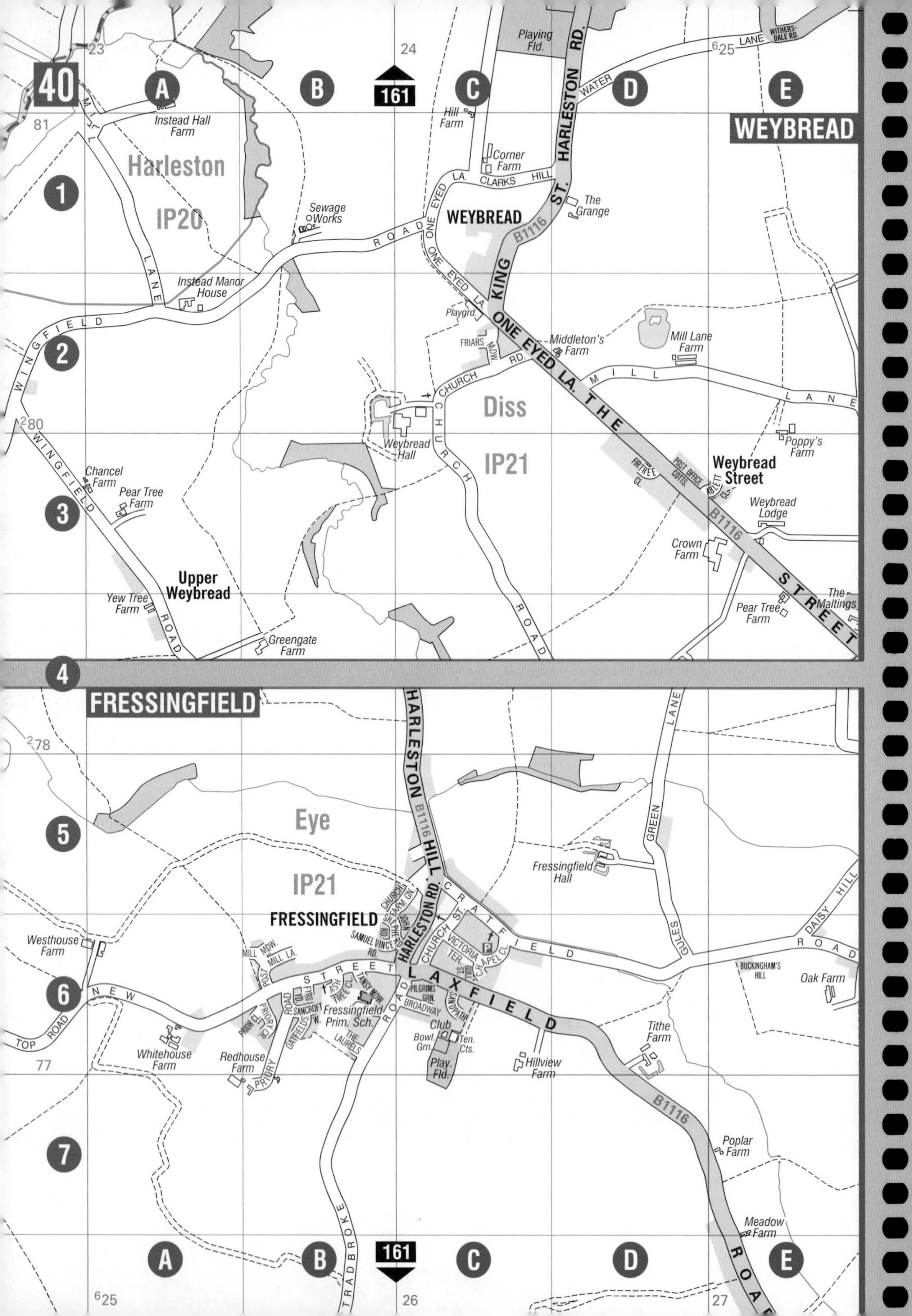

WEYBREAD
FRESSINGFIELD
161
Harleston
IP20
Diss
IP21
Eye
IP21
WEYBREAD
Weybread Street
Upper Weybread
FRESSINGFIELD
Instead Hall Farm
Sewage Works
Instead Manor House
Hill Farm
Corner Farm
The Grange
Playing Fld.
Weybread Hall
Middleton's Farm
Mill Lane Farm
Poppy's Farm
Weybread Lodge
Crown Farm
Pear Tree Farm
The Maltings
Chancel Farm
Pear Tree Farm
Yew Tree Farm
Greengate Farm
Fressingfield Hall
Westhouse Farm
Whitehouse Farm
Redhouse Farm
Fressingfield Prim. Sch.
Club
Bowl. Grn.
Ten. Cts.
Play. Fld.
Hillview Farm
Tithe Farm
Oak Farm
Poplar Farm
Meadow Farm
BUCKINGHAM'S HILL
HARLESTON RD.
KING ST.
ONE EYED LA.
THE STREET
B1116
WATER LANE
WITHERS-DALE RD.
CLARKS HILL
ROAD
MILL LANE
WINGFIELD ROAD
CHURCH RD.
FRIARS MDW.
Playgrd.
FIRTREE CL.
POST OFFICE COTTS.
ABLETT CL.
HARLESTON HILL
GREEN LANE
GILES
DAISY HILL ROAD
STRATFIELD ROAD
LAXFIELD ROAD
CHURCH ST.
VICTORIA TER.
CHAPEL CL.
NEW STREET
TOP ROAD
MILL MDW.
MILL LA.
POST
PRIORY ROAD
PRIOR CL.
OATFIELDS
SANCROFT W.
FIRS YD.
ASH TREE CL.
TANSY MDW.
THE LAURELS
PILGRIMS GRN.
BROADWAY
SANDPATH
SAMUEL VINCE RD.
JOHN SHEPHERD RD.
CHURCH FARM GN.
TRADBROKE ROAD
1 2 3 4 5 6 7
A B C D E
23 24 25 26 27
81 80 78 77

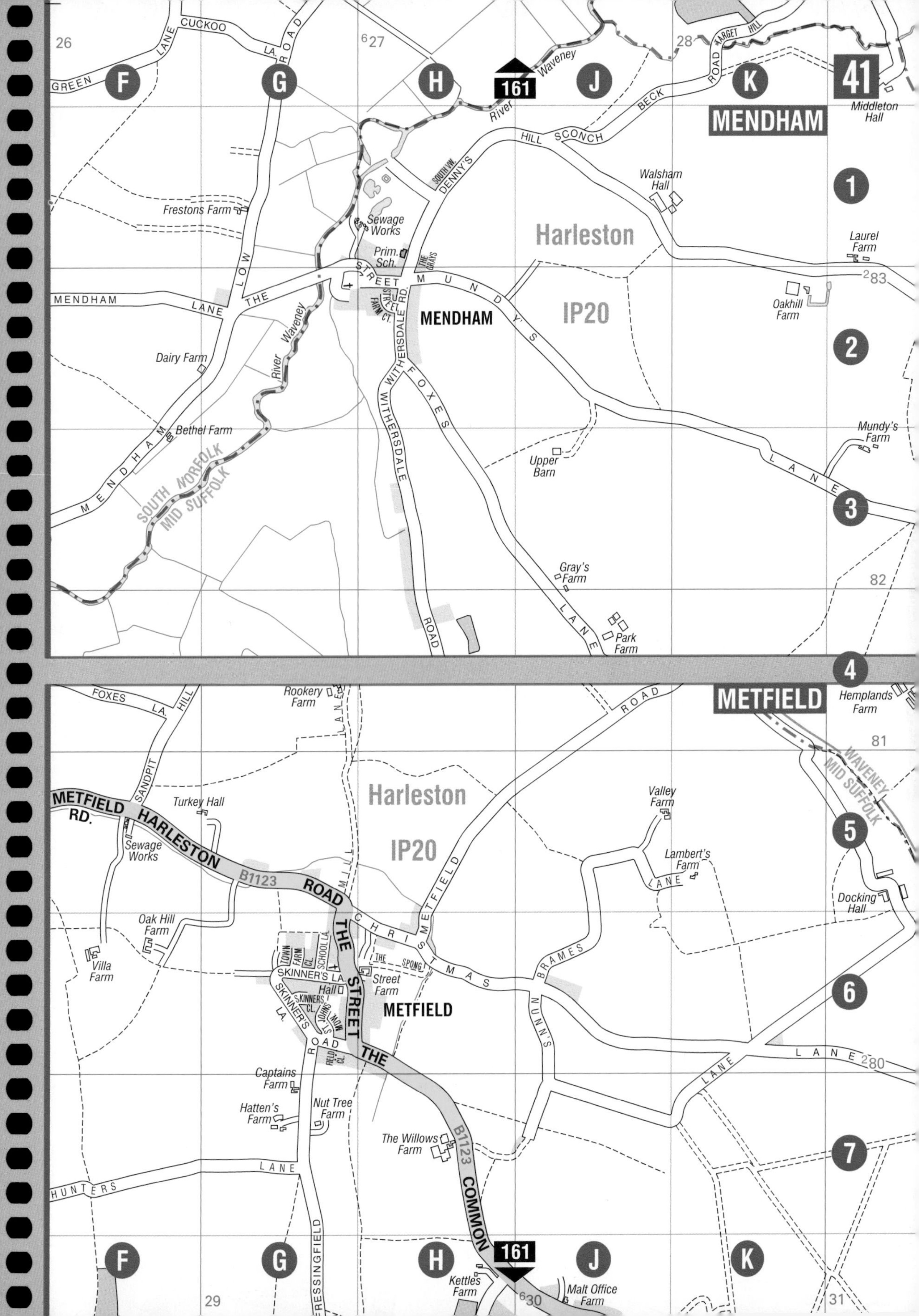

MENDHAM
METFIELD
Harleston
IP20
161
F
G
H
J
K
1
2
3
4
5
6
7
26
27
28
29
30
31
83
82
81
80
CUCKOO LA.
GREEN LANE
LOW ROAD
River Waveney
BECK ROAD
TARGET HILL
Middleton Hall
SCONCH HILL
DENNY'S
SOUTH VW.
Walsham Hall
Frestons Farm
Sewage Works
Prim. Sch.
THE GRAYS
Laurel Farm
THE STREET
MUNDY'S
STREET FARM CT.
RD.
MENDHAM LANE
MENDHAM
Oakhill Farm
WITHERSDALE
FOXES
Dairy Farm
Bethel Farm
Mundy's Farm
LANE
SOUTH NORFOLK
MID SUFFOLK
Upper Barn
WITHERSDALE ROAD
Gray's Farm
Park Farm
FOXES LA.
HILL
Rookery Farm
LANE
ROAD
Hemplands Farm
WAVENEY
MID SUFFOLK
SANDPIT
METFIELD RD.
Turkey Hall
HARLESTON ROAD
B1123
Valley Farm
Sewage Works
MILL
METFIELD
Lambert's Farm
LANE
Docking Hall
Oak Hill Farm
CHRISTMAS
BRAMES
TOWN FARM CL.
SCHOOL LA.
THE SPONG
Villa Farm
SKINNER'S LA.
Street Farm
Hall
SKINNER'S CL.
ST. JOHNS
MOW
SKINNER'S LA.
THE STREET
NUNN'S
ROAD
FIELD CL.
LANE
Captains Farm
Hatten's Farm
Nut Tree Farm
The Willows Farm
THE COMMON
HUNTERS LANE
FRESSINGFIELD
Kettles Farm
Malt Office Farm

HALESWORTH
Halesworth
IP19
HALESWORTH
Broadway
Holton
Fairstead Farm
Spexhall Manor
Hall Farm
Poultry Houses
Wissett Hall
Mill Hill
Broadway Farm
Industrial Estate
Moat Farm
Airfield (disused)
Factory
Halesworth Airfield Museum
Laurel Farm
Brick Kiln Farm
Woodside Farm
Works
Halesworth Middle Sch.
PATRICK STEAD HOSPITAL
Sports Grd.
Swim. Pool
Town Farm
Valley Farm
HOLTON HALL PARK (CARAVAN PARK)
Edgar Sewter Prim.Sch.
Halesworth Mus.
Cemetery
Town Pk.
Gallery
Saw Mill
Depot
Duckers Drift
BLYTH ROAD INDUSTRIAL ESTATE
Sewage Works
Red House Farm
Highfield Farm
Brick Kiln Farm
Mells Bridge
Bull's Corner
WAVENEY SUFFOLK COASTAL
HALESWORTH GOLF COURSE
Club House
Driving Range
Mells Court Farm
White House Farm
Wenhaston Grange
STONE ST.
NORWICH ROAD
SPARROWHAWK ROAD
BUNGAY ROAD
HOLTON ROAD
THE STREET
BECCLES RD.
SOUTHWOLD ROAD
QUAY ST.
SAXONS WAY
ROMAN WAY
LONDON RD.
BRAMFIELD ROAD
WALPOLE ROAD
CHEDISTON ST.
STATION ROAD
HARRISONS LANE
FAIRVIEW ROAD
WISSETT ROAD
OLD WISSETT
MILL HILL ROAD
SCHOOL LANE
WASH LANE
THE STREET
MILL LANE
SCALESBROOK LANE
LODGE ROAD
ORCHARD VALLEY
BLYFORD LA.
SANDY LA.
A144
B1123
B1117
B1124
161
38
39
640
79
278
77
76
A
B
C
D
E
1
2
3
4
5
6
7

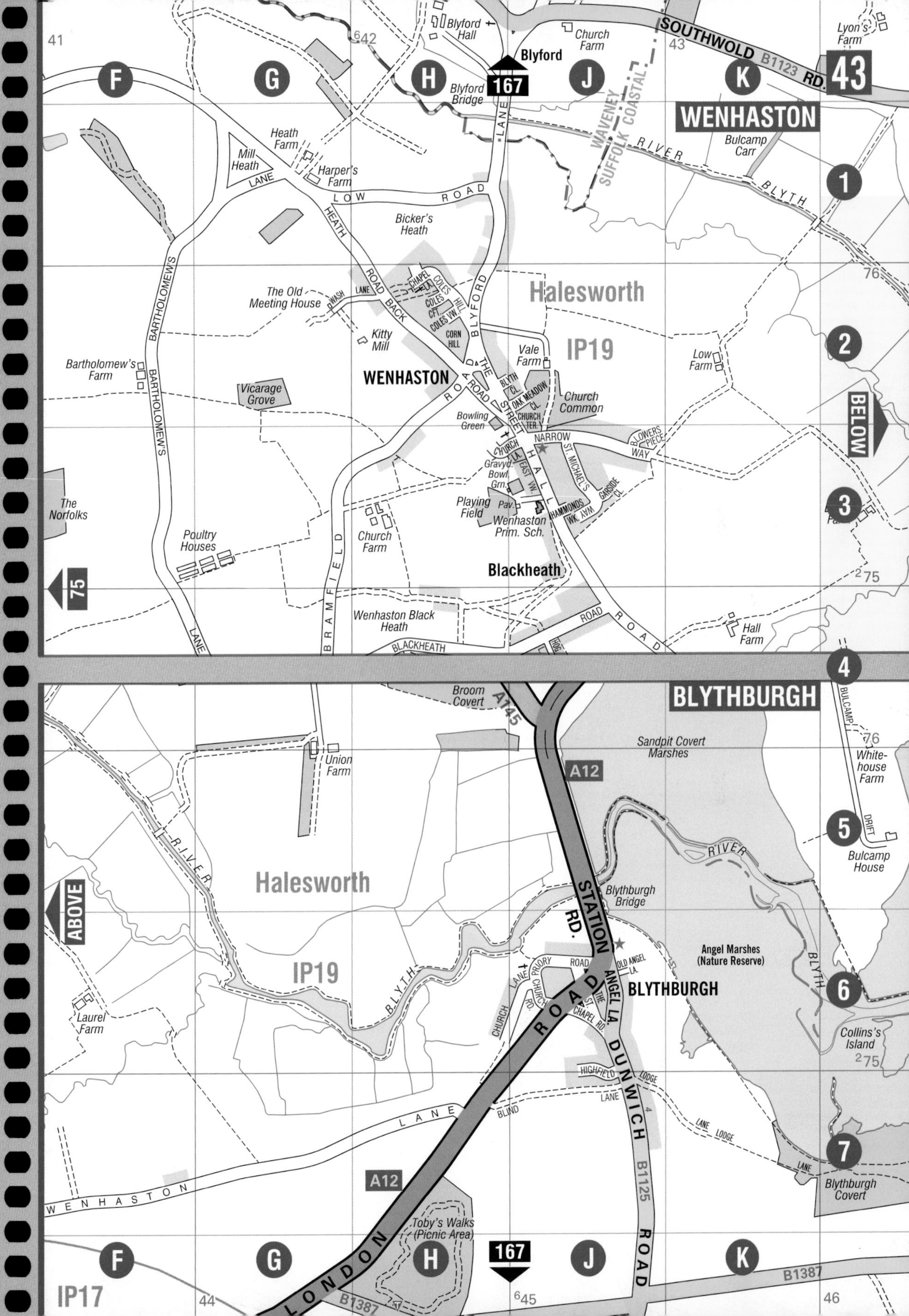
WENHASTON
Blyford
Blyford Hall
Church Farm
Lyon's Farm
SOUTHWOLD B1123 RD.
167
Blyford Bridge
Heath Farm
Mill Heath
Harper's Farm
LOW ROAD
Bicker's Heath
WAVENEY SUFFOLK COASTAL
RIVER BLYTH
Bulcamp Carr
Halesworth
IP19
The Old Meeting House
Kitty Mill
Bartholomew's Farm
WENHASTON
Vicarage Grove
Vale Farm
Church Common
Low Farm
BELOW
Bowling Green
NARROW WAY
BLOWERS PIECE
Playing Field
Wenhaston Prim. Sch.
Church Farm
The Norfolks
Poultry Houses
Blackheath
Wenhaston Black Heath
Hall Farm
75
BLYTHBURGH
Broom Covert
A145
A12
Sandpit Covert Marshes
White-house Farm
Union Farm
Bulcamp House
ABOVE
Halesworth
Blythburgh Bridge
Angel Marshes (Nature Reserve)
IP19
BLYTHBURGH
Laurel Farm
Collins's Island
DUNWICH ROAD
B1125
LONDON ROAD
WENHASTON LANE
Blythburgh Covert
Toby's Walks (Picnic Area)
IP17
B1387

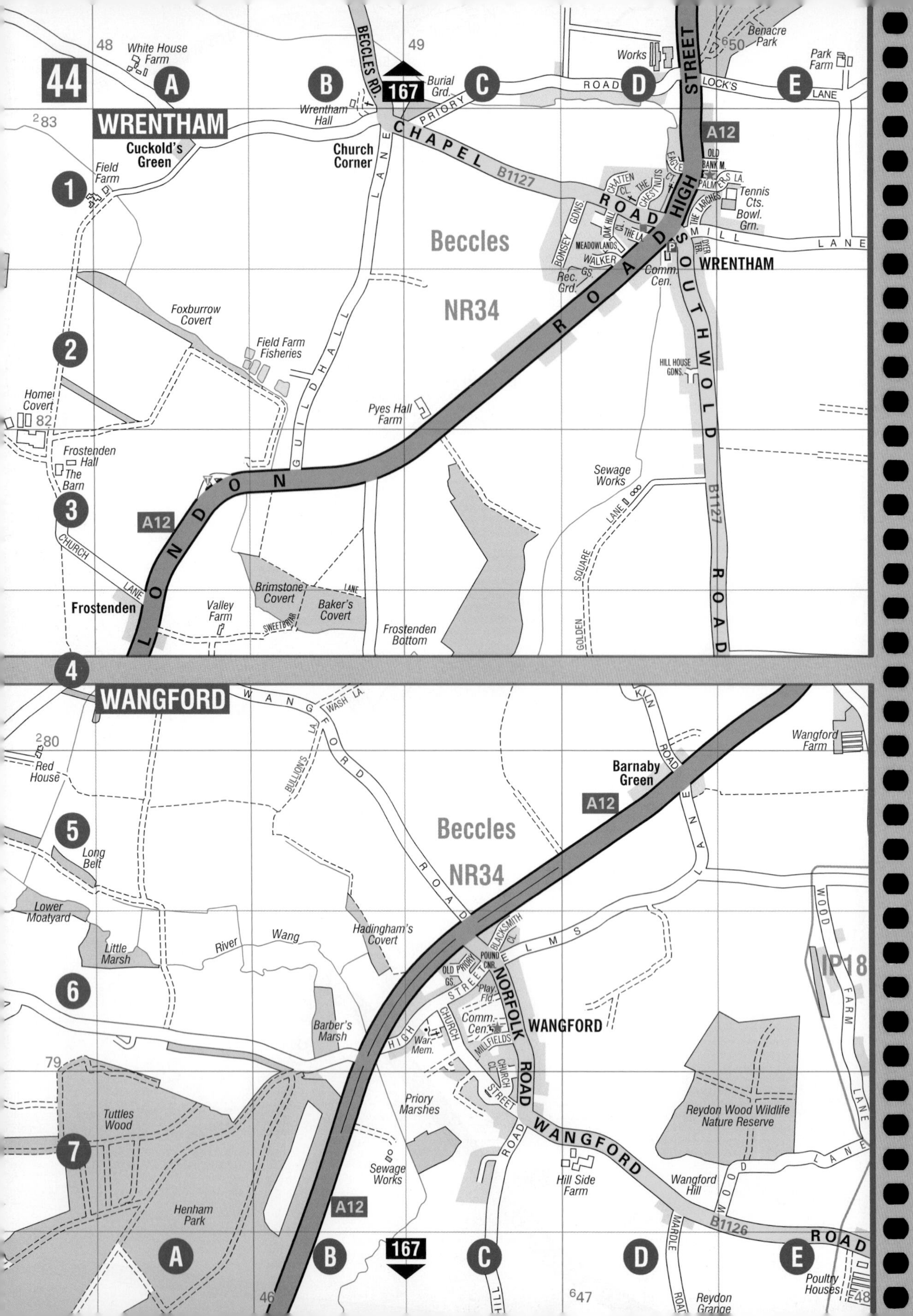
WRENTHAM
White House Farm
Cuckold's Green
Field Farm
Wrentham Hall
Burial Grd.
Church Corner
PRIORY
CHAPEL
B1127
ROAD
LOCK'S LANE
Works
Benacre Park
Park Farm
HIGH STREET
A12
OLD BANK M.
PALMER'S LA.
Tennis Cts.
Bowl. Grn.
MILL LANE
CHATTEN CL.
THE CHESTNUTS
EAGLE CT.
THE LARCHES
BONSEY GDNS.
OAK HILL CL.
THE LA.
MEADOWLANDS
WALKER GS.
DYER TER.
Rec. Grd.
Comm. Cen.
WRENTHAM
Beccles
NR34
Foxburrow Covert
Field Farm Fisheries
GUILDHALL LANE
Pyes Hall Farm
Home Covert
Frostenden Hall
The Barn
LONDON ROAD
SOUTHWOLD ROAD
HILL HOUSE GDNS.
Sewage Works
LANE
SQUARE
GOLDEN
CHURCH LANE
Frostenden
Valley Farm
SWEETBRIAR
Brimstone Covert
LANE
Baker's Covert
Frostenden Bottom
WANGFORD
WANGFORD ROAD
WASH LA.
BULLION'S LA.
KILN LANE
Red House
Wangford Farm
Barnaby Green
Beccles
NR34
Long Belt
Lower Moatyard
Little Marsh
River Wang
Hadingham's Covert
BLACKSMITH CL.
ELMS
POUND CNR.
OLD PRIORY GS.
STREET
Play. Fld.
NORFOLK ROAD
Comm. Cen.
WANGFORD
MILLFIELDS
HIGH
CHURCH
War Mem.
CHURCH CL.
CHURCH STREET
Barber's Marsh
IP18
WOOD FARM LANE
Tuttles Wood
Henham Park
Priory Marshes
Sewage Works
Hill Side Farm
WANGFORD ROAD
Reydon Wood Wildlife Nature Reserve
Wangford Hill
WOOD LANE
MARDLE ROAD
B1126
ROAD
Poultry Houses
Reydon Grange
A B C D E
1 2 3 4 5 6 7
167
48 49 650 283 82 280 79 46 647 48

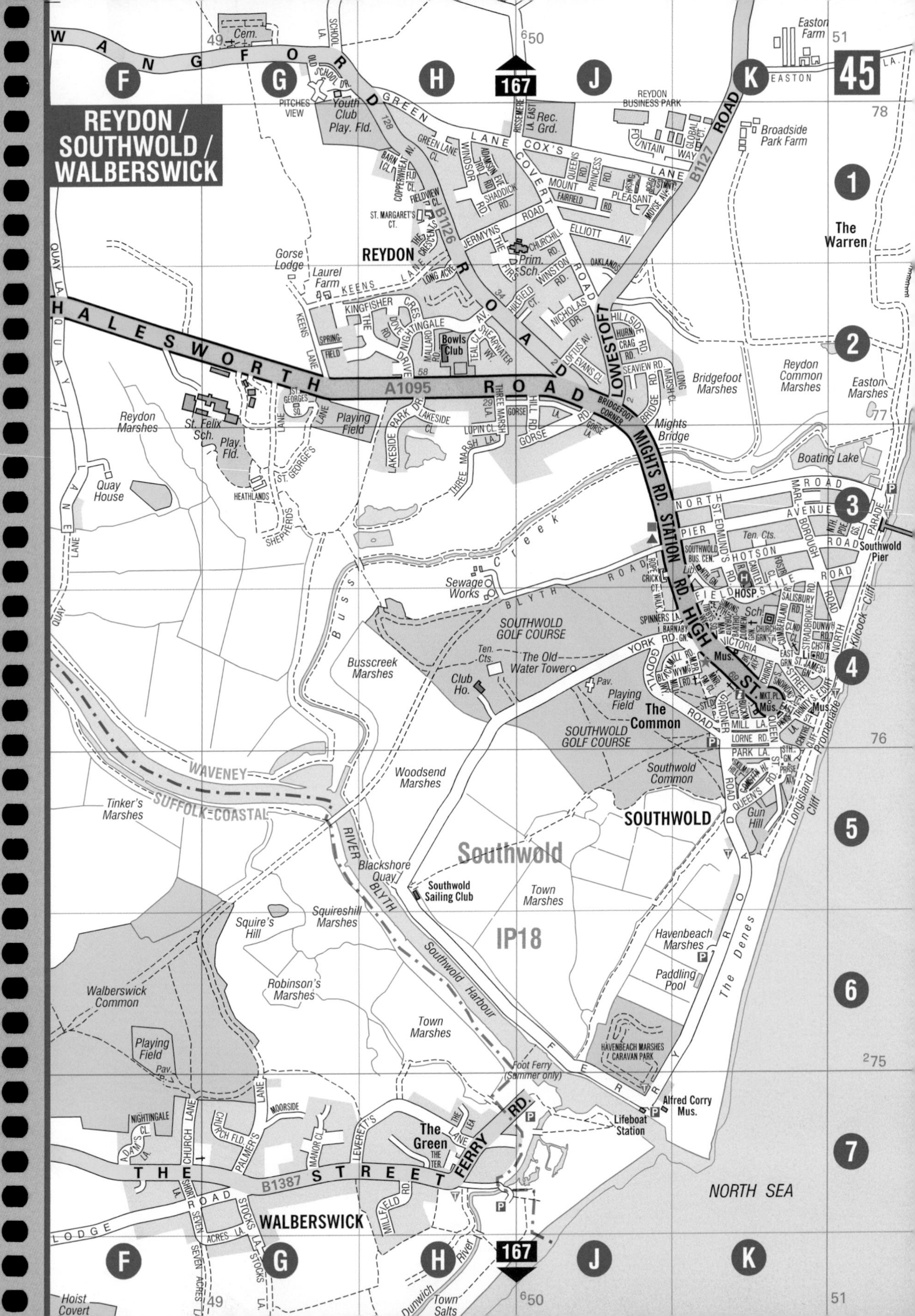

REYDON / SOUTHWOLD / WALBERSWICK
45
167
REYDON
SOUTHWOLD
WALBERSWICK
Southwold
IP18
NORTH SEA
WANGFORD ROAD
HALESWORTH ROAD
A1095
LOWESTOFT ROAD
B1127
B1126
STATION RD.
MIGHTS RD.
HIGH ST.
THE STREET
B1387
FERRY RD.
Reydon Marshes
St. Felix Sch.
Quay House
Gorse Lodge
Laurel Farm
Bowls Club
Playing Field
Youth Club Play. Fld.
Rec. Grd.
REYDON BUSINESS PARK
Broadside Park Farm
Easton Farm
The Warren
Reydon Common Marshes
Easton Marshes
Bridgefoot Marshes
Mights Bridge
Boating Lake
Southwold Pier
Buss Creek
Sewage Works
SOUTHWOLD GOLF COURSE
The Old Water Tower
Club Ho.
Busscreek Marshes
The Common
Southwold Common
Woodsend Marshes
Tinker's Marshes
WAVENEY
SUFFOLK COASTAL
RIVER BLYTH
Blackshore Quay
Southwold Sailing Club
Town Marshes
Squire's Hill
Squireshill Marshes
Robinson's Marshes
Southwold Harbour
Havenbeach Marshes
Paddling Pool
HAVENBEACH MARSHES CARAVAN PARK
The Denes
Gun Hill
Longisland Cliff
Kilcock Cliff
Alfred Corry Mus.
Lifeboat Station
Foot Ferry (Summer only)
Walberswick Common
The Green
Hoist Covert
Dunwich River
Town Salts

Northmore Cottages
Northmore Stud Farm
Orchard Farm
Rose Hall
Equine Hospital
The Mill Barn
Dog Kennel Yard
Ten. Cts.
Pavs.
Cricket Grd.
Exning House
Leveretts
Nursery Cottages
Glenmore
A142
A14
BURWELL ROAD
B1103
WINDMILL
War Meml.
Burnt Fm.
SWAN LA.
CHURCH ST.
EXNING
Priory Stables
Exeter Stables
Sch.
Play. Fld.
Rec. Grd.
Stables
Harraton Stud
Exning Football Grd.
LACEY'S LANE
DUCKS LANE
Morby's Cottages
ROAD
Sub.
Cemy.
B1103
EXNING ROAD
Brickfield Stud
Studlands Park
HANOVER CLOSE
Social Cen.
Health Club
STUDLANDS PARK INDUSTRIAL ESTATE
ENTERPRISE CT.
MINTON ENTERPRISE PARK
Ind. Est.
GOODWIN BUS. PK.
STUDLANDS BUS. CEN.
LAUREATE PADDOCKS IND. EST.
Seven Springs
New Yard
The Marsh
Charnwood Stables
Factory
Hamilton Stables
Scaltback Middle Sch. Play. Flds.
Shadowfax Stables
School
Oak Stables
Red Ho. Stables
Jamesfield Stables
Revida Pl.
Green Ridge Stables
Southfield Farm
Diomed Stables
Rathmoy Stables
Calder Park Stables
Florizel
Eve Lodge
Saffron House Stables
Marriot Stables
Loder Stables
Pav.
CB25
HEATH
Exercise Track
Exercise Track
Exercise Track
NEWMARKET HEATH
Exercise Track
Rowley Mile Course
Beacon Course
(Cesarewitch)
The Bushes
The Millennium Grandstand
NEWMARKET RACECOURSE
Cambridge Hill
A1304
BARBARA STRADBROKE
Exercise Track
158
A B C D E
1 2 3 4 5 6 7
61 62 63
66 65 64 63

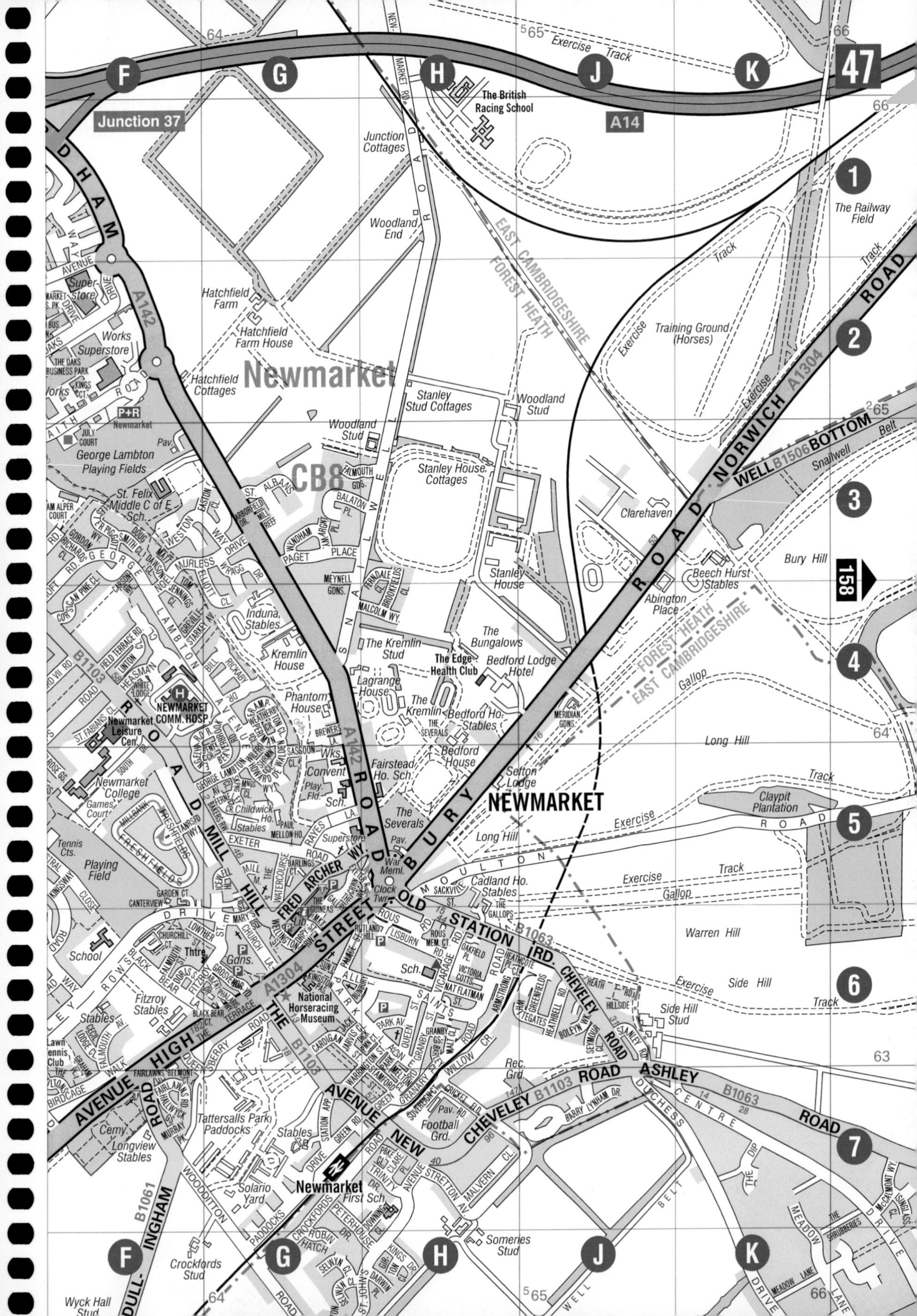
Junction 37
A14
The British Racing School
Exercise Track
Junction Cottages
Woodland End
Hatchfield Farm
Hatchfield Farm House
Hatchfield Cottages
Newmarket
CB8
EAST CAMBRIDGESHIRE
FOREST HEATH
The Railway Field
Training Ground (Horses)
Stanley Stud Cottages
Woodland Stud
Stanley House Cottages
Stanley House
Clarehaven
Beech Hurst Stables
Abington Place
Bury Hill
NORWICH ROAD
A1304
BURY ROAD
George Lambton Playing Fields
St. Felix Middle C of E Sch.
Induna Stables
Kremlin House
The Kremlin Stud
The Edge Health Club
Bedford Lodge Hotel
The Bungalows
Lagrange House
The Kremlin
Bedford Ho. Stables
Bedford House
Phantom House
NEWMARKET COMM. HOSP.
Newmarket Leisure Cen.
Newmarket College
Fairstead Ho. Sch.
Sefton Lodge
NEWMARKET
Long Hill
Claypit Plantation
Warren Hill
Side Hill
Side Hill Stud
The Severals
Playing Field
School
Fitzroy Stables
National Horseracing Museum
Tattersalls Park Paddocks
Longview Stables
Solario Yard
Newmarket
Crockfords Stud
Somerles Stud
Football Grd.
Rec. Grd.
HIGH STREET
OLD STATION RD.
CHEVELEY ROAD
ASHLEY ROAD
B1063
B1103
B1061
A142
MOULTON ROAD
Wyck Hall Stud
158

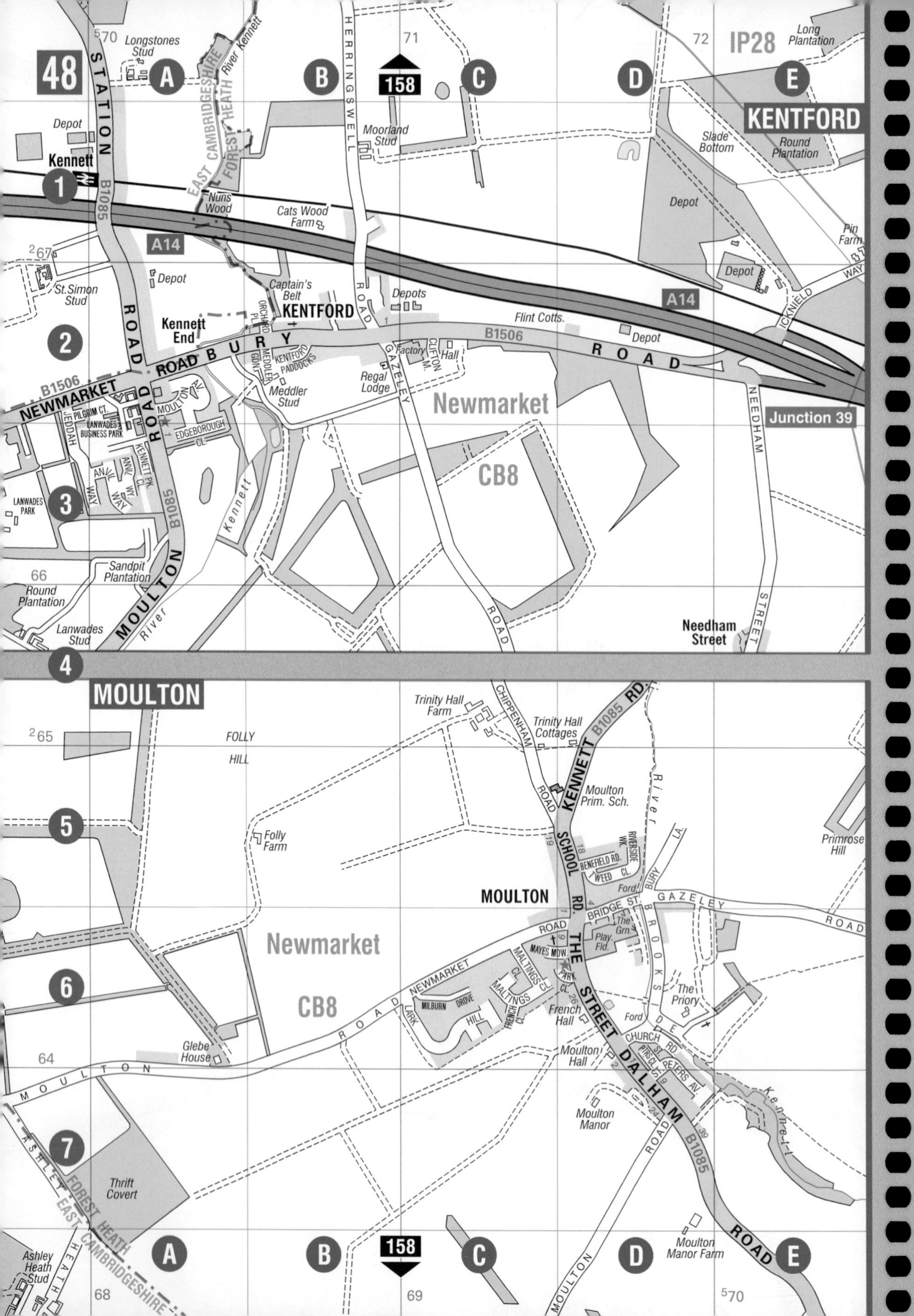
KENTFORD
MOULTON
Kennett
Kennett End
Newmarket
CB8
IP28
Junction 39
A14
B1506
B1085
158
Longstones Stud
Moorland Stud
Cats Wood Farm
Nuns Wood
Captain's Belt
St.Simon Stud
Depot
Depots
Flint Cotts.
Slade Bottom
Round Plantation
Long Plantation
Pin Farm
Needham Street
Meddler Stud
Regal Lodge
Sandpit Plantation
Lanwades Stud
LANWADES PARK
LANWADES BUSINESS PARK
Trinity Hall Farm
Trinity Hall Cottages
Moulton Prim. Sch.
FOLLY HILL
Folly Farm
Primrose Hill
Glebe House
Thrift Covert
Ashley Heath Stud
French Hall
Moulton Hall
Moulton Manor
Moulton Manor Farm
The Priory
The Grn.
Play. Fld.
EAST CAMBRIDGESHIRE
FOREST HEATH
STATION ROAD
BURY ROAD
NEWMARKET ROAD
MOULTON ROAD
HERRINGSWELL ROAD
GAZELEY ROAD
NEEDHAM STREET
ICKNIELD WAY
KENNETT RD.
SCHOOL RD.
CHIPPENHAM ROAD
THE STREET
DALHAM ROAD
GAZELEY ROAD
BRIDGE ST.
BROOKSIDE
CHURCH RD.
BURY LA.
RIVERSIDE WK.
BENEFIELD RD.
WEED CL.
MAYES MDW.
MALTINGS CL.
MILBURN DROVE
LARK HILL
FRENCH CL.
PETERS AV.
ASHLEY
River Kennett

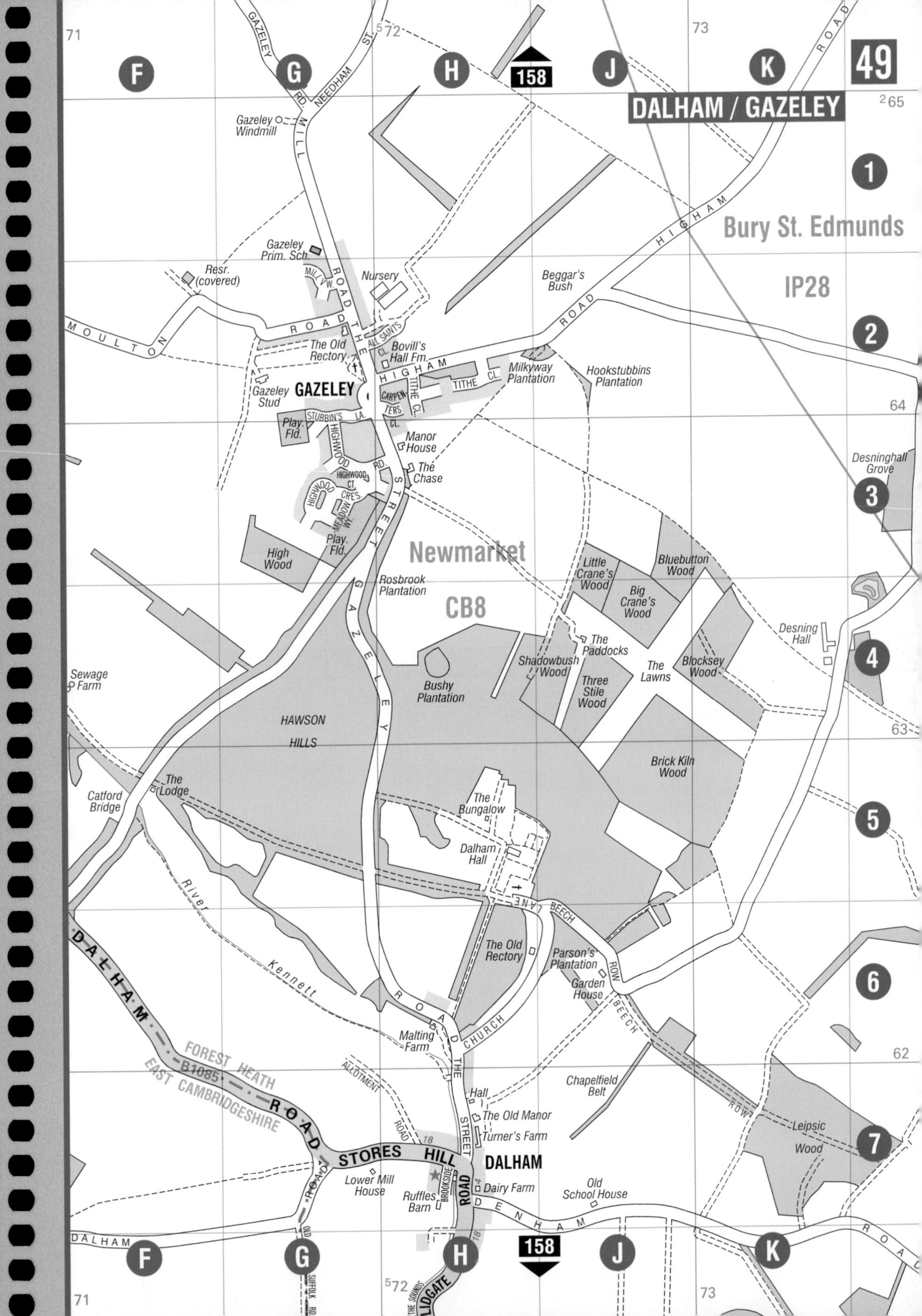
Bury St. Edmunds
IP28
Newmarket
CB8
GAZELEY
DALHAM
Gazeley Windmill
Gazeley Prim. Sch.
Resr. (covered)
Nursery
Beggar's Bush
The Old Rectory
Bovill's Hall Fm.
Milkyway Plantation
Hookstubbins Plantation
Gazeley Stud
Play. Fld.
Manor House
The Chase
Desninghall Grove
High Wood
Rosbrook Plantation
Little Crane's Wood
Bluebutton Wood
Big Crane's Wood
Desning Hall
The Paddocks
Shadowbush Wood
Three Stile Wood
The Lawns
Blocksey Wood
Bushy Plantation
Sewage Farm
HAWSON HILLS
Brick Kiln Wood
Catford Bridge
The Lodge
The Bungalow
Dalham Hall
River Kennett
The Old Rectory
Parson's Plantation
Garden House
Malting Farm
Chapelfield Belt
Hall
The Old Manor
Turner's Farm
Leipsic Wood
Lower Mill House
Dairy Farm
Old School House
Ruffles Barn
FOREST HEATH
EAST CAMBRIDGESHIRE
B1085
DALHAM ROAD
STORES HILL
DENHAM ROAD
LIDGATE ROAD
HIGHAM ROAD
MOULTON ROAD
NEEDHAM ST.
MILL RD.
GAZELEY RD.
THE STREET
GAZELEY ROAD
CHURCH ROAD
BEECH LANE
BEECH ROW
TITHE CL.
CARPENTERS CL.
STUBBIN'S LA.
HIGHWOOD RD.
HIGHWOOD CT.
HIGHWOOD CRES.
MEADOW W.
MILL W.
ALL SAINTS CL.
ALLOTMENT ROAD
BROOKSIDE
OLD SUFFOLK RD
THE SOUNDS
158
F G H J K
1 2 3 4 5 6 7
71 72 73 65 64 63 62

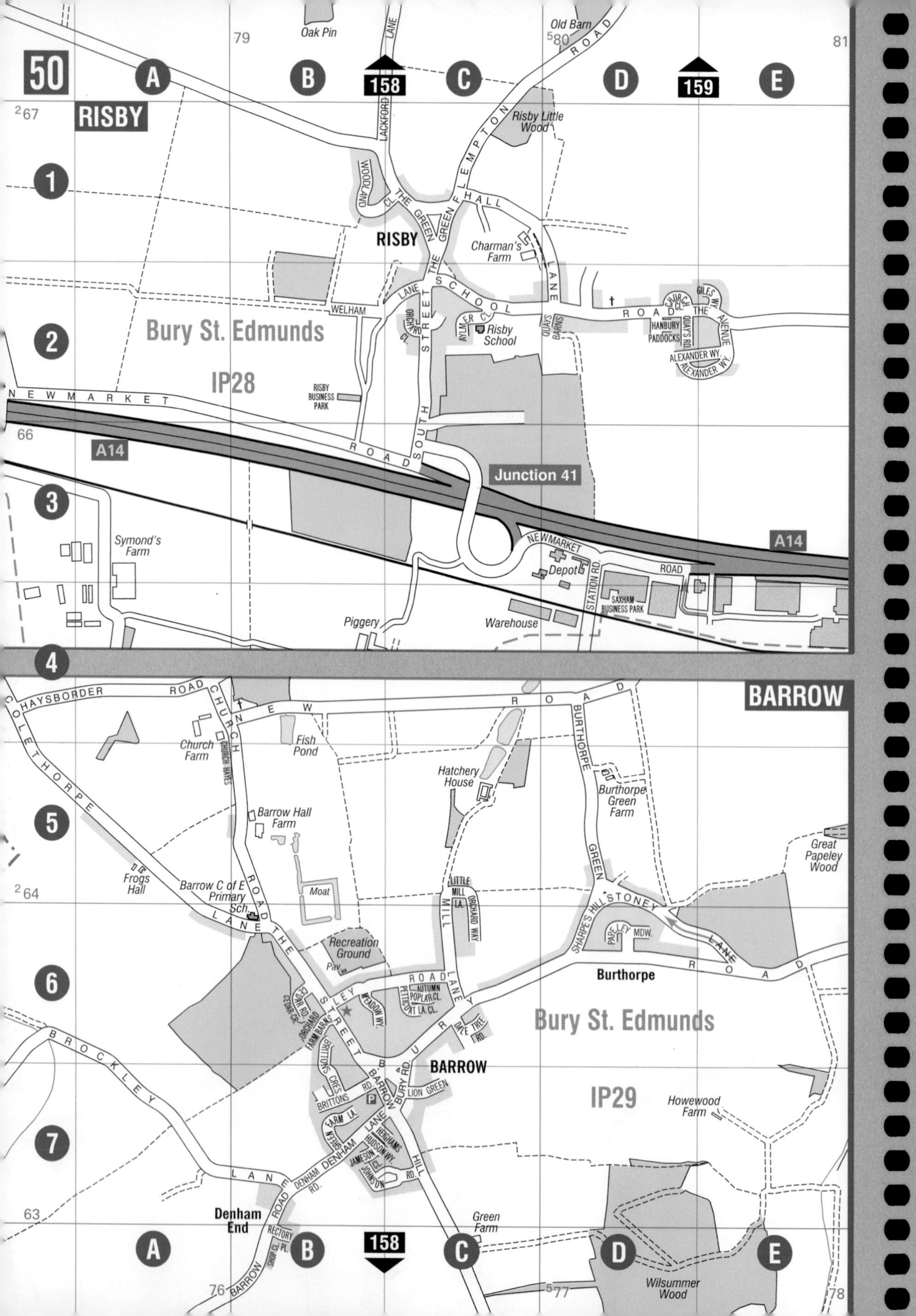
RISBY
BARROW
Oak Pin
Old Barn
LACKFORD LANE
158
159
KEMPTON ROAD
Risby Little Wood
WOODLAND CL.
THE GREEN
HALL LANE
RISBY
Charman's Farm
SCHOOL ROAD
WELHAM LANE
ORCHARD CL.
AYLMER CL.
Risby School
QUAYS BARNS
CHURCH CL.
GILES WY.
THE AVENUE
HANBURY PADDOCKS
QUAY'S RD.
ALEXANDER WY.
Bury St. Edmunds
IP28
RISBY BUSINESS PARK
NEWMARKET ROAD
SOUTH STREET
A14
Junction 41
Symond's Farm
NEWMARKET ROAD
Depot
STATION RD.
SAXHAM BUSINESS PARK
Piggery
Warehouse
HAYSBORDER ROAD
NEW ROAD
CHURCH ROAD
Church Farm
CHURCH HAYES
Fish Pond
Hatchery House
BURTHORPE GREEN
Burthorpe Green Farm
COLETHORPE LANE
Barrow Hall Farm
Frogs Hall
Barrow C of E Primary Sch.
Moat
LITTLE MILL LA.
MILL LANE
ORCHARD WAY
Great Papeley Wood
SHARPE'S HILL
STONEY LANE
PAPELEY MDW.
Recreation Ground
Pav.
ROAD
AUTUMN
POPLAR CL.
PETTIPOTT LA.CL.
MEADOW WY.
Burthorpe
ROAD
CEDAR RD.
CEDAR CR.
ORCHARD FARM BARNS
STREET
BURY ROAD
DALE TREE RD.
Bury St. Edmunds
BRITTONS CRES.
BRITTONS RD.
BARROW
BURY RD.
LION GREEN
IP29
Howewood Farm
BROCKLEY LANE
FARM LA.
HIGHAMS
HUDSON WY.
JAMESON CL.
JOHNSON RD.
DENHAM LANE
HILL
GREEN
DENHAM RD.
DENHAM ROAD
RECTORY
Denham End
Green Farm
SHOP CL.
PL.
BARROW
Wilsummer Wood
A B C D E
1 2 3 4 5 6 7
79 580 81
267 66 264 63
76 577 78

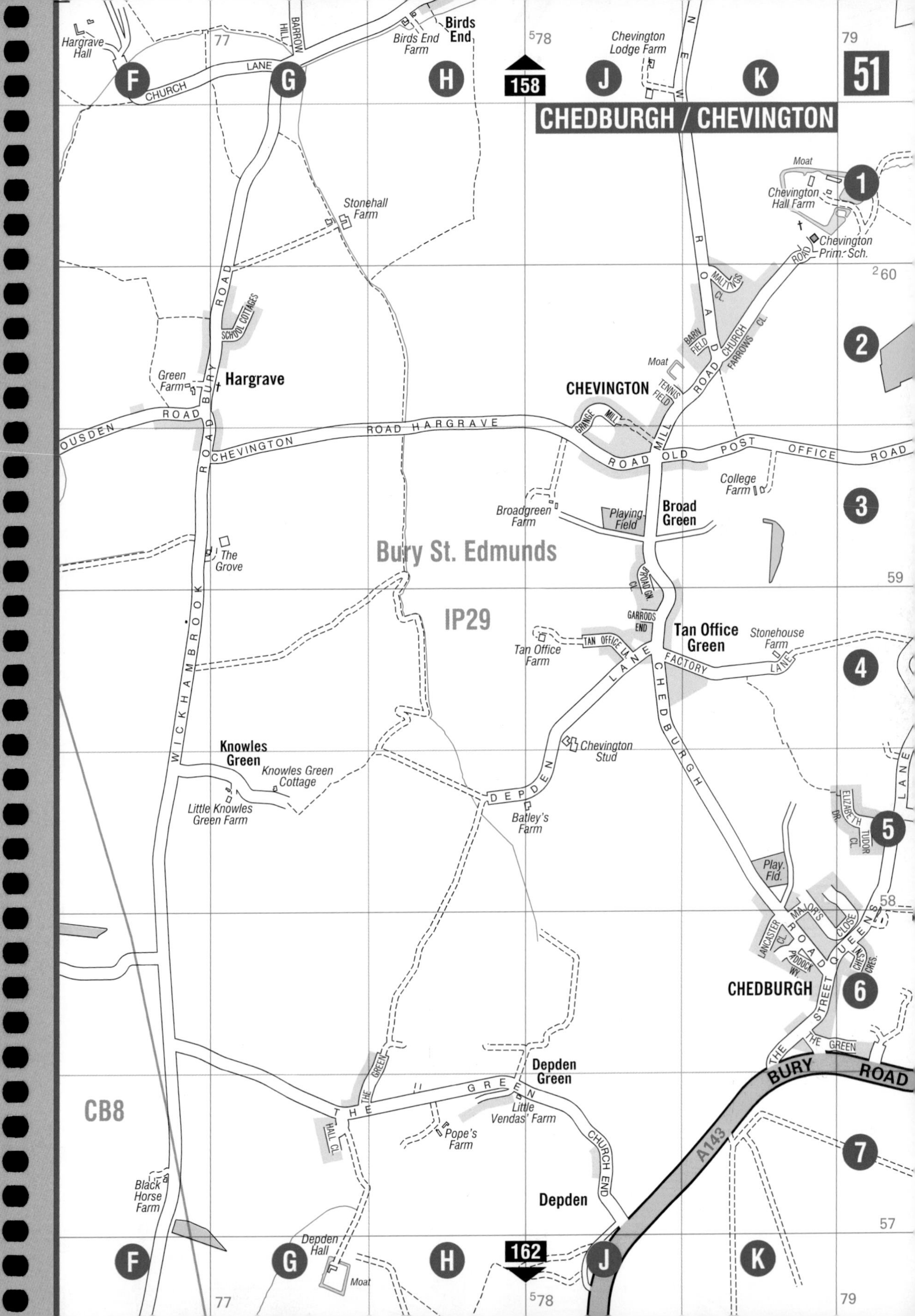
158
162
Hargrave Hall
Birds End Farm
Birds End
Chevington Lodge Farm
CHURCH LANE
BARROW HILL
NEW ROAD
Moat
Chevington Hall Farm
Chevington Prim. Sch.
Stonehall Farm
SCHOOL COTTAGES
BURY ROAD
Hargrave
Green Farm
OUSDEN ROAD
CHEVINGTON ROAD
HARGRAVE ROAD
MALTINGS CL.
BARN FIELD
CHURCH ROAD
FARROWS CL.
TENNIS FIELD
CHEVINGTON
GRANGE
MILL ROAD
OLD POST OFFICE ROAD
College Farm
Broadgreen Farm
Playing Field
Broad Green
The Grove
Bury St. Edmunds
IP29
BROAD GN. CL.
GARRODS END
Tan Office Farm
TAN OFFICE LA.
Tan Office Green
Stonehouse Farm
FACTORY LANE
WICKHAMBROOK ROAD
Knowles Green
Knowles Green Cottage
Little Knowles Green Farm
Chevington Stud
DEPDEN LANE
CHEDBURGH ROAD
Batley's Farm
ELIZABETH DR.
TUDOR CL.
Play. Fld.
MAJOR'S CLOSE
LANCASTER CL.
PADDOCK WY.
QUEENS ROAD
CHESTNUT CRES.
CHEDBURGH
THE STREET
THE GREEN
BURY ROAD
A143
Depden Green
THE GREEN
HALL CL.
Little Vendas' Farm
Pope's Farm
CHURCH END
CB8
Black Horse Farm
Depden
Depden Hall
Moat

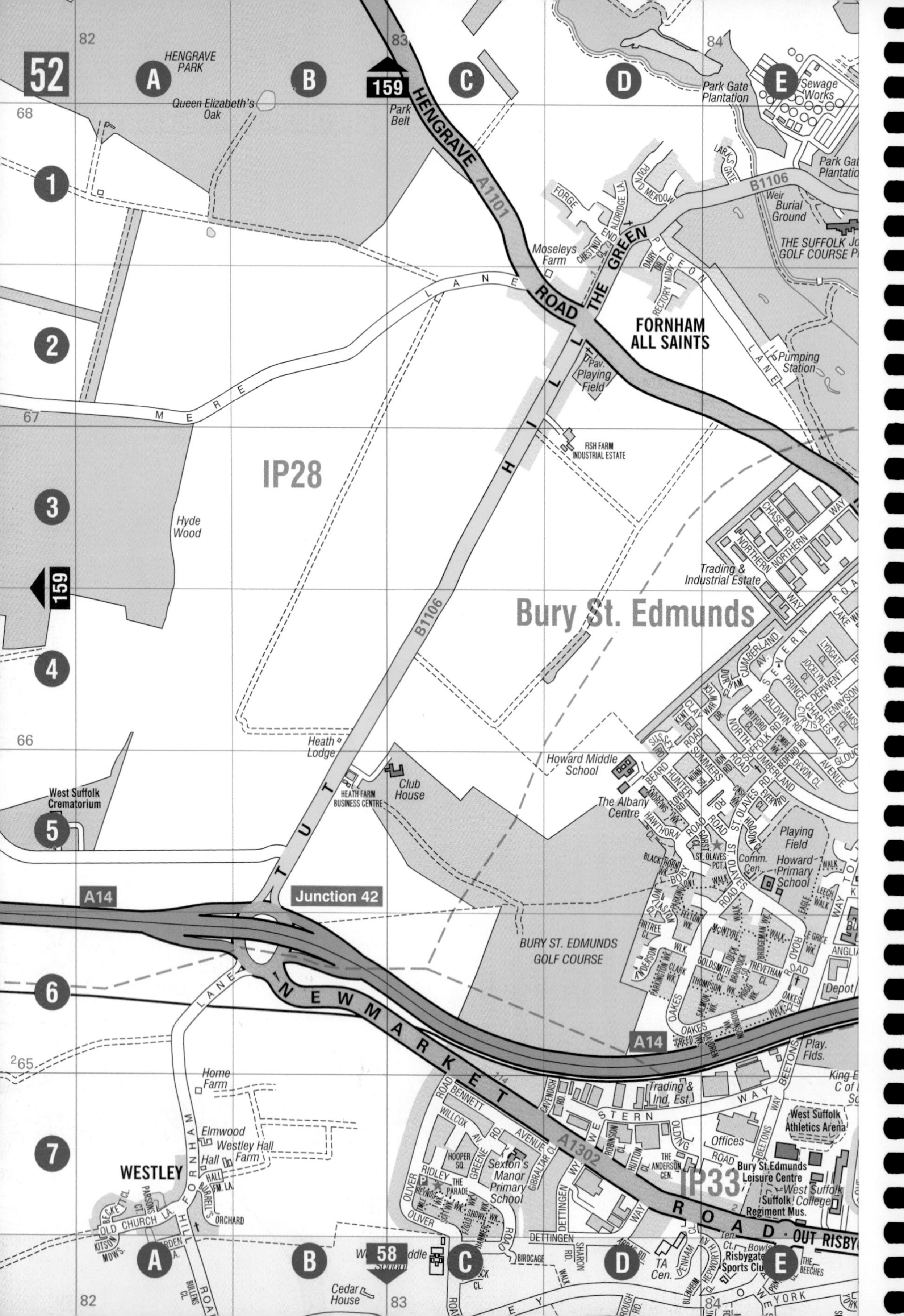
HENGRAVE PARK
Queen Elizabeth's Oak
Park Belt
HENGRAVE ROAD
A1101
Park Gate Plantation
Sewage Works
B1106
Weir
Burial Ground
THE SUFFOLK GOLF COURSE
Moseleys Farm
THE GREEN
PIGEON LANE
FORNHAM ALL SAINTS
Pumping Station
MERE LANE
Pav.
Playing Field
FISH FARM INDUSTRIAL ESTATE
IP28
Hyde Wood
HILL
Trading & Industrial Estate
Bury St. Edmunds
B1106
Heath Lodge
Howard Middle School
The Albany Centre
West Suffolk Crematorium
HEATH FARM BUSINESS CENTRE
Club House
TUT
Playing Field
Howard Primary School
A14
Junction 42
BURY ST. EDMUNDS GOLF COURSE
NEWMARKET
A14
Home Farm
Elmwood
Westley Hall Farm
WESTLEY
FORNHAM
Trading & Ind. Est.
WESTERN WAY
West Suffolk Athletics Arena
Offices
Sexton's Manor Primary School
A1302
IP33
Bury St.Edmunds Leisure Centre
West Suffolk College
Suffolk Regiment Mus.
OLD CHURCH LA.
ROAD
OUT RISBYGATE
TA Cen.
Bowls
Risbygate Sports Club
Cedar House
Depot
Play. Flds.

159
159
58

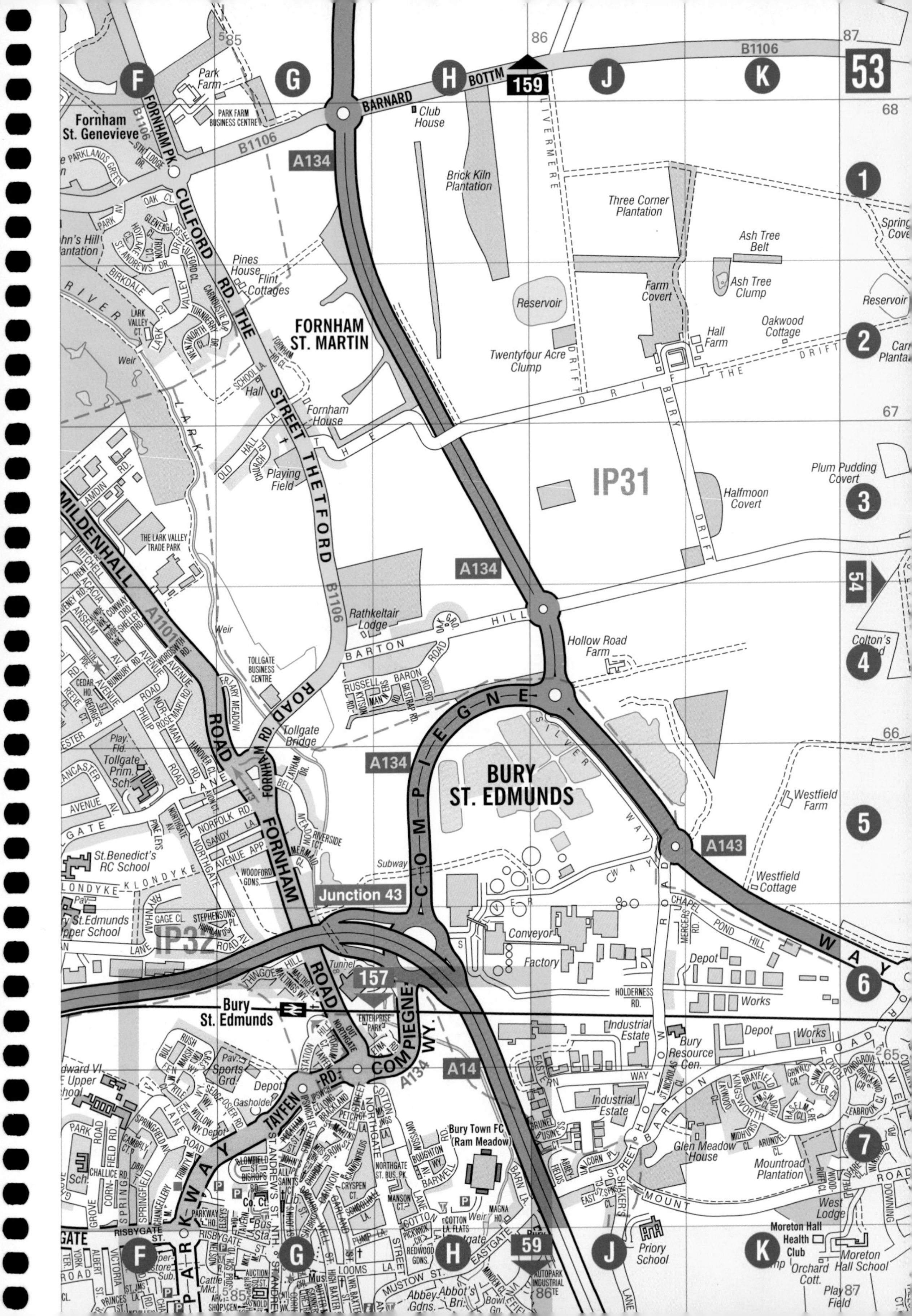

FORNHAM ST. MARTIN
Fornham St. Genevieve
BURY ST. EDMUNDS
IP31
IP32
A134
A143
A1101
B1106
Junction 43
159
157
59
54
Park Farm
Club House
Brick Kiln Plantation
Three Corner Plantation
Ash Tree Belt
Ash Tree Clump
Farm Covert
Reservoir
Oakwood Cottage
Hall Farm
Twentyfour Acre Clump
Pines House
Flint Cottages
Fornham House
Playing Field
Halfmoon Covert
Plum Pudding Covert
Rathkeltair Lodge
Hollow Road Farm
THE LARK VALLEY TRADE PARK
TOLLGATE BUSINESS CENTRE
Tollgate Bridge
Tollgate Prim. Sch.
St.Benedict's RC School
Westfield Farm
Westfield Cottage
Conveyor
Factory
Depot
Works
Industrial Estate
Bury Resource Cen.
Glen Meadow House
Mountroad Plantation
West Lodge
Moreton Hall Health Club
Moreton Hall School
Priory School
Bury Town FC (Ram Meadow)
Bury St. Edmunds
Sports Grd.
Gasholder
Orchard Cott.
Play Field

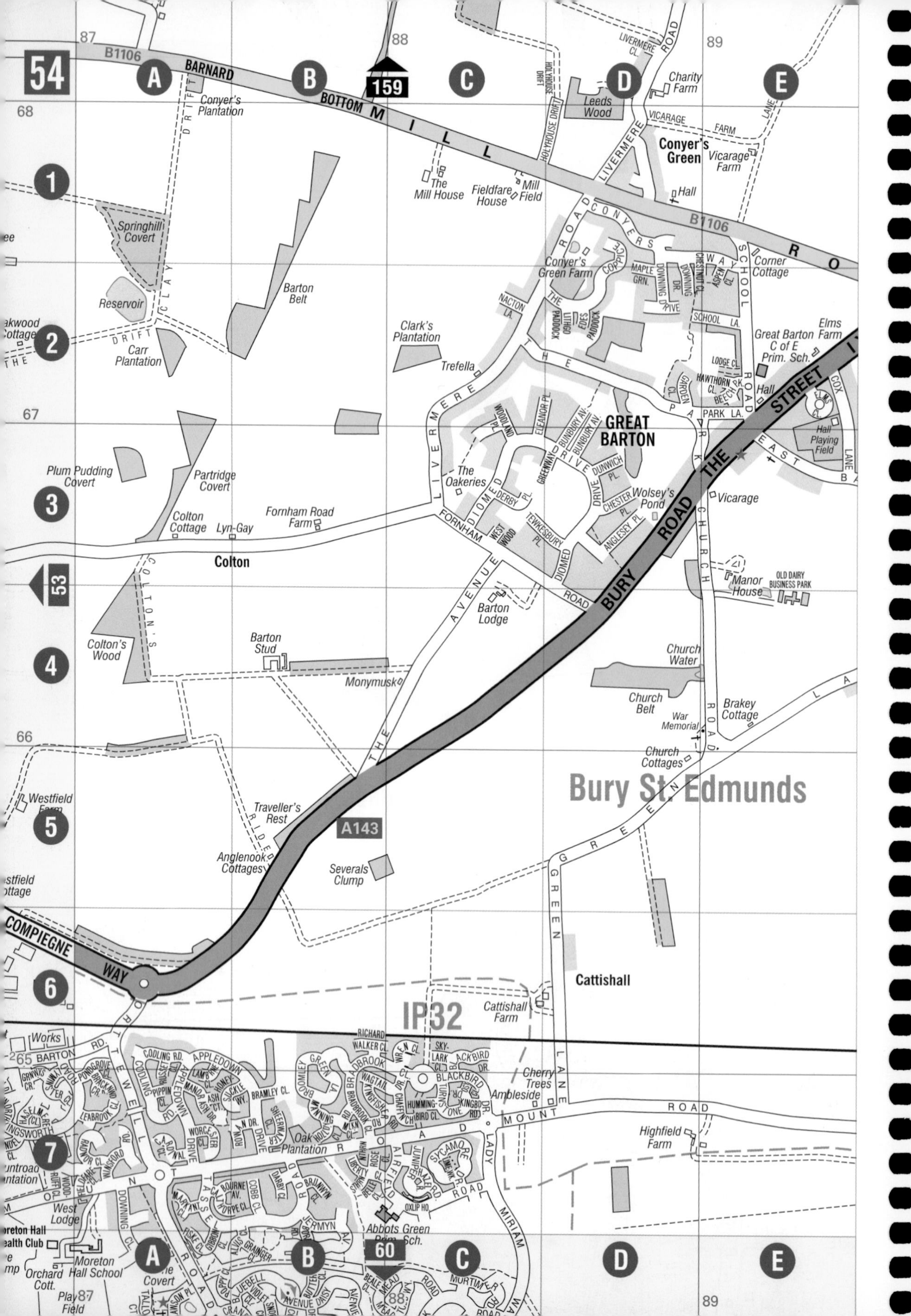

B1106
BARNARD
BOTTOM MILL
159
Conyer's Plantation
Leeds Wood
Charity Farm
Conyer's Green
Vicarage Farm
The Mill House
Fieldfare House
Mill Field
Springhill Covert
Reservoir
Barton Belt
Carr Plantation
Clark's Plantation
Trefella
Conyer's Green Farm
Corner Cottage
Great Barton C of E Prim. Sch.
Elms Farm
GREAT BARTON
Hall Playing Field
Plum Pudding Covert
Partridge Covert
The Oakeries
Wolsey's Pond
Vicarage
Colton Cottage
Lyn-Gay
Fornham Road Farm
Colton
53
Manor House
OLD DAIRY BUSINESS PARK
Barton Lodge
Colton's Wood
Barton Stud
Monymusk
Church Water
Church Belt
Brakey Cottage
War Memorial
Church Cottages
Bury St. Edmunds
Westfield Farm
Traveller's Rest
A143
Anglenook Cottages
Severals Clump
COMPIEGNE WAY
Cattishall
Cattishall Farm
IP32
Cherry Trees
Ambleside
MOUNT ROAD
Highfield Farm
Oak Plantation
West Lodge
Moreton Hall School
Orchard Cott.
Abbots Green Prim. Sch.
60

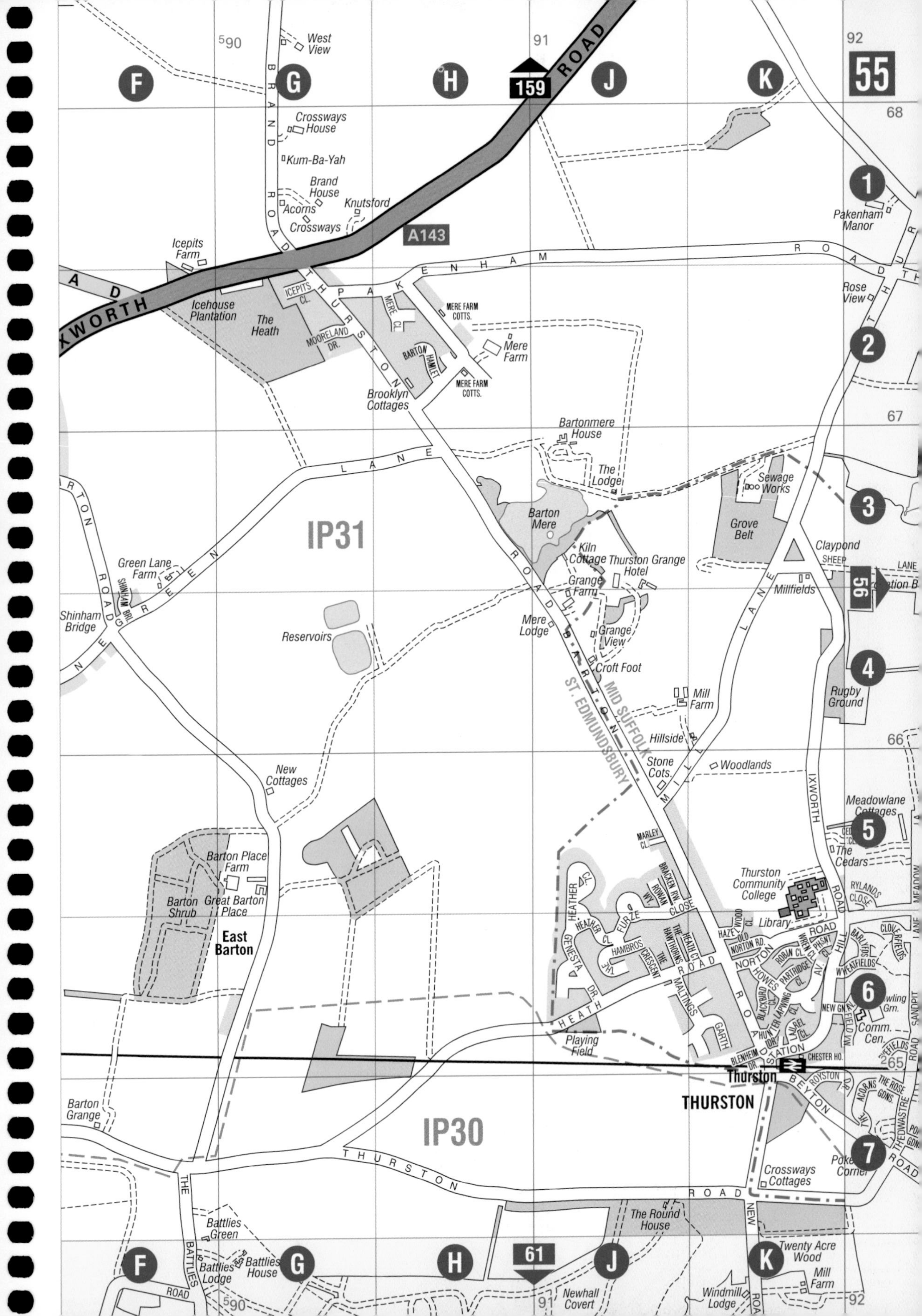

West View
Crossways House
Kum-Ba-Yah
Brand House
Knutsford
Acorns
Crossways
BRAND ROAD
A143
ROAD
159
Icepits Farm
Icehouse Plantation
The Heath
IXWORTH
ICEPITS CL.
MOORELAND DR.
THURSTON
PAKENHAM ROAD
MERE CL.
BARTON HAMLET
MERE FARM COTTS.
Mere Farm
Brooklyn Cottages
Pakenham Manor
Rose View
Bartonmere House
The Lodge
LANE
Sewage Works
Barton Mere
IP31
Grove Belt
Claypond
SHEEP LANE
Kiln Cottage
Thurston Grange Hotel
Grange Farm
Millfields
Green Lane Farm
GREEN
SHINHAM BRI.
Shinham Bridge
Reservoirs
Mere Lodge
Grange View
Croft Foot
Rugby Ground
Mill Farm
MID SUFFOLK
ST. EDMUNDSBURY
BARTON ROAD
Hillside
Stone Cots.
Woodlands
MILL LANE
IXWORTH ROAD
New Cottages
Meadowlane Cottages
The Cedars
MARLEY CL.
Barton Place Farm
Barton Shrub
Great Barton Place
East Barton
HEATHER CL.
BRACKEN RW.
ROWAN WY.
FURZE CLOSE
Thurston Community College
RYLANDS CLOSE
Library
HAMBROS CRESCENT
THE HAWTHORNS
HEATH CL.
HAZELWOOD CL.
OLD NORTON RD.
NORTON ROAD
GENESTA DR.
HEATH ROAD
MALTINGS
GARTH
HOWES
ROBIN CL.
WREN CL.
PHSNT CL.
PARTRIDGE CL.
BLACKBIRD CL.
LAPWING CL.
LAUREL CL.
HUNTER DR.
BARLYLDS
CLOVERFIELDS
WHEATFIELDS
NEW GN. AV.
Comm. Cen.
Playing Field
BLENHEIM DR.
STATION HILL
CHESTER HO.
Thurston
THURSTON
ROYSTON DR.
BEYTON ROAD
THE ACORNS
THE ROSE GDNS.
HEDWASTRE
SANDPIT
IP30
Barton Grange
THURSTON ROAD
Crossways Cottages
Poke Corner
THE BATTLIES
Battlies Green
Battlies Lodge
Battlies House
The Round House
NEW ROAD
Twenty Acre Wood
Mill Farm
61
Newhall Covert
Windmill Lodge
56
F
G
H
J
K
1
2
3
4
5
6
7
590
91
92
68
67
66
65

Upper Town
PAKENHAM
PAKENHAM FEN
Pakenham Manor
Playing Field
Rose View
Pakenham Lodge
Hall
Newe House
Home Farm
Vicarage
Pakenham Wood
Whitings Farm Cottage
Maulkin's Cottages
Maulkin's Hall
Boundary House
Moat
Beaumont Hall
CHURCH COTTAGES
Nether Hall
ST. EDMUNDSBURY
MID SUFFOLK
Claypond
Coronation Belt
Skeleton Plantation
Bella Vista
Thurston Gardens
Landimore
Rugby Ground
Poplar Farm
Elm Farm Cottages
Great Green
Elm Farm
Meadowlane Cottages
Lady Greene's Plantation
The Cedars
Manor Farm
Green Farm Cottage
Moat Farm
Green Farm
Wayside
Highfields
THURSTON
Bowling Grn.
Comm. Cen.
Play. Fld.
Sch.
The Vicarage
Thurston Lodge
Grove Farm
The Lodge
Thurston House
Stockhold Green Farm
Stockhold Green
Pokeriage Corner
Crossways Cottages
Twenty Acre Wood
Mill Farm
Hollow Lane
THURSTON ROAD
PAKENHAM ROAD
THE STREET
CHURCH HILL
SHEEP LANE
ORCHARD LANE
PAKENHAM ROAD
CHURCH ROAD
MEADOW LANE
BULL ROAD
OAK ROAD
PACKWAY LANE
POPLAR FARM LA.
GIPSIES
WYARDS
STONEY LANE
SCHOOL ROAD
BARRELLS ROAD
BIRD'S ROAD
PEPPER LANE
BEYTON ROAD
IXWORTH ROAD
SANDPIT ROAD
FIELD ROAD

159
55
62

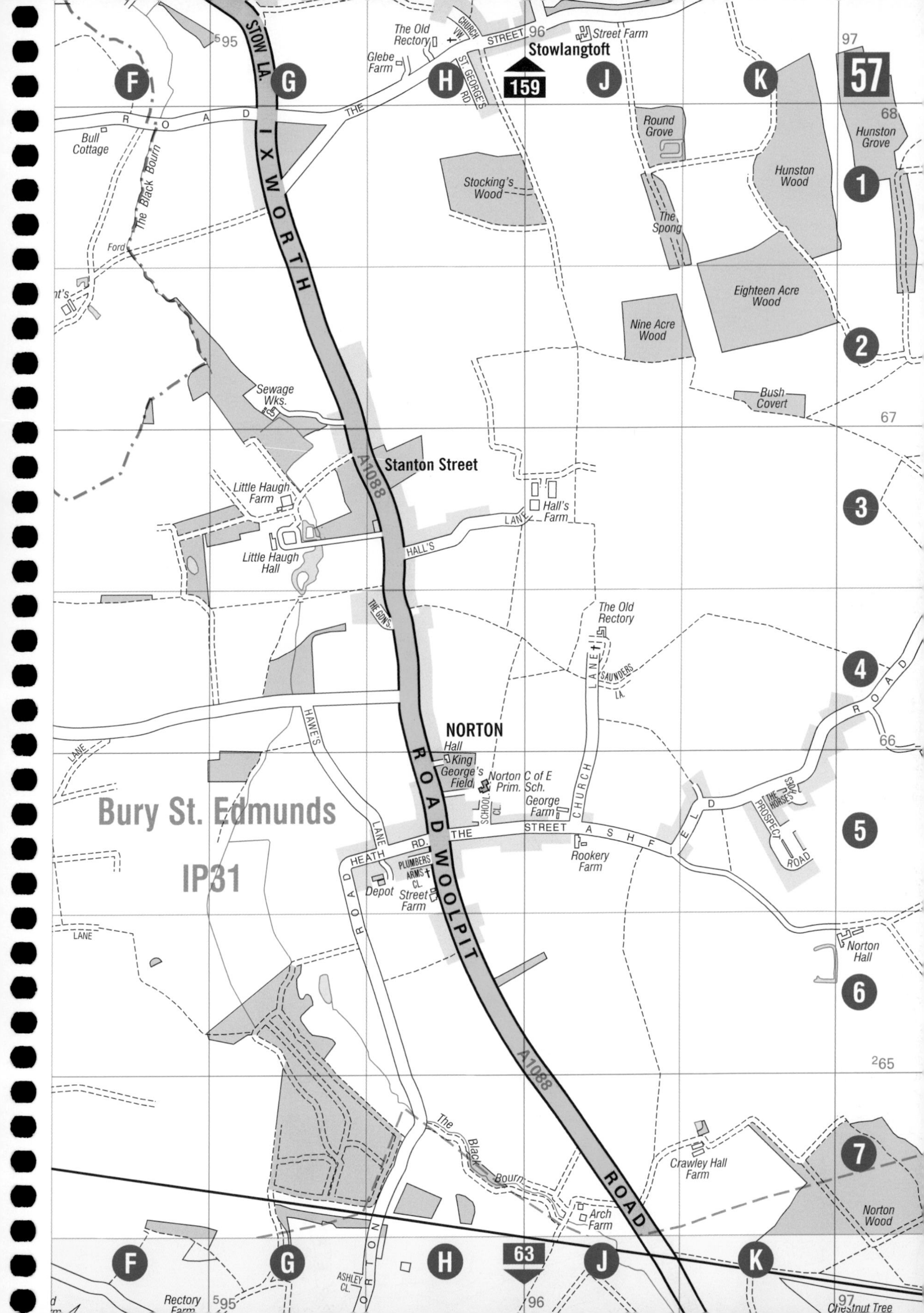

Stowlangtoft
159
Street Farm
The Old Rectory
Glebe Farm
CHURCH VW.
STREET
ST. GEORGE'S RD.
THE
ROAD
STOW LA.
IXWORTH
Bull Cottage
The Black Bourn
Ford
Round Grove
Hunston Grove
Hunston Wood
Stocking's Wood
The Spong
Eighteen Acre Wood
Nine Acre Wood
Bush Covert
Sewage Wks.
A1088
Stanton Street
Little Haugh Farm
Little Haugh Hall
HALL'S
LANE
Hall's Farm
THE GUNS
The Old Rectory
LANE
SAUNDERS LA.
HAWE'S
NORTON
Hall
King George's Field
Norton C of E Prim. Sch.
George Farm
SCHOOL CL.
CHURCH
ROAD
WOOLPIT
THE STREET
ASHFIELD
ROAD
THE HORSESHOES
PROSPECT ROAD
Bury St. Edmunds
IP31
LANE
HEATH RD.
PLUMBERS ARMS CL.
Depot
Street Farm
Rookery Farm
Norton Hall
LANE
The Black Bourn
Crawley Hall Farm
Arch Farm
Norton Wood
NORTON
ASHLEY CL.
Rectory Farm
Chestnut Tree
63
F
G
H
J
K
1
2
3
4
5
6
7
95
96
97
68
67
66
65

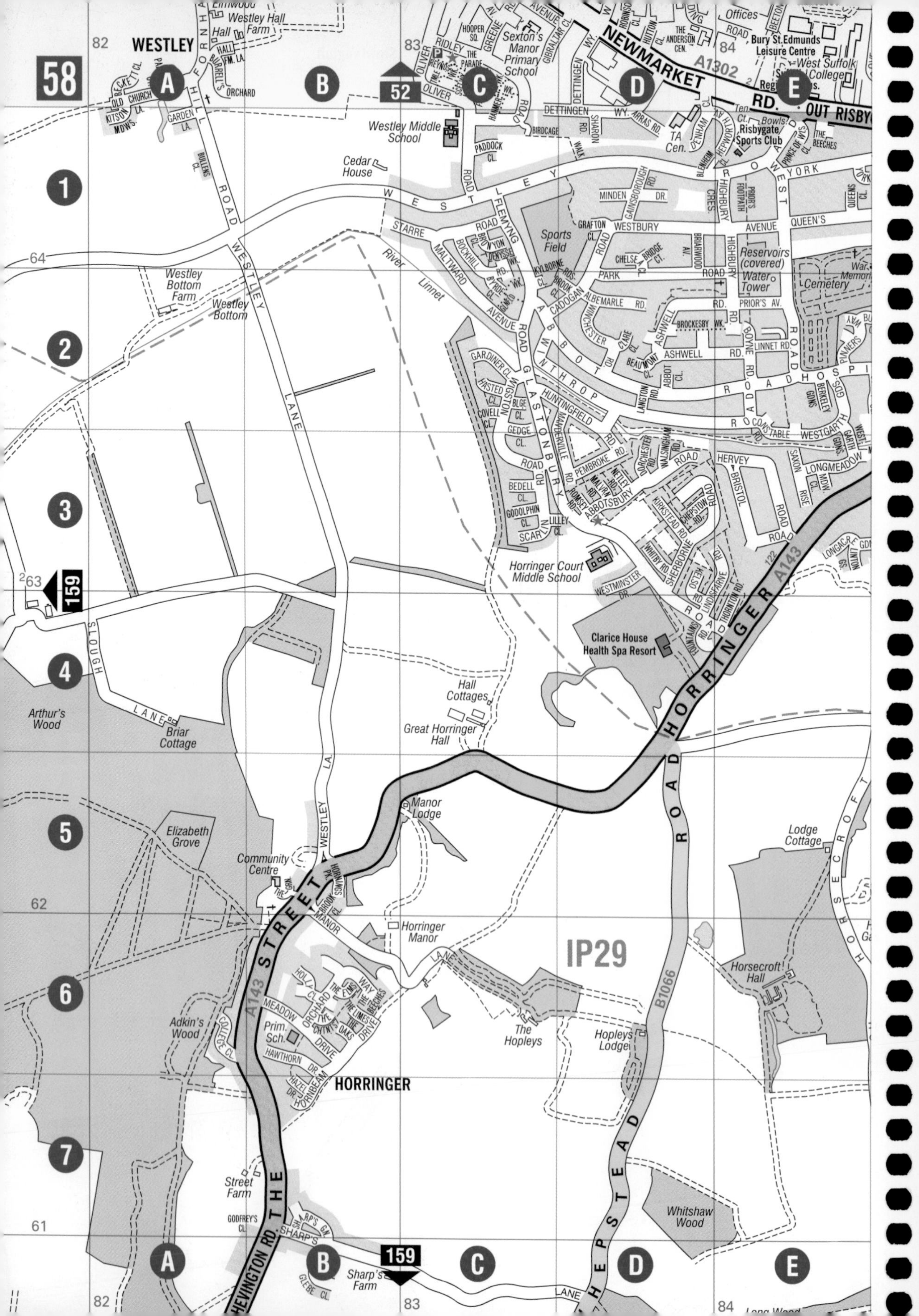
WESTLEY
Westley Hall Farm
Westley Middle School
Sexton's Manor Primary School
NEWMARKET RD.
A1302
Bury St.Edmunds Leisure Centre
West Suffolk College
OUT RISBYGATE
Risbygate Sports Club
TA Cen.
Cedar House
WESTLEY ROAD
Westley Bottom Farm
Westley Bottom
WESTLEY LANE
River Linnet
Sports Field
Reservoirs (covered)
Water Tower
Cemetery
YORK ROAD
QUEEN'S ROAD
HOSPITAL ROAD
GLASTONBURY ROAD
WINTHROP ROAD
ABBOT ROAD
Horringer Court Middle School
Clarice House Health Spa Resort
HORRINGER ROAD
A143
SLOUGH LANE
Arthur's Wood
Briar Cottage
Hall Cottages
Great Horringer Hall
Manor Lodge
Elizabeth Grove
Community Centre
Horringer Manor
IP29
B1066
Lodge Cottage
HORSECROFT ROAD
Horsecroft Hall
Adkin's Wood
Prim. Sch.
The Hopleys
Hopleys Lodge
HORRINGER
THE STREET
Street Farm
HEPSTEAD ROAD
Whitshaw Wood
Sharp's Farm
IKSWORTH ROAD
SHARP'S LANE
HEVINGTON RD.
52
159
82
83
84
64
63
62
61
A
B
C
D
E
1
2
3
4
5
6
7

59
F
G
H
J
K
53
157
159
60
BURY
ST. EDMUNDS
Bury St. Edmunds
IP33
IP32
1
2
3
4
5
6
7
Bury Town FC
(Ram Meadow)
Glen Meadow
House
Mountroad
Plantation
MOUNT ROAD
Moreton Hall
Health Club
Moreton
Hall School
West
Lodge
Priory
School
The
Clump
Orchard
Cott.
Playing
Field
RISBYGATE ST.
PARKWAY
A1302
Cattle
Mkt.
Super-
market
St.Edmundsbury
Cathedral
Abbey
Gdns.
Abbey
Gate
Remains of
St.Edmunds
Abbey
Abbot's
Bri.
Eastgate
Bri.
Courts
Theatre
Royal
HOSP.
St. James
CEVA
Mid. Sch.
AUTOPARK
INDUSTRIAL
ESTATE
A14
Junction 44
No Man's
Meadows
Layhill
Covert
Pond
Covert
Set
Wood
Prim. Sch.
BEDINGFELD WAY
Superstore
ST.EDMUNDSBURY
RETAIL PARK
WESTGATE
ROAD OUT WESTGATE
CULLUM ROAD
ROUGHAM RD.
SICKLESMERE ROAD
Westgate
Prim.Sch.
Stamford
Bridge
River
Holywater
Meadows
York
Bridge
The Grindle
Paddock
Sports
Ground
Club
House
Rugby
Football
Ground
Southgate
Bridge
ROUGHAM HILL
RUSHBROOKE
Golf Driving
Range
THE FIRS
MOBILE HOME PARK
Oak
House
Fenbrook
Farm
Kennels
HARDWICK LANE
Badger's
Place
Stonebridge
Hardwick
Prim.
Sch.
Comm.
Cen.
WEST SUFFOLK
HOSPITAL
Hardwick
Heath
Wedgwood
Unit
St. Nicholas'
Hospice
Stonebridge
Belt
Hardwick
Manor
Victory
Sports
Ground
Tennis
Courts
South
Lee
Sch.
A134
Shrub
Hill
Games
Court
Breckey Ley
House
Breckey Ley
Park
Hardwick
Middle School
Court Farm
Barn
FOX AND PIN LA.
NOWTON PARK
The
Nuttery
Hardwick
Game Farm
Hardwick
House
Beech
Grove
HENCOTE
HORSECROFT
Home
Farm
The
Paddock
NOWTON
COURT
Playing
Field
Nowton
Lodge
Play.
Fld.
GREEN
62
61
85
86
87

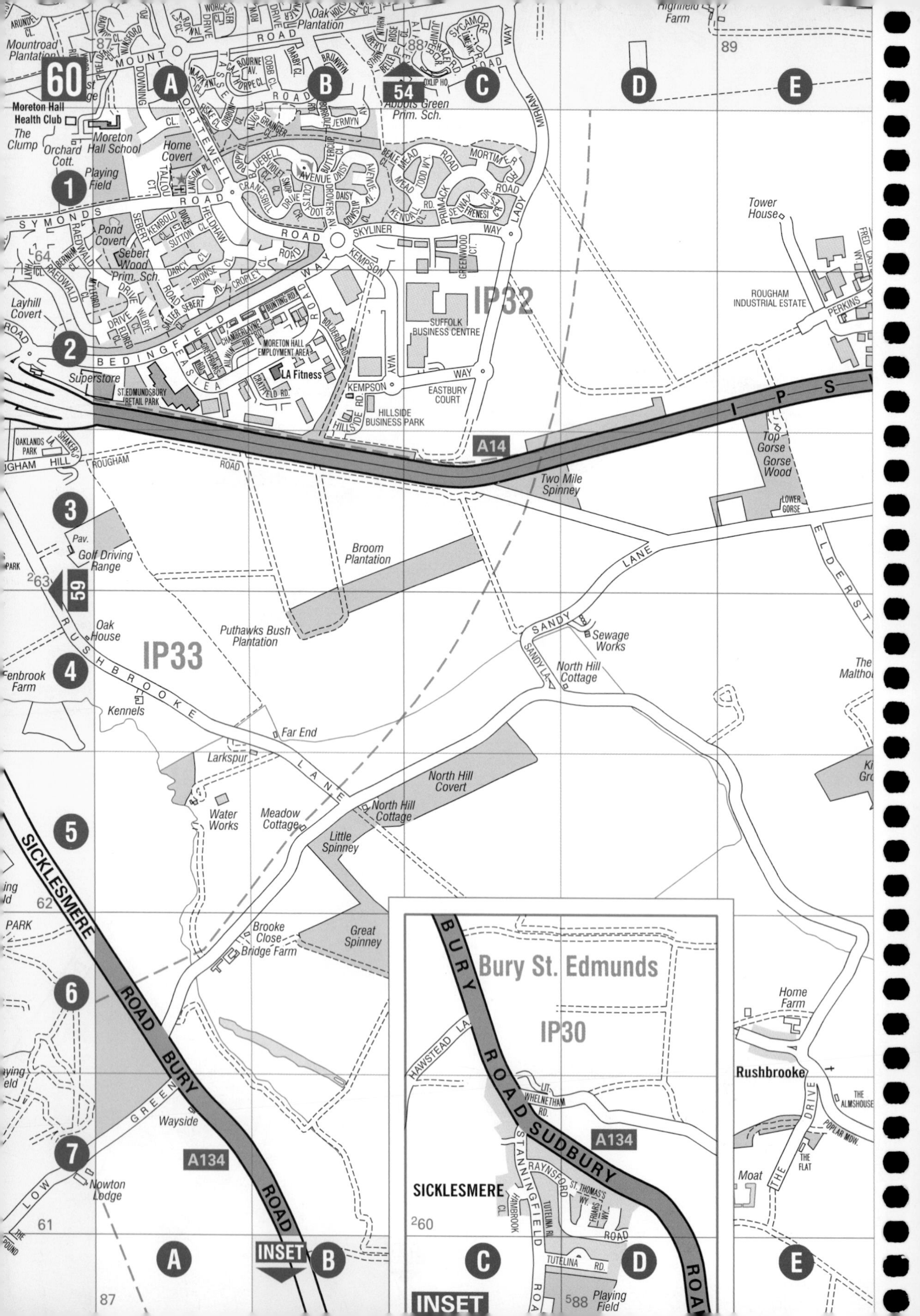
Moreton Hall Health Club
Moreton Hall School
Mountroad Plantation
Oak Plantation
Abbots Green Prim. Sch.
Home Covert
Orchard Cott.
The Clump
Playing Field
Pond Covert
Sebert Wood Prim. Sch.
Layhill Covert
Superstore
ST. EDMUNDSBURY RETAIL PARK
MORETON HALL EMPLOYMENT AREA
LA Fitness
SUFFOLK BUSINESS CENTRE
EASTBURY COURT
HILLSIDE BUSINESS PARK
IP32
Tower House
ROUGHAM INDUSTRIAL ESTATE
A14
Two Mile Spinney
Top Gorse
Gorse Wood
LOWER GORSE
Broom Plantation
Golf Driving Range
Pav.
Oak House
Puthawks Bush Plantation
IP33
Sewage Works
North Hill Cottage
Fenbrook Farm
Kennels
Far End
Larkspur
North Hill Covert
Water Works
Meadow Cottage
Little Spinney
Brooke Close
Bridge Farm
Great Spinney
Wayside
Nowton Lodge
A134
Bury St. Edmunds
IP30
SICKLESMERE
Home Farm
Rushbrooke
THE ALMSHOUSES
THE FLAT
Moat
Playing Field
INSET
54
59

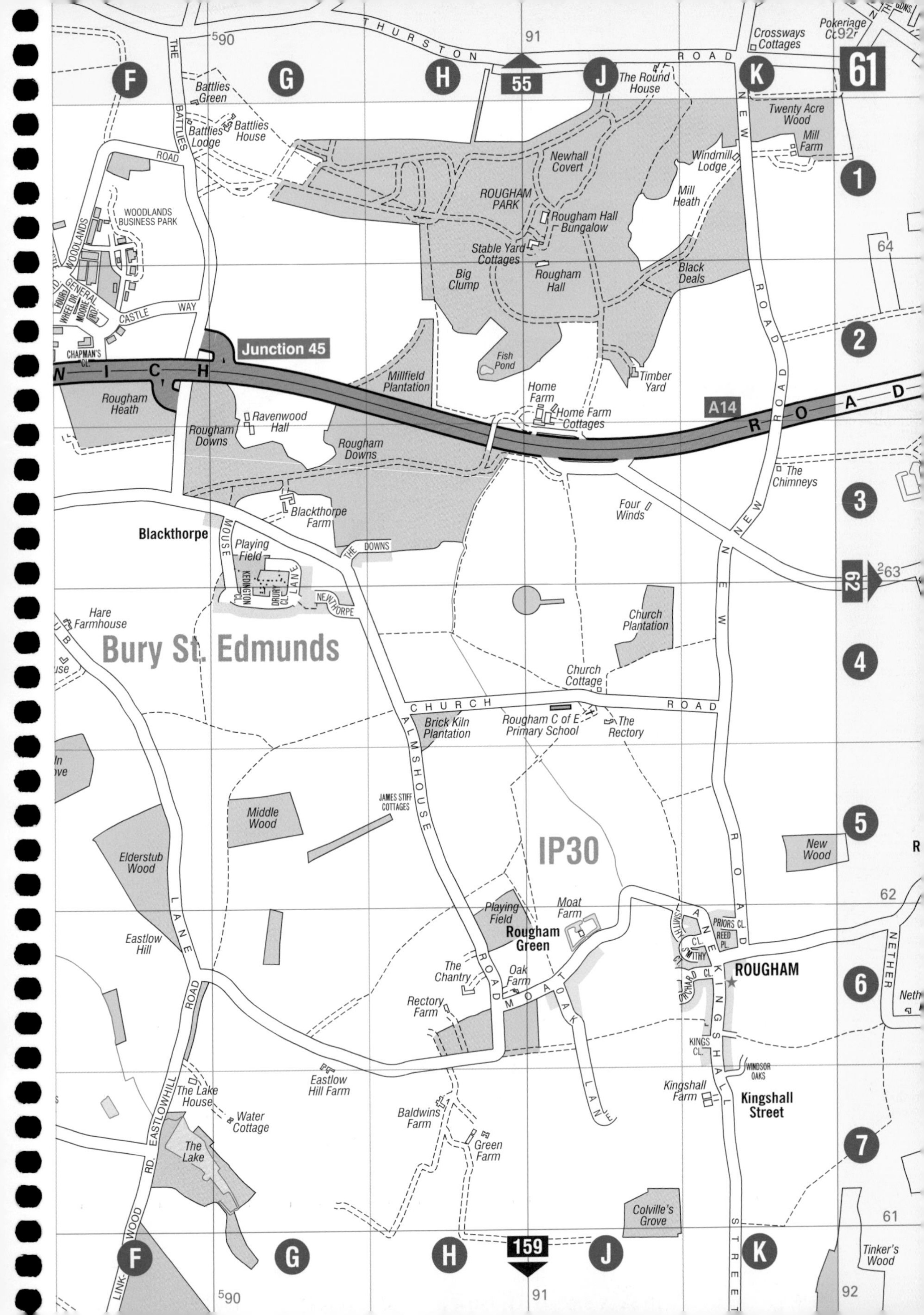

THURSTON ROAD
55
Crossways Cottages
Pokeriage Cl.
The Round House
Battlies Green
Battlies Lodge
Battlies House
THE BATTLIES ROAD
Twenty Acre Wood
Mill Farm
Windmill Lodge
Newhall Covert
ROUGHAM PARK
Rougham Hall Bungalow
Mill Heath
Stable Yard Cottages
Big Clump
Rougham Hall
Black Deals
WOODLANDS BUSINESS PARK
WOODLANDS
GENERAL
CASTLE WAY
CHAPMAN'S CL.
Junction 45
Fish Pond
Timber Yard
Millfield Plantation
Rougham Heath
Home Farm
Home Farm Cottages
A14
Ravenwood Hall
Rougham Downs
Rougham Downs
NEW ROAD
The Chimneys
Blackthorpe Farm
Blackthorpe
Four Winds
MOUSE LANE
Playing Field
THE DOWNS
KEDINGTON CL.
DRURY CL.
NEWTHORPE
Hare Farmhouse
Church Plantation
Bury St. Edmunds
Church Cottage
CHURCH ROAD
Brick Kiln Plantation
Rougham C of E Primary School
The Rectory
JAMES STIFF COTTAGES
ALMSHOUSE ROAD
Middle Wood
Elderstub Wood
IP30
New Wood
Playing Field
Moat Farm
Rougham Green
PRIORS CL.
REED PL.
SMITHY CL.
Eastlow Hill
The Chantry
Oak Farm
MOAT LANE
OAK LANE
ROUGHAM
ORCHARD CL.
KINGSHALL STREET
NETHER
Rectory Farm
KINGS CL.
WINDSOR OAKS
The Lake House
Eastlow Hill Farm
Kingshall Farm
Kingshall Street
Water Cottage
Baldwins Farm
Green Farm
The Lake
EASTLOWHILL ROAD
LINK-WOOD RD.
Colville's Grove
Tinker's Wood
159
62

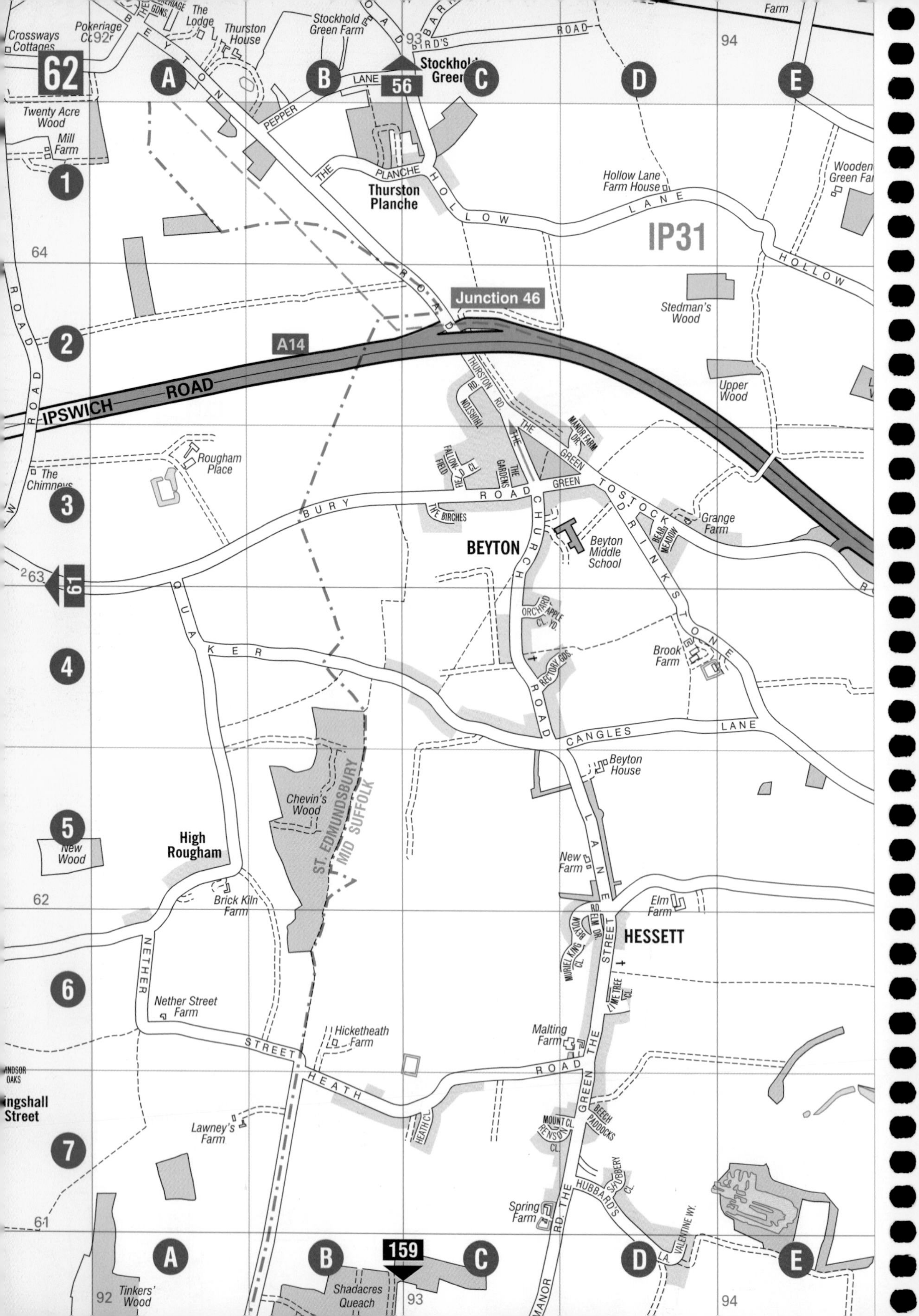

62
56
61
159
Junction 46
A14
IPSWICH ROAD
IP31
BEYTON
HESSETT
Thurston Planche
Stockhold Green
High Rougham
Crossways Cottages
Pokeriage Cotts
The Lodge
Thurston House
Stockhold Green Farm
Twenty Acre Wood
Mill Farm
Hollow Lane Farm House
Wooden Green Farm
Stedman's Wood
Upper Wood
Rougham Place
The Chimneys
Grange Farm
Beyton Middle School
Brook Farm
Beyton House
Chevin's Wood
ST. EDMUNDSBURY
MID SUFFOLK
New Wood
Brick Kiln Farm
New Farm
Elm Farm
Nether Street Farm
Hicketheath Farm
Malting Farm
Lawney's Farm
Spring Farm
Tinkers' Wood
Shadacres Queach
Windsor Oaks
ingshall Street
PEPPER LANE
THE PLANCHE
HOLLOW LANE
BIRD'S ROAD
THURSTON ROAD
THE GREEN
MANOR FARM DR.
FALLOW-FIELD CL.
THE GARDENS
BURY ROAD
THE BIRCHES
CHURCH ROAD
TOSTOCK ROAD
DRINKSTONE LANE
BEAR MEADOW
ORCHARD CL.
APPLE YD.
RECTORY GDS.
QUAKER LANE
CANGLES LANE
LANE
BEYTON RD.
ELM DR.
MURIEL KING CL.
STREET
LIME TREE CL.
NETHER STREET
HEATH ROAD
HEATH CL.
THE GREEN
BEECH PADDOCKS
MOUNT CL.
RENSON CL.
HUBBARD'S LA.
SHRUBBERY CL.
VALENTINE WY.
THE RD.
MANOR
A B C D E
1 2 3 4 5 6 7
92 93 94
64 63 62 61

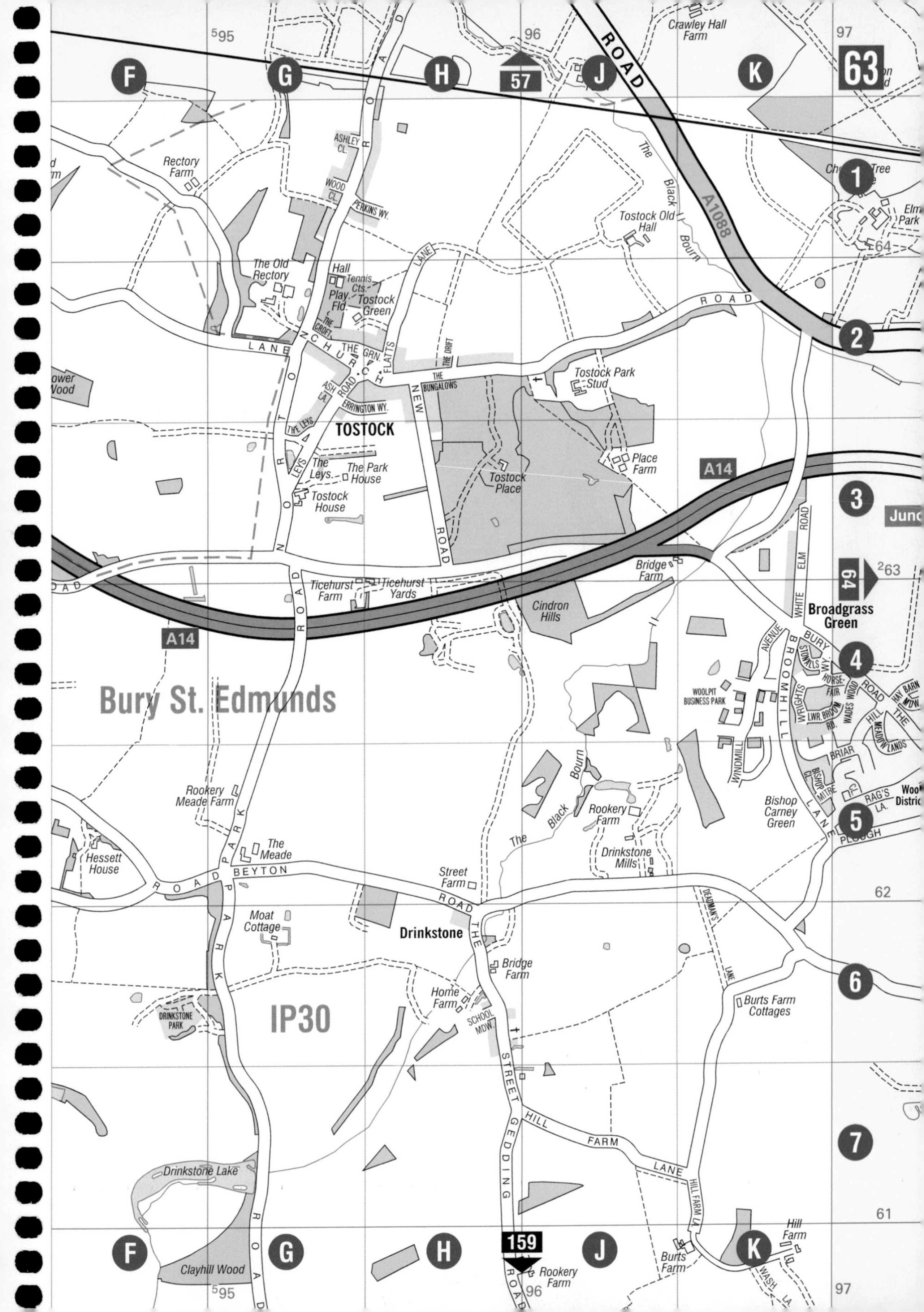

TOSTOCK
Bury St. Edmunds
IP30
Drinkstone
Broadgrass Green
Crawley Hall Farm
Rectory Farm
The Old Rectory
Hall
Tennis Cts.
Play. Fld.
Tostock Green
Tostock Old Hall
Tostock Park Stud
Place Farm
Tostock Place
The Park House
Tostock House
The Leys
Ticehurst Farm
Ticehurst Yards
Cindron Hills
Bridge Farm
Woolpit Business Park
Bishop Carney Green
Rookery Meade Farm
The Meade
Hessett House
Street Farm
Moat Cottage
Rookery Farm
Drinkstone Mills
Home Farm
Drinkstone Park
Burts Farm Cottages
Drinkstone Lake
Clayhill Wood
Burts Farm
Hill Farm
Rookery Farm
The Black Bourn
A14
A1088
57
64
159

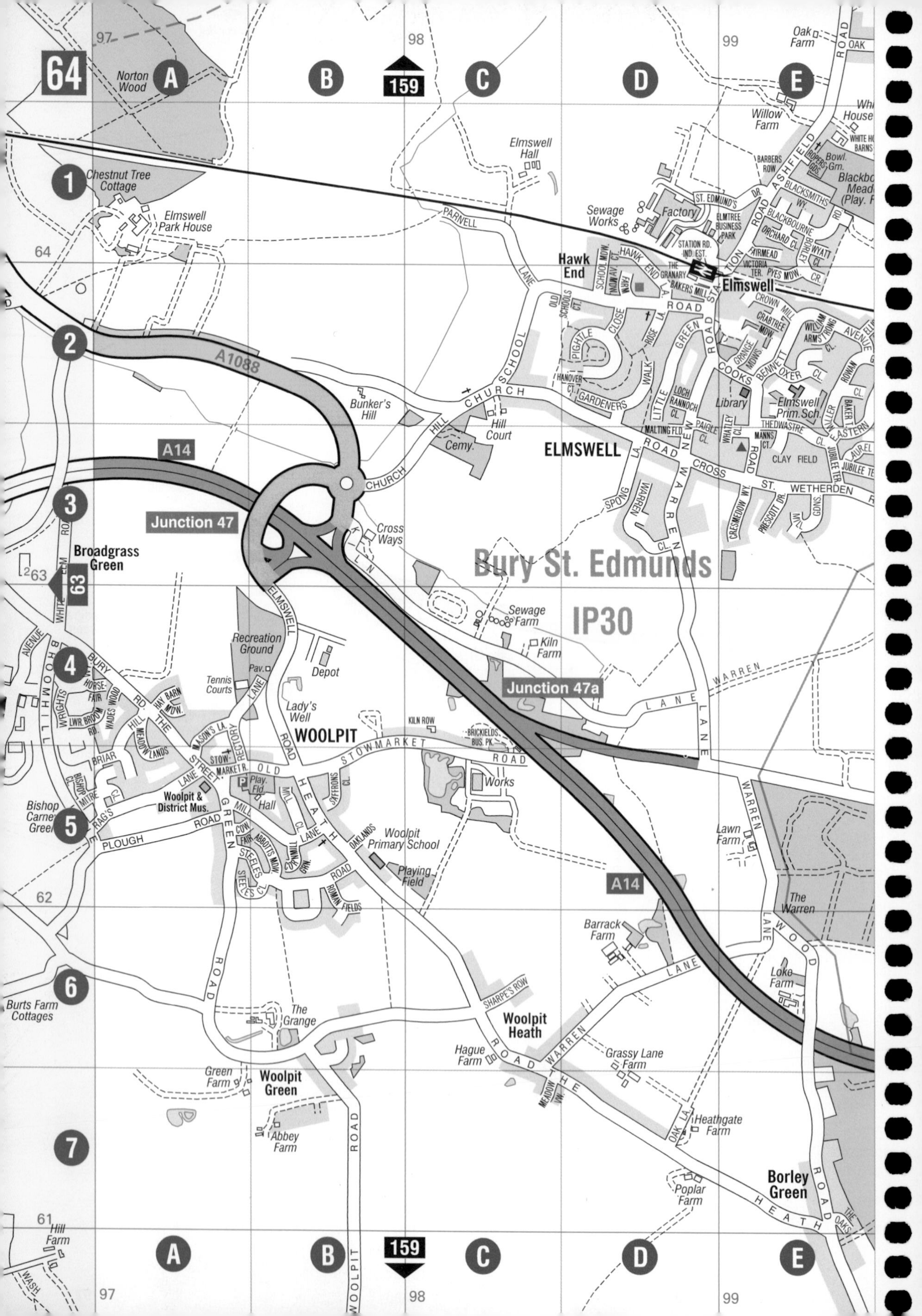

Norton Wood
Chestnut Tree Cottage
Elmswell Park House
Elmswell Hall
Parnell
Lane
Sewage Works
Factory
St. Edmund's
Elmtree Business Park
Station Rd. Ind. Est.
Hawk End
Hawk End La.
School Mdw.
Mdw. Av.
Farm Ct.
The Granary
Bakers Mill
Station
Elmswell
Willow Farm
Oak Farm
White House
Barbers Row
Ashfield
Ropers Gdns.
Bowl. Grn.
Blacksmiths Wy.
Blackbourne
Orchard Cl.
Borley
Wyatt Cl.
Fairmead
Victoria Ter.
Pyes Mdw.
Blackbourne Meadows (Play. Fd.)
Old Schools Ct.
Close
Rose La.
Green
Road
Pightle
Hanover Ct.
Gardeners
Walk
Little
Loch Rannoch Cl.
Cooks
Grange Mdws.
Crabtree Mdw.
Crown Mill
William Armstrong Cl.
Avenue
Bennett
Oxer Cl.
Rowan Cl.
Library
Elmswell Prim. Sch.
Baker
Miller
Eastern
Paigle Cl.
Whatley Cl.
Malting Fld.
New
Thedwastre Cl.
Manns Ct.
Clay Field
Jubilee Ter.
Aurel
School
Church
Hill
Bunker's Hill
Hill Court
Cemy.
ELMSWELL
Cross
St.
Wetherden
Spong La.
Warren Cl.
Warren
Cresmedow Wy.
Prescott Dr.
Mill Gdns.
A1088
A14
Junction 47
Cross Ways
Kiln Lane
Bury St. Edmunds
IP30
Sewage Farm
Kiln Farm
Junction 47a
Warren Lane
Broadgrass Green
White Elm Road
Elmswell Road
Recreation Ground
Pav.
Tennis Courts
Depot
Lady's Well
Kiln Row
Brickfields Bus. Pk.
Stowmarket Road
Old
WOOLPIT
Avenue
Broomhill
Bury Rd.
Horse-fair
Wrights
Wades Wood
Hay Barn Mdw.
Lwr. Broom Rd.
Hill
Meadow Lands
The Street
Mason's La.
Rectory Lane
Stowmarket R.
Briar
Bishop Mitre Cl.
Lane
Play. Fld.
Hall
Mill Cl.
Heath
Saffrons Cl.
Works
Woolpit & District Mus.
Bishop Carney Green
Rag's
Plough Road
Green
Mill
Cow
Fair
Abbotts Mdw.
Windmill Grn.
Lane
Steeles
Steeles Cl.
Road
Roman Fields
Oaklands
Woolpit Primary School
Playing Field
Lawn Farm
Warren Lane
The Warren
Barrack Farm
Lane
Wood Lane
Loke Farm
Burts Farm Cottages
Road
The Grange
Sharpe's Row
Woolpit Heath
Hague Farm
Road
Warren
The Meadow Vw.
Grassy Lane Farm
Green Farm
Woolpit Green
Abbey Farm
Woolpit Road
Oak La.
Heathgate Farm
Poplar Farm
Borley Green
Heath Road
The Oaks
Hill Farm
Wash
159
63
97
98
99
64
63
62
61
A B C D E
1 2 3 4 5 6 7

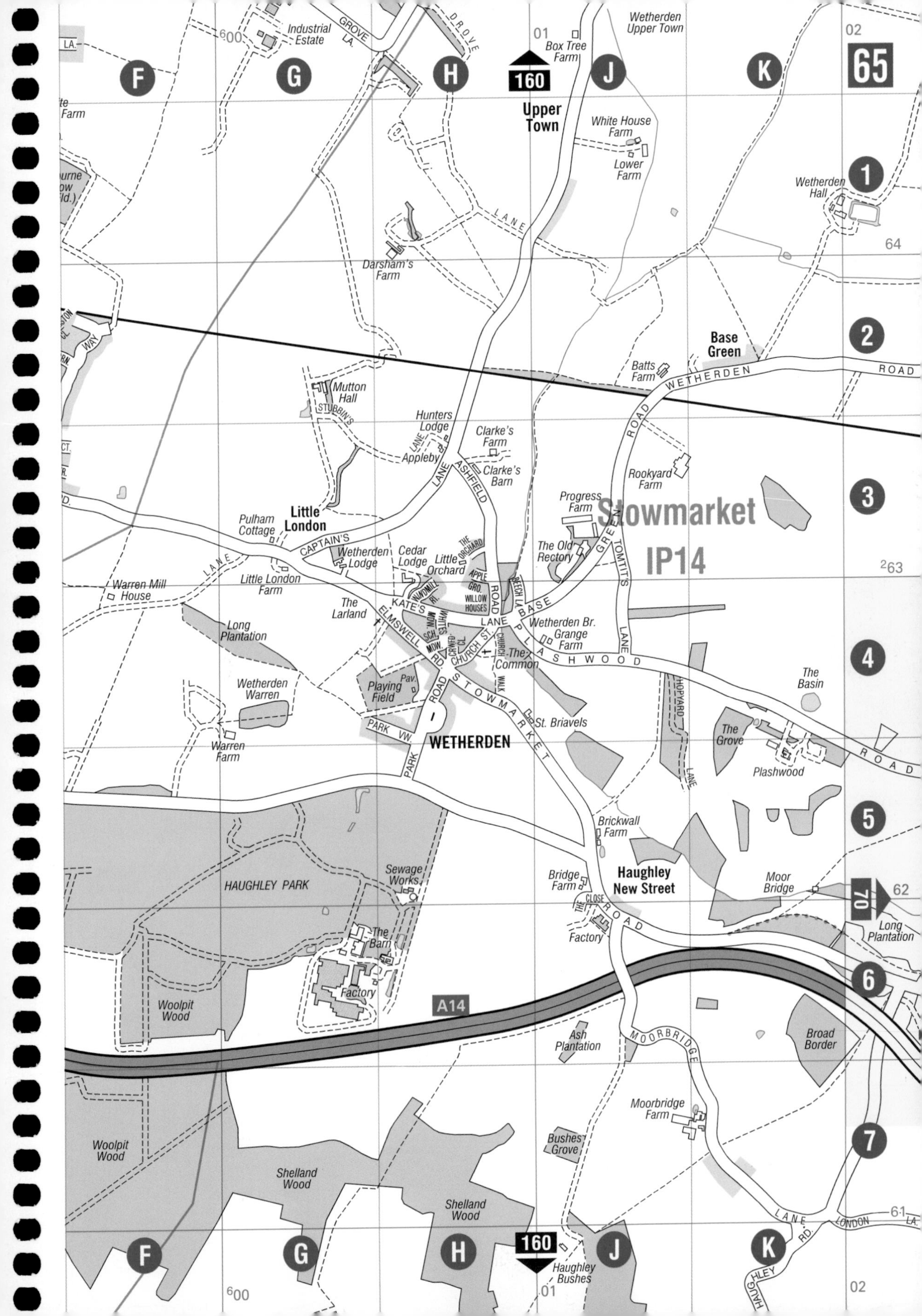
Industrial Estate
GROVE LA.
DROVE
Box Tree Farm
Wetherden Upper Town
160
Upper Town
White House Farm
Lower Farm
Wetherden Hall
LANE
Darsham's Farm
Base Green
Batts Farm
WETHERDEN ROAD
Mutton Hall
STUBBIN'S
Hunters Lodge
Clarke's Farm
Appleby
Clarke's Barn
ASHFIELD
Rookyard Farm
Progress Farm
Stowmarket
IP14
Little London
Pulham Cottage
CAPTAIN'S LANE
Wetherden Lodge
Cedar Lodge
Little Orchard
THE ORCHARD
The Old Rectory
GREEN
TOMTITS LANE
Warren Mill House
Little London Farm
The Larland
KATE'S
ELMSWELL RD.
BASE LANE
Long Plantation
Wetherden Br. Grange Farm
PLASHWOOD ROAD
CHURCH ST.
The Common
The Basin
Wetherden Warren
Playing Field
Pav.
STOWMARKET ROAD
St. Briavels
HOPYARD LANE
The Grove
Plashwood
Warren Farm
PARK VW.
WETHERDEN
PARK ROAD
Brickwall Farm
HAUGHLEY PARK
Sewage Works
Bridge Farm
Haughley New Street
Moor Bridge
THE CLOSE
Factory
70
Long Plantation
The Barn
Factory
A14
Woolpit Wood
Ash Plantation
MOORBRIDGE LANE
Broad Border
Moorbridge Farm
Woolpit Wood
Bushes Grove
Shelland Wood
Shelland Wood
LONDON RD.
HAUGHLEY
Haughley Bushes
160

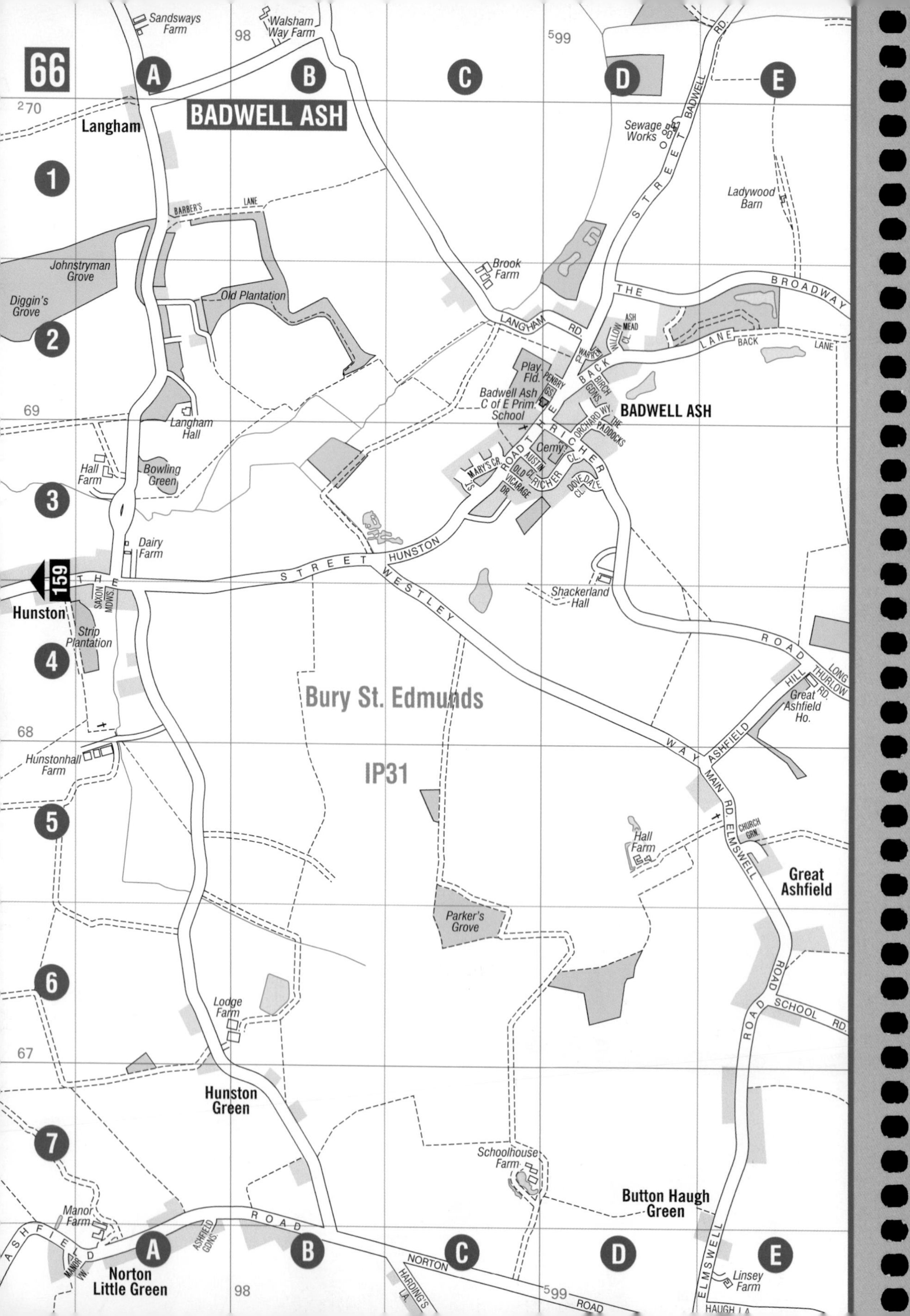
BADWELL ASH
Sandsways Farm
Walsham Way Farm
98
599
270
A
B
C
D
E
1
2
3
4
5
6
7
Langham
Sewage Works
BADWELL ST STREET
Ladywood Barn
BARBER'S LANE
Johnstryman Grove
Diggin's Grove
Old Plantation
Brook Farm
THE BROADWAY
LANGHAM RD.
ASH MEAD CL.
WILLOW CL.
WARREN CL.
BACK LANE
Play. Fld.
PENBRY GS.
BIRCH GDNS.
Badwell Ash C of E Prim. School
BADWELL ASH
69
Langham Hall
RICHER ROAD
ORCHARD WY.
THE PADDOCKS
Cemy.
Hall Farm
Bowling Green
MARY'S CR.
AUSTIN CL.
OLD VICARAGE DR.
RICHER CL.
DOVE DALE CL.
Dairy Farm
HUNSTON STREET
159
THE STREET
Hunston
SAXON MDWS.
WESTLEY WAY
Shackerland Hall
Strip Plantation
ROAD
LONG THURLOW RD.
HILL
Great Ashfield Ho.
Bury St. Edmunds
ASHFIELD
68
Hunstonhall Farm
IP31
MAIN RD.
CHURCH GRN.
Hall Farm
ELMSWELL ROAD
Great Ashfield
Parker's Grove
SCHOOL RD.
Lodge Farm
67
Hunston Green
Schoolhouse Farm
Button Haugh Green
Manor Farm
ASHFIELD ROAD
ASHFIELD GDNS.
MANOR VW.
NORTON ROAD
Norton Little Green
HARDING'S LA.
ELMSWELL
Linsey Farm
HAUGH LA.

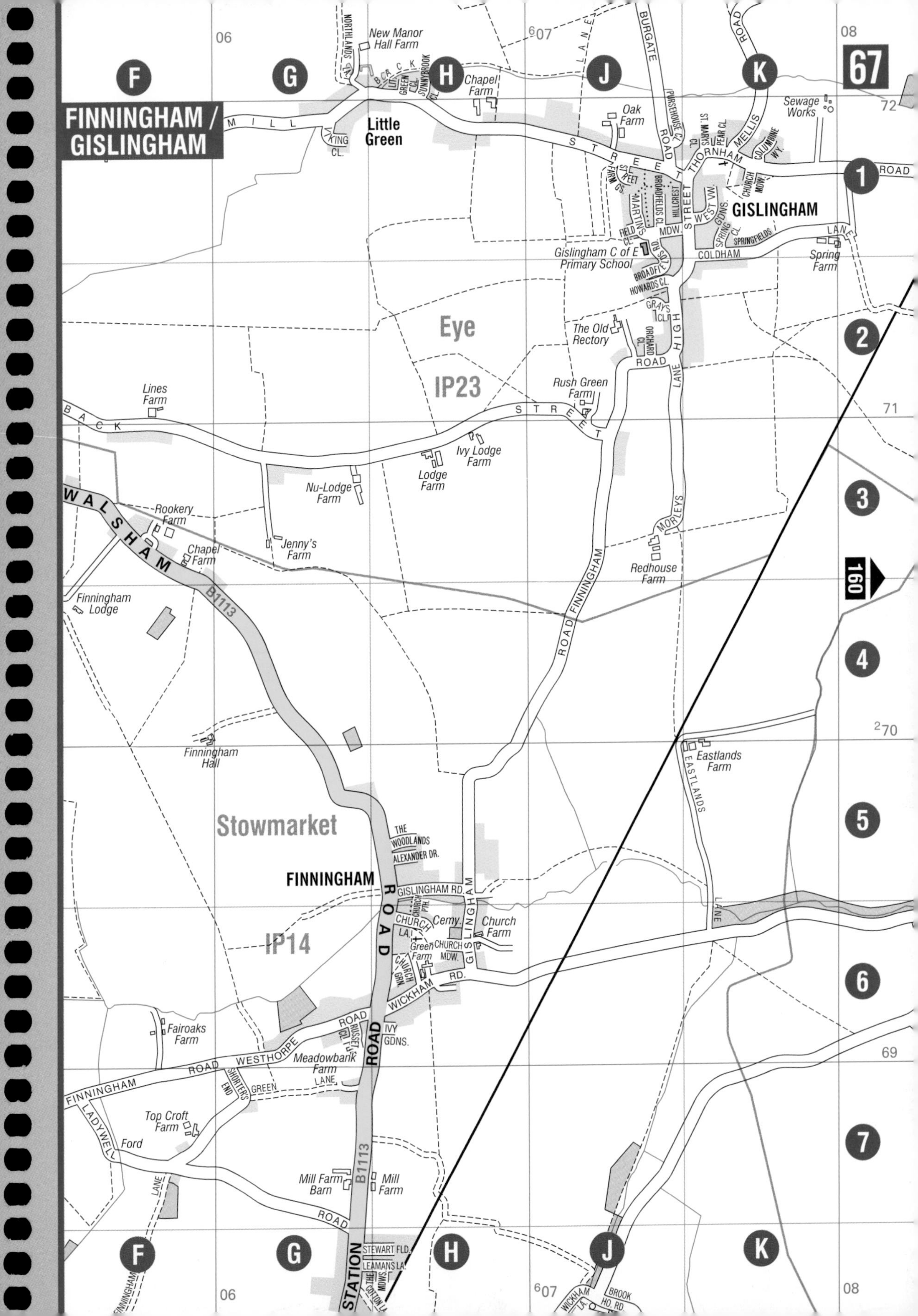
FINNINGHAM / GISLINGHAM
F
G
H
J
K
06
07
08
72
71
70
69
1
2
3
4
5
6
7
160
New Manor Hall Farm
Chapel Farm
Little Green
Oak Farm
Sewage Works
GISLINGHAM
Gislingham C of E Primary School
Spring Farm
Eye
IP23
The Old Rectory
Rush Green Farm
Lines Farm
Ivy Lodge Farm
Lodge Farm
Nu-Lodge Farm
Rookery Farm
Chapel Farm
Jenny's Farm
Redhouse Farm
Finningham Lodge
Finningham Hall
Eastlands Farm
Stowmarket
FINNINGHAM
Church Farm
Green Farm
IP14
Fairoaks Farm
Meadowbank Farm
Top Croft Farm
Ford
Mill Farm Barn
Mill Farm
MILL STREET
BACK STREET
WALSHAM ROAD
B1113
FINNINGHAM ROAD
HIGH LANE
COLDHAM LANE
THORNHAM ROAD
MELLIS ROAD
BURGATE ROAD
WESTHORPE ROAD
WICKHAM RD.
GISLINGHAM RD.
STATION ROAD
EASTLANDS LANE
LADYWELL LANE
SHORTERS END
GREEN LANE
BROOK HO. RD

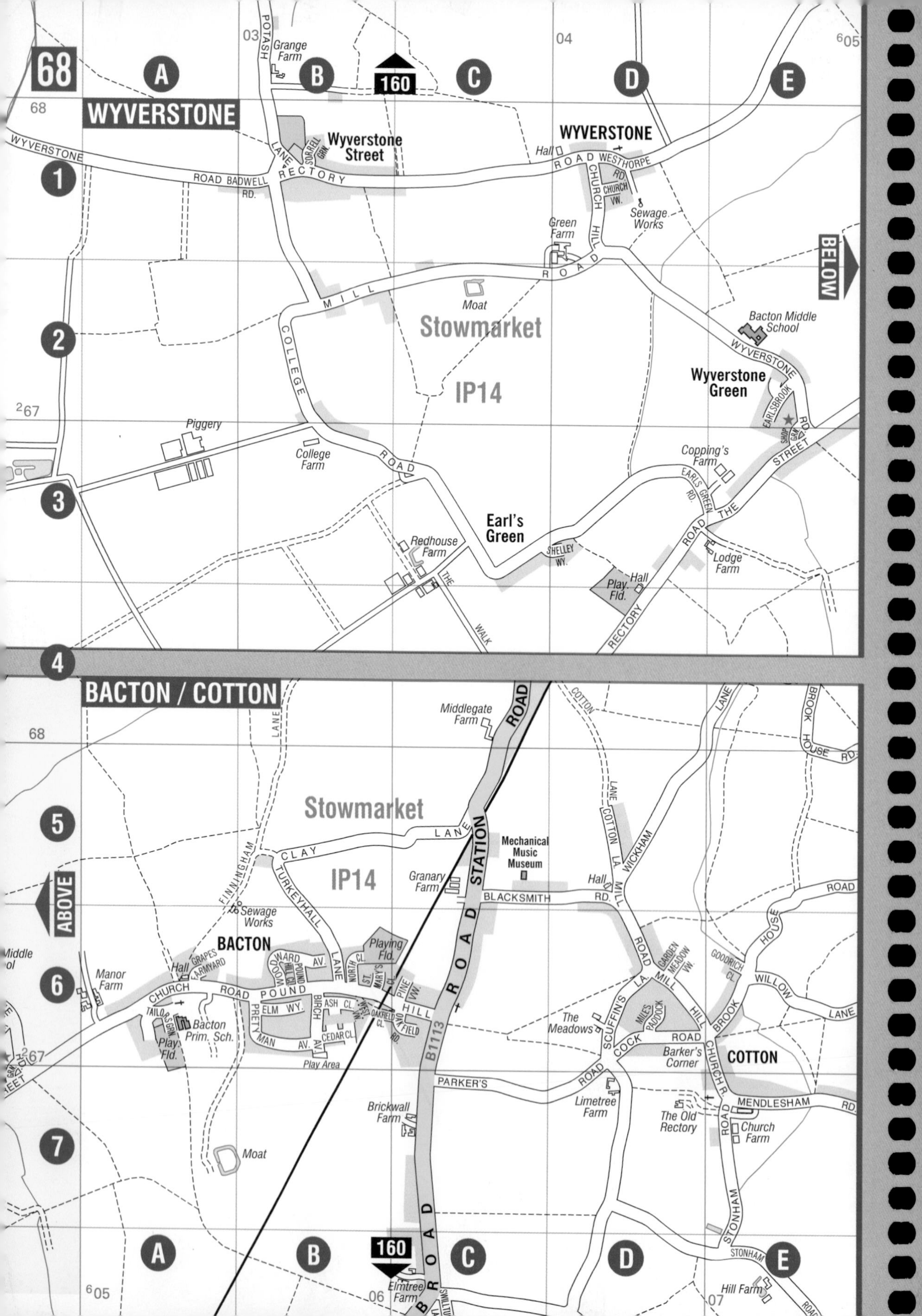
WYVERSTONE
Wyverstone Street
WYVERSTONE
Grange Farm
160
Hall
Green Farm
Sewage Works
Moat
Stowmarket
IP14
Bacton Middle School
Wyverstone Green
Piggery
College Farm
Copping's Farm
Earl's Green
Redhouse Farm
Lodge Farm
Hall
Play. Fld.
BELOW
BACTON / COTTON
Middlegate Farm
Stowmarket
IP14
Mechanical Music Museum
Granary Farm
Hall
BACTON
Sewage Works
Playing Fld.
Manor Farm
Hall
Bacton Prim. Sch.
Play. Fld.
Play Area
ABOVE
The Meadows
Barker's Corner
COTTON
Limetree Farm
The Old Rectory
Church Farm
Brickwall Farm
Moat
Elmtree Farm
Hill Farm
160
WYVERSTONE ROAD
BADWELL RD.
RECTORY
POTASH LANE
SORRELL GRN.
WESTHORPE RD.
CHURCH HILL
CHURCH VW.
MILL ROAD
COLLEGE ROAD
WYVERSTONE RD.
EARLSBROOK
SHOP GRN.
THE STREET
EARLS GREEN RD.
SHELLEY WY.
THE WALK
RECTORY ROAD
STATION ROAD
B1113
BROAD ROAD
COTTON LANE
LANE
BROOK HOUSE RD.
COTTON LA.
MILL
WICKHAM
CLAY LANE
TURKEYHALL LANE
FINNINGHAM
BLACKSMITH RD.
MILL ROAD
GARDEN MEADOW VW.
GOODRICH CL.
HOUSE ROAD
WILLOW LANE
CHURCH ROAD
POUND HILL
GRAPES FARMYARD
WOOD WARD AV.
HILL CROFT
POUND
NORTH CL.
ST. MARY'S CL.
PINE VW.
TAILORS GRN.
ELM WY.
BIRCH
ASH CL.
WEST VW.
OAKFIELD CL.
OAKFIELD RD.
PRETYMAN AV.
CEDAR CL.
SCUFFIN'S LA.
MILES PADDOCK
COCK ROAD
BROOK
CHURCH R
PARKER'S ROAD
MENDLESHAM RD.
ROAD
STONHAM

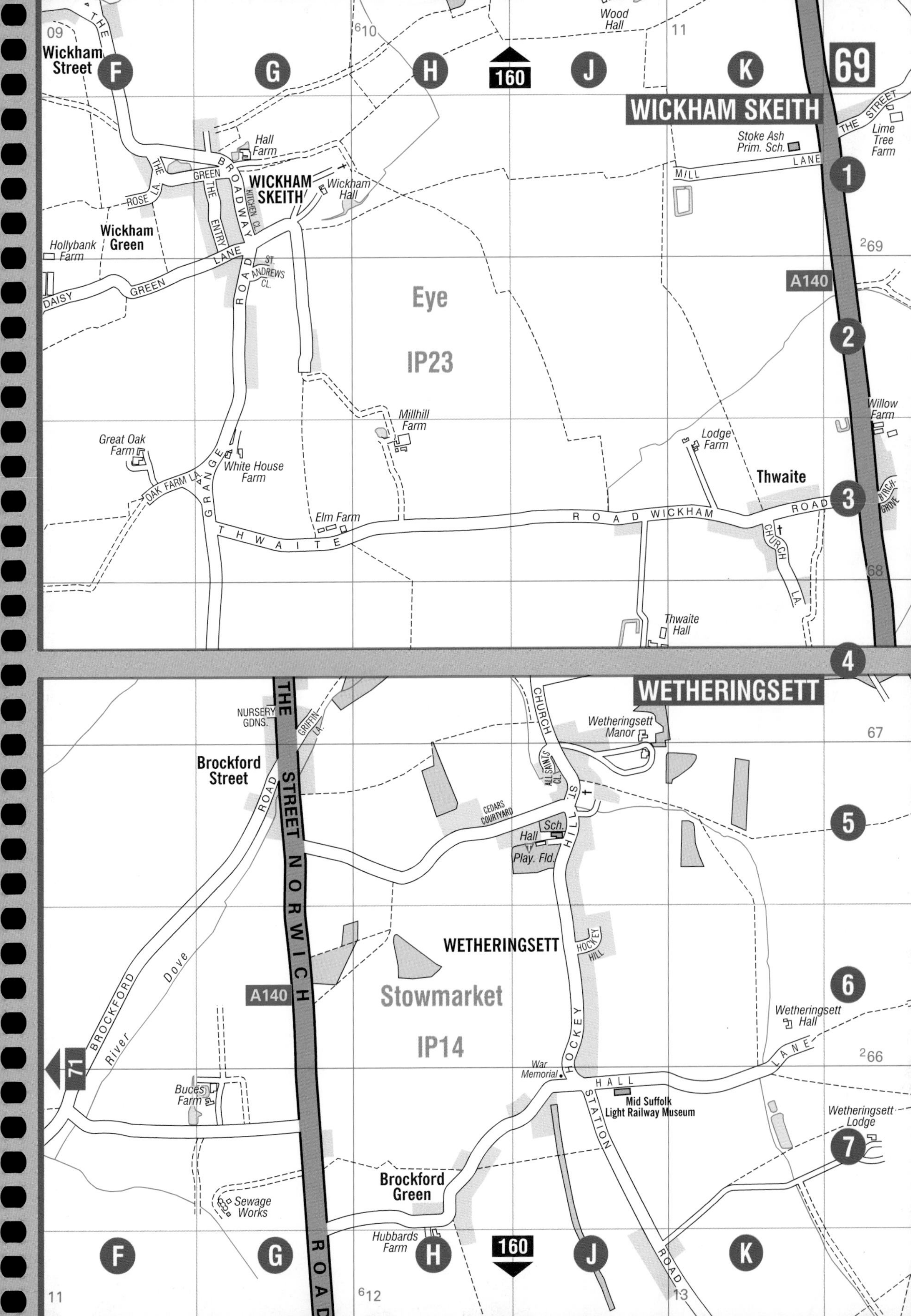

WICKHAM SKEITH
Wickham Street
Hall Farm
WICKHAM SKEITH
Wickham Hall
Wickham Green
Hollybank Farm
Stoke Ash Prim. Sch.
Lime Tree Farm
Wood Hall
Eye
IP23
Millhill Farm
Great Oak Farm
White House Farm
Elm Farm
Lodge Farm
Thwaite
Willow Farm
Thwaite Hall
A140
THE STREET
MILL LANE
ROSE LA.
THE GREEN
BROADWAY
THE ENTRY
KITCHEN CL.
ST. ANDREWS CL.
DAISY GREEN LANE
GRANGE ROAD
OAK FARM LA.
THWAITE ROAD
WICKHAM ROAD
CHURCH LA.
BIRCH GROVE
WETHERINGSETT
Wetheringsett Manor
NURSERY GDNS.
Brockford Street
THE STREET
NORWICH ROAD
GRIFFIN LA.
CHURCH ST.
ALL SAINTS CL.
CEDARS COURTYARD
Sch.
Hall
Play. Fld.
WETHERINGSETT
HOCKEY HILL
Stowmarket
IP14
BROCKFORD ROAD
River Dove
Wetheringsett Hall
HALL LANE
War Memorial
Mid Suffolk Light Railway Museum
Wetheringsett Lodge
Buces Farm
STATION ROAD
Brockford Green
Sewage Works
Hubbards Farm
160
71

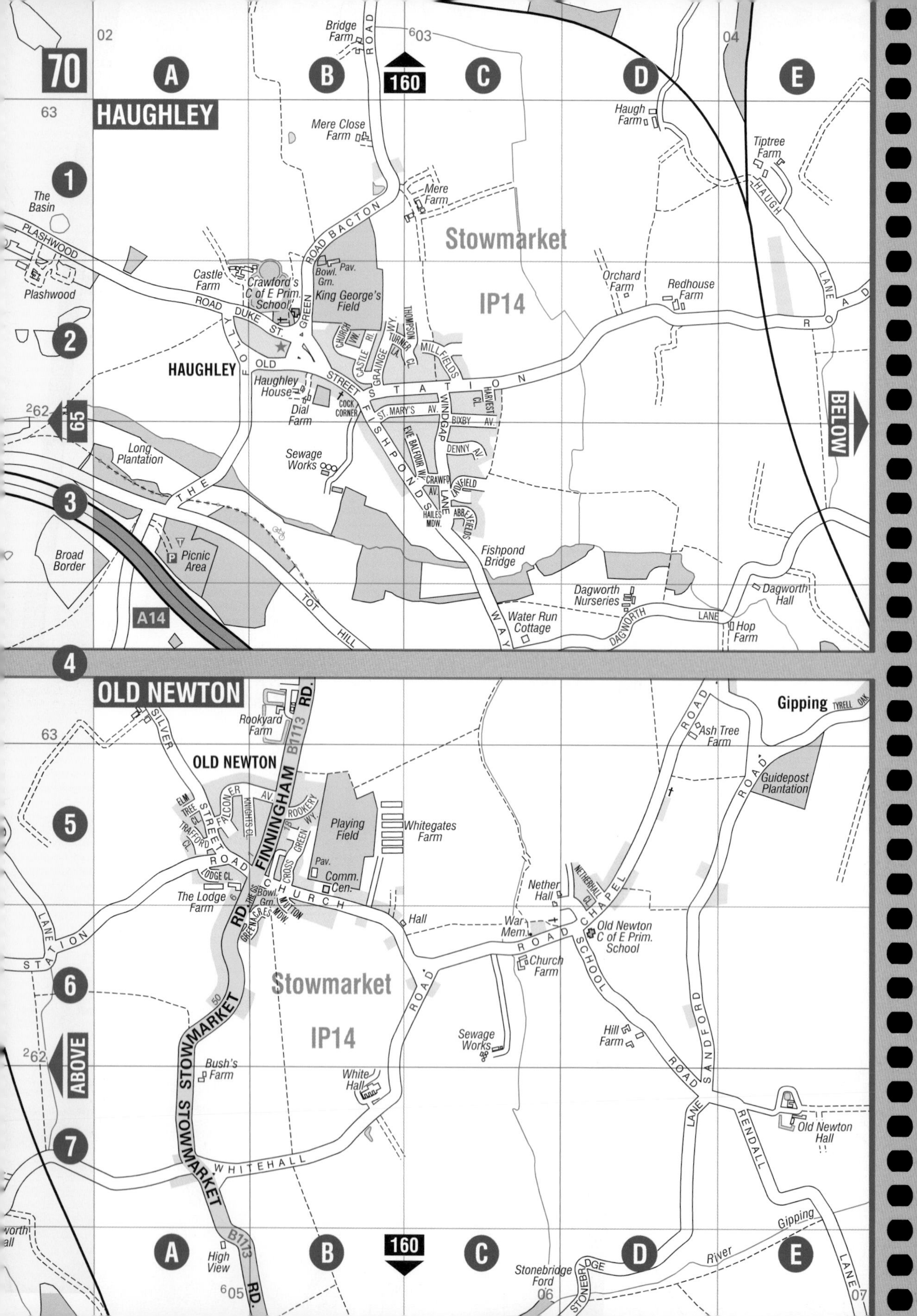
HAUGHLEY
OLD NEWTON
160
65
BELOW
ABOVE
Stowmarket
IP14
The Basin
Plashwood
Castle Farm
Crawford's C of E Prim. School
King George's Field
Mere Close Farm
Mere Farm
Bridge Farm
Haugh Farm
Tiptree Farm
Orchard Farm
Redhouse Farm
Haughley House
Dial Farm
Long Plantation
Sewage Works
Broad Border
Picnic Area
Fishpond Bridge
Dagworth Nurseries
Dagworth Hall
Hop Farm
Water Run Cottage
A14
Rookyard Farm
Playing Field
Whitegates Farm
Comm. Cen.
The Lodge Farm
Hall
Nether Hall
War Mem.
Old Newton C of E Prim. School
Church Farm
Hill Farm
Bush's Farm
White Hall
Ash Tree Farm
Gipping
Guidepost Plantation
Old Newton Hall
High View
Stonebridge Ford
River Gipping
FINNINGHAM RD.
STOWMARKET RD.
B1113
WHITEHALL
CHURCH ROAD
CHAPEL ROAD
SCHOOL ROAD
SANDFORD ROAD
RENDALL LANE
STATION ROAD
STATION LANE
FISHPONDS WAY
TOT HILL
WINDGAP LANE
DAGWORTH LANE
HAUGH LANE
PLASHWOOD ROAD
BACTON ROAD
OLD STREET
DUKE ST.
GREEN ROAD
THE FOLLY
SILVER STREET
STONEBRIDGE

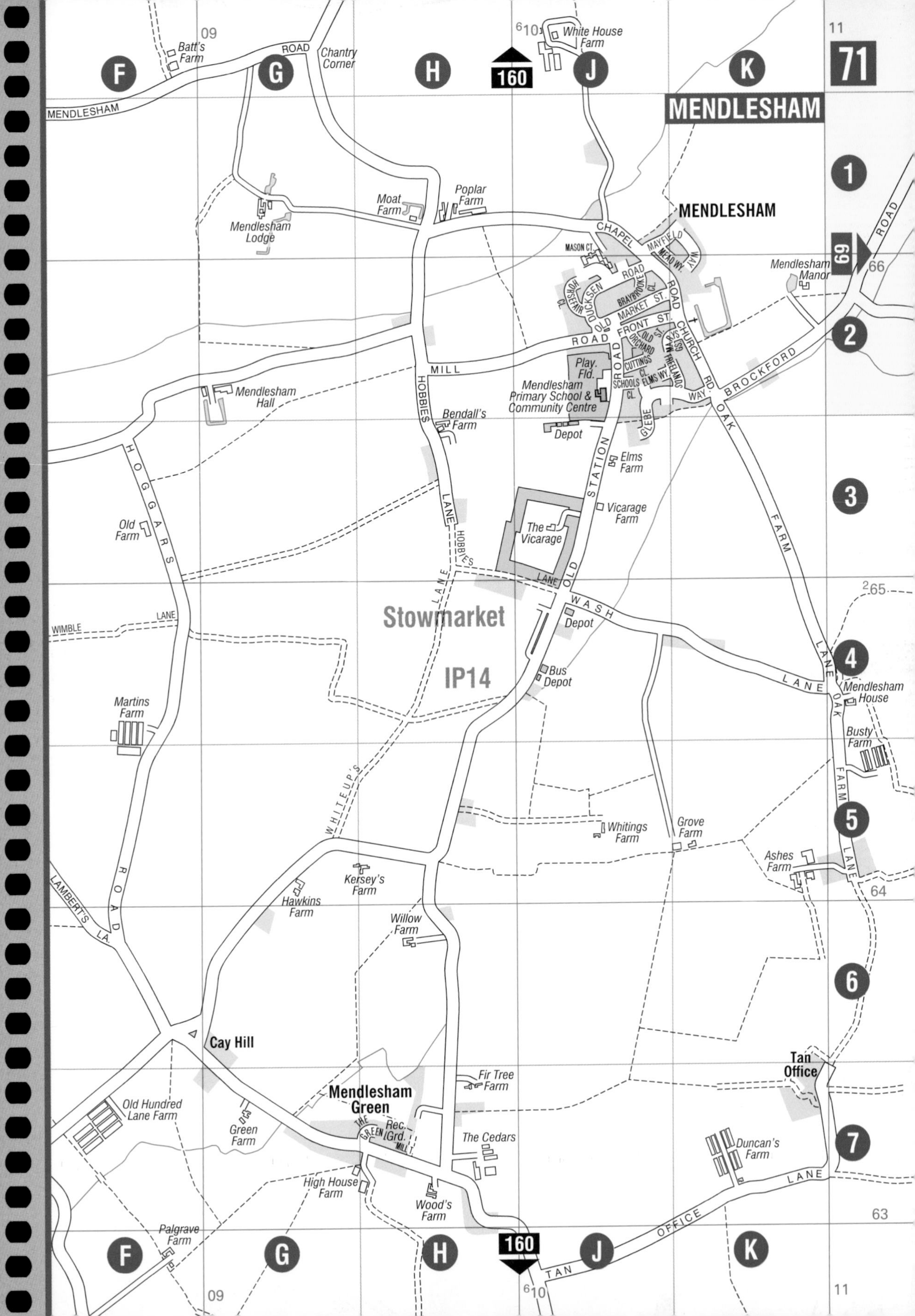

MENDLESHAM
Batt's Farm
Chantry Corner
White House Farm
160
MENDLESHAM ROAD
Moat Farm
Poplar Farm
Mendlesham Lodge
MENDLESHAM
CHAPEL
MAYFIELD
MASON CT.
MEAD WY.
WAY
Mendlesham Manor
69
66
HORSEFAIR CL.
DUCKSEN
ROAD
BRAYBROOKE CL.
MARKET ST.
OLD
FRONT ST.
ORCHARD
CUTTINGS CL.
ELMS WY.
FREELANDS
CHURCH
ROAD
MILL
Play. Fld.
SCHOOLS CL.
GLEBE
BROCKFORD
WAY
RD.
Mendlesham Primary School & Community Centre
Mendlesham Hall
HOBBIES
Bendall's Farm
Depot
Elms Farm
STATION
OAK
HOGGARS
Old Farm
LANE
The Vicarage
Vicarage Farm
FARM
HOBBIES
LANE
OLD
WASH
65
WIMBLE
LANE
Stowmarket
Depot
IP14
Bus Depot
LANE
Mendlesham House
Martins Farm
Busty Farm
FARM
WHITEUP'S
Whitings Farm
Grove Farm
Ashes Farm
LANE
LAMBERT'S LA.
ROAD
Kersey's Farm
Hawkins Farm
Willow Farm
64
Cay Hill
Tan Office
Fir Tree Farm
Old Hundred Lane Farm
Mendlesham Green
THE GREEN
Rec. Grd.
MILL
Green Farm
The Cedars
Duncan's Farm
LANE
High House Farm
Wood's Farm
63
Palgrave Farm
160
TAN
OFFICE
09
610
11

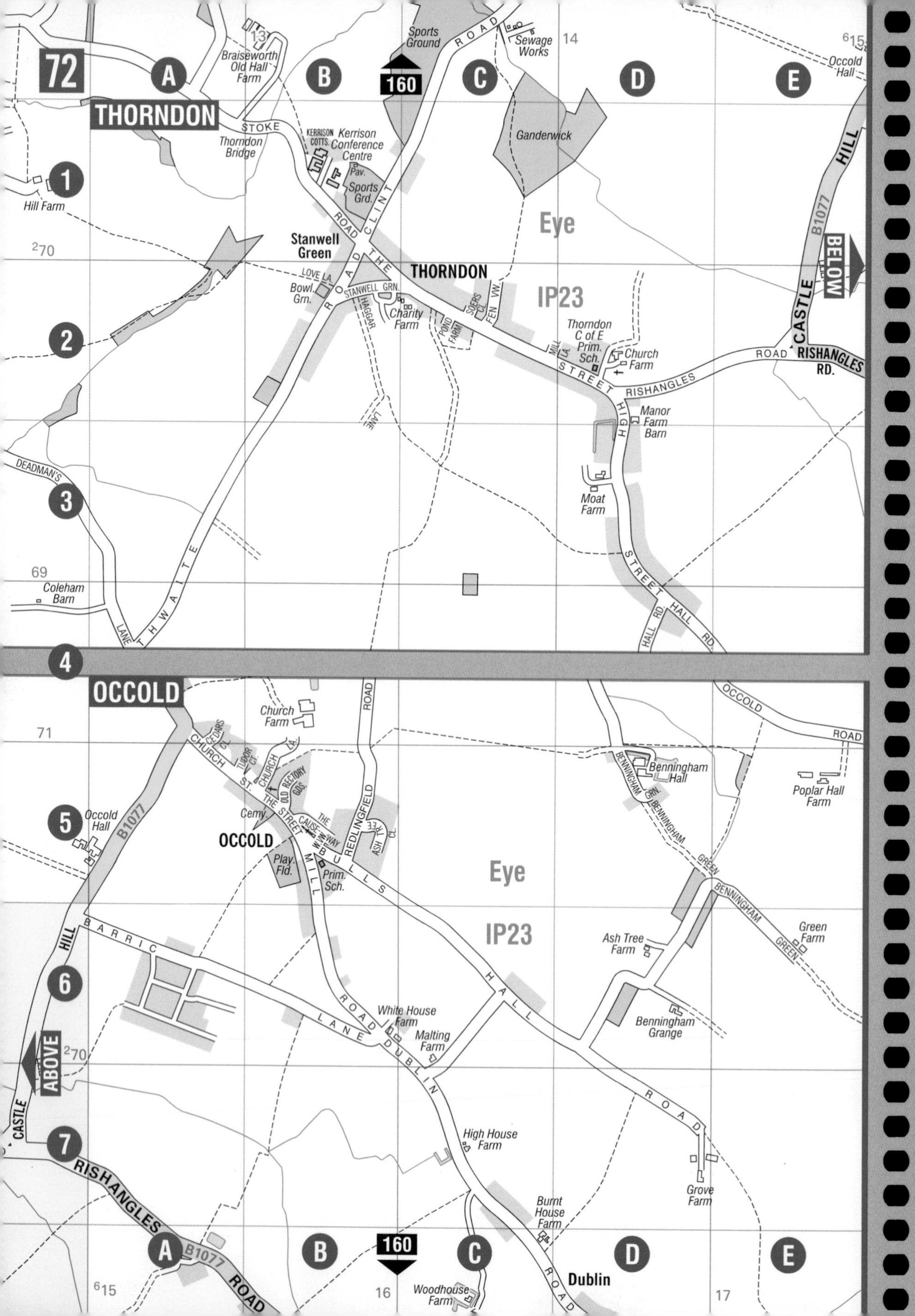
THORNDON
Braiseworth Old Hall Farm
Sports Ground
160
Sewage Works
Occold Hall
STOKE
Thorndon Bridge
KERRISON COTTS.
Kerrison Conference Centre
Pav.
Sports Grd.
Ganderwick
Hill Farm
Eye
Stanwell Green
LOVE LA.
Bowl. Grn.
STANWELL GRN.
THORNDON
Charity Farm
HAGGAR
POND FARM
SOERS CL.
FEN VW.
IP23
Thorndon C of E Prim. Sch.
MILL LA.
Church Farm
RISHANGLES
CASTLE HILL
B1077
BELOW
RISHANGLES RD.
ROAD
STREET
HIGH
Manor Farm Barn
DEADMAN'S
LANE
Moat Farm
THWAITE
ROAD
CLINT
THE
Coleham Barn
HALL RD.
HALL RD.
OCCOLD
Church Farm
ROAD
OCCOLD ROAD
CEDARS CL.
TUDOR CT.
CHURCH LA.
CHURCH ST.
OLD RECTORY GDS.
THE STREET
Benningham Hall
BENNINGHAM GRN.
Poplar Hall Farm
Occold Hall
Cemy.
OCCOLD
THE CAUSEWAY
REDLINGFIELD
ASH TREE CL.
B1077
Play. Fld.
Prim. Sch.
MILL
BULLS
Eye
BENNINGHAM GREEN
IP23
HILL
BARRIC
Ash Tree Farm
Green Farm
HALL
ROAD
LANE
White House Farm
Malting Farm
Benningham Grange
ABOVE
DUBLIN
CASTLE
High House Farm
RISHANGLES
ROAD
Grove Farm
Burnt House Farm
160
Dublin
Woodhouse Farm
A
B
C
D
E
1
2
3
4
5
6
7
13
14
615
270
69
71
16
17

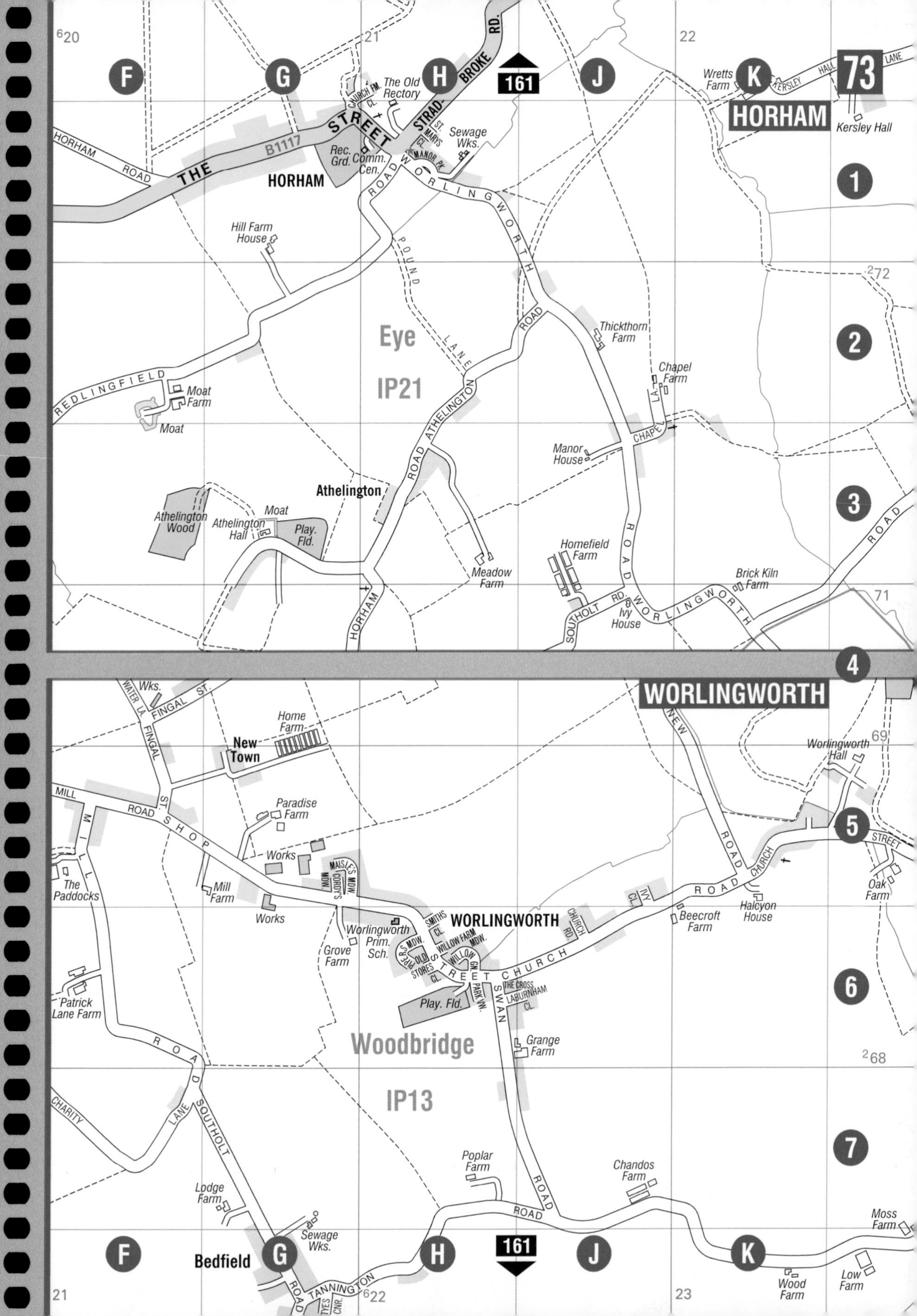
HORHAM
WORLINGWORTH
Athelington
Bedfield
New Town
Eye
IP21
Woodbridge
IP13
161
161
THE STREET
B1117
HORHAM ROAD
STRADBROKE RD.
The Old Rectory
CHURCH FM. CL.
ST. MARYS CL.
MANOR PK.
Sewage Wks.
Rec. Grd.
Comm. Cen.
Wretts Farm
KERSLEY HALL LANE
Kersley Hall
WORLINGWORTH ROAD
POUND LANE
Hill Farm House
REDLINGFIELD ROAD
Moat Farm
Moat
ATHELINGTON ROAD
Thickthorn Farm
Chapel Farm
CHAPEL LA.
Manor House
Athelington Wood
Athelington Hall
Play. Fld.
Homefield Farm
Meadow Farm
Brick Kiln Farm
SOUTHOLT RD.
Ivy House
HORHAM ROAD
Wks.
WATER LA.
FINGAL ST.
Home Farm
MILL ROAD
SHOP ST.
MILL LANE
Paradise Farm
Works
Mill Farm
The Paddocks
MAISIE'S MDW.
GORDY'S MDW.
SMITHS CL.
Worlingworth Prim. Sch.
Grove Farm
PIPERS MDW.
OLD STORES CL.
WILLOW FARM MDW.
WILLOW GN.
PARK VW.
THE CROSS
LABURNHAM CL.
SWAN ROAD
CHURCH STREET
CHURCH RD.
IVY CL.
CHURCH ROAD
NEW ROAD
Beecroft Farm
Halcyon House
Worlingworth Hall
STREET
Oak Farm
Patrick Lane Farm
Grange Farm
CHARITY LANE
SOUTHOLT ROAD
Poplar Farm
Chandos Farm
Lodge Farm
Sewage Wks.
TANNINGTON ROAD
TYES CNR.
Moss Farm
Wood Farm
Low Farm
F
G
H
J
K
1
2
3
4
5
6
7
620
21
22
23
272
71
69
268
622

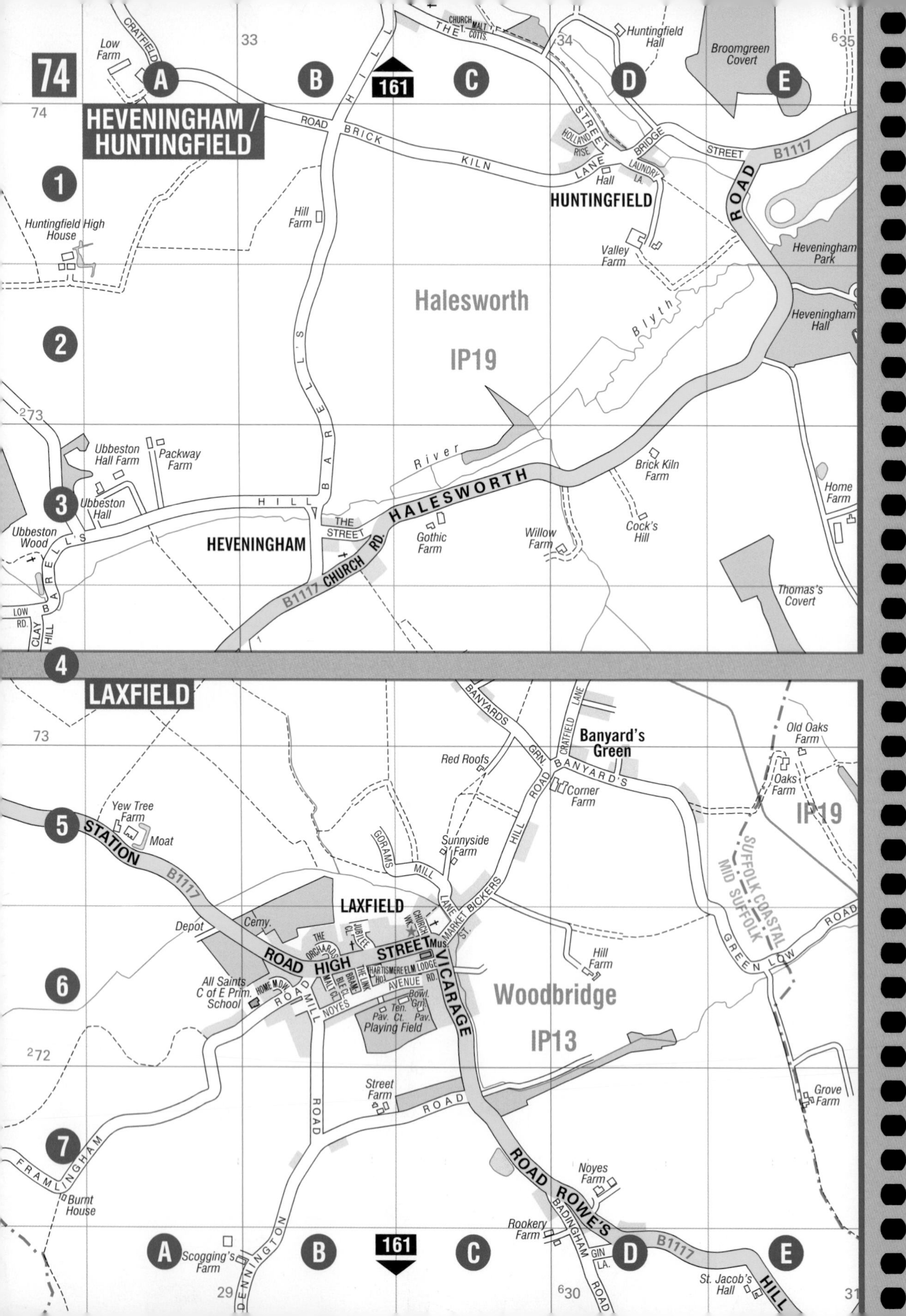

74
HEVENINGHAM / HUNTINGFIELD
LAXFIELD
161
Low Farm
Huntingfield Hall
Broomgreen Covert
Huntingfield High House
Hill Farm
HUNTINGFIELD
Valley Farm
Heveningham Park
Halesworth
IP19
Heveningham Hall
Ubbeston Hall Farm
Packway Farm
Ubbeston Hall
Ubbeston Wood
HEVENINGHAM
Gothic Farm
Willow Farm
Brick Kiln Farm
Cock's Hill
Home Farm
Thomas's Covert
BRICK KILN ROAD
HALESWORTH RD.
CHURCH RD.
B1117
Banyard's Green
Red Roofs
Corner Farm
Old Oaks Farm
Oaks Farm
Yew Tree Farm
Moat
Sunnyside Farm
STATION ROAD
HIGH STREET
VICARAGE
Depot
Cemy.
All Saints C of E Prim. School
Playing Field
Hill Farm
Woodbridge
IP13
SUFFOLK COASTAL
MID SUFFOLK
Street Farm
Grove Farm
Noyes Farm
Rookery Farm
Burnt House
Scogging's Farm
St. Jacob's Hall
ROWE'S HILL
FRAMLINGHAM
DENNINGTON ROAD

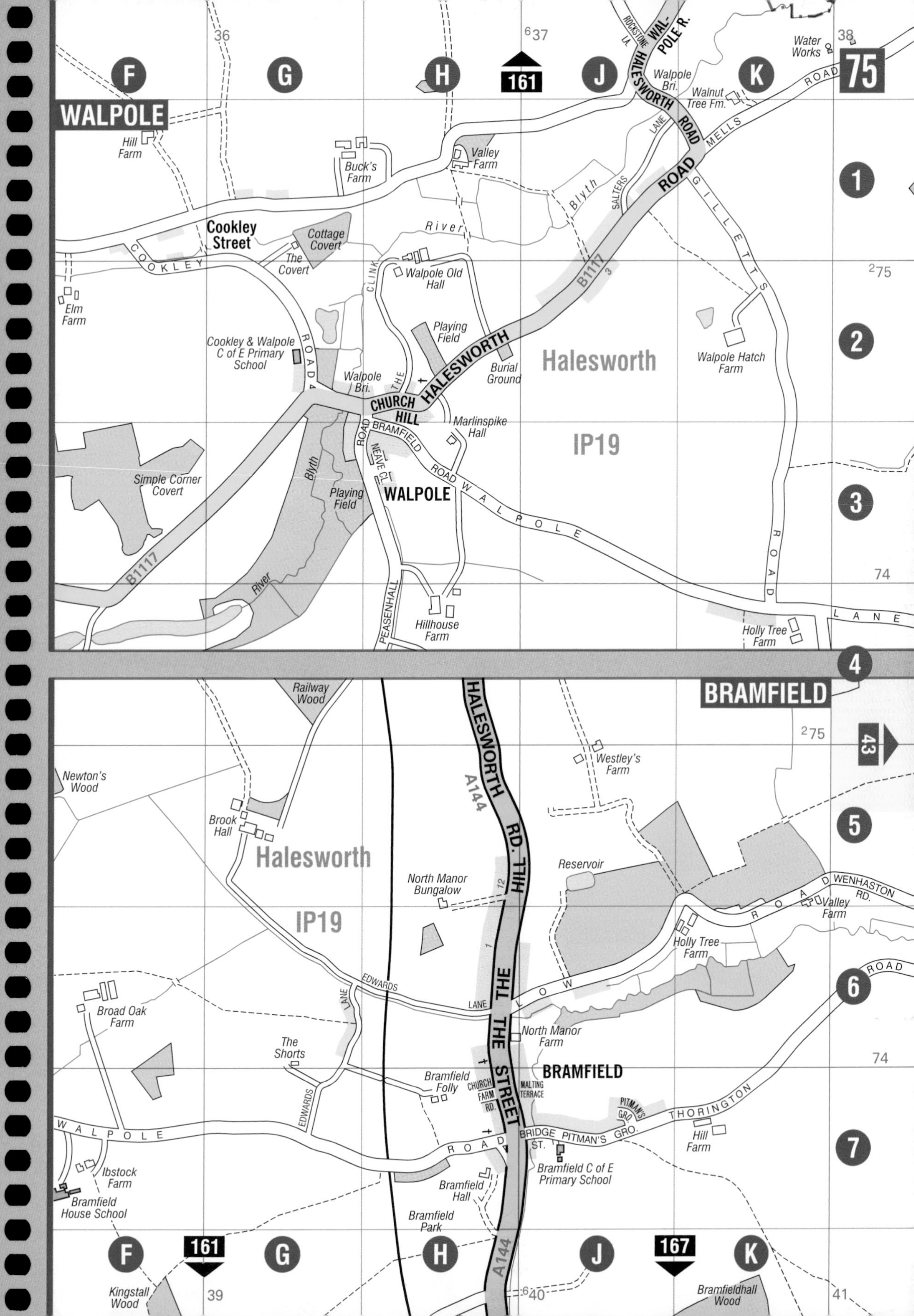
WALPOLE
BRAMFIELD
Hill Farm
Buck's Farm
Valley Farm
Cookley Street
Cottage Covert
The Covert
COOKLEY ROAD
Elm Farm
Walpole Old Hall
Playing Field
Cookley & Walpole C of E Primary School
Walpole Bri.
CHURCH HILL
HALESWORTH ROAD
Burial Ground
Halesworth
Walpole Hatch Farm
Marlinspike Hall
IP19
Simple Corner Covert
Blyth
River Blyth
WALPOLE ROAD
BRAMFIELD ROAD
NEAVE CL.
PEASENHALL ROAD
Hillhouse Farm
Holly Tree Farm
LANE
B1117
WALPOLE R.
ROCKSTONE LA.
Walpole Bri.
Walnut Tree Fm.
MELLS ROAD
SALTERS LANE
GILLETTS ROAD
Water Works
Railway Wood
Newton's Wood
Brook Hall
Westley's Farm
HALESWORTH RD.
A144
THE HILL
Reservoir
North Manor Bungalow
WENHASTON RD.
Valley Farm
Holly Tree Farm
LOW ROAD
EDWARDS LANE
Broad Oak Farm
The Shorts
North Manor Farm
THE STREET
Bramfield Folly
CHURCH FARM RD.
MALTING TERRACE
PITMAN'S GRO.
THORINGTON ROAD
BRIDGE ST.
Hill Farm
Bramfield C of E Primary School
Bramfield Hall
Bramfield Park
Ibstock Farm
Bramfield House School
Kingstall Wood
Bramfieldhall Wood
F G H J K
1 2 3 4 5 6 7
161
167
43
36 637 38 39 640 41
275 74

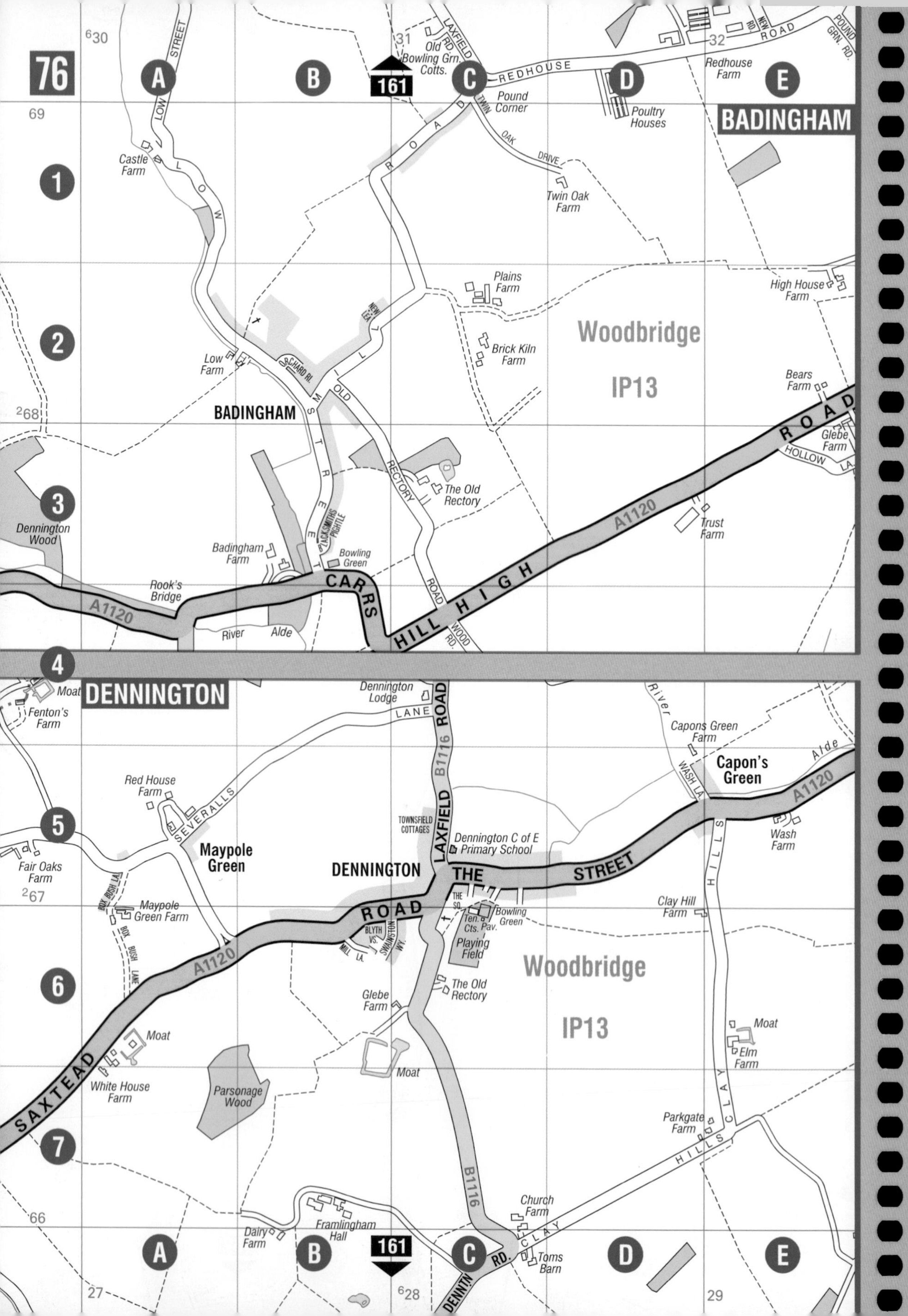
BADINGHAM
DENNINGTON
Woodbridge
IP13
Castle Farm
Low Farm
Old Bowling Grn. Cotts.
Pound Corner
Poultry Houses
Redhouse Farm
Twin Oak Farm
Plains Farm
Brick Kiln Farm
High House Farm
Bears Farm
Glebe Farm
The Old Rectory
Trust Farm
Badingham Farm
Bowling Green
Rook's Bridge
River Alde
Dennington Wood
REDHOUSE ROAD
LOW STREET
TWIN OAK DRIVE
OLD ROAD
HOLLOW LA.
HIGH ROAD
CARRS HILL
A1120
RECTORY ROAD
WOOD RD.
Dennington Lodge
LANE
LAXFIELD ROAD
B1116
Capons Green Farm
Capon's Green
WASH LA.
Wash Farm
Moat
Fenton's Farm
Red House Farm
SEVERALLS
Maypole Green
Fair Oaks Farm
Maypole Green Farm
BOX BUSH LANE
TOWNSFIELD COTTAGES
Dennington C of E Primary School
THE STREET
ROAD
Bowling Green
Ten. Cts. Pav.
Playing Field
The Old Rectory
Glebe Farm
Clay Hill Farm
CLAY HILLS
Elm Farm
Parkgate Farm
White House Farm
SAXTEAD ROAD
Parsonage Wood
Dairy Farm
Framlingham Hall
Church Farm
Toms Barn
CLAY RD.
DENNTN RD.
161
A B C D E
1 2 3 4 5 6 7

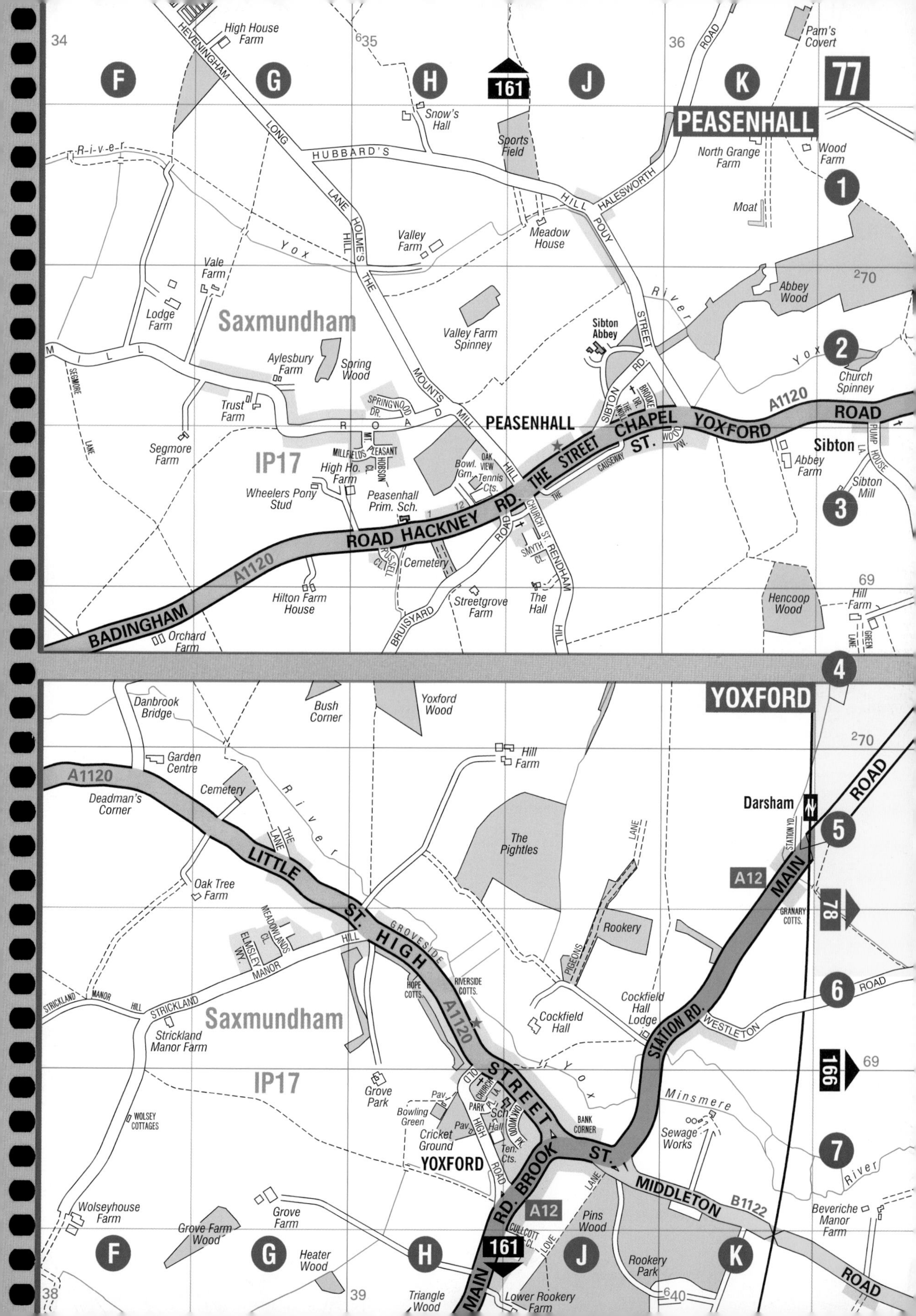
PEASENHALL
High House Farm
Pam's Covert
Snow's Hall
Sports Field
North Grange Farm
Wood Farm
HUBBARD'S HILL
HALESWORTH ROAD
LONG LANE
HEVENINGHAM
Moat
Valley Farm
Meadow House
Vale Farm
Lodge Farm
Saxmundham
Valley Farm Spinney
Sibton Abbey
Abbey Wood
Aylesbury Farm
Spring Wood
Church Spinney
Trust Farm
MILL ROAD
Segmore Farm
PEASENHALL
CHAPEL ST.
THE STREET
YOXFORD ROAD
A1120
Sibton
Abbey Farm
Sibton Mill
IP17
High Ho. Farm
Wheelers Pony Stud
Peasenhall Prim. Sch.
Bowl. Grn.
Tennis Cts.
ROAD HACKNEY RD.
Cemetery
Hilton Farm House
Streetgrove Farm
The Hall
Hencoop Wood
Hill Farm
BADINGHAM
Orchard Farm
BRUISYARD ROAD
RENDHAM HILL
YOXFORD
Danbrook Bridge
Bush Corner
Yoxford Wood
Hill Farm
Garden Centre
A1120
Deadman's Corner
Cemetery
The Pightles
Darsham
MAIN ROAD
LITTLE ST.
HIGH STREET
Oak Tree Farm
A12
Rookery
GRANARY COTTS.
Saxmundham
Strickland Manor Farm
Cockfield Hall
Cockfield Hall Lodge
STATION RD.
WESTLETON ROAD
IP17
Grove Park
Bowling Green
Cricket Ground
YOXFORD
Minsmere River
Sewage Works
BROOK ST.
MIDDLETON ROAD
B1122
WOLSEY COTTAGES
Wolseyhouse Farm
Grove Farm
Grove Farm Wood
Heater Wood
Pins Wood
Rookery Park
Beveriche Manor Farm
Triangle Wood
Lower Rookery Farm
161
166
78

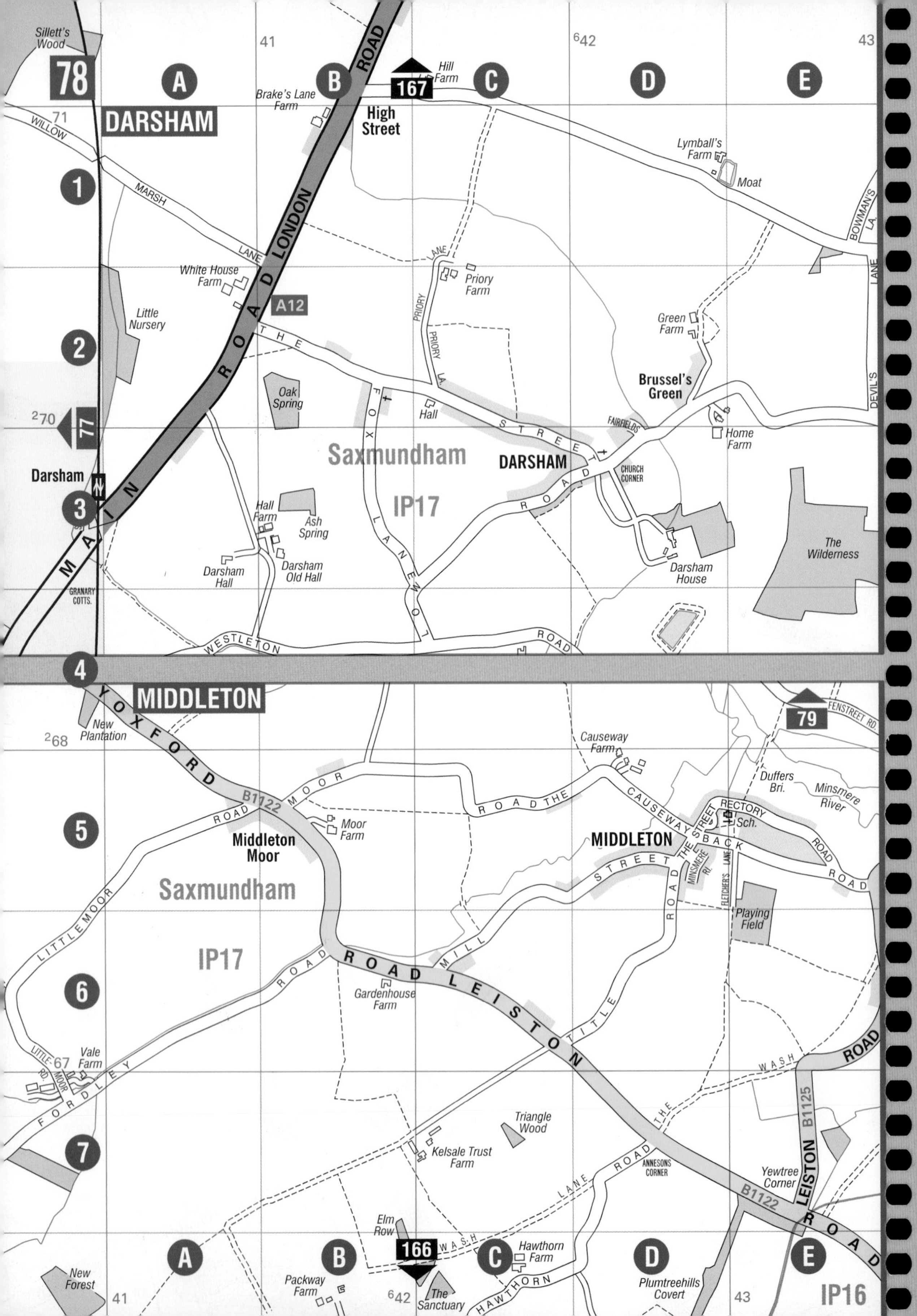

78
DARSHAM
MIDDLETON
A
B
C
D
E
1
2
3
4
5
6
7
167
166
77
79
Sillett's Wood
Brake's Lane Farm
Hill Farm
High Street
Lymball's Farm
Moat
White House Farm
Little Nursery
Priory Farm
Green Farm
Brussel's Green
Oak Spring
Hall
Home Farm
Saxmundham
DARSHAM
Darsham
Church Corner
Hall Farm
Ash Spring
IP17
Darsham Hall
Darsham Old Hall
Darsham House
The Wilderness
Granary Cotts.
New Plantation
Causeway Farm
Duffers Bri.
Minsmere River
Moor Farm
Middleton Moor
MIDDLETON
Sch.
Playing Field
Gardenhouse Farm
Vale Farm
Triangle Wood
Kelsale Trust Farm
Annesons Corner
Yewtree Corner
Elm Row
Hawthorn Farm
New Forest
Packway Farm
The Sanctuary
Plumtreehills Covert
IP16
A12
B1122
B1125

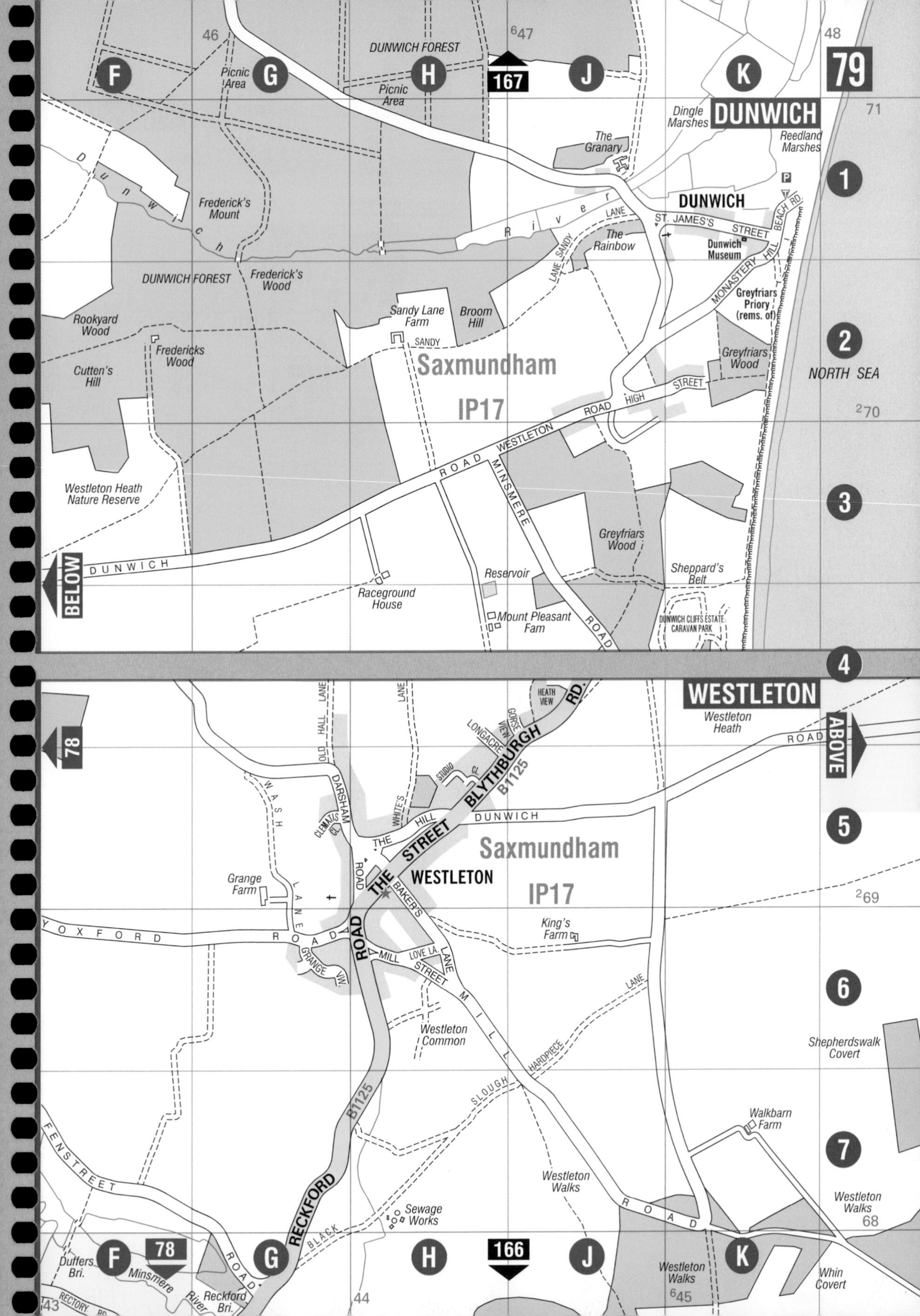
DUNWICH
DUNWICH FOREST
Picnic Area
Picnic Area
167
Dingle Marshes
Reedland Marshes
The Granary
Dunwich
Frederick's Mount
River
SANDY LANE
ST. JAMES'S STREET
The Rainbow
Dunwich Museum
BEACH RD.
MONASTERY HILL
Greyfriars Priory (rems. of)
DUNWICH FOREST
Frederick's Wood
Rookyard Wood
Sandy Lane Farm
Broom Hill
SANDY
Fredericks Wood
Cutten's Hill
Saxmundham
Greyfriars Wood
NORTH SEA
HIGH STREET
IP17
WESTLETON ROAD
MINSMERE ROAD
Westleton Heath Nature Reserve
Greyfriars Wood
DUNWICH
BELOW
Reservoir
Sheppard's Belt
Raceground House
Mount Pleasant Farm
DUNWICH CLIFFS ESTATE CARAVAN PARK
WESTLETON
Westleton Heath
78
ROAD
ABOVE
OLD HALL LANE
WHITE'S LANE
HEATH VIEW
GORSE VIEW
LONGACRE
BLYTHBURGH RD.
B1125
STUDIO CL.
WASH LANE
DARSHAM ROAD
CLEMATIS CL.
THE HILL
DUNWICH
THE STREET
Saxmundham
WESTLETON
Grange Farm
BAKER'S LANE
IP17
YOXFORD ROAD
King's Farm
GRANGE VW.
MILL STREET
LOVE LA.
LANE
MILL
Westleton Common
Shepherdswalk Covert
HARDPIECE
SLOUGH
B1125
Walkbarn Farm
FENSTREET
RECKFORD ROAD
Westleton Walks
Westleton Walks
Sewage Works
BLACK
ROAD
Duffers Bri.
78
Minsmere River
Reckford Bri.
RECTORY RD.
166
Westleton Walks
Whin Covert
F G H J K
1 2 3 4 5 6 7
46 647 48 71 270 269 68 43 44 645

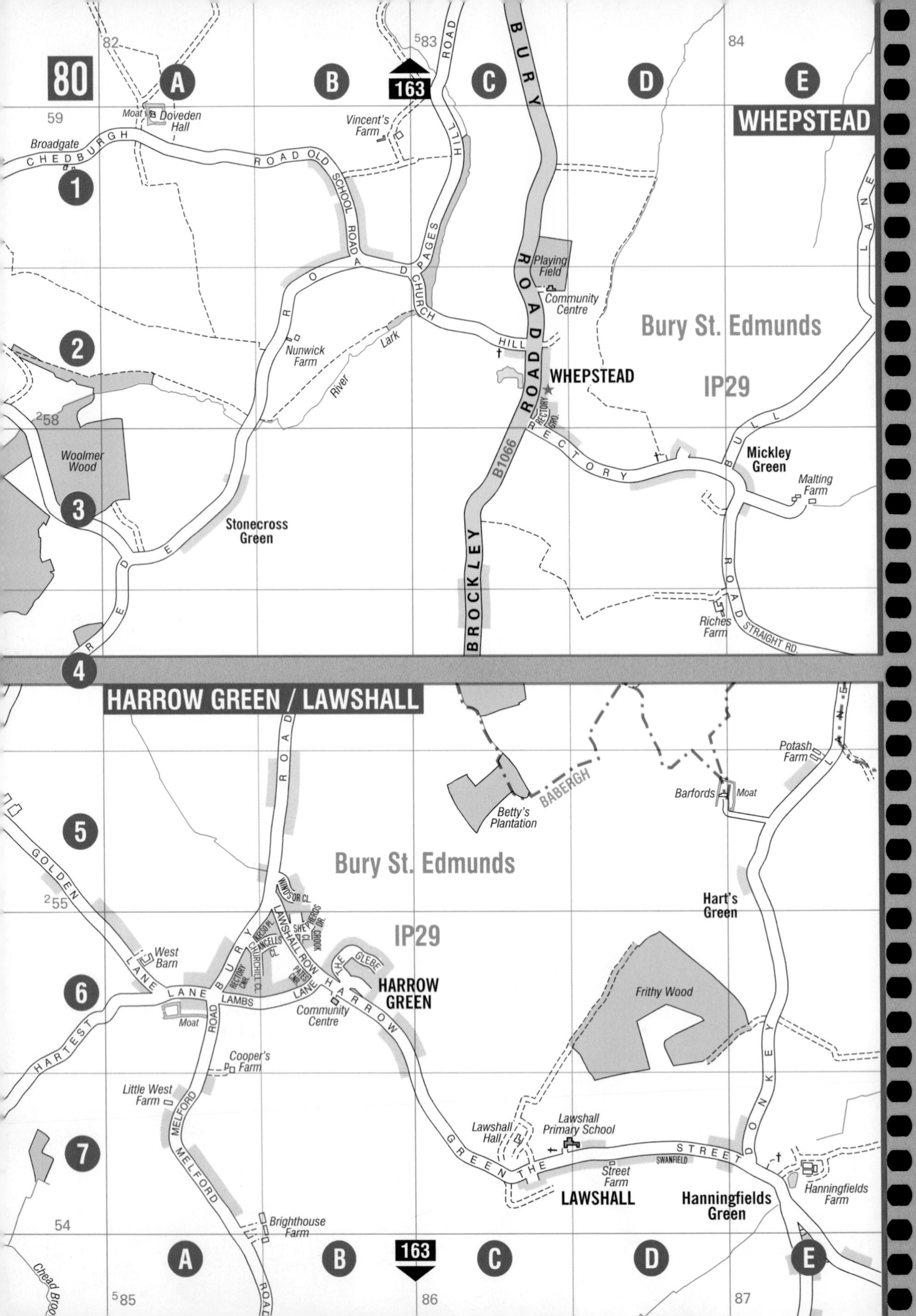
WHEPSTEAD
A
B
C
D
E
163
82
583
84
59
Moat
Doveden Hall
Vincent's Farm
Broadgate
CHEDBURGH ROAD
OLD SCHOOL ROAD
PAGES HILL
BURY ROAD
CHURCH HILL
Playing Field
Community Centre
Bury St. Edmunds
Nunwick Farm
River Lark
WHEPSTEAD
IP29
258
Woolmer Wood
RECTORY GRO.
RECTORY ROAD
B1066
Mickley Green
Malting Farm
BULL LANE
Stonecross Green
BROCKLEY ROAD
Riches Farm
STRAIGHT RD.
1
2
3
4
HARROW GREEN / LAWSHALL
Potash Farm
Barfords
Moat
BABERGH
Betty's Plantation
Bury St. Edmunds
5
GOLDEN LANE
255
WINDSOR CL.
SHEPHERDS CL.
CROOK DR.
KESO PL.
CHANCELLS CL.
LAWSHALL ROW
THE GLEBE
IP29
Hart's Green
West Barn
RECTORY CNR.
CHURCHILL CL.
PATES CNR.
HARROW GREEN
6
LAMBS LANE
Moat
Community Centre
HARTEST LANE
Frithy Wood
Cooper's Farm
Little West Farm
MELFORD ROAD
Lawshall Hall
Lawshall Primary School
THE GREEN
STREET
SWANFIELD
DONKEY LANE
7
Street Farm
LAWSHALL
Hanningfields Green
Hanningfields Farm
54
Brighthouse Farm
Chead Broo
585
86
87

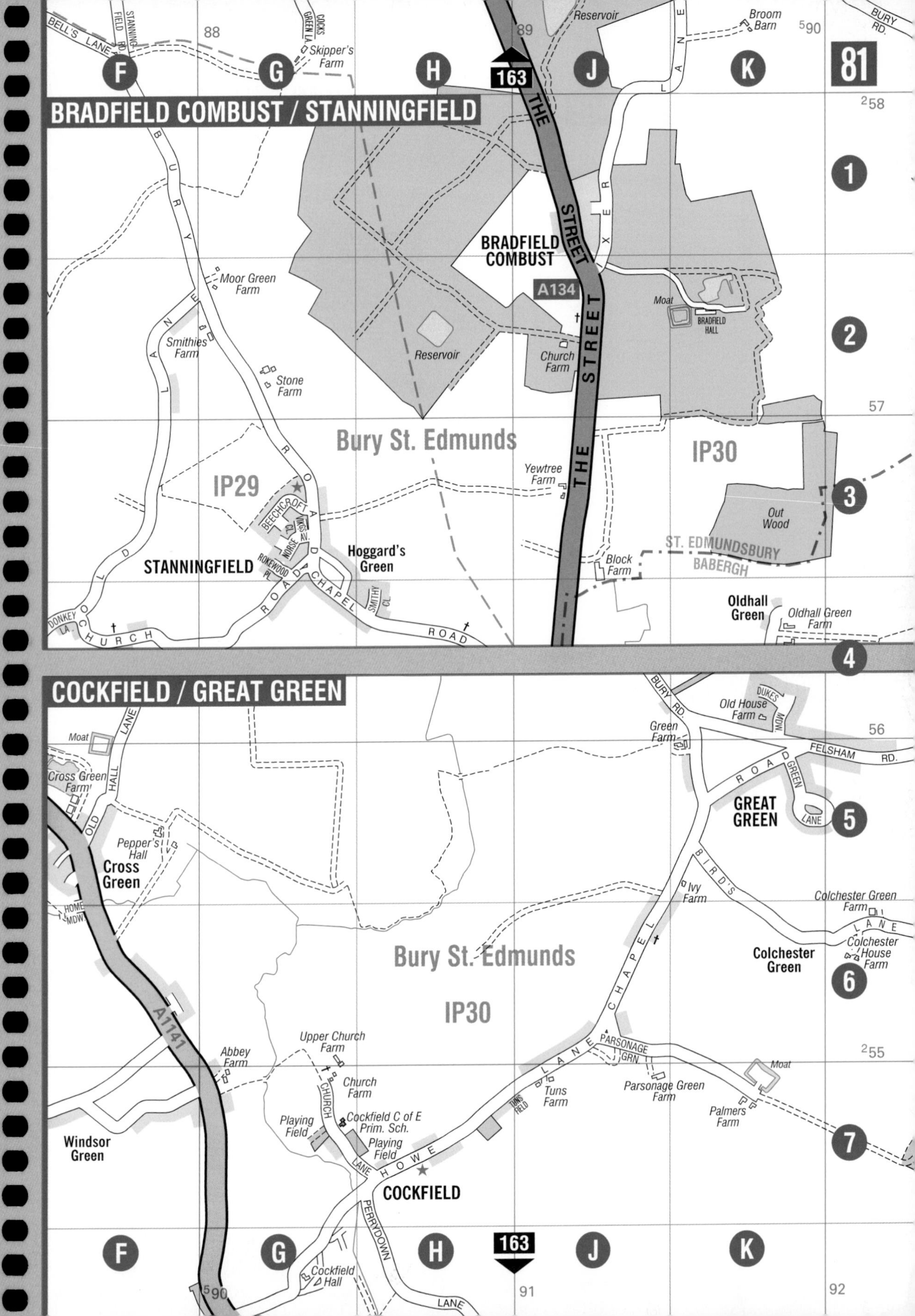
BRADFIELD COMBUST / STANNINGFIELD
BRADFIELD COMBUST
STANNINGFIELD
Hoggard's Green
Bury St. Edmunds
IP29
IP30
THE STREET
A134
BURY ROAD
OLD LANE
CHURCH ROAD
CHAPEL ROAD
Moor Green Farm
Smithies Farm
Stone Farm
Reservoir
Church Farm
Moat
BRADFIELD HALL
Yewtree Farm
Out Wood
Block Farm
ST. EDMUNDSBURY
BABERGH
Oldhall Green
Oldhall Green Farm
Broom Barn
Skipper's Farm
BELL'S LANE
163
COCKFIELD / GREAT GREEN
COCKFIELD
GREAT GREEN
Cross Green
Colchester Green
Windsor Green
Bury St. Edmunds
IP30
A1141
Cross Green Farm
Pepper's Hall
Abbey Farm
Upper Church Farm
Church Farm
Cockfield C of E Prim. Sch.
Playing Field
Tuns Farm
Parsonage Green Farm
Palmers Farm
Ivy Farm
Green Farm
Old House Farm
Colchester Green Farm
Colchester House Farm
Cockfield Hall
FELSHAM RD.
BIRD'S LANE
CHAPEL LANE
HOWE LANE
PERRYDOWN LANE
OLD HALL LANE
PARSONAGE GRN.
GREEN ROAD
163

BRADFIELD ST. GEORGE
FELSHAM
Link Wood
Linkwood Equestrian Centre
Hall Farm
Kingshall Green
Tinker's Wood
Free Wood
BRADFIELD ST. GEORGE
Bury St. Edmunds
IP30
Hollybush Corner
Frog's Hall
Maypole Green Farm
Maypole Green
Rawhall Wood
Grange Farm
Gedding
Wentis Farm
Gedding Mill
Toad Hall
Frog Hall
Play.Fld.
Bradfield Woods (Nature Reserve)
ST. EDMUNDSBURY
MID SUFFOLK
THE ORCHARD
MEADOW CL.
LIME WLK.
YEWLANDS
Felsham Hall
Rookery Farm
Poplar Farm
Moore's Farm
Rattlesden River
WHITE HORSE LANE
ROUGHAM ROAD
KINGSHALL ST.
HESSETT ROAD
STREET
CHURCH ROAD
FREEWOOD
HOLLYBUSH LANE
HOLLYBUSH LA.
OAKEY LEY
FELSHAM ROAD
DRINKSTONE ROAD
BURY ROAD
GEDDING HILL
LOWER GRN. ROAD
UPPER RD.
CHURCH ROAD
COCKFIELD ROAD
DARKINGS LA.
159
163

DRINKSTONE GREEN / RATTLESDEN

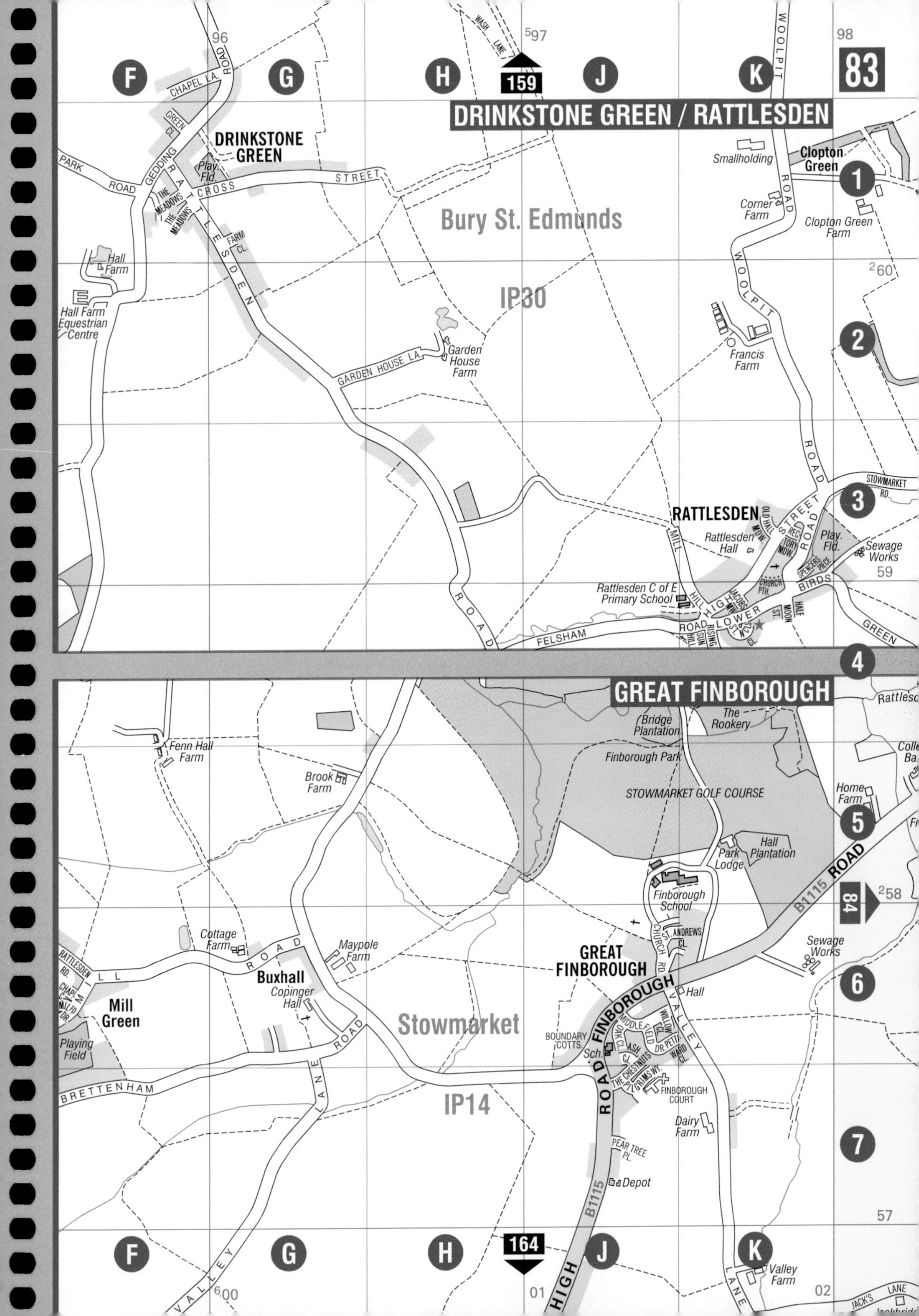

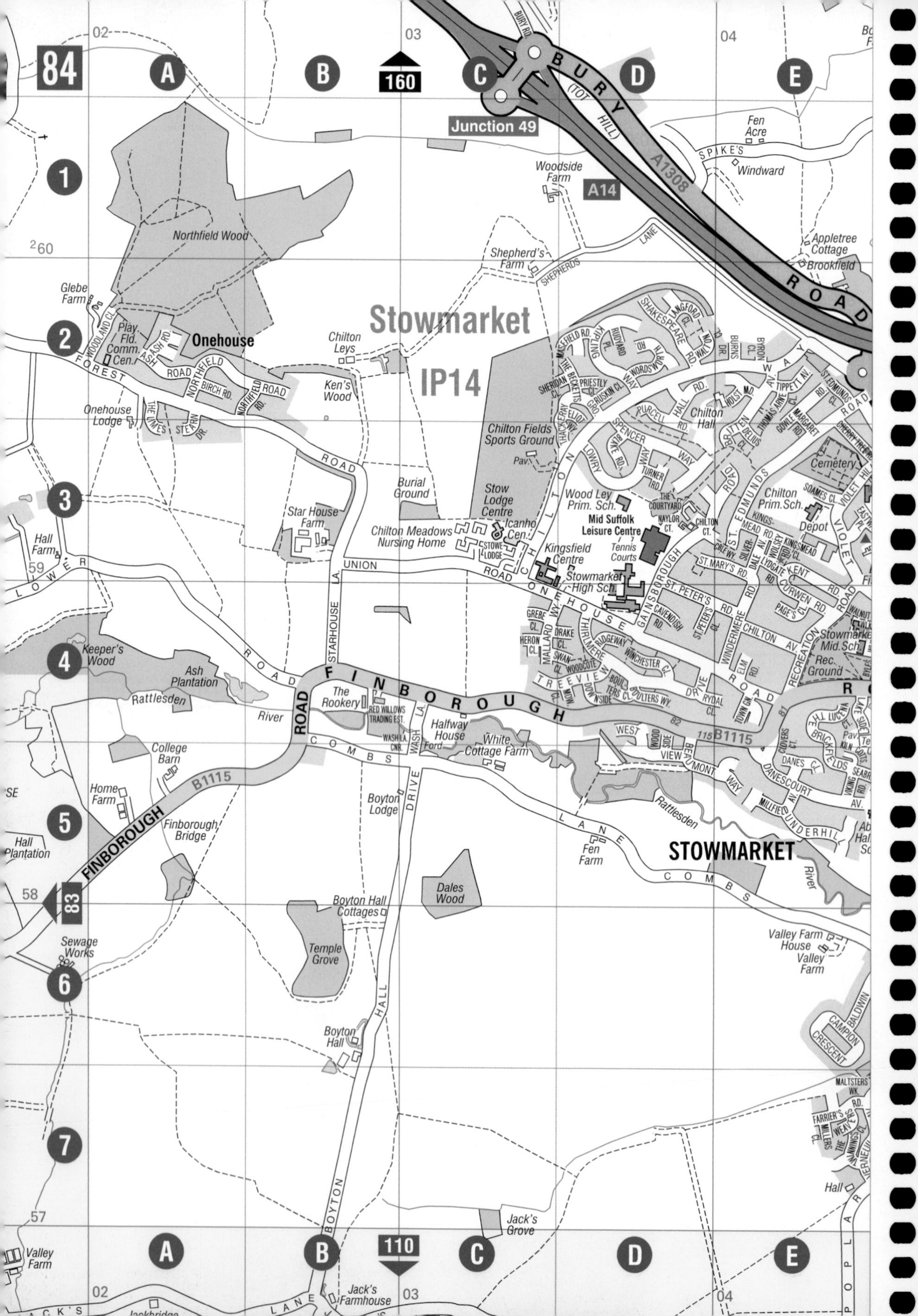

84
160
110
83
Junction 49
A14
A1308
B1115
BURY ROAD
(TOT HILL)
Stowmarket
IP14
STOWMARKET
Onehouse
Northfield Wood
Glebe Farm
Play. Fld.
Comm. Cen.
WOODLAND CL.
ASH RD.
ASH
FOREST ROAD
NORTHFIELD ROAD
BIRCH RD.
Onehouse Lodge
THE LIMES
STERN DR.
Chilton Leys
Ken's Wood
Woodside Farm
Shepherd's Farm
SHEPHERDS LANE
Fen Acre
SPIKE'S
Windward
Appletree Cottage
Brookfield
Hall Farm
LOWER ROAD
Keeper's Wood
Ash Plantation
Rattlesden River
Star House Farm
Burial Ground
UNION ROAD
STARHOUSE LA.
Chilton Meadows Nursing Home
STOWE LODGE
Stow Lodge Centre
Icanho Cen.
Chilton Fields Sports Ground
Pav.
Wood Ley Prim. Sch.
Mid Suffolk Leisure Centre
Tennis Courts
Kingsfield Centre
Stowmarket High Sch.
ONEHOUSE
CHILTON WAY
MASEFIELD RD.
KIPLING
RUDYARD
SHAKESPEARE RD.
LANGFORD CL.
WORDSWORTH RD.
WALTON
BURNS
BYRON CL.
SHERIDAN CL.
THE BECKETTS
PRIESTLY CL.
RUSKIN CL.
THACKERAY
ELIOT WAY
LOWRY
SPENCER WAY
BLAKE RD.
TURNER RD.
PURCELL RD.
HALL RD.
Chilton Hall
HOLST MD.
BRITTEN RD.
DELIUS
THOMAS ARNE
TIPPETT AV.
GOWLE RD.
MARGARET
ST. EDMUNDS RD.
ST. EDMUNDS CL.
CHERRY TREE RD.
Cemetery
Chilton Prim. Sch.
SOAMES CL.
VIOLET HILL
Depot
KINGSMEAD CL.
MEAD RD.
WOLSEY
SILVER
COLE WY.
LYDGATE
KENT RD.
CURWEN RD.
ST. MARY'S RD.
ST. PETER'S RD.
ST. PETER'S CL.
GAINSBOROUGH RD.
THE COURTYARD
NAYLOR CT.
CHILTON CT.
CAVENDISH RD.
DALE AV.
WINDERMERE RD.
PAGE'S CL.
CHILTON AV.
WALNUT
Stowmarket Mid. Sch.
Rec. Ground
RECREATION
GREBE CL.
MALLARD WY.
HERON CL.
DRAKE CL.
SWAN CL.
THIRLMERE
RIDGEWAY
WOODCOTE
WINCHESTER CL.
TREEVIEW
DOWNSIDE
BOULTERS CL.
BOULTERS WY.
RYDAL CL.
DRIVE
ELM RD.
TOWN GN.
FINBOROUGH ROAD
The Rookery
RED WILLOWS TRADING EST.
WASH LA.
WASH LA. CNR.
Halfway House
Ford
White Cottage Farm
COMBS
WEST VIEW
WOOD SIDE
BEAUMONT WAY
CLOVERS CT.
LUCENA
LAKE SIDE
BRICKFIELDS
DANES CL.
DANESCOURT AV.
MILLFIELD
UNDERHILL
VIKING
SEABROOK
Pav.
KILN
College Barn
Home Farm
Finborough Bridge
Hall Plantation
Boyton Lodge
DRIVE
HALL
BOYTON
COMBS LANE
Fen Farm
Rattlesden
River
Dales Wood
Boyton Hall Cottages
Temple Grove
Sewage Works
Valley Farm House
Valley Farm
CAMPION CRESCENT
BALDWIN
Boyton Hall
MALTSTERS WK.
FARRIER'S RD.
MILLERS CL.
THE WEAVERS
MANNINGS
VERNEUIL
Hall
POPLAR
Jack's Grove
Jack's Farmhouse
Jackbridge
JACK'S LANE
Valley Farm
02
03
04
260
59
58
57
82
81
115
A
B
C
D
E
1
2
3
4
5
6
7

85
160
164
F
G
H
J
K
1
2
3
4
5
6
7
05
06
07
60
59
58
57
STOWUPLAND
Thorney Green
Stowmarket
Combs Ford
Columbyne Hall Cottages
Bridge Cottages
Bridge Farm
Newton Bridge
Corner Farm
Green Farm
Century Cottages
Thorney Green
Poole's Farm
Freeman Prim. Sch.
Playing Field
Stowupland Sports Centre
Stowupland High School
War Meml.
Cemetery
Mount Pleasant Farm
Football Ground
The Ashes
Elm House
Hilversum
Alibaba
Millgreen Farm
Bramford Farm
VIOLET HILL DAY HOSP.
Evelyn
Hill Farm
CHARLES IND. EST.
Pickerel Bri.
Cedars Park Prim. Sch.
A14
Junction 50
TOMO INDUSTRIAL ESTATE
TOMO BUS. PARK
Sewage Works
Superstore
Cedars Park
Abbot's Hall
Museum of East Anglian Life
Ford Bri.
Weir
Works
Bowling Green
Stowmarket Meadlands Rec. Club
Factory
Combs Ford Prim. Sch.
Combs Middle School
Church Meadow
Play Fld.
Combs Wood Nature Reserve
Fir Covert
STOWMARKET BUSINESS PARK
NEEDHAM ROAD (EAST) INDUSTRIAL ESTATE
Mill Farm
The Woodlands
Badley Mill Farm
Clamp Farm
Clamp Farm Cottages
RIVER GIPPING
STOWMARKET ROAD
NEWTON ROAD
B1113
B1115
A1120
A1308
CHURCH ROAD
STOWUPLAND RD.
NAVIGATION APPROACH
MORTIMER RD.
GIPPING WAY
BURY ROAD
NEEDHAM RD.
NEEDHAM ROAD
STOWMARKET RD.
COMBS LANE
GREEN ROAD
THORNEY GREEN
MILL STREET
CREETING ROAD
GUN COTTON WAY
EAST DRIVE
TEMPLE ROAD
LOCKINGTON RD.
BRIDGE STREET
IPSWICH ST.
STATION RD.
ELIZABETH
LIME TREE PL.
HOLLINGSWORTH RD.
WOODFIELD DR.
GLEMSFORD RD.
LAVENHAM
LINDSEY WAY
JUBILEE
EDGAR AVENUE
SPRING RW
REGENT ST.
BOND ST.
CROWN ST.

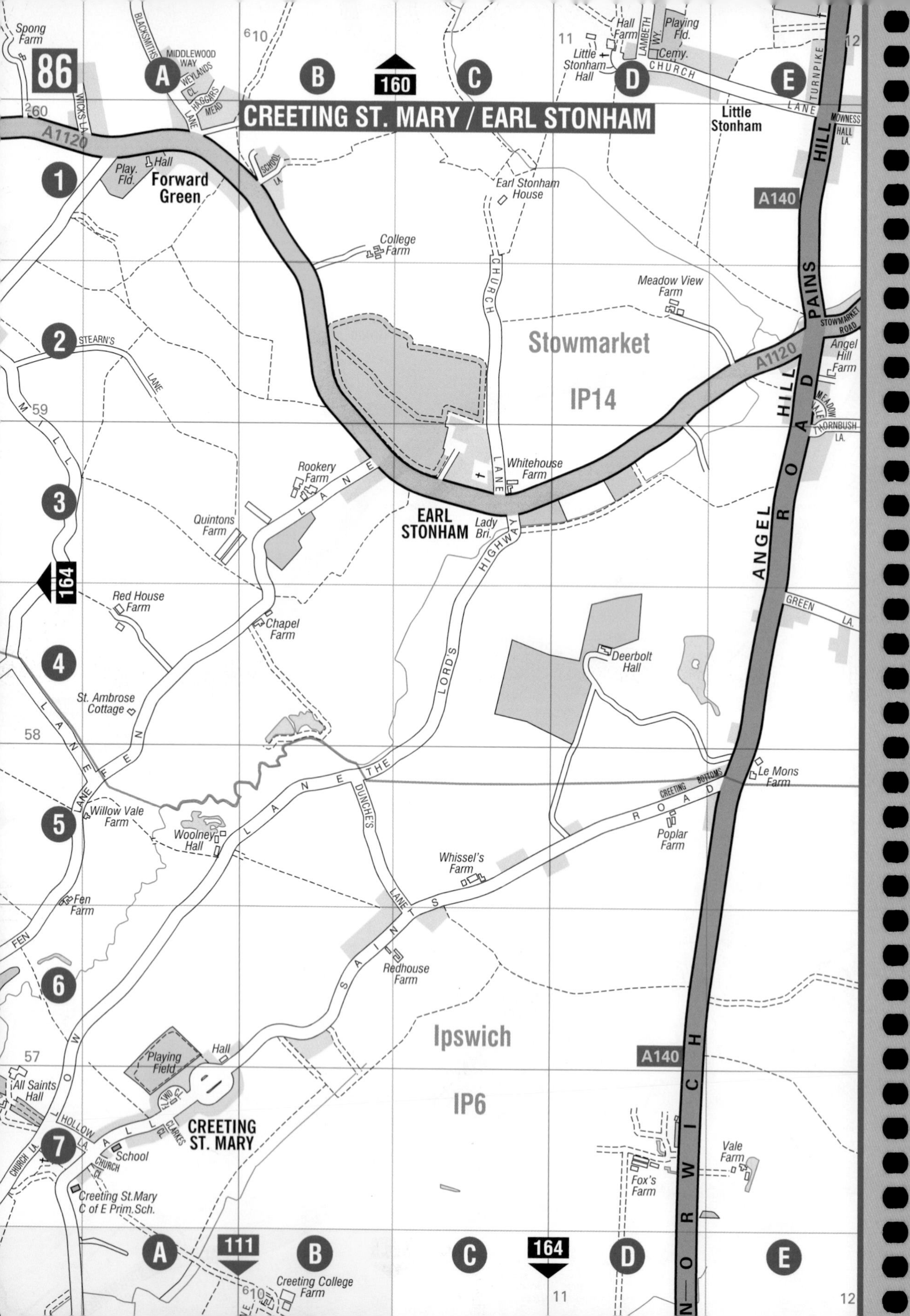
CREETING ST. MARY / EARL STONHAM
160
164
111
164
A1120
A140
Forward Green
EARL STONHAM
CREETING ST. MARY
Little Stonham
Stowmarket
IP14
Ipswich
IP6
Spong Farm
Play. Fld.
Hall
Earl Stonham House
College Farm
Little Stonham Hall
Hall Farm
Playing Fld.
Cemy.
Meadow View Farm
Angel Hill Farm
Rookery Farm
Whitehouse Farm
Quintons Farm
Lady Bri.
Red House Farm
Chapel Farm
Deerbolt Hall
St. Ambrose Cottage
Le Mons Farm
Willow Vale Farm
Woolney Hall
Poplar Farm
Whissel's Farm
Fen Farm
Redhouse Farm
Playing Field
Hall
All Saints Hall
School
Creeting St.Mary C of E Prim.Sch.
Vale Farm
Fox's Farm
Creeting College Farm
MIDDLEWOOD WAY
WEYLANDS CL.
HAGGARS MEAD
BLACKSMITHS LANE
WICKS LA.
SCHOOL LA.
LAMBETH WY.
CHURCH
TURNPIKE LANE
MOWNESS HALL LA.
PAINS HILL
STOWMARKET ROAD
STEARN'S LANE
MILL
CHURCH LANE
LANE
MEADOW VALE
THORNBUSH LA.
ANGEL HILL ROAD
LORD'S HIGHWAY
GREEN LA.
FEN LANE
LANE
THE LANE
DUNCHE'S LANE
CREETING BOTTOMS ROAD
SAINTS
FEN
HOLLOW LA.
CLARKES CL.
CHURCH CL.
CHURCH LA.
NORWICH ROAD
A B C D E
1 2 3 4 5 6 7
610
11
12
60
59
58
57

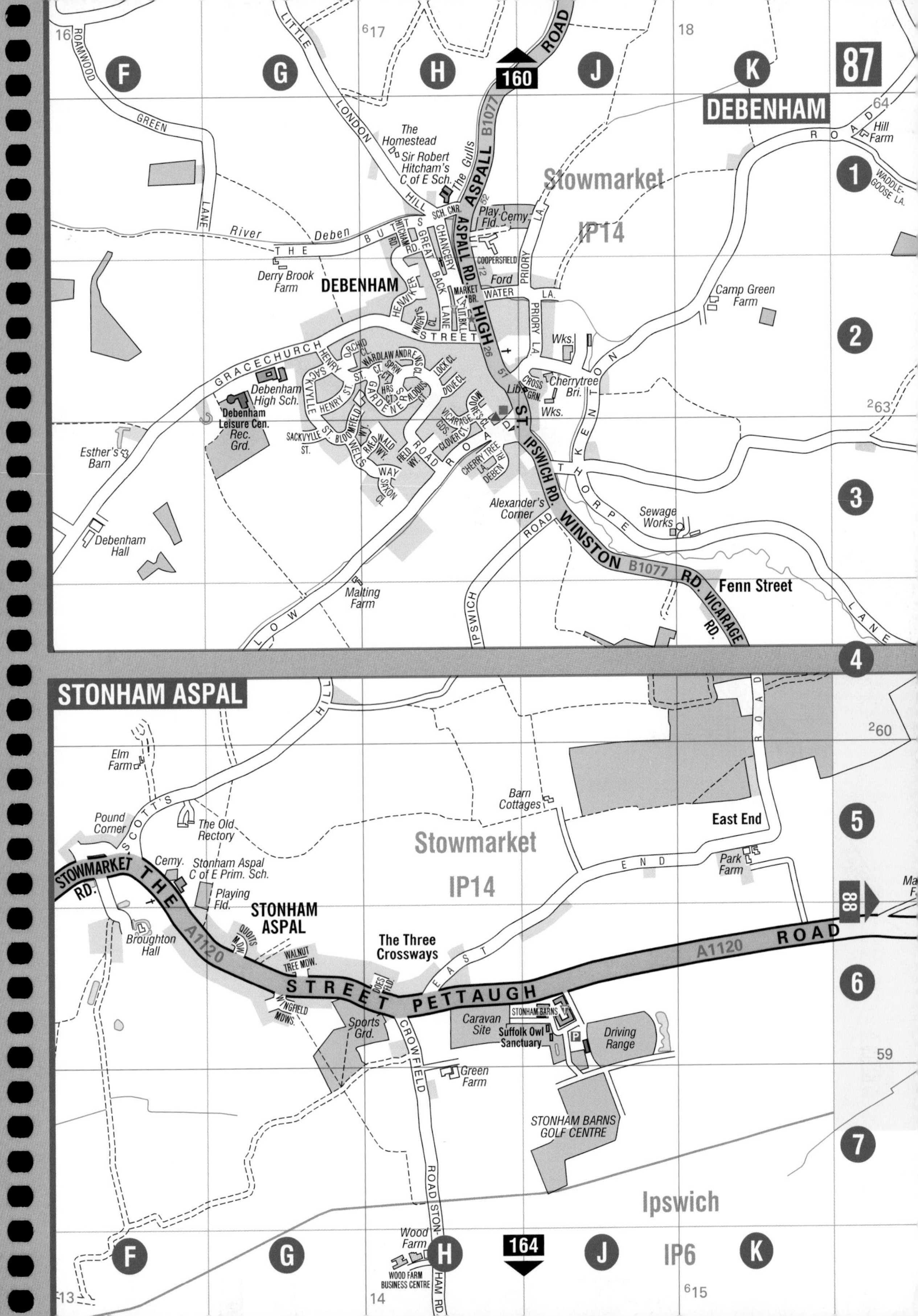

DEBENHAM
160
F
G
H
J
K
1
2
3
4
5
6
7
Stowmarket
IP14
DEBENHAM
The Homestead
Sir Robert Hitcham's C of E Sch.
The Gulls
ASPALL ROAD
ASPALL RD.
HIGH ST.
B1077
LITTLE LONDON HILL
GREEN LANE
ROAMWOOD
River Deben
THE BUTTS
Play. Fld.
Cemy.
COOPERSFIELD
Ford
WATER LA.
PRIORY LA.
Derry Brook Farm
Camp Green Farm
Hill Farm
WADDLE-GOOSE LA.
GRACECHURCH STREET
Debenham High Sch.
Debenham Leisure Cen.
Rec. Grd.
Esther's Barn
Debenham Hall
Wks.
Cherrytree Bri.
Lib.
KENTON ROAD
THORPE LANE
Sewage Works
Alexander's Corner
IPSWICH RD.
WINSTON RD.
VICARAGE RD.
Fenn Street
Malting Farm
LOW ROAD
IPSWICH ROAD
STONHAM ASPAL
Elm Farm
Pound Corner
SCOTTS HILL
The Old Rectory
Cemy.
Stonham Aspal C of E Prim. Sch.
Playing Fld.
STONHAM ASPAL
Broughton Hall
STOWMARKET RD.
THE STREET
PETTAUGH ROAD
A1120
The Three Crossways
Barn Cottages
Stowmarket
IP14
East End
EAST END ROAD
Park Farm
88
Sports Grd.
Caravan Site
STONHAM BARNS
Suffolk Owl Sanctuary
Driving Range
CROWFIELD ROAD
Green Farm
STONHAM BARNS GOLF CENTRE
Ipswich
IP6
Wood Farm
WOOD FARM BUSINESS CENTRE
STONHAM RD.
164

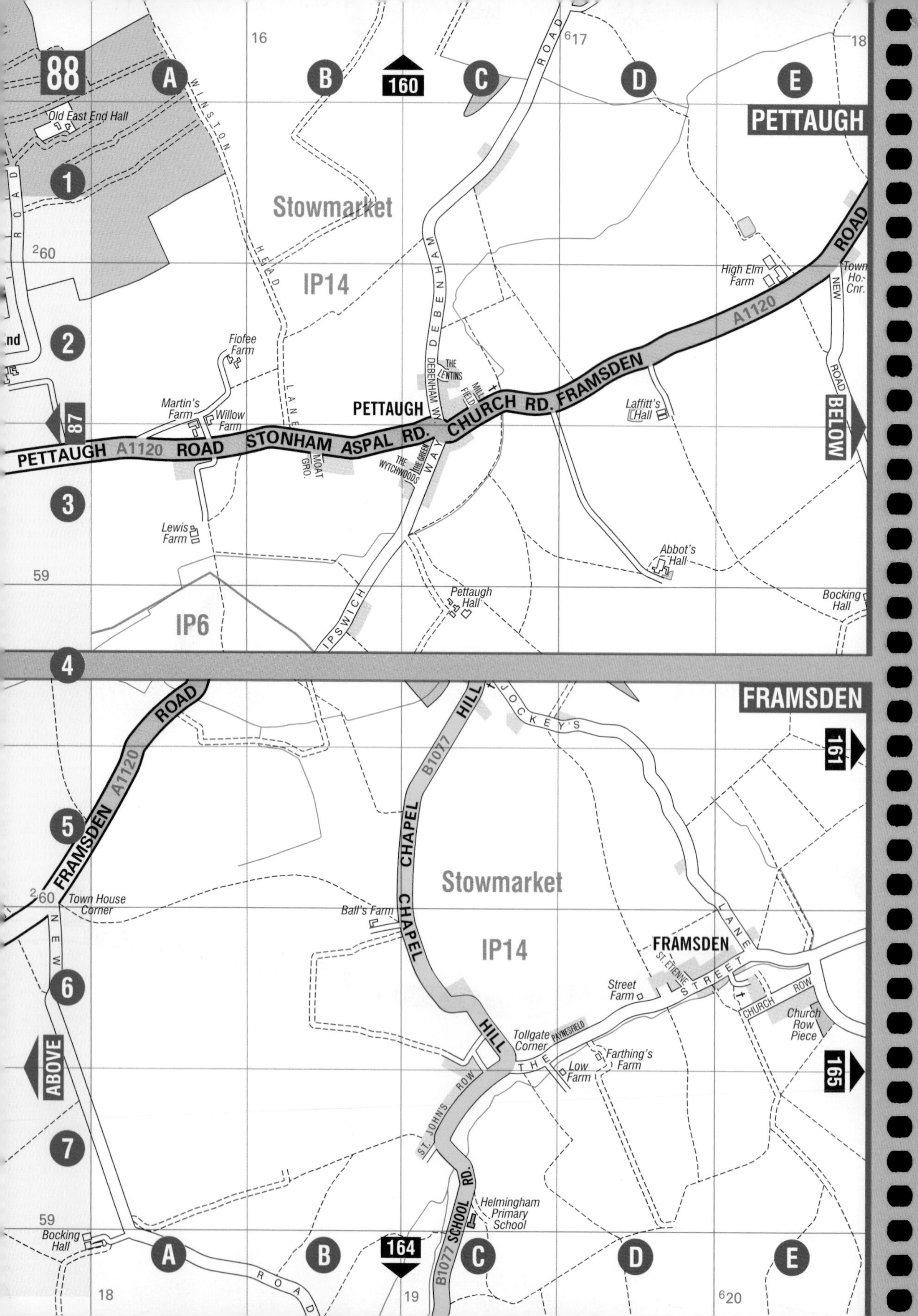
PETTAUGH
FRAMSDEN
Stowmarket
IP14
IP6
PETTAUGH
FRAMSDEN
Old East End Hall
Fiofee Farm
Martin's Farm
Willow Farm
Lewis Farm
Pettaugh Hall
Abbot's Hall
Laffitt's Hall
High Elm Farm
Town Ho. Cnr.
Bocking Hall
PETTAUGH A1120 ROAD STONHAM ASPAL RD. CHURCH RD. FRAMSDEN ROAD
WINSTON
HEAD LANE
DEBENHAM
DEBENHAM WAY
IPSWICH
MOAT GRO.
THE WYTCHWOODS
THE GREEN
THE LENTINS
MILL FIELD
NEW ROAD
FRAMSDEN A1120 ROAD
Town House Corner
NEW
Ball's Farm
CHAPEL HILL
B1077
JOCKEY'S LANE
ST. ETIENNE
STREET
CHURCH ROW
Church Row Piece
Street Farm
Tollgate Corner
PAYNESFIELD
THE
Low Farm
Farthing's Farm
ST. JOHN'S ROW
SCHOOL RD.
Helmingham Primary School
Bocking Hall
ROAD
A B C D E
1 2 3 4 5 6 7
16 617 18 260 59 18 19 620
160 87 BELOW 161 165 ABOVE 164

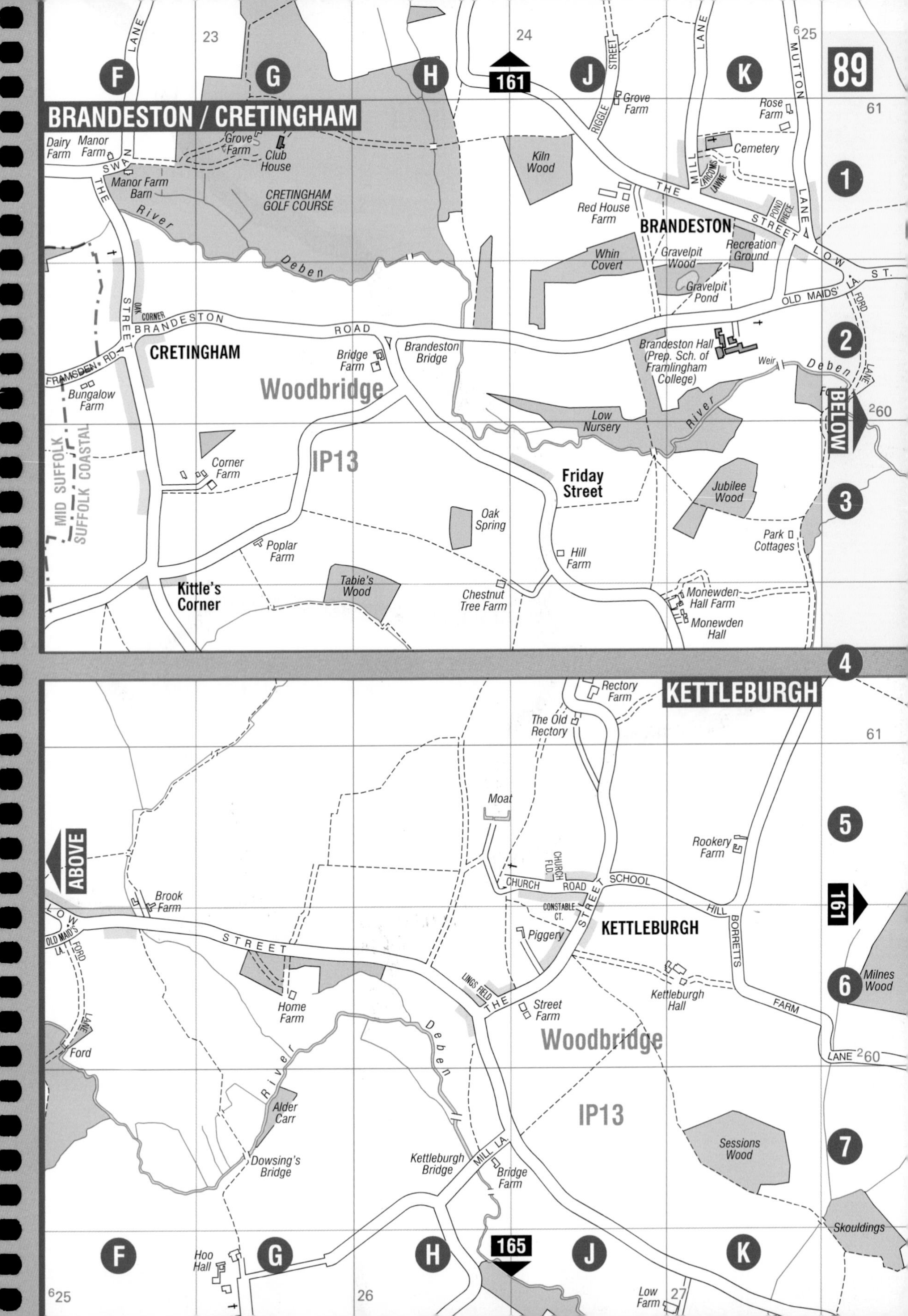

161
165
ABOVE
BELOW

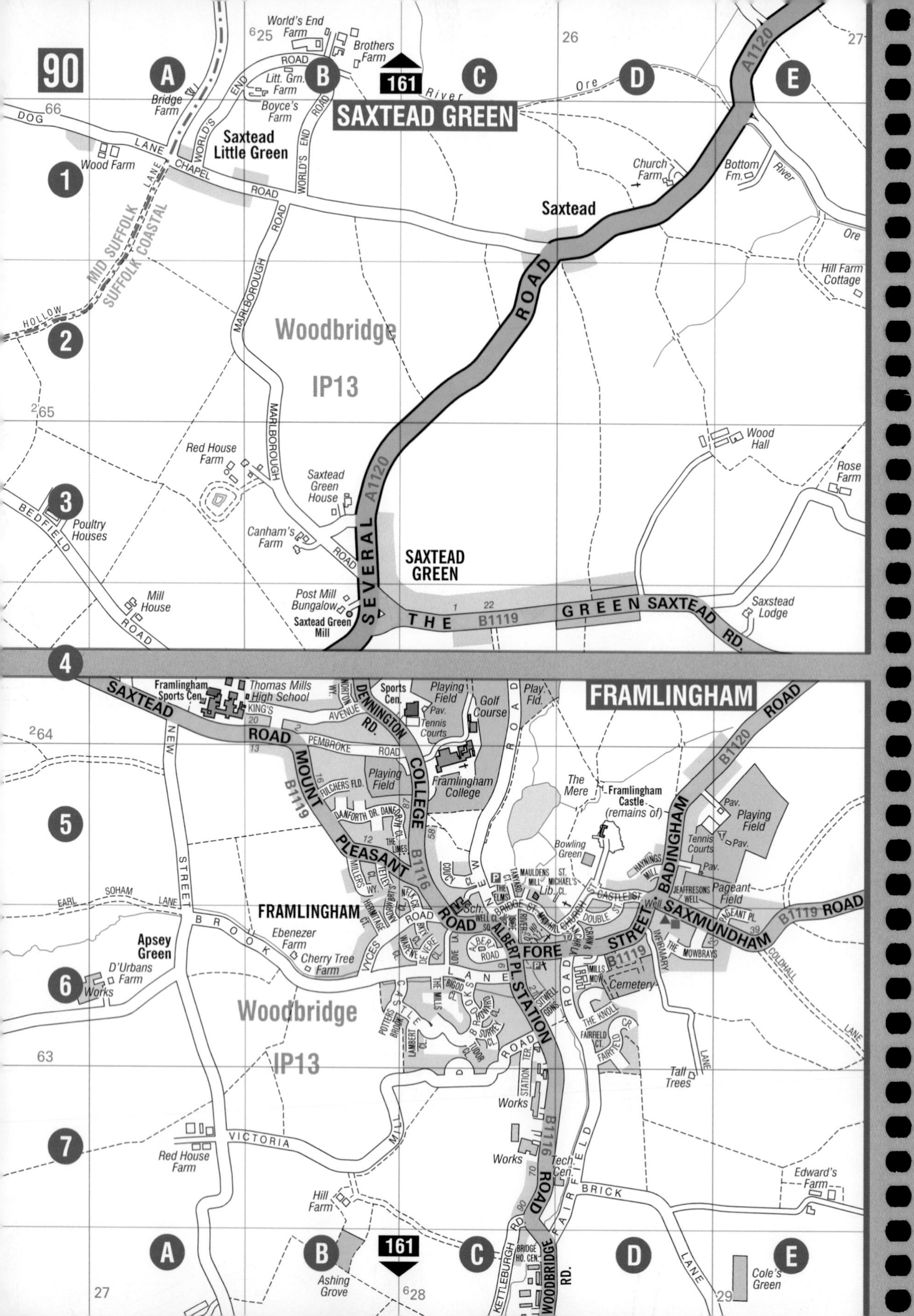
SAXTEAD GREEN
161
Saxtead Little Green
World's End Farm
Brothers Farm
Litt. Grn. Farm
Boyce's Farm
Bridge Farm
Wood Farm
DOG LANE
CHAPEL ROAD
WORLD'S END ROAD
MARLBOROUGH ROAD
MID SUFFOLK
SUFFOLK COASTAL
HOLLOW LANE
Church Farm
Bottom Fm.
Saxtead
River Ore
Hill Farm Cottage
Woodbridge
IP13
Wood Hall
Rose Farm
Red House Farm
Saxtead Green House
Poultry Houses
Canham's Farm
SAXTEAD GREEN
Mill House
Post Mill Bungalow
Saxtead Green Mill
SEVERAL ROAD
A1120
THE GREEN
B1119
SAXTEAD RD.
Saxtead Lodge
BEDFIELD ROAD
FRAMLINGHAM
Framlingham Sports Cen.
Thomas Mills High School
Sports Cen.
Playing Field
Golf Course
Play. Fld.
SAXTEAD ROAD
DENNINGTON RD.
COLLEGE ROAD
MOUNT PLEASANT
PEMBROKE ROAD
Framlingham College
The Mere
Framlingham Castle (remains of)
Bowling Green
BADINGHAM ROAD
Pageant Field
SAXMUNDHAM ROAD
FORE STREET
NEW STREET
EARL SOHAM LANE
BROOK LANE
Apsey Green
D'Urbans Farm
Works
Ebenezer Farm
Cherry Tree Farm
ALBERT ROAD
STATION ROAD
Cemetery
THE KNOLL
Tall Trees
Woodbridge
IP13
VICTORIA
Red House Farm
Works
Tech. Cen.
B1116
FAIRFIELD ROAD
BRICK LANE
Edward's Farm
Hill Farm
Ashing Grove
161
KETTLEBURGH RD.
WOODBRIDGE RD.
Cole's Green

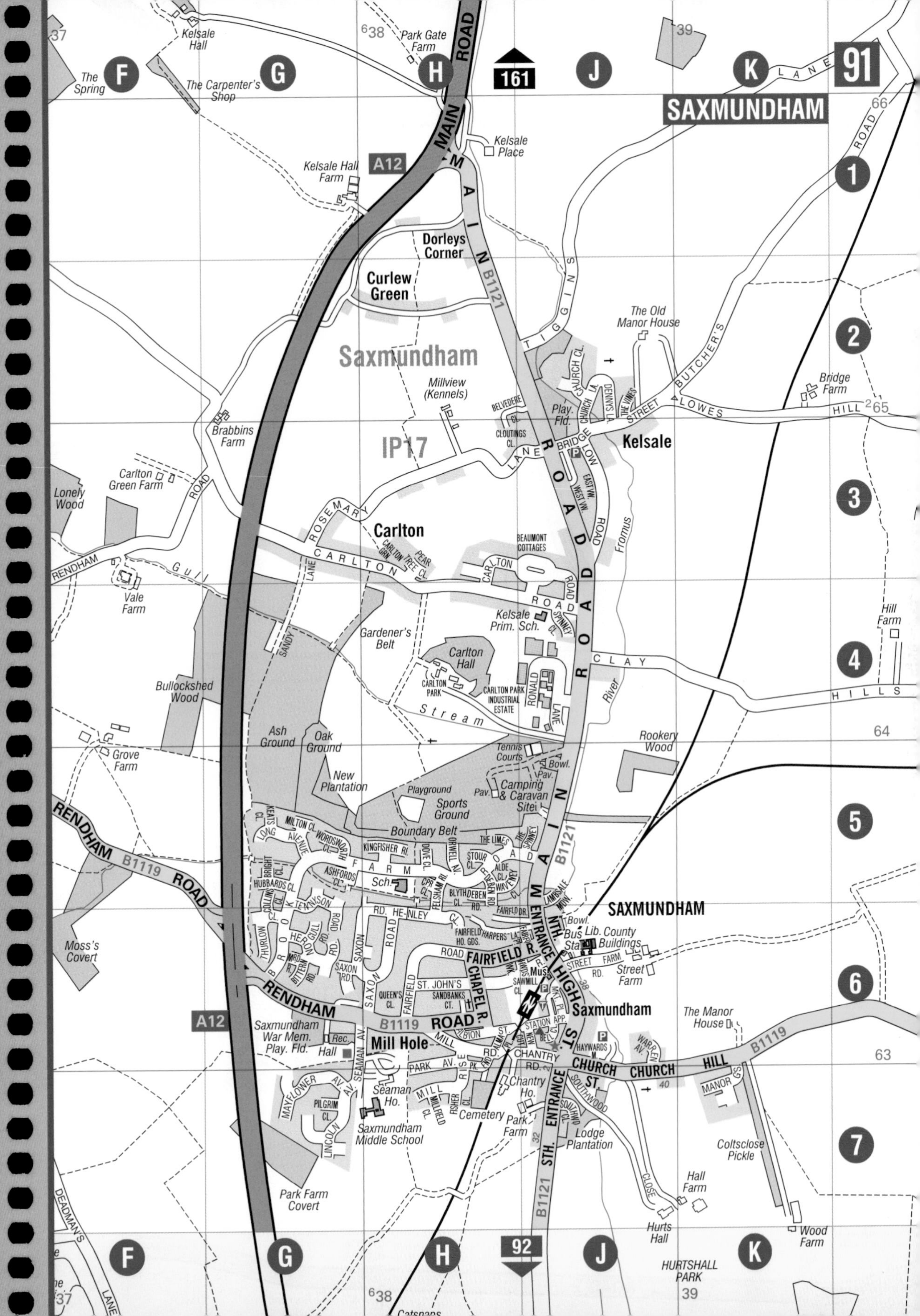
SAXMUNDHAM
161
92
F
G
H
J
K
1
2
3
4
5
6
7
Saxmundham
IP17
Kelsale
Carlton
SAXMUNDHAM
Dorleys Corner
Curlew Green
Kelsale Hall
The Spring
The Carpenter's Shop
Park Gate Farm
Kelsale Place
Kelsale Hall Farm
Brabbins Farm
Carlton Green Farm
Lonely Wood
Vale Farm
Bullockshed Wood
Grove Farm
Moss's Covert
Millview (Kennels)
The Old Manor House
Bridge Farm
Hill Farm
Rookery Wood
Gardener's Belt
Carlton Hall
Carlton Park Industrial Estate
Kelsale Prim. Sch.
Ash Ground
Oak Ground
New Plantation
Playground
Sports Ground
Camping & Caravan Site
Tennis Courts
Boundary Belt
Saxmundham War Mem. Play. Fld.
Mill Hole
Seaman Ho.
Saxmundham Middle School
Cemetery
Chantry Ho.
Park Farm
Lodge Plantation
Park Farm Covert
The Manor House
Street Farm
County Buildings
Coltsclose Pickle
Hall Farm
Hurts Hall
Wood Farm
HURTSHALL PARK
MAIN ROAD
A12
B1121
B1119
RENDHAM ROAD
CARLTON ROAD
ROSEMARY LANE
SANDY LANE
TIGGINS LANE
BUTCHER'S ROAD
LOWES HILL
CLAY HILLS
CHURCH HILL
FAIRFIELD R.
CHAPEL R.
HIGH ST.
NTH. ENTRANCE
STH. ENTRANCE
FARM ROAD
BROOK FARM ROAD
LONG AVENUE
MILL ROAD
CHANTRY RD.
STREET FARM RD.
River Fromus
Gull
Stream
Bus Sta.
Lib.
Mus.
63
64
65
66
37
638
39

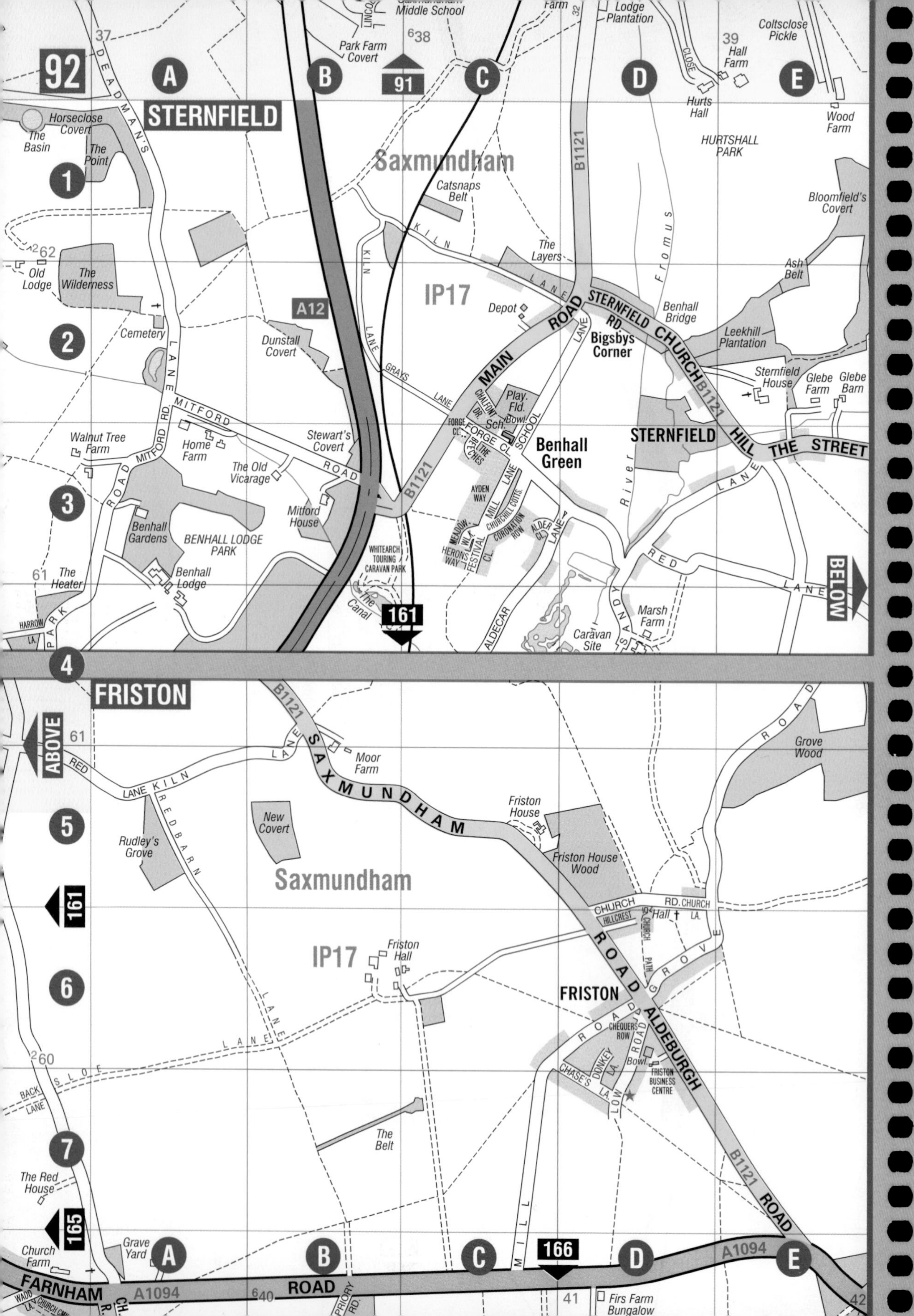
STERNFIELD
Saxmundham
IP17
Benhall Green
Bigsbys Corner
STERNFIELD
FRISTON
Saxmundham
IP17
FRISTON
Horseclose Covert
The Basin
The Point
Old Lodge
The Wilderness
Cemetery
Walnut Tree Farm
Home Farm
The Old Vicarage
Benhall Gardens
BENHALL LODGE PARK
Benhall Lodge
The Heater
Dunstall Covert
Stewart's Covert
Mitford House
Catsnaps Belt
The Layers
Depot
Park Farm Covert
Lodge Plantation
Hall Farm
Hurts Hall
HURTSHALL PARK
Coltsclose Pickle
Wood Farm
Bloomfield's Covert
Ash Belt
Benhall Bridge
Leekhill Plantation
Sternfield House
Glebe Farm
Glebe Barn
WHITEARCH TOURING CARAVAN PARK
The Canal
Caravan Site
Marsh Farm
Moor Farm
New Covert
Rudley's Grove
Friston House
Friston House Wood
Friston Hall
Grove Wood
The Belt
The Red House
Church Farm
Grave Yard
FRISTON BUSINESS CENTRE
Firs Farm Bungalow
DEADMAN'S LANE
MITFORD RD.
MITFORD ROAD
KILN LANE
GRAYS LANE
MAIN ROAD
STERNFIELD RD.
CHURCH HILL
THE STREET
RED LANE
SANDY LANE
ALDECAR LANE
SCHOOL LANE
FORGE CL.
MILL LANE
SAXMUNDHAM ROAD
ALDEBURGH ROAD
CHURCH RD.
GROVE ROAD
FARNHAM ROAD
A1094
A12
B1121
161
91
166
165
BELOW
ABOVE

Leiston Abbey (remains of)
Abbey Farm
166
Spring Covert
Tennis Court
Playing Field
Aldhurst Farm
Old Abbey Farm
Leiston Old Abbey
Dunwich Forest
CAKES & ALE CARAVAN PARK
Fisher's Farm
Buckle's Wood
Leiston
IP16
Brick Kiln Farm
Sewage Works
Wood Farm
West End Nurseries
Summerhill School
Football Ground
Cemetery
Playing Field
HIGHBURY COTTS.
MASTERLORD INDUSTRIAL ESTATE
EASTLANDS INDUSTRIAL ESTATE
ARCHWAY COTTS.
SAXMUNDHAM RD
WATERLOO AVENUE
B1119
MAIN S.
HIGH STREET
B1122
KING GEORGE'S AVENUE
Sizewell Sports & Social Club
Sports Ground
Rec. Grd.
Play Area
Leiston Prim. Sch.
Leiston Mid. Sch.
Leiston Hall Farm
Dunn's Hole
The Cupola
Sports Grd.
Club
Community Education Centre
Leiston High School
Leiston Leisure Centre
LEISTON
RED HOUSE LANE
GRIMSEY'S LANE
Hawsell's Farm
HAYLINGS ROAD
B1069
ALDEBURGH ROAD
GOLDING'S LANE
OGILVIE HOMES
Depot
Saxmundham
IP17
KNODISHALL
Coldfair Green
ALDRINGHAM
ALDRINGHAM LANE
B1353
Keepers Cottages
Aldringham House
Elm Tree Farm
Rec. Grd.
Playing Field
Knodishall Common
Sewage Works
Hundred River
MILL HILL ESTATE
Aldringham Green
Little Beauties Wood
Coldfair Grn. Prim. Sch.
School Plantation
Aldringham Square
Square Plantation
Church Farm Wood
SNAPE ROAD
FITCHE'S LANE
GIPSY LA.
Billeaford Hall
THE OGILVIE ALMSHOUSES
94
F
G
H
J
K
1
2
3
4
5
6
7

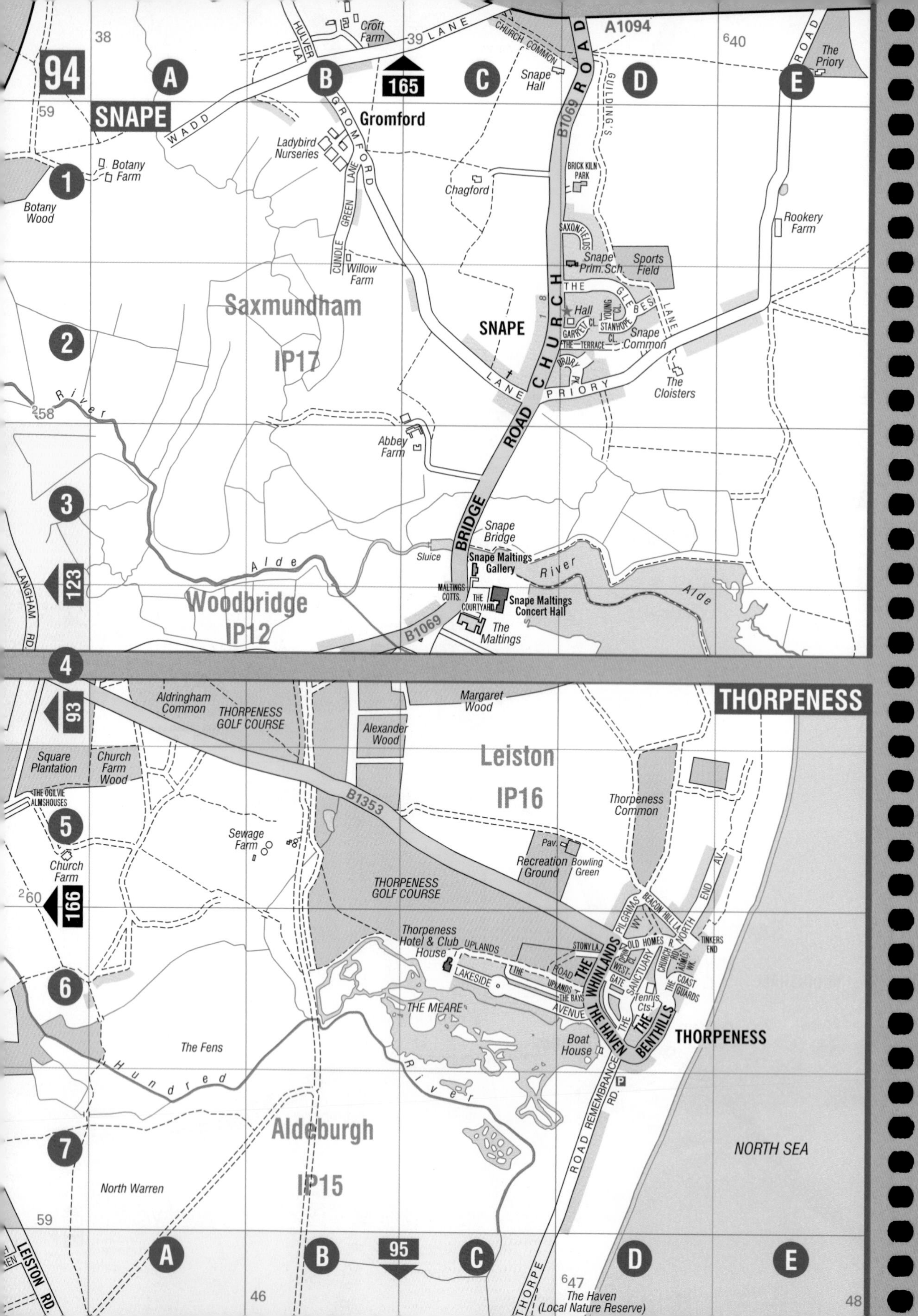

165
123
93
166
95

ALDEBURGH
North Warren
94
Chapel Farm
Triangle Covert
Round Plantation
Eight Acre Covert
ALDEBURGH GOLF COURSE
LEISTON ROAD
B1122
WARREN HILL LA.
SAXMUNDHAM ROAD
A1094
Club Ho.
Watering Forest
Sewage Pumping Station
LINDEN ROAD
LINDEN CLOSE
Playing Field
THE MAYOR'S FIELD CARAVAN PARK
CHURCH FARM CARAVAN PARK
THE PLANTATION
VICTORIA ROAD
Aldeburgh Brickworks
Aldeburgh
IP15
Aldeburgh Comm. & Sports Cen.
Sports Grd.
King's Field (Recreation Ground)
Lib.
Cin.
HIGH STREET
CRABBE STREET
Aldeburgh Museum (Moot Hall)
War Meml.
ALDEBURGH
Lifeboat Station
NORTH SEA
ALDEBURGH BAY
ALDEBURGH COMMUNITY HOSPITAL
Tennis Cts.
Stanny Point
Cob Island
Aldeburgh Marshes
Sewage Works
Fort Green
THORPE ROAD
CRAG PATH
Hundred River
The Haven (Local Nature Reserve)
Short Reach
Westrow Reach
RIVER ALDE
Slaughden Sailing Club
Slaughden
Boatbuilding Yard
Aldeburgh Yacht Club
Sudbourne Marshes
166

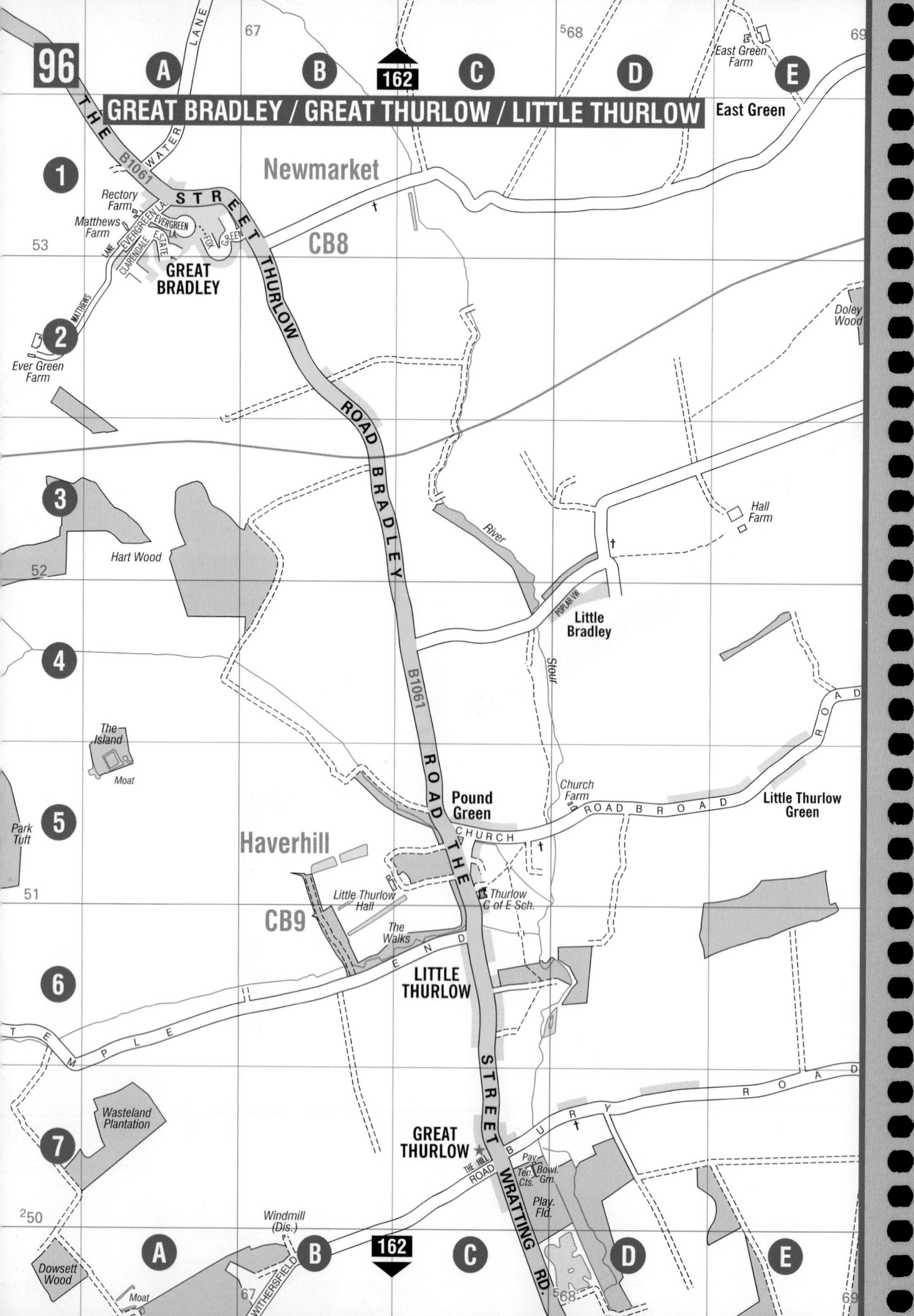
96
GREAT BRADLEY / GREAT THURLOW / LITTLE THURLOW
162
East Green
East Green Farm
Newmarket
CB8
Rectory Farm
Matthews Farm
GREAT BRADLEY
Ever Green Farm
THE STREET
THURLOW ROAD
BRADLEY ROAD
B1061
WATER LANE
MATTHEWS LANE
EVERGREEN LA.
CLARENDALE ESTATE
FOX GREEN
Doley Wood
Hall Farm
River Stour
Hart Wood
Little Bradley
POPLAR VW.
The Island
Moat
Park Tuft
Church Farm
Pound Green
CHURCH ROAD
BROAD ROAD
Little Thurlow Green
Haverhill
CB9
Little Thurlow Hall
Thurlow C of E Sch.
The Walks
TEMPLE END
LITTLE THURLOW
THE STREET
BURY ROAD
GREAT THURLOW
THE HILL
Pav.
Ten. Cts.
Bowl. Grn.
Play. Fld.
WRATTING RD.
Wasteland Plantation
Windmill (Dis.)
WITHERSFIELD ROAD
Dowsett Wood
Moat
67
568
69
53
52
51
250

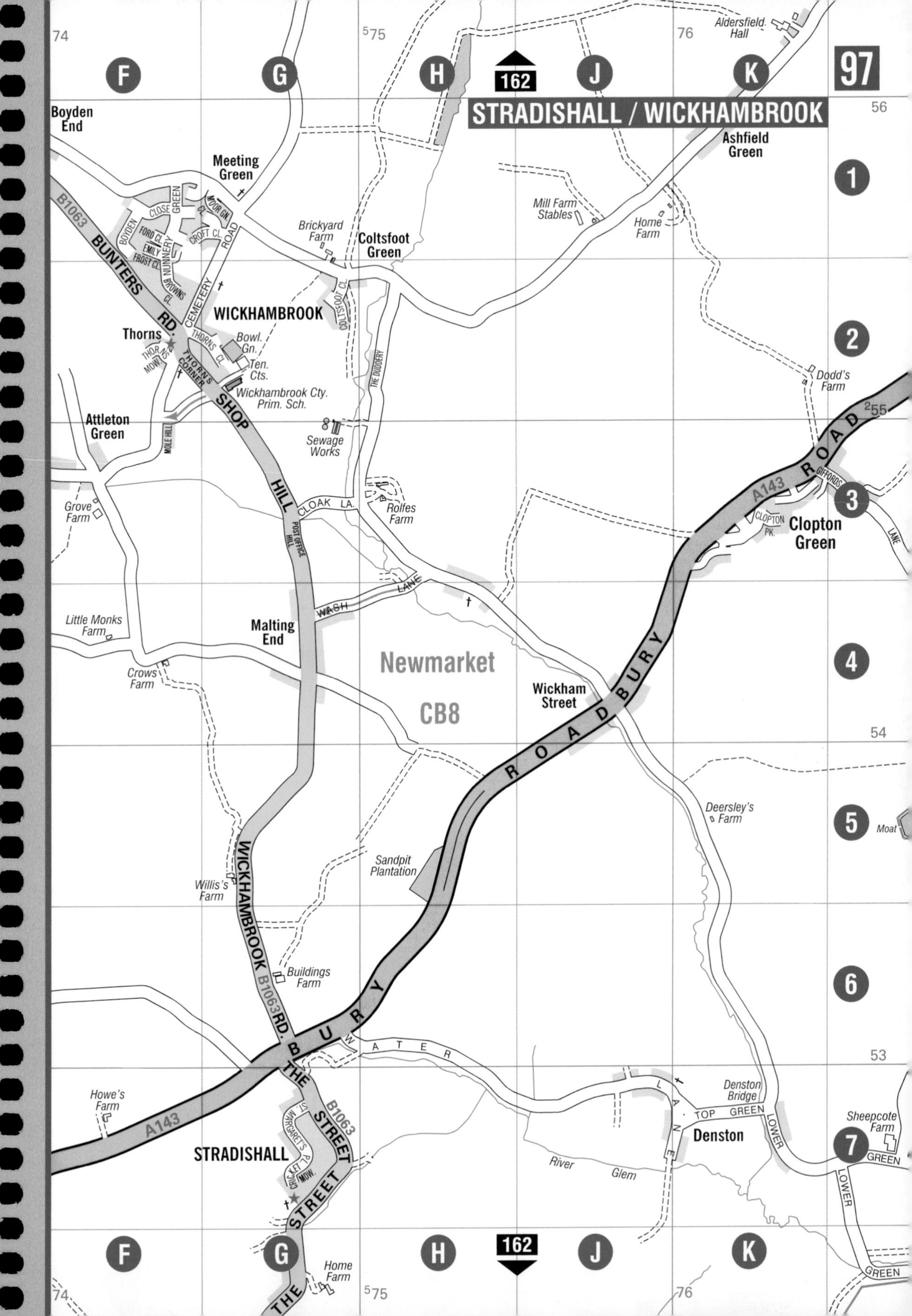
Boyden End
Meeting Green
Brickyard Farm
Coltsfoot Green
Mill Farm Stables
Home Farm
Ashfield Green
Aldersfield Hall
WICKHAMBROOK
Thorns
Bowl. Gn.
Ten. Cts.
Wickhambrook Cty. Prim. Sch.
Attleton Green
Sewage Works
Dodd's Farm
Grove Farm
Rolfes Farm
Clopton Green
Little Monks Farm
Malting End
Newmarket
CB8
Crows Farm
Wickham Street
Deersley's Farm
Moat
Sandpit Plantation
Willis's Farm
Buildings Farm
Howe's Farm
STRADISHALL
Denston Bridge
Denston
Sheepcote Farm
River Glem
Home Farm
BUNTERS RD.
SHOP HILL
CLOAK LA.
POST OFFICE HILL
WASH LANE
BURY ROAD
A143
B1063
WICKHAMBROOK RD.
THE STREET
WATER LANE
TOP GREEN
LOWER GREEN
THE DUDDERY
COLTSFOOT CL.
CEMETERY ROAD
MOLE HILL
162

WITHERSFIELD
565
66
67
A
B
C
D
E
162
1
2
3
4
5
6
7
248
47
247
46
Lawn Farm
SKIPPER'S LANE
HORSEHEATH RD.
HOLLOW HILL
CHURCH STREET
HOMESTEAD CRES.
QUEEN ST.
TURNPIKE HILL
THURLOW RD.
PARK VW.
SCHOOL TER.
WITHERSFIELD
Haverhill
CB9
Hall Farm
Sewage Works
Howe Wood
BURTON GRN.
BURTON HILL
ROSE HILL
Charity Farm
WITHERSFIELD ROAD
Pav.
Sports Grd.
Paradise Farm
Norney Plantation
100
HALES BARN RD
BRICKFIELDS DR.
MASON CL.
KEDINGTON
Taylor's Farm
OLD HAVERHILL RD.
B1061
A143
Factory
Bowling Green
Sports Ground
HAVERHILL ROAD
TAYLORS FARM ROAD
Hall Farm
HALL ROAD
CO10
Poplar Farm
Stonebridge Farm
CORDWAINER CL.
RISBRIDGE DRIVE
STOURMEAD CL.
BARHAM CL.
MILL ROAD
SCHOOL ROAD
SCHOOL CRES.
Play. Fld.
Kedington Primary Sch.
CHURCH WLK.
WESTEND LANE
DASH END
DASH END LANE
UNDON ROAD
WESTWARD DEALS
THE PARADE
BARTON DR.
BARTON GRO.
KEDINGTON
WHITE HORSE RD.
DANE CL.
MEADOW ROAD
RAILWAY TER.
KING'S HILL
SILVER ST.
RECTORY ROAD
ARMS LANE
Comm. Cen. & Lib.
Playing Field
COCK ROAD
SIMM'S LANE
Simm's Farm
Whyberries Farm
Stour Farm
River Stour
Sewage Works
Ruse's Farm
STURMER ROAD
101
570
71
72
Jolly's Wood

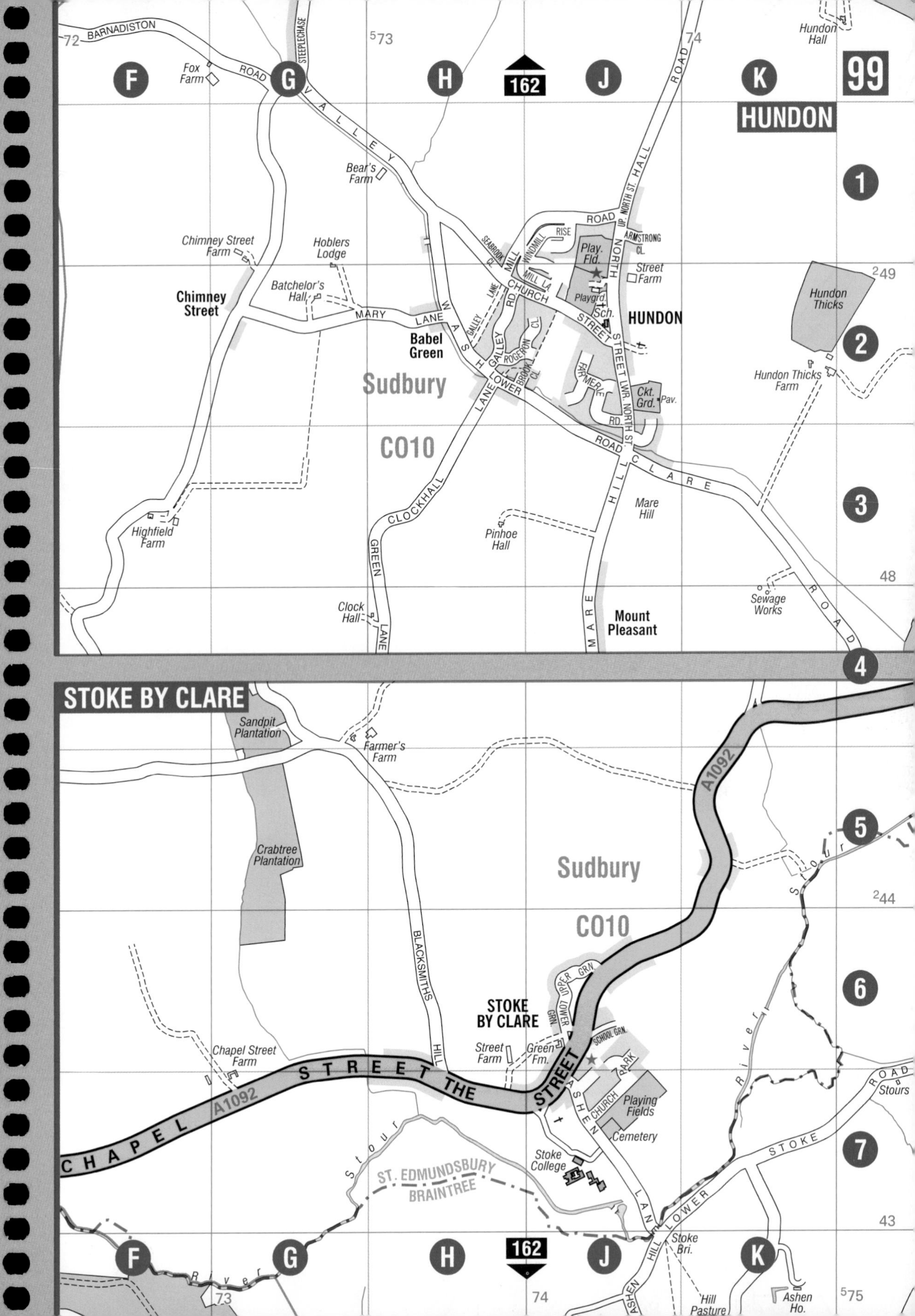

HUNDON
STOKE BY CLARE
162
F
G
H
J
K
1
2
3
4
5
6
7
BARNADISTON
ROAD
STEEPLECHASE
VALLEY
Fox Farm
Bear's Farm
Hundon Hall
Chimney Street Farm
Hoblers Lodge
Batchelor's Hall
Chimney Street
MARY LANE
Babel Green
WASH
Sudbury
CO10
Highfield Farm
CLOCKHALL
GREEN LANE
Clock Hall
Pinhoe Hall
Mare Hill
MARE HILL
Mount Pleasant
HUNDON
Play. Fld.
Playgrd.
Sch.
Street Farm
ARMSTRONG CL.
UP. NORTH ST.
HALL ROAD
NORTH STREET
LWR. NORTH ST.
CHURCH STREET
SEABROOK CL.
MILL RD.
WINDMILL RISE
MILL LA.
GALLEY LANE
GALLEY RD.
ROGERON CL.
BROOK CL.
LOWER
FARMERIE RD.
Ckt. Grd.
Pav.
CLARE ROAD
Hundon Thicks
Hundon Thicks Farm
Sewage Works
Sandpit Plantation
Farmer's Farm
Crabtree Plantation
BLACKSMITHS HILL
Chapel Street Farm
CHAPEL STREET
A1092
THE STREET
STOKE BY CLARE
UPPER GRN.
LOWER GRN.
SCHOOL GRN.
Street Farm
Green Fm.
PARK
CHURCH
ASHEN LANE
Playing Fields
Cemetery
Stoke College
Stour
River Stour
ST. EDMUNDSBURY
BRAINTREE
STOKE ROAD
LOWER
Stours
Stoke Bri.
HILL
ASHEN
Hill Pasture
Ashen Ho.
572
573
74
575
249
48
244
43

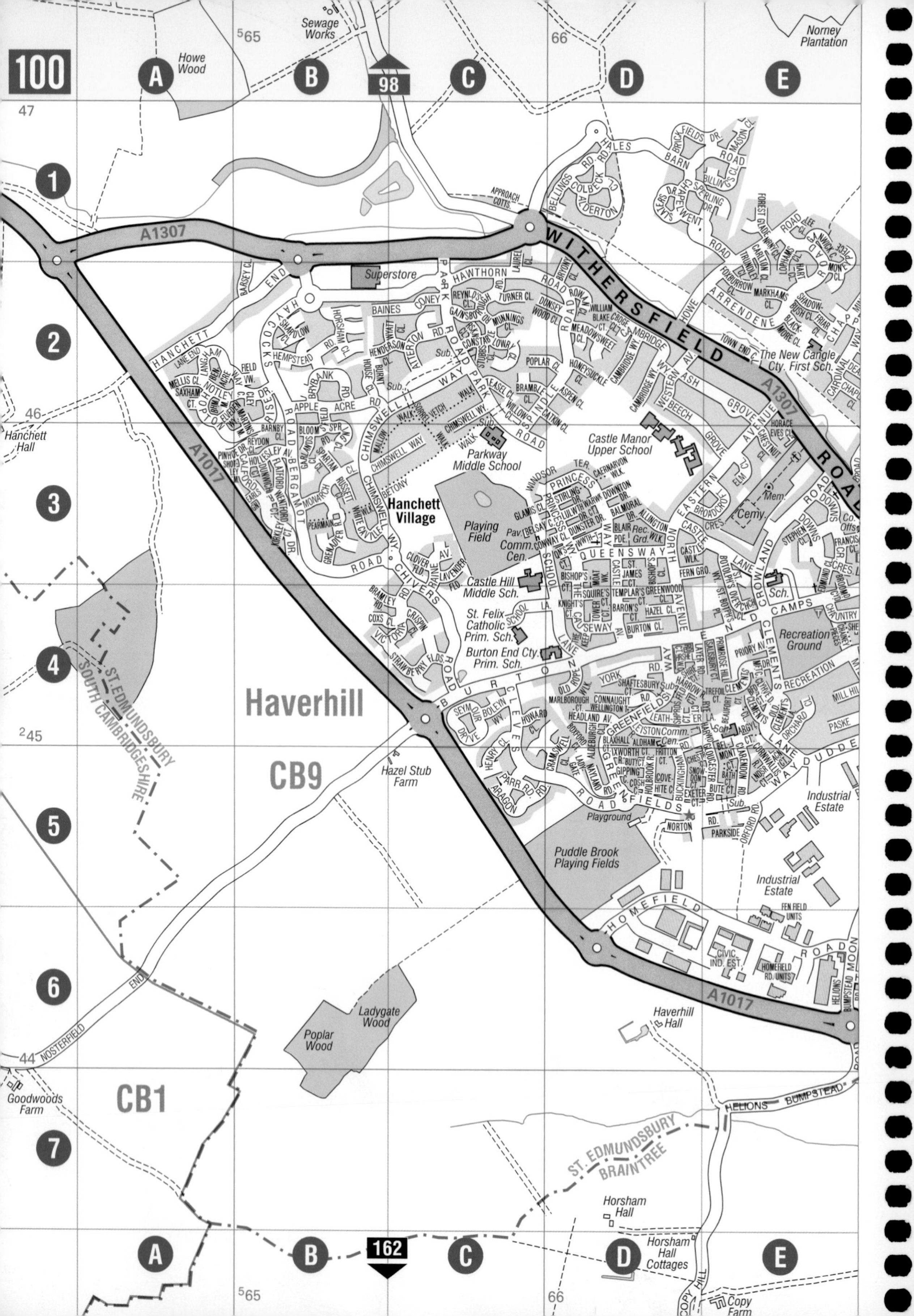

Haverhill
CB9
CB1
Hanchett Village
A1307
A1017
WITHERSFIELD ROAD
Superstore
Sewage Works
Howe Wood
Norney Plantation
Hanchett Hall
Castle Manor Upper School
Parkway Middle School
Playing Field
Castle Hill Middle Sch.
St. Felix Catholic Prim. Sch.
Burton End Cty. Prim. Sch.
Recreation Ground
Industrial Estate
Puddle Brook Playing Fields
Hazel Stub Farm
Ladygate Wood
Poplar Wood
Goodwoods Farm
Haverhill Hall
Horsham Hall
Horsham Hall Cottages
Copy Farm
ST. EDMUNDSBURY
SOUTH CAMBRIDGESHIRE
BRAINTREE
The New Cangle Cty. First Sch.
98
162

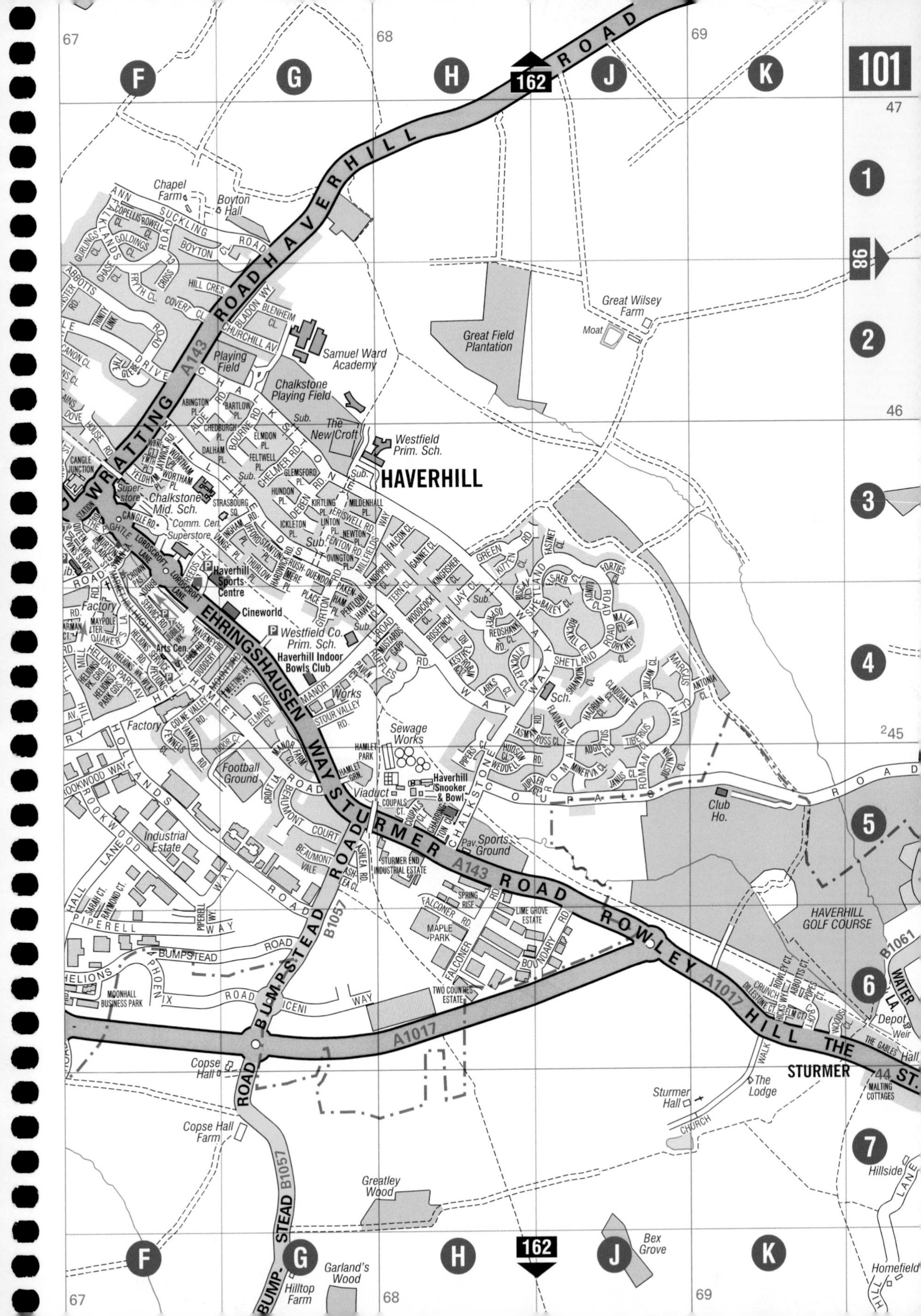
HAVERHILL
STURMER
Great Field Plantation
Great Wilsey Farm
Moat
Samuel Ward Academy
Chalkstone Playing Field
Westfield Prim. Sch.
Playing Field
Chalkstone Mid. Sch.
Haverhill Sports Centre
Cineworld
Westfield Co. Prim. Sch.
Haverhill Indoor Bowls Club
Sewage Works
Haverhill Snooker & Bowl
Sports Ground
Football Ground
Industrial Estate
MOONHALL BUSINESS PARK
TWO COUNTIES ESTATE
MAPLE PARK
LIME GROVE ESTATE
STURMER END INDUSTRIAL ESTATE
HAVERHILL GOLF COURSE
Club Ho.
Chapel Farm
Boyton Hall
Copse Hall
Copse Hall Farm
Greatley Wood
Bex Grove
Garland's Wood
Hilltop Farm
Sturmer Hall
The Lodge
Hillside
Homefield
Depot
Weir
MALTING COTTAGES
WRATTING ROAD
HAVERHILL ROAD
EHRINGSHAUSEN WAY
STURMER ROAD
ROWLEY HILL
THE ST.
BUMPSTEAD ROAD
CHALKSTONE WAY
COUPALS ROAD
ROMAN WAY
A143
A1017
B1057
B1061
162
98
F G H J K
1 2 3 4 5 6 7
67 68 69
47 46 45 44

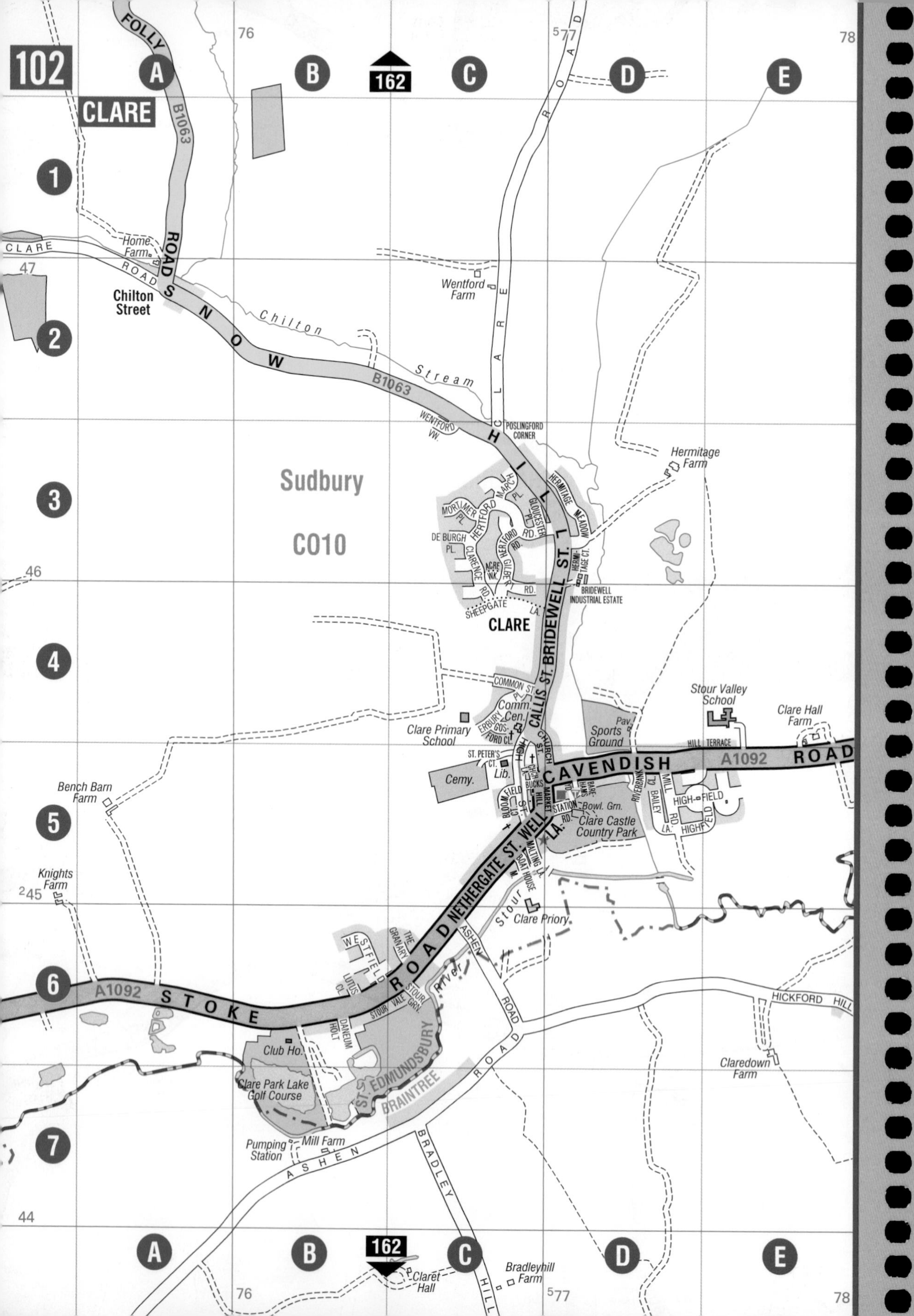
CLARE
A
B
C
D
E
162
1
2
3
4
5
6
7
76
577
78
47
46
245
44
FOLLY
B1063
ROAD
CLARE ROAD
Home Farm
Chilton Street
SNOW HILL
Chilton Stream
B1063
CLARE ROAD
Wentford Farm
WENTFORD VW.
POSLINGFORD CORNER
Sudbury
CO10
Hermitage Farm
MORTIMER PL.
HERTFORD
MARCH PL.
GLOUCESTER PL.
HERMITAGE MEADOW
DE BURGH PL.
CLARENCE RD.
ACRE WK.
HERTFORD RD.
GILBERT RD.
HERMITAGE CT.
BRIDEWELL ST.
BRIDEWELL INDUSTRIAL ESTATE
SHEEPGATE LA.
CLARE
COMMON ST.
Comm. Cen.
CALLIS ST.
Clare Primary School
Stour Valley School
Clare Hall Farm
Pav.
Sports Ground
HILL TERRACE
A1092
CAVENDISH ROAD
ST. PETER'S CT.
Lib.
Cemy.
CHURCH ST.
MARKET HILL
BUCKS
RIVERBANK
BAILEY LA.
MILL RD.
HIGHFIELD
Bench Barn Farm
BLOOMFIELD CT.
STATION RD.
Bowl. Grn.
Clare Castle Country Park
NETHERGATE ST.
WELL LA.
MALTING LA.
BOAT HOUSE
Knights Farm
Stour
Clare Priory
WESTFIELD
THE GRANARY
ASHEN ROAD
LUTUS CL.
STOUR GRN.
River
A1092
STOKE ROAD
STOUR VALE
DANEUM HOLT
HICKFORD HILL
Club Ho.
ST. EDMUNDSBURY
BRAINTREE
Claredown Farm
Clare Park Lake Golf Course
Pumping Station
Mill Farm
ASHEN ROAD
BRADLEY HILL
Claret Hall
Bradleyhill Farm

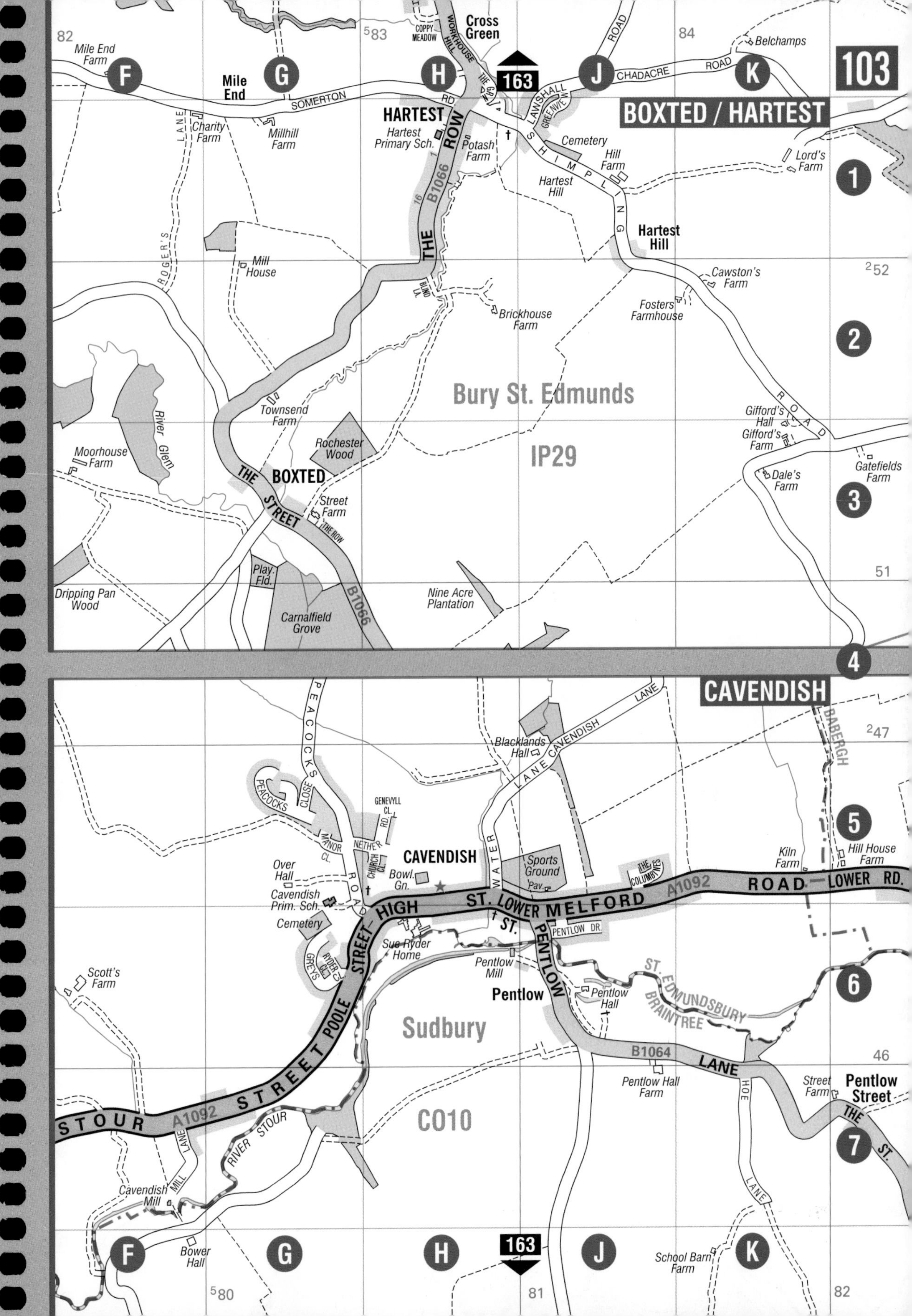
BOXTED / HARTEST
Mile End Farm
Mile End
Cross Green
Coppy Meadow
Workhouse Hill
Somerton Rd
Chadacre Road
Belchamps
Lawshall Road
163
HARTEST
Hartest Primary Sch.
Charity Farm
Millhill Farm
Potash Farm
Cemetery
Hill Farm
Lord's Farm
Hartest Hill
Shimpling Road
Hartest Hill
The Row
B1066
Mill House
Rogers Lane
Blind La.
Brickhouse Farm
Cawston's Farm
Fosters Farmhouse
Bury St. Edmunds
IP29
Townsend Farm
River Glem
Rochester Wood
Gifford's Hall
Gifford's Farm
Gatefields Farm
Dale's Farm
Moorhouse Farm
BOXTED
The Street
Street Farm
The Row
Play. Fld.
Carnalfield Grove
Dripping Pan Wood
Nine Acre Plantation
CAVENDISH
Peacocks Close
Peacocks
Blacklands Hall
Lane
Cavendish Lane
Babergh
Genevyll Cl.
Rd.
Manor Cl.
Nether Road
Church Cl.
CAVENDISH
Bowl. Gn.
Over Hall
Water Lane
Sports Ground
Pav.
The Columbines
Kiln Farm
Hill House Farm
Cavendish Prim. Sch.
High St.
Lower St.
Melford Road
A1092
Lower Rd.
Cemetery
Pentlow Dr.
Sue Ryder Home
Greys
Ryder Cl.
Pentlow Mill
Pentlow
St. Edmundsbury
Braintree
Pentlow Hall
Scott's Farm
Poole Street
Sudbury
B1064
Lane
Hoe Lane
Pentlow Hall Farm
Street Farm
Pentlow Street
The St.
Stour Street
A1092
CO10
River Stour
Mill Lane
Cavendish Mill
Bower Hall
School Barn Farm
F G H J K
1 2 3 4 5 6 7
82 583 84 252 51 247 46 580 81 82

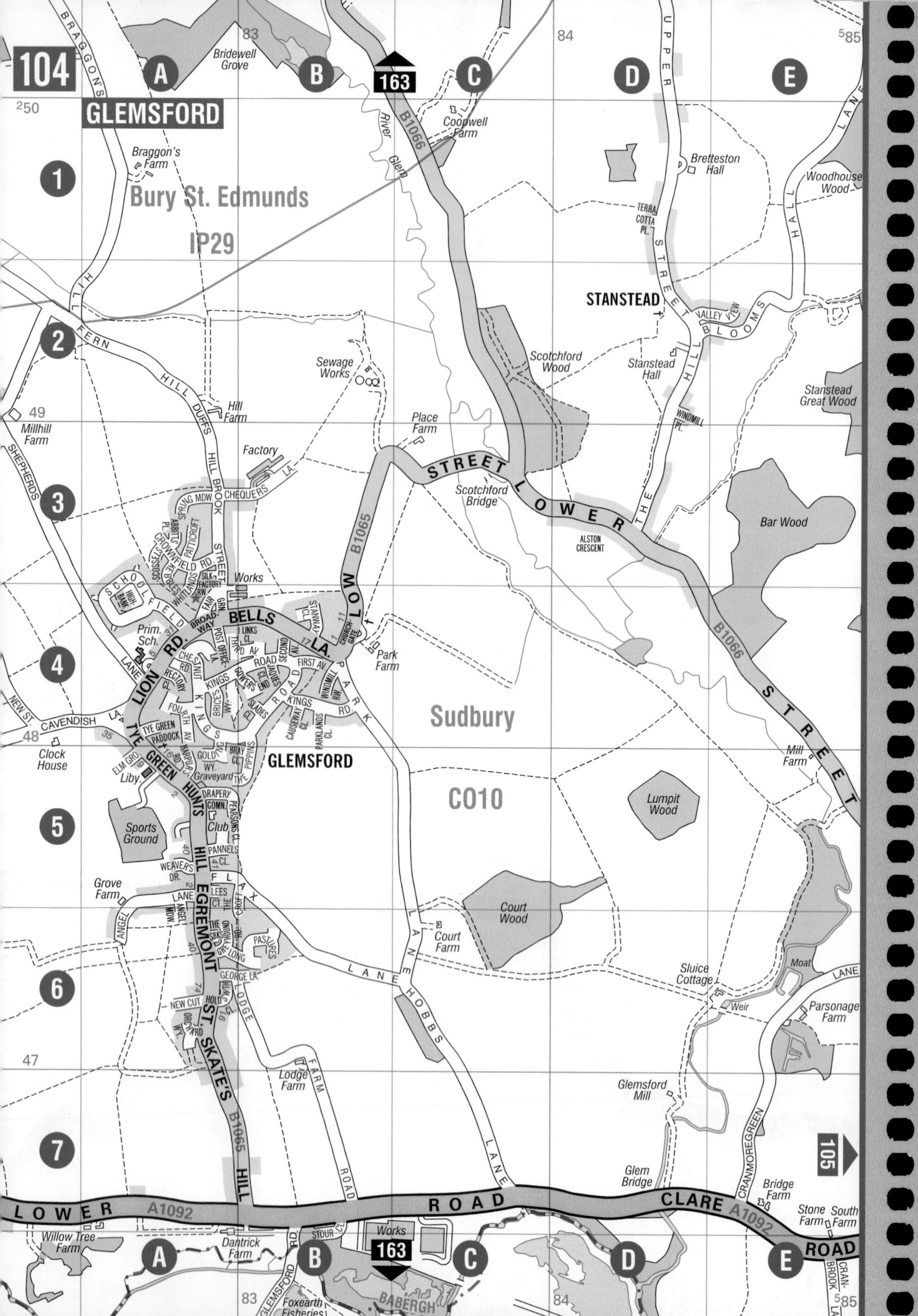
GLEMSFORD
Bridewell Grove
163
Coopwell Farm
Braggon's Farm
Bury St. Edmunds
IP29
Bretteston Hall
Woodhouse Wood
TERRA COTTA PL.
STANSTEAD
VALLEY VIEW
BLOOMS
Scotchford Wood
Sewage Works
Stanstead Hall
Stanstead Great Wood
Hill Farm
Millhill Farm
Place Farm
WINDMILL PL.
Factory
STREET
Scotchford Bridge
LOWER
Bar Wood
ALSTON CRESCENT
CHEQUERS
B1065
B1066
Works
BELLS LA.
LION RD.
Prim. Sch.
Park Farm
Sudbury
CAVENDISH LA.
Clock House
GLEMSFORD
Mill Farm
Liby.
CO10
Lumpit Wood
Sports Ground
Club
Grove Farm
Court Wood
Court Farm
EGREMONT
HILL
Sluice Cottage
Moat
Weir
Parsonage Farm
HOBBS LANE
Lodge Farm
Glemsford Mill
ST. SKATE'S HILL
CRANMOREGREEN
105
Glem Bridge
Bridge Farm
LOWER ROAD A1092
CLARE ROAD
Stone Farm
South Farm
Willow Tree Farm
Dantrick Farm
Works
163
BABERGH
Foxearth Fisheries

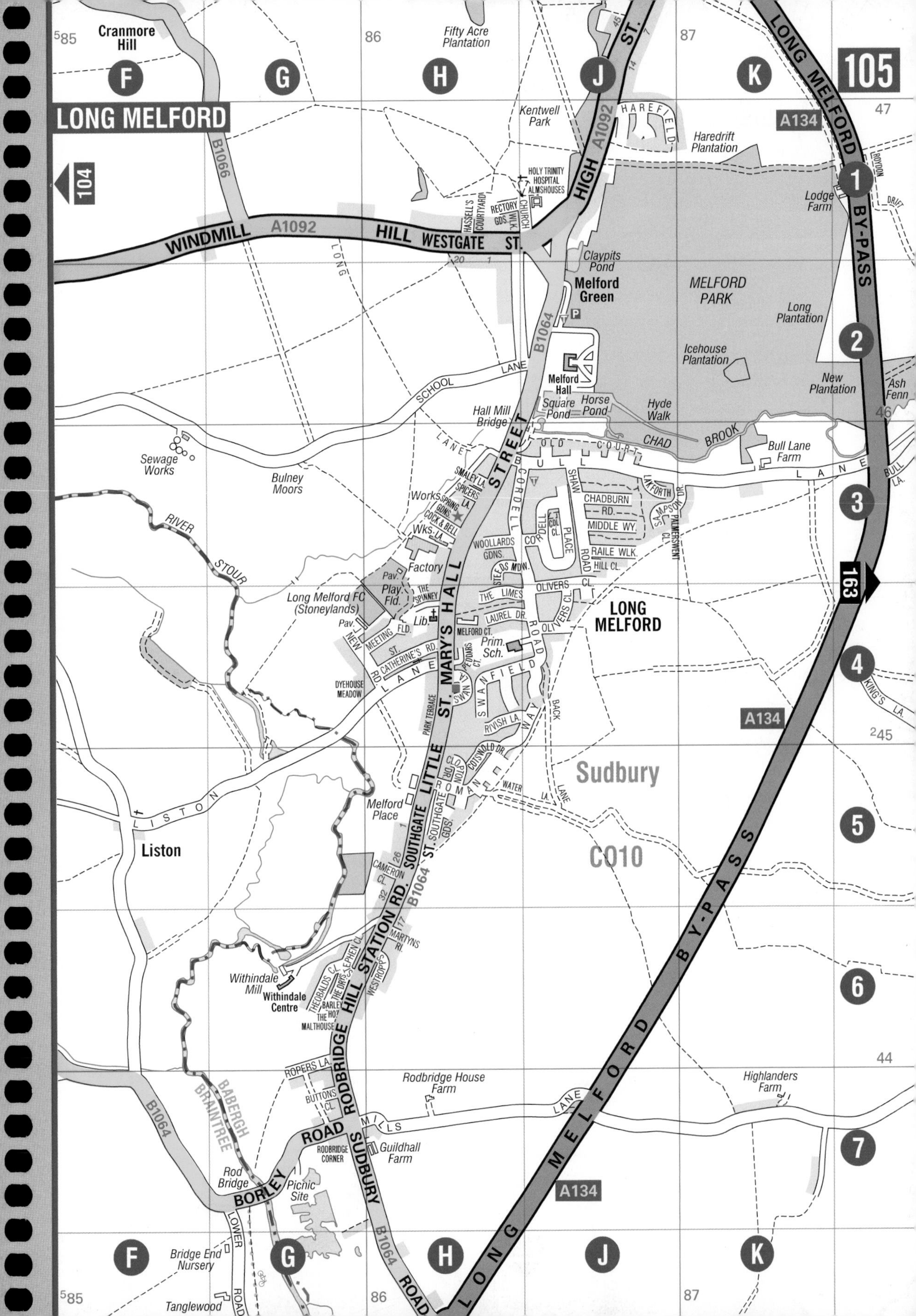

LONG MELFORD
Cranmore Hill
Fifty Acre Plantation
Kentwell Park
Haredrift Plantation
HOLY TRINITY HOSPITAL ALMSHOUSES
WINDMILL HILL
WESTGATE ST.
HIGH ST.
LONG MELFORD BY-PASS
Lodge Farm
Claypits Pond
Melford Green
MELFORD PARK
Long Plantation
Icehouse Plantation
Melford Hall
New Plantation
Ash Fenn
SCHOOL LANE
Hall Mill Bridge
Square Pond
Horse Pond
Hyde Walk
CHAD BROOK
OLD COURT
Bull Lane Farm
BULL LANE
Sewage Works
Bulney Moors
RIVER STOUR
Works
Factory
Long Melford FC (Stoneylands)
Play. Fld.
Lib.
CHADBURN RD.
MIDDLE WY.
RAILE WLK.
HILL CL.
WOOLLARDS GDNS.
OLIVERS CL.
THE LIMES
LAUREL DR.
LONG MELFORD
Prim. Sch.
ST. CATHERINE'S RD.
MEETING FLD.
DYEHOUSE MEADOW
ST. MARY'S HALL STREET
LITTLE ST.
SWANFIELD
RIVISH LA.
BACK LANE
PARK TERRACE
COTSWOLD DR.
CLOPTON DR.
ROMAN WAY
WATER LA.
Sudbury
CO10
Melford Place
LISTON LANE
Liston
SOUTHGATE
CAMERON CL.
MARTYNS RI.
Withindale Mill
Withindale Centre
THEOBALDS CL.
WESTROPPS
THE MALTHOUSE
RODBRIDGE HILL
STATION RD.
ROPERS LA.
BUTTONS CL.
Rodbridge House Farm
MILLS LANE
Highlanders Farm
BABERGH
BRAINTREE
RODBRIDGE CORNER
Guildhall Farm
BORLEY ROAD
Rod Bridge
Picnic Site
SUDBURY ROAD
A134
A1092
B1064
B1066
Bridge End Nursery
LOWER ROAD
Tanglewood
104
163

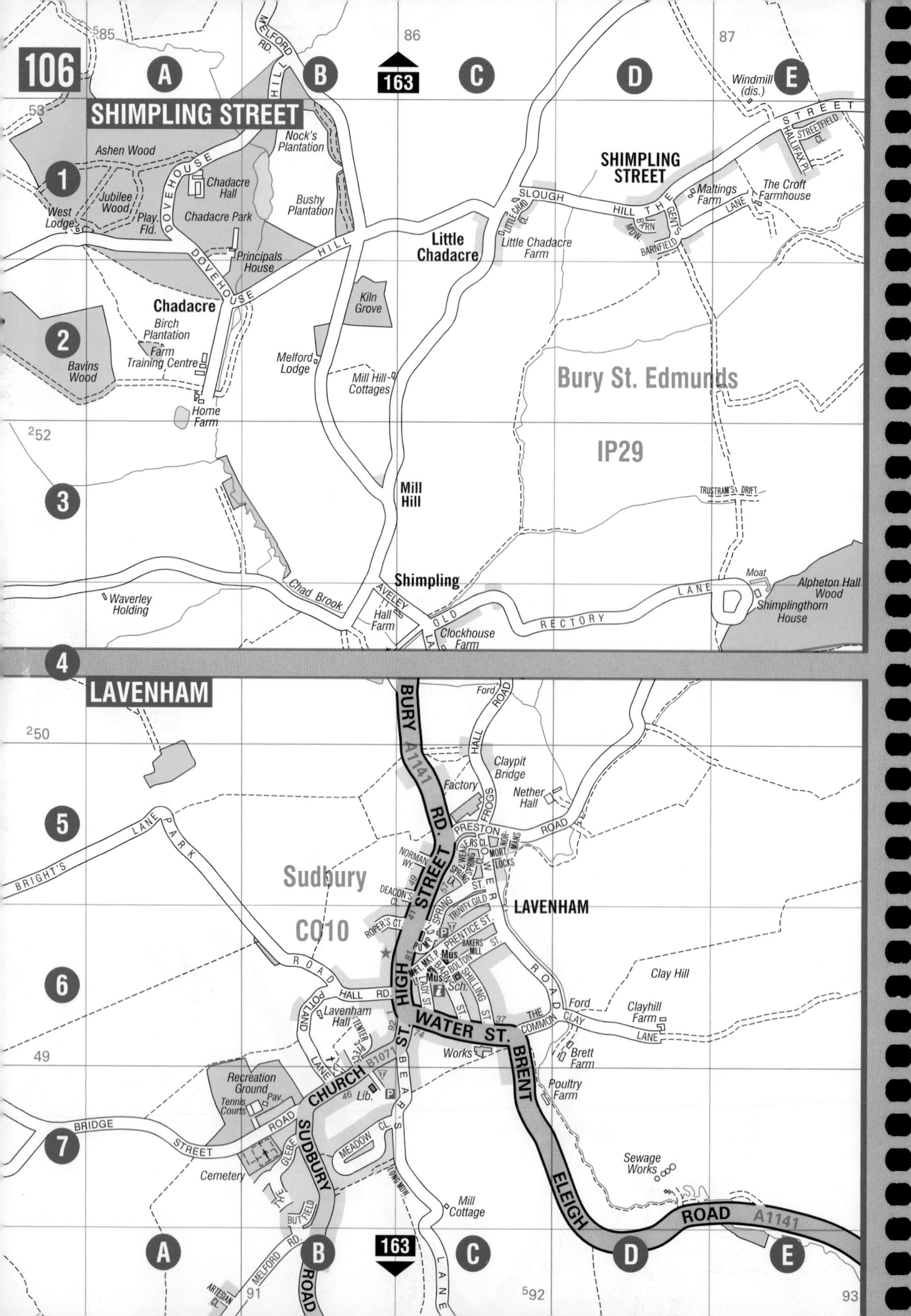

SHIMPLING STREET
LAVENHAM
Ashen Wood
Jubilee Wood
West Lodge
Play. Fld.
Chadacre Hall
Chadacre Park
Principals House
Nock's Plantation
Bushy Plantation
Chadacre
Birch Plantation
Farm Training Centre
Bavins Wood
Home Farm
Kiln Grove
Melford Lodge
Mill Hill Cottages
Little Chadacre
Little Chadacre Farm
SHIMPLING STREET
Maltings Farm
The Croft Farmhouse
Windmill (dis.)
Bury St. Edmunds
IP29
Mill Hill
Shimpling
Chad Brook
Waverley Holding
Hall Farm
Clockhouse Farm
Moat
Shimplingthorn House
Alpheton Hall Wood
RECTORY LANE
SLOUGH HILL
DOVEHOUSE HILL
MELFORD RD.
TRUSTRAM'S DRIFT
Ford
Claypit Bridge
Factory
Nether Hall
PRESTON ROAD
BURY RD. A1141
HIGH STREET
Sudbury
CO10
LAVENHAM
BRIGHT'S LANE
PARK ROAD
Clay Hill
Clayhill Farm
CLAY LANE
Brett Farm
Poultry Farm
Works
WATER ST.
BRENT ELEIGH ROAD
A1141
Sewage Works
Lavenham Hall
HALL RD.
POTLAND LANE
CHURCH ST.
B1071
Lib.
Recreation Ground
Tennis Courts
Pav.
Cemetery
BRIDGE STREET
SUDBURY ROAD
MEADOW CL.
BEAR'S LANE
Mill Cottage
MELFORD RD.
ARTESIAN CL.

163
163

107
ACTON / GREAT WALDINGFIELD
163
108
127
F
G
H
J
K
1
2
3
4
5
6
7
89
590
91
46
245
44
43
Bassett's Farm
Slough Farm
LAVENHAM ROAD
Sand & Gravel Pit
B1071
SLOUGH HILL
LANE
PEAKHALL
Red House Farm
Clay Hall
Lavenham Road Farm
MELFORD
ACTON PLACE INDUSTRIAL ESTATE
Acton Hall
Barrowhill Farm
Playing Field
BARROW
HIGH STREET
WALNUT CL.
GOTSFIELD CL.
POST OFFICE ROW
ACTON
Sudbury
CO10
QUEENSWAY
COBLERS WY.
DANIELS CL.
Sch.
WALDINGFIELD
CLAYHALL
GORDON PL.
Babergh Hall
Dyer's Green Farm
LAVENHAM
TAMAGE RD.
SUDBURY
VICARAGE LANE
JENNENS
LIME
LAMBERT
DRIVE
CEDAR WK.
BABERGH CL.
WALK
Babergh Heath Farm
ACTON ROAD
TENTREE ROAD
Babergh Place Farm
Northfields Farm
THE STREET
Ovens Green
VICARAGE LA.
Green Farm
Newman's Green
LAVENHAM ROAD
B1115
HEATHWAY
CORONATION RISE
HEATH ESTATE
GREEN ACRE
Works
FORTRESS FLDS.
KEIFFER CL.
RECTORY
CHESTNUT CL.
FOLLY ROAD
CHAPEL CL.
The Garrison
ALEXANDER DR.
KENYON DR.
ABBOTTS HALL CL.
NETHER HALL CL.
New Farm
GREAT WALDINGFIELD
GARRISON LA.
CARBONELS
BANTOCKS
BRAND CL.
LYNN'S HALL CL.
WHITE HALL CL.
CHILTON GROVE
Chilton Priory
The Lodge
Grain Stores
CHILTON CORNER
Hall Gate Cott.
ROAD
White Hall Farm
VALLEY RD.
Chilton Hall Fm.
Chilton Hall Farm Cottages
Greenacres
Moat
FIELD

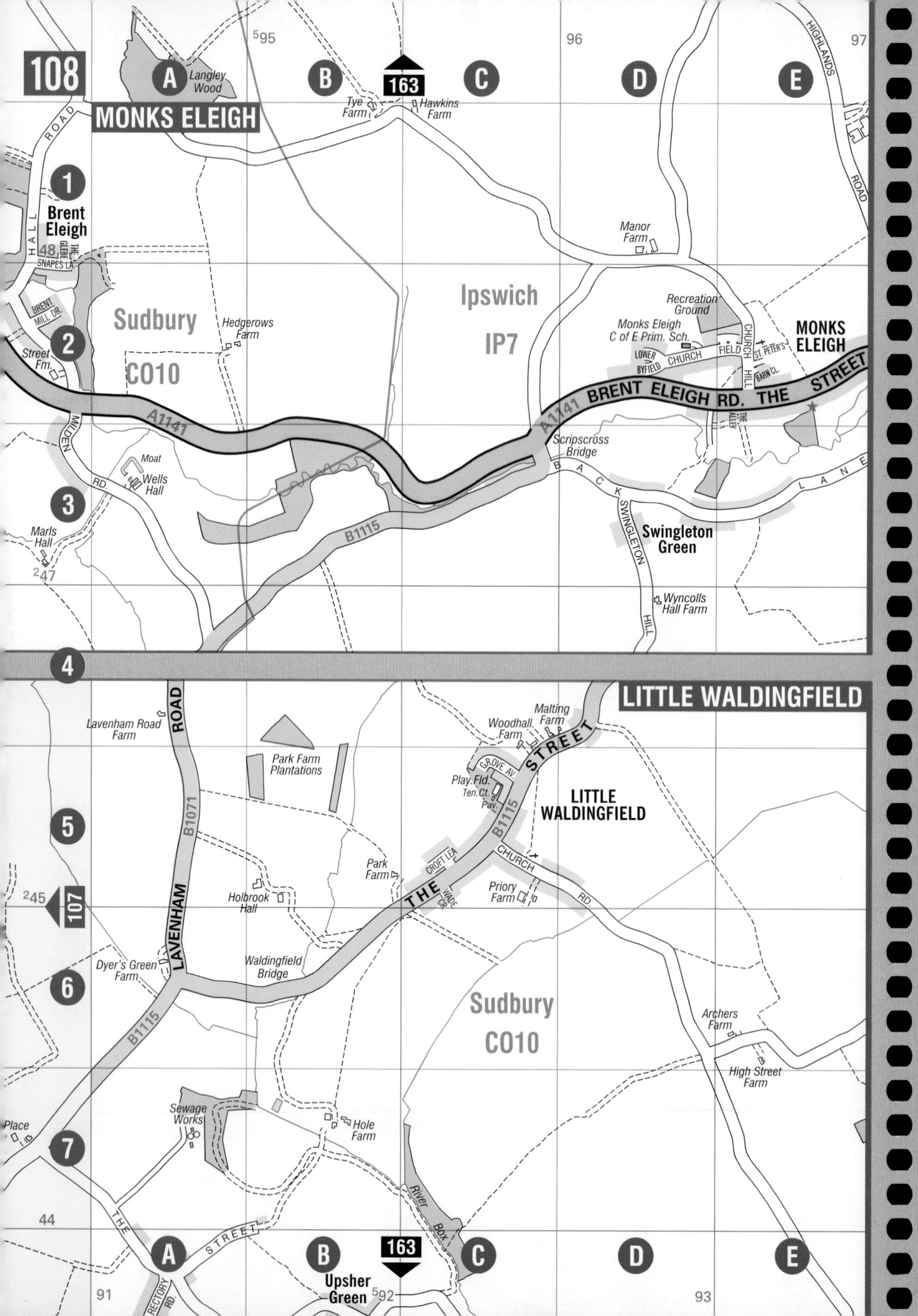

MONKS ELEIGH
Langley Wood
Tye Farm
Hawkins Farm
163
Brent Eleigh
Sudbury
CO10
Hedgerows Farm
Ipswich
IP7
Manor Farm
Recreation Ground
Monks Eleigh C of E Prim. Sch.
MONKS ELEIGH
BRENT ELEIGH RD. THE STREET
A1141
Street Fm.
Moat
Wells Hall
Marls Hall
Scripscross Bridge
BACK LANE
B1115
Swingleton Green
Wyncolls Hall Farm
LITTLE WALDINGFIELD
Lavenham Road Farm
LAVENHAM ROAD
B1071
Park Farm Plantations
Woodhall Farm
Malting Farm
THE STREET
Play.Fld.
Ten.Ct.
Pav.
LITTLE WALDINGFIELD
Park Farm
Holbrook Hall
CHURCH RD.
Priory Farm
107
Dyer's Green Farm
Waldingfield Bridge
Sudbury
CO10
Archers Farm
High Street Farm
Sewage Works
Hole Farm
Place
River Box
THE STREET
RECTORY RD.
Upsher Green
163

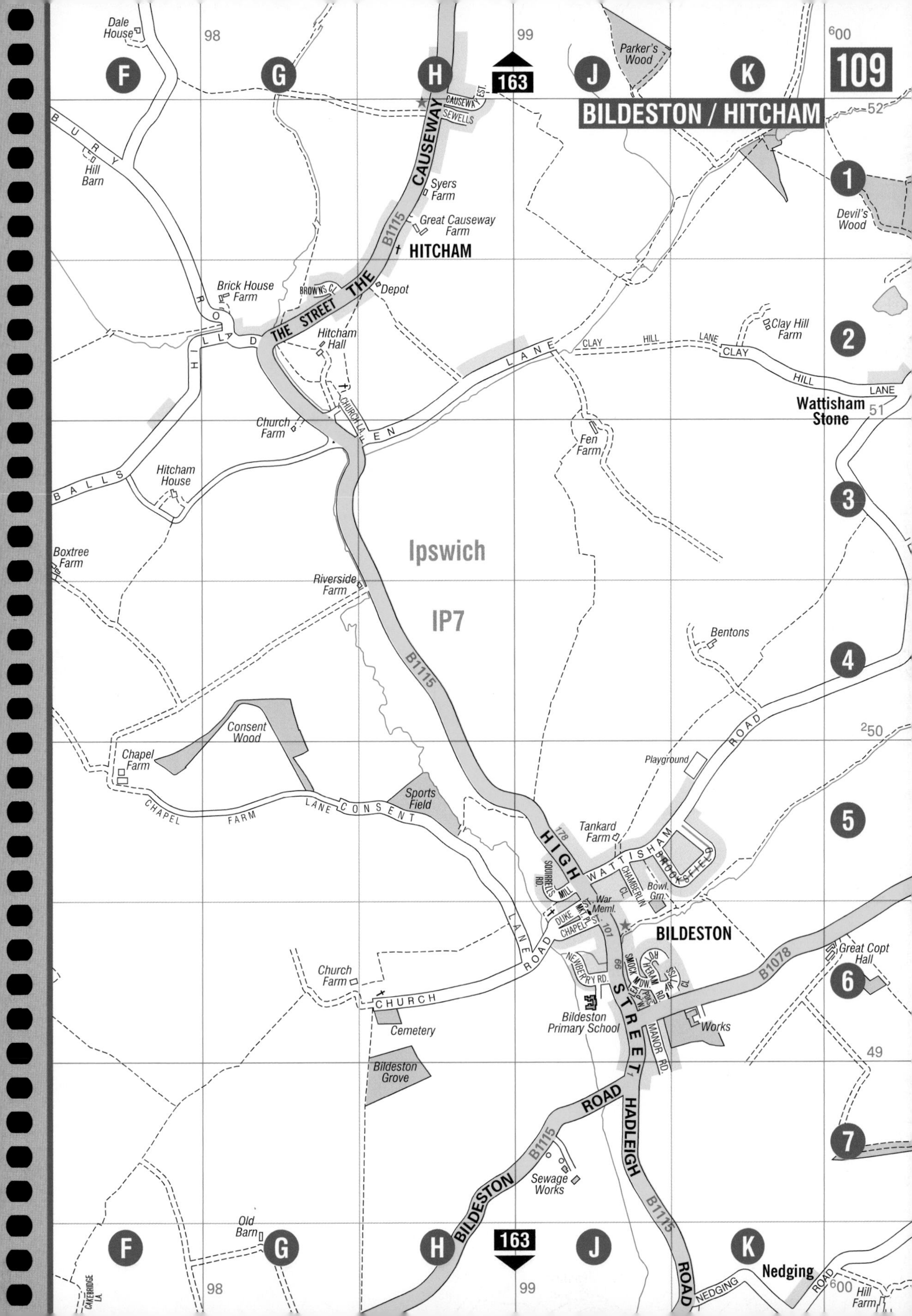
Dale House
98
99
600
Parker's Wood
F
G
H
163
J
K
52
CAUSEWAY EST.
SEWELLS
BURY ROAD
Hill Barn
THE CAUSEWAY
Syers Farm
B1115
Great Causeway Farm
HITCHAM
1
Devil's Wood
Brick House Farm
BROWNS CL.
THE STREET
Depot
Hitcham Hall
CLAY HILL LANE
Clay Hill Farm
2
HILL ROAD
LANE
Wattisham Stone
51
CHURCH LA.
FEN LANE
Church Farm
Fen Farm
BALLS
Hitcham House
3
Ipswich
Boxtree Farm
Riverside Farm
IP7
Bentons
B1115
4
Consent Wood
250
Chapel Farm
Playground
ROAD
Sports Field
5
CHAPEL FARM LANE
CONSENT
Tankard Farm
HIGH
WATTISHAM
BROOKSFIELD
SQUIRRELS RD.
MILL
CHAMBERLIN CL.
Bowl. Grn.
War Meml.
DUKE ST.
CHAPEL ST.
BILDESTON
LANE ROAD
NEWBERRY RD.
SMOCK MDW.
B1078
Great Copt Hall
Church Farm
6
CHURCH
Bildeston Primary School
STREET
Works
Cemetery
MANOR RD.
49
Bildeston Grove
ROAD
HADLEIGH
7
B1115
Sewage Works
BILDESTON
B1115
Old Barn
F
G
H
163
J
K
Nedging
CAKEBRIDGE LA.
98
99
NEDGING
ROAD
600
Hill Farm

BATTISFORD TYE / COMBS

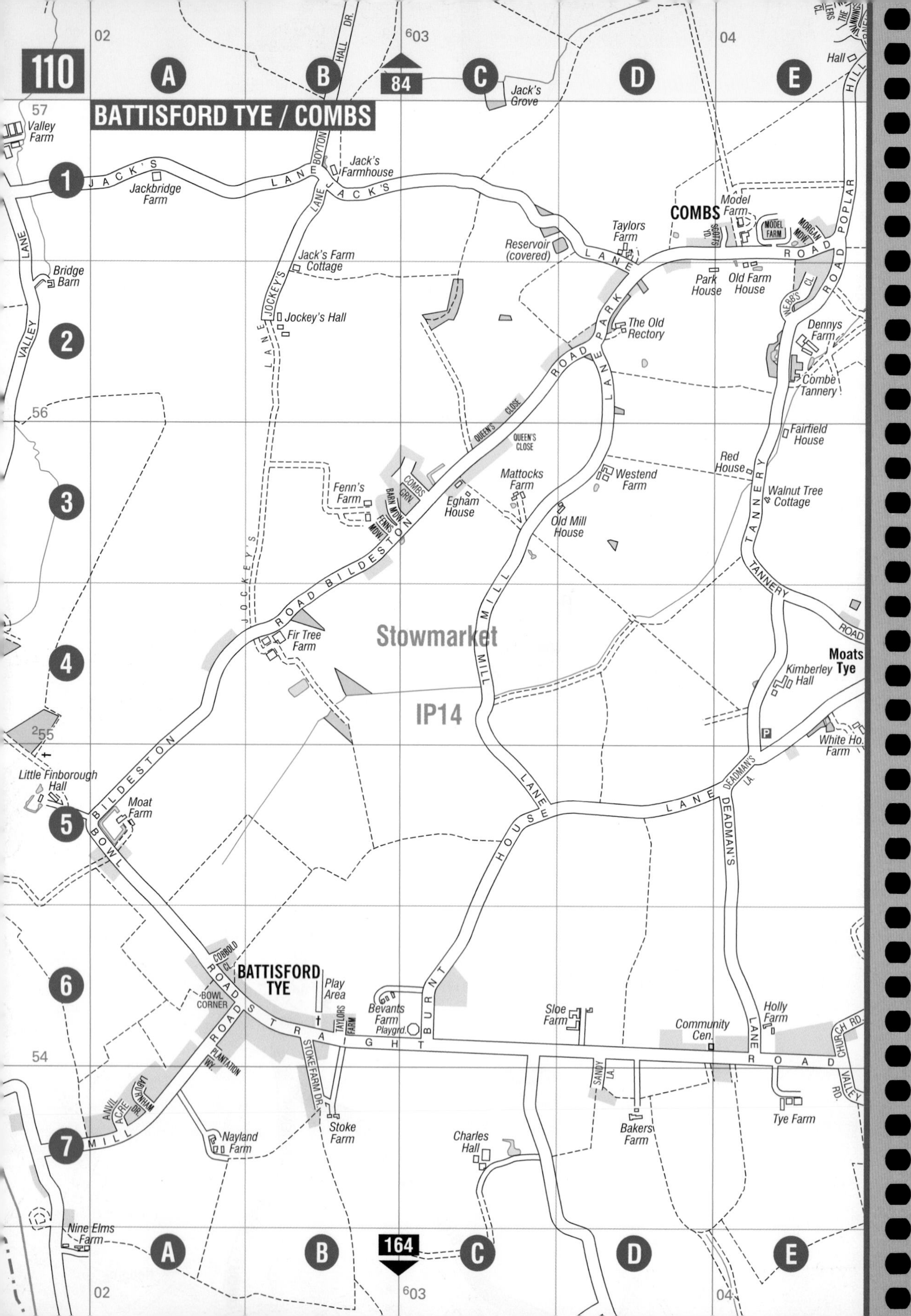

84
164

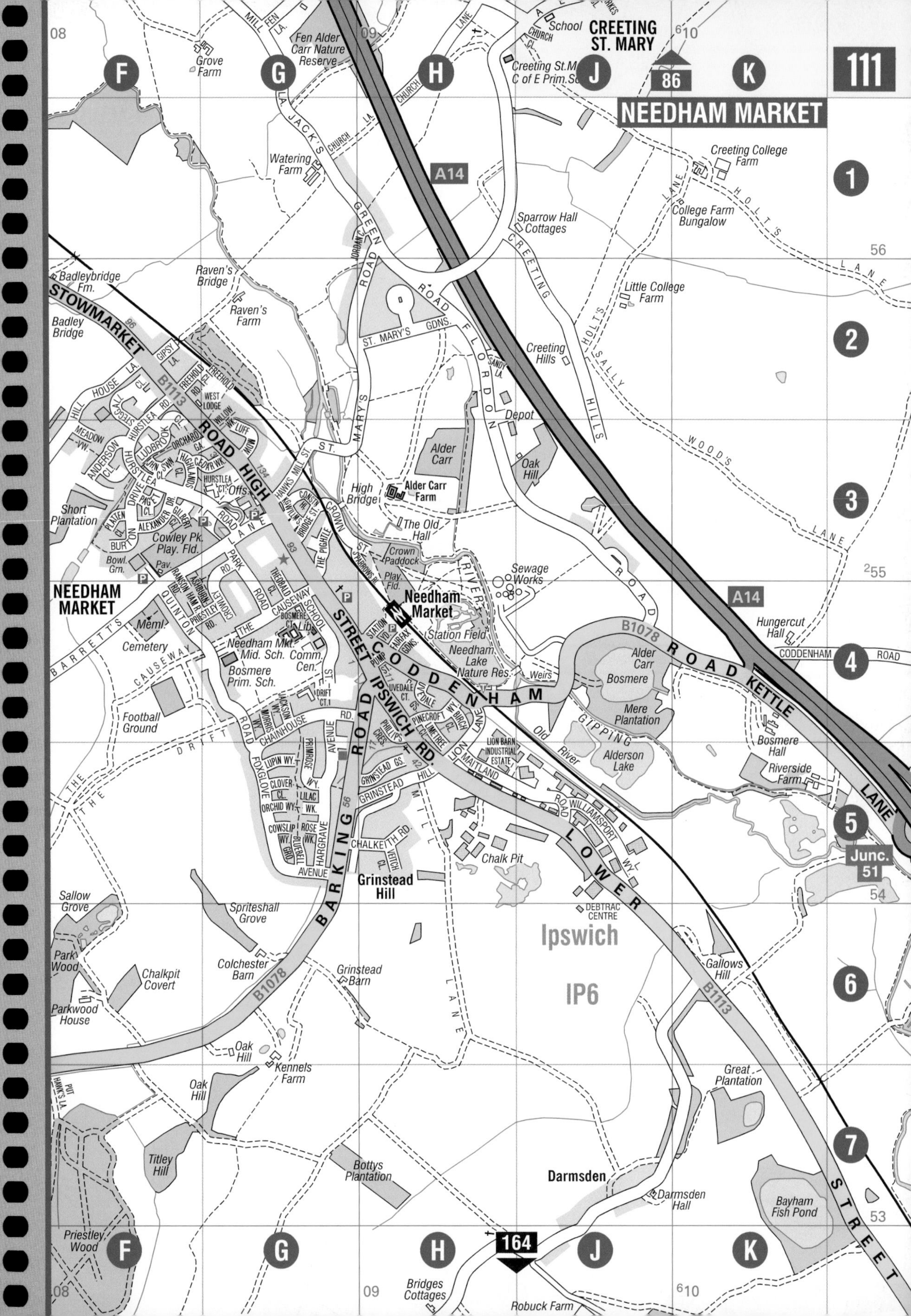
NEEDHAM MARKET
CREETING ST. MARY
86
164
F
G
H
J
K
1
2
3
4
5
6
7
Junc. 51
A14
Fen Alder Carr Nature Reserve
Grove Farm
Watering Farm
Creeting College Farm
College Farm Bungalow
Sparrow Hall Cottages
Little College Farm
Badleybridge Fm.
Badley Bridge
Raven's Bridge
Raven's Farm
Creeting Hills
Depot
Alder Carr
Oak Hill
High Bridge
Alder Carr Farm
The Old Hall
Short Plantation
Cowley Pk. Play. Fld.
Sewage Works
NEEDHAM MARKET
Needham Market
Station Field
Needham Lake Nature Res.
Hungercut Hall
Alder Carr
Bosmere
Mere Plantation
Alderson Lake
Bosmere Hall
Riverside Farm
Cemetery
Needham Mkt. Mid. Sch.
Bosmere Prim. Sch.
Football Ground
Chalk Pit
Grinstead Hill
Sallow Grove
Spriteshall Grove
Ipswich
IP6
Park Wood
Colchester Barn
Chalkpit Covert
Grinstead Barn
Gallows Hill
Parkwood House
Oak Hill
Kennels Farm
Great Plantation
Titley Hill
Bottys Plantation
Darmsden
Darmsden Hall
Bayham Fish Pond
Priestley Wood
Bridges Cottages
Robuck Farm
STOWMARKET ROAD
HIGH ROAD
B1113
B1078
CODDENHAM ROAD
KETTLE LANE
BARKING ROAD
IPSWICH RD.
LOWER STREET
STREET
CREETING ROAD
HOLT'S LANE
SALLY HILLS
WOOD'S LANE
DEBTRAC CENTRE
LION BARN INDUSTRIAL ESTATE

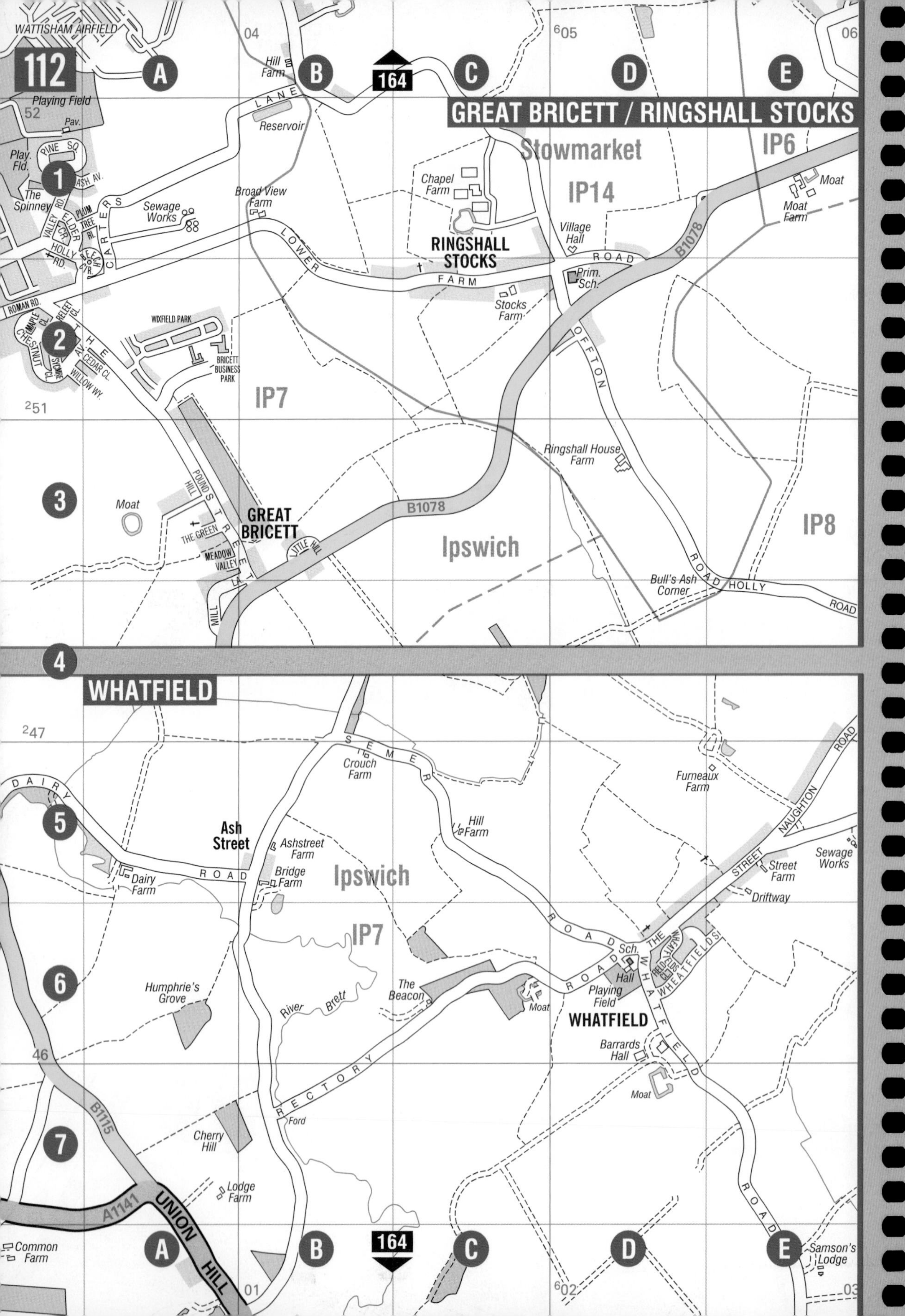
GREAT BRICETT / RINGSHALL STOCKS
WHATFIELD
164
WATTISHAM AIRFIELD
Playing Field
Pav.
Play. Fld.
The Spinney
Reservoir
Hill Farm
Broad View Farm
Sewage Works
Chapel Farm
RINGSHALL STOCKS
Village Hall
Prim. Sch.
Stocks Farm
Stowmarket
IP14
IP6
IP7
IP8
Moat
Moat Farm
WIXFIELD PARK
BRICETT BUSINESS PARK
Ringshall House Farm
GREAT BRICETT
Ipswich
Bull's Ash Corner
B1078
Ash Street
Ashstreet Farm
Bridge Farm
Dairy Farm
Crouch Farm
Hill Farm
Furneaux Farm
Street Farm
Sewage Works
Driftway
Humphrie's Grove
River Brett
The Beacon
Playing Field
Hall
WHATFIELD
Barrards Hall
Cherry Hill
Lodge Farm
Common Farm
Ford
Samson's Lodge
B1115
A1141
UNION HILL

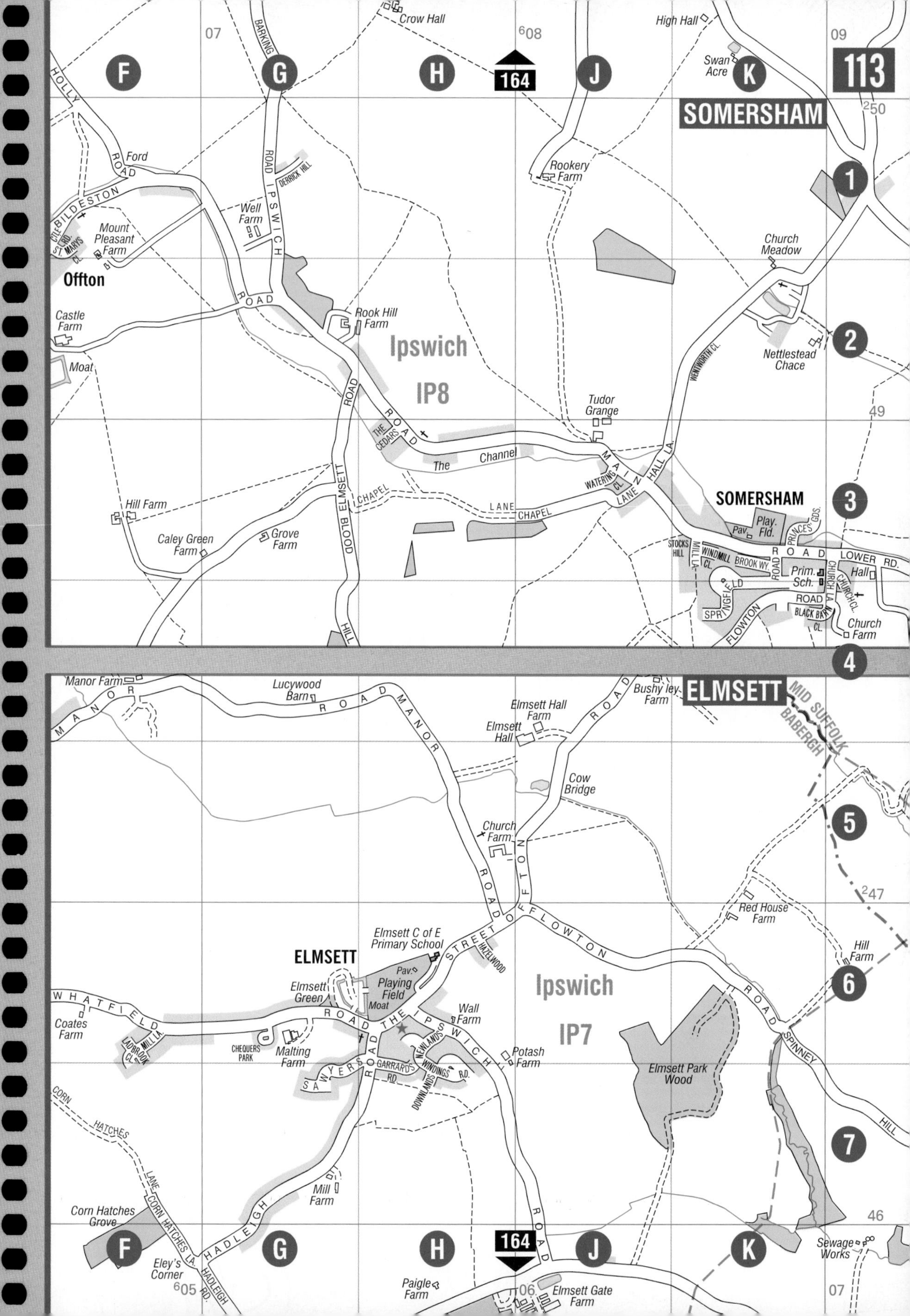
SOMERSHAM
ELMSETT
Offton
Ipswich IP8
Ipswich IP7
MID SUFFOLK
BABERGH
Crow Hall
High Hall
Swan Acre
Rookery Farm
Well Farm
Mount Pleasant Farm
Castle Farm
Moat
Rook Hill Farm
Church Meadow
Nettlestead Chace
Tudor Grange
The Channel
Hill Farm
Caley Green Farm
Grove Farm
Play. Fld.
Pav.
Prim. Sch.
Hall
Church Farm
Manor Farm
Lucywood Barn
Elmsett Hall Farm
Elmsett Hall
Bushy ley Farm
Cow Bridge
Church Farm
Red House Farm
Hill Farm
Elmsett C of E Primary School
Playing Field
Elmsett Green
Coates Farm
Malting Farm
Wall Farm
Potash Farm
Elmsett Park Wood
Mill Farm
Corn Hatches Grove
Eley's Corner
Paigle Farm
Elmsett Gate Farm
Sewage Works
164

114
CLAYDON / GREAT BLAKENHAM
SHRUBLAND PARK
Barham Plantation
Queech Wood
Broomfield Pit
The Ferns
Malting Farm
STOWMARKET
SHARPSTONE ST.
SORREL CL.
SHRUB-LAND CL.
SAUMAREZ DR.
MAPLE GRO.
SANDY LANE
JACKSON PL.
Hall Farm
LWR. CRESCENT
THE CRESCENT
QUEECH PL.
QUEECH WOOD CL.
PESTHOUSE LANE
Hall Farm Cotts.
NORWICH
Hop Ground
Honeymoon Cottages
Great Wood
BLUEIGHS PARK
B1113
CHALK HILL
CHEQUERS RISE
KILN HILL RI.
CHURCH RD.
KINGSMILL DR.
HOOD LANE
MILL LA.
Rec. Grd. Hall
PLUMMERS DELL
MULBERRY GDNS.
Warehouses
A14
Lower Farm Cottages
Barham Hall
IP6
Cemetery
WAINWRIGHT GDNS.
DR. KYTS WY.
HACKNEY'S CORNER
ASPEN CL.
LAUREL DR.
Works
CLAYDON BUSINESS PARK
Lower Farm
Henry VIII Farm
GIPPING
Depot
CLAYDON INDUSTRIAL PARK
BRIDGE TRADING ESTATE
GREAT BLAKENHAM
BRAMFORD ROAD
CHURCH
RECTORY CL.
THORNHILL
GLEBE WY.
WINCHESTER GDNS.
PHILLIPPS RD.
MIDDLETON RD.
EDDOWES RD.
KIRBY RISE
BACON RD.
LINCOLN GS.
ELY RD.
HEREFORD DR.
EXETER RD.
The Slade
Slade Cottages
Recreation Grd.
WEAVERS WY.
MN CT.
FLETCHER CL.
COOPERS WY.
MILLERS CT.
FORESTERS
WOODTIMER CL.
TOLLGATE CT.
YORK ROAD
JUBILEE CL.
EDINBURGH GDNS.
LANCASTER WY.
Playing Field
Claydon Prim. Sch.
Claydon High Sch.
Comm. Cen.
HIGHFIELD DR.
Depot
Works
STATION ROAD
ST. PETER'S AV.
ST. PETER'S CT.
THE ST.
GILES CT. RD.
THE PINES
QUOITS FLD.
BACK LA.
CRESCENT
LANE
Playing Field
Bowling Green
Pav.
Column Field Quarry
164
115
CHAPEL
BLUE BARN LANE
WAY
Factory
Ipswich
LODGE LA.
ORION CT.
ORION AV.
ADDISON
CHURCH LANE
ALASDAIR PL.
CHESTNUT DR.
HAZEL WY.
POPLAR CL.
FIR TREE LA.
ROWAN CL.
MORGAN CT.
IPSWICH RD.
NEWELL PL.
LARCH DR.
DRURY R.
ASPEN CL.
WILLOW CL.
THE BEECHES
RISE
CLAYDON
Junction 52
Lodge Cott.
B1113
Blackacre Hill
Warehouse
KILN CL.
LIME
OLD PAPER MILL LA.
ORCHARD GRO.
Tennis Courts
Claydon Hill
Stanfield House
BROOMVALE BUSINESS PARK
The Meadows
PAPER MILL LANE
IPSWICH
Broomvale Farm
Football Grd.
HILL VIEW BUSINESS PARK
ROAD
The Common
Broomvale Cottages
RIVER GIPPING
POUND LANE
IP8
The Rookery
A14
Mill Lade
Mockbeggars Hall
OLD NORWICH ROAD
Ash Pollard
Blood Hill
B1113
LORAINE WAY
Hill Top
Lower Dairy Farm
Suffolk Water Park
The Old Paper Mill
Paper Mill Farm
Alder Carr
Broom Hill
IP1
Pitch & Putt
The Grove Cottage
Fisk Grove
Junction 53
130
Works
SOMERSHAM RD.
WOODLAND WY.
WHITTON
ANGLIA
A
B
C
D
E
1
2
3
4
5
6
7
12
613
14
51
250
49
48

CODDENHAM
164
F
G
H
J
K
13
14
615
255
1
2
3
4
5
6
7
Needham Plantation
Valley Farm
Rec. Grd.
THE POPLARS
BLACKSMITHS LA.
SCHOOL RD.
LOWER ROAD
SCHOOL LA.
GREEN HILL
SPRING LA.
CATHERINES HILL
MARY DAY CL.
CODDENHAM
Nucleus Plantation
Coddenham Comm. & Sports Hall
Coddenham House
Vicarage Farm
THE DRIFT
Ivy Farm
Hall Farm
COOPER ROAD
Sky Hall Wood
Ipswich
IP6
HIGH STREET
LOWER RD.
B1078
MILL LA.
LOVE LA.
Broom Hill
NEEDHAM ROAD
CHURCH RD.
Cemetery
SANDY HILL
The Shrubbery
RECTORY ROAD
Church Farm
CHURCH LANE
BULL'S ROAD
GRANVILLE CT.
54
Hemingstone
Hillcrest Fm.
MAIN RD.
HENLEY
Skeet's Green
BELL'S CROSS RD.
North Corner
White Cottage
The Cottage
MAIN ROAD
Rose Lodge
River Fynn
252
The Croft
Barham Green
DANGEROUS LA.
Queech Wood
Green Farm
Pond Farm
LANE
Barrack Cottages
MILL LANE
Chestnut Farm
Walnut Tree Farm
Home Farm
Henley Watering
SCHOOL ROAD
HARVEY'S
Barham House
Red House
Community Centre
The Cottage
Headlands
Henley Prim. Sch.
PEARSONS PL.
The Firs
Sewage Works
The Lodge
BULLS RD.
Barham
Nursery Wood
The Cottage
COOPER'S ROAD
Mill House
WELL FIELD
CHURCH MEADOWS
POND END
ASHBOCKING
Royal Beech Cottage
Eastwood Cottages
Church Farm
ST. PETER'S CL.
HENLEY
CHURCH
Kewland Hall
Kewland Hall Farm
OLD HALL CL.
GASCOIGNE DR.
FREEMAN AV.
THE DRIFT
HENLEY ROAD
Whitelodge Farm
CHURCH LA.
114
Barham Manor
51
Rectory Farm
Rectory Farm Cottages
Dameron's Farm
Red Barn Farm
Glebe Plantation
Rede Wood (Local Nature Reserve)
Redewood Cottage
LANE
Rede Wood Farm
High House Farm
REDE
615
16

TUDDENHAM ST. MARTIN / WITNESHAM

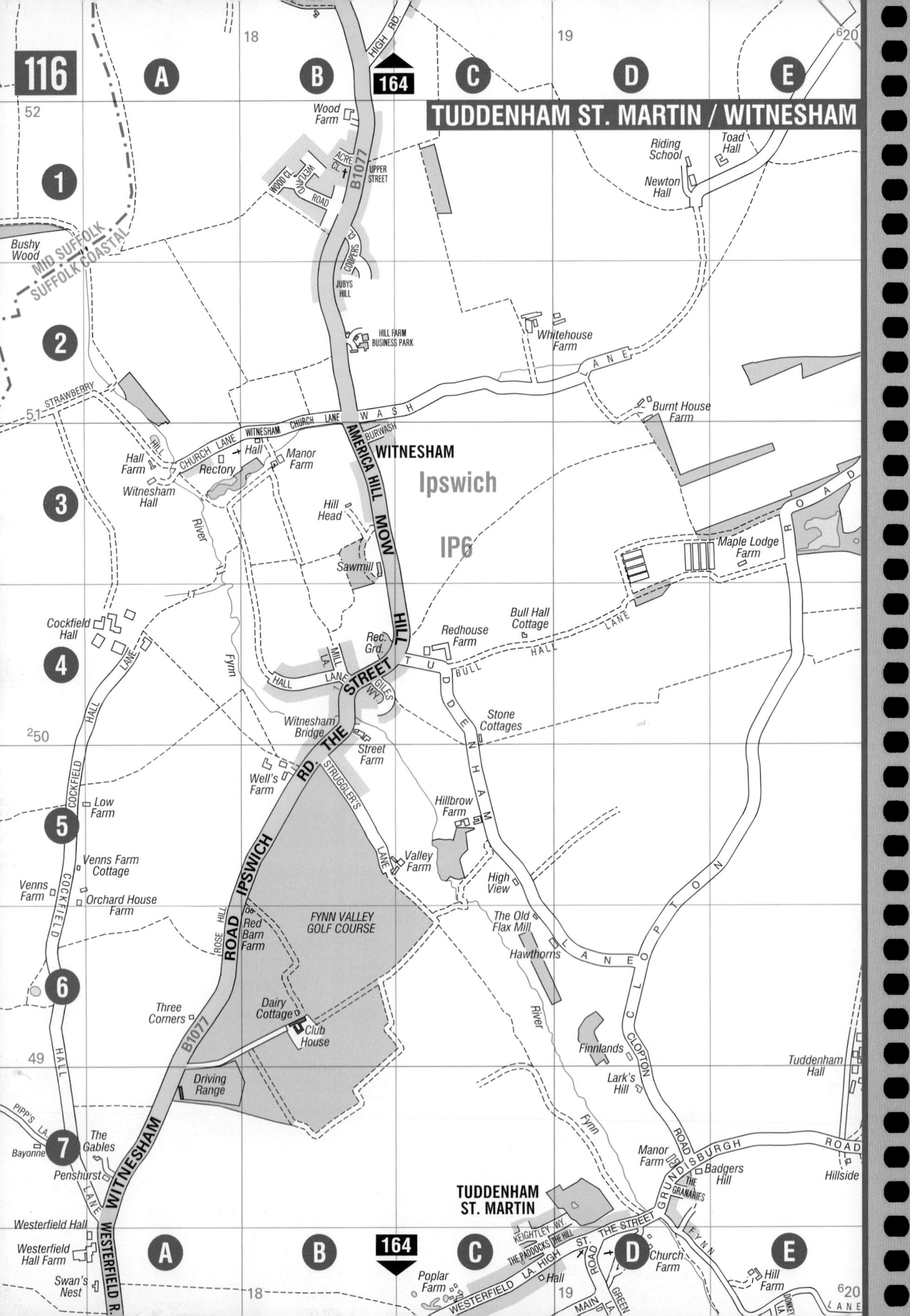

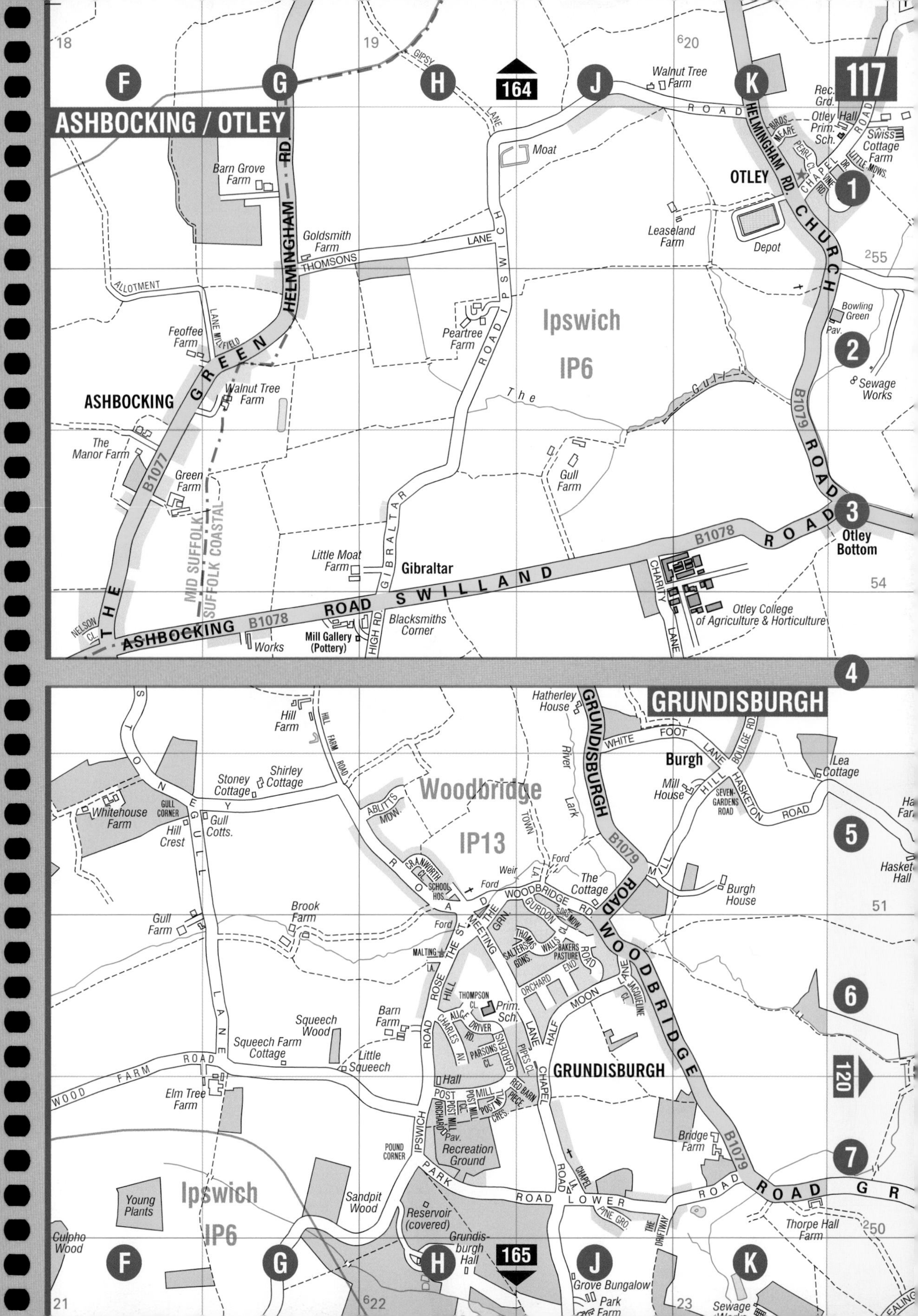
ASHBOCKING / OTLEY
GRUNDISBURGH
164
165
120
F
G
H
J
K
1
2
3
4
5
6
7
18
19
620
255
54
51
250
21
622
23
Walnut Tree Farm
Barn Grove Farm
Moat
Goldsmith Farm
THOMSONS LANE
HELMINGHAM RD.
ALLOTMENT LANE
MILLFIELD
Feoffee Farm
GREEN
ASHBOCKING
Walnut Tree Farm
The Manor Farm
Green Farm
B1077
THE
MID SUFFOLK
SUFFOLK COASTAL
NELSON CL.
ASHBOCKING ROAD
B1078
SWILLAND ROAD
Works
Mill Gallery (Pottery)
HIGH RD.
Blacksmiths Corner
Little Moat Farm
Gibraltar
GIBRALTAR
IPSWICH ROAD
Peartree Farm
Ipswich
IP6
The Gull
Gull Farm
Leaseland Farm
Depot
OTLEY
HELMINGHAM RD.
CHURCH ROAD
B1079
Rec. Grd.
Otley Hall
Prim. Sch.
Swiss Cottage Farm
BIRDS MEARE
PEARL CL.
CHAPEL RD.
VINE
LITTLE MOWS.
Bowling Green
Pav.
Sewage Works
Otley Bottom
CHARITY LANE
Otley College of Agriculture & Horticulture
Hill Farm
HILL FARM ROAD
Stoney Cottage
Shirley Cottage
Whitehouse Farm
GULL CORNER
Gull Cotts.
Hill Crest
STONEY
GULL LANE
Woodbridge
IP13
ABLITTS MDW.
CRANWORTH CL.
SCHOOL HOS.
ROAD
Weir
Ford
Brook Farm
Gull Farm
Hatherley House
GRUNDISBURGH
WHITE FOOT LANE
Burgh
BOULGE RD.
HASKETON ROAD
Lea Cottage
Mill House
HILL
SEVEN-GARDENS ROAD
River Lark
TOWN
B1079
MILL
The Cottage
Burgh House
Hasketon Hall
WOODBRIDGE RD.
GURDON
SORREL MDW.
THE GRN.
THE ST.
MEETING
MALTING LA.
THOMAS WALLS CL.
SALTERS GDNS.
BAKERS PASTURE
END ROAD
ORCHARD
WOODBRIDGE ROAD
ROSE HILL
THOMPSON CL.
Prim. Sch.
MOON LANE
JACQUELINE CL.
HALF
Barn Farm
Squeech Wood
Squeech Farm Cottage
Little Squeech
ALICE DRIVER RD.
CHARLES AV.
PARSONS CL.
GARDENS
PIPES CL.
CHAPEL LANE
GRUNDISBURGH
WOOD FARM ROAD
Elm Tree Farm
Hall
POST MILL
POST MILL ORCHARD
POST MILL CL.
POST MILL CRES.
RED BARN PIECE
Pav.
Recreation Ground
POUND CORNER
IPSWICH ROAD
PARK ROAD
LOWER ROAD
CHAPEL LA.
PINE GRO.
THE DRIFTWAY
Bridge Farm
Young Plants
Ipswich
IP6
Sandpit Wood
Reservoir (covered)
Grundisburgh Hall
Culpho Wood
Thorpe Hall Farm
Grove Bungalow
Park Farm
Sewage
EALING

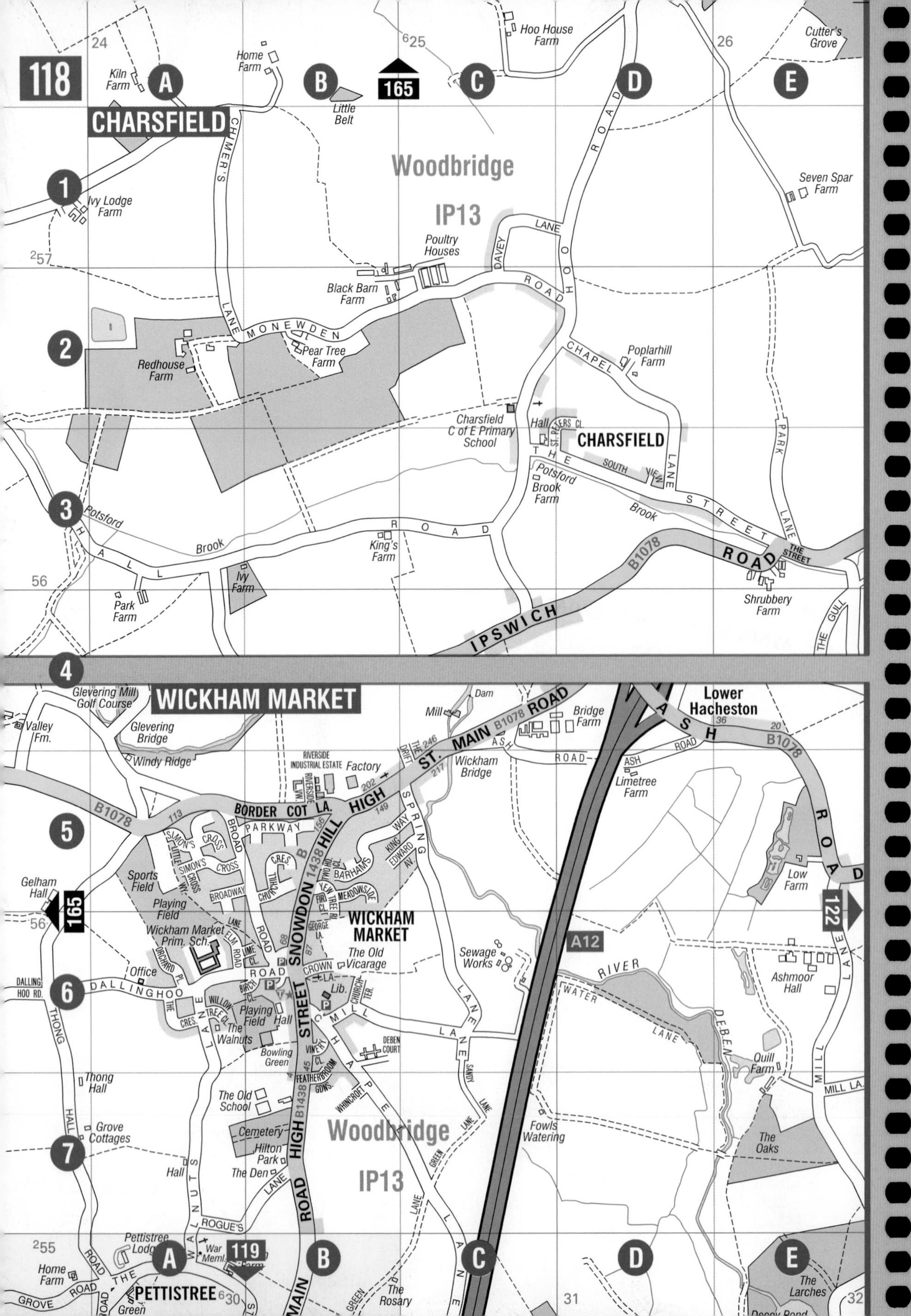
CHARSFIELD
Kiln Farm
Home Farm
Little Belt
165
Hoo House Farm
Cutter's Grove
Woodbridge
IP13
Ivy Lodge Farm
Seven Spar Farm
Poultry Houses
Black Barn Farm
Redhouse Farm
Pear Tree Farm
MONEWDEN
CHIMER'S LANE
DAVEY LANE
HOO ROAD
CHAPEL
Poplarhill Farm
Charsfield C of E Primary School
Hall
ST. PETERS CL.
CHARSFIELD
SOUTH VIEW
THE STREET
Potsford Brook Farm
Brook
PARK LANE
Potsford
HALL
ROAD
King's Farm
Brook
Ivy Farm
Park Farm
IPSWICH ROAD
B1078
Shrubbery Farm
THE GULL
WICKHAM MARKET
Glevering Mill Golf Course
Valley Fm.
Glevering Bridge
Windy Ridge
Mill
Dam
Bridge Farm
Lower Hacheston
ASH ROAD
RIVERSIDE INDUSTRIAL ESTATE
Factory
THE DRIFT
MAIN ROAD
HIGH ST.
Wickham Bridge
Limetree Farm
BORDER COT LA.
PARKWAY
SIMON'S CROSS
LITTLE SIMON'S CROSS
BROAD ROAD
BROADWAY
HILL
SNOWDON HILL
SPRING LANE
KING EDWARD AV.
BARHAMS WAY
MEADOWSIDE
Low Farm
Gelham Hall
Sports Field
Playing Field
Wickham Market Prim. Sch.
WICKHAM MARKET
The Old Vicarage
Sewage Works
A12
RIVER DEBEN
Ashmoor Hall
122
Office
DALLINGHOO ROAD
ORCHARD PL.
CROWN LA.
CHURCH TER.
Lib.
Playing Field
Hall
The Walnuts
Bowling Green
MILL LANE
DEBEN COURT
WATER LANE
Quill Farm
MILL LA.
THONG HALL ROAD
Thong Hall
Grove Cottages
The Old School
Cemetery
Hilton Park
The Den
HIGH STREET
B1438
Woodbridge
IP13
SANDY LANE
GREEN LANE
Fowls Watering
The Oaks
Hall
ROGUE'S LANE
WALNUTS
Pettistree Lodge
War Meml.
119
Home Farm
GROVE ROAD
THE GREEN
PETTISTREE
The Rosary
The Larches
Decoy Pond

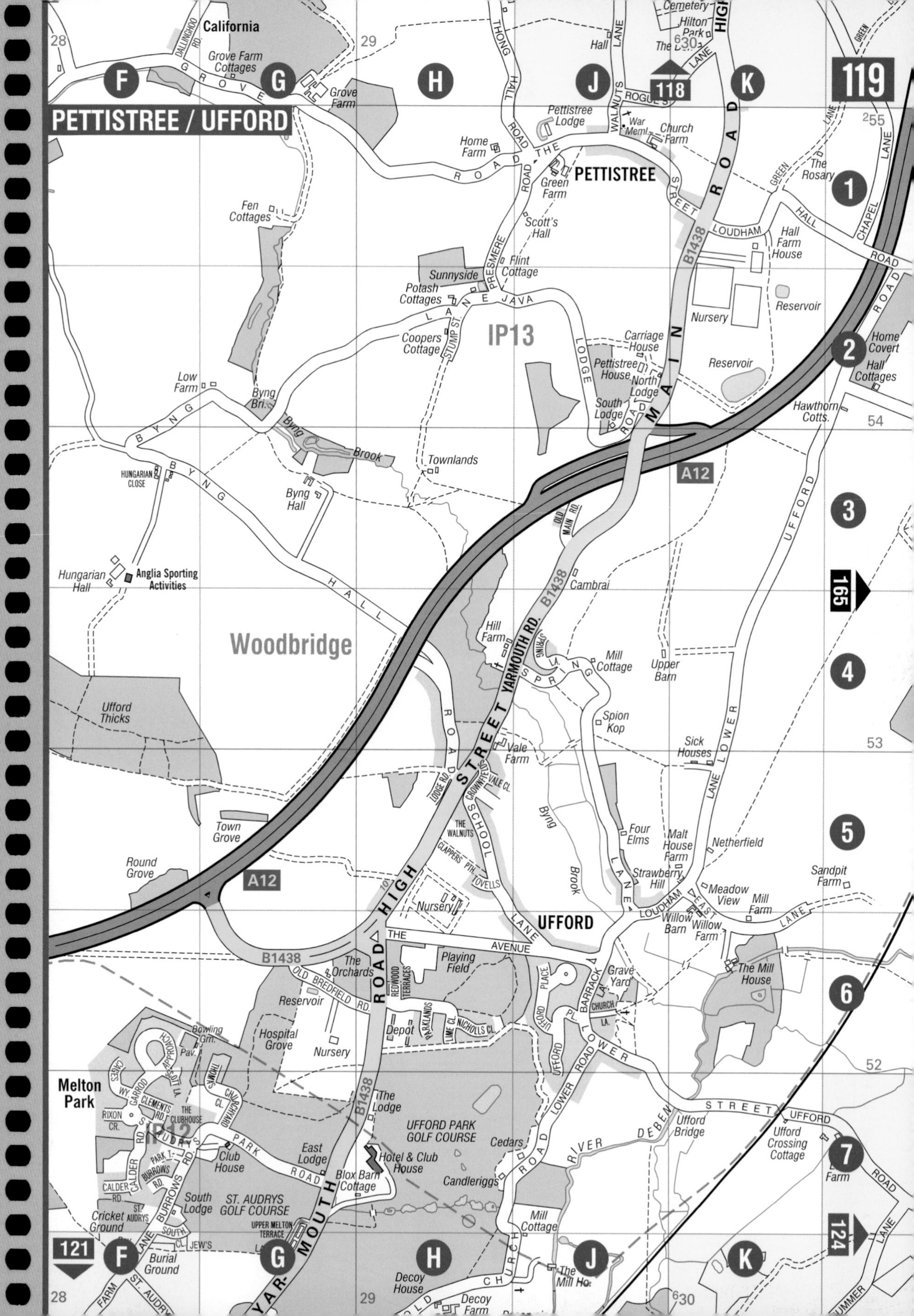
PETTISTREE / UFFORD
California
Grove Farm Cottages
Grove Farm
Pettistree Lodge
Home Farm
Church Farm
PETTISTREE
Green Farm
Scott's Hall
Flint Cottage
Sunnyside
Potash Cottages
Coopers Cottage
IP13
Fen Cottages
Low Farm
Byng Bri.
Byng Brook
Townlands
Byng Hall
Carriage House
Pettistree House
North Lodge
South Lodge
Nursery
Reservoir
The Rosary
Hall Farm House
Home Covert
Hall Cottages
Hawthorn Cotts.
HUNGARIAN CLOSE
Hungarian Hall
Anglia Sporting Activities
Woodbridge
Ufford Thicks
Town Grove
Round Grove
Cambrai
Hill Farm
Mill Cottage
Upper Barn
Spion Kop
Vale Farm
Sick Houses
Four Elms
Malt House Farm
Netherfield
Strawberry Hill
Meadow View
Mill Farm
Sandpit Farm
Willow Barn
Willow Farm
UFFORD
The Mill House
The Orchards
Playing Field
Reservoir
Hospital Grove
Nursery
Depot
Grave Yard
Bowling Grn.
Pav.
Melton Park
IP12
THE CLUBHOUSE
Club House
East Lodge
The Lodge
UFFORD PARK GOLF COURSE
Hotel & Club House
Cedars
Blox Barn Cottage
Candleriggs
South Lodge
ST. AUDRYS GOLF COURSE
Cricket Ground
Burial Ground
UPPER MELTON TERRACE
Mill Cottage
The Mill Ho.
Decoy House
Decoy Farm
Ufford Bridge
Ufford Crossing Cottage
Farm
RIVER DEBEN
A12
B1438
MAIN ROAD
HIGH STREET
YARMOUTH RD.
YARMOUTH ROAD
OLD MAIN RD
THE AVENUE
OLD BREDFIELD RD.
SCHOOL LANE
LOWER ROAD
LOWER STREET
UFFORD ROAD
LOUDHAM HALL ROAD
LOUDHAM LANE
EAST LANE
LOWER LANE
UFFORD ROAD
BYNG HALL ROAD
JAVA LANE
STUMP ST.
PRESMERE ROAD
THE STREET
THONG HALL ROAD
GROVE ROAD
DALLINGHOO RD.
WALNUTS LANE
ROGUES LANE
CHAPEL LANE
GREEN LANE
SPRING LA.
LODGE ROAD
LODGE RD.
CROWNFIELDS
VALE CL.
THE WALNUTS
CLAPPERS PTH.
TOVELLS
REDWOOD TERRACES
PARKLANDS
LIME CL.
NICHOLLS CL.
UFFORD PLACE
BARRACK LA.
CHURCH LA.
PARK ROAD
CALDER RD.
BURROWS RD.
JEW'S LA.
ST. AUDRYS RD.
CHURCH LANE
118
121
124
165
F G H J K
1 2 3 4 5 6 7
28 29 6 30 2 55 54 53 52

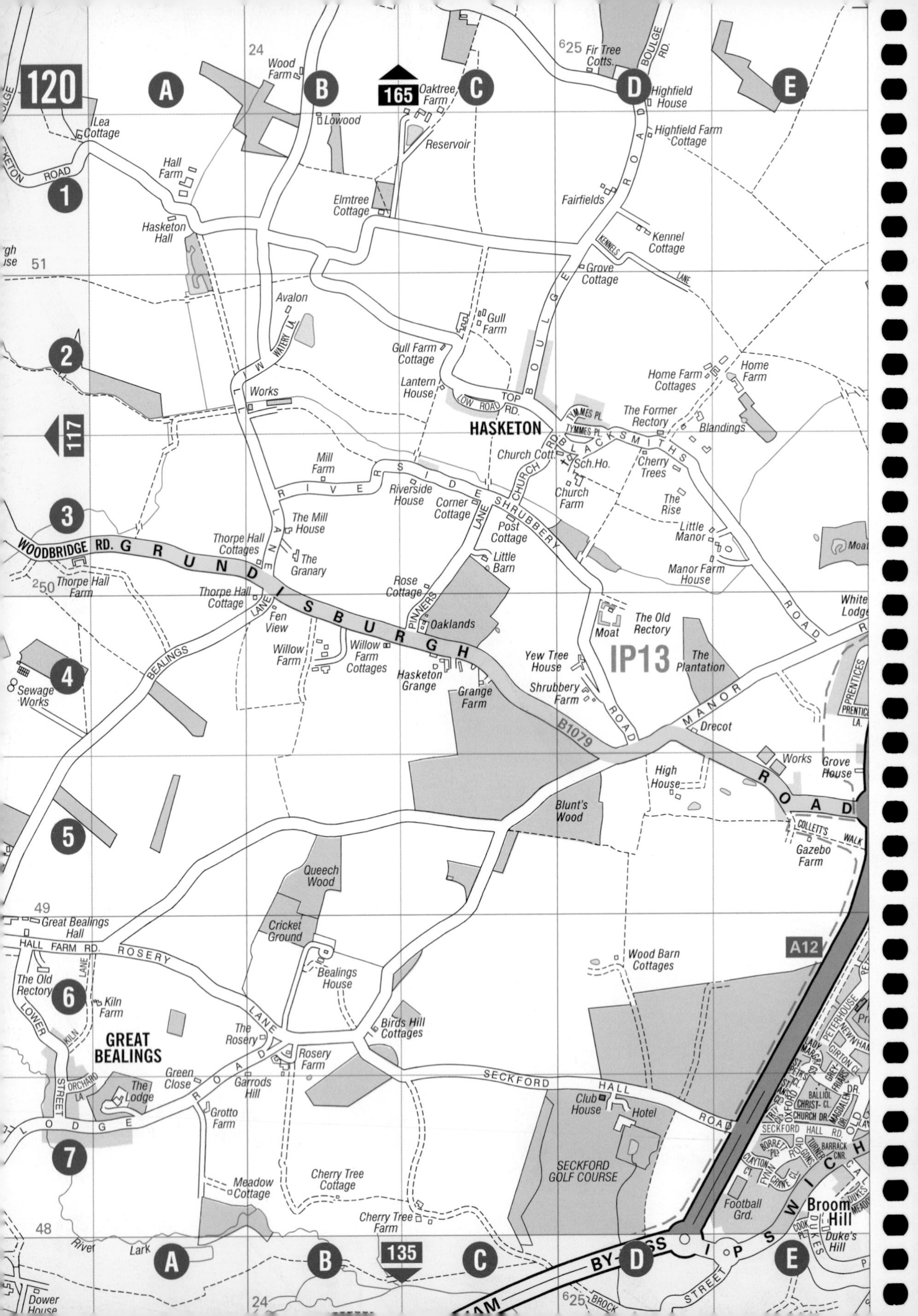
Wood Farm
Lea Cottage
Lowood
Oaktree Farm
165
Fir Tree Cotts.
Highfield House
Highfield Farm Cottage
Reservoir
Hall Farm
Hasketon Hall
Elmtree Cottage
Fairfields
Kennel Cottage
Kennels Lane
Grove Cottage
Avalon
Watery La.
Gull Farm
Gull Farm Cottage
Lantern House
Home Farm Cottages
Home Farm
Works
Low Road
Top Rd.
HASKETON
Tymmes Pl.
The Former Rectory
Blandings
Blacksmiths
Mill Farm
Riverside
Riverside House
Church Cott.
Sch.Ho.
Cherry Trees
Church Farm
Corner Cottage
The Rise
The Mill House
Thorpe Hall Cottages
The Granary
Post Cottage
Little Manor
Shrubbery
Moat
Woodbridge Rd.
Grundisburgh
Little Barn
Manor Farm House
Thorpe Hall Farm
Thorpe Hall Cottage
Rose Cottage
Pinners
Oaklands
The Old Rectory
White Lodge
Fen View
Willow Farm
Willow Farm Cottages
Bealings
Hasketon Grange
Yew Tree House
IP13
The Plantation
Prentices La.
Sewage Works
Grange Farm
Shrubbery Farm
Road
B1079
Manor Road
Drecot
Works
Grove House
High House
Blunt's Wood
Collett's Walk
Gazebo Farm
Queech Wood
Cricket Ground
Great Bealings Hall
Hall Farm Rd.
Rosery
Wood Barn Cottages
A12
The Old Rectory
Lane
Bealings House
Kiln Farm
GREAT BEALINGS
The Rosery
Birds Hill Cottages
Lower Kiln
Rosery Farm
Green Close
Garrods Hill
Seckford Hall Road
Orchard La.
Street
The Lodge
Club House
Hotel
Grotto Farm
Lodge
Seckford Hall Rd.
Peterhouse
Newnham
Girton Cl.
Grey Friars Dr.
Balliol
Christ- Cl.
Church Dr.
Magdalen Dr.
Oxford
Borrett Pl.
Barrack Cnr.
Clayton Ct.
Fynn
Grange Cl.
Turner Gdns.
Seckford Golf Course
Meadow Cottage
Cherry Tree Cottage
Football Grd.
Broom Hill
Cherry Tree Farm
Dukes Meadow
Cook Pl.
Duke's Hill
River Lark
135
By-pass
Ipswich
Brock
Street
Dower House
24
25
51
50
49
48
117
A B C D E
1 2 3 4 5 6 7

Woodbridge
WOODBRIDGE
MELTON
Drybridge Hill
Mill Hills
Maidensgrave
IP12
A12
A1152
B1438
B1079
165
119
Foxburrow Farm
Manor Farm
Fitzgerald Cottage
Bradfield House
Pear Tree Cottage
Foxboro Hall Cottage
Club House
Burial Ground
Lodge Farm
The Retreat
Long Wood
Red Cott.
Old Rectory
Tollgate Cottages
Melton Lodge
Block Field
Witchpit Farm
Valley Farm Bungalows
Slaughter House
The Woodlands
Greylands
Potash Farm
Long Springs
Works
Hasketon Manor
Melton Hall
Tennis Court
Boat Yard
Recreation Ground
Leek's Hill
Farlingaye High Sch.
Turnpike Ho.
Laundry
Spring Farm
Sewage Works
Playing Fields
Woodbridge School
Home Wood
Council Offices
Wharf
Sun Wharf
Buttrum's Mill
St. Mary's Prim.Sch.
Seckford Foundation
Elmhurst Park
Little Haugh
Garden Wood
Sutton Hoo Farm
Slipways
Fen Meadow
Abbey Grounds
Abbey Sch.
Little Sutton Hoo
Pontoon
Warren Hill
Tide Mill
Tide Mill Yacht Harbour
Apricot Hill Plantation
Top Hat Wood
Tidemill Quay
Jetty
Woodbridge
DEBEN
Ferry Cliff
Ferry Hill
Kingston Field
Sailing Club
Jetties
Slipway
Tempe
Kingston Farm
Long Tongue
Reservoir
Deben Wood
Cheveley Links
Porter's Wood
Tempe Field
Crosstrees
Kingston Nurseries
Arundel Belt
Anchor Ho.
Hill House
Heath Lodge
Broom Heath
Broom Hill
Ferry Farm
Shaftesbury
Allenby
Heath Cottages
RIVER
WOODS LANE
GROVE ROAD
BURKITT RD.
GRUNDISBURGH RD.
SECKFORD STREET
STATION ROAD
QUAY
MELTON HILL
MELTON ROAD
WILFORD BRIDGE R.
YARMOUTH ROAD
WARREN HILL ROAD
BROOM HEATH
PYTCHES ROAD
F G H J K
1 2 3 4 5 6 7
26 27 28
48 49 50 51

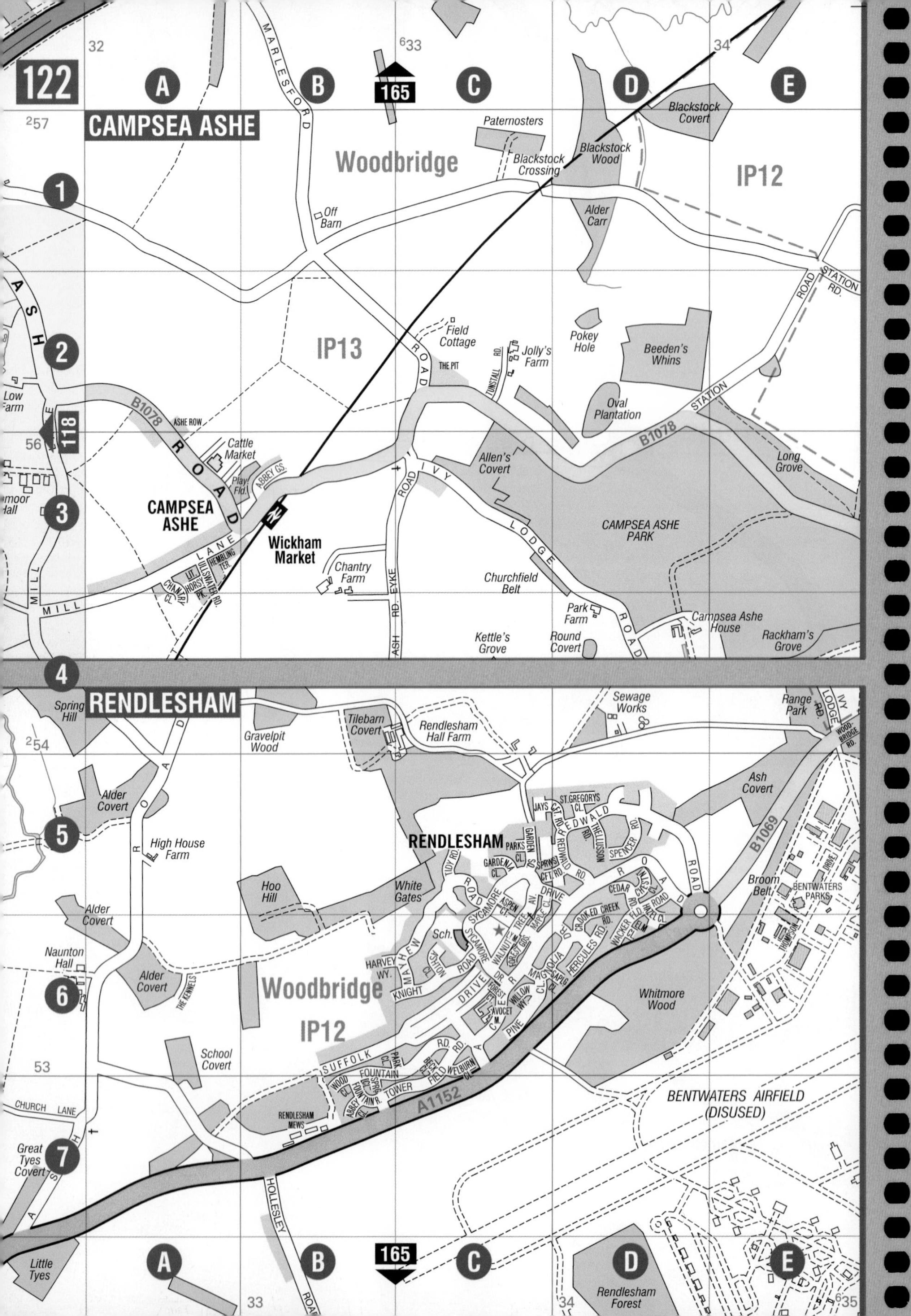
CAMPSEA ASHE
Woodbridge
IP12
IP13
Paternosters
Blackstock Crossing
Blackstock Wood
Blackstock Covert
Alder Carr
Off Barn
Field Cottage
THE PIT
Jolly's Farm
Pokey Hole
Beeden's Whins
Oval Plantation
Low Farm
B1078 ROAD
ASHE ROW
Cattle Market
Play Fld.
ABBEY GS.
CAMPSEA ASHE
Wickham Market
Allen's Covert
Long Grove
CAMPSEA ASHE PARK
STATION RD.
Chantry Farm
Churchfield Belt
Park Farm
Kettle's Grove
Round Covert
Campsea Ashe House
Rackham's Grove
MILL LANE
HEMBLING TER.
ULLSWATER RD.
LT. HORSY PK.
CHANTRY CL.
ASH RD.
EYKE
IVY LODGE ROAD
TUNSTALL RD.
MARLESFORD ROAD
RENDLESHAM
Spring Hill
Gravelpit Wood
Tilebarn Covert
Rendlesham Hall Farm
Sewage Works
Range Park
WOODBRIDGE RD.
Ash Covert
Alder Covert
High House Farm
Hoo Hill
White Gates
RENDLESHAM
Broom Belt
BENTWATERS PARKS
B1069
Naunton Hall
Alder Covert
THE KENNELS
Woodbridge
IP12
Whitmore Wood
School Covert
CHURCH LANE
RENDLESHAM MEWS
A1152
BENTWATERS AIRFIELD (DISUSED)
Great Tyes Covert
HOLLESLEY ROAD
Little Tyes
Rendlesham Forest
SUFFOLK DRIVE
FOUNTAIN
TOWER
SYCAMORE
MAYHEW
HARVEY WY.
KNIGHT
CEDAR RD.
CROOKED CREEK RD.
HERCULES RD.
MAGNOLIA
EDWALD
SPENCER RD.
JAYS CFT.
ST. GREGORYS CL.
THELLUSSON RD.
Sch.
PINE
AVOCET
WILLOW WY.
WALNUT TREE AV.
FOREST
GARDENIA CL.
PARKS
Campsea Ashe
Rendlesham
165
118
A B C D E
1 2 3 4 5 6 7
32 33 34 35
53 54 56 57

BLAXHALL / TUNSTALL

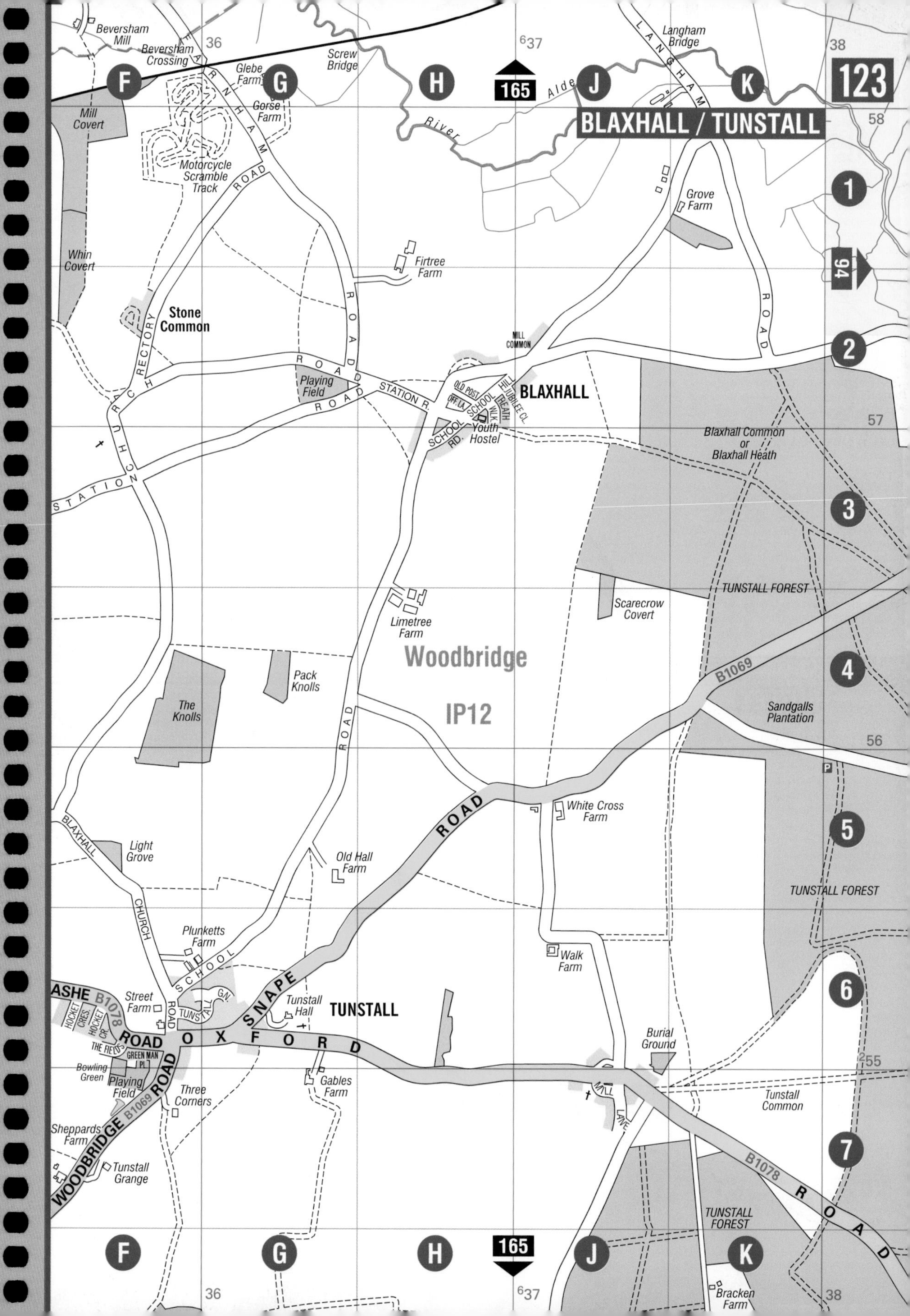

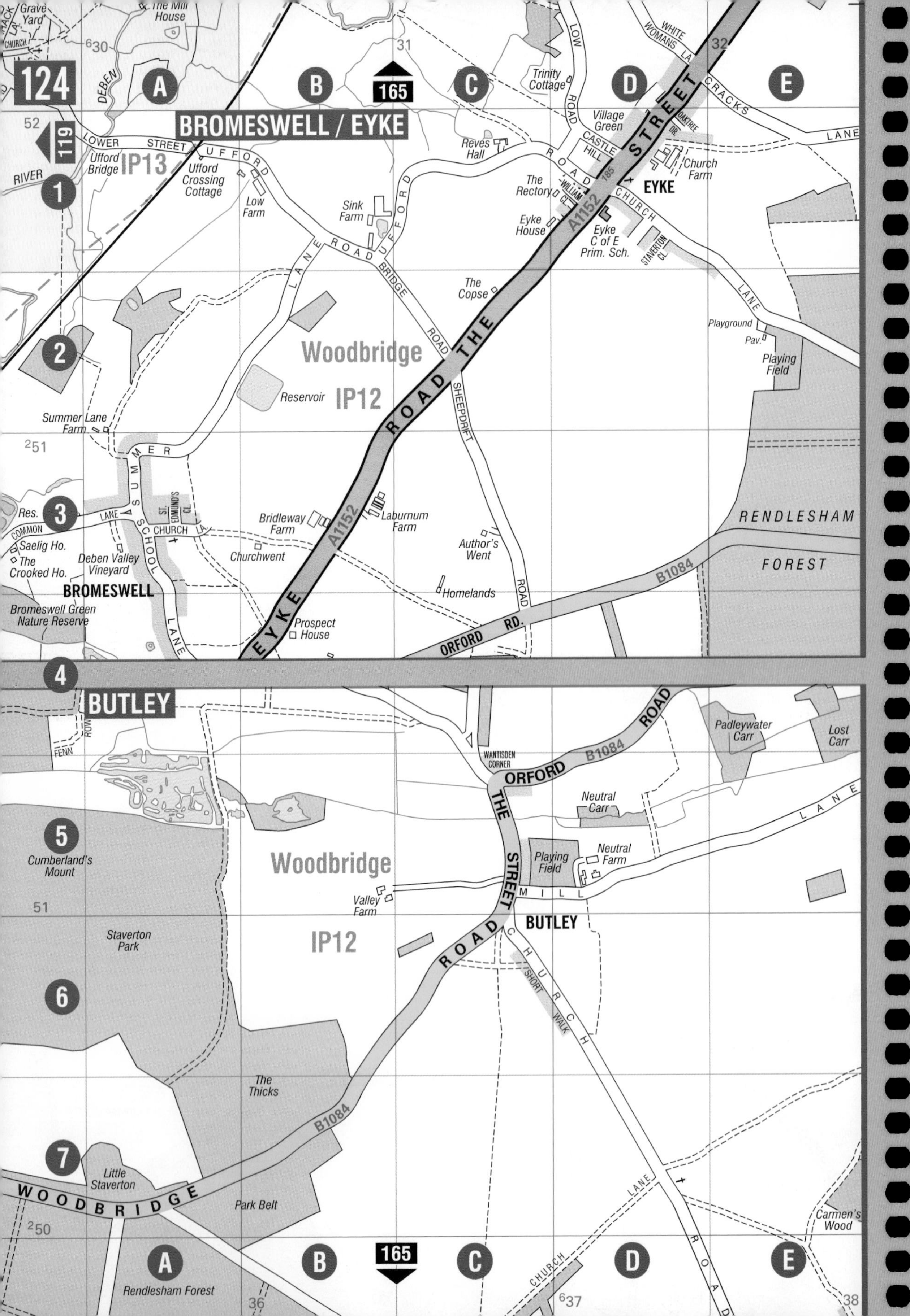
BROMESWELL / EYKE
119
165
IP13
IP12
Woodbridge
Ufford Bridge
Ufford Crossing Cottage
Low Farm
Sink Farm
Reves Hall
Trinity Cottage
Village Green
The Rectory
Eyke House
Eyke C of E Prim. Sch.
EYKE
Church Farm
The Copse
Playground
Pav.
Playing Field
Reservoir
Summer Lane Farm
Res.
Saelig Ho.
The Crooked Ho.
Deben Valley Vineyard
BROMESWELL
Bromeswell Green Nature Reserve
Churchwent
Bridleway Farm
Laburnum Farm
Author's Went
Homelands
Prospect House
RENDLESHAM
FOREST
LOWER STREET
UFFORD ROAD
LANE ROAD
UFFORD BRIDGE ROAD
EYKE ROAD
THE STREET
A1152
SHEEPDRIFT ROAD
ORFORD RD.
B1084
CHURCH LANE
STAVERTON CL.
WILLIAM CL.
CASTLE HILL
OAKTREE DR.
WHITE WOMANS LA.
CRACKS LANE
LOW ROAD
COMMON LANE
SUMMER LANE
SCHOOL LANE
ST. EDMUND'S CL.
CHURCH LA.
BUTLEY
Padleywater Carr
Lost Carr
WANTISDEN CORNER
ORFORD ROAD
Neutral Carr
Neutral Farm
Playing Field
Cumberland's Mount
Valley Farm
Staverton Park
The Thicks
Little Staverton
Park Belt
Rendlesham Forest
Carmen's Wood
THE STREET
MILL LANE
CHURCH ROAD
SHORT WALK
CHURCH LANE
WOODBRIDGE ROAD
FENN ROW

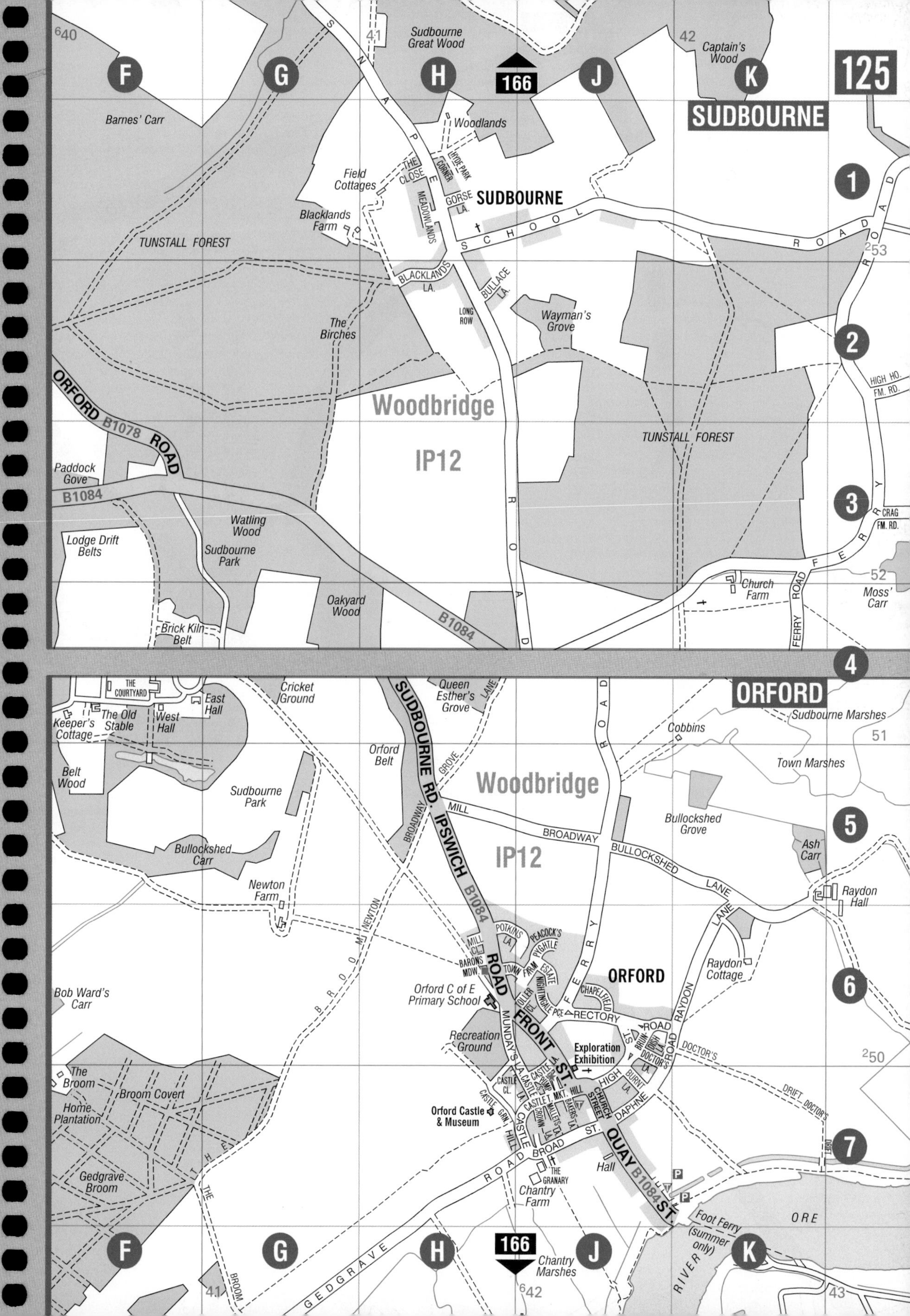

SUDBOURNE
Sudbourne Great Wood
Captain's Wood
166
Barnes' Carr
Woodlands
Field Cottages
THE CLOSE
CORNER
HYDE PARK
MEADOWLANDS
GORSE LA.
SUDBOURNE
SCHOOL ROAD
Blacklands Farm
TUNSTALL FOREST
BLACKLANDS LA.
BULLACE LA.
LONG ROW
Wayman's Grove
The Birches
HIGH HO. FM. RD.
ORFORD B1078 ROAD
Woodbridge
IP12
TUNSTALL FOREST
Paddock Gove
B1084
Watling Wood
Sudbourne Park
Lodge Drift Belts
CRAG FM. RD.
FERRY ROAD
Church Farm
Moss' Carr
Oakyard Wood
Brick Kiln Belt
B1084
ORFORD
THE COURTYARD
East Hall
Cricket Ground
Queen Esther's Grove
LANE
Keeper's Cottage
The Old Stable
West Hall
Sudbourne Marshes
Cobbins
Belt Wood
Orford Belt
Town Marshes
SUDBOURNE RD.
IPSWICH
GROVE
Woodbridge
Sudbourne Park
MILL BROADWAY
BROADWAY
Bullockshed Grove
Bullockshed Carr
IP12
BULLOCKSHED LANE
Ash Carr
Newton Farm
B1084
Raydon Hall
NEWTON
POTKINS LA.
PEACOCK'S PYGHTLE
MILL CL.
BARONS MDW.
TOWN FARM ESTATE
Raydon Cottage
ORFORD
Bob Ward's Carr
Orford C of E Primary School
JOLLEY CL.
NIGHTINGALE PCE
CHAPELFIELD
RECTORY ROAD
RAYDON
BROOM
Recreation Ground
MUNDAY'S LA.
FRONT ST.
Exploration Exhibition
DOCTOR'S
DOCTOR'S LA.
The Broom
Broom Covert
CASTLE CL.
CASTLE LA.
HIGH ST.
BURNT LA.
DRIFT DOCTOR'S
Home Plantation
Orford Castle & Museum
CASTLE GDN.
CASTLE HILL
MKT. HILL
CHURCH STREET
DAPHNE
THE
BROAD ST.
QUAY ST.
B1084
Hall
DRIFT
Gedgrave Broom
ROAD
THE GRANARY
Chantry Farm
ORE
Foot Ferry (summer only)
RIVER
GEDGRAVE
Chantry Marshes
166
BROOM

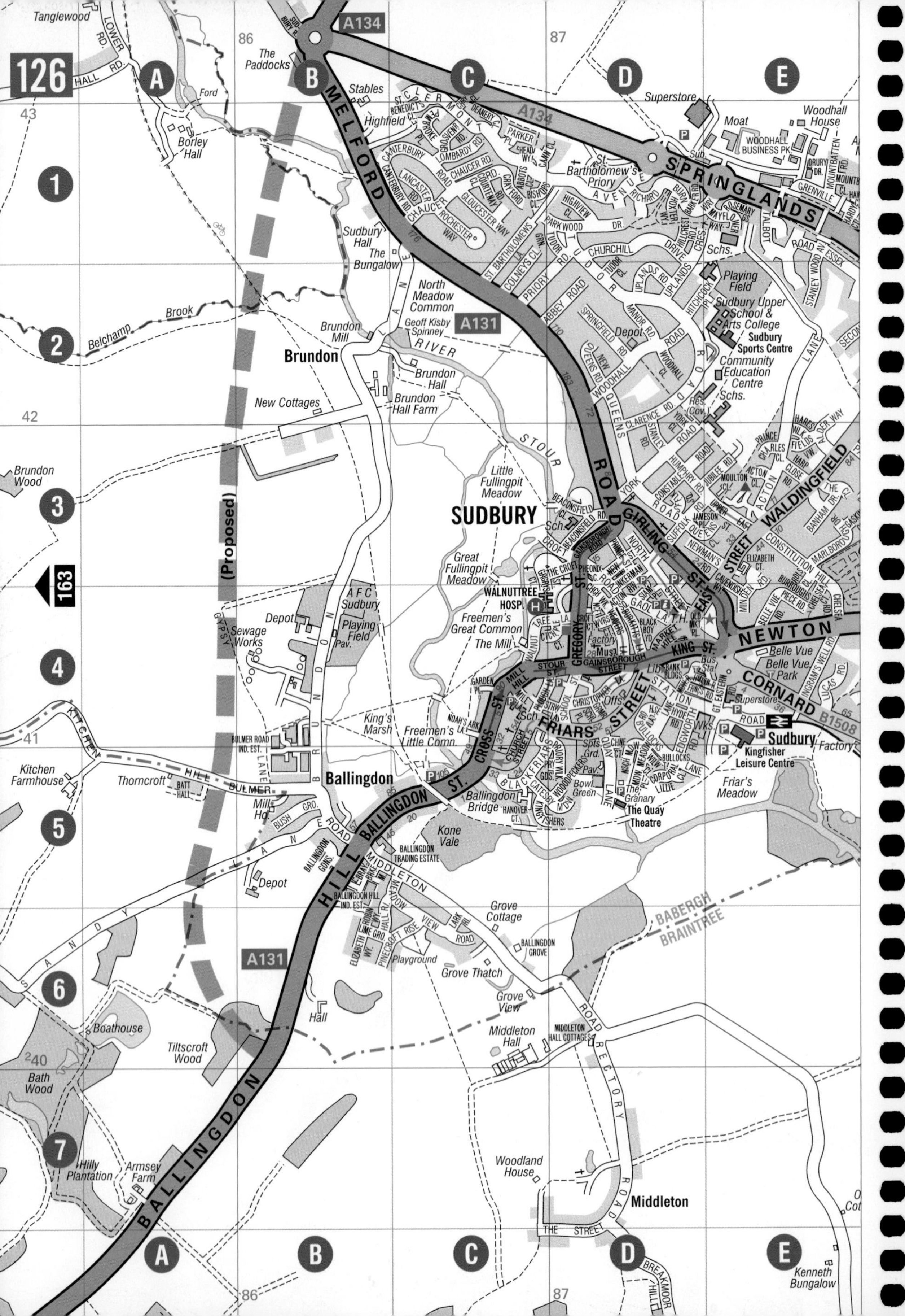

A
B
C
D
E
1
2
3
4
5
6
7
86
87
43
42
41
40
A134
A131
B1508
163
Tanglewood
Lower Rd.
Hall Rd.
Ford
Borley Hall
The Paddocks
Stables
Highfield
Melford
Superstore
Moat
Woodhall House
Woodhall Business Pk.
Springlands
St. Bartholomew's Priory
Avenue
Canterbury Rd.
Lancaster Rd.
Chaucer Rd.
Rochester Way
Gloucester Way
Lombardy Rd.
Deanery
Parker
Sudbury Hall
The Bungalow
Belchamp Brook
North Meadow Common
Geoff Kisby Spinney
Brundon Mill
Brundon
River
Brundon Hall
Brundon Hall Farm
New Cottages
Stour
Churchill
Tudor Rd.
Priory Rd.
Abbey Road
Springfield Rd.
Manor Rd.
Depot
Uplands Rd.
Playing Field
Sudbury Upper School & Arts College
Sudbury Sports Centre
Community Education Centre
Schs.
Queens Rd.
Woodhall Rd.
Clarence Rd.
York Road
Humphry Rd.
Jubilee Rd.
Constable Rd.
Moulton Cl.
Acton Cl.
Acton
Waldingfield
Stanley Wood Av.
Essex
Talbot Road
Mountbatten Rd.
Brundon Wood
Little Fullingpit Meadow
SUDBURY
Beaconsfield Cl.
Sch.
Girling
Road
(Proposed)
Great Fullingpit Meadow
Walnuttree Hosp.
AFC Sudbury
Playing Field
Pav.
Depot
Sewage Works
Gypsy
Freemen's Great Common
The Mill
Gregory St.
North St.
East St.
Old Mkt. Pl.
Market Hill
King St.
Gainsborough Street
Stour St.
Mill Hill
Newton
Constitution Hill
Cornard
Belle Vue
Belle Vue Park
Bus Sta.
Station
Superstore
Sudbury
Factory
Kingfisher Leisure Centre
Friar's Meadow
Friars
Street
Cross St.
Church Street
School St.
Christopher
Quay Lane
Bowl. Green
The Granary
The Quay Theatre
King's Marsh
Freemen's Little Comn.
Brundon Lane
Bulmer Road Ind. Est.
Kitchen Farmhouse
Thorncroft
Kitchen Hill
Bulmer
Batt Hall
Mill Ho.
Ballingdon
Bush Gro.
Ballingdon St.
Ballingdon Bridge
Kingfishers
Kone Vale
Ballingdon Trading Estate
Ballingdon Hill Ind. Est.
Sandy Lane
Depot
Middleton
Grove Cottage
Babergh
Braintree
Pinecroft Rise
View Road
Playground
Ballingdon Grove
Grove Thatch
Grove View
Boathouse
Hall
Tiltscroft Wood
Middleton Hall
Middleton Hall Cottages
Rectory Road
Bath Wood
Hilly Plantation
Armsey Farm
Ballingdon
Hill
Woodland House
Middleton
The Street
Breakmoor Hill
Kenneth Bungalow

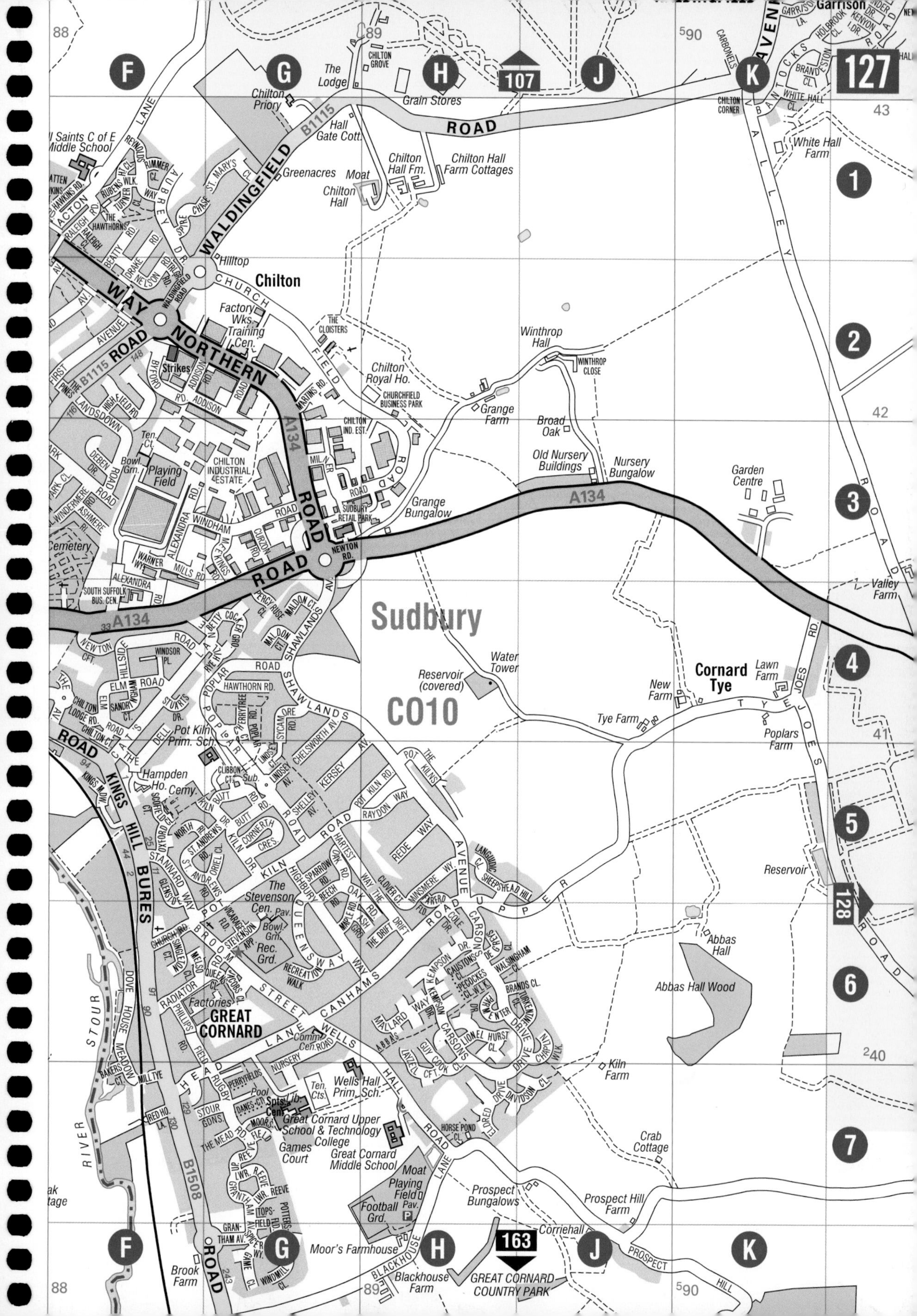
Sudbury
CO10
Chilton
Cornard Tye
GREAT CORNARD
Chilton Priory
The Lodge
Chilton Grove
Grain Stores
Hall Gate Cott.
Greenacres
Moat
Chilton Hall
Chilton Hall Fm.
Chilton Hall Farm Cottages
White Hall Farm
Hilltop
Factory Wks.
Training Cen.
Strikes
The Cloisters
Chilton Royal Ho.
Churchfield Business Park
Chilton Ind. Est.
Chilton Industrial Estate
Playing Field
Winthrop Hall
Winthrop Close
Grange Farm
Broad Oak
Old Nursery Buildings
Nursery Bungalow
Garden Centre
Grange Bungalow
Sudbury Retail Park
Cemetery
South Suffolk Bus. Cen.
Valley Farm
Water Tower
Reservoir (covered)
New Farm
Lawn Farm
Tye Farm
Poplars Farm
Pot Kiln Prim. Sch.
Hampden Ho.
Cemy.
The Stevenson Cen.
Rec. Grd.
Factories
Reservoir
Abbas Hall
Abbas Hall Wood
Kiln Farm
Wells Hall Prim. Sch.
Great Cornard Upper School & Technology College
Games Court
Great Cornard Middle School
Crab Cottage
Moat
Playing Field
Football Grd.
Prospect Bungalows
Prospect Hill Farm
Corriehall
Moor's Farmhouse
Brook Farm
Blackhouse Farm
GREAT CORNARD COUNTRY PARK
River Stour
Waldingfield Road
Northern Road
Church Field Road
Shawlands Avenue
Pot Kiln Road
Queensway
Canhams Road
Wells Hall Road
Kings Hill
Bures Road
Upper Road
Joes Road
Valley Road
Prospect Hill
Blackhouse Lane
Head Lane
A134
B1115
B1508
107
163
128

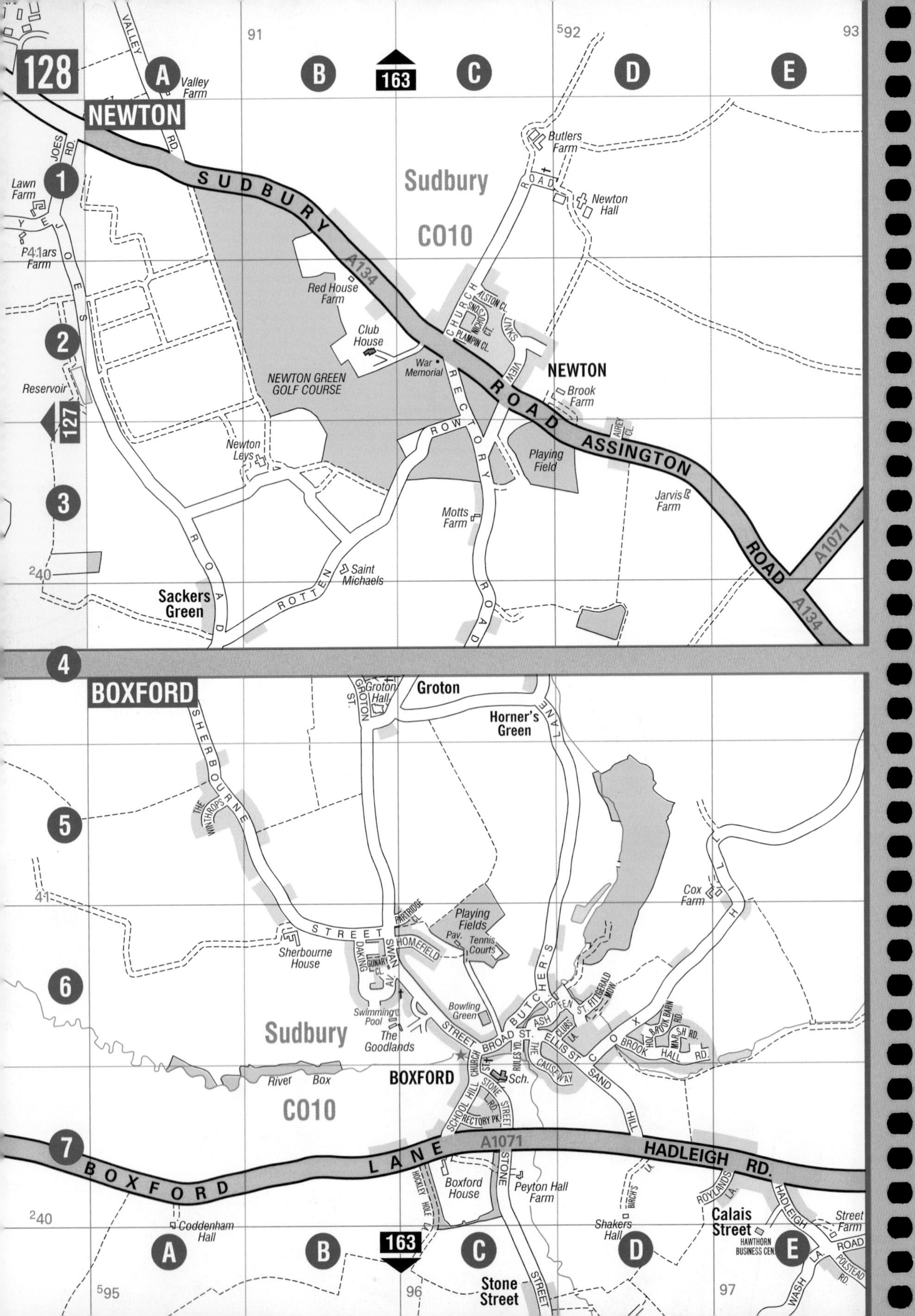

NEWTON
Valley Farm
Butlers Farm
Newton Hall
Lawn Farm
Friars Farm
Sudbury
CO10
SUDBURY ROAD
A134
Red House Farm
Club House
War Memorial
NEWTON GREEN GOLF COURSE
Reservoir
NEWTON
Brook Farm
ASSINGTON ROAD
Playing Field
Newton Leys
Jarvis Farm
Motts Farm
Saint Michaels
Sackers Green
ROTTEN ROAD
RECTORY ROAD
A1071
BOXFORD
Groton Hall
Groton
Horner's Green
SHERBOURNE
THE WINTHROPS
Cox Farm
Playing Fields
Tennis Courts
Sherbourne House
Swimming Pool
Bowling Green
The Goodlands
Sudbury
River Box
BOXFORD
CO10
Sch.
BOXFORD LANE
HADLEIGH RD.
Boxford House
Peyton Hall Farm
Coddenham Hall
Shakers Hall
Calais Street
HAWTHORN BUSINESS CEN.
Street Farm
Stone Street

163
127
163

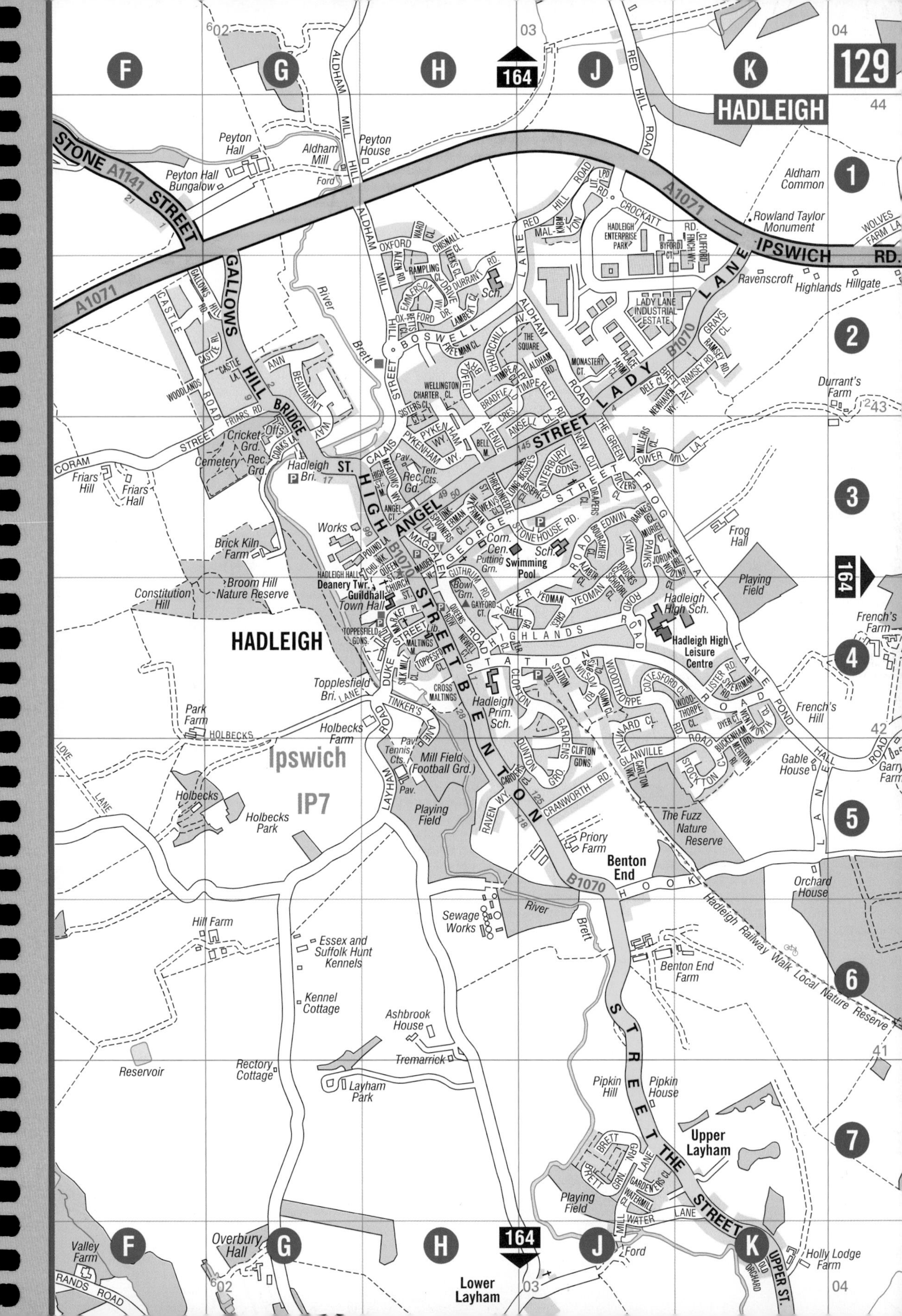
HADLEIGH
F
G
H
J
K
164
1
2
3
4
5
6
7
02
03
04
44
43
42
41
Peyton Hall
Peyton House
Aldham Mill
Ford
Peyton Hall Bungalow
STONE STREET
A1141
A1071
ALDHAM MILL HILL
RED HILL ROAD
Aldham Common
Rowland Taylor Monument
IPSWICH RD.
WOLVES FARM LA.
Ravenscroft
Highlands
Hillgate
HADLEIGH ENTERPRISE PARK
CROCKATT RD.
LADY LANE INDUSTRIAL ESTATE
LADY LANE
B1070
GALLOWS HILL
CASTLE RD.
WOODLANDS ROAD
FRIARS RD.
BRIDGE STREET
River Brett
BOSWELL LA.
ALDHAM ROAD
THE SQUARE
WELLINGTON CL.
CHARTER CL.
PYKENHAM WY.
ANGEL STREET
Durrant's Farm
TOWER MILL LA.
FROG HALL LANE
CORAM STREET
Friars' Hill
Friars Hall
Cricket Grd.
Cemetery
Rec. Grd.
Hadleigh Bri.
HIGH STREET
Pav.
Ten. Cts.
Rec. Gd.
GEORGE STREET
STONEHOUSE RD.
Com. Cen.
Swimming Pool
Sch.
Works
Brick Kiln Farm
Broom Hill Nature Reserve
Constitution Hill
Deanery Twr.
Guildhall
Town Hall
Putting Grn.
Bowl. Grn.
Frog Hall
Playing Field
Hadleigh High Sch.
Hadleigh High Leisure Centre
HIGHLANDS ROAD
YEOMAN WAY
French's Farm
HADLEIGH
Lib.
Topplesfield Bri.
DUKE STREET
STATION ROAD
Hadleigh Prim. Sch.
CROSS MALTINGS
TINKER'S LANE
Park Farm
HOLBECKS
Holbecks Farm
Ipswich
IP7
Mill Field (Football Grd.)
Tennis Cts.
Pav.
LAYHAM ROAD
BENTON STREET
French's Hill
POND HALL ROAD
Gable House
Garry Farm
Holbecks
Holbecks Park
Playing Field
CRANWORTH RD.
The Fuzz Nature Reserve
Priory Farm
Benton End
HOOK LANE
Orchard House
Hadleigh Railway Walk Local Nature Reserve
Hill Farm
Sewage Works
River Brett
Essex and Suffolk Hunt Kennels
Benton End Farm
Kennel Cottage
Ashbrook House
Tremarrick
Reservoir
Rectory Cottage
Layham Park
Pipkin Hill
Pipkin House
THE STREET
Upper Layham
BRETT GRN.
Playing Field
WATER LANE
Ford
Valley Farm
RANDS ROAD
Overbury Hall
Lower Layham
UPPER ST.
Holly Lodge Farm
LOVE LANE

114
136
164
BRAMFORD
SPROUGHTON
IP8
Broom Hill
Lower Dairy Farm
Suffolk Water Park
Alder Carr
The Old Paper Mill
Paper Mill Farm
Pitch & Putt
Sycamore House
Dairy Farm
SOMERSHAM ROAD
LORAINE WAY
B1113
RIVER GIPPING
Bramford Common
Works
The Grove Cottage
Fisk Grove
The Grove
A14
Superstore
Brickkiln Farm
WESTERN BY-PASS
IPSWICH
Rutters Cottages
Rutters Farm
TYE LANE
THE ROW
Pav.
Play Fld.
Tennis Courts
Bowling Green
Bushman's Bridge
Grove Ho.
PAPER MILL LANE
Cem.
THE STREET
BRAMFORD PARK
HALL WALK
Keepers Cottage
BULLEN LANE
Bramford Bri.
SHIP LANE
B1067
The Gables
BRAMFORD RD.
By-pass Nurseries
Clarice Ho. Day Spa
Prim. Sch.
Hall
Cemy.
DUCKAMERE
FITZGERALD
VICARAGE LA.
Figdeon's Farm
Runcton Farm
Thornbush Hall
THORNBUSH LANE
Runcton Cottage
Hazel Wood
Sproughton Manor
Manor View
Langham House
Anglia Kart Racing
Junction 54
Grindle Farm
THE GRINDLE
MID SUFFOLK
BABERGH
Hope Farm
Sproughton Hall
Hall Field Cottage
SPROUGHTON ROAD
Sproughton Bri.
LOWER STREET
CHURCH LANE
HIGH ST.
Perry Barn
Laurel Farm
Oakdene
BURSTALL LANE
Abbey Oaks
Abbey Oaks Farmhouse
Oak House
Sproughton Lodge
Tennis Cts.
Play. Fld.
Prim. Sch.
Bowling Green
Burial Ground
Rookery Farm
Sewage Works
RIVER
The Rookery
The Old Dairy
Bungalow Farm
Clay Shooting
The Grove
Chantry Gro.
Sub.
A
B
C
D
E
1
2
3
4
5
6
7
11
12
13
45
46
47
48

Junction 53
164
132
137
4
Whitton
Castle Hill
White House
Ipswich
Westbourne
IPSWICH
IP1
IP2
The Dales
Broomhill Park
Sherrington Road Park
MID SUFFOLK
IPSWICH
Ormiston Endeavour Academy
Westbourne Sports College
Whitehouse Prim. Sch.
Dale Hale Prim. Sch.
Castle Hill Jun.& Inf. Schs.
NORWICH ROAD
BURY ROAD
VALLEY ROAD
HANDFORD ROAD
YARMOUTH RD.
BRAMFORD ROAD
CHEVALLIER ST.
A1156
A1214
A1071
B1067
GIPPING

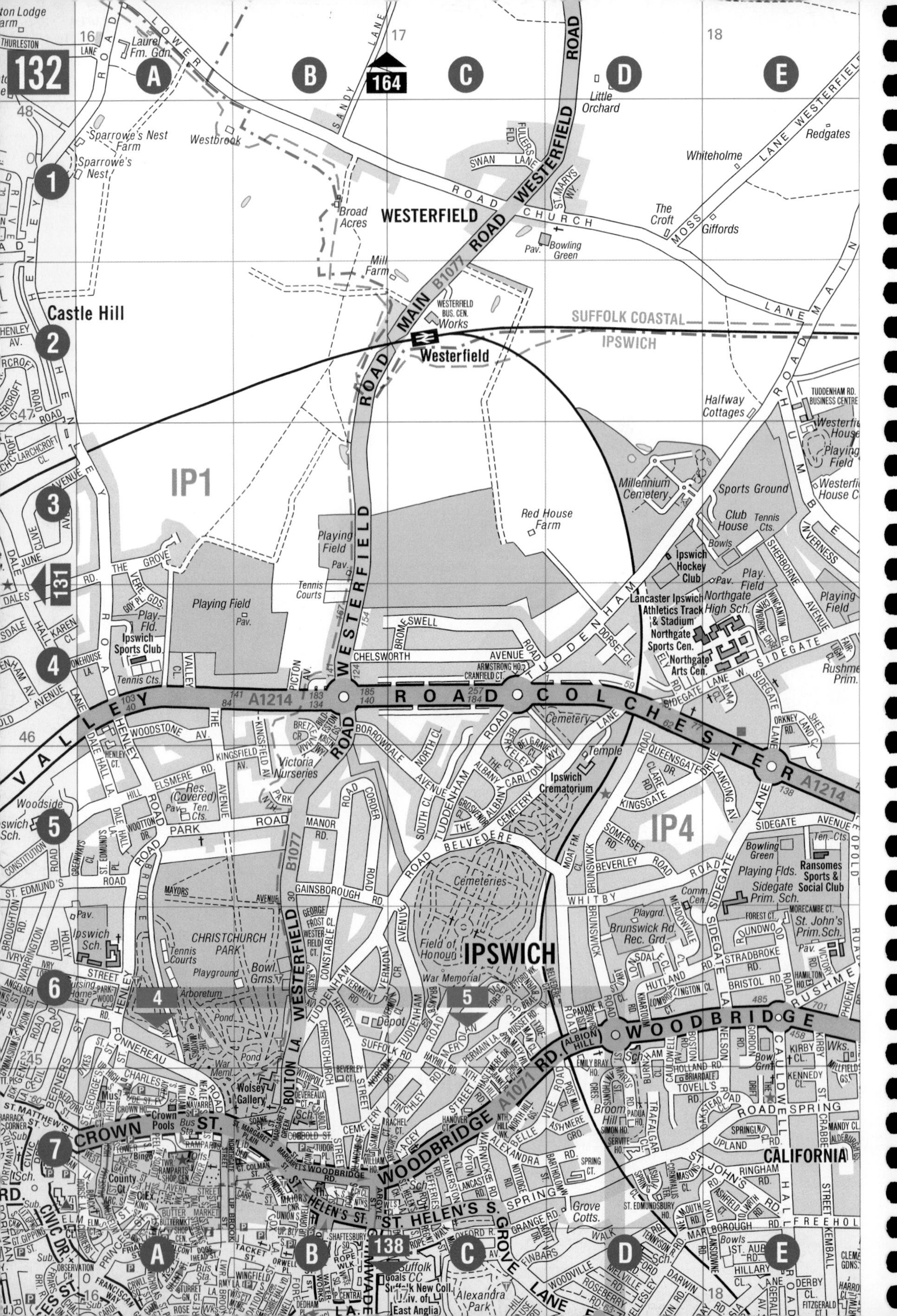

132
164
131
138
A
B
C
D
E
1
2
3
4
5
6
7
16
17
18
48
47
46
45
WESTERFIELD
Castle Hill
IP1
IP4
IPSWICH
CALIFORNIA
Westerfield
SUFFOLK COASTAL
IPSWICH
Laurel Fm. Gdn.
Sparrowe's Nest Farm
Sparrowe's Nest
Westbrook
Broad Acres
Mill Farm
Little Orchard
Redgates
Whiteholme
The Croft
Giffords
Bowling Green
Pav.
Works
WESTERFIELD BUS. CEN.
Halfway Cottages
TUDDENHAM RD. BUSINESS CENTRE
Westerfield House
Playing Field
Millennium Cemetery
Sports Ground
Club House
Tennis Cts.
Red House Farm
Ipswich Hockey Club
Lancaster Ipswich Athletics Track & Stadium
Northgate High Sch.
Northgate Sports Cen.
Northgate Arts Cen.
Rushmere Prim.
Ipswich Sports Club
Tennis Courts
Victoria Nurseries
Ipswich Crematorium
Temple
Cemetery
Cemeteries
Field of Honour
War Memorial
CHRISTCHURCH PARK
Arboretum
Pond
Playground
Bowl. Grns.
Wolsey Gallery
Crown Pools
Bus St.
County Ct.
Bingo
Depot
Ransomes Sports & Social Club
Sidegate Prim. Sch.
St. John's Prim. Sch.
Brunswick Rd. Rec. Grd.
Playgrd.
Comm. Cen.
Grove Cotts.
Suffolk New Coll. / Univ. of East Anglia
Alexandra Park
Suffolk CC Goals
LOWER ROAD
SANDY LANE
WESTERFIELD ROAD
MAIN ROAD B1077
CHURCH LANE
SWAN LANE
FULLERS FLD.
ST. MARYS WY.
MOSS LANE
LANE WESTERFIELD
MAIN ROAD
HUMBER DOUCY LANE
TUDDENHAM ROAD
COLCHESTER ROAD A1214
VALLEY ROAD A1214
HENLEY ROAD
BROMESWELL
CHELSWORTH AVENUE
ARMSTRONG HO.
CRANFIELD CT.
DORSET CL.
SIDEGATE LANE
SIDEGATE AVENUE
INVERNESS
SHERBORNE AVENUE
WINCANTON CL.
QUEENSGATE DR.
KINGSGATE
LANCING AV.
SOMERSET RD.
BEVERLEY ROAD
WHITBY ROAD
BRUNSWICK ROAD
BELVEDERE ROAD
CEMETERY ROAD
ALBANY
CARLTON WY.
BORROWDALE AVENUE
NORTH CL.
SOUTH CL.
MANOR RD.
CORDER ROAD
GAINSBOROUGH RD.
BOLTON LA.
PARK ROAD
CONSTITUTION HILL
ST. EDMUND'S ROAD
WOODSTONE AV.
KINGSFIELD AV.
ELSMERE RD.
DALE HALL LA.
WOOTTON DR.
MAYORS AVENUE
FONNEREAU ROAD
CROWN ST.
WOODBRIDGE ROAD
WOODBRIDGE RD. A1071
ST. HELEN'S ST.
GROVE LANE
SPRING ROAD
ALEXANDRA RD.
ST. JOHN'S ROAD
UPLAND RD.
RINGHAM RD.
FREEHOLD
RUSHMERE ROAD
CAULDWELL HALL ROAD
KIRBY CL.
SPRING ROAD
TUDDENHAM AVENUE
SUFFOLK RD.
CHRISTCHURCH ST.
STRADBROKE RD.
BRISTOL RD.
HUTLAND
TOVELL'S
BROOM HILL
MARLBOROUGH
TENNYSON RD.
DARWIN
WOODVILLE
CIVIC DR.
ST. MATTHEW'S ST.
ELM ST.
PRINCES ST.

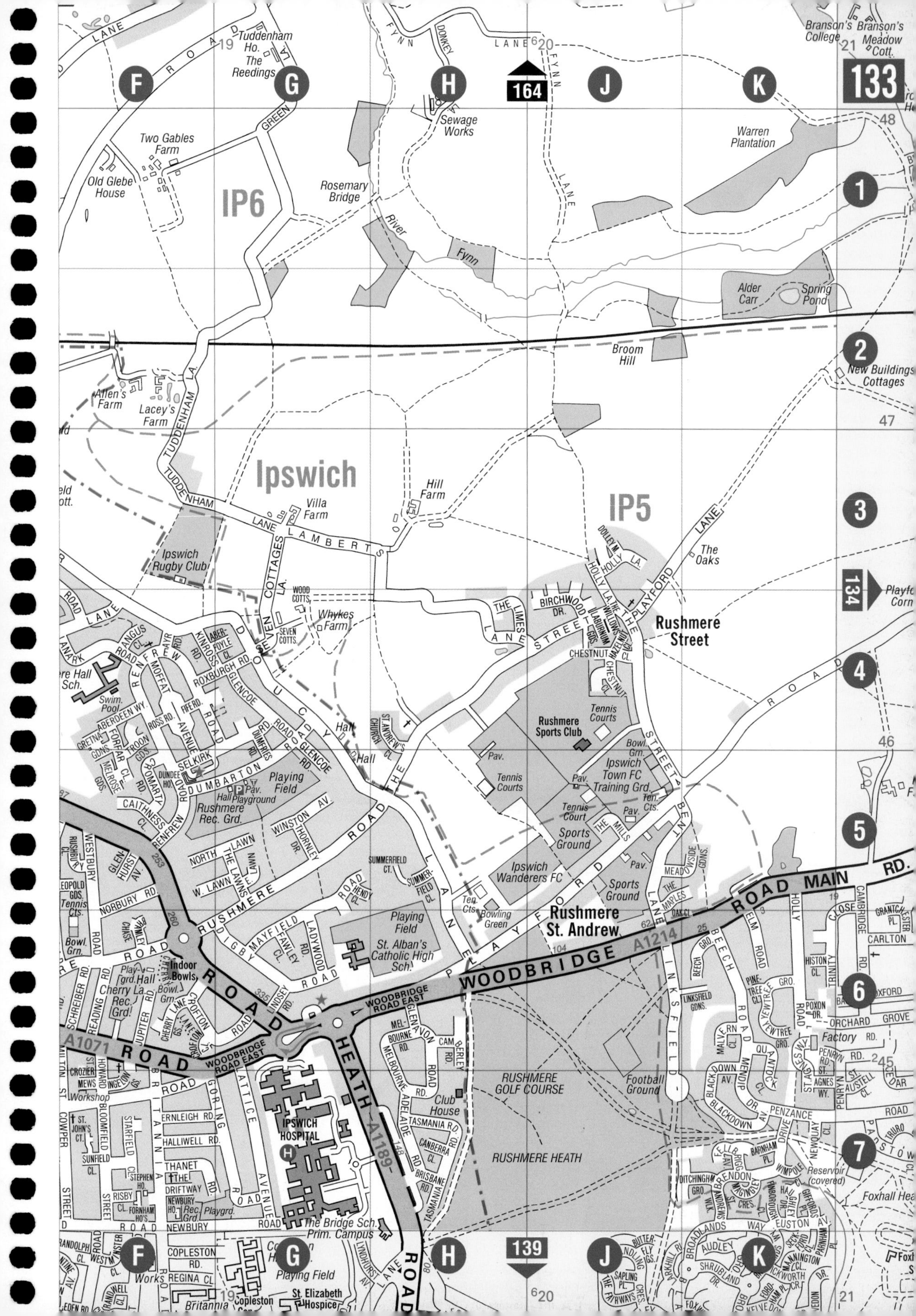

133
164
134
139
Playford Corner
Branson's College
Branson's Meadow Cott.
Tuddenham Ho.
The Reedings
Two Gables Farm
Old Glebe House
IP6
Rosemary Bridge
Sewage Works
Warren Plantation
River Fynn
Alder Carr
Spring Pond
Broom Hill
New Buildings Cottages
Allen's Farm
Lacey's Farm
Ipswich
Hill Farm
Villa Farm
IP5
The Oaks
Ipswich Rugby Club
Whykes Farm
Wood Cotts.
Seven Cotts.
Rushmere Street
Rushmere Sports Club
Tennis Courts
Ipswich Town FC Training Grd.
Sports Ground
Ipswich Wanderers FC
Bowling Green
Playing Field
Rushmere Rec. Grd.
Rushmere St. Andrew
St. Alban's Catholic High Sch.
Indoor Bowls
Cherry La. Rec. Grd.
Swim. Pool
Ipswich Hospital
The Bridge Sch. Prim. Campus
Club House
Rushmere Golf Course
Rushmere Heath
Football Ground
Reservoir (covered)
Factory
Foxhall Heath
St. Elizabeth Hospice
Copleston
Britannia
Workshop
Woodbridge Road
Woodbridge Road East
Main Road
A1214
A1071
A1189
Heath Road
Playford Road
Tuddenham Road
Tuddenham Lane
Lamberts Lane
Seven Cottages La.
Fynn Lane
Donkey Lane
Green La.
Holly La.
Dolly La.
Birchwood Dr.
The Limes
Chestnut Cl.
Bent Lane
Linksfield
Humber Doucy Lane
Renfrew Road
Rushmere Road
Dumbarton Road
Selkirk Road
Glencoe Road
Roxburgh Rd.
Lanark
Angus Cl.
Aberdeen Wy.
Gretna Gdns.
Forfar Cl.
Melrose Gdns.
Cromarty Rd.
Caithness Cl.
Mayfield Rd.
Digby Road
Ladywood Rd.
Fawley Cl.
Lindsey Rd.
Winston Av.
Thorney Dr.
North Lawn
W. Lawn
The Lawns
Norbury Rd.
Westbury Road
Glenhurst Av.
Leopold Gds.
Chase
Schreiber Rd.
Reading Rd.
Jupiter Rd.
Crofton
Melbourne Rd.
Glenavon Rd.
Cambridge Rd.
Adelaide Rd.
Tasmania Rd.
Canberra Cl.
Brisbane Rd.
Britannia Road
Goring Road
Lattice Avenue
Ernleigh Rd.
Halliwell Rd.
Thanet Rd.
The Driftway
Newbury Road
Copleston Rd.
Regina Cl.
Starfield Cl.
Bloomfield St.
Cowper Street
Milton St.
Howard St.
Crozier Mews
Beech Grove
Elm Road
Holly Road
Cambridge Road
Carlton
Trinity
Histon Cl.
Pinetree Cl.
Yewtree Grove
Malvern Rd.
Mendip Dr.
Blackdown Av.
Quantock Cl.
Penzance Road
Newquay Cl.
St. Agnes Wy.
Penryn Rd.
St. Austell Cl.
Cedar
Truro
Padstow Road
Orchard Grove
Poxon Dr.
Ditchingham Gro.
Brendon Dr.
Barnham Pl.
Wimpole Cl.
Euston Av.
Broadlands Way
Audley Gro.
Shrubland Dr.
Sapling Pl.
The Fairways
Butterfly Gdns.
Lyndhurst Ave.
Meadowside Gdns.
The Maples
Oak Cl.
The Mills
Hendy Cl.
Summerfield Ct.
Summerfield Cl.
St. Andrew's Church Cl.
Moffat Av.
Kinross Rd.
Aberfoyle Cl.
Dunfries Rd.
Dundee Ho.
Cherry Lane Gdns.

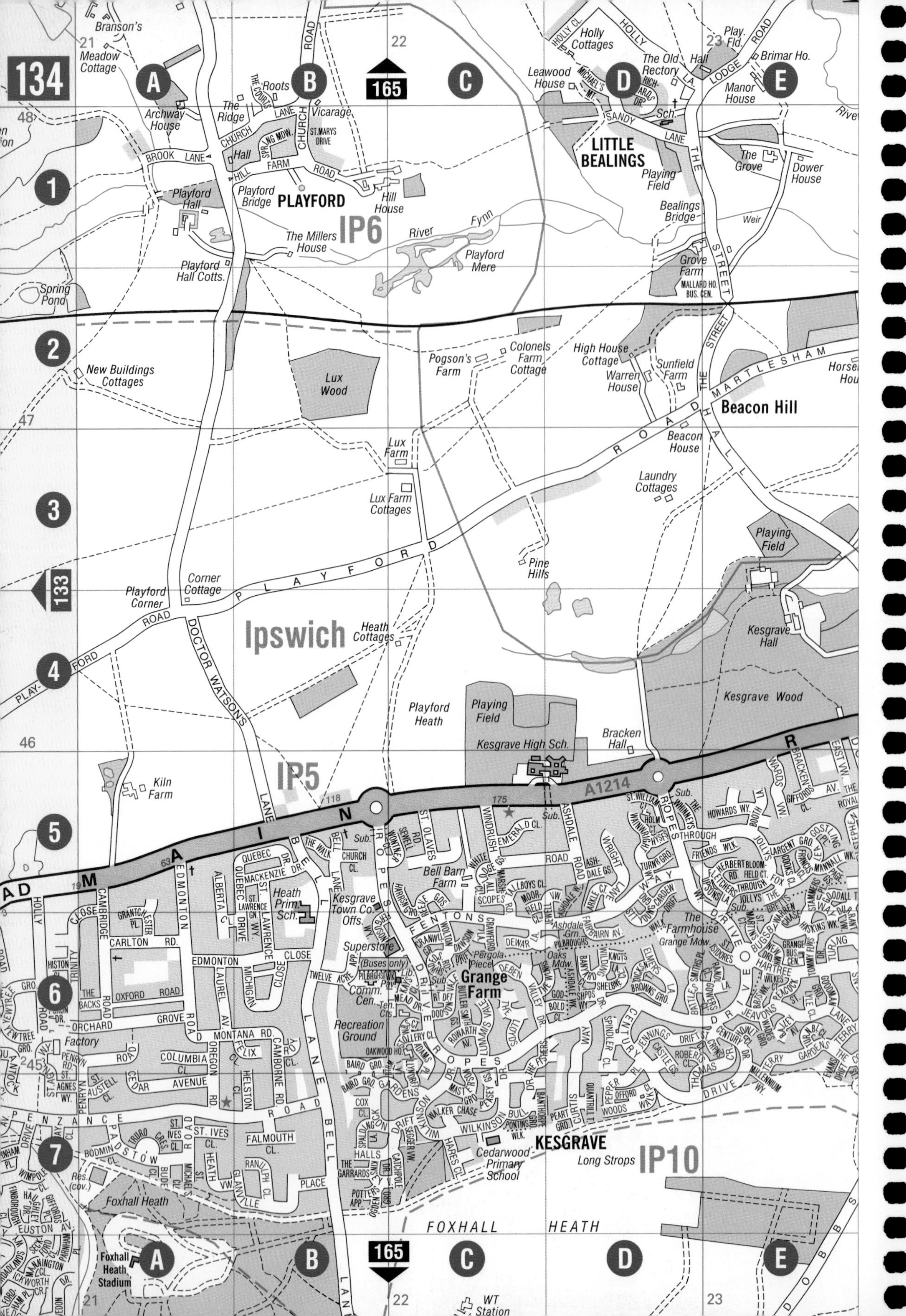

165
133
PLAYFORD
LITTLE BEALINGS
Beacon Hill
Ipswich
IP6
IP5
IP10
KESGRAVE
Grange Farm
Branson's
Meadow Cottage
Archway House
The Ridge
Roots
Vicarage
Hall
Playford Hall
Playford Bridge
Hill House
The Millers House
River Fynn
Playford Mere
Playford Hall Cotts.
Spring Pond
Leawood House
Holly Cottages
The Old Rectory
Hall
Play. Fld.
Brimar Ho.
Manor House
Sch.
The Grove
Dower House
Playing Field
Bealings Bridge
Weir
Grove Farm
MALLARD HO. BUS. CEN.
New Buildings Cottages
Lux Wood
Pogson's Farm
Colonels Farm Cottage
High House Cottage
Warren House
Sunfield Farm
Beacon House
Lux Farm
Lux Farm Cottages
Laundry Cottages
Pine Hills
Playing Field
Corner Cottage
Playford Corner
Heath Cottages
Kesgrave Hall
Kesgrave Wood
Playford Heath
Playing Field
Kesgrave High Sch.
Bracken Hall
Kiln Farm
A1214
BROOK LANE
CHURCH LANE
HILL FARM ROAD
SANDY LANE
THE STREET
LODGE LA.
HOLLY LA.
PLAYFORD ROAD
MARTLESHAM ROAD
HALL ROAD
DOCTOR WATSONS LANE
MAIN ROAD
BELL LANE
ROPES DRIVE
EDMONTON ROAD
Heath Prim. Sch.
Kesgrave Town Co. Offs.
Superstore
Bell Barn Farm
Comm. Cen.
Recreation Ground
The Farmhouse
Grange Mdw.
Factory
Cedarwood Primary School
Long Strops
Foxhall Heath
FOXHALL HEATH
Foxhall Heath Stadium
WT Station
21
22
23
48
47
46
45

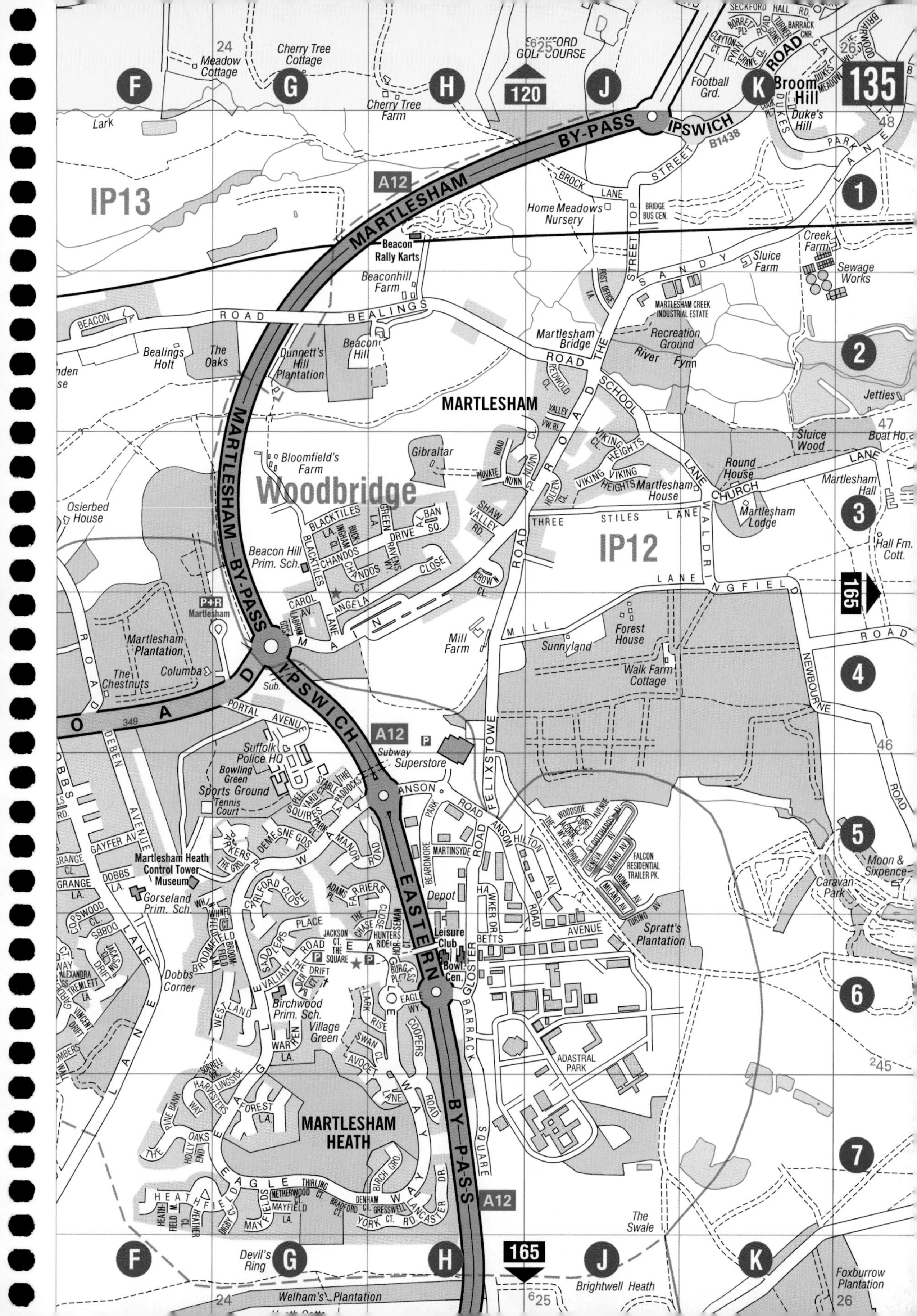

IP13
IP12
Woodbridge
MARTLESHAM
MARTLESHAM HEATH
MARTLESHAM BY-PASS
IPSWICH BY-PASS
EASTERN BY-PASS
A12
B1438
Broom Hill
Duke's Hill
Football Grd.
SECKFORD GOLF COURSE
Meadow Cottage
Cherry Tree Cottage
Cherry Tree Farm
Lark
Home Meadows Nursery
Bridge Bus Cen.
Beacon Rally Karts
Beaconhill Farm
Creek Farm
Sluice Farm
Sewage Works
Martlesham Creek Industrial Estate
Recreation Ground
Martlesham Bridge
River Fynn
Bealings Holt
The Oaks
Dunnett's Hill Plantation
Beacon Hill
Jetties
Sluice Wood
Boat Ho.
Round House
Martlesham Hall
Martlesham House
Martlesham Lodge
Hall Fm. Cott.
Bloomfield's Farm
Gibraltar
Osierbed House
Beacon Hill Prim. Sch.
P+R Martlesham
Martlesham Plantation
The Chestnuts
Columba
Mill Farm
Sunnyland
Forest House
Walk Farm Cottage
Suffolk Police HQ
Bowling Green
Sports Ground
Tennis Court
Subway
Superstore
Martlesham Heath Control Tower Museum
Gorseland Prim. Sch.
Depot
Leisure Club
Bowl. Cen.
Falcon Residential Trailer Pk.
Spratt's Plantation
Moon & Sixpence
Caravan Park
Dobbs Corner
Birchwood Prim. Sch.
Village Green
Adastral Park
The Swale
Devil's Ring
Brightwell Heath
Welham's Plantation
Foxburrow Plantation
120
165

SPROUGHTON
Sproughton Lodge
130
Abbey Oaks
Abbey Farm
Oak House
Tennis Cts.
Play. Fld.
Prim. Sch.
Bowling Green
Burial Ground
Rookery Farm
Sewage Works
RIVER
Chantry
The Rookery
Bungalow Farm
The Old Dairy
Clay Shooting Range
Garden Cottage
River's Farm
B1113
The Grove
Chantry Gro.
Red House Cottages
Red House Farm
Red House
BABERGH
IPSWICH
A14
Ivywell Farm
HURDLE MAKERS HILL
A1071
HADLEIGH ROAD
Springvale Cotts.
Springvale
WESTERN BY-PASS
Valley Farm Lodge
VALLEY
DRIVE
Hermitage Farm
Valley Farm
Valley Lodge Farm
West Ridge
Poplar Farm Cottages
Poplar Farm
POPLAR LANE
Hotel
Depot
FARM
Washbrook Street
LANE
HILL
Pigeons
164
PIGEON'S
The Grange
Cookshop Corner
IP8
Belstead Brook
Spring
London Rd. P+R
LONDON RD.
A1214
LONDON
Suffolk One
Works
SPRITES
GOLDCREST
MERLIN
SWALLOW
Sprites Prim. Sch.
Comm. Hall
COPDOCK INTERCHANGE
Superstores
Belstead Sch.
Hill Farm
Commerce Ho.
Washbrook Bri.
SWAN
STREET
THE MARVENS
CHAPEL LA.
White Cottage
Amor Hall
LONDON ROAD
Junction 55 (A14)
Junction 33 (A12)
Copdock Mill
MILL LANE
Belstead House Education & Conference Cen.
Belstead Brook
Sub.
Fen Farm
CHURCH LANE
SPRING RD.
CHARLOTTE'S
PEARSONS WY.
PHEASANT RI.
Highfield
CHERRY WOOD
Hall
Sch.
WASHBROOK
Hillbrook
DALES VW.
VIEW
Football Grd.
BACK LANE
HOLLOW RD.
COPDOCK MILL INTERCHANGE
IPSWICH
A14
A12
Copdock Hall
Ryecroft
ELM ROAD
WENHAM
POUND LANE
COPDOCK
Tennis Courts
Pav.
Playing Field
Felcourt Lodge
Rockwood
Copdock Lodge
Belstead Rise
Belstead Hall
BELSTEAD
Holly House
HOLLY LANE
The Gro
THE AVENUE
Felcourt
Green Close
OAKFIELD
Glebe Farm
Scot's Field
BUCK'S HORNS LA.
Buck's Horns
Mill Poultry Farm
Hall
Eight Elms Farm
164

F
G
H
J
K
1
2
3
4
5
6
7
131
4
138
149
IPSWICH
CHANTRY
MAIDENHALL
STOKE PARK
IP1
IP2
IP9
Ipswich
CHANTRY PARK
GIPPESWYK PARK
BOURNE PARK
HANDFORD RD.
CROWN
LONDON ROAD
A1214
CRANE HILL
HADLEIGH ROAD
RANELAGH ROAD
B1075
WEST END ROAD
A137
BURRELL ROAD
PRINCES ST.
GRAFTON W.
BELSTEAD ROAD
STONE LODGE LANE
HAWTHORN DRIVE
BIRKFIELD DRIVE
MALLARD WY.
SHELDRAKE DR.
CAMBRIDGE DR.
CORPORATION AVENUE
WHERSTEAD ROAD
SOUTHERN BY-PASS
A14
IPSWICH
Junction 56
North Lodge
The Chantry (Sue Ryder Home)
Nursery Lodge
Beech Lawn
Avenue Lodge
South Lodge
Horley Cott.
Gipeswyk Hall
Tennis Courts
Playground
Chantry High Sch.
Chantry High Sports Cen.
Beacon Hill Sch.
St.Joseph's Coll. with the Sch.of Jesus & Mary
St. Joseph's College Playing Field
Stone Lodge Park
Halifax Prim. Sch.
Maidenhall Sports Cen.
Ipswich Town FC (Portman Rd.)
Endeavour Ho.
Klick Fitness
Crown Ct.
Bus Depot
Gala Bingo
Orwell Retail Park
Superstore
Sea Scout Hut
Waste Covert
Gusford Prim. Sch.
Ellenbrook Open Space
Playing Field
Belstead Bridge
Belstead Brook
Spinney Covert
Paddling Pool
Bourne Bridge
Ashground Plantation
Alder Carr
Spring Wood Nature Reserve
Sewage Works
Braky Wood
Sandpit Covert
Thorington Hall
Chapman's Grove
Lodge Grove
Camp Yard
Bourne Hall Farm
Ski Slope
Ipswich Golf Range
Suffolk Ski Cen.
North Lodge
Home Covert
North Clump
Monmouth Ct. Nursing Home
Lombardy Pk. Res. Home
People's Comm. Pav. Gdn.
WHERSTEAD PARK

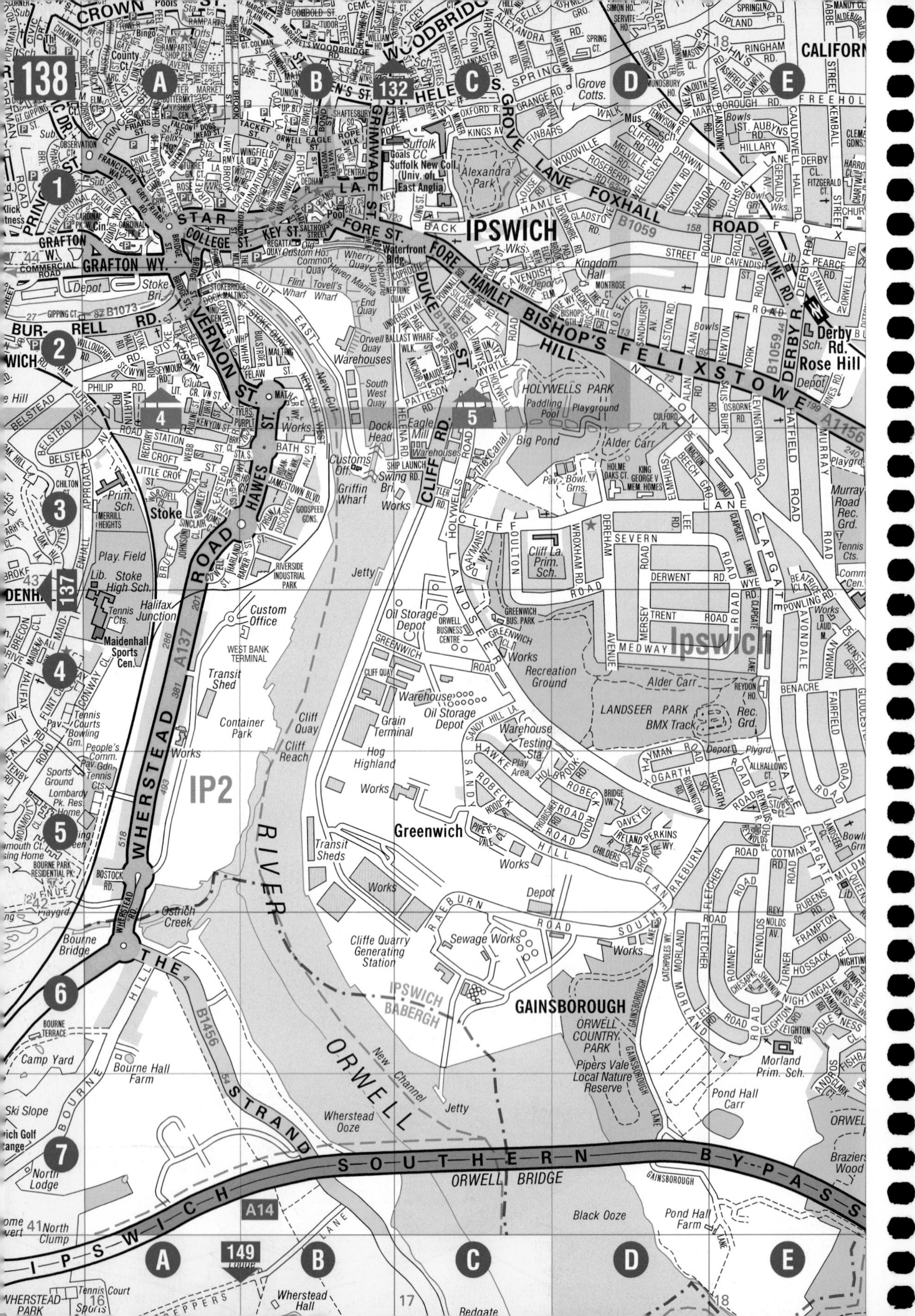

A
B
C
D
E
1
2
3
4
5
6
7
132
4
5
137
149
IPSWICH
Ipswich
IP2
CALIFORN
Greenwich
GAINSBOROUGH
Stoke
CROWN
WOODBRIDGE
ST. HELENS
SPRING
GROVE LANE
FOXHALL ROAD
FELIXSTOWE
BISHOP'S HILL
NACTON
FORE ST.
FORE HAMLET
STAR
COLLEGE ST.
KEY ST.
GRAFTON WY.
BURRELL RD.
VERNON ST.
HAWES ST.
CLIFF RD.
DUKE ST.
WHERSTEAD ROAD
THE STRAND
LANDSEER
CLIFF LANE
CLAPGATE LANE
RAEBURN ROAD
IPSWICH SOUTHERN BYPASS
ORWELL BRIDGE
RIVER ORWELL
New Channel
Alexandra Park
HOLYWELLS PARK
Paddling Pool
Playground
Big Pond
Alder Carr
Recreation Ground
LANDSEER PARK
BMX Track
Cliff La. Prim. Sch.
Oil Storage Depot
Grain Terminal
Container Park
Transit Shed
Cliff Quay
Cliff Reach
Hog Highland
Transit Sheds
Sewage Works
Cliffe Quarry Generating Station
IPSWICH
BABERGH
ORWELL COUNTRY PARK
Pipers Vale Local Nature Reserve
Pond Hall Carr
Pond Hall Farm
Black Ooze
Wherstead Ooze
Jetty
Ostrich Creek
Bourne Bridge
Bourne Hall Farm
Camp Yard
Ski Slope
North Lodge
Stoke High Sch.
Play. Field
Maidenhall Sports Cen.
Halifax Junction
Griffin Wharf
Dock Head
Customs Off.
Orwell Quay
South West Quay
Waterfront Bldg.
Suffolk New Coll.
Morland Prim. Sch.
Derby Rd.
Rose Hill
Murray Road Rec. Grd.
Kingdom Hall
A14
A137
A1156
B1059
B1073
B1456
B1458

139
133
165
164
F
G
H
J
K
1
2
3
4
5
6
7
19
20
21
41
42
43
44
RUSHMERE HEATH
HOSPITAL
HALLIWELL RD.
THANET RD.
THE DRIFTWAY
NEWBURY RD.
CANBERRA CL.
BRISBANE RD.
The Bridge Sch. Prim. Campus
Copleston High Sch.
Playing Field
Copleston Cen.
St. Elizabeth Hospice
Britannia Prim. Sch.
IP4
Works
REGINA CL.
COPLESTON RD.
SUFFOLK COASTAL
IPSWICH
Broke Hall Primary School
Play. Fld.
BROADLANDS WY.
AUDLEY GRO.
SHRUBLAND DR.
Foxhall Heath Stadium
Bixley Fm.
Hall
THE PASTURES
BIXLEY DR.
KELVEDON DR.
BIXLEY LANE
Brookhill Cottage
FOXHALL ROAD
ROAD
CHILTON ROAD
CHAPLAIN GDNS.
CLAVERTON WAY
CHATSWORTH DRIVE
GWENDOLINE DRIVE
GLEMHAM
HEATH ROAD
BIXLEY ROAD
A1189
ST. CLEMENTS HOSPITAL
Playing Field
Bowls
Tennis Ct.
CAMDEN
DOVER RD.
EXETER RD.
THE PIPPINS
TEMPLE RD.
PRINCETHORPE RD.
PENSHURST RD.
WIMBORNE AV.
HEATHLANDS PARK
HEATHLAND RETREAT CARAVAN PARK
Brook Hill
THE GREENS
EASTERN CL.
WESTERN CL.
VALLEYVIEW DR.
BROOKHILL
THE SPINNEY
Hospital (private) Golf Course
Robert Milne Ho.
Broke Hall
IPSWICH (PURDIS HEATH) GOLF COURSE
ST. AUGUSTINE RD.
RYE CL.
WINFRITH RD.
BODIAM RD.
MELPLASH RD.
BRIDPORT AV.
WAREHAM AV.
ARUNDEL WAY
Racecourse
LULWORTH AV.
POOLE CL.
BLANDFORD RD.
HORSHAM AV.
CUCKFIELD AV.
Decoy Pond
Black Heath
IP3
Treehouse Hospice
ASHDOWN WAY
DORCHESTER RD.
WADHURST RD.
SALEHURST RD.
LEWES CL.
Decoypond Wood
Decoy House
Bixley Heath
BROKE HALL HO.
Mill
River
Club House
Hillingdon
Purdis Rise
PURDIS FARM LA.
RAMSGATE DR.
MARGATE RD.
ASCOT DRIVE
MALVERN CL.
KING EDWARD RD.
HAMILTON RD.
SHACKLETON RD.
ROAD
COBHAM RD.
KING'S WAY
QUEEN'S WAY
RANSOME RD.
Rec. Grd.
BUCKLESHAM ROAD
The Chase
PURDIS FARM LANE
Ipswich Transport Mus.
WARREN HEATH RD.
WARREN HEATH AV.
FELIXSTOWE ROAD
Purdis Farm
Purdis Croft
PURDIS AVENUE
St. Augustines Rec. Grd.
Pav.
Bowl. Grn.
Sports Grd.
BADER CL.
GIBSON CL.
Superstores
WOODRUSH RD.
ROWAN CL.
DOGWOOD CL.
Warren Heath
FOXGLOVE RD.
MURRILLS RD.
ESSEX WAY
HAZEL DR.
ACACIA CRES.
PINE DR.
MEADOW CRESCENT
ASH CL.
Ipswich Academy
HOLYWELLS CT.
CLARENCE RD.
NACTON ROAD
GROSVENOR CT.
MILDMAY RD.
WYNTERTON
HILTON RD.
CRANWELL CR.
CAMPBELL RD.
LINDBERGH RD.
Depot
Warehouse
ALTITUDE BUSINESS PARK
Priory Heath
THE DRIFT
UXBRIDGE CRES.
RANSOMES WAY
A1156
Suffolk Showground
SHENLEY RD.
THEBERTON RD.
CORTON RD.
BOYTON RD.
MARYON RD.
LESLIE RD.
ALSTON'S CT.
THE QUADRANGLE CENTRE
EURO RETAIL PARK
EPSILON T.
DELTA T.
GAMMA T.
BETA T.
ALPHA T.
WEST RD.
Engineering Works
RANSOMES EUROPARK
CENTRAL AVENUE
FRONT RD.
Nacton Heath
Driving Test Cen.
LATIMER CL.
WENTWORTH
Cattle Pens
ROAD
Gainsborough Sports & Comm. Cen.
Gymnastics Centre
RAVENSWOOD
BONNY CR.
WITNEY CL.
HENING AV.
RANSOMES WY.
ROAD
Playing Field
Ravenswood Prim. Sch.
PASHFORD PL.
AVENUE
CRESCENT
FOXTAIL RD.
BLUESTEM RD.
RANSOMES EUROPARK
Superstore
BASEPOINT CENTRE
LYTHAM RD.
HAVENS
FRESTON ROAD
NACTON RD.
BERMUDA RD.
Fox's Heath
David Lloyd Ipswich
BELFRY RD.
Round Plantation
ALNESBOURN CRES.
Halfway House
AUGUSTA CL.
MELFORD CT.
MEDITE HO.
Airport Farm
Playgrd.
CIRCLE
SOUTHERN BY-PASS
IPSWICH
A14
IP10
Junction 57
MANSBROOK VILLAS
NACTON RD.
IPSWICH ROAD
Square Covert
ORWELL MEADOWS CARAVAN SITE
ALNESBOURNE PRIORY
Robert's Grove
Broom Hill
Reservoir
Whin Covert
COUNTRY PARK
PLATTERS RD.
BRAZIER'S WOOD RD.

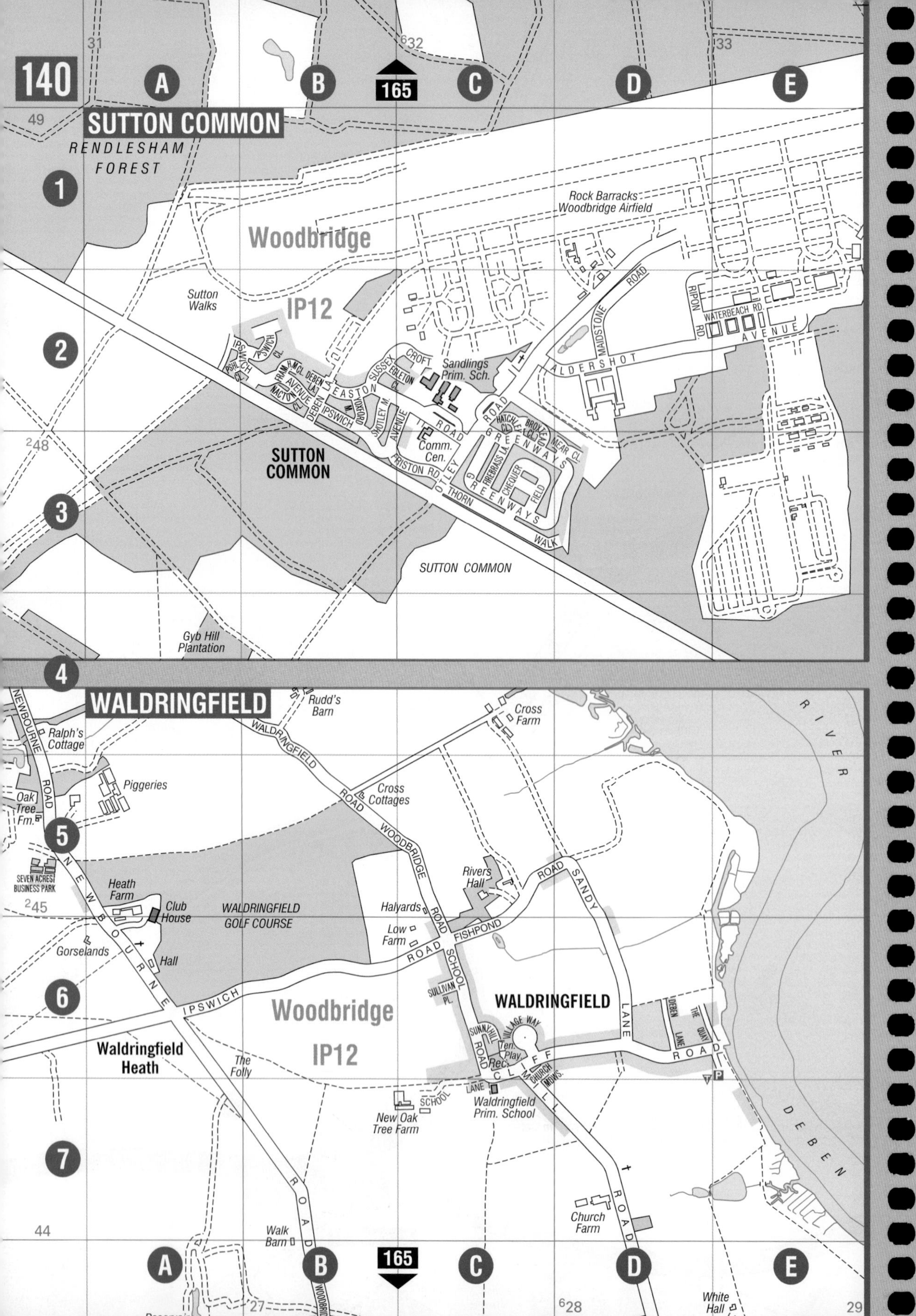
SUTTON COMMON
RENDLESHAM FOREST
Woodbridge
Rock Barracks
Woodbridge Airfield
Sutton Walks
IP12
Sandlings Prim. Sch.
Comm. Cen.
SUTTON COMMON
SUTTON COMMON
Gyb Hill Plantation
IPSWICH ROAD
OTLEY ROAD
MAIDSTONE ROAD
ALDERSHOT
WATERBEACH RD.
RIPON RD.
AVENUE
GREENWAYS
THORN WALK
FRISTON RD.
CROFT
SUSSEX
EGLETON CL.
EASTON
DEBEN AVENUE
NACTON CL.
HATCHLEY CL.
BROXTED
NEAR CL.
FIREBRASS LA.
CHEQUER FIELD
WALDRINGFIELD
Rudd's Barn
Cross Farm
Ralph's Cottage
Piggeries
Cross Cottages
Oak Tree Fm.
SEVEN ACRES BUSINESS PARK
Heath Farm
Club House
Hall
Gorselands
WALDRINGFIELD GOLF COURSE
WALDRINGFIELD ROAD
WOODBRIDGE ROAD
NEWBOURNE ROAD
Rivers Hall
Halyards
Low Farm
FISHPOND ROAD
SANDY LANE
SCHOOL ROAD
SULLIVAN PL.
WALDRINGFIELD
VILLAGE WAY
SUNNYHILL
Ten. Play.
Rec.
CLIFF ROAD
CHURCH MDWS.
MILL ROAD
SCHOOL LANE
Waldringfield Prim. School
Woodbridge
IP12
Waldringfield Heath
The Folly
New Oak Tree Farm
Church Farm
Walk Barn
DEBEN LANE
THE QUAY
RIVER DEBEN
White Hall
165
165
A
B
C
D
E
1
2
3
4
5
6
7
31
32
33
49
48
45
44
27
28
29

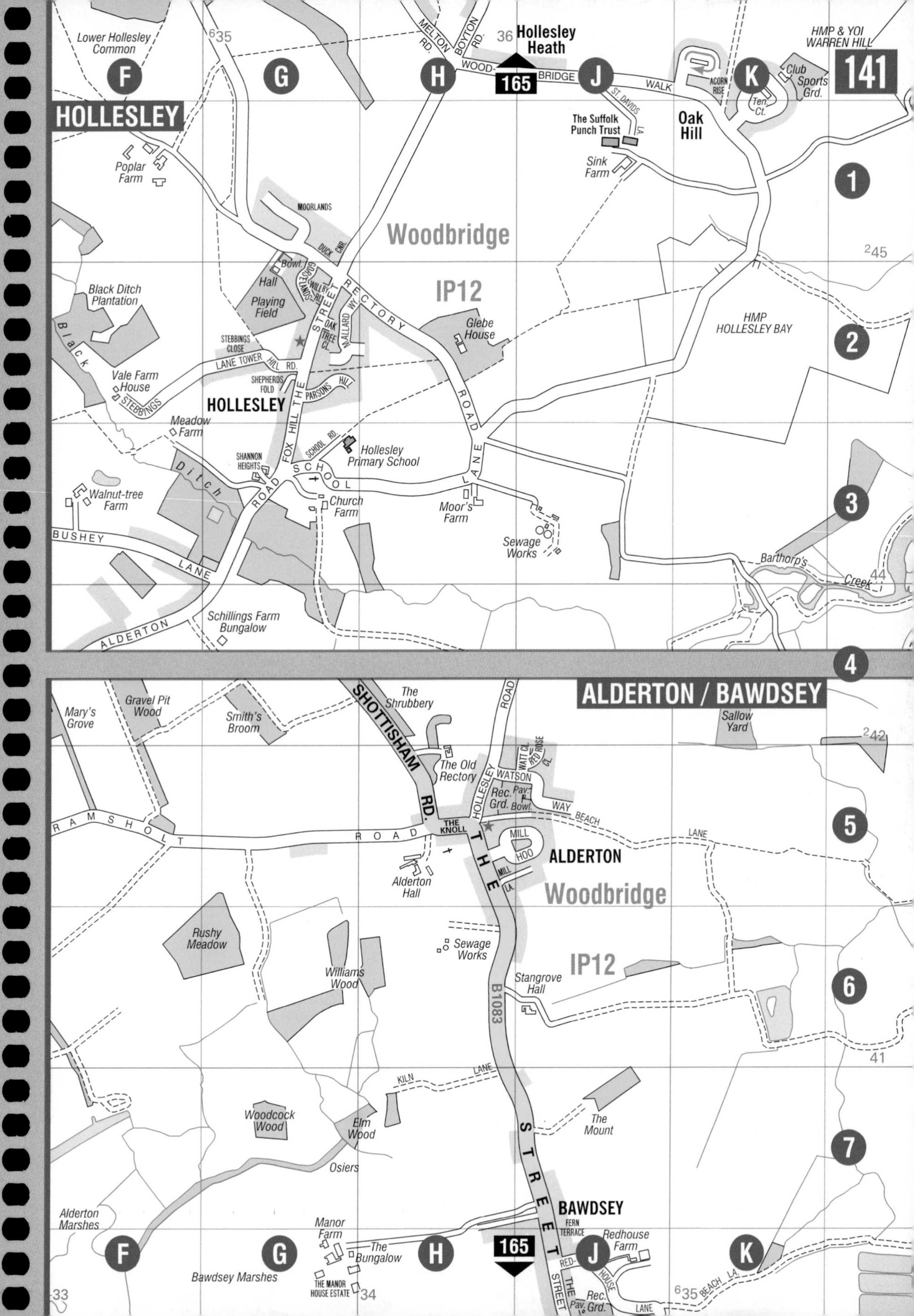
HOLLESLEY
ALDERTON / BAWDSEY
Lower Hollesley Common
Hollesley Heath
165
HMP & YOI WARREN HILL
The Suffolk Punch Trust
Oak Hill
Sink Farm
Poplar Farm
Woodbridge
IP12
Black Ditch Plantation
Playing Field
Glebe House
HMP HOLLESLEY BAY
Vale Farm House
HOLLESLEY
Meadow Farm
Hollesley Primary School
Walnut-tree Farm
Church Farm
Moor's Farm
Sewage Works
Barthorp's Creek
Schillings Farm Bungalow
Mary's Grove
Gravel Pit Wood
Smith's Broom
The Shrubbery
Sallow Yard
The Old Rectory
ALDERTON
Alderton Hall
Rushy Meadow
Williams Wood
Stangrove Hall
Woodcock Wood
Elm Wood
The Mount
Osiers
BAWDSEY
Alderton Marshes
Manor Farm
The Bungalow
Bawdsey Marshes
Redhouse Farm
THE MANOR HOUSE ESTATE
F
G
H
J
K
1
2
3
4
5
6
7

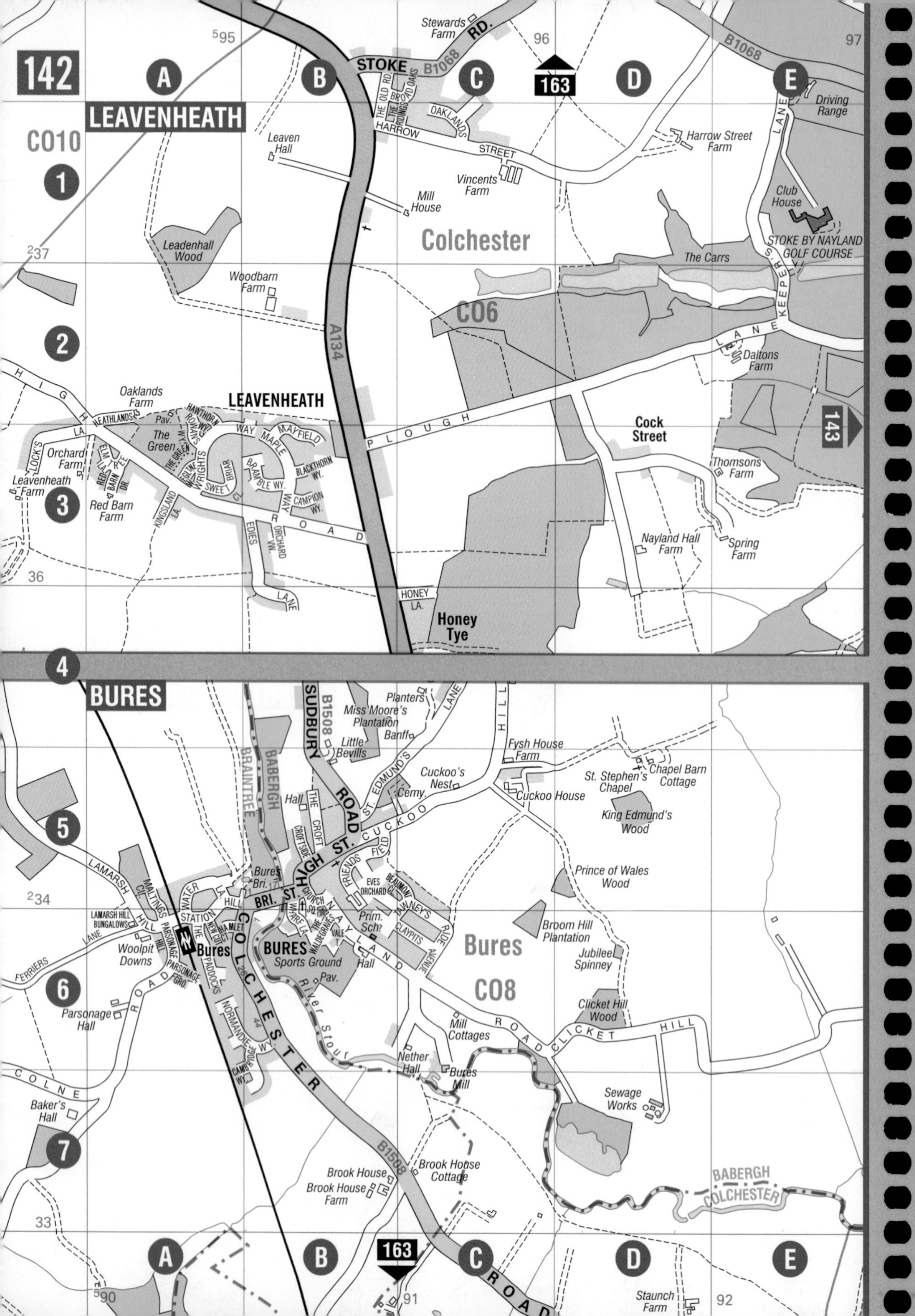

LEAVENHEATH
CO10
Stewards Farm
STOKE
B1068
RD.
163
Driving Range
Leaven Hall
Harrow Street Farm
HARROW STREET
OAKLANDS
Vincents Farm
Mill House
Club House
STOKE BY NAYLAND GOLF COURSE
Colchester
Leadenhall Wood
The Carrs
Woodbarn Farm
CO6
A134
KEEPERS LANE
Daltons Farm
Oaklands Farm
LEAVENHEATH
HIGH ROAD
PLOUGH LANE
Cock Street
143
Orchard Farm
The Green
Leavenheath Farm
Red Barn Farm
Thomsons Farm
Nayland Hall Farm
Spring Farm
HONEY LA.
Honey Tye
BURES
Planters
Miss Moore's Plantation
Little Bevills
Banff
SUDBURY ROAD
B1508
BABERGH
BRAINTREE
Fysh House Farm
Cuckoo's Nest
Cemy.
St. Stephen's Chapel
Chapel Barn Cottage
Cuckoo House
King Edmund's Wood
HIGH ST.
CUCKOO
Prince of Wales Wood
LAMARSH HILL
Bures Bri.
BRI. ST.
Station
Bures
BURES
Sports Ground
Pav.
Prim. Sch.
Hall
Broom Hill Plantation
Bures
Jubilee Spinney
CO8
Woolpit Downs
FERRIERS LANE
Parsonage Hall
COLCHESTER
NAYLAND ROAD
CLICKET HILL
Clicket Hill Wood
Mill Cottages
River Stour
Nether Hall
Bures Mill
COLNE
Baker's Hall
Sewage Works
Brook House
Brook House Farm
Brook House Cottage
B1508
BABERGH
COLCHESTER
COLCHESTER ROAD
Staunch Farm

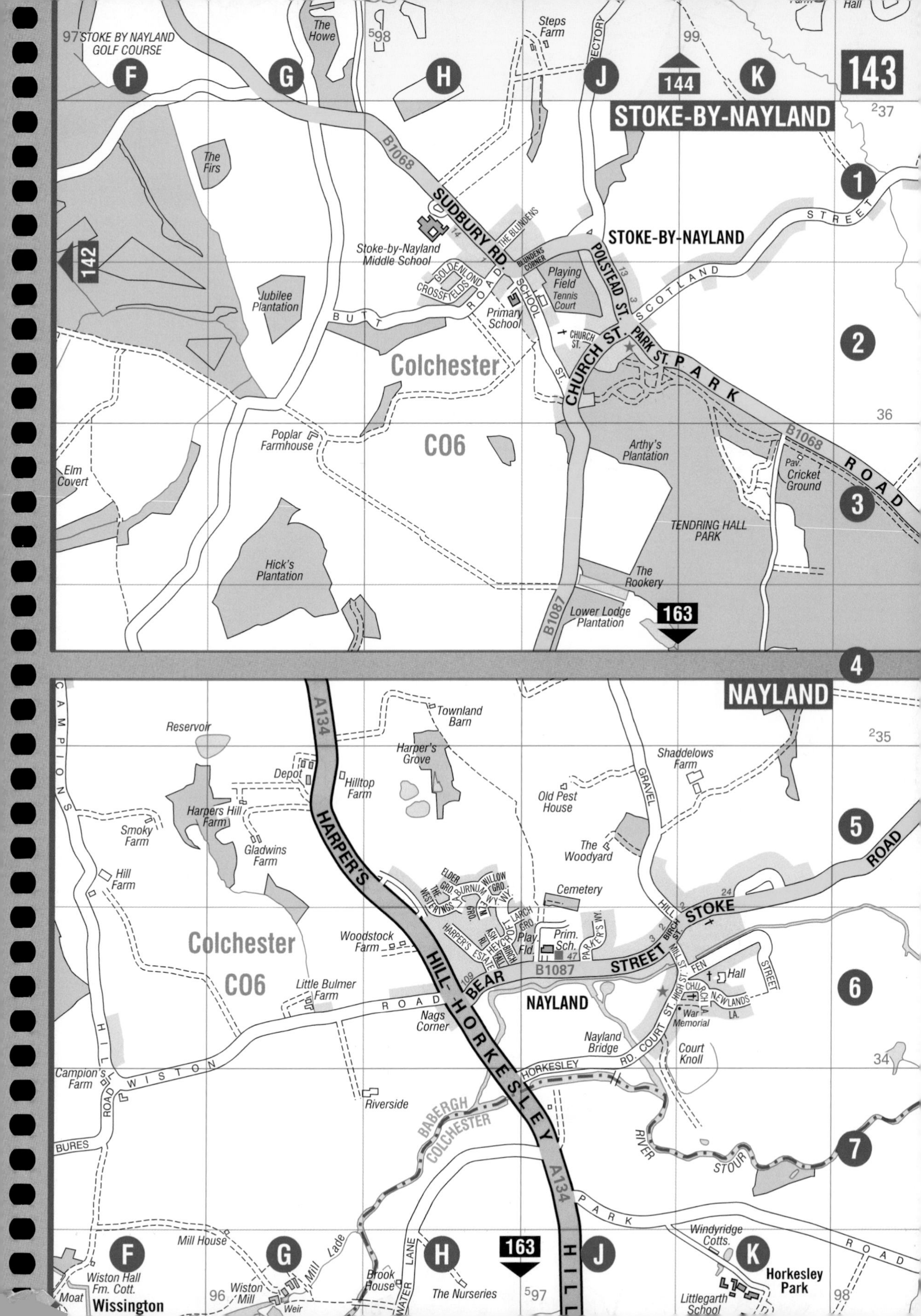
STOKE-BY-NAYLAND
NAYLAND
STOKE BY NAYLAND GOLF COURSE
The Howe
Steps Farm
The Firs
Stoke-by-Nayland Middle School
Jubilee Plantation
SUDBURY RD.
THE BLUNDENS
BLUNDENS CORNER
GOLDENLOND
CROSSFIELDS
BUTT ROAD
Playing Field
Tennis Court
Primary School
SCHOOL ST.
CHURCH ST.
POLSTEAD ST.
SCOTLAND STREET
PARK ST.
PARK ROAD
Colchester
CO6
Poplar Farmhouse
Elm Covert
Arthy's Plantation
Cricket Ground
Pav.
TENDRING HALL PARK
Hick's Plantation
The Rookery
Lower Lodge Plantation
B1068
B1087
A134
Townland Barn
Reservoir
Harper's Grove
Depot
Hilltop Farm
Shaddelows Farm
Old Pest House
Harpers Hill Farm
Smoky Farm
Gladwins Farm
The Woodyard
Hill Farm
HARPER'S HILL
Cemetery
ELDER GRO.
WILLOW GRO.
LABURNUM WY.
THE WESTERINGS
HARPER'S ESTATE
HEYCROFT
LARCH GRO.
Play. Fld.
Prim. Sch.
PARKER'S WY.
Woodstock Farm
BEAR STREET
STOKE ROAD
GRAVEL HILL
BIRCH ST.
MILL ST.
HIGH ST.
FEN ST.
Hall
CHURCH LA.
NEWLANDS LA.
War Memorial
Little Bulmer Farm
Nags Corner
NAYLAND
Nayland Bridge
COURT ST.
Court Knoll
HORKESLEY RD.
HORKESLEY
CAMPIONS HILL
Campion's Farm
WISTON ROAD
BURES ROAD
Riverside
BABERGH
COLCHESTER
RIVER STOUR
PARK ROAD
Mill House
Mill Lade
WATER LANE
Brook House
The Nurseries
Windyridge Cotts.
Horkesley Park
Littlegarth School
Wiston Hall Fm. Cott.
Moat
Wissington
Wiston Mill
Weir
F G H J K
1 2 3 4 5 6 7
142 144 163

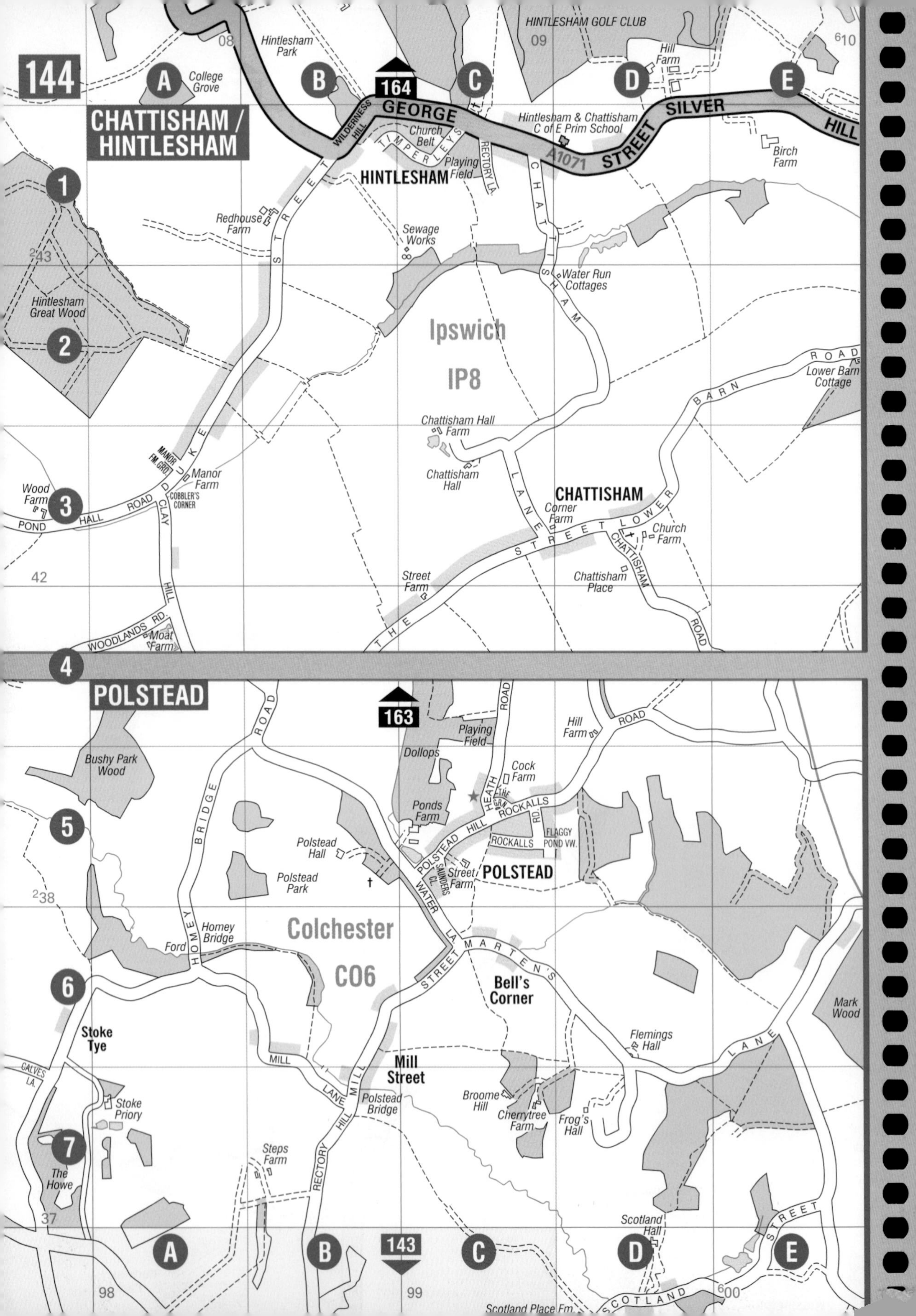
CHATTISHAM / HINTLESHAM
POLSTEAD
164
163
143
HINTLESHAM GOLF CLUB
Hintlesham Park
College Grove
Hill Farm
GEORGE
SILVER
STREET
HILL
A1071
Hintlesham & Chattisham C of E Prim School
Birch Farm
WILDERNESS HILL
Church Belt
TIMPERLEYS
Playing Field
RECTORY LA.
HINTLESHAM
Redhouse Farm
Sewage Works
Water Run Cottages
Hintlesham Great Wood
Ipswich
IP8
CHATTISHAM
DUKE STREET
ROAD
BARN
Lower Barn Cottage
Chattisham Hall Farm
Chattisham Hall
LANE
MANOR FM. GRD.
Manor Farm
COBBLER'S CORNER
Wood Farm
POND HALL ROAD
CLAY HILL
Corner Farm
THE STREET
LOWER
Church Farm
Chattisham Place
Street Farm
WOODLANDS RD.
Moat Farm
Bushy Park Wood
HOMEY BRIDGE ROAD
HEATH ROAD
Hill Farm
Playing Field
Dollops
Cock Farm
Ponds Farm
THE GRN
ROCKALLS RD.
POLSTEAD HILL
FLAGGY POND VW.
Polstead Hall
Polstead Park
SAUNDERS CL.
Street Farm
POLSTEAD
WATER LA.
Colchester
CO6
Homey Bridge
Ford
MARTEN'S
Bell's Corner
Stoke Tye
Mark Wood
Flemings Hall
LANE
MILL
Mill Street
MILL HILL
CALVES LA.
Stoke Priory
Polstead Bridge
Broome Hill
Cherrytree Farm
Frog's Hall
The Howe
Steps Farm
RECTORY HILL
Scotland Hall
STREET
SCOTLAND
Scotland Place Fm.

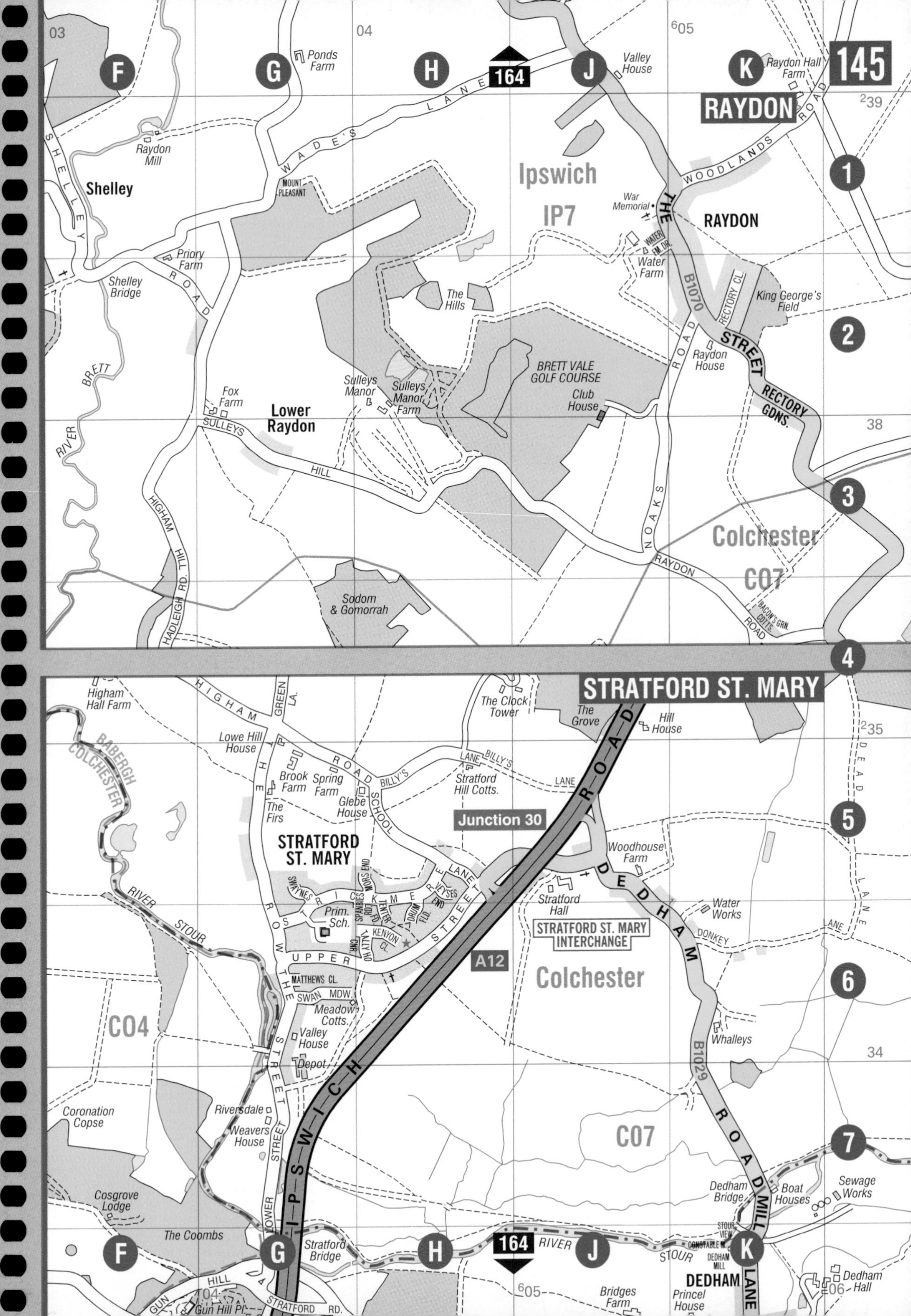
RAYDON
Shelley
Raydon Mill
Ponds Farm
Valley House
Raydon Hall Farm
WADE'S LANE
SHELLEY
Ipswich
IP7
RAYDON
WOODLANDS ROAD
War Memorial
THE STREET
Priory Farm
ROAD
Shelley Bridge
Water Farm
The Hills
King George's Field
RECTORY CL.
B1070
RIVER BRETT
BRETT VALE GOLF COURSE
Club House
Raydon House
RECTORY GDNS.
Fox Farm
Lower Raydon
Sulleys Manor
Sulleys Manor Farm
SULLEYS HILL
HIGHAM HILL
HADLEIGH RD.
NOAKS ROAD
RAYDON ROAD
Colchester
CO7
Sodom & Gomorrah
BACON'S GRN. COTTS.
STRATFORD ST. MARY
Higham Hall Farm
HIGHAM
GREEN LA.
The Clock Tower
The Grove
Hill House
Lowe Hill House
BABERGH COLCHESTER
Brook Farm
Spring Farm
Glebe House
The Firs
BILLY'S LANE
Stratford Hill Cotts.
SCHOOL LANE
Junction 30
STRATFORD ST. MARY
Woodhouse Farm
Stratford Hall
DEDHAM ROAD
Water Works
DONKEY LANE
DEAD LANE
STRATFORD ST. MARY INTERCHANGE
RIVER STOUR
Prim. Sch.
KENYON CL.
UPPER STREET
A12
Colchester
MATTHEWS CL.
SWAN MDW.
Meadow Cotts.
CO4
Valley House
Depot
Whalleys
B1029
THE STREET
IPSWICH ROAD
Coronation Copse
Riversdale
Weavers House
CO7
Dedham Bridge
Boat Houses
Sewage Works
MILL LANE
Cosgrove Lodge
The Coombs
TOWER
Stratford Bridge
RIVER STOUR
164
STOUR VIEW
DEDHAM MILL
DEDHAM
Dedham Hall
Bridges Farm
Princel House
GUN HILL
Gun Hill Pl.
STRATFORD RD.

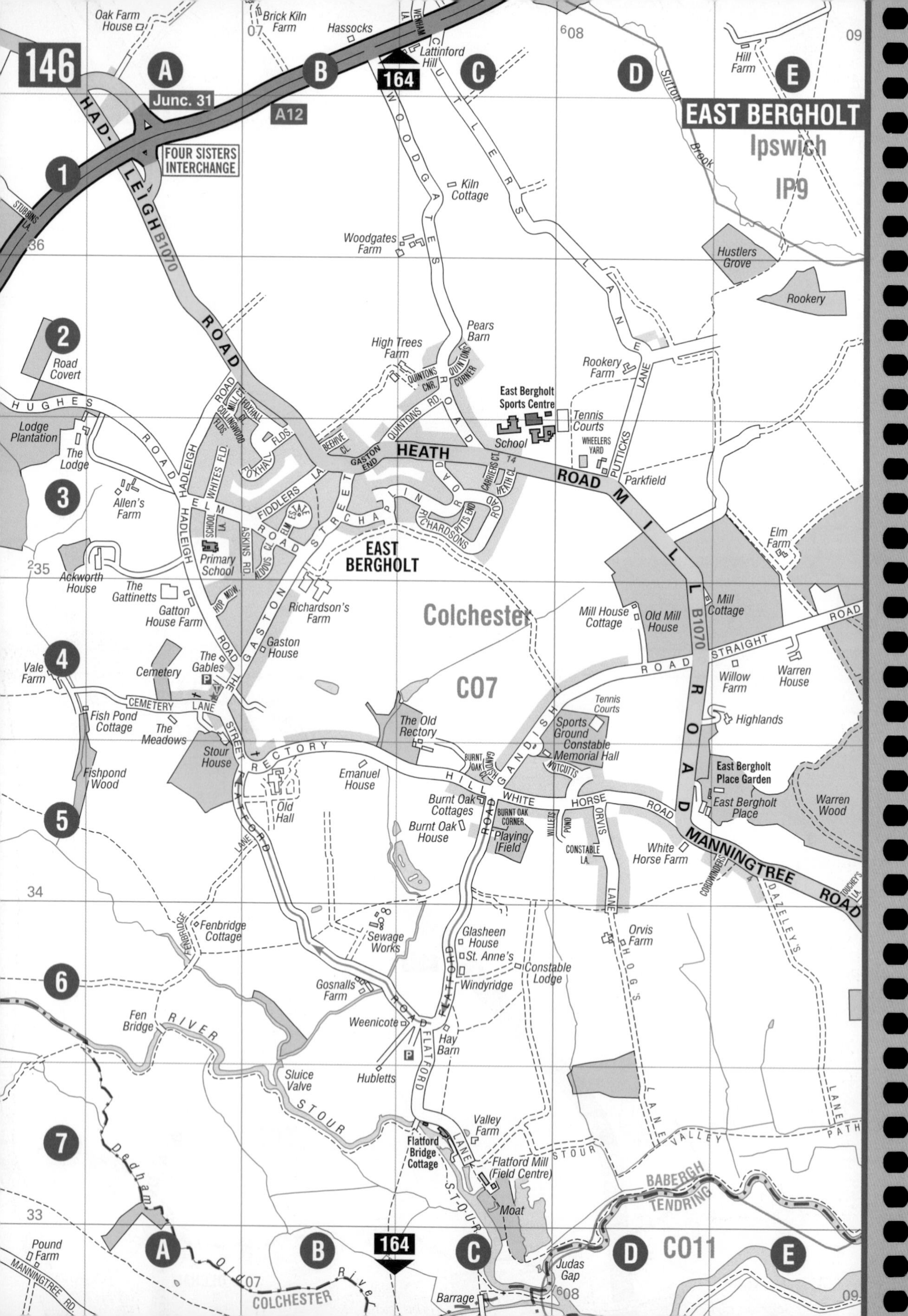
EAST BERGHOLT
Ipswich
IP9
Colchester
CO7
CO11
EAST BERGHOLT
Junc. 31
FOUR SISTERS INTERCHANGE
A12
HADLEIGH ROAD
B1070
HEATH ROAD
MILL ROAD
MANNINGTREE ROAD
STRAIGHT ROAD
RECTORY HILL
WHITE HORSE ROAD
GASTON STREET
FLATFORD ROAD
FLATFORD LANE
CUTLERS LANE
WOODGATES ROAD
HUGHES ROAD
CEMETERY LANE
CHAPLIN ROAD
ELM ROAD
GANDISH ROAD
HOG'S LANE
VALLEY LANE
RIVER STOUR
Oak Farm House
Brick Kiln Farm
Hassocks
Lattinford Hill
Hill Farm
Kiln Cottage
Woodgates Farm
Hustlers Grove
Rookery
Pears Barn
High Trees Farm
Rookery Farm
East Bergholt Sports Centre
Tennis Courts
School
Parkfield
Road Covert
Lodge Plantation
The Lodge
Allen's Farm
Primary School
Ackworth House
The Gattinetts
Gatton House Farm
Richardson's Farm
Gaston House
Mill House Cottage
Old Mill House
Mill Cottage
Elm Farm
Willow Farm
Warren House
Highlands
Vale Farm
Cemetery
The Gables
Fish Pond Cottage
The Meadows
Stour House
Fishpond Wood
The Old Rectory
Emanuel House
Old Hall
Sports Ground
Constable Memorial Hall
East Bergholt Place Garden
East Bergholt Place
Warren Wood
Burnt Oak Cottages
Burnt Oak House
Playing Field
White Horse Farm
Fenbridge Cottage
Sewage Works
Glasheen House
St. Anne's
Constable Lodge
Windyridge
Orvis Farm
Gosnalls Farm
Fen Bridge
Weenicote
Hay Barn
Hubletts
Sluice Valve
Valley Farm
Flatford Bridge Cottage
Flatford Mill (Field Centre)
Moat
Judas Gap
Barrage
Pound Farm
BABERGH
TENDRING
Dedham
Old River
COLCHESTER
164
164
A B C D E
1 2 3 4 5 6 7

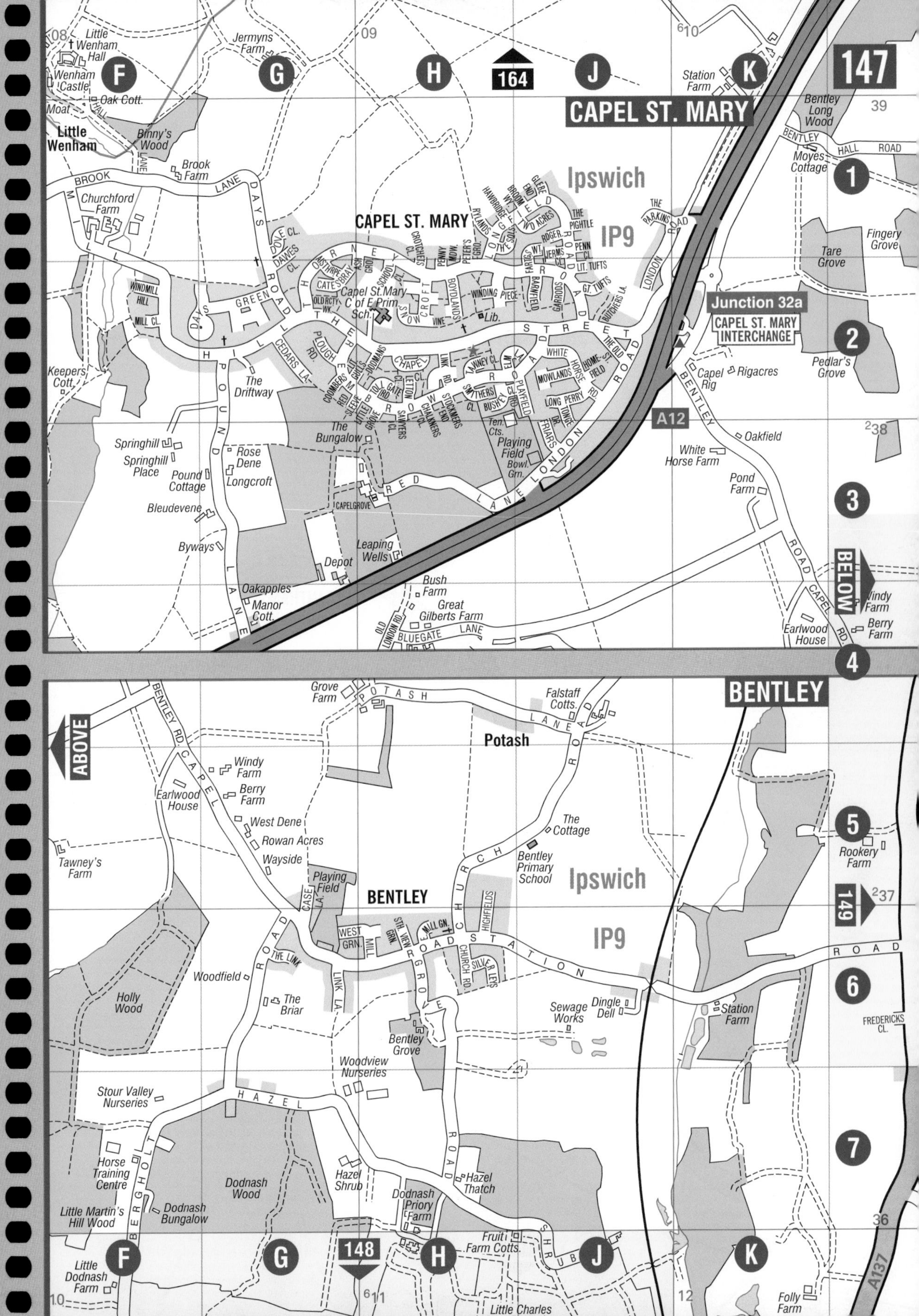
147
164
CAPEL ST. MARY
Little Wenham Hall
Wenham Castle
Moat
Oak Cott.
Little Wenham
Binny's Wood
Jermyns Farm
Station Farm
Bentley Long Wood
BENTLEY HALL ROAD
Moyes Cottage
Brook Farm
BROOK LANE
Churchford Farm
DAYS ROAD
Ipswich
IP9
CAPEL ST. MARY
THE PARKINS ROAD
Fingery Grove
Tare Grove
Capel St.Mary C of E Prim. Sch.
Lib.
WINDING PIECE
THE STREET
LONDON ROAD
Junction 32a
CAPEL ST. MARY INTERCHANGE
Capel Rig
Rigacres
Pedlar's Grove
Keepers Cott.
The Driftway
Springhill
Springhill Place
Rose Dene
Longcroft
Pound Cottage
The Bungalow
Playing Field
Bowl. Grn.
Ten. Cts.
A12
White Horse Farm
Oakfield
Pond Farm
RED LANE
CAPELGROVE
Bleudevene
Byways
POUND LANE
Leaping Wells
Depot
Oakapples
Manor Cott.
Bush Farm
Great Gilberts Farm
BLUEGATE LANE
OLD LONDON RD.
BELOW
Windy Farm
Berry Farm
Earlwood House
CAPEL RD.
BENTLEY
ABOVE
Grove Farm
POTASH LANE
Falstaff Cotts.
Potash
BENTLEY RD.
Windy Farm
Berry Farm
Earlwood House
West Dene
Rowan Acres
Wayside
Tawney's Farm
The Cottage
Bentley Primary School
CHURCH ROAD
Ipswich
IP9
Playing Field
BENTLEY
Rookery Farm
149
STATION ROAD
Woodfield
The Briar
Holly Wood
Sewage Works
Dingle Dell
Station Farm
FREDERICKS CL.
Bentley Grove
Woodview Nurseries
Stour Valley Nurseries
HAZEL SHRUB
Horse Training Centre
Dodnash Wood
Hazel Shrub
Hazel Thatch
Dodnash Priory Farm
Little Martin's Hill Wood
Dodnash Bungalow
BERGHOLT ROAD
148
Fruit Farm Cotts.
Little Dodnash Farm
Little Charles
Folly Farm
A137

BRANTHAM / CATTAWADE

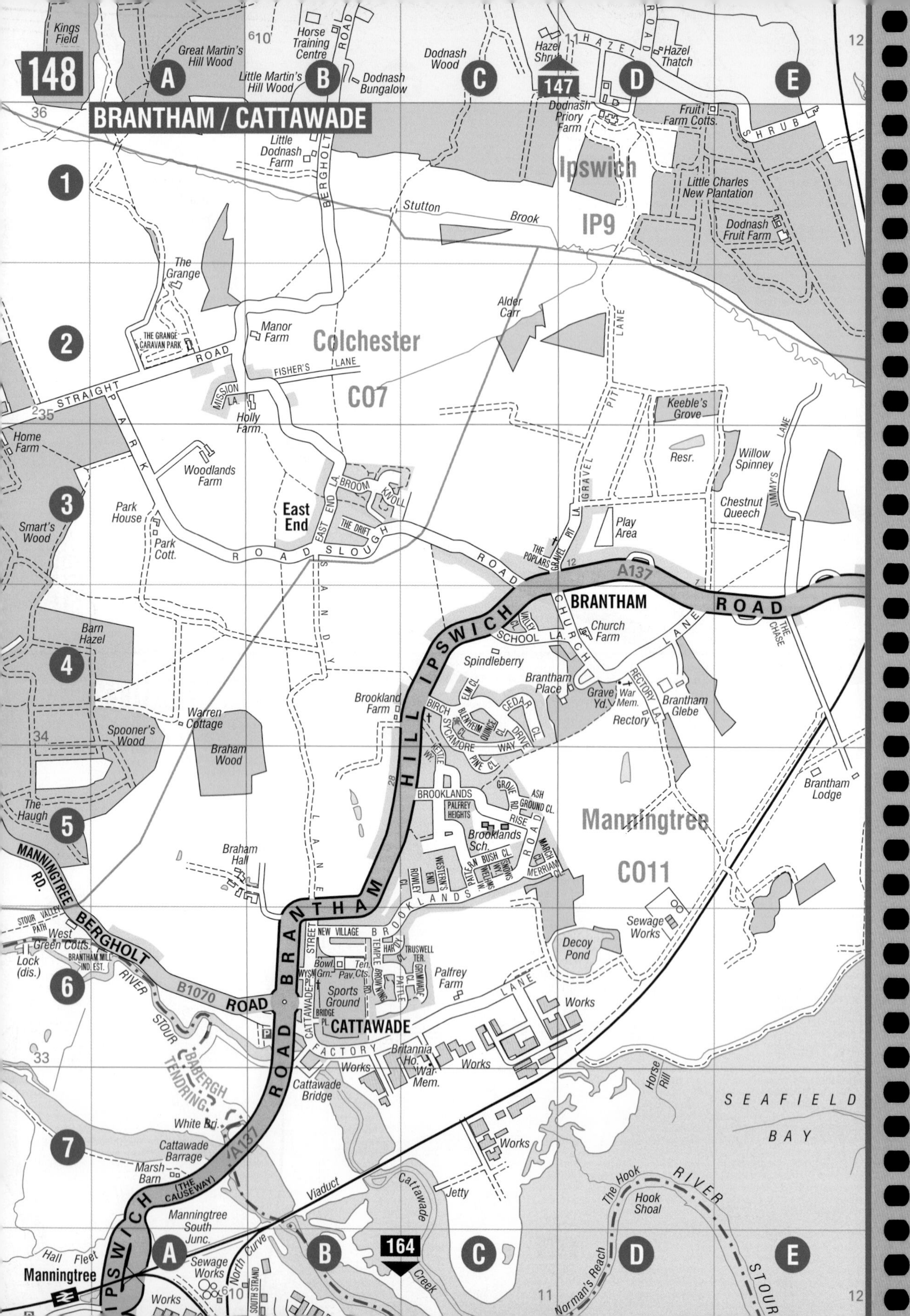

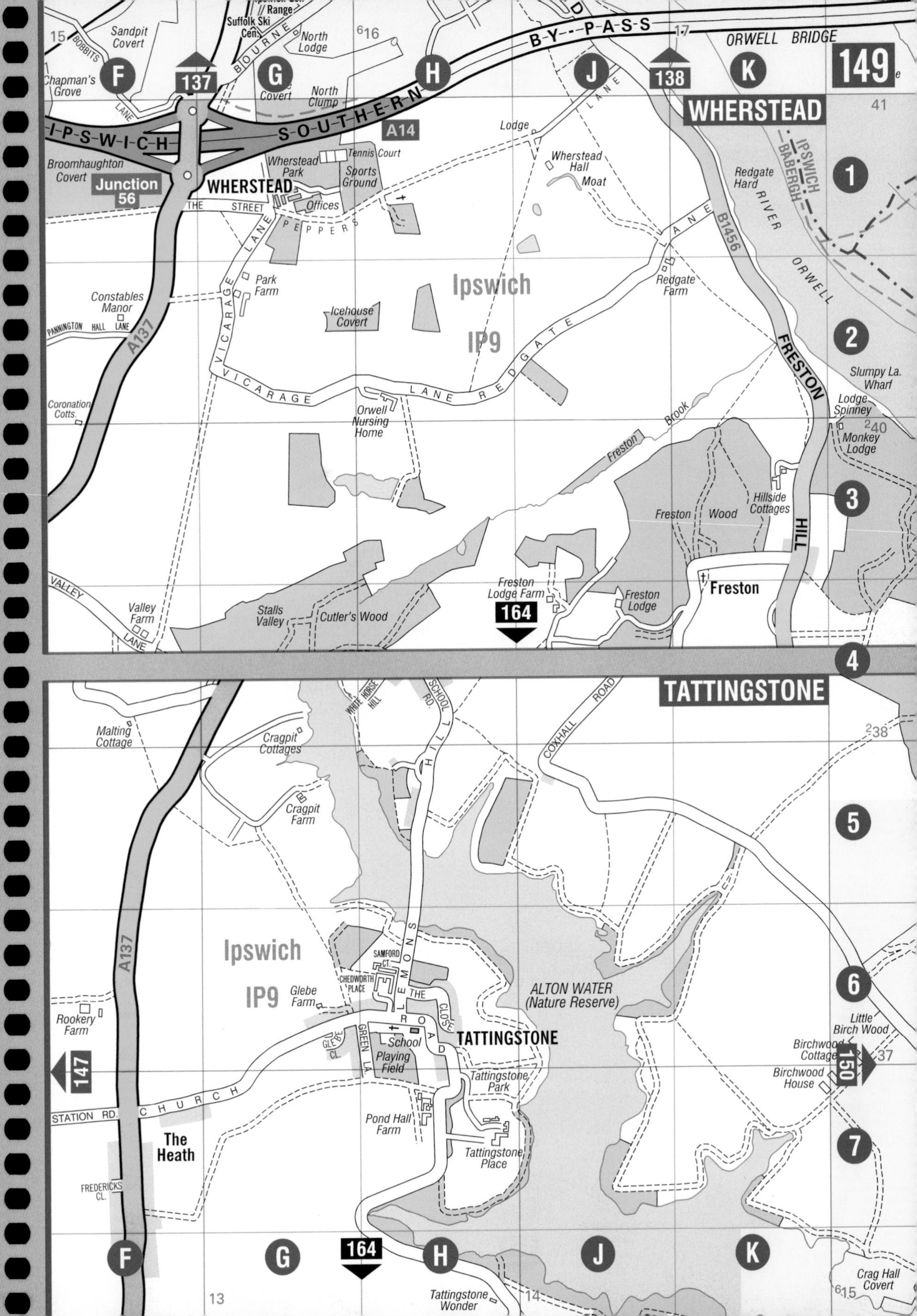
WHERSTEAD
TATTINGSTONE
IPSWICH SOUTHERN BY-PASS
ORWELL BRIDGE
Junction 56
A14
A137
B1456
Ipswich
IP9
Sandpit Covert
Suffolk Ski Cen.
Range
North Lodge
Chapman's Grove
Covert
North Clump
Broomhaughton Covert
Wherstead Park
Tennis Court
Sports Ground
Offices
THE STREET
PEPPERS LANE
VICARAGE LANE
REDGATE LANE
Lodge
Wherstead Hall
Moat
Redgate Hard
RIVER ORWELL
IPSWICH
BABERGH
Redgate Farm
Park Farm
Constables Manor
PANNINGTON HALL LANE
Icehouse Covert
Coronation Cotts.
Orwell Nursing Home
FRESTON HILL
Slumpy La. Wharf
Lodge Spinney
Monkey Lodge
Freston Brook
Hillside Cottages
Freston Wood
Freston
Freston Lodge
Freston Lodge Farm
Stalls Valley
Cutler's Wood
Valley Farm
VALLEY LANE
WHITE HORSE HILL
SCHOOL RD.
COXHALL ROAD
Malting Cottage
Cragpit Cottages
Cragpit Farm
HILL
LEMONS
SAMFORD CT.
CHEDWORTH PLACE
THE CLOSE
Glebe Farm
Rookery Farm
ALTON WATER (Nature Reserve)
GLEBE CL.
GREEN LA.
ROAD
School
Playing Field
Tattingstone Park
Pond Hall Farm
Tattingstone Place
CHURCH
STATION RD.
The Heath
FREDERICKS CL.
Little Birch Wood
Birchwood Cottage
Birchwood House
Crag Hall Covert
Tattingstone Wonder
137
138
164
147
150
F G H J K
1 2 3 4 5 6 7
15 16 17 41 40 38 37 13 14 15

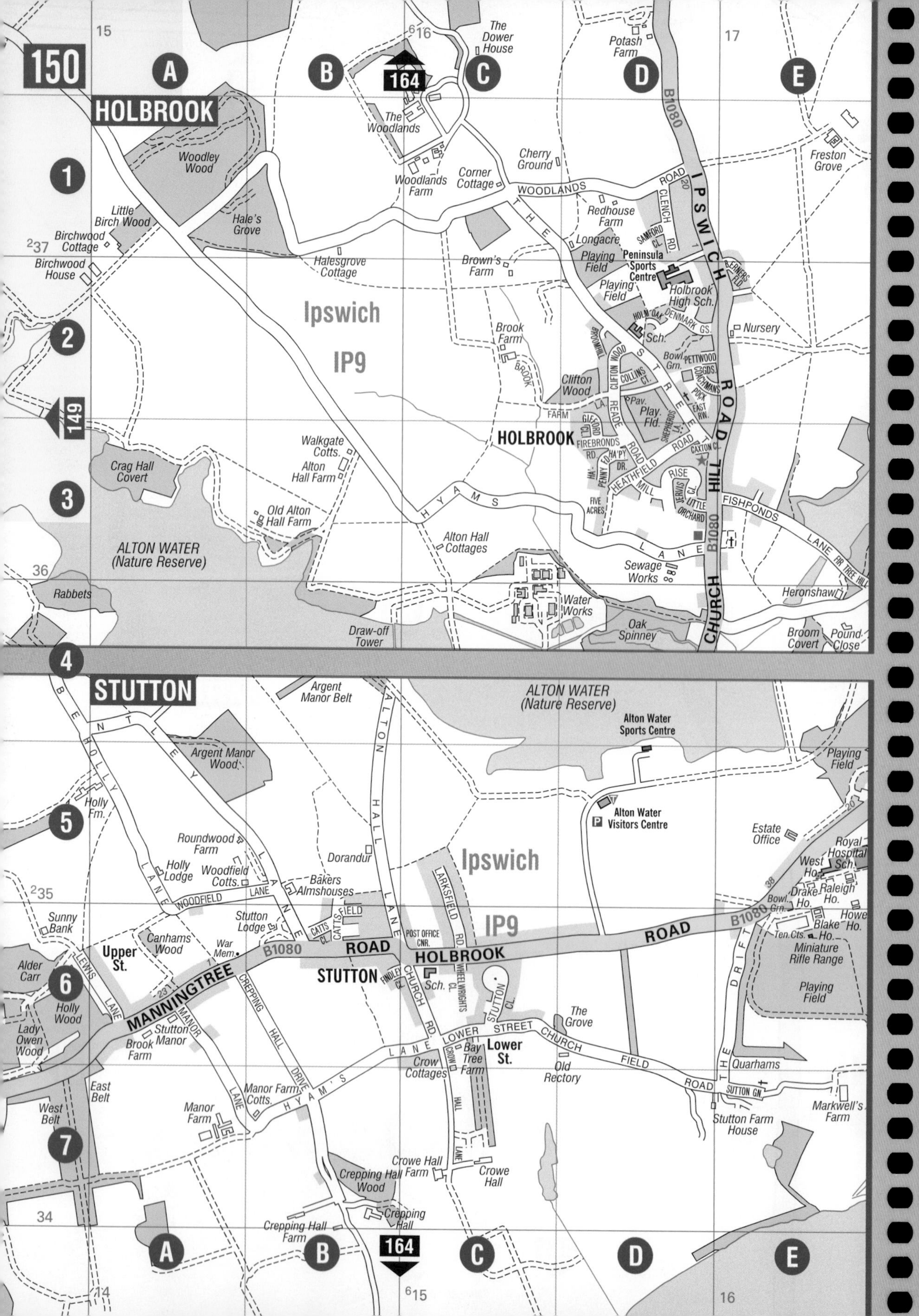
HOLBROOK
Woodley Wood
Little Birch Wood
Birchwood Cottage
Birchwood House
Hale's Grove
Halesgrove Cottage
The Woodlands
The Dower House
Woodlands Farm
Corner Cottage
Cherry Ground
Potash Farm
Freston Grove
Redhouse Farm
Longacre
Playing Field
Peninsula Sports Centre
Holbrook High Sch.
Brown's Farm
Ipswich
IP9
Brook Farm
Nursery
Clifton Wood
Play. Fld.
HOLBROOK
Walkgate Cotts.
Alton Hall Farm
Crag Hall Covert
Old Alton Hall Farm
Alton Hall Cottages
ALTON WATER (Nature Reserve)
Rabbets
Sewage Works
Heronshaw
Water Works
Oak Spinney
Draw-off Tower
Broom Covert
Pound Close
STUTTON
Argent Manor Belt
Argent Manor Wood
Alton Water Sports Centre
Alton Water Visitors Centre
Playing Field
Holly Fm.
Roundwood Farm
Dorandur
Holly Lodge
Woodfield Cotts.
Bakers Almshouses
Estate Office
Royal Hospital Sch.
West Ho.
Drake Ho.
Raleigh Ho.
Howe Ho.
Blake Ho.
Sunny Bank
Stutton Lodge
Canhams Wood
Upper St.
War Mem.
Alder Carr
Holly Wood
Lady Owen Wood
Stutton Manor
Brook Farm
Miniature Rifle Range
STUTTON
Sch.
Lower St.
Bay Tree Farm
Crow Cottages
The Grove
Old Rectory
Quarhams
Manor Farm Cotts.
East Belt
West Belt
Manor Farm
Markwell's Farm
Stutton Farm House
Crowe Hall Farm
Crowe Hall
Cropping Hall Wood
Crepping Hall
Crepping Hall Farm
WOODLANDS ROAD
IPSWICH ROAD
CHURCH HILL
HYAMS LANE
FISHPONDS LANE
BENTLEY LANE
HOLLY LANE
WOODFIELD LANE
ALTON HALL LANE
MANNINGTREE ROAD
HOLBROOK ROAD
B1080
LOWER STREET
CHURCH FIELD ROAD
THE DRIFT
CREPPING HALL DRIVE
MANOR LANE
LEWIS LANE
CHURCH RD.
CROWN LANE
LARKSFIELD RD.
STUTTON CL.
SUTTON GN.
CATTS CL.
POST OFFICE CNR.
164
149

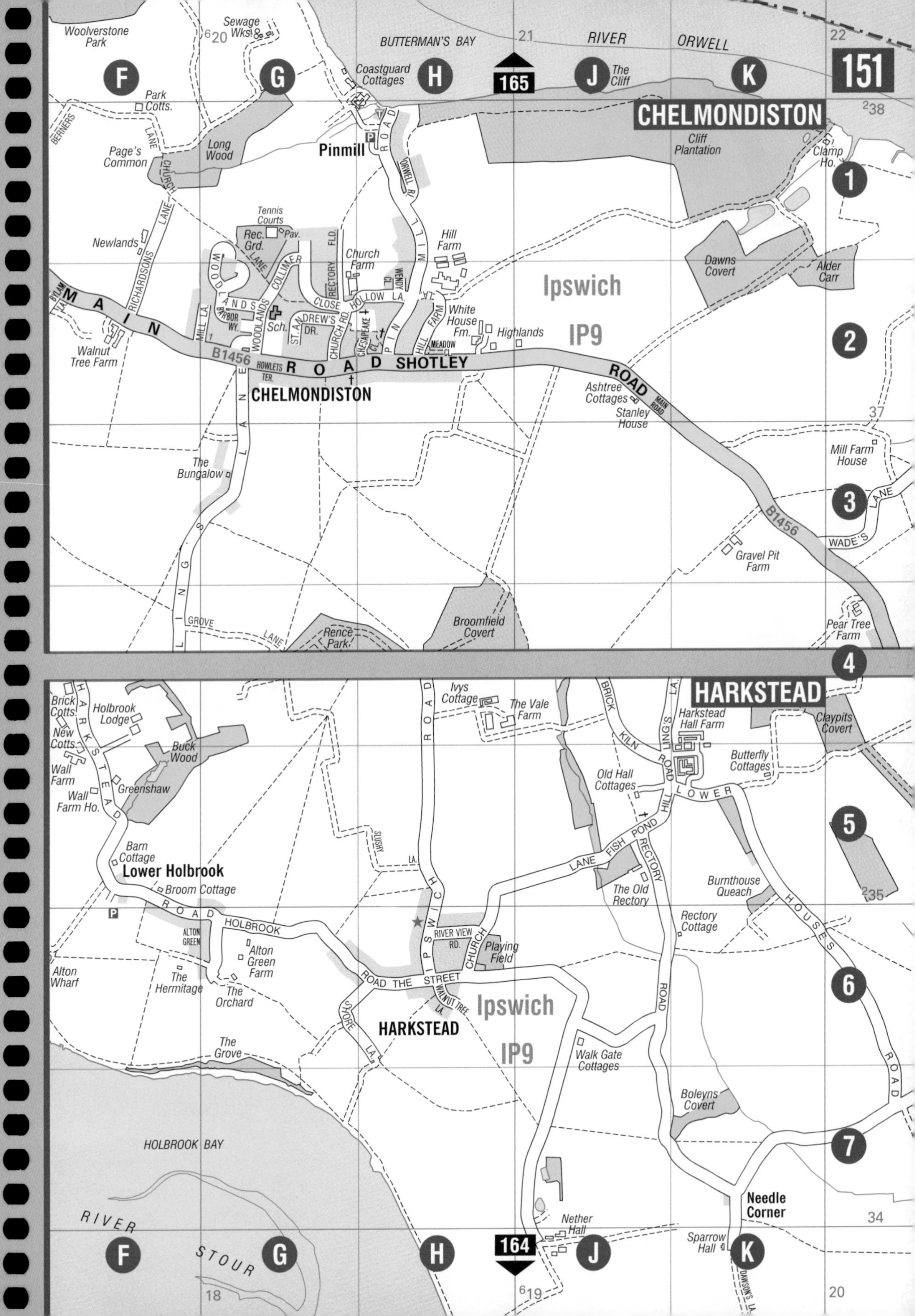

CHELMONDISTON
HARKSTEAD
Woolverstone Park
Sewage Wks.
BUTTERMAN'S BAY
RIVER ORWELL
Coastguard Cottages
165
The Cliff
Park Cotts.
Long Wood
Pinmill
Page's Common
Cliff Plantation
Clamp Ho.
Tennis Courts
Rec. Grd.
Pav.
Newlands
Church Farm
Hill Farm
Ipswich
Dawns Covert
Alder Carr
White House Fm.
Highlands
IP9
Sch.
Walnut Tree Farm
MAIN ROAD
B1456
SHOTLEY ROAD
CHELMONDISTON
Ashtree Cottages
Stanley House
The Bungalow
Mill Farm House
WADE'S LANE
Gravel Pit Farm
GROVE LANE
Rence Park
Broomfield Covert
Pear Tree Farm
Brick Cotts.
Holbrook Lodge
Ivys Cottage
The Vale Farm
Harkstead Hall Farm
Claypits Covert
New Cotts.
Buck Wood
Butterfly Cottages
Wall Farm
Greenshaw
Old Hall Cottages
Wall Farm Ho.
LOWER
FISH POND HILL LANE
RECTORY ROAD
Barn Cottage
Lower Holbrook
Broom Cottage
Burnthouse Queach
The Old Rectory
HOLBROOK ROAD
ALTON GREEN
Alton Green Farm
RIVER VIEW RD.
Playing Field
Rectory Cottage
HOUSES ROAD
Alton Wharf
The Hermitage
The Orchard
THE STREET
WALNUT TREE LA.
SHORE LA.
HARKSTEAD
Ipswich
IP9
The Grove
Walk Gate Cottages
Boleyns Covert
HOLBROOK BAY
RIVER STOUR
Needle Corner
Nether Hall
164
Sparrow Hall
DAWSON'S LA.
F G H J K
1 2 3 4 5 6 7

BUCKLESHAM
LEVINGTON / NACTON
165
Waddling Duck
Valley Farm
Street Farm Cottages
Brightwell
Belee
Dairy Farm
Hill Cottages
Lewis Cottages
KENNELS RD.
KENNELS ROAD
HALL R.
EASTERN BY-PASS
IPSWICH
A12
Depot
Brightwell House
The Bungalow
IP12
Ipswich
IP10
Mousehole Carr
BUCKLESHAM ROAD
Steel's Farm
The Bungalow
The Old Rectory
Brunlea
MAIN ROAD
FORGE CL.
MDW. VW.
The White Ho.
CHURCH CL.
CHURCH
ST. MARYS PK.
LANE
Street Farm
STREET FM. CL.
Hall
LANE
GREEN CR.
BUCKLESHAM
Bucklesham Primary School
Playing Field
FIELD VW.
LEVINGTON LA.
SLIP PONDS
LEVINGTON
NACTON
Junction 58
A14
CHAPEL RD.
Park Farm
Lady Wood Cottages
Sorrel Grove
MILL PIECE
SAWMILL LA.
WORK SHOP LA.
THE STREET
FINNEY'S DRIFT
Amberfield School
Manor Ponds (Decoy)
Sports Ground
Lady Wood Cottage
Lady Wood
Lady Wood Cotts.
TOM LINE CT.
Home Farm
CAMILLA CT.
NACTON
Decoy Cottage
Lark Hill
Meml.
Nacton C of E Primary School
Ipswich
The Hangings
Rec.
SCHOOL HILL
Anchor House
The Belt
The Barn
ROAD
CHURCH
LEVINGTON
IP10
WOODLAND HOUSES
Levington Park
Lower Farm Cottages
Orwell Park Gardens
ROAD
Burnaville Hall
RED HO. WLK.
Red House Farm
Sewage Works
Pav.
Orwell Park School
SHORE
Broke Hall Woods
BRIDGE
LEVINGTON
LANE
P
THE DRIFT
BARRACK ROW
Rackhams Farm
CHURCH
LANE
Broke Hall
RIVER
ORWELL
Home Wood
The Oaks
Sewage Works
STRATTONHALL DRIFT
Levington Creek
165
A B C D E
1 2 3 4 5 6 7
24 25 26 43 242 240 39 22 623 24

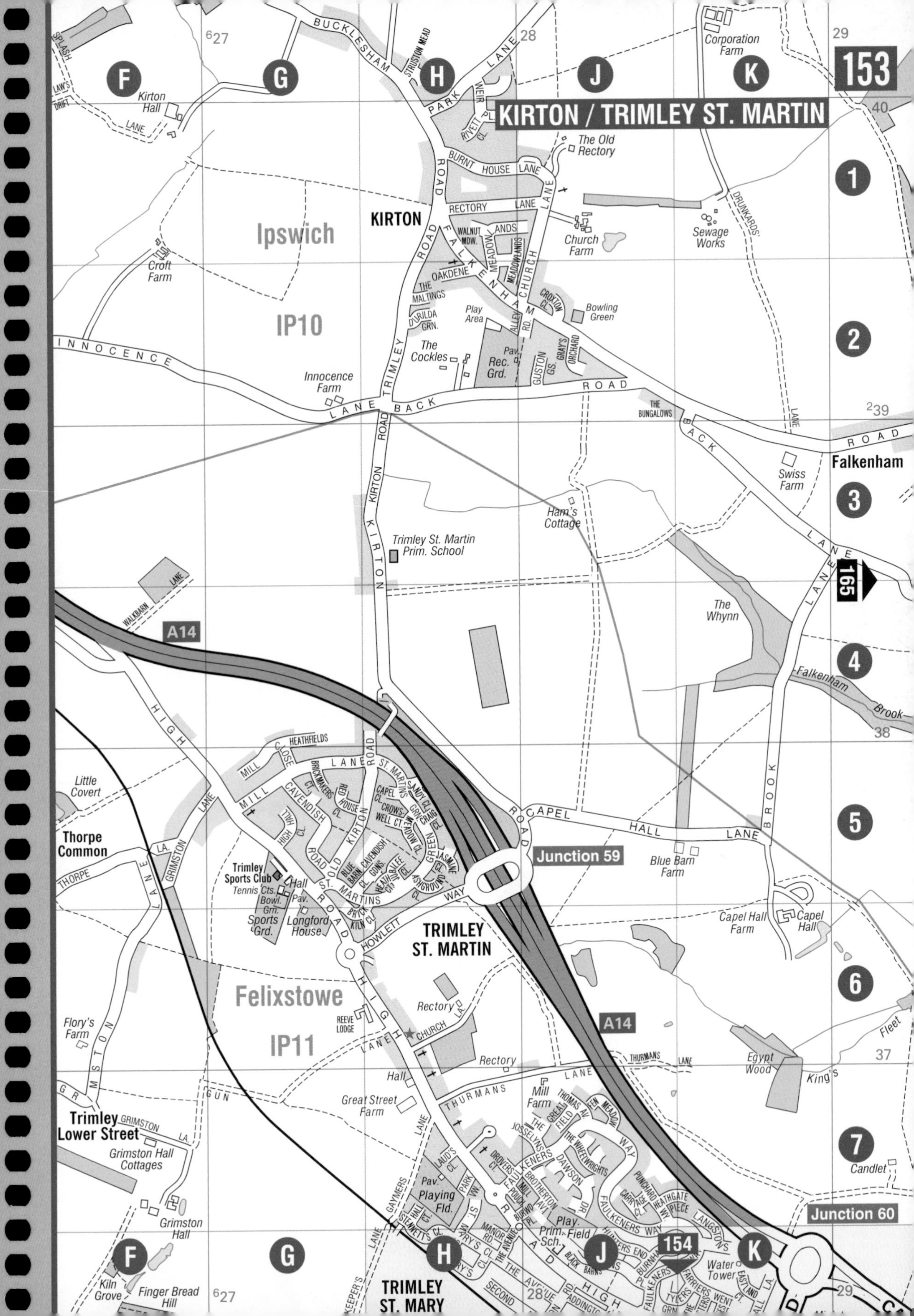
KIRTON
Ipswich
IP10
Felixstowe
IP11
TRIMLEY ST. MARTIN
TRIMLEY ST. MARY
Trimley Lower Street
Thorpe Common
Falkenham
Kirton Hall
Croft Farm
Innocence Farm
The Old Rectory
Church Farm
Sewage Works
Corporation Farm
Bowling Green
Play Area
The Cockles
Rec. Grd.
Pav.
The Bungalows
Swiss Farm
Ham's Cottage
Trimley St. Martin Prim. School
The Whynn
Falkenham Brook
Blue Barn Farm
Capel Hall Farm
Capel Hall
Junction 59
Junction 60
A14
Little Covert
Trimley Sports Club
Tennis Cts.
Bowl. Grn.
Sports Grd.
Longford House
Hall
Rectory
Reeve Lodge
Flory's Farm
Great Street Farm
Mill Farm
Egypt Wood
Candlet
Grimston Hall Cottages
Grimston Hall
Kiln Grove
Finger Bread Hill
Playing Fld.
Play. Field
Prim. Sch.
Water Tower
Bucklesham
Innocence Lane
Back Road
Kirton Road
Burnt House Lane
Rectory Lane
Church Lane
Falkenham Road
High Road
Mill Lane
Old Kirton Road
St. Martins Road
Howlett Way
Capel Hall Lane
Brook Lane
Thurmans Lane
Grimston Lane
Church Lane
Faulkeners Way
Gaymers Lane
Walkbarn Lane
Drunkards' Lane
King's Fleet
154
165

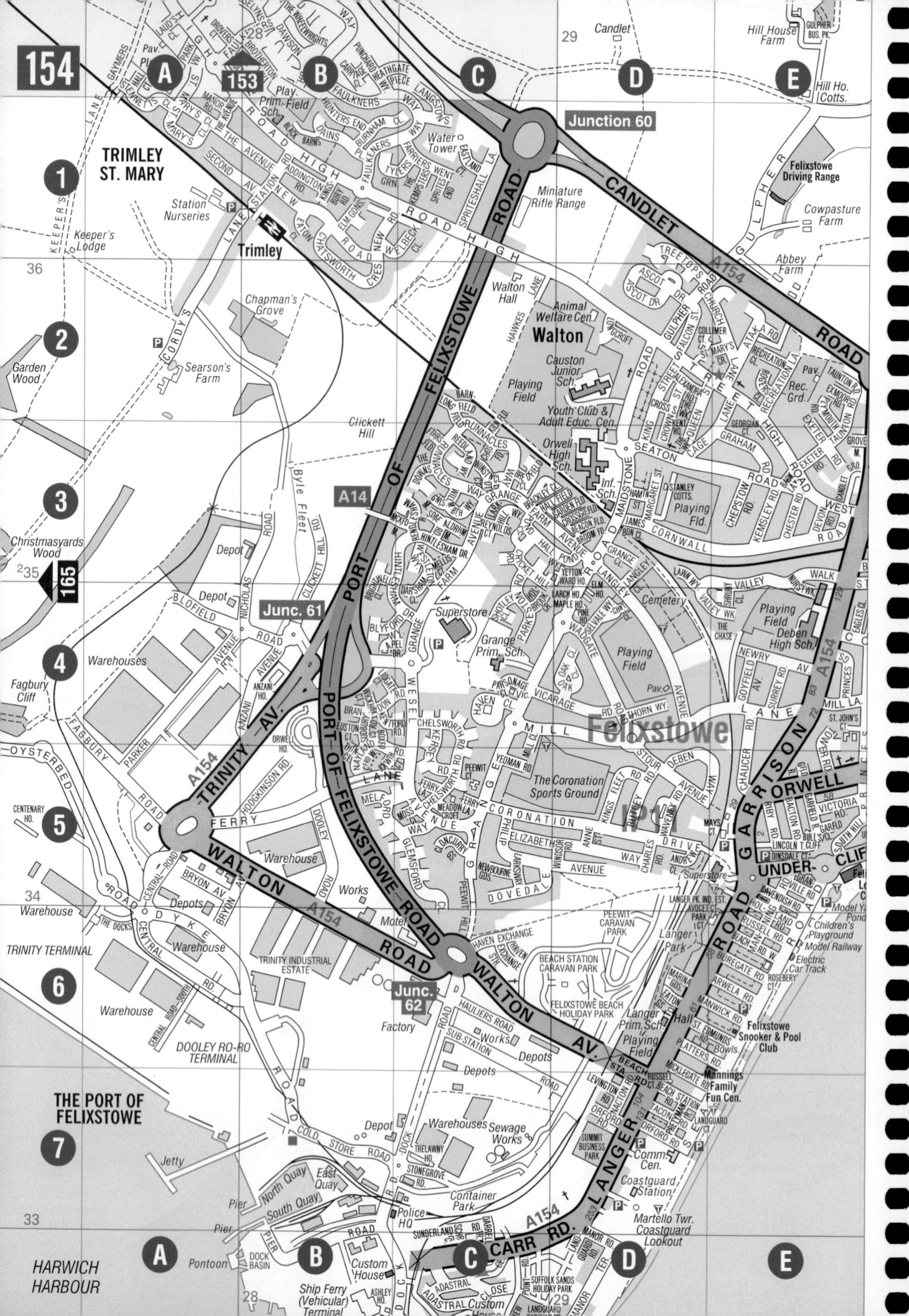

TRIMLEY ST. MARY
Trimley
Walton
Felixstowe
IP11
Junction 60
Junc. 61
Junc. 62
153
165
CANDLET ROAD
PORT OF FELIXSTOWE ROAD
TRINITY AV.
WALTON ROAD
WALTON AV.
GARRISON LANE
LANGER RD.
CARR RD.
HIGH ROAD
A154
A14
THE PORT OF FELIXSTOWE
HARWICH HARBOUR
TRINITY TERMINAL
DOOLEY RO-RO TERMINAL
TRINITY INDUSTRIAL ESTATE
Felixstowe Driving Range
Cowpasture Farm
Abbey Farm
Hill House Farm
Candlet
Miniature Rifle Range
Chapman's Grove
Searson's Farm
Garden Wood
Christmasyards Wood
Fagbury Cliff
Clickett Hill
Keeper's Lodge
Station Nurseries
Walton Hall
Animal Welfare Cen.
Causton Junior Sch.
Orwell High Sch.
Youth Club & Adult Educ. Cen.
Grange Prim. Sch.
Deben High Sch.
Cemetery
The Coronation Sports Ground
BEACH STATION CARAVAN PARK
FELIXSTOWE BEACH HOLIDAY PARK
PEEWIT CARAVAN PARK
Langer Park
Langer Prim. Sch.
Felixstowe Snooker & Pool Club
Mannings Family Fun Cen.
Children's Playground
Model Railway
Electric Car Track
Coastguard Station
Martello Twr. Coastguard Lookout
Container Park
Police HQ
Custom House
Ship Ferry (Vehicular) Terminal
North Quay
South Quay
East Quay
Jetty
Pontoon
DOCK BASIN
Sewage Works
SUMMIT BUSINESS PARK
Superstore
Warehouses
Depots
Factory
Motel

FELIXSTOWE FERRY GOLF COURSE
KINGSFLEET GOLF COURSE
165
Laurel Farm
Nursery
Fleet House
Whitehouse Cotts.
Fleet Ho. Corner
East End Farm
Club House
Park Farm
The Grove
Playing Field
Playground
Pav.
Colneis Jun. Sch.
Felixstowe Port & Town FC
Dellwood Sports Grd.
Old Felixstowe
Felixstowe College
Brackenbury Sports Cen.
Allenby Park
Felixstowe
Cinema & Bingo
HOSP.
Tennis Courts
Cliff Gardens
The Spa Pavilion Theatre
FELIXSTOWE
Cobbolds Point
Martello Place
NORTH SEA
F
G
H
J
K
1
2
3
4
5
6
7
30
31
32
33
34
35
36

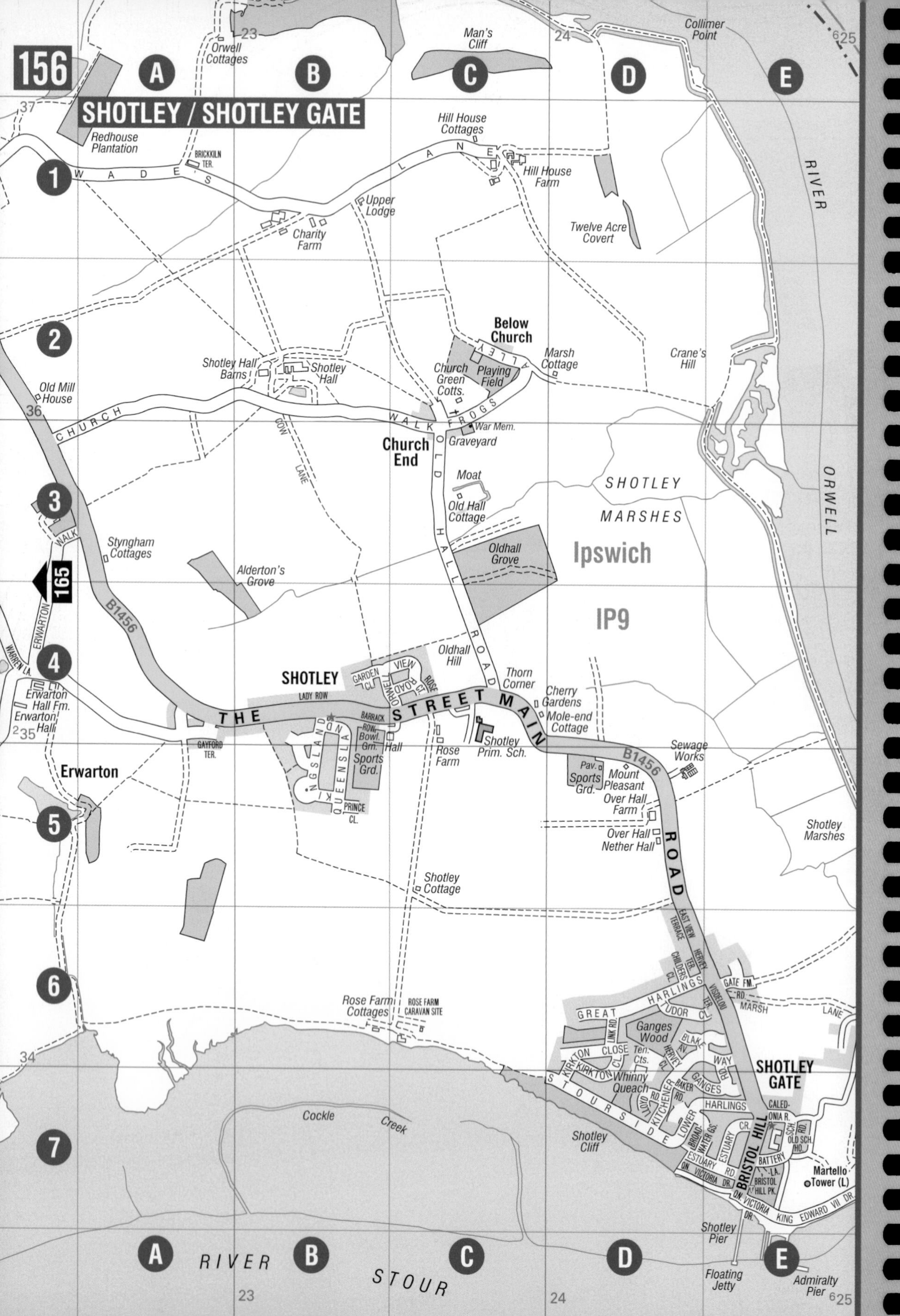
SHOTLEY / SHOTLEY GATE
Redhouse Plantation
Orwell Cottages
Man's Cliff
Collimer Point
Hill House Cottages
Hill House Farm
WADE'S LANE
BRICKKILN TER.
Upper Lodge
Charity Farm
Twelve Acre Covert
RIVER ORWELL
Below Church
Shotley Hall Barns
Shotley Hall
Church Green Cotts.
Playing Field
ALLEY
Marsh Cottage
Crane's Hill
Old Mill House
CHURCH WALK
FROGS
War Mem.
Graveyard
Church End
COW LANE
OLD HALL ROAD
Moat
Old Hall Cottage
SHOTLEY MARSHES
Styngham Cottages
Oldhall Grove
Ipswich
Alderton's Grove
165
ERWARTON WALK
B1456
IP9
WARREN LA.
Erwarton Hall Fm.
Erwarton Hall
Oldhall Hill
SHOTLEY
GARDEN CL.
VIEW
ORWELL ROAD
ROSE CT.
LADY ROW
THE STREET
MAIN ROAD
Thorn Corner
Cherry Gardens
Mole-end Cottage
BARRACK ROW
KINGSLAND
QUEENSLAND
Bowl. Grn.
Hall
Sports Grd.
GAYFORD TER.
Rose Farm
Shotley Prim. Sch.
Sewage Works
Pav.
Sports Grd.
Mount Pleasant
Over Hall Farm
Erwarton
PRINCE CL.
Over Hall
Nether Hall
Shotley Marshes
Shotley Cottage
EAST VIEW TERRACE
HERVEY TER.
CHILDERS CL.
GATE FM. RD.
MARSH LANE
HARLINGS
VISDELOU TER.
Rose Farm Cottages
ROSE FARM CARAVAN SITE
GREAT TUDOR CL.
LINK RD.
Ganges Wood
BLAKE AV.
HERVEY CL.
KIRKTON CLOSE
Ten. Cts.
WAY
KIRKTON CL.
Whinny Queach
GANGES
SHOTLEY GATE
STOURSIDE
BAKER RD.
LLOYD RD.
KITCHENER
HARLINGS
CALEDONIA R.
LOWER BROAD WATER GS.
ESTUARY CR.
BRISTOL HILL
SCH. RD.
OLD SCH. HO.
Cockle Creek
Shotley Cliff
ESTUARY RD.
BATTERY LA.
ON. VICTORIA DR.
BRISTOL HILL PK.
Martello Tower (L)
ON VICTORIA DR.
KING EDWARD VII DR.
Shotley Pier
RIVER STOUR
Floating Jetty
Admiralty Pier
A B C D E
1 2 3 4 5 6 7
23 24 625
37 36 35 34

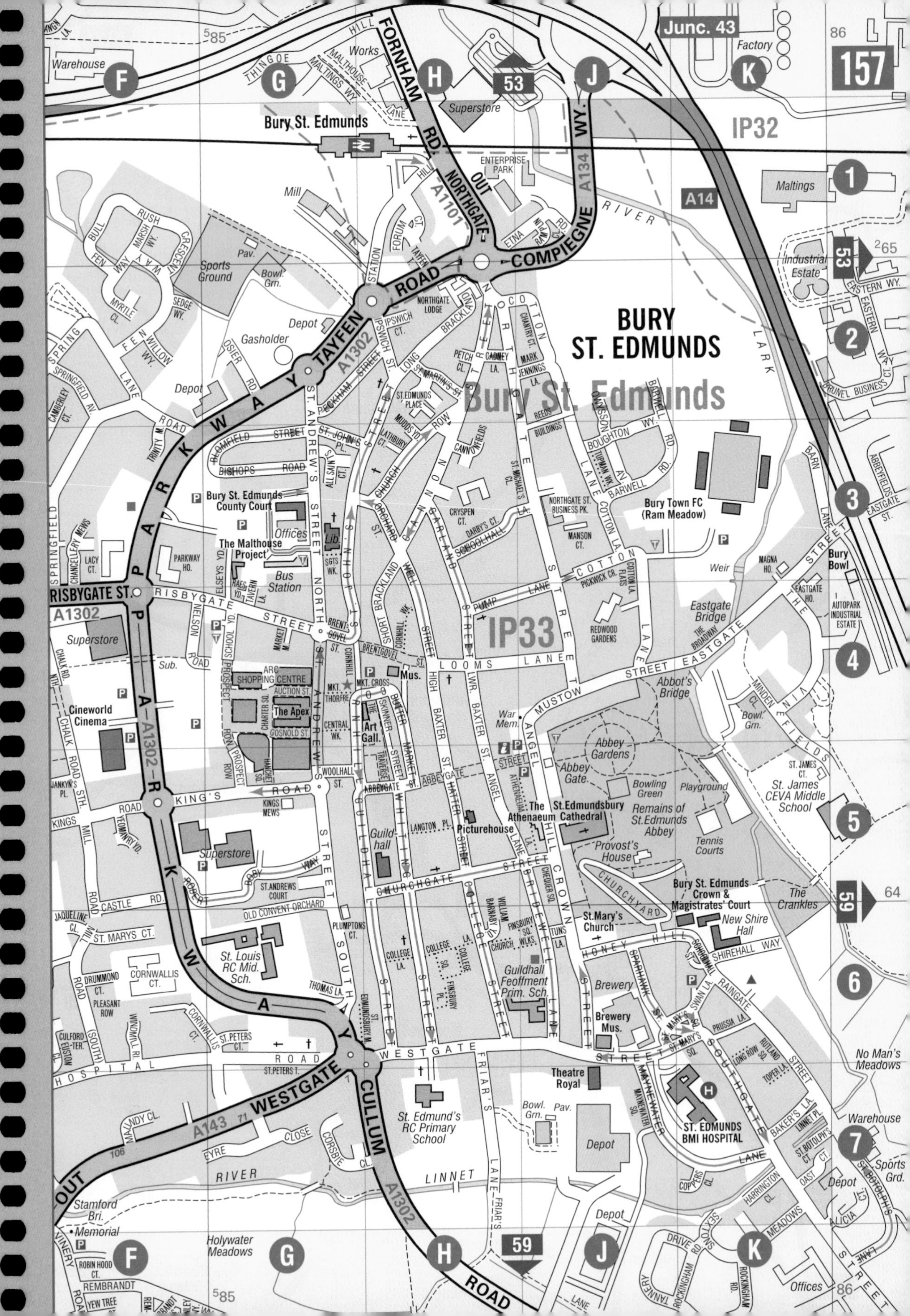
157
Junc. 43
BURY ST. EDMUNDS
Bury St. Edmunds
IP32
IP33
Bury St. Edmunds
Warehouse
Works
Factory
Superstore
Maltings
Industrial Estate
ENTERPRISE PARK
Mill
Sports Ground
Bowl. Grn.
Pav.
Gasholder
Depot
NORTHGATE LODGE
Bury St. Edmunds County Court
Offices
Lib.
The Malthouse Project
PARKWAY HO.
Bus Station
LACY CT.
Superstore
Cineworld Cinema
ARC SHOPPING CENTRE
The Apex
Mus.
MKT. CROSS
Art Gall.
Guildhall
Picturehouse
The Athenaeum
St.Edmundsbury Cathedral
War Mem.
Abbey Gardens
Abbey Gate
Bowling Green
Playground
Remains of St.Edmunds Abbey
Tennis Courts
Provost's House
Bury Town FC (Ram Meadow)
NORTHGATE ST. BUSINESS PK.
REDWOOD GARDENS
Eastgate Bridge
Abbot's Bridge
Weir
MAGNA HO.
EASTGATE HO.
Bury Bowl
AUTOPARK INDUSTRIAL ESTATE
St. James CEVA Middle School
The Crankles
Bury St. Edmunds Crown & Magistrates' Court
New Shire Hall
St.Mary's Church
Guildhall Feoffment Prim. Sch.
Brewery
Brewery Mus.
St. Louis RC Mid. Sch.
Theatre Royal
ST. EDMUNDS BMI HOSPITAL
St. Edmund's RC Primary School
Bowl. Grn.
Depot
Warehouse
Sports Grd.
No Man's Meadows
Stamford Bri.
Memorial
Holywater Meadows
Offices
PARKWAY
TAYFEN ROAD
NORTHGATE
COMPIEGNE WY.
FORNHAM RD.
RISBYGATE ST.
WESTGATE
CULLUM ROAD
EASTGATE STREET
MUSTOW STREET
SOUTHGATE STREET
HOSPITAL ROAD
KING'S ROAD
CHURCHGATE STREET
ABBEYGATE ST.
HONEY HILL
SHIREHALL WAY
RIVER LINNET
RIVER LARK
A1302
A1101
A134
A14
A143
53
59
F
G
H
J
K
1
2
3
4
5
6
7
585
86
265
64

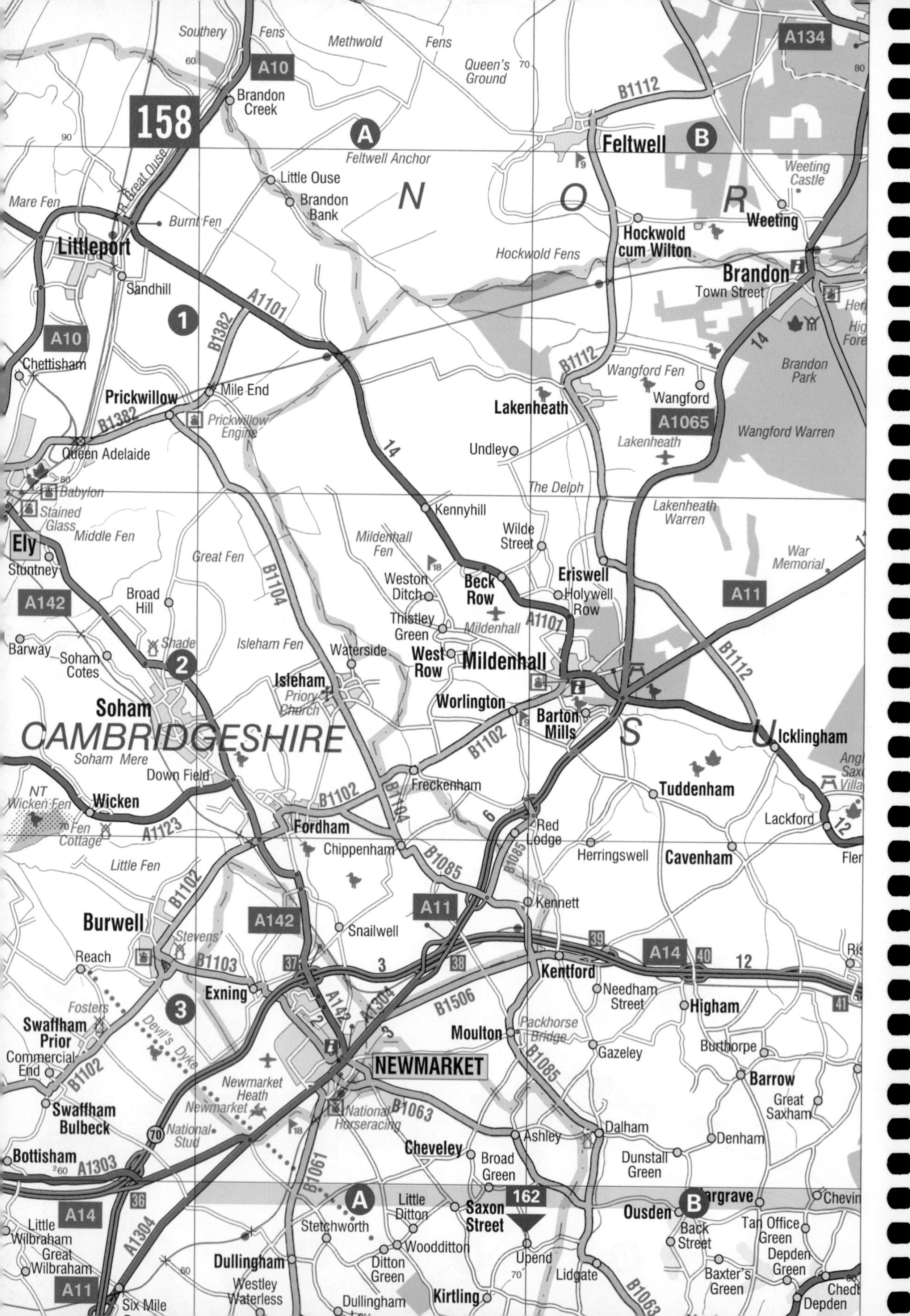

Southery
Fens
Methwold
Fens
Queen's Ground
A134
A10
158
Brandon Creek
B1112
A
Feltwell
B
Feltwell Anchor
Little Ouse
Brandon Bank
N
O
R
Weeting Castle
Weeting
Mare Fen
R. Great Ouse
Burnt Fen
Hockwold cum Wilton
Littleport
Hockwold Fens
Brandon
Town Street
Sandhill
A1101
1
B1382
A10
Chettisham
14
B1112
Wangford Fen
Brandon Park
Mile End
Prickwillow
Wangford
Lakenheath
B1382
Prickwillow Engine
A1065
Wangford Warren
Queen Adelaide
Lakenheath
14
Undley
Babylon
The Delph
Stained Glass
Kennyhill
Lakenheath Warren
Middle Fen
Ely
Mildenhall Fen
Wilde Street
Great Fen
Stuntney
War Memorial
Eriswell
B1104
Weston Ditch
Beck Row
Holywell Row
A142
Broad Hill
A11
Thistley Green
Mildenhall
A1101
Shade
Barway
Isleham Fen
Waterside
B1112
Soham Cotes
2
West Row
Mildenhall
Isleham
Priory Church
Worlington
Soham
Barton Mills
CAMBRIDGESHIRE
S
U
Icklingham
Soham Mere
B1102
Down Field
Freckenham
Tuddenham
NT Wicken Fen
Wicken
B1102
B1104
Lackford
Fen Cottage
A1123
Fordham
6
Red Lodge
12
Chippenham
Herringswell
Cavenham
Little Fen
B1085
B1085
B1102
A11
Kennett
Burwell
A142
Snailwell
Stevens'
39
A14
40
12
Reach
B1103
37
3
38
Kentford
Exning
A142
A1304
B1506
Needham Street
Higham
Fosters
3
41
Swaffham Prior
Devil's Dyke
Moulton
Packhorse Bridge
Commercial End
Gazeley
Burthorpe
B1102
NEWMARKET
B1085
Barrow
Newmarket Heath
Great Saxham
Swaffham Bulbeck
National Horseracing
B1063
National Stud
Dalham
70
Ashley
Denham
Cheveley
Broad Green
Bottisham
A1303
Dunstall Green
36
B1061
A
162
B
Hargrave
Chevin
A14
Little Ditton
Saxon Street
Ousden
Tan Office Green
Little Wilbraham
Stetchworth
Back Street
Woodditton
Depden Green
Great Wilbraham
A1304
Dullingham
Ditton Green
Upend
Lidgate
Baxter's Green
Westley Waterless
B1063
A11
Six Mile
Dullingham
Kirtling
Depden

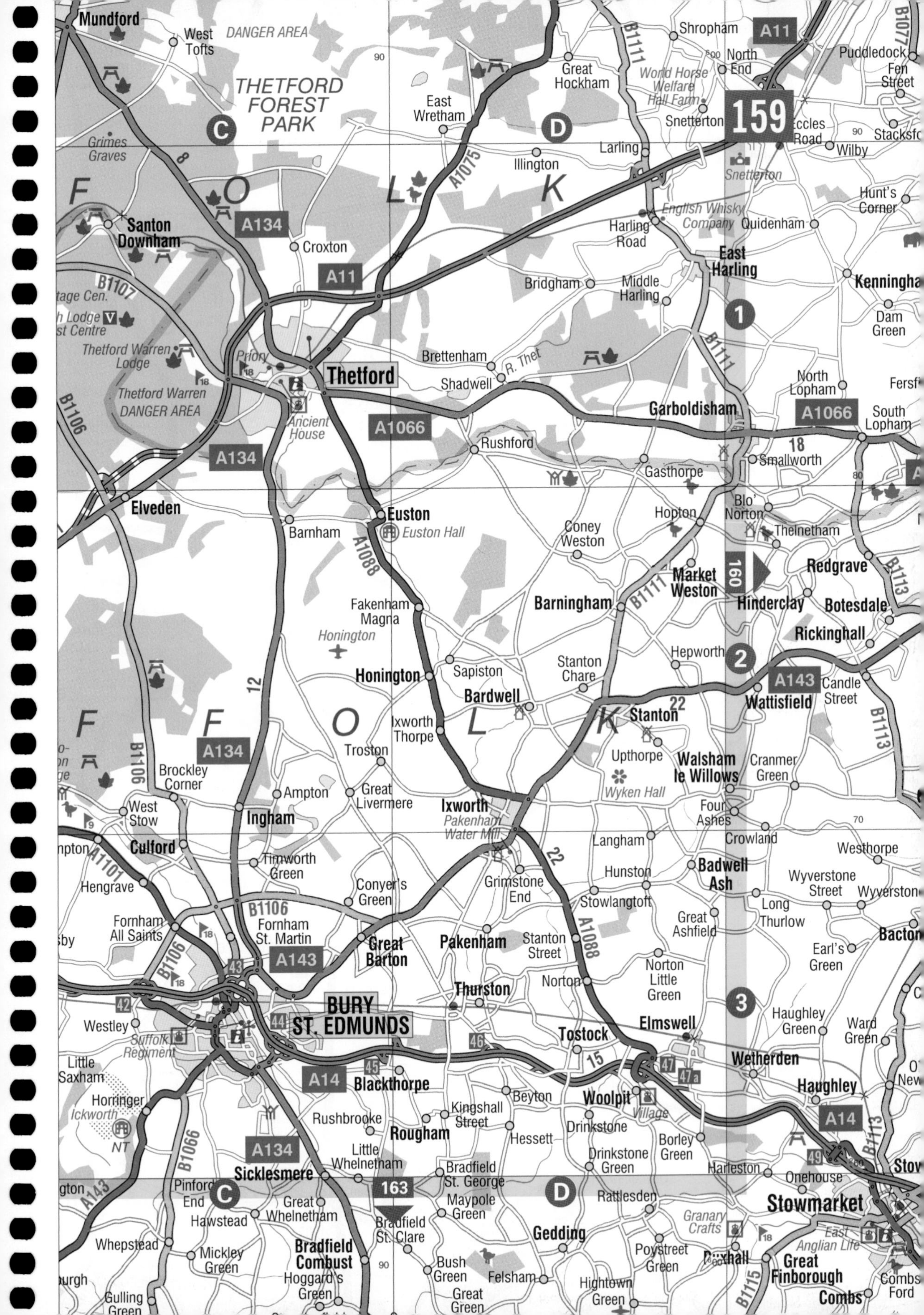
159
Mundford
West Tofts
DANGER AREA
THETFORD FOREST PARK
Grimes Graves
East Wretham
Great Hockham
Shropham
North End
World Horse Welfare Hall Farm
Snetterton
Eccles Road
Wilby
Stacksford
Puddledock
Fen Street
B1077
A11
B1111
Illington
Larling
Snetterton
Hunt's Corner
Quidenham
English Whisky Company
Harling Road
East Harling
Kenninghall
Dam Green
Santon Downham
Croxton
A134
A1075
A11
Bridgham
Middle Harling
B1107
Thetford Warren Lodge
Thetford Warren
DANGER AREA
Priory
Thetford
Ancient House
Brettenham
R. Thet
Shadwell
North Lopham
Fersfield
Garboldisham
A1066
South Lopham
Smallworth
Gasthorpe
Rushford
A1066
A134
B1106
Elveden
Euston
Euston Hall
Barnham
A1088
Hopton
Blo' Norton
Thelnetham
Coney Weston
Market Weston
160
Redgrave
B1113
Barningham
B1111
Hinderclay
Botesdale
Rickinghall
Fakenham Magna
Honington
Hepworth
Honington
Sapiston
Stanton Chare
Bardwell
A143
Candle Street
Wattisfield
Stanton
Ixworth Thorpe
Troston
Upthorpe
Walsham le Willows
Cranmer Green
Wyken Hall
A134
B1106
Brockley Corner
Ampton
Great Livermere
Ixworth
Pakenham Water Mill
Four Ashes
Crowland
West Stow
Ingham
Langham
Westhorpe
Culford
Timworth Green
A1101
Hengrave
Conyer's Green
Grimstone End
Hunston
Badwell Ash
Wyverstone Street
Wyverstone
Stowlangtoft
Long Thurlow
Fornham All Saints
B1106
Fornham St. Martin
Great Barton
Pakenham
Stanton Street
A1088
Great Ashfield
Earl's Green
Bacton
A143
Norton Little Green
Norton
Thurston
Westley
BURY ST. EDMUNDS
Suffolk Regiment
Tostock
Elmswell
Haughley Green
Ward Green
Little Saxham
Blackthorpe
A14
Wetherden
Haughley
Beyton
Woolpit
Village
Horringer
Ickworth
NT
Rushbrooke
Kingshall Street
Rougham
Hessett
Drinkstone
Borley Green
A14
A134
B1066
Little Whelnetham
Sicklesmere
Bradfield St. George
Drinkstone Green
Harleston
Onehouse
Pinford End
Great Whelnetham
163
Maypole Green
Rattlesden
Stowmarket
Hawstead
Bradfield St. Clare
Gedding
Granary Crafts
East Anglian Life
Whepstead
Mickley Green
Bradfield Combust
Bush Green
Poystreet Green
Buxhall
Great Finborough
Hoggard's Green
Felsham
Hightown Green
B1115
Combs Ford
Combs
Gulling Green
Great Green

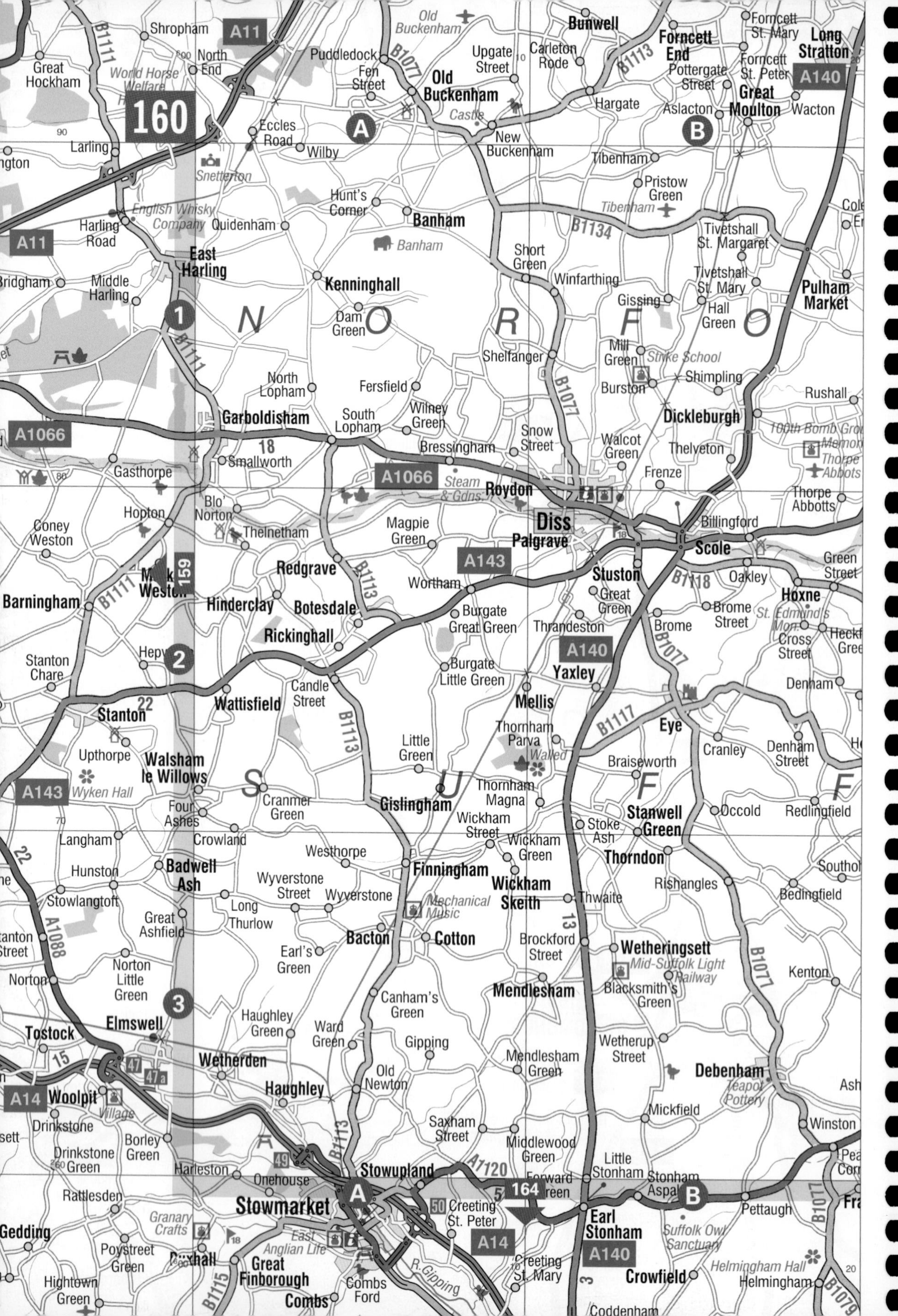

160
Shropham
A11
Old Buckenham
Bunwell
Forncett St. Mary
Long Stratton
B1111
Great Hockham
North End
World Horse Welfare
Puddledock
Fen Street
B1077
Upgate Street
Carleton Rode
B1113
Forncett End
Pottergate Street
Forncett St. Peter
A140
Old Buckenham
Castle
Hargate
Aslacton
Great Moulton
Wacton
A
B
Larling
Eccles Road
Wilby
New Buckenham
Tibenham
Snetterton
Pristow Green
Hunt's Corner
Banham
Tibenham
English Whisky Company
Harling Road
Quidenham
A11
B1134
Tivetshall St. Margaret
Banham
East Harling
Short Green
Bridgham
Middle Harling
Kenninghall
Winfarthing
Tivetshall St. Mary
Pulham Market
Gissing
Hall Green
1
N
Dam Green
O
R
F
O
Mill Green
Strike School
Shelfanger
Shimpling
B1111
North Lopham
Fersfield
Burston
Rushall
B1077
Dickleburgh
A1066
Garboldisham
South Lopham
Wilney Green
100th Bomb Group Memorial
Snow Street
Walcot Green
18
Bressingham
Thelveton
Gasthorpe
Smallworth
Thorpe Abbots
80
A1066
Steam & Gdns.
Frenze
Royndon
Roydon
Thorpe Abbotts
Blo' Norton
Hopton
Diss
Billingford
Coney Weston
Thelnetham
Magpie Green
Palgrave
18
Scole
159
Redgrave
A143
Green Street
B1113
Stuston
B1118
Oakley
Market Weston
Wortham
Great Green
Hoxne
B1111
Barningham
Hinderclay
Botesdale
Burgate Great Green
Brome Street
Brome
St. Edmund's Mon.
Thrandeston
Cross Street
Rickinghall
B1077
A140
Hepworth
2
Stanton Chare
Burgate Little Green
Yaxley
Candle Street
Denham
Wattisfield
Stanton
22
Mellis
B1113
B1117
Eye
Thornham Parva
Little Green
Walled
Braiseworth
Cranley
Denham Street
Upthorpe
Walsham le Willows
S
U
F
F
Thornham Magna
A143
Wyken Hall
Cranmer Green
Gislingham
Stanwell Green
Occold
Redlingfield
Four Ashes
70
Wickham Street
Stoke Ash
Langham
Crowland
Wickham Green
Thorndon
Westhorpe
Finningham
22
Hunston
Badwell Ash
Wickham Skeith
Rishangles
Bedingfield
Wyverstone Street
Wyverstone
Thwaite
Stowlangtoft
Long Thurlow
Mechanical Music
Great Ashfield
A1088
13
Bacton
Cotton
Brockford Street
Wetheringsett
Earl's Green
Mid-Suffolk Light Railway
B1077
Norton
Norton Little Green
Kenton
Mendlesham
Blacksmith's Green
Canham's Green
3
Haughley Green
Ward Green
Gipping
Tostock
Elmswell
Wetherup Street
15
47
47a
Wetherden
Mendlesham Green
Old Newton
Debenham
A14
Woolpit
Haughley
Teapot Pottery
Village
Mickfield
Drinkstone
Saxham Street
Winston
Borley Green
Middlewood Green
B1113
Drinkstone Green
49
Little Stonham
Harleston
Stowupland
A1120
Stonham Aspal
Onehouse
164
Forward Green
A
B
Rattlesden
Stowmarket
50
Creeting St. Peter
Pettaugh
Granary Crafts
B1077
Gedding
East Anglian Life
Earl Stonham
18
A14
Suffolk Owl Sanctuary
Poystreet Green
Buxhall
A140
Helmingham Hall
Great Finborough
Creeting St. Mary
R. Gipping
Hightown Green
B1115
Crowfield
Helmingham
Combs Ford
Combs
B1079
Coddenham
20

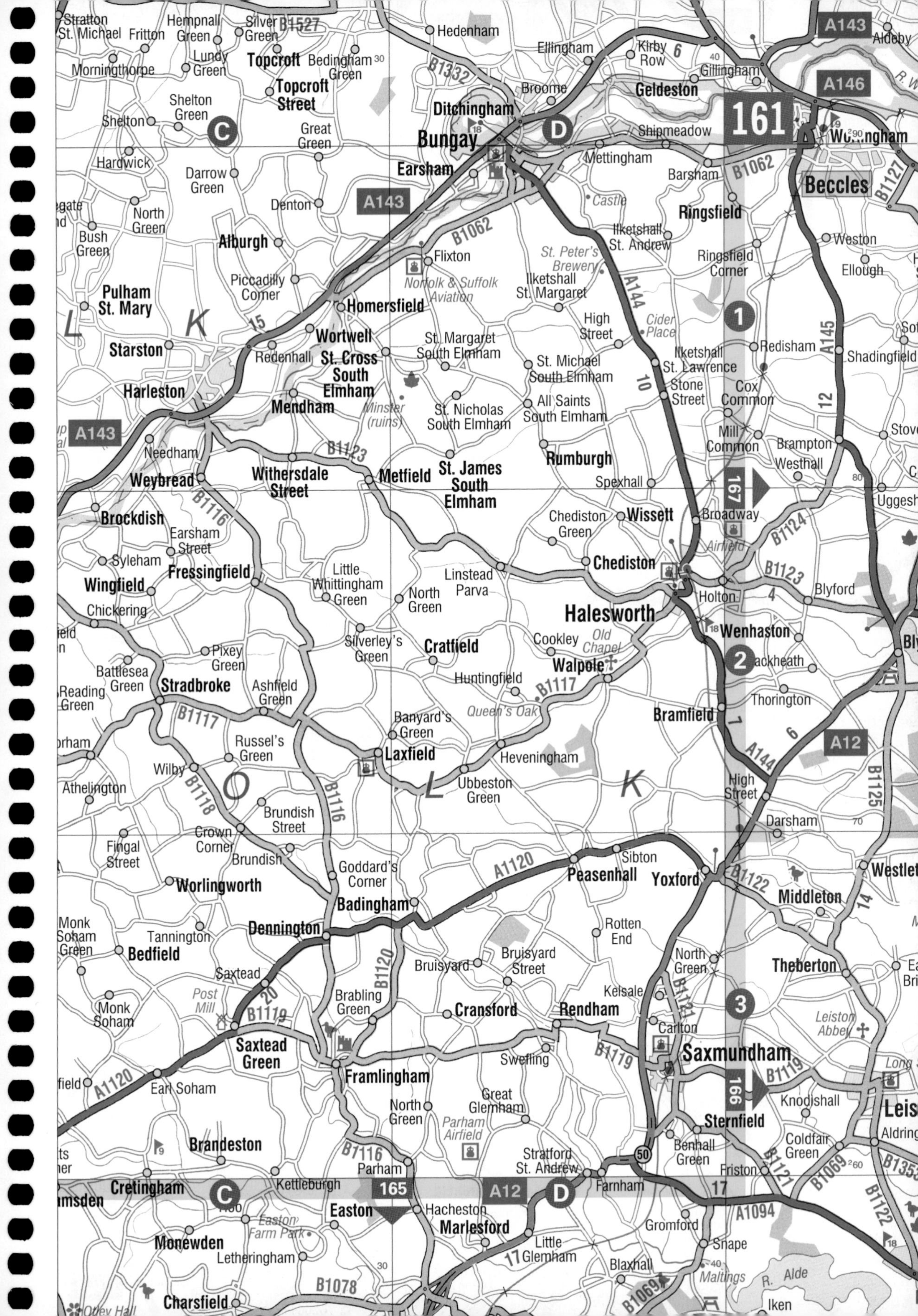
161
Bungay
Beccles
Halesworth
Saxmundham
Framlingham
Harleston
Ditchingham
Earsham
Geldeston
Stradbroke
Laxfield
Yoxford
Peasenhall
Wenhaston
Bramfield
Metfield
Fressingfield
Wingfield
Weybread
Brockdish
Homersfield
Mendham
Wortwell
Starston
Alburgh
Ringsfield
Wissett
Chediston
Rumburgh
Cratfield
Walpole
Heveningham
Dennington
Badingham
Worlingworth
Bedfield
Saxtead Green
Cransford
Rendham
Sternfield
Middleton
Theberton
Brandeston
Cretingham
Easton
Marlesford
Monewden
Charsfield
165
166
167
A143
A146
A144
A145
A12
A1120
A1094
B1062
B1123
B1117
B1116
B1118
B1119
B1120
B1121
B1122
B1124
B1125
B1069
B1078
B1527
B1332
C
D
1
2
3

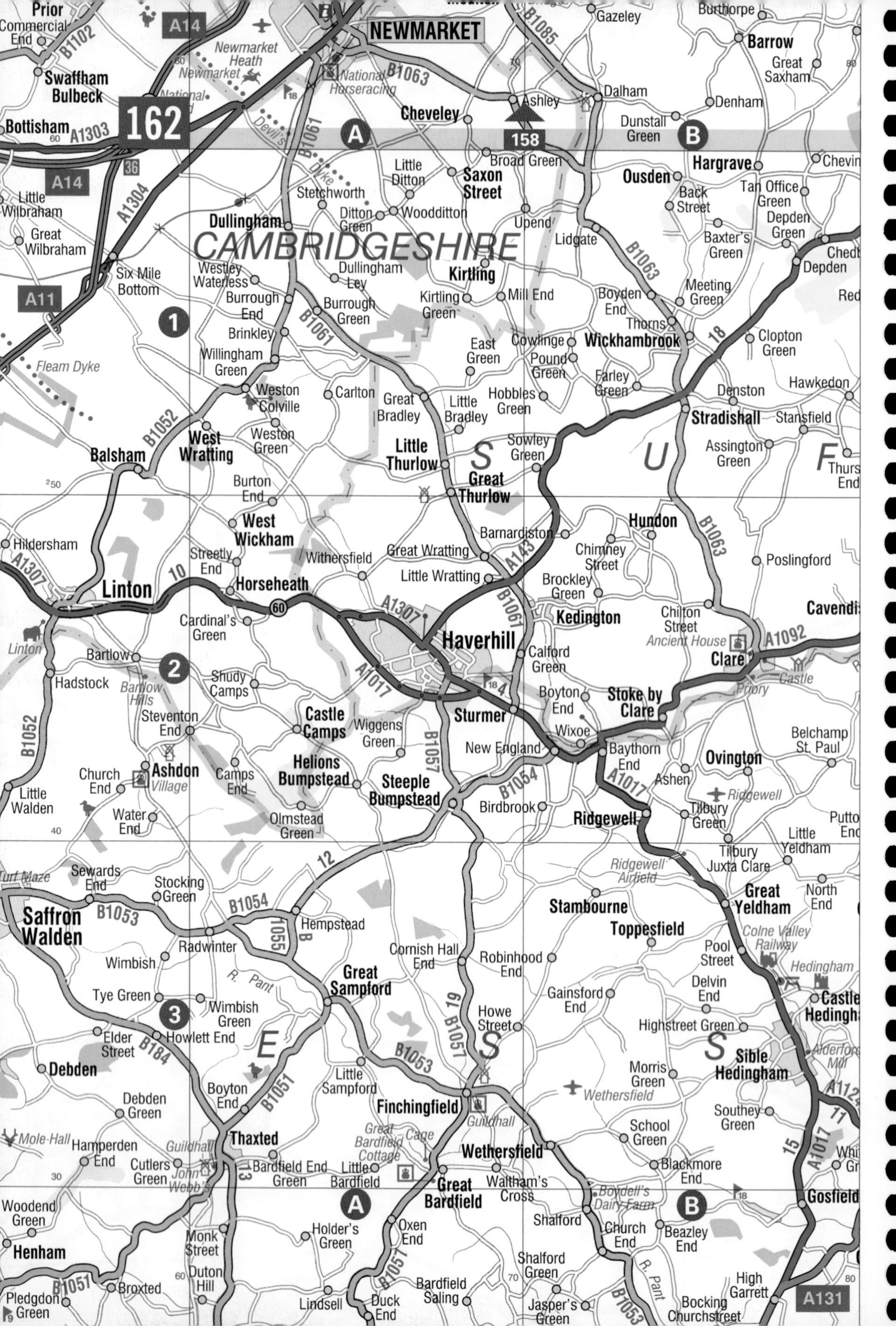

162
158
NEWMARKET
Prior Commercial End
Swaffham Bulbeck
Bottisham
A14
A1303
A1304
A11
B1102
Newmarket Heath
National Horseracing
B1063
B1085
Gazeley
Burthorpe
Barrow
Great Saxham
Dalham
Denham
Ashley
Cheveley
Dunstall Green
Broad Green
Little Ditton
Saxon Street
Hargrave
Ousden
Chevington
Tan Office Green
Back Street
Depden Green
Baxter's Green
Devil's Dyke
B1061
Stetchworth
Ditton Green
Woodditton
Upend
Lidgate
Dullingham
CAMBRIDGESHIRE
Little Wilbraham
Great Wilbraham
Six Mile Bottom
Westley Waterless
Dullingham Ley
Kirtling
Kirtling Green
Mill End
Boyden End
Meeting Green
Depden
Burrough End
Burrough Green
Thorns
Brinkley
East Green
Cowlinge
Wickhambrook
Clopton Green
Willingham Green
Pound Green
Farley Green
Fleam Dyke
Weston Colville
Carlton
Great Bradley
Little Bradley
Hobbles Green
Denston
Hawkedon
Stradishall
Stansfield
B1052
Balsham
West Wratting
Weston Green
Little Thurlow
Sowley Green
Assington Green
Great Thurlow
Thurston End
Burton End
West Wickham
Barnardiston
Hundon
Hildersham
Streetly End
Withersfield
Great Wratting
Little Wratting
Chimney Street
Poslingford
A1307
Linton
Horseheath
A143
Brockley Green
Kedington
Chilton Street
Cavendish
Cardinal's Green
Haverhill
Calford Green
Ancient House
Clare
A1092
Castle
Priory
Bartlow
Hadstock
Bartlow Hills
Shudy Camps
A1017
Boyton End
Stoke by Clare
Steventon End
Castle Camps
Wiggens Green
Sturmer
Wixoe
Belchamp St. Paul
Ashdon
Ashdon Village
Church End
Camps End
Helions Bumpstead
B1057
Steeple Bumpstead
New England
B1054
Baythorn End
Ashen
Ovington
Little Walden
Water End
Olmstead Green
Birdbrook
Ridgewell
Tilbury Green
Putts End
Little Yeldham
Tilbury Juxta Clare
Turf Maze
Sewards End
Stocking Green
Ridgewell Airfield
North End
Great Yeldham
Saffron Walden
B1053
Hempstead
Stambourne
Toppesfield
Colne Valley Railway
Radwinter
B1055
Cornish Hall End
Robinhood End
Pool Street
Wimbish
R. Pant
Great Sampford
Gainsford End
Delvin End
Hedingham
Castle Hedingham
Tye Green
Wimbish Green
Howe Street
Highstreet Green
Elder Street
Howlett End
B184
Debden
Little Sampford
Morris Green
Sible Hedingham
Alderford Mill
Boyton End
B1051
Wethersfield
Debden Green
Finchingfield
Guildhall
Southey Green
A1124
School Green
Mole Hall
Hamperden End
Thaxted
Great Bardfield Cage
Great Bardfield Cottage
Blackmore End
Cutlers Green
John Webb's
Bardfield End Green
Little Bardfield
Great Bardfield
Waltham's Cross
Boydell's Dairy Farm
Gosfield
Woodend Green
Monk Street
Holder's Green
Oxen End
Shalford
Church End
Beazley End
Henham
Duton Hill
Shalford Green
Bardfield Saling
High Garrett
Pledgdon Green
Broxted
Lindsell
Duck End
Jasper's Green
Bocking Churchstreet
A131
A120

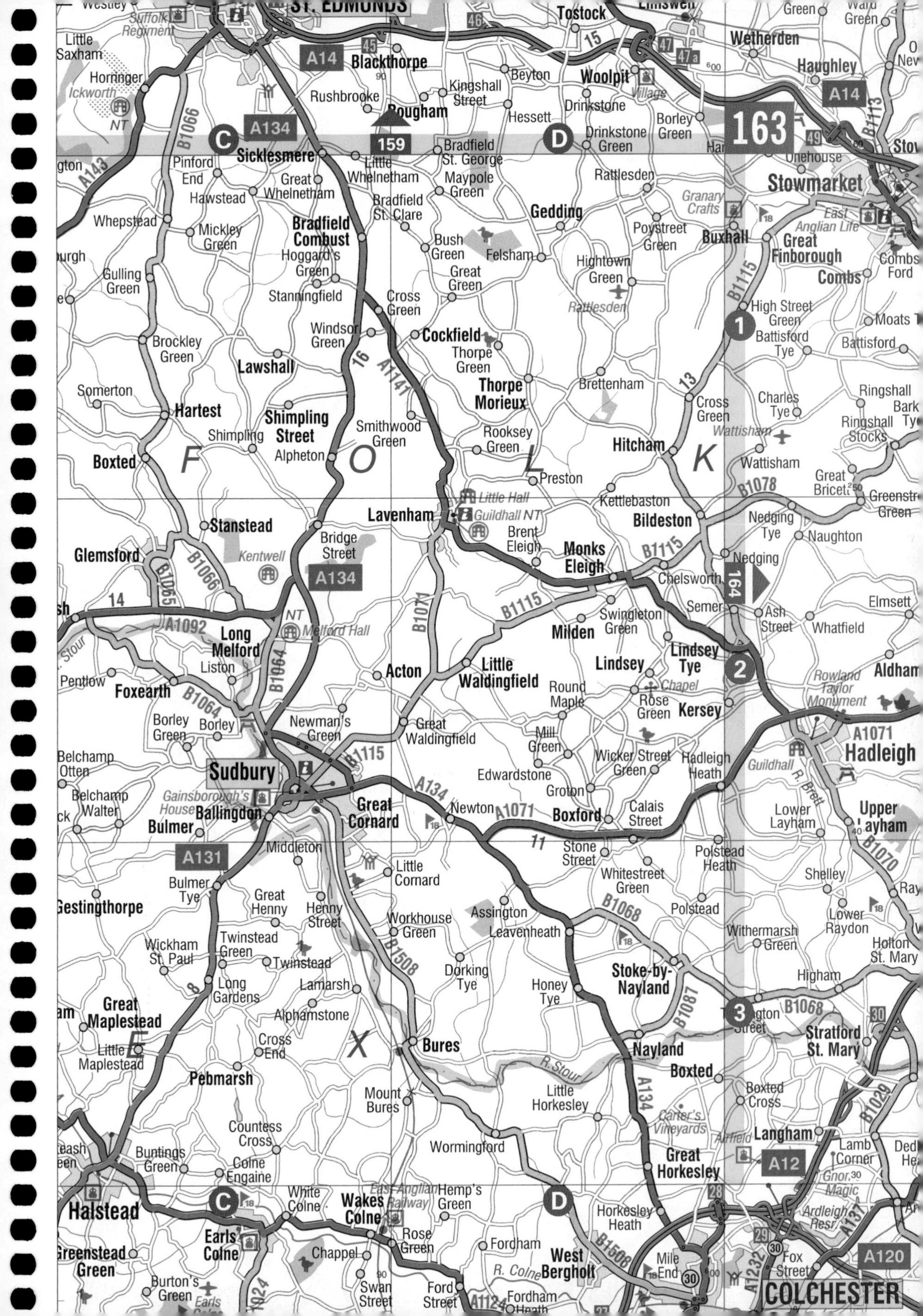

ST. EDMUNDS
Westley
Suffolk Regiment
Tostock
Elmswell
Green
Ward Green
Little Saxham
A14
Blackthorpe
Beyton
Woolpit
Wetherden
Haughley
Horringer
Ickworth
NT
Rushbrooke
Kingshall Street
Village
Rougham
Hessett
Drinkstone
Borley Green
A14
163
B1066
C
A134
159
Bradfield St. George
D
Drinkstone Green
Onehouse
Stowmarket
A143
Sicklesmere
Pinford End
Little Whelnetham
Great Whelnetham
Maypole Green
Rattlesden
Hawstead
Bradfield St. Clare
Granary Crafts
East Anglian Life
Whepstead
Mickley Green
Bradfield Combust
Gedding
Poystreet Green
Buxhall
Great Finborough
Hoggard's Green
Bush Green
Felsham
Hightown Green
Combs Ford
Gulling Green
Great Green
Combs
Stanningfield
Cross Green
Rattlesden
B1115
High Street Green
Moats Tye
Windsor Green
Cockfield
1
Battisford Tye
Battisford
Brockley Green
Lawshall
Thorpe Green
A1141
Thorpe Morieux
Brettenham
Ringshall
Somerton
Hartest
Shimpling Street
Smithwood Green
Cross Green
Charles Tye
Ringshall Stocks
Shimpling
Alpheton
Rooksey Green
Hitcham
Wattisham
Boxted
F
O
L
K
Preston
Wattisham
Great Bricett
Little Hall
Kettlebaston
B1078
Greenstreet Green
Lavenham
Guildhall NT
Bildeston
Stanstead
Brent Eleigh
Nedging Tye
Naughton
Glemsford
Bridge Street
Monks Eleigh
B1115
Nedging
Kentwell
B1066
A134
B1071
Chelsworth
164
B1065
14
NT
B1115
Semer
Elmsett
Melford Hall
Swingleton Green
Ash Street
Whatfield
A1092
Long Melford
Milden
Lindsey Tye
Stour
B1064
Liston
Acton
Little Waldingfield
Lindsey
2
Rowland Taylor Monument
Aldham
Pentlow
Foxearth
Round Maple
Chapel
B1064
Rose Green
Kersey
Borley Green
Borley
Newman's Green
Great Waldingfield
Mill Green
A1071
Hadleigh
Belchamp Otten
B1115
Wicker Street Green
Hadleigh Heath
Guildhall
R. Brett
Sudbury
Edwardstone
Belchamp Walter
Gainsborough's House
Ballingdon
Great Cornard
A134
Groton
Calais Street
Lower Layham
Upper Layham
Bulmer
Newton
A1071
Boxford
A131
Middleton
11
Stone Street
Polstead Heath
B1070
Little Cornard
Whitestreet Green
Shelley
Bulmer Tye
Great Henny
Henny Street
Gestingthorpe
Assington
B1068
Polstead
Lower Raydon
Workhouse Green
Leavenheath
Withermarsh Green
Holton St. Mary
Wickham St. Paul
Twinstead Green
Twinstead
B1508
Dorking Tye
Stoke-by-Nayland
Higham
Long Gardens
Lamarsh
Honey Tye
B1087
Great Maplestead
Alphamstone
3
Street
B1068
E
Cross End
X
Bures
Nayland
Stratford St. Mary
Little Maplestead
R. Stour
Boxted
Pebmarsh
Mount Bures
Little Horkesley
Boxted Cross
A134
Countess Cross
Carter's Vineyards
Airfield
Langham
B1029
Wormingford
Lamb Corner
Buntings Green
Colne Engaine
Great Horkesley
A12
Halstead
C
White Colne
Wakes Colne
East Anglian Railway
Hemp's Green
D
Horkesley Heath
28
Ardleigh Resr.
Earls Colne
Rose Green
Fordham
29
A137
Greenstead Green
Chappel
West Bergholt
B1508
Mile End
30
A1232
Fox Street
A120
Burton's Green
Earls Colne
Swan Street
R. Colne
Ford Street
A1124
Fordham Heath
COLCHESTER

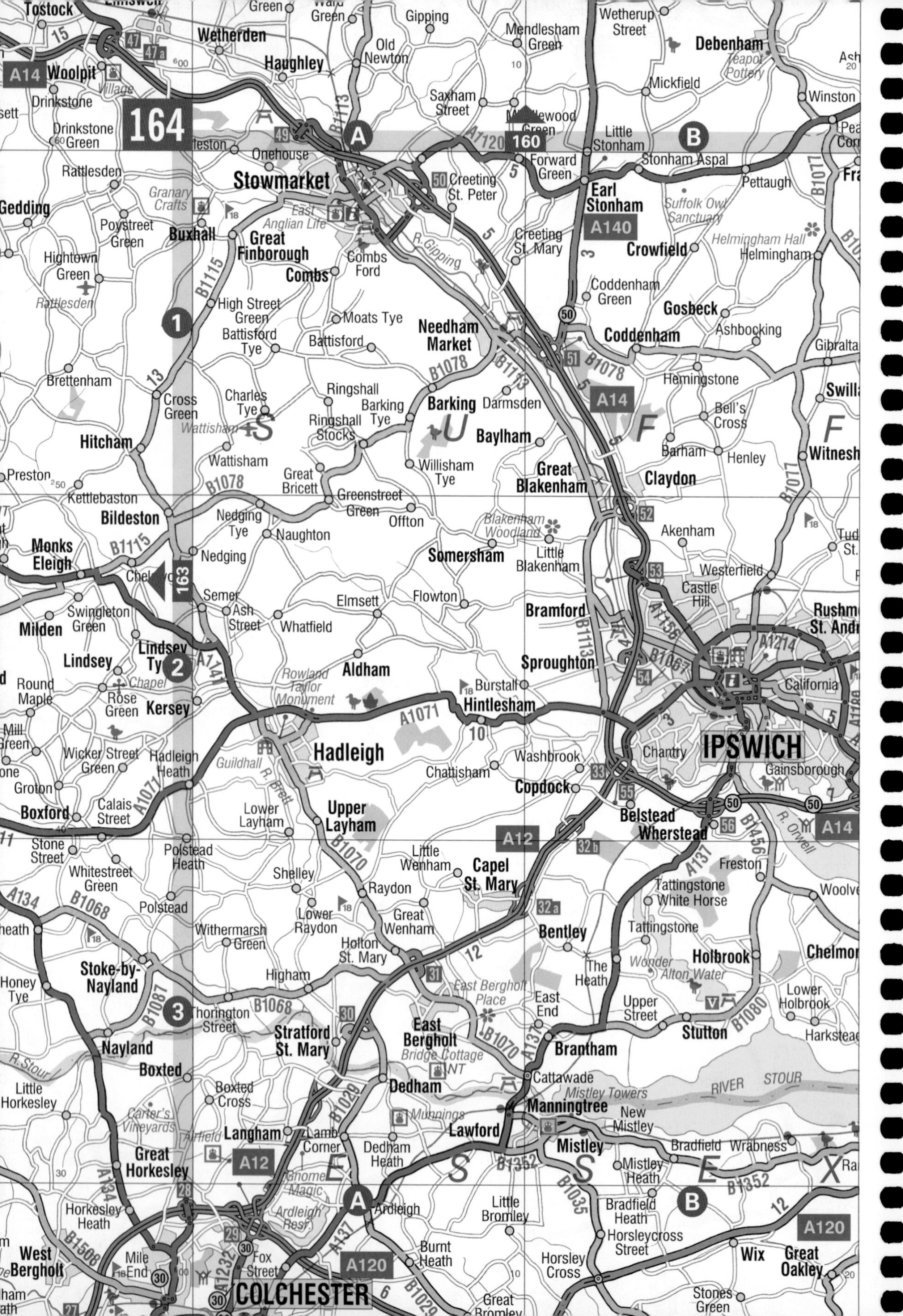
164
160
163
Stowmarket
Needham Market
Hadleigh
IPSWICH
COLCHESTER
Manningtree
Woolpit
Haughley
Wetherden
Debenham
Mendlesham Green
Gipping
Old Newton
Mickfield
Wetherup Street
Winston
Onehouse
Creeting St. Peter
Forward Green
Little Stonham
Stonham Aspal
Earl Stonham
Pettaugh
Rattlesden
Gedding
Buxhall
Great Finborough
Combs
Combs Ford
Crowfield
Helmingham Hall
Helmingham
Creeting St. Mary
Coddenham Green
Gosbeck
Coddenham
Ashbocking
Hightown Green
High Street Green
Moats Tye
Battisford Tye
Battisford
Brettenham
Hemingstone
Cross Green
Charles Tye
Ringshall
Barking Tye
Ringshall Stocks
Barking
Darmsden
Baylham
Bell's Cross
Hitcham
Wattisham
Willisham Tye
Barham
Henley
Great Blakenham
Claydon
Witnesham
Preston
Kettlebaston
Great Bricett
Greenstreet Green
Offton
Bildeston
Nedging Tye
Naughton
Blakenham Woodland
Akenham
Monks Eleigh
Nedging
Somersham
Little Blakenham
Westerfield
Castle Hill
Milden
Swingleton Green
Semer
Ash Street
Whatfield
Elmsett
Flowton
Bramford
Lindsey
Lindsey Tye
Aldham
Sproughton
Rowland Taylor Monument
Burstall
Round Maple
Rose Green
Chapel
Kersey
Hintlesham
California
Mill Green
Wicker Street Green
Hadleigh Heath
Guildhall
Chattisham
Washbrook
Chantry
Gainsborough
Groton
Calais Street
Copdock
Boxford
Lower Layham
Upper Layham
Belstead
Wherstead
Stone Street
Polstead Heath
Little Wenham
Capel St. Mary
Freston
Whitestreet Green
Shelley
Raydon
Tattingstone White Horse
Woolverstone
Polstead
Lower Raydon
Great Wenham
Tattingstone
Withermarsh Green
Holton St. Mary
Bentley
Holbrook
Chelmondiston
Stoke-by-Nayland
Honey Tye
Higham
The Heath
Alton Water
East Bergholt Place
Lower Holbrook
Thorington Street
East End
Upper Street
Stutton
Harkstead
Nayland
Stratford St. Mary
East Bergholt
Brantham
Boxted
Bridge Cottage
Cattawade
Dedham
Mistley Towers
River Stour
R. Stour
Little Horkesley
Boxted Cross
New Mistley
Munnings
Lawford
Carter's Vineyards
Langham
Lamb Corner
Dedham Heath
Mistley
Bradfield
Wrabness
Great Horkesley
Mistley Heath
Horkesley Heath
Ardleigh
Ardleigh Resr.
Little Bromley
Bradfield Heath
Horsleycross Street
West Bergholt
Mile End
Fox Street
Burnt Heath
Horsley Cross
Wix
Great Oakley
Stones Green
Great Bromley
Suffolk Owl Sanctuary
Granary Crafts
East Anglian Life
Teapot Pottery
Saxham Street
Little Stonham
R. Gipping
R. Brett
R. Orwell
Gnome Magic
Mendlewood Green
A14
A140
A12
A120
A1071
A1141
A134
A137
A1214
A1156
A1189
B1113
B1115
B1078
B1077
B1070
B1068
B1087
B1029
B1035
B1352
B1080
B1456
B1067
B1508
A1232
SUFFOLK
ESSEX

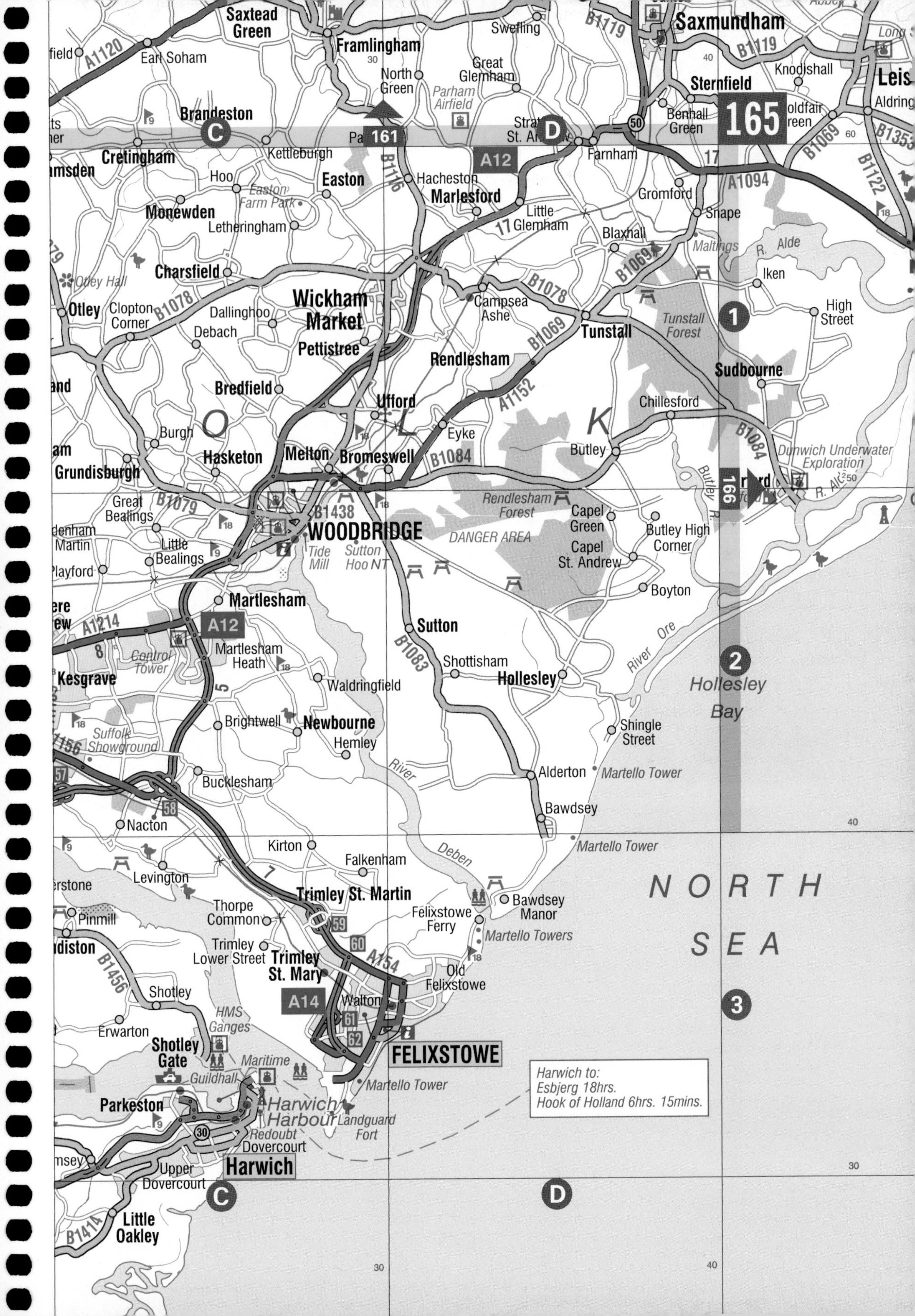

Saxtead Green
Framlingham
Swefling
B1119
Saxmundham
Earl Soham
A1120
North Green
Great Glemham
Parham Airfield
Sternfield
Knodishall
Leis
Aldring
Benhall Green
165
Brandeston
C
Kettleburgh
161
Stratford St. Andrew
D
Farnham
A12
A1094
B1122
B1069
Cretingham
Hoo
Easton
Easton Farm Park
Hacheston
Marlesford
Gromford
Snape
Monewden
Letheringham
Little Glemham
Blaxhall
Maltings
R. Alde
Iken
Charsfield
Otley Hall
Otley
Clopton Corner
B1078
Dallinghoo
Debach
Wickham Market
Pettistree
Campsea Ashe
Tunstall
Tunstall Forest
High Street
1
Rendlesham
Sudbourne
Bredfield
Ufford
A1152
Chillesford
B1084
Burgh
Hasketon
Eyke
Butley
Dunwich Underwater Exploration
Grundisburgh
Melton
Bromeswell
166
Butley R.
R. Alde
Great Bealings
B1079
B1438
Rendlesham Forest
Capel Green
Butley High Corner
WOODBRIDGE
DANGER AREA
Little Bealings
Tide Mill
Sutton Hoo NT
Capel St. Andrew
Playford
Boyton
Martlesham
A1214
A12
Sutton
Control Tower
Martlesham Heath
B1083
Shottisham
River Ore
2
Kesgrave
Hollesley
Hollesley Bay
Waldringfield
Brightwell
Newbourne
Shingle Street
Suffolk Showground
Hemley
River
Bucklesham
Alderton
Martello Tower
Nacton
Bawdsey
Kirton
Martello Tower
Deben
Falkenham
Levington
NORTH SEA
Trimley St. Martin
Bawdsey Manor
Pinmill
Thorpe Common
Felixstowe Ferry
Martello Towers
Trimley Lower Street
Trimley St. Mary
A154
B1456
Shotley
Old Felixstowe
A14
Walton
3
HMS Ganges
Erwarton
Shotley Gate
FELIXSTOWE
Maritime
Guildhall
Martello Tower
Harwich to:
Esbjerg 18hrs.
Hook of Holland 6hrs. 15mins.
Parkeston
Harwich Harbour
Landguard Fort
Redoubt
Dovercourt
Upper Dovercourt
Harwich
C
D
Little Oakley
B1414

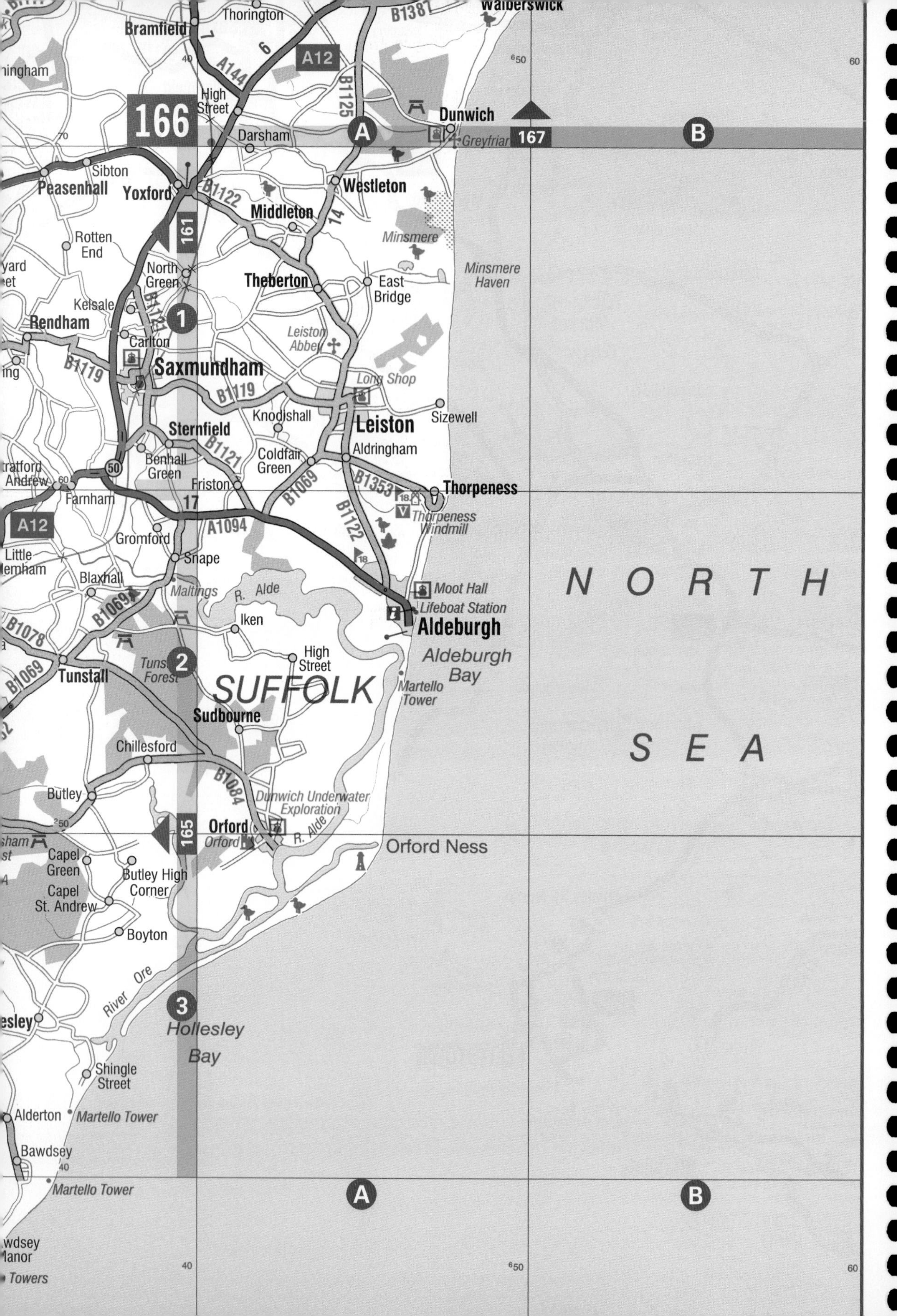

166
167
165
161
Walberswick
Thorington
Bramfield
Dunwich
Greyfriars
Darsham
High Street
Sibton
Peasenhall
Yoxford
Westleton
Middleton
Minsmere
Minsmere Haven
Rotten End
North Green
Theberton
East Bridge
Kelsale
Rendham
Carlton
Leiston Abbey
Saxmundham
Long Shop
Sizewell
Knodishall
Leiston
Sternfield
Aldringham
Coldfair Green
Benhall Green
Friston
Thorpeness
Thorpeness Windmill
Farnham
Gromford
Snape
Little Glemham
Blaxhall
Maltings
R. Alde
Moot Hall
Lifeboat Station
Aldeburgh
Iken
Aldeburgh Bay
Tunstall
Tunstall Forest
High Street
SUFFOLK
Martello Tower
Sudbourne
Chillesford
Butley
Dunwich Underwater Exploration
Orford
Orford Ness
Capel Green
Butley High Corner
Capel St. Andrew
Boyton
River Ore
Hollesley Bay
Shingle Street
Alderton
Martello Tower
Bawdsey
Martello Tower
Bawdsey Manor
Towers
NORTH SEA
A12
A144
A1094
B1387
B1125
B1122
B1121
B1119
B1069
B1078
B1353
B1084

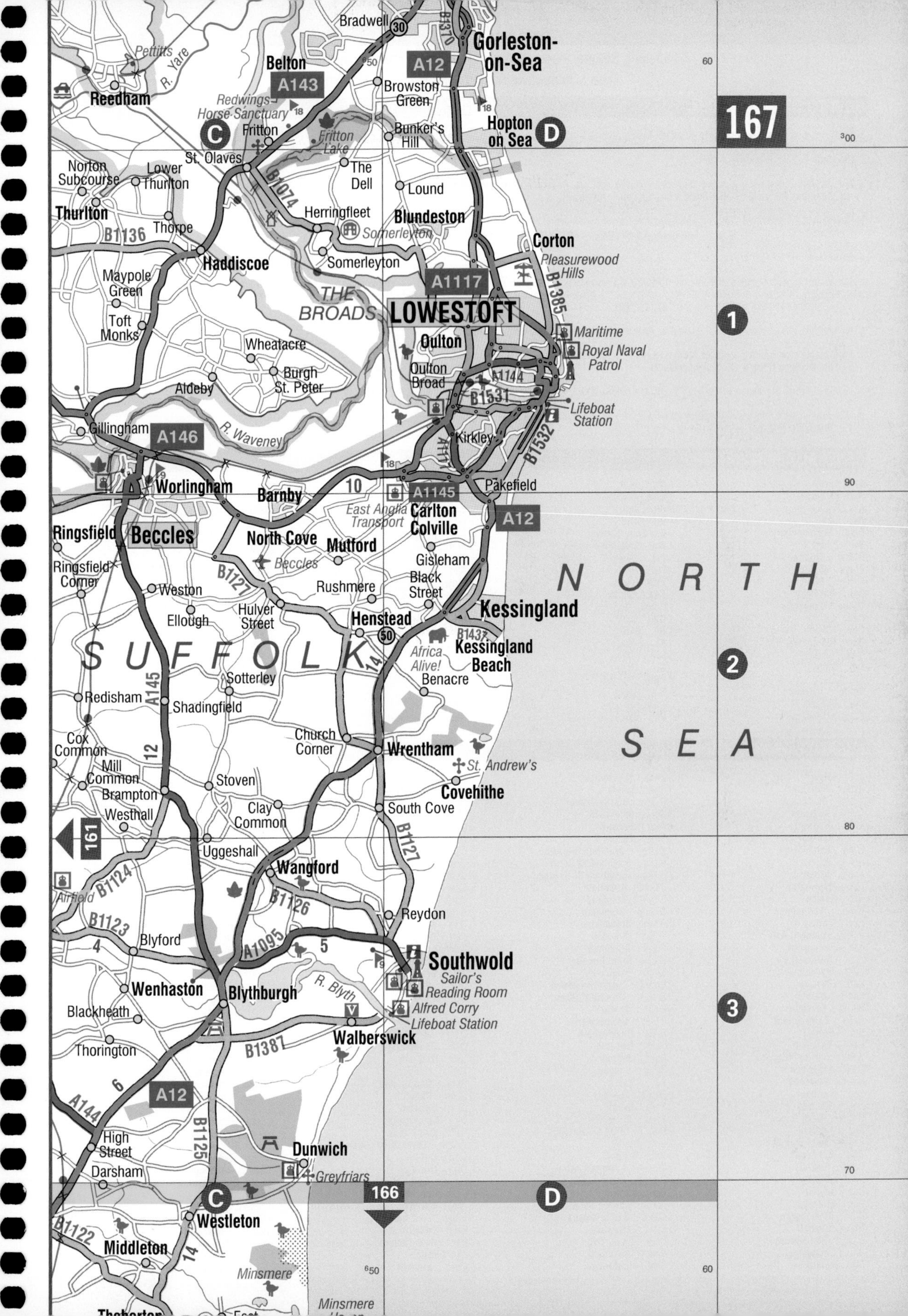
Bradwell
Gorleston-on-Sea
Belton
A12
A143
Reedham
Pettitts
R. Yare
Browston Green
Redwings Horse Sanctuary
Fritton
Fritton Lake
Bunker's Hill
Hopton on Sea
St. Olaves
Norton Subcourse
Lower Thurlton
The Dell
Lound
Thurlton
B1074
Herringfleet
Blundeston
Thorpe
B1136
Somerleyton
Corton
Haddiscoe
Pleasurewood Hills
Maypole Green
A1117
B1385
THE BROADS
LOWESTOFT
Toft Monks
Oulton
Maritime
Wheatacre
Royal Naval Patrol
Oulton Broad
Burgh St. Peter
A1144
Aldeby
B1531
Lifeboat Station
Gillingham
A146
R. Waveney
Kirkley
B1532
Worlingham
Barnby
Pakefield
A1145
East Anglia Transport
Carlton Colville
A12
Ringsfield
Beccles
North Cove
Mutford
Gisleham
NORTH
Ringsfield Corner
B1127
Black Street
Rushmere
Weston
Kessingland
Ellough
Hulver Street
Henstead
B1437
Kessingland Beach
SUFFOLK
Africa Alive!
Benacre
Sotterley
A145
Redisham
Shadingfield
Church Corner
Wrentham
SEA
Cox Common
St. Andrew's
Mill Common
Stoven
Covehithe
Brampton
Clay Common
South Cove
Westhall
161
B1127
Uggeshall
Wangford
B1124
Airfield
B1126
Reydon
B1123
Blyford
A1095
Southwold
Sailor's Reading Room
Wenhaston
Blythburgh
R. Blyth
Alfred Corry Lifeboat Station
Blackheath
Walberswick
B1387
Thorington
A12
A144
High Street
B1125
Dunwich
Darsham
Greyfriars
166
Westleton
B1122
Middleton
Minsmere
C
D
1
2
3
60
90
80
70
650
300

Including Streets, Places & Areas, Industrial Estates, Junction Names, Flats & Walkways, Stations and Places of Interest.

HOW TO USE THIS INDEX

1. Each street name is followed by its Postcode District, then by its Locality abbreviation(s) and then by its map reference; e.g. **Abbey Hill** IP21: Hox . . . .2C **38** is in the IP21 Postcode District and the Hoxne Locality and is to be found in square 2C on page **38**. The page number is shown in bold type.

2. A strict alphabetical order is followed in which Av., Rd., St., etc. (though abbreviated) are read in full and as part of the street name; e.g. **Adamson Rd.** appears after **Adam's La.** but before **Adams Pl.**

3. Streets and a selection of flats and walkways that cannot be shown on street map pages **4-157**, appear in the index with the thoroughfare to which they are connected shown in brackets; e.g. **Adrian Ct.** *NR32: Low . . . . 6J **9** (off Alexandra Rd.)*

4. Addresses that are in more than one part are referred to as not continuous.

5. Places and areas are shown in the index in **BLUE TYPE** and the map reference is to the actual map square in which the town centre or area is located and not to the place name shown on the map. Map references for entries that appear on street map pages **4-157** are shown first, with references to road map pages **158-167** shown in brackets; e.g. **ACTON . . . .4G 107 (2C 163)**

6. An example of a selected place of interest is **Aldeburgh Museum (Moot Hall) 5K 95**

7. An example of a station is **Beccles Station (Rail) . . . . 3F 13**, also included is **Park & Ride**. e.g. **Martlesham (Park & Ride) 4G 135**

8. Junction names are shown in the index in **BOLD CAPITAL TYPE**; e.g. **CAPEL ST MARY INTERCHANGE. . . .2K 147**

9. Map references for entries that appear on large scale pages **4**, **5** & **157** are shown first, with small scale map references shown in brackets; e.g. **Abbey Ct.** IP1: Ips 1A **4** (6J **131**)

GENERAL ABBREVIATIONS

All. : Alley
App. : Approach
Av. : Avenue
Bk. : Back
Blvd. : Boulevard
Bri. : Bridge
B'way. : Broadway
Bldgs. : Buildings
Bungs. : Bungalows
Bus. : Business
C'way. : Causeway
Cen. : Centre
Chu. : Church
Chyd. : Churchyard
Circ. : Circle
Cir. : Circus
Cl. : Close
Comn. : Common
Cnr. : Corner
Cotts. : Cottages
Ct. : Court
Cres. : Crescent
Cft. : Croft
Dr. : Drive
E. : East
Ent. : Enterprise
Est. : Estate
Fld. : Field
Flds. : Fields
Gdn. : Garden
Gdns. : Gardens
Gth. : Garth
Ga. : Gate
Gt. : Great
Grn. : Green
Gro. : Grove
Hgts. : Heights
Ho. : House
Ho's. : Houses
Ind. : Industrial
Info. : Information
Junc. : Junction
La. : Lane
Lit. : Little
Lwr. : Lower
Mnr. : Manor
Mans. : Mansions
Mkt. : Market
Mdw. : Meadow
Mdws. : Meadows
M. : Mews
Mt. : Mount
Mus. : Museum
Nth. : North
Pde. : Parade
Pk. : Park
Pas. : Passage
Pl. : Place
Pct. : Precinct
Res. : Residential
Ri. : Rise
Rd. : Road
Shop. : Shopping
Sth. : South
Sq. : Square
Sta. : Station
St. : Street
Ter. : Terrace
Trad. : Trading
Up. : Upper
Va. : Vale
Vw. : View
Vs. : Villas
Vis. : Visitors
Wlk. : Walk
W. : West
Yd. : Yard

LOCALITY ABBREVIATIONS

Act : **Acton**
Aken : **Akenham**
Aldeb : **Aldeburgh**
Alder : **Alderton**
Aldh : **Aldham**
Aldr : **Aldringham**
A'ing : **Ashbocking**
Ashb : **Ashby**
Ashe : **Ashen**
Ath : **Athelington**
Bac : **Bacton**
B'ham : **Badingham**
Badl : **Badley**
B Ash : **Badwell Ash**
Ball : **Ballingdon**
Bard : **Bardwell**
Barh : **Barham**
Bark : **Barking**
Barnb : **Barnby**
Barnh : **Barnham**
Barni : **Barningham**
Barr : **Barrow**
Bars : **Barsham**
B Mil : **Barton Mills**
Batt : **Battisford**
Bawd : **Bawdsey**
Bay : **Baylham**
Becc : **Beccles**
B Row : **Beck Row**
Bed : **Bedfield**
Bel P : **Belchamp St Paul**
Bels : **Belstead**
Benh : **Benhall**
Bent : **Bentley**
Bey : **Beyton**
Bild : **Bildeston**
Blac : **Blackthorpe**
Blax : **Blaxhall**
B Nor : **Blo' Norton**
Blun : **Blundeston**
Bly : **Blyford**
Blyth : **Blythburgh**
Borl : **Borley**
B Grn : **Borley Green**
Bote : **Botesdale**
Boxf : **Boxford**
Boxt : **Boxted**
B Com : **Bradfield Combust**
B Cla : **Bradfield St Clare**
B Geo : **Bradfield St George**
B'field : **Bramfield**
B'ford : **Bramford**
Bramp : **Brampton**
B'ton : **Brandeston**
B'don : **Brandon**
Brant : **Brantham**
B Ele : **Brent Eleigh**
Brigh : **Brightwell**
Broc G : **Brockford Green**
Broc S : **Brockford Street**
Brom : **Brome**
B'well : **Bromeswell**
Buck : **Bucklesham**
Bulc : **Bulcamp**
Bulm : **Bulmer**
Bung : **Bungay**
Bure : **Bures**
B'gate : **Burgate**
Burg : **Burgh**
Burw : **Burwell**
Bury E : **Bury St Edmunds**
But : **Butley**
Bux : **Buxhall**
Cam A : **Campsea Ashe**
Cap M : **Capel St Mary**
Carl : **Carlton**
Car C : **Carlton Colville**
Cas C : **Castle Camps**
Catt : **Cattawade**
Cave : **Cavendish**
Char : **Charsfield**
Chat : **Chattisham**
Chedb : **Chedburgh**
Chelm : **Chelmondiston**
Chels : **Chelsworth**
Chev : **Chevington**
Clar : **Clare**
Clay : **Claydon**
C'field : **Cockfield**
Cod : **Coddenham**
Comb : **Combs**
Con W : **Coney Weston**
Cook : **Cookley**
Cop : **Copdock**
Cort : **Corton**
Cott : **Cotton**
C Mary : **Creeting St Mary**
C Pet : **Creeting St Peter**
Cret : **Cretingham**
Crow : **Crowfield**
Cul : **Culford**
Dalh : **Dalham**
Dall : **Dallinghoo**
Dars : **Darsham**
Deb : **Debenham**
Ded : **Dedham**
Denh : **Denham**
Denn : **Dennington**
Dens : **Denston**
Dep : **Depden**
Dit : **Ditchingham**
Drin : **Drinkstone**
Drin G : **Drinkstone Green**
Dub : **Dublin**
Dun : **Dunwich**
E Soh : **Earl Soham**
E Sto : **Earl Stonham**
Ears : **Earsham**
E Ber : **East Bergholt**
East : **Easton**
Edw : **Edwardstone**
Ell : **Ellough**
E'sett : **Elmsett**
E'well : **Elmswell**
Elv : **Elveden**
Eris : **Eriswell**
Erw : **Erwarton**
Exn : **Exning**
Eye : **Eye**
Eyk : **Eyke**
F Mag : **Fakenham Magna**
Falk : **Falkenham**
Farn : **Farnham**
Felix : **Felixstowe**
Fels : **Felsham**
Finn : **Finningham**
Flix : **Flixton**
Flow : **Flowton**
Ford : **Fordham**
Forn S : **Fornham All Saints**
Forn G : **Fornham St Genevieve**
Forn M : **Fornham St Martin**
Forw G : **Forward Green**
Foxe : **Foxearth**
Foxh : **Foxhall**
F'ham : **Framlingham**
Fram : **Framsden**
Frec : **Freckenham**
Fress : **Fressingfield**
Frest : **Freston**
Fris : **Friston**
Fros : **Frostenden**
Gar : **Garboldisham**
Gaz : **Gazeley**
Ged : **Gedding**
Geld : **Geldeston**
Gill : **Gillingham**
Gipp : **Gipping**
Gisle : **Gisleham**
Gisli : **Gislingham**
Glem : **Glemsford**
Gos : **Gosbeck**
Gt Ash : **Great Ashfield**
Gt Bar : **Great Barton**

Gt Bea : **Great Bealings**
Gt Bla : **Great Blakenham**
Gt Bra : **Great Bradley**
Gt Bri : **Great Bricett**
Gt Cor : **Great Cornard**
Gt Fin : **Great Finborough**
Gt Liv : **Great Livermere**
Gt Thu : **Great Thurlow**
Gt Wal : **Great Waldingfield**
Gt Whe : **Great Whelnetham**
Gt Wra : **Great Wratting**
Gro : **Groton**
Gru : **Grundisburgh**
Hach : **Hacheston**
Hadl : **Hadleigh**
H'orth : **Halesworth**
Harg : **Hargrave**
Hark : **Harkstead**
Harl : **Harleston**
Hart : **Hartest**
Hask : **Hasketon**
Haug : **Haughley**
Have : **Haverhill**
Haws : **Hawstead**
Hel B : **Helions Bumpstead**
Helm : **Helmingham**
Hemi : **Hemingstone**
Henl : **Henley**
Hens : **Henstead**
Hep : **Hepworth**
Herr : **Herringfleet**
H'well : **Herringswell**
Hess : **Hessett**
Hev : **Heveningham**
High : **Higham**
Hind : **Hinderclay**
Hint : **Hintlesham**
Hit : **Hitcham**
Holb : **Holbrook**
Holl : **Hollesley**
Holt : **Holton**
H Mar : **Holton St Mary**
Holy R : **Holywell Row**
Home : **Homersfield**
Honi : **Honington**
Hoo : **Hoo**
Hop : **Hopton**
Horh : **Horham**
Horr : **Horringer**
Hox : **Hoxne**
Hund : **Hundon**
Huns : **Hunston**
Hunt : **Huntingfield**
Ick : **Icklingham**
Ilk A : **Ilketshall St Andrew**
Ilk J : **Ilketshall St John**
Ilk L : **Ilketshall St Lawrence**
Ing : **Ingham**
Ips : **Ipswich**
Ixw : **Ixworth**
Ixw T : **Ixworth Thorpe**
Ked : **Kedington**
Kel : **Kelsale**
Kenn : **Kennett**
Ken H : **Kenny Hill**
Kent : **Kentford**
Kesg : **Kesgrave**
Kess : **Kessingland**
Ket : **Kettleburgh**
Kirt : **Kirton**
Knod : **Knodishall**
Lake : **Lakenheath**
Lang : **Langham**
Lave : **Lavenham**
Lawf : **Lawford**
Laws : **Lawshall**
Laxf : **Laxfield**
Lay : **Layham**
Leav : **Leavenheath**
Leis : **Leiston**
Levi : **Levington**
Lis : **Liston**
L Bea : **Little Bealings**
L Bla : **Little Blakenham**
L Brad : **Little Bradley**
L Cor : **Little Cornard**
L Fin : **Little Finborough**
L Sax : **Little Saxham**
L Sto : **Little Stonham**
L Thu : **Little Thurlow**
L Wal : **Little Waldingfield**
L Wen : **Little Wenham**
L Wrat : **Little Wratting**
L Mel : **Long Melford**
Lou : **Lound**
L Hac : **Lower Hacheston**
Low : **Lowestoft**
M Wes : **Market Weston**
Marl : **Marlesford**
Martl : **Martlesham**
Martl H : **Martlesham Heath**
Melli : **Mellis**
Mells : **Mells**
Melt : **Melton**
Mendh : **Mendham**
Mendl : **Mendlesham**
Men G : **Mendlesham Green**
Metf : **Metfield**
Mett : **Mettingham**
Midd : **Middleton**
Mide : **Mildenhall**
M Ele : **Monks Eleigh**
Mou : **Moulton**
M Bur : **Mount Bures**
Mut : **Mutford**
Nac : **Nacton**
Nay : **Nayland**
Ned : **Nedging**
Nee : **Needham**
Nee M : **Needham Market**
Nett : **Nettlestead**
Newb : **Newbourne**
New G : **Newman's Green**
Newm : **Newmarket**
Newt : **Newton**
Nor C : **North Cove**
Nort : **Norton**
Now : **Nowton**
Oak : **Oakley**
Occ : **Occold**
Off : **Offton**
Old N : **Old Newton**
One : **Onehouse**
Orf : **Orford**
Otl : **Otley**
Oul : **Oulton**
Oul B : **Oulton Broad**
Pake : **Pakenham**
Pal : **Palgrave**
Pea : **Peasenhall**
Pent : **Pentlow**
Petta : **Pettaugh**
Petti : **Pettistree**
Play : **Playford**
Pols : **Polstead**
Posl : **Poslingford**
Pur F : **Purdis Farm**
RAF L : **RAF Lakenheath**
RAF M : **RAF Mildenhall**
Rat : **Rattlesden**
Ray : **Raydon**
Rede : **Redenhall**
Redg : **Redgrave**
Red L : **Red Lodge**
Rend : **Rendlesham**
Rey : **Reydon**
Rick : **Rickinghall**
R'field : **Ringsfield**
R'hall : **Ringshall**
Ris : **Risby**
Roug : **Rougham**
Rushb : **Rushbrooke**
Rushm : **Rushmere**
Rush A : **Rushmere St Andrew**
San D : **Santon Downham**
Sap : **Sapiston**
Saxm : **Saxmundham**
Saxt : **Saxtead**
Sax G : **Saxtead Green**
Scole : **Scole**
Sem : **Semer**
Shel : **Shelley**
Shim : **Shimpling**
Shot : **Shotley**
Shot G : **Shotley Gate**
Sib : **Sibton**
S'mere : **Sicklesmere**
Size : **Sizewell**
Snail : **Snailwell**
Snap : **Snape**
S'ton : **Somerleyton**
S'ham : **Somersham**
Sou : **Southwold**
Spex : **Spexhall**
Spro : **Sproughton**
Stann : **Stanningfield**
Stans : **Stanstead**
Stant : **Stanton**
Ster : **Sternfield**
Stoke A : **Stoke Ash**
Stoke C : **Stoke by Clare**
Stoke N : **Stoke-by-Nayland**
Ston A : **Stonham Aspal**
Stov : **Stoven**
Stowl : **Stowlangtoft**
Stowm : **Stowmarket**
Stowu : **Stowupland**
Stradb : **Stradbroke**
Stradi : **Stradishall**
Strat M : **Stratford St Mary**
Stur : **Sturmer**
Stus : **Stuston**
Stut : **Stutton**
Sud : **Sudbourne**
S'bury : **Sudbury**
Sutt : **Sutton**
Swil : **Swilland**
Syle : **Syleham**
Tan : **Tannington**
Tatt : **Tattingstone**
Theb : **Theberton**
Thel : **Thelnetham**
Thorn : **Thorndon**
Thor : **Thorpeness**
Thran : **Thrandeston**
Thur : **Thurston**
Thw : **Thwaite**
Tim : **Timworth**
Tost : **Tostock**
T Mart : **Trimley St Martin**
T Mary : **Trimley St Mary**
Tros : **Troston**
Tud : **Tuddenham**
Tun : **Tunstall**
Ubb : **Ubbeston**
Uff : **Ufford**
Ugg : **Uggeshall**
U Hol : **Upper Holton**
Walb : **Walberswick**
Wald : **Waldringfield**
Wal : **Walpole**
Wals W : **Walsham le Willows**
Wang : **Wangford**
Wash : **Washbrook**
W'field : **Wattisfield**
W'ham : **Wattisham**
Weet : **Weeting**
Wen : **Wenhaston**
W Row : **West Row**
Weste : **Westerfield**
W'hall : **Westhall**
W'orpe : **Westhorpe**
Westl : **Westleton**
W'ley : **Westley**
Westo : **Weston**
W'den : **Wetherden**
W'sett : **Wetheringsett**
Wey : **Weybread**
What : **Whatfield**
Whep : **Whepstead**
Wher : **Wherstead**
W'rook : **Wickhambrook**
Wick M : **Wickham Market**
Wick S : **Wickham Skeith**
Wilb : **Wilby**
Will : **Willisham**
Wing : **Wingfield**
Wins : **Winston**
Wins G : **Winston Green**
Wiss : **Wissett**
With : **Withersfield**
Witn : **Witnesham**
Wood : **Woodbridge**
Wool : **Woolpit**
Worl : **Worlingham**
W'ton : **Worlington**
W'orth : **Worlingworth**
Wort : **Wortham**
W'well : **Wortwell**
Wrent : **Wrentham**
Wyve : **Wyverstone**
Yax : **Yaxley**
Yox : **Yoxford**

A

Abbas Wlk. CO10: Gt Cor 6H **127**
Abbey Cl. IP12: Rend 7B **122**
IP21: Thran 4F **37**
IP31: Ixw 5H **29**
Abbey Ct. IP1: Ips 1A **4** (6J **131**)
Abbeydale NR33: Car C 7D **10**
Abbeyfields IP14: Haug 3C **70**
IP33: Bury E 3K **157** (7J **53**)
Abbey Gardens
Bury St Edmunds . . .5J 157 (1H 59)
Abbey Gdns. IP13: Cam A 3B **122**
Abbey Gate
Bury St Edmunds . . .5J 157 (1H 59)
Abbeygate Picturehouse
Bury St Edmunds . . .5H 157 (1G 59)
Abbeygate St.
IP33: Bury E 5H **157** (1G **59**)
Abbey Hill IP21: Hox 2C **38**
Abbey La. IP16: Leis 1F **93**
Abbey Rd. CO10: S'bury 2D **126**
IP16: Leis 2H **93**
Abbitts Pl. CO10: Glem 3A **104**
Abbot Cl. IP33: Bury E 2D **58**
Abbot Rd. IP33: Bury E 2D **58**
Abbotsbury Cl. IP2: Ips 5J **137**
Abbotsbury Rd. IP33: Bury E 3D **58**
Abbots Cl. CO10: S'bury 1C **126**
Abbots Ga. IP33: Bury E 3H **59**
Abbot's Hall Rd. IP14: Stowm 5F **85**
Abbot's Wlk. IP14: Stowm 5F **85**
Abbotts Ct. CB9: Stur 6K **101**
Abbotts Hall Cl. CO10: Gt Wal 7K **107**
Abbotts Mdw. IP30: Wool 5B **64**
Abbotts Rd. CB9: Have 2F **101**
Abercorn Ct. CB9: Have 5E **100**
Aberdare Cl. IP2: Ips 4K **137**
Aberdeen Way IP4: Ips 4F **133**
Aberfoyle Cl. IP4: Ips 4G **133**
Abernant Dr. CB8: Newm 6G **47**
Abigail Ct. NR32: Low 5K **9**
Abingdon Cl. IP2: Ips 5J **137**
Abington Pl. CB9: Have 2F **101**
Ablett Cl. IP21: Wey 3E **40**
Ablitts Mdw. IP13: Gru 5H **117**
Acacia Av. IP32: Bury E 4F **53**
Acacia Cl. IP3: Pur F 5J **139**
IP28: Red L 6G **25**
Acer Gro. IP8: Ips 5E **136**
Acer Rd. IP12: Rend 6C **122**
Acer Way IP28: Red L 6J **25**
Acheson Way IP15: Aldeb 4J **95**
Acorn Bus. Cen. CB8: Newm 2E **46**
Acorn Cl. IP2: Ips 4E **136**
Acorn Ri. IP12: Holl 1K **141**
Acorns, The IP31: Thur 7A **56**
Acorn Way IP5: Martl H 5J **135**
IP28: Red L 5J **25**
Acre Cl. IP6: Witn 1B **116**
Acre Wlk. CO10: Clar 3C **102**
ACTON 4G 107 (2C 163)
Acton Cl. CO10: S'bury 3E **126**
IP8: B'ford 3C **130**
Acton Gdns. IP8: B'ford 3C **130**
Acton La. CO10: S'bury 1F **127**
(Hawkins Rd.)
CO10: S'bury 3E **126**
(Waldingfield Rd.)
Acton Pl. Ind. Est. CO10: Act 2F **107**
Acton Rd. CO10: Gt Wal 5J **107**
IP8: B'ford 3C **130**
NR33: Low 5G **11**
Acton Sq. CO10: S'bury 4D **126**
Adair Rd. IP1: Ips 5F **131**
Adams Cl. IP2: Ips 3A **138**
Adam's La. IP18: Walb 7F **45**
Adamson Rd. IP18: Rey 1H **45**
Adams Pl. IP5: Kesg 6C **134**
Adams Wlk. IP12: Wood 5J **121**
Adastral Cl. CB8: Newm 5E **46**
IP11: Felix 7C **154**
Adastral Pk. IP5: Martl H 6J **135**
Addington Rd. IP11: T Mary 1B **154**
Addison Rd. CO10: S'bury 2F **127**
Addison Way IP6: Gt Bla 4A **114**
Adelaide Rd. IP4: Ips 7H **133**
Admiral Rd. IP8: Ips 6G **137**
Admirals Wlk. IP12: Wood 3G **121**
IP16: Thor 6D **94**
Adrian Ct. *NR32: Low 6J* ***9***
(off Alexandra Rd.)
Adrian Rd. NR32: Low 6J **9**
Africa Alive! 5G 17
Agate Cl. IP1: Ips 4F **131**
Aggas Acre IP23: Melli 6A **36**
Ailmar Cl. NR32: Low 3F **9**
Ailwin Rd. IP32: Bury E 2A **60**
Ainslie Rd. IP1: Ips 2A **4** (7J **131**)
Airedale NR33: Car C 6D **10**
Airey Cl. CO10: Newt 3D **128**
NR32: Oul 3E **8**
Airfield Ind. Pk. IP23: Eye 6G **37**
Airfield Rd. IP32: Bury E 7C **54**
Aisthorpe IP9: Cap M 2G **147**
AKENHAM 2B 164
Akenham Cl. IP1: Ips 1H **131**
Akethorpe Way NR32: Low 5F **9**
Alabaster Cl. IP7: Hadl 3J **129**
Alandale Dr. NR33: Kess 5K **17**
Alan Rd. IP3: Ips 2D **138**
Alasdair Pl. IP6: Clay 4D **114**
Alban Sq. IP12: Martl 3H **135**
Albany, The IP4: Ips 5C **132**
Albany Rd. NR32: Low 6K **9**

Albemarle Rd. IP33: Bury E ... 2D 58
Alberta Cl. IP5: Kesg ... 5A 134
Albert Cl. IP22: Rick ... 6G 35
Albert Cres. IP33: Bury E ... 1F 59
Albert Pl. IP13: F'ham ... 6C 90
Albert Rd. IP13: F'ham ... 6C 90
Albert Rolph Dr. IP27: Lake ... 7C 20
Albert St. IP33: Bury E ... 1F 59
Albert Wlk. *IP11: Felix ... 4F 155*
(off Hamilton Rd.)
Albion Ct. CB8: Newm ... 2E 46
Albion Hill IP4: Ips ... 1K 5 (6D 132)
Albion Rd. NR35: Bung ... 3D 14
Albion St. IP17: Saxm ... 6H 91
ALBURGH ... 1C 161
Alconbury IP27: RAF L ... 4J 21
ALDEBURGH ... 5J 95 (2A 166)
Aldeburgh Cinema ... 5J 95
Aldeburgh Cl. CB9: Have ... 4D 100
Aldeburgh Community & Sports Cen. ... 5H 95
Aldeburgh Gdns. IP4: Ips ... 7E 132
Aldeburgh Golf Course ... 3F 95
Aldeburgh Lodge IP15: Aldeb ... 4J 95
Aldeburgh Lodge Gdns.
IP15: Aldeb ... 4K 95
Aldeburgh Museum (Moot Hall) ... 5K 95
Aldeburgh Rd. IP16: Aldr, Leis ... 4J 93
IP17: Fris ... 6D 92
Aldeburgh Yacht Club ... 7J 95
ALDEBY ... 1C 167
Aldecar La. IP17: Benh ... 4C 92
Alde Cl. IP17: Saxm ... 5H 91
Alde Ho. IP15: Aldeb ... 5J 95
Alde Ho. Dr. IP15: Aldeb ... 5J 95
Alde La. IP15: Aldeb ... 5J 95
Alder Carr Farm ... 3H 111
Alder Cl. IP17: Benh ... 3C 92
Aldercroft Cl. IP1: Ips ... 2K 131
Aldercroft Rd. IP1: Ips ... 3K 131
Alder Dr. NR33: Car C ... 5B 10
Aldergrove Cl. IP19: H'orth ... 5A 42
Alderlee IP2: Ips ... 6H 137
Alderman Rd. IP1: Ips ... 3B 4 (1K 137)
Alde Rd. CB9: Have ... 2F 101
Aldershot Av. IP12: Sutt ... 2D 140
ALDERTON ... 5H 141 (2D 165)
Alderton Cl. CB9: Have ... 1D 100
Alderton Rd. IP12: Holl ... 4F 141
Alder Way CO10: S'bury ... 3E 126
ALDHAM ... 2A 164
Aldham Ct. CB9: Have ... 4D 100
Aldham Gdns. IP14: Stowm ... 6G 85
Aldham Mill Hill IP7: Hadl ... 1G 129
Aldham Rd. IP7: Hadl ... 2J 129
Aldis Av. IP14: Stowm ... 6F 85
Aldous Cl. CO7: E Ber ... 3B 146
Aldous Ct. IP14: Deb ... 2H 87
Aldridge La. IP28: Forn S ... 1D 52
ALDRINGHAM ... 7H 93 (1A 166)
Aldringham La. IP16: Aldr ... 6G 93
IP17: Knod ... 6G 93
Aldringham M. IP11: Felix ... 3C 154
Aldringham Pk. IP16: Aldr ... 6J 93
Aldringham Rd. IP17: Knod ... 6G 93
Aldwyck Way NR33: Oul B ... 5E 10
Alexander Cl. NR34: Becc ... 6F 13
Alexander Dr. CO10: Gt Wal ... 7K 107
IP6: Nee M ... 3F 111
IP14: Finn ... 5H 67
Alexander Way IP28: Ris ... 2D 50
Alexandra Gdns. IP5: Kesg ... 6F 135
Alexandra Rd. CO10: S'bury ... 4F 127
(Newton Rd.)
CO10: S'bury ... 3F 127
(Windham Rd.)
IP4: Ips ... 2J 5 (7C 132)
IP11: Felix ... 2D 154
NR32: Low ... 7J 9
NR34: Becc ... 3E 12
Alfred Corry Mus. ... 7J 45
Alice Driver Rd. IP13: Gru ... 6H 117
Alicia Ct. IP33: Bury E ... 7K 157 (2J 59)
Allenby Rd. IP2: Ips ... 7H 131
Allen Rd. IP7: Hadl ... 2H 129
NR32: Oul B ... 7C 8
Alley, The IP7: M Ele ... 2E 108
Alley Rd. IP10: Kirt ... 2J 153
All Fired Up Ceramics ... 3D 4
Allhallows Ct. IP3: Ips ... 5E 138
Allington Cl. IP4: Ips ... 6D 132
Allington Rd. IP19: H'orth ... 5A 42
Allington-Smith Cl. NR32: Oul ... 3D 8
Allington Wlk. CB9: Have ... 3D 100
Allotment La. IP6: A'ing ... 2F 117
Allotment Rd. CB8: Dalh ... 6G 49
All Saints Cl. CB8: Gaz ... 2H 49
IP14: W'sett ... 5J 69
All Saints Ct.
IP33: Bury E ... 3G 157 (7G 53)
All Saints Dr. NR34: Becc ... 6F 13
All Saints Grn. NR34: Worl ... 4J 13
All Saints Rd. CB8: Newm ... 6G 47
IP1: Ips ... 6J 131
IP6: C Mary ... 7A 86
NR33: Low ... 5G 11
ALL SAINTS SOUTH ELMHAM ... 1D 161
All Saints Wlk. IP28: W'ton ... 2B 24
Alma Cl. IP4: Ips ... 4E 132
Alma Pl. IP17: Saxm ... 6H 91
Alma Rd. NR32: Low ... 7H 9
Alma St. NR32: Low ... 7J 9
Almond Dr. IP28: Frec, Red L ... 5J 25
Almondhayes IP2: Ips ... 3K 137
Almshouse Rd. IP30: Roug ... 4H 61
Almshouses, The IP30: Rushb ... 7E 60
Alnesbourn Cres. IP3: Ips ... 7G 139
Alnesbourne Priory IP10: Nac ... 7G 139
Alpe St. IP1: Ips ... 1B 4 (6K 131)
Alpha Bus. Pk. IP1: Ips ... 2G 131
ALPHAMSTONE ... 3C 163
Alpha Ter. IP3: Ips ... 5J 139
ALPHETON ... 1C 163
Alston Cl. CO10: Newt ... 2C 128
Alston Cres. CO10: Stans ... 3D 104
Alston Rd. IP3: Ips ... 6K 5 (2D 138)
Alston's Ct. IP3: Ips ... 5H 139
Altitude Bus. Pk. IP3: Ips ... 5H 139
Alton Grn. IP9: Holb ... 6F 151
Alton Hall La. IP9: Stut ... 4B 150
Alton Water (Nature Reserve)
... 6J 149, 3A 150 & 4C 150
Alton Water Sports Cen. ... 4D 150
Alton Water Vis. Cen. ... 5D 150
Alvis Cl. IP32: Bury E ... 1B 60
Alvis Wlk. IP1: Ips ... 4E 130
Amber Dr. NR33: Kess ... 4H 17
Amberley Ct. NR32: Oul B ... 4E 8
Amber Mus. ... 4K 45
Ambleside Gdns. NR32: Low ... 4F 9
America Hill IP6: Witn ... 3B 116
Amis Ct. IP27: Lake ... 7B 20
AMPTON ... 2C 159
Amy Ct. NR32: Low ... 6G 9
Amy Johnson Ct. IP28: Mide ... 6H 23
Ancaster Rd. IP2: Ips ... 6B 4 (2K 137)
Ancells Cl. IP29: Laws ... 6B 80
Anchorage, The NR32: Low ... 5K 9
Anchor La. IP27: Lake ... 5A 20
Anchor St. IP3: Ips ... 7H 5
NR33: Low ... 3H 11
Anchor Way NR33: Car C ... 5A 10
Anderson Centre, The
IP33: Bury E ... 7D 52
Anderson Cl. IP6: Nee M ... 3F 111
Andersons Way IP12: Wood ... 6F 121
Anderson Wlk. IP32: Bury E ... 6D 52
Andrew Burtt's Cl. IP13: F'ham ... 6B 90
Andrew Cl. IP11: Felix ... 5D 154
IP16: Leis ... 4J 93
Andrew Johnston Way
IP19: H'orth ... 6B 42
Andrew Rd. CB8: Newm ... 4E 46
Andrews Cl. IP14: Deb ... 2H 87
Andrews Wlk. IP32: Bury E ... 5D 52
Andrew Way NR33: Oul B ... 3C 10
Andros Cl. IP3: Ips ... 7E 138
Angela Cl. IP12: Martl ... 4G 135
Angel Cl. IP31: Stant ... 7D 32
Angel Ct. IP7: Hadl ... 3H 129
Angel Hill IP14: E Sto ... 3E 86
IP33: Bury E ... 4J 157 (1H 59)
Angel La. CO10: Glem ... 6A 104
IP4: Ips ... 5G 5 (1B 138)
IP12: Wood ... 5H 121
IP19: Blyth ... 6J 43
IP33: Bury E ... 5H 157 (1G 59)
Angel Link IP19: H'orth ... 5B 42
Angel Marshes (Nature Reserve) ... 6K 43
Angel Mdw. CO10: Glem ... 6A 104
Angel Rd. IP8: B'ford ... 3C 130
Angel St. IP7: Hadl ... 3H 129
Anglesea Rd. IP1: Ips ... 1A 4 (6J 131)
Anglesey Pl. IP31: Gt Bar ... 3D 54
Anglia Kart Racing ... 5E 130
Anglian La.
IP32: Bury E ... 1F 157 (6E 52)
Anglia Parkway Nth. IP1: Ips ... 1F 131
Anglia Parkway Sth. IP1: Ips ... 1F 131
Anglia Sporting Activities ... 3F 119
Angus Cl. IP4: Ips ... 4F 133
Anita Cl. E. IP2: Ips ... 1G 137
Anita Cl. W. IP2: Ips ... 1G 137
Annandale Dr. NR34: Becc ... 4G 13
Ann Beaumont Way IP7: Hadl ... 2G 129
Annbrook Rd. IP2: Ips ... 5G 137
Anne's Cl. CB8: Exn ... 1B 46
Annesons Cnr. IP17: Midd ... 7D 78
Anne St. IP11: Felix ... 5D 154
Anni Healey Cl. IP12: Wood ... 4G 121
Annis Hill NR35: Bung ... 3D 14
Annis Hill La. NR35: Bung ... 3D 14
Annis Hill Rd. NR35: Bung ... 3E 14
Annison Cl. NR33: Low ... 4G 11
Ann St. IP1: Ips ... 1B 4 (6K 131)
Ann Suckling Rd. CB9: L Wrat ... 1F 101
Ansell Cl. IP7: Hadl ... 3H 129
Anselm Av. IP32: Bury E ... 4F 53
Anson Rd. IP5: Martl H ... 5H 135
Anson Way NR34: Ell ... 7K 13
Antonia Cl. CB9: Have ... 4K 101
Antonine Way IP19: H'orth ... 2D 42
Antrim Rd. IP1: Ips ... 4F 131
Anvil Acre IP14: Batt ... 7A 110
Anvil Way CB8: Kenn ... 3A 48
Anzani Av. IP11: Felix ... 4B 154
Anzani Ho. IP11: Felix ... 4B 154
Apex, The ... 4G 157
Apollo Ho. IP2: Ips ... 5F 137
Apple Acre Rd. CB9: Have ... 2B 100
Appleby Cl. IP2: Ips ... 5E 136
Apple Cl. IP27: RAF L ... 5G 21
Appledore Dr. NR33: Car C ... 5C 10
Appledown Dr.
IP32: Bury E ... 6A 54
Apple Gro. IP14: W'den ... 3H 65
Apple Tree Cl. NR33: Low ... 3G 11
Appletrees, The IP23: Eye ... 7C 38
Approach Cotts. CB9: With ... 1C 100
APSEY GREEN ... 6A 90
Aragon Rd. CB9: Have ... 5C 100
Arborfield Dr. CB8: Newm ... 3G 47
Arbor La. NR33: Low ... 7F 11
Arcade St. IP1: Ips ... 3D 4 (7A 132)
Archangel Gdns. IP2: Ips ... 2G 137
Arches, The IP12: Wood ... 5H 121
Archway, The NR33: Kess ... 4H 17
Archway Cotts. IP16: Leis ... 3J 93
Arc Shop. Cen.
IP33: Bury E ... 4G 157 (1G 59)
ARDLEIGH ... 3A 164
Argent Pl. CB8: Newm ... 3G 47
Argyle St. IP4: Ips ... 3G 5 (7B 132)
Argyll Ct. CB9: Have ... 4E 100
Ark Cl. NR33: Kess ... 4H 17
Arkle Ct. IP5: Kesg ... 5D 134
Arkwright Rd. IP2: Ips ... 7G 131
Arlington Ct. *CB8: Newm ... 6G 47*
(off Church La.)
Arms La. CB9: Ked ... 7C 98
Armstrong Cl. CB8: Newm ... 6H 47
CO10: Hund ... 1J 99
Armstrong Ho. IP4: Ips ... 4C 132
Arnhem Ct. NR32: Low ... 4H 9
Arnhem Rd. IP16: Leis ... 4J 93
Arnold Cl. IP1: Ips ... 2H 131
Arnold Gdns. *NR32: Low ... 5J 9*
(off Osborne St.)
Arnold St. NR32: Low ... 7K 9
Arnold Walk, The *NR32: Low ... 5K 9*
(off Jubilee Way)
Arras Rd. IP33: Bury E ... 1D 58
Arras Sq. IP1: Ips ... 3E 4
Arrendene Rd. CB9: Have ... 2E 100
Arrowhead Dr. IP27: Lake ... 4A 20
Artesian Cl. CO10: Lave ... 7A 106
Arthur Leonard Cl. *IP28: Mide ... 6H 23*
(off Folly Rd.)
Arthur's Ter. IP4: Ips ... 3H 5 (7C 132)
Artillery Way NR32: Low ... 6K 9
Artiss Cl. IP7: Bild ... 6K 109
Arundel Cl. IP32: Bury E ... 7K 53
Arundel Wlk. *CB9: Have ... 3D 100*
(off Princess Way)
Arundel Way IP3: Ips ... 3H 139
NR33: Car C ... 5C 10
Arwela Rd. IP11: Felix ... 6E 154
Ascot Cl. CB8: Exn ... 1B 46
Ascot Dr. IP3: Ips ... 3F 139
IP11: Felix ... 2D 154
Ash Av. IP7: Gt Bri ... 1A 112
ASHBOCKING ... 3F 117 (1B 164)
Ashbocking Rd. IP6: A'ing, Swil ... 4F 117
IP6: Henl ... 6J 115
Ashbourne Ct. *CB8: Newm ... 6H 47*
(off All Saints Rd.)
Ashburnham Rd. IP6: Nee M ... 4F 111
Ashburnham Way
NR33: Car C ... 5C 10
Ashby Rd. NR32: Low ... 7H 9
Ash Cl. IP3: Pur F ... 5K 139
IP12: Wood ... 6G 121
IP14: Bac ... 6B 68
IP14: Gt Fin ... 6J 83
IP27: B'don ... 4H 19
IP27: RAF L ... 4G 21
NR33: Car C ... 4C 10
Ash Ct. IP28: Red L ... 6J 25
Ashcroft La. IP1: Ips ... 4H 131
Ashcroft Rd. IP1: Ips ... 4H 131
Ashdale Dr. NR34: Worl ... 4H 13
Ashdale Gdns. IP5: Kesg ... 5D 134
Ashdale Pk. IP27: B'don ... 5D 18
Ashdale Rd. IP5: Kesg ... 5D 134
Ashdale Wlk. IP5: Kesg ... 5D 134
(Ashdale Rd.)
IP5: Kesg ... 6D 134
(Banyard Cl.)
ASHDON ... 2A 162
Ashdown Way IP3: Ips ... 3H 139
Ash Dr. IP23: Eye ... 6D 38
ASHEN ... 2B 162
Ashen CO10: Clar ... 6C 102
Ashen Hill CO10: Ashe ... 7J 99
Ashen La. CO10: Stoke C ... 7J 99
Ashen Rd. CO10: Clar ... 7B 102
Ashe Rd. IP12: Tun ... 6F 123
Ashe Row IP13: Cam A ... 2A 122
ASHFIELD ... 3C 161
Ashfield Ct. IP4: Ips ... 7E 132
Ashfield Cres. NR33: Oul B ... 2E 10
Ashfield Dr. IP16: Leis ... 4H 93
Ashfield Gdns. IP31: Nort ... 7A 66
ASHFIELD GREEN
Newmarket ... 1K 97
Stradbroke ... 2C 161
Ashfield Hill IP31: B Ash ... 5E 66
Ashfield Rd. IP14: W'den ... 3H 65
IP30: E'well ... 1E 64
IP31: Nort ... 5J 57 & 7A 66
Ashfords Cl. IP17: Saxm ... 5G 91
Ash Ground Cl. CO11: Brant ... 5C 148
Ashground Cl. IP11: T Mart ... 5H 153
Ash Gro. CB9: Have ... 2D 100
CO10: Gt Cor ... 6H 127
IP9: Cap M ... 2H 147
Ash Ho. IP2: Ips ... 4F 137
Ashhurst Pl. NR33: Low ... 6F 11
Ash La. IP30: Tost ... 2G 63
Ashlea Cl. CB9: Have ... 5G 101
Ashlea Rd. CB9: Have ... 5G 101
ASHLEY ... 3A 158
Ashley Cl. IP30: Tost ... 1G 63
Ashley Downs NR32: Low ... 5H 9
Ashley Heath CB8: Newm ... 7A 48
Ashley Ho. IP11: Felix ... 7B 154
Ashley Rd. CB8: Newm ... 7J 47
Ashley St. IP2: Ips ... 7E 4
Ashman's Rd. NR34: Becc ... 4D 12
Ash Mead IP31: B Ash ... 2D 66
Ashmere Gro. IP4: Ips ... 2K 5 (7D 132)
Ashmere Ri. CO10: S'bury ... 3F 127
Ashness Cl. NR32: Low ... 4F 9
Ash Plough IP21: Stradb ... 4G 39
Ash Ri. CO6: Nay ... 6H 143
Ash Rd. IP12: Rend ... 7A 122 & 4B 122
IP13: Cam A, L Hac ... 4C 118
(not continuous)
IP14: One ... 2A 84
ASH STREET ... 5B 112 (2A 164)
Ash St. CO10: Boxf ... 6C 128
Ashton Cl. IP2: Ips ... 4E 136
IP12: Rend ... 6C 122
Ashton Rd. IP23: Eye ... 6C 38
Ash Tree Cl. IP16: Leis ... 3G 93
IP21: Fress ... 6B 40
IP23: Occ ... 5B 72
NR34: Worl ... 5K 13
Ashtree Gdns. NR33: Car C ... 6C 10
Ashwell Rd. IP33: Bury E ... 2D 58
Askins Rd. CO7: E Ber ... 3B 146
ASLACTON ... 1B 160
Aspal Cl. IP28: B Row ... 1F 23
Aspal Hall Rd. IP28: B Row ... 1F 23
Aspal La. IP28: B Row ... 1G 23
Aspall Rd. IP14: Deb ... 1H 87
Aspal Pk. IP28: B Row ... 1F 23
Aspal Pl. *IP28: B Row ... 1F 23*
(off Aspal Cl.)
Aspal Way IP28: B Row ... 1F 23
Aspen Cl. CB9: Have ... 2D 100
IP6: Clay ... 4E 114
IP6: Gt Bla ... 2A 114
IP12: Melt ... 4J 121
IP31: Gt Bar ... 2E 54
Aspen Coppice NR32: Oul ... 2E 8
Aspen Ct. IP12: Rend ... 5C 122
Aspen Way IP28: Red L ... 7J 25
Aspinall Cl. NR33: Oul B ... 5E 10
Aspley Ct. IP1: Ips ... 1A 4
ASSINGTON ... 3D 163
ASSINGTON GREEN ... 1B 162
Assington Rd. CO10: Newt ... 3D 128
Astbury Rd. NR32: Low ... 3G 9
Aster Cl. IP28: Red L ... 7G 25
Aster Rd. IP2: Ips ... 3G 137
Aston Cl. IP1: Ips ... 4E 130
Astor Ct. IP27: B'don ... 3G 19
Ataka Rd. IP11: Felix ... 2E 154
ATHELINGTON ... 3H 73 (2C 161)
Athelington Rd. IP21: Horh ... 3H 73
Athenaeum, The
Bury St Edmunds ... 5J 157
Athenaeum La.
IP33: Bury E ... 5H 157 (1H 59)
Athenrye Ct. IP12: Wood ... 6H 121

Atherton Rd. IP2: Ips ... 4F 137
Athroll M. IP5: Kesg ... 5E 134
(off Howards Way)
Atlas Ho. IP4: Ips ... 3G 5
Atterton Rd. CB9: Have ... 2C 100
ATTLETON GREEN ... 3F 97
Aubretia Cl. NR33: Oul B ... 2E 10
Aubrey Dr. CO10: S'bury ... 1F 127
Auction St.
IP33: Bury E ... 4G 157 (1G 59)
Audley Gro. IP4: Rush A ... 1K 139
Augusta Cl. IP3: Ips ... 7J 139
Augustus Cl. CB9: Have ... 5J 101
Aureole Wlk. CB8: Newm ... 1E 46
Austin Cl. IP31: B Ash ... 3C 66
Austin St. IP2: Ips ... 6E 4 (2A 138)
Autopark Ind. Est.
IP33: Bury E ... 4K 157 (1J 59)
Autumn Cl. IP29: Barr ... 6C 50
Aveley La. IP29: Shim ... 4B 106
Aveling Way NR33: Car C ... 6A 10
Avenue, The CB8: Newm ... 6G 47
CO10: S'bury ... 4F 127
IP1: Ips ... 4A 132
IP5: Martl H ... 5J 135
IP8: Cop ... 7B 136
IP11: T Mary ... 1A 154
IP12: Wood ... 6H 121
IP13: Uff ... 6H 119
IP19: H'orth ... 3B 42
IP28: Ris ... 2E 50
IP31: Gt Bar ... 4B 54
NR33: Kess ... 4H 17
NR33: Low ... 4F 11
NR34: Becc ... 2F 13
Avenue App. IP32: Bury E ... 5G 53
Avenue Mans. NR32: Low ... 5J 9
Avenue Rd. IP27: Lake ... 7C 20
Avocet Cl. NR33: Oul B ... 4C 10
Avocet Ct. IP11: Felix ... 5D 154
IP17: Saxm ... 6G 91
(off Brook Farm Rd.)
Avocet Gdns. IP14: Stowm ... 4H 85
Avocet La. IP5: Martl H ... 6G 135
Avocet M. IP12: Rend ... 6C 122
Avon Ct. IP32: Bury E ... 5F 53
Avondale Rd. IP3: Ips ... 4E 138
NR32: Low ... 7H 9
Avondale Wlk. IP32: Bury E ... 4F 53
Ayden Way IP17: Benh ... 3C 92
Aylmer Cl. IP28: Ris ... 2C 50
Aylward Cl. IP7: Hadl ... 5J 129
Ayr Rd. IP4: Ips ... 4F 133
Azure Seas Caravan Pk.
NR32: Low ... 7K 7

B

BABEL GREEN ... 2H 99
Babergh Cl. CO10: Act ... 4H 107
Babington Dr. IP19: H'orth ... 6B 42
Back Hamlet IP3: Ips ... 5H 5 (1C 138)
Back Hills IP22: Bote ... 5J 35
Back La. CO10: L Mel ... 4J 105
IP6: Clay ... 4D 114
IP7: M Ele ... 3D 108
IP8: Wash ... 6A 136
IP10: Falk ... 3K 153
IP11: Felix ... 3E 154
IP17: Snap ... 7A 92
IP23: Gisli ... 1H 67
IP31: B Ash ... 2D 66
Bk. of Market Pl. IP17: Saxm ... 6J 91
(off Market Pl.)
Back Rd. IP10: Kirt ... 2H 153
IP17: Midd ... 5D 78
IP19: Wen ... 2H 43
Backs, The IP5: Kesg ... 6A 134
BACK STREET ... 1B 162
Back St. IP23: Gisli ... 2F 67
IP27: Lake ... 5A 20
Bacon Rd. IP6: Barh, Clay ... 3D 114
Bacon's Grn. Cotts.
CO7: H Mar ... 4K 145
Bacon's Grn. Rd. NR34: W'hall ... 7F 15
BACTON ... 6B 68 (3A 160)
Bacton Rd. IP11: Felix ... 5E 154
IP14: Haug ... 1B 70
Baden Powell Wlk. IP5: Kesg ... 6E 134
(off Ropes Dr.)
Bader Cl. IP3: Ips ... 4G 139
Bader Ct. IP5: Martl H ... 6G 135
Badgers Bank IP2: Ips ... 5G 137
Badger's Holt NR33: Kess ... 4H 17
Badgerwood Cl. NR33: Low ... 4G 11
BADINGHAM ... 2B 76 (3D 161)
Badingham Rd. IP13: F'ham ... 5D 90
IP13: Laxf ... 7D 74
IP17: Pea ... 4F 77
Badleys Cl. CO10: Gt Wal ... 7K 107
BADLINGHAM ... 7E 24
Badshah Av. IP3: Ips ... 3F 139
BADWELL ASH ... 3C 66 (3D 159)
Badwell Rd. IP14: Wyve ... 1A 68
IP31: Wals W ... 1D 66 & 7F 33
Bagsham La. IP28: W Row ... 6C 22
Bahram Cl. CB8: Newm ... 5E 46
Bailey Av. IP5: Kesg ... 6E 134
Bailey Cl. CB9: Have ... 4J 101
IP2: Ips ... 7G 131
Bailey La. CO10: Clar ... 5D 102
Baileypool La. IP31: Pake ... 7J 29
Baines Coney CB9: Have ... 2B 100
Baird Cl. IP2: Ips ... 6H 131
Baird Gro. IP5: Kesg ... 6B 134
Baker Rd. IP9: Shot G ... 7D 156
Bakers Ct. CO10: Gt Cor ... 7F 127
Bakers La. IP12: Orf ... 7J 125
IP12: Wood ... 6H 121
IP17: Westl ... 5H 79
IP33: Bury E ... 7K 157 (2H 59)
Bakers Mill CO10: Lave ... 6C 106
IP30: E'well ... 2D 64
Bakers Pasture IP13: Gru ... 6J 117
Bakers Row CB8: Newm ... 5G 47
Baker's Score NR32: Cort ... 5J 7
Bakers Way IP28: Tud ... 6C 26
Balaton Pl. CB8: Newm ... 3G 47
Baldry Cl. IP8: Ips ... 5E 136
Baldwin Av. IP32: Bury E ... 4E 52
Baldwin Rd. IP14: Stowm ... 6E 84
Ballast Wharf Wlk.
IP3: Ips ... 6H 5 (2C 138)
Ballater Cl. IP1: Ips ... 1G 131
BALLINGDON ... 5B 126 (2C 163)
Ballingdon Gdns. CO10: Ball ... 5B 126
Ballingdon Gro. CO10: Ball ... 6C 126
Ballingdon Hill CO10: Ball ... 7A 126
Ballingdon Hill Ind. Est.
CO10: Ball ... 5B 126
Ballingdon St. CO10: Ball ... 5B 126
Ballingdon Trad. Est.
CO10: Ball ... 5C 126
Balliol Cl. IP12: Wood ... 7E 120
Balls Hill IP7: Hit ... 3F 109
Ballygate NR34: Becc ... 3D 12
Balmoral Cl. IP2: Ips ... 5H 137
Balmoral Dr. CB9: Have ... 3D 100
BALSHAM ... 1A 162
Bangor Ct. IP27: RAF L ... 4H 21
Bangor Rd. IP27: RAF L ... 4H 21
BANHAM ... 1A 160
Banham Dr. CO10: S'bury ... 3E 126
Banham M. CB9: Have ... 2A 100
Banham Rd. NR34: Becc ... 6G 13
Bank All. IP18: Sou ... 4K 45
Bank Bldgs. CO10: S'bury ... 4D 126
Bank Corner IP17: Yox ... 7J 77
Bank Rd. IP4: Ips ... 2J 5 (7C 132)
BANKS, THE ... 1A 34
Banks Cl. IP7: Hadl ... 4J 129
Banks Wlk. IP33: Bury E ... 5J 59
Bannatyne's Health Club
Lowestoft ... 7F 9
Banner Ct. NR33: Low ... 3H 11
Banters La. NR34: Ilk A ... 2H 15
Banthorpe Gro. IP5: Kesg ... 7C 134
Bantocks Rd. CO10: Gt Wal ... 1K 127
Bantoft Ter. IP3: Ips ... 4G 139
Banyard Cl. IP5: Kesg ... 6D 134
BANYARD'S GREEN ... 5D 74 (2D 161)
Banyard's Grn. IP13: Laxf ... 4C 74
Barbara Stradbroke Av.
CB8: Newm ... 7D 46
Barber Cl. NR33: Kess ... 4H 17
Barber's La. IP31: Lang ... 1A 66
Barbers Row IP30: E'well ... 1E 64
BARDFIELD END GREEN ... 3A 162
BARDFIELD SALING ... 3A 162
Bardolph Rd. NR35: Bung ... 3B 14
BARDWELL ... 2D 32 (2D 159)
Bardwell Rd. IP31: Bard, Ixw T ... 2A 32
IP31: Barni ... 4C 30
IP31: Ixw ... 5J 29
IP31: Sap ... 2J 29
IP31: Stant ... 5A 32
Bardwell Windmill ... 2D 32
Barehams Yd. CO10: Clar ... 5D 102
Barell's Hill IP19: Hunt, Ubb ... 4A 74
Bargate La. IP28: W Row ... 7B 22
Bargate Rd. IP28: W Row ... 6B 22
BARHAM ... 6F 115 (1B 164)
BARHAM GREEN ... 5G 115
Barhams Way IP13: Wick M ... 5B 118
Barker Cl. IP2: Ips ... 1F 137
Barker Rd. CO10: S'bury ... 1D 126
BARKING ... 1A 164
Barking Rd. IP6: Nee M ... 5G 111
IP8: Will ... 1G 113
BARKING TYE ... 1A 164
Barkis Mdw. NR32: Blun ... 1J 7
Barley Cl. CB8: Newm ... 6H 47
IP14: Stowu ... 1K 85
Barleycorn Way IP28: B Row ... 1D 22
Barleyfields IP31: Thur ... 6A 56
Barleyhayes Cl. IP2: Ips ... 4K 137
Barley Ho. CO10: L Mel ... 6G 105
Barley Lands IP15: Aldeb ... 4H 95
Barley Mdw. IP19: H'orth ... 6A 42
Barley Way NR33: Low ... 7E 10
Barlings Ct. CB8: Newm ... 5G 47
BARNABY GREEN ... 5D 44
Barnaby Grn. IP18: Sou ... 4J 45
Barnadiston Rd. CO10: Hund ... 1F 99
Barnard Bottom
IP31: Gt Bar, Tim ... 1H 53
(not continuous)
BARNARDISTON ... 2B 162
Barnards Centre Point ... 7F 9
Barnards Way NR32: Low ... 7G 9
BARNBY ... 7C 6 (2C 167)
Barnby Cl. CB9: Have ... 3B 100
Barn Cl. IP7: M Ele ... 2E 108
IP18: Rey ... 1H 45
NR33: Car C ... 4C 10
Barnes Cl. IP7: Hadl ... 3J 129
IP27: B'don ... 5E 18
Barn Fld. IP29: Chev ... 2K 51
Barnfield IP9: Cap M ... 2J 147
IP11: Felix ... 2C 154
IP29: Shim ... 1D 106
BARNHAM ... 6H 27 (2C 159)
Barnham Pl. IP5: Rush A ... 7K 133
BARNINGHAM ... 3D 30 (2D 159)
Barningham Rd. IP31: Stant ... 6C 32
(not continuous)
Barn La. IP33: Bury E ... 3K 157 (7H 53)
Barn Mdw. IP14: Comb ... 3B 110
IP29: Shim ... 1D 106
Barn St. CO10: Lave ... 6C 106
Barons Cl. IP11: Felix ... 2J 155
IP19: H'orth ... 6A 42
Baron's Ct. CB9: Have ... 4D 100
Baronsdale Cl. IP1: Ips ... 4K 131
Barons Mdw. IP12: Orf ... 6H 125
Barons Rd. IP33: Bury E ... 3G 59
Barrack Cnr. IP1: Ips ... 2C 4 (7K 131)
IP12: Wood ... 7E 120
Barrack La. IP1: Ips ... 2C 4 (7K 131)
IP13: Uff ... 6J 119
Barrack Row IP9: Shot ... 4B 156
IP10: Levi ... 7D 152
Barrack Sq. IP5: Martl H ... 6H 135
Barr Dr. IP27: Lake ... 3B 20
Barrell's Rd. IP31: Thur ... 7C 56
Barrett's La. IP6: Nee M ... 4F 111
Barric La. IP23: Occ ... 6A 72
BARROW ... 6B 50 (3B 158)
Barrow Hill CO10: Act ... 3G 107
IP29: Barr ... 7B 50
IP29: Harg ... 1G 51
Barrow Rd. IP29: Denh ... 7B 50
Barry Lynham Dr. CB8: Newm ... 7J 47
Barsey Cl. CB9: Have ... 2B 100
BARSHAM ... 1D 161
BARSHAM HILL ... 4B 12
Bartholomew Grn. IP18: Sou ... 4K 45
(not continuous)
Bartholomew's La. IP19: Wen ... 2F 43
Bartholomew St.
IP4: Ips ... 3K 5 (7D 132)
BARTLOW ... 2A 162
Bartlow Pl. CB9: Have ... 2G 101
Barton Cl. IP2: Ips ... 4G 137
Barton Dr. CB9: Ked ... 6C 98
Barton Gro. CB9: Ked ... 6C 98
Barton Hamlet IP31: Gt Bar ... 2H 55
Barton Hill IP31: Forn M ... 4G 53
Barton Ho. IP28: B Mil ... 2H 25
BARTON MILLS ... 2G 25 (2B 158)
Barton Mills Rd.
IP28: B Mil, Tud ... 3J 25 & 4A 26
Barton Rd. IP11: Felix ... 4G 155
IP12: Wood ... 3G 121
IP31: Thur ... 4J 55
IP32: Bury E ... 7J 53
Bartons Pl. CB8: Newm ... 4E 46
Bartrum La. IP5: Kesg ... 6C 134
BARWAY ... 2A 158
Barwell Rd.
IP33: Bury E ... 3J 157 (7H 53)
BASE GREEN ... 2K 65
Base Grn. Rd. IP14: W'den ... 4H 65
Basepoint Cen. IP3: Ips ... 6K 139
Basil Brown Cl. IP22: Rick ... 5J 35
Bassingbourn IP27: RAF L ... 4H 21
Bath Hill IP11: Felix ... 4G 155
Bath Rd. IP11: Felix ... 4G 155
Bath St. IP2: Ips ... 7F 5 (3B 138)
Battery Grn. Rd. NR32: Low ... 1J 11
Battery La. IP9: Shot G ... 7E 156
Batt Hall CO10: Bulm ... 5A 126
BATTISFORD ... 1A 164
BATTISFORD TYE ... 6B 110 (1A 164)
BATTLESEA GREEN ... 2C 161
Battles La. IP5: Kesg ... 6D 134
Battlies, The IP30: Roug ... 7F 55
BAWDSEY ... 7J 141 (2D 165)
Bawdsey Cl. IP11: Felix ... 1J 155
BAWDSEY MANOR ... 3D 165
BAXTER'S GREEN ... 1B 162
Bayberry Cl. IP28: Red L ... 6J 25
Bayles Way IP21: Stradb ... 7G 39
BAYLHAM ... 1B 164
Bays, The IP16: Thor ... 6D 94
Bayswater Cl. IP1: Ips ... 6H 131
BAYTHORN END ... 2B 162
Beach Farm Residential & Holiday Pk.
NR33: Low ... 7F 11
Beach Ind. Est. NR32: Low ... 6K 9
(not continuous)
Beach La. IP12: Alder ... 5J 141
IP12: Bawd ... 7K 141
Beachmans Ct. NR33: Low ... 5H 11
Beach M. NR32: Low ... 1J 11
(off Beach Rd.)
Beach Pl. IP11: Felix ... 4H 155
Beach Rd. IP17: Dun ... 1K 79
NR32: Low ... 1J 11
NR33: Kess ... 7K 17
Beach Rd. E. IP11: Felix ... 4H 155
Beach Rd. W. IP11: Felix ... 6E 154
Beach Station Caravan Pk.
IP11: Felix ... 6C 154
Beach Sta. Rd. IP11: Felix ... 6D 154
Beacon Fld. IP11: Felix ... 3D 154
BEACON HILL ... 2E 134
Beacon Hill La. IP16: Thor ... 5D 94
Beacon La. IP13: L Bea ... 2F 135
Beacon Rally Karts ... 1H 135
Beaconsfield Cl. CO10: S'bury ... 3D 126
Beaconsfield Ct. CB9: Have ... 4E 100
(off Clements Cl.)
Beaconsfield Rd.
CO10: S'bury ... 3D 126
IP1: Ips ... 6H 131
IP12: Wood ... 5H 121
IP15: Aldeb ... 6J 95
NR33: Kess ... 5K 17
NR33: Low ... 3H 11
Beale Cl. IP32: Bury E ... 1B 60
Bealings La. IP13: Hask ... 4A 120
Bealings Rd. IP12: Martl ... 2G 135
Bean's La. IP22: Wort ... 2K 35
Beardmore Pk. IP5: Martl H ... 5H 135
Beard Rd. IP32: Bury E ... 5D 52
Bear Mdw. IP30: Bey ... 3D 62
Bear's La. CO10: Lave ... 7C 106
Bear St. CO6: Nay ... 6H 143
Beatrice Av. IP11: Felix ... 2F 155
Beatrice Cl. IP3: Ips ... 3E 138
Beatty Rd. CO10: S'bury ... 2F 127
IP3: Ips ... 4F 139
Beauford Rd. IP31: Ing ... 5D 28
Beaufort Ct. CB9: Have ... 4E 100
Beaufort St. IP1: Ips ... 1A 4 (6J 131)
Beaumont Cl. CO8: Bure ... 5B 142
IP33: Bury E ... 2D 58
Beaumont Cotts. IP17: Kel ... 3J 91
Beaumont Ct. CB9: Have ... 5G 101
IP27: B'don ... 6E 18
Beaumont Rd. NR33: Car C ... 7B 10
Beaumont Va. CB9: Have ... 5G 101
Beaumont Way IP14: Stowm ... 5D 84
Beaverbrook Rd. CB8: Newm ... 5G 47
Beavor La. IP27: B'don ... 4F 19
BEAZLEY END ... 3B 162
BECCLES ... 3E 12 (2C 167)
Beccles Amateur Sailing Club ... 1E 12
Beccles Bus. Pk. NR34: Ell ... 6K 13
Becclesgate NR34: Becc ... 1E 12
Beccles Golf Course ... 2G 13
Beccles Indoor Bowls Club ... 3F 13
Beccles Lido ... 3D 12
BECCLES MARSHES ... 1F 13
Beccles Mus. ... 3D 12
Beccles Rd. IP19: Holt ... 4E 42
NR33: Car C, Oul B ... 5A 10
NR34: Barnb, Nor C, Worl
... 4K 13 & 7A 6
NR34: Mut ... 2A 16
NR34: Wrent ... 1B 44
NR35: Bung ... 2C 14
Beccles Sports Cen. ... 5D 12
Beccles Station (Rail) ... 3F 13
Beck Cl. IP12: Rend ... 6C 122
Beckett Cl. IP33: W'ley ... 7A 52
Becketts, The IP14: Stowm ... 2D 84
Beckham Rd. NR32: Low ... 7H 9
BECK ROW ... 2F 23 (2A 158)
Beck St. IP22: Hep ... 4C 30
Bedell Cl. IP33: Bury E ... 3C 58
Bederic Cl. IP32: Bury E ... 2K 59
BEDFIELD ... 7G 73 (3C 161)
Bedfield Rd. IP13: E Soh ... 3A 90
Bedford Ct. CB9: Have ... 4E 100
Bedford Rd. IP32: Bury E ... 5E 52

Bedford St. IP1: Ips . . . 2C 4 (7K 131)
Bedingfeld Way IP32: Bury E . . . 2K 59
BEDINGFIELD . . . 3B 160
Bedingfield Cres. IP19: H'orth . . . 7A 42
BEDINGHAM GREEN . . . 1C 161
Beech Cir. IP7: Gt Bri . . . 1A 112
Beech Cl. IP8: Spro . . . 7C 130
IP19: H'orth . . . 5A 42
IP21: Scole . . . 1K 37
IP27: RAF L . . . 4G 21
Beechcroft IP29: Stann . . . 3G 81
Beechcroft Rd. IP1: Ips . . . 4H 131
Beech Dr. IP28: Red L . . . 6J 25
Beeches, The IP3: Ips . . . 6K 5 (2D 138)
IP6: Clay . . . 4D 114
IP17: Benh . . . 3C 92
IP29: Horr . . . 6B 58
IP33: Bury E . . . 1E 58
Beeches Cl. IP28: W Row . . . 4A 22
IP31: Ixw . . . 5H 29
Beeches Mobile Home Park, The
NR33: Oul B . . . 2D 10
Beeches Rd. IP28: W Row . . . 5A 22
Beechfields IP27: B'don . . . 3J 19
Beech Gro. CB9: Have . . . 2D 100
IP3: Ips . . . 3D 138
IP5: Rush A . . . 6K 133
Beech Ho. IP2: Ips . . . 4F 137
Beeching Dr. NR32: Low . . . 3J 9
Beech La. IP14: W'den . . . 4H 65
Beech Paddocks IP30: Hess . . . 7D 62
Beech Pk. IP31: Gt Bar . . . 2E 54
Beech Ri. IP33: Bury E . . . 3J 59
Beech Rd. CO10: Gt Cor . . . 5G 127
IP5: Rush A . . . 6K 133
NR33: Car C . . . 6C 10
Beech Row CB8: Dalh . . . 6J 49
Beech Ter. IP14: Stowm . . . 3F 85
Beech Tree Cl. NR34: Becc . . . 4E 12
Beech Wlk. IP16: Leis . . . 4H 93
Beech Way IP12: Wood . . . 7G 121
Beechwood Cl. CB8: Exn . . . 1C 46
Beechwood Gdns. NR33: Oul B . . . 3F 11
Beehive Cl. CO7: E Ber . . . 3B 146
Beetons Way IP32: Bury E . . . 7E 52
IP33: Bury E . . . 7E 52
Belaugh Av. NR33: Oul B . . . 4E 10
BELCHAMP OTTEN . . . 2C 163
BELCHAMP ST PAUL . . . 2B 162
BELCHAMP WALTER . . . 2C 163
Belcher Grn. IP18: Rey . . . 1J 45
Belfry Rd. IP3: Ips . . . 7K 139
Belgrave Cl. IP4: Ips . . . 4C 132
Bellands Way IP23: Eye . . . 6C 38
Bell Cl. IP2: Ips . . . 6E 4 (2A 138)
IP17: Saxm . . . 6J 91
Bell Cnr. IP31: Pake . . . 2B 56
Belle Vue Cl. NR32: Low . . . 5K 9
Belle Vue Rd. CO10: S'bury . . . 4E 126
IP4: Ips . . . 2J 5 (7C 132)
Bellflower Cres. IP28: Red L . . . 6J 25
Bellings Rd. CB9: Have . . . 1D 100
Bell La. IP2: Ips . . . 6E 4 (2A 138)
IP5: Kesg . . . 5B 134
IP28: B Mil . . . 2G 25
IP28: W'ton . . . 2B 24
Bell Lodge *IP16: Thor . . . 6D 94*
(off The Benthills)
Bell Mdw. IP22: Bote . . . 5J 35
IP32: Bury E . . . 5G 53
Bell M. IP7: Hadl . . . 3H 129
BELL'S CORNER . . . 6C 144
BELL'S CROSS . . . 1B 164
Bell's Cross Rd. IP6: Barh . . . 4G 115
Bells La. CO10: Glem . . . 4B 104
IP22: Hind . . . 7K 31
IP29: Stann . . . 1F 81
Bell Trees IP27: Lake . . . 7B 20
Belmont Ct. CB8: Newm . . . 7F 47
CB9: Have . . . 5E 100
Belmont Gdns. NR32: Low . . . 5G 9
Belmont Rd. IP2: Ips . . . 4E 136
IP8: Ips . . . 4E 136
BELOW CHURCH . . . 2C 156
Belsay Ct. CB9: Have . . . 3C 100
BELSTEAD . . . 7E 136 (2B 164)
Belstead Av. IP2: Ips . . . 7C 4 (3K 137)
Belstead Rd. IP2: Ips . . . 7B 4 (5G 137)
BELTON . . . 1C 167
Belvedere Cl. IP17: Kel . . . 2H 91
Belvedere Ct. IP4: Ips . . . 1K 5 (6D 132)
Belvedere Dr. NR33: Kess . . . 5K 17
Belvedere Rd. IP4: Ips . . . 1K 5 (5C 132)
NR33: Low . . . 1H 11
Belvoir Ct. *CB9: Have . . . 3D 100*
(off Princess Way)
BENACRE . . . 2D 167
Benacre CB9: Have . . . 2A 100
Benacre Rd. IP3: Ips . . . 4E 138
NR34: Ell . . . 7J 13
NR34: Hens . . . 7D 16
Benefield Rd. CB8: Mou . . . 5D 48
Benezet St. IP1: Ips . . . 2B 4 (7K 131)
BENHALL GREEN . . . 3C 92 (3D 161)
Bennett Av. IP30: E'well . . . 2E 64
IP33: Bury E . . . 7C 52
Bennett Rd. IP1: Ips . . . 5F 131
IP28: Red L . . . 6J 25
Benningham Grn. IP23: Occ . . . 5D 72
Benouville NR33: Car C . . . 6D 10
Bensly's Drift IP19: H'orth . . . 4C 42
Bentham La. IP12: Wood . . . 4H 121
Bent Hill IP11: Felix . . . 5F 155
Benthills, The IP16: Thor . . . 6D 94
Bentinck Cres. CB8: Newm . . . 5G 47
Bent La. IP4: Rush A . . . 5J 133
BENTLEY . . . 6H 147 (3B 164)
Bentley Dr. NR32: Low . . . 2F 9
Bentley Hall Rd.
IP9: Cap M, Bent . . . 1K 147
Bentley La. IP9: Stut . . . 4A 150
Bentley Rd. IP1: Ips . . . 3E 130
IP9: Cap M . . . 2K 147 & 4F 147
BENTON END . . . 5J 129
Benton St. IP7: Hadl, Lay . . . 4H 129
Benton Way IP19: H'orth . . . 4B 42
Bentwaters IP27: RAF L . . . 4H 21
(not continuous)
Bentwaters Parks IP12: Rend . . . 5E 122
Benyon Gdns. IP28: Cul . . . 7A 28
Berberis Dr. IP28: Red L . . . 7G 25
Beresford Dr. IP12: Wood . . . 3G 121
Beresford Rd. NR32: Low . . . 6J 9
Bergamot Cl. IP28: Red L . . . 5J 25
Bergamot Rd. CB9: Have . . . 3B 100
Bergholt Rd. CO11: Brant . . . 6A 148
IP9: Bent . . . 1B 148
Berkeley Cl. IP4: Ips . . . 4C 132
IP13: F'ham . . . 6C 90
Berkeley Gdns. IP33: Bury E . . . 2E 58
NR32: Oul B . . . 4F 9
Bermuda Rd. IP3: Ips . . . 7J 139
Bernard Cres. IP3: Ips . . . 4F 139
Bernards Cl. IP28: W Row . . . 4A 22
Berners Fld. IP9: Holb . . . 2E 150
Berners La. IP9: Chelm . . . 1F 151
Berners Rd. IP11: Felix . . . 4H 155
Berners St. IP1: Ips . . . 2C 4 (7K 131)
Bernham Cl. IP32: Bury E . . . 1K 59
Berry Cl. IP3: Pur F . . . 5K 139
NR32: Oul B . . . 7D 8
Beta Ter. IP3: Ips . . . 5J 139
Bethel Dr. NR33: Kess . . . 5K 17
Betony Wlk. CB9: Have . . . 3B 100
Betts Av. IP5: Martl H . . . 6H 135
Betts Cl. IP7: Hadl . . . 2H 129
Betty Cocker Gro.
CO10: S'bury . . . 4G 127
Bevan St. E. NR32: Low . . . 7J 9
Bevan St. W. NR32: Low . . . 7H 9
Beverley Cl. IP28: B Row . . . 2F 23
NR33: Oul B . . . 3C 10
Beverley Ct. IP4: Ips . . . 2G 5
NR33: Car C . . . 7A 10
Beverley Rd. IP4: Ips . . . 5D 132
Bevis Wlk. IP33: Bury E . . . 4J 59
BEYTON . . . 3C 62 (3D 159)
Beyton Rd. IP30: Drin . . . 5G 63
IP30: Hess . . . 6D 62
IP31: Thur . . . 7K 55
Bibb Way IP1: Ips . . . 4A 4 (1J 137)
Bickers Hill Rd. IP13: Laxf . . . 5C 74
Bier La. IP22: Redg . . . 1E 34
Bigod Cl. IP13: F'ham . . . 6C 90
IP19: H'orth . . . 6B 42
Bigod Rd. NR35: Bung . . . 3D 14
BIGSBYS CORNER . . . 2D 92
Bilberry Cl. IP28: Red L . . . 5K 25
Bilberry Rd. IP3: Ips . . . 7G 139
BILDESTON . . . 6J 109 (2D 163)
Bildeston Gdns. IP4: Ips . . . 4B 132
Bildeston Rd. IP7: Chels . . . 7H 109
IP8: Off . . . 1F 113
IP14: Comb, L Fin . . . 5A 110
BILLINGFORD . . . 2B 160
Billings Cl. CB9: Have . . . 1E 100
Bill Rickaby Dr. CB8: Newm . . . 4G 47
Billy's La. CO7: Strat M . . . 5H 145
Bilney Rd. IP12: Wood . . . 5F 121
Birch Av. IP14: Bac . . . 6B 68
Birch Cl. IP12: Wood . . . 7G 121
IP13: Wick M . . . 6B 118
IP14: Stowu . . . 2J 85
NR32: Oul . . . 6C 8
Birch Cres. IP27: Lake . . . 4B 20
Birchcroft Rd. IP1: Ips . . . 3K 131
Birch Dr. CO11: Brant . . . 4C 148
Birches, The IP15: Aldeb . . . 4H 95
IP28: Red L . . . 7J 25
IP30: Bey . . . 3C 62
Birch Fall CO6: Nay . . . 6H 143
Birch Gdns. IP31: B Ash . . . 2D 66
Birch Gro. IP5: Martl H . . . 7H 135
Birchgrove IP23: Thw . . . 3K 69
Birch Rd. IP14: One . . . 2A 84
IP31: Thur . . . 6A 56
Birch's La. CO10: Boxf . . . 7D 128
Birch St. CO6: Nay . . . 6J 143
Birch Wlk. IP27: RAF L . . . 5G 21
IP28: B Row . . . 1F 23
Birchwood Dr. IP5: Rush A . . . 4J 133
BIRDBROOK . . . 2B 162
Birdcage Wlk. CB8: Newm . . . 7F 47
IP33: Bury E . . . 1C 58
Birds Cft. IP31: Gt Liv . . . 3B 28
BIRDS END . . . 1H 51
Birds Grn. IP30: Rat . . . 4K 83
Birds La. IP30: C'field . . . 5K 81
NR33: Low . . . 3F 11
Birds Meare IP6: Otl . . . 1K 117
Bird's Rd. IP31: Thur . . . 7C 56
Birkdale Av. IP28: Mide . . . 6H 23
Birkdale Ct. IP28: Forn M . . . 2F 53
Birkfield Cl. IP2: Ips . . . 7A 4 (2J 137)
Birkfield Dr. IP2: Ips . . . 7A 4 (5G 137)
Birkfield Gdns. *IP2: Ips . . . 3H 137*
(off Emmanuel Cl.)
Biscay Cl. CB9: Have . . . 4H 101
Bishop M. IP8: Ips . . . 4D 136
Bishops Cl. CB9: Have . . . 3D 100
CO10: S'bury . . . 1C 126
IP11: Felix . . . 2J 155
Bishop's Ct. CB9: Have . . . 3D 100
Bishops Cft. IP31: Barni . . . 2D 30
Bishopsgarth IP3: Ips . . . 6K 5 (2D 138)
Bishop's Hill IP3: Ips . . . 6J 5 (2C 138)
Bishops Rd.
IP33: Bury E . . . 3G 157 (7G 53)
Bishops Wlk. NR32: Low . . . 3H 9
Bishops Way IP21: Stradb . . . 6G 39
Bittern Cl. IP2: Ips . . . 3G 137
Bittern Grn. NR33: Oul B . . . 4B 10
Bittern Rd. IP17: Saxm . . . 6G 91
Bixby Av. IP14: Haug . . . 2C 70
Bixley Dr. IP4: Rush A . . . 1J 139
BIXLEY HEATH . . . 3H 139
Bixley La. IP4: Rush A . . . 1J 139
Bixley Rd. IP3: Ips . . . 3G 139
NR33: Low . . . 3H 11
Black Arches *IP8: Ips . . . 6G 137*
(off Ellenbrook Rd.)
Black Barn Cl. IP8: S'ham . . . 4K 113
Black Barns IP11: T Mary . . . 1B 154
Black Bear Ct. CB8: Newm . . . 6F 47
Black Bear La. CB8: Newm . . . 6F 47
Blackberry Way IP28: Red L . . . 6J 25
NR32: Oul . . . 6D 8
Blackbird Av. IP27: B'don . . . 4J 19
Blackbird Cl. IP31: Thur . . . 6K 55
Blackbird Dr. IP32: Bury E . . . 7C 54
Blackbird Rd. IP28: B Row . . . 1C 22
Blackbird Way IP14: Stowm . . . 4J 85
Blackbourne Rd. IP30: E'well . . . 1E 64
Blackbourne Vw. IP31: Ixw . . . 5H 29
Black Boy Mdw. NR34: Becc . . . 4E 12
Black Boy Yd. CO10: S'bury . . . 4D 126
Blackdown Av. IP5: Rush A . . . 7K 133
Blackfriars CO10: S'bury . . . 5C 126
Blackfriars Ct. IP4: Ips . . . 4F 5 (1B 138)
BLACKHEATH . . . 3J 43 (3C 167)
Blackheath Rd. IP19: Wen . . . 4H 43
NR33: Low . . . 4F 11
Black Horse La.
IP1: Ips . . . 3D 4 (7A 132)
Black Horse Wlk. IP1: Ips . . . 3D 4
Blackhouse La.
CO10: Gt Cor, L Cor . . . 7H 127
Blacklands La. IP12: Sud . . . 2H 125
Blackmill Rd. IP18: Sou . . . 4J 45
Blackmore Cl. CB9: Have . . . 2E 100
BLACKMORE END . . . 3B 162
Black Slough IP17: Westl . . . 7G 79
Blacksmith Cl. NR34: Wang . . . 6C 44
Blacksmith La. IP24: Barnh . . . 6G 27
Blacksmith Rd. IP14: Cott . . . 5C 68
BLACKSMITH'S GREEN . . . 3B 160
Blacksmiths Hill CO10: Stoke C . . . 6H 99
Blacksmiths La. IP6: Cod . . . 1G 115
IP14: Forw G . . . 1A 86
Blacksmith's Loke NR32: S'ton . . . 2C 6
Blacksmiths Pightle
IP13: B'ham . . . 3B 76
Blacksmiths Rd. IP13: Hask . . . 3D 120
Blacksmiths Way IP30: E'well . . . 1E 64
BLACK STREET . . . 4F 17 (2D 167)
Black St. NR33: Gisle . . . 4E 16 & 4F 17
Blackthorn Cl. IP3: Pur F . . . 5J 139
IP28: Red L . . . 7J 25
Blackthorn Wlk. IP32: Bury E . . . 5D 52
Blackthorn Way CO6: Leav . . . 3B 142
BLACKTHORPE . . . 4G 61 (3C 159)
Blacktiles La. IP12: Martl . . . 3G 135
Bladen Dr. IP4: Rush A . . . 1J 139
Bladon Way CB9: Have . . . 2G 101
Blagge Cl. IP33: Bury E . . . 2C 58
Blair Cl. IP4: Rush A . . . 1J 139
Blair Pde. CB9: Have . . . 3D 100
Blake Av. IP9: Shot G . . . 6D 156
Blakenham Cl. NR32: Oul B . . . 4E 8
Blakenham Woodland Garden . . . 2B 164
Blake Rd. IP1: Ips . . . 2H 131
IP14: Stowm . . . 3D 84
Blakes Cl. IP12: Melt . . . 3K 121
Blanche St. IP4: Ips . . . 3G 5 (7B 132)
Blandford Rd. IP3: Ips . . . 3H 139
Blands Farm Cl. IP22: Pal . . . 2D 36
BLAXHALL . . . 2H 123 (1D 165)
Blaxhall Church Rd. IP12: Tun . . . 5F 123
Blaxhall Common . . . 3K 123
Blaxhall Ct. CB9: Have . . . 4D 100
Blaxhall Heath . . . 3K 123
BLEACH GREEN . . . 1K 39
Blenheim Cl. CB9: Have . . . 2G 101
CO11: Brant . . . 4C 148
IP28: W Row . . . 4A 22
IP33: Bury E . . . 1D 58
Blenheim Ct. IP1: Ips . . . 1A 4
Blenheim Dr. IP31: Thur . . . 6K 55
Blenheim Rd. IP1: Ips . . . 6J 131
Blickling Cl. IP2: Ips . . . 4K 137
Blinco Rd. NR32: Oul B . . . 7B 8
Blind La. IP19: Blyth . . . 7H 43
IP29: Hart . . . 2H 103
Blofield Rd. IP11: Felix . . . 4A 154
Blomfield St.
IP33: Bury E . . . 3G 157 (7G 53)
BLO' NORTON . . . 2A 160
Blood Hill IP8: S'ham . . . 3G 113
Bloodmoor La. NR33: Car C . . . 6D 10
NR33: Gisle . . . 7D 10
Bloodmoor Rd.
NR33: Low, Oul B . . . 5D 10
Bloomfield Cl. IP31: Sap . . . 2J 29
Bloomfield Ct. CO10: Clar . . . 5C 102
IP5: Kesg . . . 5E 134
Bloomfield St. IP4: Ips . . . 7F 133
Bloomfield Way IP14: Deb . . . 3G 87
NR33: Car C . . . 6D 10
Bloomsbury Cl. NR32: Oul . . . 4D 8
Blooms Ct. IP28: Mide . . . 6K 23
Bloomsfield Rd. CB9: Have . . . 3B 100
Blooms Hall La. CO10: Stans . . . 2E 104
Blower's La. NR33: Rushm . . . 3D 16
Blowers Piece IP19: Wen . . . 3J 43
Blue Barn Cl. IP11: T Mart . . . 5G 153
Blue Barn La. IP6: Gt Bla . . . 4A 114
Bluebell Av. IP32: Bury E . . . 1B 60
Bluebell Cl. IP2: Ips . . . 2G 137
NR33: Low . . . 6E 10
Bluebell Gdns. IP27: Lake . . . 5B 20
Bluebell Gro. IP6: Nee M . . . 5G 111
Bluebell Wlk. IP27: B'don . . . 5D 18
Bluebell Way NR34: Worl . . . 5H 13
Bluegate La. IP9: Cap M . . . 4H 147
Blueleighs Pk. IP6: Gt Bla . . . 2A 114
Bluestem Rd. IP3: Ips . . . 6H 139
Bluetail Cl. IP14: Stowm . . . 3J 85
Blundens, The CO6: Stoke N . . . 1H 143
Blundens Cnr. CO6: Stoke N . . . 1J 143
BLUNDESTON . . . 2J 7 (1D 167)
Blundeston Rd. NR32: Cort . . . 7F 7
NR32: S'ton . . . 2D 6 & 2F 7
Blyburgate NR34: Becc . . . 3E 12
BLYFORD . . . 1J 43 (3C 167)
Blyford La. IP19: Bly, Wen . . . 2H 43
IP19: Holt . . . 4E 42
Blyford Rd. NR32: Low . . . 2F 9
Blyford Way IP11: Felix . . . 4B 154
BLYTHBURGH . . . 6J 43 (3C 167)
Blythburgh Rd. IP17: Westl . . . 5H 79
Blyth Cl. IP2: Ips . . . 5J 137
IP17: Saxm . . . 5H 91
IP19: Wen . . . 2H 43
Blything Ct. NR34: Worl . . . 4J 13
Blyth M. IP19: H'orth . . . 4B 42
Blyth Rd. IP18: Sou . . . 4J 45
IP19: H'orth . . . 6B 42
Blyth Rd. Ind. Est.
IP19: H'orth . . . 5B 42
Blyth Vs. IP13: Denn . . . 6B 76
Boasts Ind. Pk. NR34: Worl . . . 5K 13
Boathouse La. NR32: Oul B . . . 1A 10
Boat Ho. M. CO10: Clar . . . 5C 102
Boatman Cl. *IP8: Ips . . . 6G 137*
(off Marbled White Dr.)
Bobbits La. IP8: Ips . . . 6G 137
IP9: Wher . . . 7H 137
BOBBY HILL . . . 1H 33
Boby Rd. IP32: Bury E . . . 5D 52
Bockhill Rd. IP33: Bury E . . . 1C 58
Bodiam Cl. IP3: Ips . . . 2H 139
Bodiam Rd. IP3: Ips . . . 2H 139
Bodiam Wlk. *CB9: Have . . . 3D 100*
(off Dunster Dr.)
Bodiam Way NR33: Car C . . . 5C 10
Bodmin Cl. IP5: Kesg . . . 7A 134
Boeing Way IP28: Mide . . . 6H 23
Boldero Rd. IP32: Bury E . . . 2B 60

Boleyn Wlk. CB8: Newm 6J 47
Boleyn Way CB9: Have 4C 100
Bollard Way NR33: Oul B 4D 10
Bolton La. IP4: Ips 2F 5 (7B 132)
Bolton St. CO10: Lave 6C 106
Bonds Mdw. NR32: Oul B 6D 8
Bond St. IP4: Ips 4G 5 (1B 138)
IP14: Stowm 3F 85
Bon Marche NR32: Low 1J 11
Bonnington Rd. IP3: Ips 5D 138
Bonny Cres. IP3: Ips 6G 139
Bonsey Gdns. NR34: Wrent 1D 44
Boon Cl. IP33: Bury E 3G 59
Boon Dr. NR33: Oul B 3D 10
Booth Ct. IP1: Ips 3B 4 (7K 131)
Booth La. IP5: Kesg 5E 134
Border Cot La. IP13: Wick M 5B 118
Borehamgate *CO10: S'bury* *4E 126*
(off King St.)
BORLEY 2C 163
Borley Cl. IP31: Honi 3H 29
Borley Cres. IP30: E'well 1E 64
BORLEY GREEN
Bury St Edmunds . . .7E 64 (3D 159)
Sudbury 2C 163
Borley Rd. CO10: L Mel 7G 105
Borough End NR34: Becc 5F 13
Borradale Rd. IP32: Bury E 1B 60
Borrett Pl. IP12: Wood 7E 120
Borretts Farm La.
IP13: East, Ket 6K 89
Borrow Cl. NR33: Car C 6B 10
Borrowdale Av. IP4: Ips 4B 132
Borrow Rd. NR32: Oul B 7B 8
Bosmere Ct. IP6: Nee M 4G 111
Bosquet Cl. NR32: Oul 3E 8
Boss Hall Bus. Pk. IP1: Ips 6G 131
Boss Hall Rd. IP1: Ips 6F 131
Bostock Rd. IP2: Ips 5A 138
Boston Rd. IP4: Ips 6D 132
NR32: Low 6J 9
Boswell La. IP7: Hadl 2H 129
BOTESDALE 5K 35 (2A 160)
BOTTISHAM 3A 158
Bouchain Ct. IP19: H'orth 5A 42
Boughton Way
IP33: Bury E 3J 157 (7H 53)
Boulevard, The NR33: Oul B 1C 10
Boulge Rd. IP13: Burg 4K 117
IP13: Hask 2C 120
Boulters Cl. IP14: Stowm 4D 84
Boulters Way IP14: Stowm 4D 84
Boundary Cotts. IP14: Gt Fin 6J 83
Boundary Rd. CB9: Stur 6H 101
IP28: Red L 5J 25
Bourchier Cl. IP7: Hadl 3J 129
Bourne Av. IP32: Bury E 7A 54
Bourne Hill IP2: Wher 7K 137
Bourne Pk. Res. Pk. IP2: Ips 5K 137
Bourne Rd. CB9: Have 3G 101
NR32: Low 5G 9
Bourne Ter. IP2: Wher 6K 137
Bovingdon IP27: RAF L 4J 21
Bowland Dr. IP8: Ips 5E 136
Bowl Cnr. IP14: L Fin 6A 110
Bowling All. *IP23: Gisli* *1J 67*
(off Martins Mdw.)
Bowl Rd. IP14: Batt, L Fin 5A 110
Bowman's La. IP17: Westl 1E 78
Bowthorpe Cl. IP1: Ips 1B 4 (6K 131)
Box Bush La. IP13: Denn 5A 76
(not continuous)
BOXFORD 6C 128 (2D 163)
Boxford Cl. IP14: Stowm 7G 85
Boxford Ct. CB9: Have 4D 100
IP11: Felix 4B 154
Boxford La. CO10: Boxf 7A 128
BOXTED
Bury St Edmunds
...............3G 103 (1C 163)
Nayland 3D 163
BOXTED CROSS 3A 164
Boyden Cl. CB8: W'rook 1F 97
BOYDEN END 1F 97 (1B 162)
Boydlands IP9: Cap M 2H 147
Boyne Rd. IP33: Bury E 2E 58
Boyscott La. NR35: Bung 3B 14
Boysenberry Wlk. *IP3: Ips* *7G 139*
(off Sloeberry Rd.)
BOYTON 2D 165
Boyton Cl. CB9: Have 1F 101
BOYTON END
Haverhill 2B 162
Thaxted 3A 162
Boyton Hall Dr. IP14: Stowm 1B 110
Boyton Rd. IP3: Ips 6F 139
IP12: Holl 1H 141
BRABLING GREEN 3C 161
Bracken Av. IP5: Kesg 5E 134
Brackenbury Cl. IP1: Ips 5K 131
Brackenbury Sports Cen. 3H 155
Brackenhayes Cl. IP2: Ips 3K 137
Bracken Ri. IP27: B'don 4H 19
Bracken Row IP31: Thur 5J 55
Brackenwood Cres.
IP32: Bury E 7A 54
Brackley Cl. IP11: Felix 3C 154
Bradbrook Cl. IP32: Bury E 7B 54
Braddock Sq. IP32: Bury E 6E 52
BRADFIELD 3B 164
Bradfield Av. IP7: Hadl 2H 129
BRADFIELD COMBUST . . .2J 81 (1C 163)
Bradfield Cres. IP7: Hadl 2H 129
Bradfield Hall IP30: B Com 2K 81
BRADFIELD HEATH 3B 164
BRADFIELD ST CLARE 1D 163
BRADFIELD ST GEORGE
...............1C 82 (3D 159)
Bradfield Woods (Nature Reserve)
...........................5A 82
Bradford Ct. IP5: Martl H 7G 135
Bradley Hill CO10: Ashe 7C 102
Bradley Rd. CB9: L Thu 3B 96
Bradley St. IP2: Ips 7E 4
BRADWELL 1D 167
Braeburn Cl. IP4: Ips 1J 5 (6C 132)
Braggon's Hill IP29: Boxt 1A 104
BRAISEWORTH 2B 160
Braithwaite Dr. CO10: Gt Wal 7K 107
Bramble Cl. CB9: Have 2C 100
IP13: Laxf 6B 74
Bramble Dr. IP3: Pur F 5J 139
Bramble Grn. NR32: Low 5G 9
Brambles, The IP15: Aldeb 3G 95
Bramble Wlk. *IP28: B Row* *1F 23*
(off Broom Wlk.)
IP28: Red L 7J 25
Bramble Way CO6: Leav 3B 142
Bramblewood IP8: Ips 4E 136
Bramblewood Way IP19: H'orth ...4B 42
Brambling Cl. IP14: Stowm 5J 85
Brames La. IP20: Metf 6J 41
BRAMFIELD 7J 75 (2D 161)
Bramfield Rd. IP19: H'orth 6B 42
IP19: Wal 3H 75
IP19: Wen 4G 43
NR32: Low 5F 9
BRAMFORD 3C 130 (2B 164)
Bramford Ct. IP14: Stowm 6G 85
Bramford La. IP1: Ips 4F 131
Bramford Pl. IP1: Ips 5G 131
Bramford Rd. IP1: Ips 1A 4 (4E 130)
IP6: Gt Bla 3A 114
IP8: B'ford 4E 130
Bramhall Cl. IP2: Ips 5F 137
Bramley Chase IP4: Ips 6F 133
Bramley Cl. IP32: Bury E 7B 54
Bramley Hill IP4: Ips 1J 5 (6C 132)
Bramley Ri. NR34: Becc 5F 13
Bramley Rd. CB9: Have 4B 100
BRAMPTON 5H 15 (2C 167)
Brampton Gro. NR32: Oul B 4E 8
BRAMPTON STREET 6F 15
BRANDESTON 1K 89 (3C 161)
Brandeston Cl. CO10: Gt Wal 7J 107
Brandeston Rd. IP13: Cret 2F 89
BRANDON 3F 19 (1B 158)
BRANDON BANK 1A 158
Brandon Bus. Cen. IP27: B'don ...6D 18
Brandon Country Pk. 7E 18
BRANDON CREEK 1A 158
BRANDON FIELDS 5A 18
Brandon Heritage Cen. 3G 19
Brandon Leisure Cen. 4E 18
Brandon Rd. IP11: Felix 4B 154
IP24: Elv 1F 27
IP27: B'don 7B 18
IP27: Eris, RAF L 7J 21
IP27: Weet 1F 19
IP28: B Mil 1J 25
IP28: Mide 7K 23
Brandon Station (Rail) 2F 19
Brandon St. IP27: RAF L 3H 21
Brand Rd. IP31: Gt Bar 1G 55
Brands Cl. CO10: Gt Cor 6J 127
Bransby Gdns. IP4: Ips ...1H 5 (6C 132)
BRANTHAM 4C 148 (3B 164)
Brantham Hill
CO11: Catt, Brant 6B 148
Brantham Mill Ind. Est.
CO11: Brant 6A 148
Braodway, The IP23: Wick S 1F 69
Braybrooke Cl. IP14: Mendl 2J 71
Braybrooke M. CO10: Ball 5B 126
Brayfield Cl. IP32: Bury E 7K 53
Brazier's Wood Rd. IP3: Ips 6F 139
Brazilian Ter. *CB8: Newm* *6F 47*
(off Black Bear La.)
Breakmoor Hill CO10: Midd 7D 126
Breck Gdns. IP28: Mide 7J 23
Breckland Av. IP27: Lake 4B 20
Breckland Way IP28: Mide 6J 23
NR32: Low 5F 9
Brecon Cl. IP2: Ips 4K 137
BREDFIELD 1C 165
Bredfield Cl. IP11: Felix 3C 154
Bredfield Rd. IP12: Wood 3G 121
Bredfield St. IP12: Wood 5G 121
Brendon Cl. NR32: Oul 6D 8
Brendon Dr. IP5: Rush A 7K 133
Brent Cl. IP28: Mide 7K 23
BRENT ELEIGH 1A 108 (2D 163)
Brent Eleigh Rd. CO10: Lave 6C 106
IP7: M Ele 2D 108
Brentgovel St.
IP33: Bury E 4G 157 (1G 59)
Brent Mill Dr. CO10: B Ele 2A 108
BRESSINGHAM 1A 160
Brett Av. IP7: Hadl 2J 129
Brett Cl. IP1: Ips 5G 131
BRETTENHAM
Thetford 1D 159
Thorpe Morieux 1D 163
Brettenham Cres. IP4: Ips 4B 132
Brettenham Rd. IP14: Bux 7F 83
Brett Grn. IP7: Lay 7J 129
Bretts, The IP5: Kesg 5E 134
Brett Vale Golf Course 2J 145
Brewers Cl. IP27: Lake 5A 20
Brewers La. CB8: Newm 4G 47
Breydon Way IP3: Ips 7H 139
NR33: Oul B 3E 10
Briar Cl. IP19: H'orth 4C 42
NR32: Low 3G 9
Briardale IP4: Ips 7D 132
Briarhayes Cl. IP2: Ips 3K 137
Briar Hill IP30: Wool 5A 64
Briar La. IP22: Rick 7F 35
Briarwood Av. IP33: Bury E 1D 58
Briarwood Rd. IP12: Wood 7F 121
NR33: Oul B 4E 10
Brices Way CO10: Glem 4A 104
Bricett Bus. Pk. IP7: Gt Bri 2A 112
Brickfield Cl. IP2: Ips 7F 5 (3A 138)
Brickfields NR32: S'ton 3B 6
Brickfields, The IP14: Stowm 4E 84
Brickfields Av. CB8: Newm 3D 46
Brickfields Bus. Pk. IP30: Wool ...4C 64
Brickfields Cotts. NR32: S'ton 2B 6
Brickfields Dr. CB9: Have 1D 100
Brick Kiln Av. NR34: Becc 3F 13
Brick Kiln Cl. IP11: T Mart 6G 153
Brick Kiln La. IP19: Hunt 1B 74
Brick Kiln Pk. IP17: Snap 1D 94
Brick Kiln Rd. IP9: Hark 4J 151
IP28: Mide 6K 23
Brickkiln Ter. IP9: Shot 1A 156
Brick La. IP13: F'ham 7D 90
Brickmakers Ct. IP11: T Mart 5G 153
Bridewell Cl. IP28: Mide 7H 23
Bridewell Ind. Est. CO10: Clar ...4D 102
Bridewell La. IP22: Bote, Rick 5J 35
IP33: Bury E 5J 157 (1H 59)
Bridewell St. CO10: Clar 4D 102
Bridewell Wlk. IP12: Wood 5G 121
Bridge Bus. Cen. IP12: Martl 1J 135
Bridge End Rd. IP28: Red L 6G 25
Bridge Farm Cl. IP28: Mide 1E 24
Bridgefoot Cnr. IP18: Rey 2J 45
Bridge Ho. Cen. IP13: F'ham 7C 90
Bridgeman Wlk. IP32: Bury E 6E 52
Bridge Pl. CO11: Catt 6B 148
Bridge Rd. IP10: Levi 7D 152
IP11: Felix 3F 155
IP12: B'well 2B 124
IP17: Snap 3C 94
IP18: Rey 2J 45
IP21: Scole 1K 37
NR32: Oul B 1D 10
NR33: Oul B 2C 10
BRIDGE STREET 2C 163
Bridge St. CB8: Mou 6D 48
CO8: Bure 5B 142
IP1: Ips 5E 4 (1A 138)
IP6: Nee M 3G 111
IP7: Hadl 2G 129
IP13: F'ham 6C 90
IP14: Stowm 5G 85
(not continuous)
IP17: Kel 3J 91
IP19: B'field 7J 75
IP19: H'orth 4B 42
IP19: Hunt 1D 74
NR34: Becc 1E 12
NR35: Bung 2B 14
Bridge St. Rd. CO10: Lave 7A 106
Bridge Trad. Est. IP6: Gt Bla 3C 114
Bridge Vw. IP3: Ips 5D 138
Bridgewood Rd. IP12: Wood 5F 121
BRIDGHAM 1D 159
Bridgwater Rd. IP2: Ips 4F 137
Bridlemere Ct. *CB8: Newm* *6F 47*
(off Queensbury Rd.)
Bridles, The NR34: Worl 4J 13
Bridle Way IP1: Ips 5A 132
Bridport Av. IP3: Ips 3H 139
Bright Cl. IP17: Saxm 5G 91
IP33: Bury E 4J 59
Brighton St. IP27: RAF L 4H 21
Bright's La. CO10: Lave 5A 106
Brights Wlk. IP5: Kesg 6E 134
BRIGHTWELL 1C 152 (2C 165)
Brightwell Cl. IP11: Felix 4B 154
Brimstone Rd. IP8: Ips 6G 137
Brindles, The NR33: Car C 5D 10
BRINKLEY 1A 162
Brinkley Way IP11: Felix 1J 155
Brisbane Rd. IP4: Ips 7H 133
Briscoe Ter. IP12: Wood 5F 121
Briscoe Way IP27: Lake 3A 20
Bristol Hill IP9: Shot G 7E 156
Bristol Hill Pk. IP9: Shot G 7E 156
Bristol Rd. IP4: Ips 6E 132
IP33: Bury E 3E 58
Bristol St. IP27: RAF L 3J 21
Britannia Rd. IP4: Ips 7F 133
British Racing School, The 1H 47
Britten Av. IP14: Stowm 3E 84
Britten Cl. IP15: Aldeb 4H 95
Britten Ho. NR34: Becc 3F 13
Britten Rd. NR33: Oul B 3F 11
Britten Shop. Cen. NR32: Low 7J 9
Brittons Cres. IP29: Barr 6B 50
Brittons Rd. IP29: Barr 7B 50
Brize Norton IP27: RAF L 5H 21
Broadcroft Cres. CB9: Have 3D 100
Broadfields Cl. IP23: Gisli 1J 67
Broadfields Rd. IP23: Gisli 2J 67
Broad Fleet Cl. NR32: Oul 4D 8
BROADGRASS GREEN 3K 63
BROAD GREEN
Bury St Edmunds 3J 51
Saxon Street 1A 162
Broad Grn. Cl. IP29: Chev 3J 51
BROAD HILL 2A 158
Broadhurst Ter. *IP5: Kesg* *6E 134*
(off Hartree Way)
Broadland Cl. NR33: Oul B 2C 10
NR34: Worl 4H 13
Broadland Holiday Village
NR33: Oul B 2C 10
Broadland Rd. IP33: Bury E 5H 59
Broadlands Way IP4: Rush A 1K 139
Broad Mdw. IP8: Ips 4E 136
IP31: Wals W 5H 33
Broadmere Rd. IP1: Ips 5G 131
Broadoak Cl. NR33: Car C 5B 10
Broad Oaks CO6: Leav 1C 142
Broad Oke IP1: Ips 3B 4
Broad Rd. CB9: L Thu 5D 96
IP13: Wick M 5A 118
IP14: Bac, Cott 7C 68
NR32: Oul B 7C 8
Broads, The 2A 6
Broadside NR32: Oul B 7D 8
Broad St. CB9: Have 3E 100
CO10: Boxf 6C 128
IP12: Orf 7J 125
IP23: Eye 7D 38
NR35: Bung 1A 14
Broadview Rd. NR32: Oul B 1B 10
Broadwater Gdns. IP9: Shot G ...7D 156
Broadwaters Rd. NR33: Oul B 5D 10
BROADWAY 2C 42 (2D 161)
Broadway CO10: Glem 4A 104
IP13: Wick M 5A 118
IP21: Fress 6C 40
IP23: Wick S 1G 69
Broadway, The IP31: B Ash 2D 66
IP33: Bury E 4K 157
Broadway Dr. IP19: H'orth 2C 42
Broadway La. IP1: Ips 3G 131
Broadway Vs. *IP1: Ips* *3G 131*
(off Broadway La.)
BROCKDISH 2C 161
Brockesby Wlk. IP33: Bury E 2D 58
BROCKFORD GREEN 7H 69
Brockford Rd.
IP14: Broc S, Mendl 2K 71
BROCKFORD STREET . . .5G 69 (3B 160)
Brock La. IP12: Martl 1J 135
BROCKLEY CORNER 4A 28 (2C 159)
Brockley Cres. IP1: Ips 4F 131
BROCKLEY GREEN
Hartest 1C 163
Haverhill 2B 162
Brockley La. IP29: Denh 6A 50
Brockley Rd. IP29: Whep 4C 80
Brock Rd. NR34: Nor C 7B 6
Broke Av. IP8: B'ford 3D 130
BROKE HALL 1K 139
Broke Hall Gdns. IP3: Ips 2H 139
Broke Hall Ho. IP3: Ips 3H 139
BROME 5G 37 (2B 160)
Brome Av. IP23: Eye 5C 38
Brome Ind. Est. IP23: Eye 6G 37
Bromelands IP23: Brom 4K 37
Brome Rd. IP21: Thran 4F 37

BROME STREET . . . 2B 160
BROMESWELL . . . 3A 124 (1D 165)
Bromeswell Green Nature Reserve . . . 4A 124
Bromeswell Rd. IP4: Ips . . . 4C 132
Bromley Cl. IP2: Ips . . . 3A 138
Bronyon Cl. IP33: Bury E . . . 1C 58
Brook Cl. CO10: Hund . . . 2H 99
IP29: Horr . . . 5B 58
IP31: Stant . . . 7D 32
NR33: Car C . . . 5C 10
Brooke Business & Industrial Pk.
NR33: Oul B . . . 1F 11
Brooke Dr. IP17: Pea . . . 2J 77
Brook Farm La. IP9: Holb . . . 2C 150
Brook Farm Rd. IP17: Saxm . . . 6G 91
Brookfield Rd. IP1: Ips . . . 5H 131
Brookfields Cl. CB8: Newm . . . 4H 47
Brook Hall Rd. CO10: Boxf . . . 6D 128
Brookhill Way IP4: Rush A . . . 2K 139
Brookhouse Bus. Pk. IP2: Ips . . . 7H 131
Brook Ho. Rd.
IP14: Cott . . . 7J 67, 4E 68 & 6E 68
Brooklands Cl. IP33: Bury E . . . 2F 59
Brooklands Ri. CO11: Brant . . . 5C 148
Brooklands Rd. CO11: Brant . . . 6B 148
Brook La. IP6: Play . . . 1A 134
IP9: Cap M . . . 1F 147
IP10: Falk . . . 5K 153
IP11: Felix . . . 3G 155
IP13: F'ham . . . 6A 90
IP22: B'gate . . . 4J 35
Brook Pk. IP22: Rick . . . 6G 35
Brook Service Rd. CB9: Have . . . 3F 101
Brooksfield IP7: Bild . . . 5J 109
Brooks Hall Rd. IP1: Ips . . . 6J 131
Brookside CB8: Dalh . . . 7H 49
CB8: Exn . . . 1C 46
CB8: Mou . . . 6D 48
Brook St. CO10: Glem . . . 3A 104
IP12: Wood . . . 5H 121
IP17: Yox . . . 7J 77
Brookview IP8: Ips . . . 5G 137
Brook Way IP8: S'ham . . . 3K 113
Brookwood Cl. NR34: Worl . . . 5K 13
Broom, The IP12: Orf . . . 7G 125
Broom Cres. IP3: Ips . . . 5D 138
BROOME . . . 1D 161
Broom Fld. IP11: Felix . . . 3D 154
Broomfield IP5: Martl H . . . 6F 135
Broomfield Comn. IP8: Spro . . . 7D 130
Broomfield Courtyard
CB9: Have . . . 3E 100
Broomfield M. IP5: Martl H . . . 6G 135
Broomhayes IP2: Ips . . . 4J 137
Broomheath IP12: Wood . . . 7F 121
BROOM HILL
Ipswich . . . 7C 114
Woodbridge . . . 7E 120
Broomhill IP9: Holb . . . 2D 150
Broomhill Cl. IP28: Red L . . . 6J 25
Broomhill La. IP30: Wool . . . 4K 63
Broom Hill Nature Reserve . . . 4G 129
Broom Hill Rd. IP1: Ips . . . 5J 131
Broom Knoll CO7: E Ber . . . 3B 148
Broomley Grn. La. IP32: Bury E . . . 7B 54
Broom Rd. IP27: Lake . . . 6B 20
NR32: Low . . . 6G 9
Broom Rd. Cl. IP27: Lake . . . 6C 20
Broomspath Rd. IP14: Stowu . . . 2J 85
Broom St. CO10: Gt Cor . . . 6G 127
Broomvale Bus. Pk. IP8: L Bla . . . 5B 114
Broomwade Cl. IP2: Ips . . . 5A 4 (1J 137)
Broom Wlk. IP28: B Row . . . 1F 23
Broom Way IP9: Cap M . . . 1J 147
Brotherton Av. IP11: T Mary . . . 7J 153
Broughton Rd. IP1: Ips . . . 1C 4 (6K 131)
Browning Rd. CO11: Brant . . . 6B 148
IP1: Ips . . . 2H 131
Brownlow Rd. IP11: Felix . . . 4G 155
Brownrigg Wlk. *IP2: Ips . . . 3B 138*
(off Jamestown Blvd.)
Browns Acre IP23: Melli . . . 5A 36
Browns Cl. CB8: W'rook . . . 2F 97
CO10: Act . . . 4G 107
IP7: Hit . . . 2G 109
Brownsea Ct. *IP5: Kesg . . . 6E 134*
(off Ropes Dr.)
Browns Gro. IP5: Kesg . . . 6D 134
Browse Cl. IP32: Bury E . . . 2A 60
BROWSTON GREEN . . . 1C 167
Broxtead Cl. IP12: Sutt . . . 2C 140
BROXTED . . . 3A 162
Bruce St. NR33: Low . . . 2H 11
Brudenell St. IP15: Aldeb . . . 6J 95
Bruff Rd. IP2: Ips . . . 7E 4 (3A 138)
BRUISYARD . . . 3D 161
Bruisyard Rd. IP17: Pea . . . 4H 77
BRUISYARD STREET . . . 3D 161
BRUNDISH . . . 3C 161
Brundish La. IP12: Orf . . . 6J 125
BRUNDISH STREET . . . 2C 161
BRUNDON . . . 2B 126
Brundon La. CO10: Ball, S'bury . . . 5B 126
Brunel Bus. Ct.
IP32: Bury E . . . 2K 157 (7J 53)
Brunel Rd. IP2: Ips . . . 7G 131
Brunswick Rd. IP4: Ips . . . 1K 5 (5D 132)
Bruntingthorpe IP27: RAF L . . . 5H 21
Brunwyn Cl. IP32: Bury E . . . 7B 54
BRUSSEL'S GREEN . . . 2D 78
Brybank Rd. CB9: Have . . . 2B 100
Bryntirion Ct. *CB8: Newm . . . 6J 47*
(off Boleyn Wlk.)
Bryon Av. IP11: Felix . . . 5A 154
Bryony Cl. CB9: Have . . . 2D 100
NR33: Low . . . 6E 10
Buckenham Cl. NR34: Worl . . . 5H 13
Buckenham Ct. IP18: Sou . . . 4K 45
Buckenham Rd. IP7: Hadl . . . 5K 129
Buckfast Cl. IP2: Ips . . . 4J 137
Buckingham Cl. IP12: Martl . . . 3G 135
Buckingham Rd. CB9: Have . . . 5D 100
Buckingham's Hill IP21: Fress . . . 6E 40
Buck La. IP21: Oak . . . 2K 37
IP23: Brom . . . 2K 37
Buckles Fld. IP31: Stant . . . 6D 32
BUCKLESHAM . . . 2B 152 (2C 165)
Bucklesham Rd. IP3: Ips . . . 4H 139
IP10: Buck, Foxh . . . 2A 152
IP10: Kirt . . . 1G 153
Buckleswood Rd. IP16: Leis . . . 1F 93
Bucknam Cl. NR33: Kess . . . 4K 17
Buckshorn La. IP23: Eye . . . 7D 38
Bucks Horn Pl. IP8: Bels . . . 7E 136
Buck's Horns La. IP8: Bels . . . 7D 136
Bucks La. CO10: Clar . . . 5C 102
Buddleia Cl. IP2: Ips . . . 2G 137
Bude Cl. IP5: Kesg . . . 7A 134
Buggs Hole La.
IP22: Thel . . . 2K 31 & 4F 31
Bugsby Way IP5: Kesg . . . 6E 134
Bulcamp Drift IP19: Bulc . . . 4K 43
Bullace La. IP12: Sud . . . 2H 125
Bullard's La. IP12: Wood . . . 5F 121
Bull Dr. IP5: Kesg . . . 7C 134
Bullen Cl. IP8: B'ford . . . 3C 130
IP33: Bury E . . . 2F 59
Bullen La. IP8: B'ford . . . 4A 130
Bullens Cl. IP33: W'ley . . . 1A 58
Buller Rd. IP16: Leis . . . 3H 93
Bullfinch Cl. IP14: Stowm . . . 4J 85
Bull Hall La. IP6: Witn . . . 4C 116
Bullion's La. NR34: Ugg . . . 5B 44
Bull La. CO10: Act, L Mel . . . 3J 105
IP29: Haws, Whep . . . 3E 80
Bullockshed La. IP12: Orf . . . 5J 125
Bullocks La. CO10: S'bury . . . 4D 126
Bullocks Ter. CO10: S'bury . . . 5D 126
Bull Rd. IP3: Ips . . . 2E 138
IP31: Pake, Stowl . . . 2C 56
Bull Rush Cres.
IP33: Bury E . . . 1F 157 (6F 53)
Bull's Cliff IP11: Felix . . . 5E 154
Bulls Hall Rd. IP23: Occ . . . 5B 72
Bull's Rd. IP6: Barh . . . 6F 115
IP6: Hemi . . . 3J 115
BULMER . . . 2C 163
Bulmer Rd. CO10: Ball . . . 5B 126
Bulmer Rd. Ind. Est.
CO10: Ball . . . 4B 126
BULMER TYE . . . 3C 163
Bulstrode Rd. IP2: Ips . . . 7F 5 (2B 138)
Bulwer Rd. IP1: Ips . . . 1A 4 (6J 131)
Bumpstead Rd. CB9: Have . . . 7G 101
Bunbury Av. IP28: Mide . . . 6J 23
IP31: Gt Bar . . . 3D 54
(not continuous)
Bunbury Rd. IP32: Bury E . . . 4F 53
Bunbury Ter. CB8: Newm . . . 6G 47
Bungalows, The IP10: Falk . . . 2J 153
IP30: Tost . . . 2H 63
BUNGAY . . . 2A 14 (1D 161)
Bungay & Waveney Valley Golf Course . . . 1A 14
Bungay Castle . . . 2A 14
Bungay Mus. . . . 2B 14
Bungay Pool . . . 4D 14
Bungay Riverside Cen. . . . 2C 14
Bungay Rd. IP19: Holt . . . 3D 42
IP19: H'orth . . . 3B 42
NR34: Bars, Becc . . . 5A 12
Bungay Sports Cen. . . . 4C 14
Bunker Cl. NR33: Low . . . 4F 11
BUNKER'S HILL . . . 1D 167
Bunters Rd. CB8: W'rook . . . 1F 97
Bunting Rd. IP2: Ips . . . 3F 137
IP32: Bury E . . . 2B 60
Buntings, The IP14: Stowm . . . 5K 85
BUNTINGS GREEN . . . 3C 163
BUNWELL . . . 1B 160
Bunyan Cl. IP1: Ips . . . 2J 131
Burch's Cl. IP17: Knod . . . 7F 93
Buregate Rd. IP11: Felix . . . 6E 154
BURES . . . 6B 142 (3D 163)
Bures Cl. IP14: Stowm . . . 6G 85
Bures Ct. *CB9: Have . . . 4D 100*
(off Leather La.)
Bures Rd. CO6: Nay . . . 7F 143
CO10: Gt Cor . . . 5F 127
Bures Station (Rail) . . . 6A 142
BURGATE GREAT GREEN . . . 4H 35 (2A 160)
BURGATE LITTLE GREEN . . . 2A 160
Burgate Rd. IP23: Gisli . . . 1J 67
Burgess Cl. NR32: Oul B . . . 6E 8
Burgess Pl. IP5: Martl H . . . 6H 135
BURGH . . . 5K 117 (1C 165)
Burghley Cl. IP2: Ips . . . 4J 137
BURGH ST PETER . . . 1C 167
Burke Cl. IP1: Ips . . . 2J 131
Burke Rd. IP1: Ips . . . 2H 131
Burkitt Ho. IP12: Wood . . . 5H 121
Burkitt Rd. IP12: Wood . . . 5G 121
Burkitts La. CO10: S'bury . . . 4D 126
Burlingham Dr. NR33: Car C . . . 6A 10
Burlingham Ho. IP2: Ips . . . 7B 4
Burlington Cl. IP22: Pal . . . 2D 36
Burlington Rd. IP1: Ips . . . 3B 4 (7K 131)
Burls Yd. *IP6: Nee M . . . 3H 111*
(off Crown St.)
Burnet Cl. IP8: Ips . . . 6F 137
Burnham Cl. IP4: Ips . . . 2K 5 (7D 132)
IP11: T Mary . . . 1B 154
Burnham Way NR33: Oul B . . . 2F 11
Burns Cl. IP23: Yax . . . 6C 36
Burns Dr. IP14: Stowm . . . 2E 84
Burns Rd. IP1: Ips . . . 2G 131
BURNT HEATH . . . 3A 164
Burnt Hill La. NR33: Car C . . . 1A 10
Burnt Hill Way NR33: Oul B . . . 3B 10
Burnt Ho. Cl. CB9: Have . . . 2B 100
Burnt Ho. La. IP10: Kirt . . . 1H 153
IP14: Batt, Comb . . . 6C 110
Burnt La. IP12: Orf . . . 7J 125
Burnt Oak CO7: E Ber . . . 5C 146
Burnt Oak Cnr. CO7: E Ber . . . 5C 146
Burrell Cres. IP28: B Mil . . . 2G 25
Burrell Rd. IP2: Ips . . . 6C 4 (2K 137)
Burrells Cotts. IP17: Knod . . . 7F 93
Burrell's Orchard IP33: W'ley . . . 7A 52
Burr La. IP22: Hind . . . 5C 34
BURROUGH END . . . 1A 162
BURROUGH GREEN . . . 1A 162
Burroughs Piece Rd.
CO10: S'bury . . . 4E 126
Burrow Dr. IP27: Lake . . . 3A 20
Burrows Rd. IP12: Melt . . . 7F 119
BURSTALL . . . 2A 164
Burstall La. IP8: Spro . . . 7A 130
BURSTON . . . 1B 160
BURTHORPE . . . 6D 50 (3B 158)
Burthorpe Grn. IP29: Barr . . . 4D 50
Burton Cl. CB9: Have . . . 4D 100
Burton Dr. IP6: Nee M . . . 3F 111
BURTON END . . . 2A 162
Burton End CB9: Have . . . 4C 100
Burton Hill CB9: With . . . 1C 98
BURTON'S GREEN . . . 3C 163
Burton St. NR32: Low . . . 6J 9
Burtonwood IP27: RAF L . . . 4J 21
Burwash IP6: Witn . . . 3B 116
BURWELL . . . 3A 158
Burwell Rd. CB8: Exn . . . 1A 46
Burwood Pl. IP11: T Mary . . . 7J 153
NR32: Low . . . 2G 9
Bury Bowl
Bury St Edmunds . . . 3K 157 (1J 59)
Bury Drift IP31: Forn M . . . 2J 53
Bury Hill IP12: Wood . . . 3H 121
Bury Hill Cl. IP12: Wood . . . 3H 121
Bury La. CB8: Mou . . . 5D 48
IP31: Stant . . . 7C 32
Bury Pk. Dr. IP33: Bury E . . . 4J 59
Bury Rd. CB8: Kent . . . 2A 48
CB8: Newm . . . 5H 47
CB8: Stradi, W'rook . . . 6G 97
CB9: Gt Thu . . . 7C 96
CO10: Lave . . . 4C 106
IP1: Ips . . . 1F 131
IP7: Hit . . . 1F 109
IP14: Stowm . . . 1C 84
IP22: B'gate, Wort . . . 4G 35
IP22: Hep, W'field . . . 2F 33
IP22: Hop, M Wes . . . 4G 31
IP22: Rick . . . 7F 35
IP27: B'don . . . 4G 19
IP28: B Mil, Mide . . . 7K 23 & 1H 25
IP29: Barr . . . 6C 50
IP29: Chedb . . . 7K 51
IP29: Harg . . . 2F 51
IP29: Laws . . . 6A 80
IP29: Stann . . . 1F 81
IP29: Whep . . . 1C 80
IP30: B Cla . . . 1K 81
IP30: Bey . . . 3B 62
Bury Rd. IP30: C'field . . . 4J 81
IP30: Fels, Ged . . . 5B 82
IP30: Rushb, S'mere . . . 7A 60
IP30: Wool . . . 4K 63
IP31: Gt Bar . . . 3D 54
IP31: Ixw . . . 6H 29
IP31: Stant . . . 7B 32
BURY ST EDMUNDS . . . 4G 157 (3C 159)
Bury St Edmunds Golf Course . . . 5C 52
Bury St Edmunds Leisure Cen. . . . 7E 52
Bury St Edmunds Station (Rail) . . . 1H 157 (6G 53)
Bury St. IP14: Stowm . . . 4F 85
Bury Town FC . . . 3J 157 (7H 53)
Bushey Cl. IP9: Cap M . . . 2H 147
Bushey La. IP12: Holl . . . 3F 141
BUSH GREEN
Gedding . . . 1D 163
Pulham St Mary . . . 1C 161
Bush Gro. CO10: Ball . . . 5B 126
Bushman Gdns. IP8: B'ford . . . 3C 130
BUSTARD GREEN . . . 3A 162
Butchers La. CO10: Boxf, Gro . . . 6C 128
IP9: Cap M . . . 2J 147
Butcher's Rd. IP17: Kel . . . 2K 91
Bute Ct. CB9: Have . . . 5E 100
Butfield CO10: Lave . . . 7B 106
Butler Smith Gdns. IP5: Kesg . . . 6C 134
BUTLEY . . . 5C 124 (1D 165)
Butley Cl. IP2: Ips . . . 6H 137
Butley Ct. CB9: Have . . . 5D 100
Butley Dr. NR32: Oul B . . . 5E 8
BUTLEY HIGH CORNER . . . 2D 165
Butley Rd. IP11: Felix . . . 5D 154
Buttercup Cl. IP8: Ips . . . 5E 136
IP32: Bury E . . . 1B 60
NR33: Car C . . . 5B 10
Buttercup Wlk. IP28: Red L . . . 7J 25
Butterfly Gdns. IP4: Rush A . . . 1J 139
Butter Mkt. IP1: Ips . . . 3E 4 (7A 132)
IP14: Stowm . . . 4F 85
(off Market Pl.)
IP33: Bury E . . . 4H 157 (1G 59)
Buttermarket Shop. Cen.
IP1: Ips . . . 3E 4 (7A 132)
Buttermere Grn. IP11: Felix . . . 2J 155
Buttermere Way NR33: Car C . . . 7C 10
BUTTON HAUGH GREEN . . . 7E 66
Buttons Cl. CO10: L Mel . . . 7G 105
Butt Rd. CO6: Stoke N . . . 2G 143
CO10: Gt Cor . . . 5G 127
Buttrum's Mill . . . 5F 121
Butts, The IP14: Deb . . . 1G 87
BUXHALL . . . 6G 83 (1A 164)
Buxlow Cl. IP17: Knod . . . 7G 93
Buzzard Ri. IP14: Stowu . . . 4K 85
Byfield Way IP33: Bury E . . . 3J 59
Byford Ct. IP7: Hadl . . . 1J 129
Byford Rd. CO10: S'bury . . . 2F 127
Byford Wlk. IP4: Ips . . . 1J 5 (6C 132)
Bylam La. IP9: Chelm . . . 2F 151
Byland Cl. IP2: Ips . . . 4J 137
Byles Wlk. IP14: Stowm . . . 4E 84
Byng Hall Rd. IP13: Petti, Uff . . . 3F 119
Byng La. IP13: Petti . . . 3F 119
Byrde Cl. IP33: Bury E . . . 2C 58
Byron Cl. IP14: Stowm . . . 2E 84
Byron Rd. IP1: Ips . . . 1G 131

C

Cabin Cl. NR33: Car C . . . 5A 10
Cable La. IP15: Aldeb . . . 4J 95
Caddie's Wlk. NR33: Low . . . 5F 11
Cadney La.
IP33: Bury E . . . 2H 157 (7G 53)
Cadogan Rd. IP33: Bury E . . . 2D 58
Caernarvon Wlk. CB9: Have . . . 3D 100
Cage La. IP11: Felix . . . 3D 154
Cages Way IP12: Melt . . . 7F 119
Caie Wlk. IP33: Bury E . . . 4H 59
Caithness Cl. IP4: Ips . . . 5F 133
Cakebridge La. IP7: Chels . . . 7F 109
Cakes & Ale Caravan Pk.
IP16: Leis . . . 1F 93
Cake St. Cl. IP28: B Row . . . 2F 23
CALAIS STREET . . . 7E 128 (2D 163)
Calais St. IP7: Hadl . . . 3H 129
Caldecott Rd. NR32: Oul B . . . 7C 8
Calder Rd. IP12: Melt . . . 7F 119
Caledonia Rd. IP9: Shot G . . . 7E 156
Calford Dr. CB9: Have . . . 3B 100
CALFORD GREEN . . . 2A 162
CALIFORNIA
Ipswich . . . 7E 132 (2B 164)
Woodbridge . . . 1G 119
California IP12: Wood . . . 7E 120
Calkewood La. IP22: W'field . . . 1K 33
Calledge Drove IP27: Lake . . . 2D 20
Callis St. CO10: Clar . . . 4C 102
Callisto Ct. IP1: Ips . . . 6F 131

Callowhill La. IP31: Gt Liv 3C **28**
Calthorpe Cl. IP32: Bury E 7A **54**
Calves La. CO6: Stoke N 7A **144**
Camberley Ct.
IP33: Bury E 2F **157** (7F **53**)
Camberley Rd. IP4: Ips 6H **133**
Camborne Rd. IP5: Kesg 6B **134**
Cambria, The *IP4: Ips 5F 5*
(off Key St.)
Cambrian Cres. NR32: Oul 6C **8**
Cambridge Cl. CB9: Have 2D **100**
Cambridge Dr. IP2: Ips 4H **137**
Cambridge Rd. IP5: Kesg 5A **134**
IP11: Felix 4G **155**
NR32: Low 5J **9**
Cambridge Wlk. IP32: Bury E 4E **52**
Cambridge Way CB9: Have 2D **100**
CO8: Bure 6B **142**
Camden Rd. IP3: Ips 2F **139**
Camden St. NR32: Low 5K **9**
Cameron Cl. CO10: L Mel 5H **105**
Camilla Ct. IP10: Nac 5A **152**
Campbell Cl. IP28: Mide 5H **23**
Campbell Rd. IP3: Ips 4G **139**
Campion Cres. IP14: Stowm 6E **84**
Campion Rd. IP2: Ips 2H **137**
Campions Hill CO6: Nay 4F **143**
Campion Way CO6: Leav 3B **142**
Camp Rd. NR32: Low 7J **9**
CAMPSEA ASHE 3A **122** (1D **165**)
CAMPS END 2A **162**
CAMPS HEATH 6C **8**
Camps Rd. CB9: Have 4E **100**
Camwood Gdns. IP3: Ips 2F **139**
Canaletto Cl. NR32: Low 2G **9**
Canberra Cl. IP4: Ips 7H **133**
IP28: RAF M 1D **22**
CANDLE STREET 7G **35** (2A **160**)
Candlet Gro. IP11: Felix 3E **154**
Candlet Rd. IP11: Felix 1D **154**
Cangle Junc. CB9: Have 3F **101**
Cangle Rd. CB9: Have 3F **101**
Cangles La. IP30: Bey 4D **62**
CANHAM'S GREEN 3A **160**
Canhams Rd. CO10: Gt Cor 6G **127**
Canham St. IP1: Ips 3C **4** (7K **131**)
Cann Cl. CO10: S'bury 1C **126**
Canning Rd. NR33: Low 2G **11**
Cannonfields
IP33: Bury E 3H **157** (7G **53**)
Cannon St.
IP33: Bury E 3H **157** (7G **53**)
Canon Cl. CB9: Have 2F **101**
Canon Pugh Dr. CO10: Act 4G **107**
Canterbury Cl. IP2: Ips 6H **137**
Canterbury Gdns. IP7: Hadl 3J **129**
Canterbury Grn. IP33: Bury E 3G **59**
Canterbury Rd. CO10: S'bury 1C **126**
Canterview CB8: Newm 5F **47**
Capel Cl. IP11: T Mart 5H **153**
IP31: Tros 1D **28**
Capel Dr. IP11: Felix 4B **154**
CAPEL GREEN 2D **165**
Capelgrove IP9: Cap M 3G **147**
Capel Hall La. IP11: T Mart 5J **153**
Capell Wlk. IP31: Stant 6C **32**
Capel Rd. IP9: Bent 5F **147**
CAPEL ST ANDREW 2D **165**
CAPEL ST MARY 2H **147** (3A **164**)
CAPEL ST MARY INTERCHANGE
. . . . 2K **147**
Capital Trad. Est. NR32: Low 6K **9**
CAPON'S GREEN 5E **76**
Capstan Way NR33: Car C 5A **10**
Captain's La. IP14: W'den 3G **65**
Carbonels CO10: Gt Wal 7J **107**
Carders Cl. IP7: Hadl 5H **129**
Cardew Drift IP5: Kesg 5D **134**
Cardiff Av. IP2: Ips 5K **137**
Cardigan St. CB8: Newm 6G **47**
IP1: Ips 1B **4**
Cardinal Cl. IP32: Bury E 7A **54**
Cardinal Lofts IP4: Ips 5E **4**
Cardinalls Rd. IP14: Stowm 3F **85**
Cardinal Pk. E. IP1: Ips 5D **4**
Cardinal Pk. W. IP1: Ips 5C **4**
Cardinals Ct. IP11: Felix 5F **155**
CARDINAL'S GREEN 2A **162**
Cardinal St. IP1: Ips 5D **4** (1A **138**)
Cardinal Way CB9: Have 2E **100**
CARLETON RODE 1B **160**
Carlford Cl. IP5: Martl H 5G **135**
Carlford Ct. IP4: Ips 1F **139**
NR34: Worl 4K **13**
Carlow M. IP12: Wood 5H **121**
CARLTON
Little Thurlow 1A **162**
Saxmundham 3H **91** (3D **161**)
Carlton Cl. CB9: Have 1E **100**
CARLTON COLVILLE 6C **10** (1D **167**)
Carlton Cross NR33: Car C 7B **10**
Carlton Grn. IP17: Carl 3H **91**
Carlton Pk. IP17: Carl 4H **91**
Carlton Pk. Ind. Est. IP17: Carl 4H **91**
Carlton Rd. IP5: Kesg 6A **134**
IP17: Carl, Kel 3G **91**
NR33: Low 3G **11**
Carlton Sq. NR33: Car C 7B **10**
Carlton Wlk. IP7: Hadl 5J **129**
Carlton Way IP4: Ips 5C **132**
Carlyle Cl. IP1: Ips 1H **131**
Carmarthen Cl. IP2: Ips 5J **137**
Carmelite Pl. IP12: Wood 6H **121**
Carnation Way IP28: Red L 7H **25**
Carnoustie Dr. IP28: Forn M 2F **53**
NR33: Oul B 5E **10**
Carol Av. IP12: Martl 4G **135**
Carolbrook Rd. IP2: Ips 5G **137**
Carol Cl. IP11: Felix 3H **155**
Carpenter Cl. IP31: Ixw 6J **29**
Carpenters Cl. CB8: Gaz 2H **49**
Carr Av. IP16: Leis 3H **93**
Carriage Cl. IP11: T Mary 7J **153**
Carriers Ct. CO7: E Ber 3C **146**
Carr La. IP31: Bard 4C **32**
Carrops, The CB8: Kenn 7H **25**
IP28: Red L 7H **25**
Carr Rd. IP11: Felix 7C **154**
Carrs Hill IP13: B'ham 3B **76**
Carr St. IP4: Ips 3F **5** (7B **132**)
Carsons Dr. CO10: Gt Cor 6H **127**
Carson Wlk. CB8: Newm 3F **47**
Carters La. IP7: Gt Bri 1A **112**
Carthew Ct. IP12: Wood 6H **121**
Cart Score NR32: Low 5K **9**
Case La. IP9: Bent 5G **147**
Castle Av. CB9: Have 3D **100**
Castle Brooks IP13: F'ham 6C **90**
CASTLE CAMPS 2A **162**
Castle Cl. IP11: Felix 2J **155**
IP12: Orf 7H **125**
Castle Ct. IP1: Ips 2J **131**
Castle Cres. IP21: Wing 2J **39**
Castle Gdns. IP5: Kesg 6D **134**
Castle Grn. IP12: Orf 7H **125**
CASTLE HEDINGHAM 3B **162**
CASTLE HILL 2K **131** (2B **164**)
Castle Hill IP12: Eyk 1D **124**
IP12: Orf 7J **125**
IP19: H'orth 5C **42**
IP23: Eye 7D **38**
IP23: Occ, Thorn 2E **72**
NR34: Becc 4F **13**
Castle La. CB9: Have 3D **100**
IP7: Hadl 2G **129**
IP12: Orf 7J **125**
NR35: Bung 2A **14**
Castle Orchard NR35: Bung 2B **14**
Castle Ri. IP7: Hadl 2G **129**
IP14: Haug 2B **70**
Castle Rd. IP1: Ips 4G **131**
IP7: Hadl 2F **129**
IP8: Off 1F **113**
IP33: Bury E 5F **157** (1F **59**)
Castle St. IP12: Wood 5H **121**
IP13: F'ham 5D **90**
IP23: Eye 7D **38**
Castle Ter. IP12: Orf 7J **125**
Castleton Av. NR33: Car C 6A **10**
Castleton Cl. NR32: Low 4G **9**
Castleton Way IP23: Eye 6A **38**
Castle Wlk. CB9: Have 3D **100**
Catchpole Cl. NR33: Kess 4J **17**
Catchpole Ct. CO10: S'bury 4D **126**
Catchpole Dr. IP5: Kesg 7C **134**
Catchpoles Way IP3: Ips 6D **138**
Catchpole Way IP31: Stant 6D **32**
Catesbray IP9: Cap M 2G **147**
Catesby Mdw. CO10: S'bury 5C **126**
Cathcart St. NR32: Low 6J **9**
Catherine Rd. IP12: Wood 5F **121**
Catherines Hill IP6: Cod 1H **115**
Catkin Cl. CB9: Have 2D **100**
Cat's La. CO10: S'bury 5F **127**
CATTAWADE 6B **148** (3B **164**)
Cattawade St. CO11: Catt 6B **148**
CATTISHALL 6D **54**
Catts Cl. IP9: Stut 6B **150**
Cattsfield IP9: Stut 6B **150**
Caudle Av. IP27: Lake 7C **20**
Cauldwell Av. IP4: Ips 7D **132**
Cauldwell Hall Rd. IP4: Ips 6E **132**
Caulfield Cl. IP33: Bury E 3F **59**
Causeway IP27: Lake 6A **20**
NR33: Low 5G **11**
Causeway, The CB9: Have 4D **100**
CO10: Boxf 6C **128**
CO11: Catt 7A **148**
IP6: Bark, Nee M 5F **111**
IP7: Hit 2H **109**
IP17: Midd 5C **78**
IP17: Pea 3J **77**
IP23: Occ 5B **72**
IP31: Wals W 6F **33**
Causeway Cl. CO10: Glem 4B **104**
Causeway Est. IP7: Hit 1H **109**
Caustons Cl. CO10: Gt Cor 6H **127**
Cautley Rd. IP18: Sou 3K **45**
Cavan Rd. IP1: Ips 3F **131**
CAVENDISH 5H **103** (2C **163**)
Cavendish Cl. IP31: Thur 6B **56**
NR32: Oul B 5F **9**
Cavendish Ct. CB9: Have 5D **100**
Cavendish Gdns. IP11: T Mart . . . 5H **153**
Cavendish La. CO10: Cave 5J **103**
CO10: Glem 4A **104**
Cavendish Rd. CO10: Clar 5D **102**
IP11: Felix 5E **154**
IP11: T Mart 5G **153**
IP14: Stowm 4D **84**
IP33: Bury E 7D **52**
Cavendish St. IP3: Ips 6J **5** (2C **138**)
Cavendish Way CO10: S'bury 3E **126**
CAVENHAM 3B **158**
Cavenham Heath Nature Reserve
. . . . 4A **26**
Cavenham Rd. IP28: Tud 6C **26**
Cawseyhorn Drove IP27: Lake 3E **20**
Caxton Cl. IP9: Holb 3D **150**
Caxton M. NR34: Becc 2E **12**
Caxton Rd. NR34: Becc 2E **12**
Cayford Ter. IP9: Shot 4A **156**
CAY HILL 6F **71**
Cecilia St. IP1: Ips 5D **4** (1A **138**)
Cecil Lodge Cl. CB8: Newm 6F **47**
Cecil Rd. IP1: Ips 2C **4** (7K **131**)
Cedar Av. IP5: Kesg 7A **134**
Cedar Cl. CO11: Brant 4C **148**
IP7: Gt Bri 2A **112**
IP14: Bac 6B **68**
IP21: Stradb 6H **39**
IP27: RAF L 4G **21**
Cedar Ct. IP28: B Row 1D **22**
Cedar Cres. IP29: Barr 6B **50**
Cedarcroft Rd. IP1: Ips 3H **131**
Cedar Dr. NR33: Oul B 4D **10**
NR34: Worl 5H **13**
Cedar Ho. IP2: Ips 3J **137**
IP32: Bury E 4F **53**
Cedar Rd. IP12: Rend 5D **122**
IP29: Barr 6B **50**
Cedars, The IP8: Off 3H **113**
IP27: Lake 6C **20**
Cedars Cl. IP23: Occ 4A **72**
IP31: Thur 5A **56**
Cedars Courtyard IP14: W'sett 5H **69**
Cedars La. IP9: Cap M 2G **147**
Cedar Wlk. CO10: Act 4H **107**
IP6: Nee M 3G **111**
Cedar Way IP27: B'don 5G **19**
Celandine Cl. NR33: Car C 4B **10**
Celestion Dr. IP3: Ips 2F **139**
Cemetery Hill CB8: Exn 2D **46**
Cemetery La. CO7: E Ber 4A **146**
IP4: Ips 5C **132**
IP12: Wood 6F **121**
Cemetery Rd. CB8: W'rook 2F **97**
IP4: Ips 2G **5** (7B **132**)
IP27: Lake 5B **20**
Centenary Ho. IP11: Felix 5A **154**
Central Av. IP3: Ips 6H **139**
Central Maltings *IP12: Wood 6H 121*
(off Crown Pl.)
Central Rd. IP11: Felix 5A **154**
IP16: Leis 4H **93**
Central Rd. Sth. IP11: Felix 6A **154**
Central Wlk.
IP33: Bury E 4G **157** (1G **59**)
Centre, The IP2: Ips 5J **137**
Centre Cliff IP18: Sou 4K **45**
Centre Cl. NR34: Becc 5F **13**
Centre Dr. CB8: Newm 7K **47**
Centrum Ct. IP2: Ips 6B **4**
Century Dr. IP5: Kesg 6D **134**
Century Rd. IP23: Eye 5C **38**
CHADACRE 2A **106**
Chadacre Rd. IP29: Hart 1J **103**
Chadburn Rd. CO10: L Mel 3J **105**
Chadwick Gdns. NR33: Car C 5B **10**
Chaffinch Rd. IP32: Bury E 7C **54**
Chaffinch Way IP14: Stowm 3H **85**
Chainey Pieces CB9: Have 4E **100**
Chainhouse Rd. IP6: Nee M 4G **111**
Chalfont Dr. IP17: Benh 2C **92**
Chalfont Sq. IP4: Ips 3F **5**
Chalkeith Rd. IP6: Nee M 5H **111**
Chalk Hill La. IP6: Gt Bla 2A **114**
Chalk Hill Ri. IP6: Gt Bla 2A **114**
Chalk La. IP31: Ixw 5H **29**
Chalkners Cl. IP9: Cap M 2H **147**
Chalk Rd. IP27: B'don 4B **18**
Chalk Rd. Nth.
IP33: Bury E 4F **157** (1F **59**)
Chalk Rd. Sth.
IP33: Bury E 4F **157** (1F **59**)
Chalkstone Way CB9: Have 2G **101**
Chalk Ter. IP31: Ixw 5J **29**
Challice Rd. IP33: Bury E 7F **53**
Chalmers Grn. NR33: Car C 5B **10**
Chalon St. IP1: Ips 5C **4** (1K **137**)
Chamberlain Way IP8: Ips 4D **136**
Chamberlayne Rd. IP32: Bury E . . . 2A **60**
Chamberlin Cl. IP7: Bild 5J **109**
Champion Rd. IP15: Aldeb 6J **95**
Chancellery M.
IP33: Bury E 3F **157** (7F **53**)
Chancellor Wlk. IP4: Ips 1F **139**
Chancery La. IP14: Deb 1H **87**
Chancery Rd. IP1: Ips 5B **4** (1K **137**)
Chandler Ct. *IP5: Kesg 6E 134*
(off Hartree Way)
Chandlers Wlk. IP14: Stowm 6F **85**
Chandlers Way IP16: Aldr 6H **93**
Chandos Ct. IP12: Martl 3G **135**
Chandos Dr. IP12: Martl 3G **135**
CHANTRY 3G **137** (2B **164**)
Chantry Cl. CO10: S'bury 1C **126**
IP2: Ips 2G **137**
IP13: Cam A 3A **122**
Chantry Ct. IP33: Bury E 2J **157**
Chantry Grn. IP2: Ips 3F **137**
Chantry High Sports Cen. 3H **137**
Chantry Home Farm Pk.
IP2: Ips 1G **137**
Chantry La. IP6: Otl 3J **117**
Chantry M. IP2: Ips 1F **137**
Chantry Rd. IP17: Saxm 6J **91**
Chapel Cl. CO10: Gt Wal 7J **107**
IP9: Cap M 2H **147**
IP14: Bux 6F **83**
IP21: Fress 6C **40**
IP21: Stradb 6H **39**
Chapel Ct. *NR32: Low 6J 9*
(off St Peter's St.)
Chapel Farm La. IP7: Bild 5F **109**
Chapel Fld. IP8: B'ford 3C **130**
Chapelfield IP12: Orf 6J **125**
Chapel Hill IP14: Fram 5C **88**
Chapel La. IP6: Gt Bla 4B **114**
IP8: Bels 7E **136**
IP8: S'ham 3H **113**
IP8: Wash 5C **136**
IP13: Char 2D **118**
IP13: Gru 7J **117**
IP13: Petti, Wick M
. . . . 6B **118** & 1K **119**
IP14: Stowu 2K **85**
IP19: Wen 2H **43**
IP21: Horh 3J **73**
IP22: Bote 5J **35**
(not continuous)
IP22: Wort 3J **35**
IP28: Tud 5B **26**
IP30: Drin G 1F **83**
Chapel M. IP4: Ips 2F **5**
Chapel Pond Hill IP32: Bury E 5J **53**
Chapel Rd. IP6: Otl 1K **117**
IP10: Buck 4D **152**
IP13: Gru 7J **117**
IP13: Saxt 1A **90**
IP14: Mendl 1J **71**
IP14: Old N 6D **70**
IP17: Saxm 6H **91**
IP19: Blyth 6J **43**
IP22: W'field 4H **33**
IP28: W Row 5A **22**
IP29: Stann 4G **81**
IP30: C'field 6J **81**
NR33: Car C 6A **10**
NR34: Mut 1B **16**
NR34: Wrent 1C **44**
Chapel St. CB8: Exn 1B **46**
CO10: Stoke C 7F **99**
IP7: Bild 6J **109**
IP12: Wood 5H **121**
IP17: Pea 3J **77**
NR32: Low 6J **9**
Chapel Wlk. *IP31: Stant 7D 32*
(off Upthorpe Rd.)
Chapelwent Rd. CB9: Have 1D **100**
Chaplain Gdns. IP3: Ips 2G **139**
Chaplains Cl. CB9: Have 2E **100**
Chaplin Rd. CO7: E Ber 3B **146**
Chaplin Wlk. CO10: Gt Cor 6J **127**
Chapman La. IP1: Ips 2C **4** (7K **131**)
Chapman's Cl. IP30: Roug 2F **61**
CHAPPEL 3C **163**
Chapple Dr. CB9: Have 2E **100**
Chare La. IP31: Stant 5B **32**
Chare Rd. IP31: Stant 5B **32**
Charity La. IP13: Bed 7F **73**
Charles Adams Cl. IP16: Leis 3J **93**
Charles Av. IP13: Gru 6H **117**
Charles Cl. CB8: Newm 6E **46**
Charles Graven Ct. *CB8: Newm . . . 7H 47*
(off St John's Av.)
Charles Ind. Est. IP14: Stowm 3G **85**
Charles Melrose Cl. IP28: Mide . . . 6H **23**

Charles Miller Ct. *IP16: Leis* 4H **93**
(off Cross St.)
Charles Rd. IP11: Felix 5D **154**
Charles St. IP1: Ips 2D **4** (7A **132**)
CHARLES TYE 1A **164**
Charlotte's IP8: Wash 5B **136**
Charlton Av. IP1: Ips 3H **131**
Charnwood Ct. IP2: Ips 7C **4**
Charrington Cl. CB9: Have 5H **101**
CHARSFIELD . . . . **.3C 118 (1C 165)**
Charter Cl. IP7: Hadl 2H **129**
Charter Sq.
IP33: Bury E 4G **157** (1G **59**)
Charter Way NR33: Car C 4B **10**
Chartwell Cl. IP4: Ips 1E **138**
Chase, The CO11: Brant 4E **148**
IP5: Martl H 6G **135**
IP11: Felix 4E **154**
IP27: B'don 5H **19**
IP31: Stant 6D **32**
NR34: Worl 4H **13**
Chase Cl. CB9: Have 2F **101**
Chaser Cl. IP3: Ips 6G **139**
Chase Rd. IP32: Bury E 3E **52**
Chase's La. IP17: Fris 7D **92**
Chatsworth Cl. NR32: Low 5F **9**
Chatsworth Cres. IP2: Ips 4J **137**
IP11: T Mary 1B **154**
Chatsworth Dr. IP4: Rush A 1J **139**
Chatten Cl. NR34: Wrent 1D **44**
CHATTISHAM . . . . **.3D 144 (2A 164)**
Chattisham Cl. IP14: Stowm 7G **85**
Chattisham La. IP8: Chat, Hint . . .1C **144**
Chattisham Rd. IP8: Chat 3D **144**
Chaucer Rd. CO10: S'bury 1C **126**
IP1: Ips 2H **131**
IP11: Felix 5E **154**
Chaucer St. NR35: Bung 2A **14**
Chauker's Cres. NR33: Car C 3B **10**
Chauntry Rd. CB9: Have 4E **100**
CHEDBURGH . . . . **.6K 51 (1B 162)**
Chedburgh Pl. CB9: Have 3F **101**
Chedburgh Rd.
IP29: Chedb, Chev 4J **51**
IP29: Whep 1A **80**
Chedgrave Rd. NR33: Oul B 4E **10**
CHEDISTON . . . . **.2D 161**
CHEDISTON GREEN . . . . **.2D 161**
Chediston St. IP19: H'orth 5A **42**
Chedworth Pl. IP9: Tatt 6G **149**
Chelmer Rd. CB9: Have 3G **101**
CHELMONDISTON . . . . **.2H 151 (3C 165)**
Chelsea Cl. IP1: Ips 4H **131**
IP33: Bury E 1D **58**
Chelsea Ct. CO10: S'bury 4E **126**
Chelsea Rd. CO10: S'bury 4E **126**
CHELSWORTH . . . . **.2D 163**
Chelsworth Av. CO10: Gt Cor 5G **127**
IP4: Ips 4B **132**
Chelsworth Rd. IP11: Felix 4C **154**
Chelsworth Way IP14: Stowm 7G **85**
Cheltenham Av. IP1: Ips 4K **131**
Chepstow Rd. IP1: Ips 1K **131**
IP11: Felix 3E **154**
IP33: Bury E 3D **58**
Chequer Fld. IP12: Sutt 3C **140**
Chequers La. CO10: Glem 3A **104**
Chequers Pk. IP7: E'sett 6G **113**
Chequer Sq. IP33: Bury E 5J **157**
Chequers Ri. IP6: Gt Bla 2A **114**
Chequers Row IP17: Fris 6D **92**
Cherry Blossom Cl. IP8: Ips 4D **136**
Cherry Ct. IP28: Red L 6J **25**
Cherryfields IP8: B'ford 4C **130**
Cherry Hill Cl. NR34: Worl 4J **13**
Cherry La. IP4: Ips 6F **133**
IP15: Aldeb 4H **95**
IP27: RAF L 4G **21**
Cherry La. Gdns. IP4: Ips 6F **133**
Cherry Tree Cl. IP23: Yax 6E **36**
IP27: B'don 5G **19**
Cherry Tree La. IP14: Deb 3H **87**
IP22: Bote 4J **35**
Cherry Tree Rd. IP12: Wood 6G **121**
IP14: Stowm 3E **84**
Cherrytree Rd. CO10: Gt Cor 4G **127**
Cherrytree Row IP31: Wals W 6H **33**
Cherry Wood IP8: Wash 6B **136**
Chesapeake Cl. IP9: Chelm 2H **151**
Chesapeake Rd. IP3: Ips 6E **138**
Chesham Rd. IP2: Ips 7C **4** (2K **137**)
Chessington Gdns. IP1: Ips 5H **131**
Chester Ct. CB9: Have 5D **100**
Chesterfield Dr. IP1: Ips 3H **131**
Chester Ho. IP31: Thur 6K **55**
Chester Pl. IP31: Gt Bar 3D **54**
Chester Rd. IP11: Felix 3E **154**
IP18: Sou 4K **45**
Chester St. IP27: RAF L 3J **21**
Chesterton Cl. IP2: Ips 4G **137**
Chestnut Av. IP7: Gt Bri 2A **112**
NR32: Oul B 6D **8**
Chestnut Cl. CB9: Have 3E **100**
CO10: Gt Wal 7J **107**
IP5: Rush A 4J **133**
IP11: Felix 4D **154**
IP12: Rend 5D **122**
IP14: Stowu 2J **85**
IP27: B'don 5H **19**
IP28: B Mil 2H **25**
IP28: Forn S 1D **52**
IP28: Mide 7K **23**
IP31: Gt Bar 1D **54**
NR34: Worl 5H **13**
Chestnut Ct. IP28: W'ton 2B **24**
Chestnut Cres. IP29: Chedb 6K **51**
NR33: Car C 6B **10**
Chestnut Dr. IP6: Clay 4D **114**
Chestnut Gro. IP14: Stowm 5G **85**
Chestnut M. *CO10: S'bury* *4D 126*
(off Friars St.)
Chestnut Rd. CO10: Glem 4A **104**
Chestnuts, The IP2: Ips 4E **136**
IP14: Gt Fin 7J **83**
IP22: Rick 6H **35**
(not continuous)
IP29: Horr 6B **58**
NR34: Wrent 1D **44**
Chestnut Tree Cl.
IP22: Redg 2C **34**
Chestnut Way IP27: RAF L 5G **21**
CHETTISHAM . . . . **.1A 158**
Chevalier Rd. IP11: Felix 4G **155**
Chevallier St. IP1: Ips 1A **4** (6J **131**)
CHEVELEY . . . . **.3A 158**
Cheveley Rd. CB8: Newm 6J **47**
CHEVINGTON . . . . **.2J 51 (1B 162)**
Chevington Rd. IP29: Harg 3G **51**
IP29: Horr 7A **58**
Cheviot Rd. NR32: Oul 6C **8**
Cheyne Ct. CO10: S'bury 4D **126**
Chichester Cl. IP33: Bury E 3H **59**
Chichester Dr. NR33: Oul B 3C **10**
Chichester Rd. IP19: H'orth 3A **42**
CHICKERING . . . . **.2C 161**
Chickering Rd. IP21: Hox 3D **38**
(Denham Rd.)
IP21: Hox 1E **38**
(Syleham Rd.)
Childer Rd. IP14: Stowm 4F **85**
Childers Cl. IP9: Shot G 6D **156**
Childers Ct. IP3: Ips 5D **138**
Childers Fld. IP11: Felix 3C **154**
Child's Yd. *IP18: Sou* *4K 45*
(off Market Pl.)
CHILLESFORD . . . . **.1D 165**
Chiltern Cres. NR32: Oul 6D **8**
CHILTON . . . . **.2G 127**
Chilton Av. IP14: Stowm 4E **84**
Chilton Cnr. CO10: Gt Wal 1K **127**
Chilton Ct. CO10: S'bury 4F **127**
IP2: Ips 7C **4** (3K **137**)
IP14: Stowm 3D **84**
Chilton Gro. CO10: S'bury 7G **107**
Chilton Ind. Est. CO10: S'bury . . .3G **127**
(not continuous)
Chilton Lodge Rd.
CO10: S'bury 4F **127**
Chilton Rd. IP3: Ips 1G **139**
CHILTON STREET . . . . **.2A 102 (2B 162)**
Chilton Way IP14: Stowm 3C **84**
Chimer's La. IP13: Char, Hoo 1A **118**
CHIMNEY STREET . . . . . **.2G 99 (2B 162)**
Chimswell Way CB9: Have 3B **100**
(not continuous)
CHIPPENHAM . . . . **.3A 158**
Chippenham Rd. CB8: Mou 4C **48**
IP28: Frec 7B **24**
Chipperfield Rd. NR33: Kess 5K **17**
Chippings, The IP15: Aldeb 3G **95**
Chislehurst Rd. NR33: Car C 5C **10**
Chisnall Cl. IP7: Hadl 1H **129**
Chiswick Av. IP28: Mide 5J **23**
Chivers Ct. IP4: Ips 1J **5** (7C **132**)
Chivers Rd. CB9: Have 3C **100**
Christchurch Ct. IP4: Ips 2F **5**
Christchurch Dr. IP12: Wood 7E **120**
Christchurch Mansion & Wolsey Gallery
. . . . **.2F 5 (7B 132)**
Christ Church Sq. NR32: Low 7K **9**
Christchurch St.
IP4: Ips 1G **5** (6B **132**)
Christmas La. IP20: Metf 6H **41**
NR32: Oul B 7B **8**
Christopher Ct. *CO10: S'bury* *4D 126*
(off Christopher La.)
Christopher La. CO10: S'bury 4D **126**
Church Av. NR32: Oul 6B **8**
Church Cl. CB8: Exn 1C **46**
CO10: Cave 5H **103**
IP5: Kesg 5B **134**
IP6: C Mary 7A **86**
IP8: S'ham 4K **113**
IP8: Spro 7C **130**
Church Cl. IP10: Buck 2B **152**
IP15: Aldeb 5J **95**
IP17: Kel 2J **91**
IP21: Hox 1C **38**
IP22: Hep 7D **30**
IP27: B'don 4E **18**
IP28: B Row 1E **22**
IP28: Ris 2D **50**
IP31: Forn M 3G **53**
IP31: Stant 7C **32**
NR34: Wang 6C **44**
Church Comn. IP17: Snap 1C **94**
CHURCH CORNER . . . . . **.1B 44 (2C 167)**
Church Cnr. IP17: Dars 3D **78**
Church Cotts. IP31: Pake 3B **56**
Church Cres. IP8: Spro 7C **130**
CHURCH END
Ashdon . . . . **.2A 162**
Ipswich . . . . **.2C 156**
Wethersfield . . . . **.3B 162**
Church End IP27: B'don 4E **18**
IP29: Dep 7J **51**
Church Farm Caravan Pk.
IP15: Aldeb 4J **95**
Church Farm Cl. IP21: Horh 1G **73**
IP22: Pal 1C **36**
IP22: Rick 6G **35**
Church Farm Grn. IP21: Fress 5B **40**
Church Farm La. IP19: H'orth 5A **42**
IP22: Thel 6H **31**
Church Farm Ri. IP15: Aldeb 4J **95**
Church Farm Rd. IP15: Aldeb 4H **95**
IP19: B'field 7H **75**
Church Farm Way IP27: Lake 5A **20**
Church Fld. IP6: Gt Bla 2A **114**
IP7: M Ele 2D **108**
IP13: Ket 5J **89**
IP18: Walb 7G **45**
Churchfield Bus. Pk.
CO10: S'bury 2H **127**
Church Fld. Rd. CO10: S'bury 2G **127**
IP9: Stut 6C **150**
Church Gdns. IP28: W Row 6B **22**
IP31: Barni 2D **30**
Churchgate CO10: Glem 4B **104**
Churchgate St.
IP33: Bury E 5H **157** (1G **59**)
Church Grn. IP8: B'ford 4D **130**
IP14: Finn 6H **67**
IP18: Sou 4K **45**
IP31: Gt Ash 5E **66**
IP31: Pake 2B **56**
NR32: Low 5H **9**
Church Grn. La. IP22: W'field 2J **33**
Church Hayes IP29: Barr 5A **50**
Church Hill IP7: M Ele 2E **108**
IP9: Holb 4D **150**
IP14: Wyve 1D **68**
IP17: Saxm 7J **91**
IP17: Ster 2D **92**
IP19: Wal 2H **75**
IP21: Hox 1C **38**
IP29: Whep 2C **80**
IP30: E'well 3B **64**
IP31: Pake 2B **56**
Churchill Av. CB8: Newm 4D **46**
CB9: Have 2G **101**
IP4: Ips 1E **138**
IP7: Hadl 2H **129**
Churchill Cl. *CO10: Clar* *4C 102*
(off Erbury Pl.)
IP12: Wood 6F **121**
IP29: Laws 6A **80**
NR32: Low 4H **9**
Churchill Cotts. IP17: Benh 3C **92**
Churchill Ct. CB8: Newm 6F **47**
Churchill Cres. IP13: Wick M 5B **118**
Churchill Dr. CO10: S'bury 1D **126**
IP28: Mide 6H **23**
Churchill Rd. IP18: Rey 1J **45**
IP19: H'orth 3B **42**
Church La. CB8: Dalh 6H **49**
CB8: Exn 1B **46**
CB8: Newm 6G **47**
CO6: Nay 6K **143**
CO10: Clar 5C **102**
CO11: Brant 4D **148**
IP6: Barh . . . . .2D **114** & 6F **115**
(not continuous)
IP6: C Mary . . . . . . .1G **111** & 7A **86**
(not continuous)
IP6: Clay 4D **114**
IP6: Hemi 3J **115**
IP6: Henl 6K **115**
IP6: Play 1B **134**
IP6: Weste 1C **132**
IP6: Witn 3A **116**
IP7: Hit 2G **109**
IP8: S'ham 3K **113**
IP8: Spro 7D **130**
(not continuous)
IP8: Wash 5A **136**
Church La. IP9: Chelm 1F **151**
IP9: Hark 6H **151**
IP10: Buck 2B **152**
IP10: Kirt 2J **153**
IP10: Levi 7D **152**
IP11: Felix 2D **154**
IP11: T Mart 6H **153**
IP12: But 7C **124**
IP12: B'well 3A **124**
IP12: Eyk 1D **124**
IP12: Martl 3K **135**
IP12: Rend 7A **122**
IP13: Uff 6J **119**
IP14: E Sto 2C **86**
IP14: Finn 6H **67**
IP14: L Sto 1D **86**
IP14: Stowm 4F **85**
IP17: Fris 5D **92**
IP17: Kel 2J **91**
IP17: Yox 7H **77**
IP18: Walb 7F **45**
IP19: Blyth 6H **43**
IP19: Wen 3H **43**
IP21: Stus 2G **37**
IP22: Hep 7D **30**
IP22: Rick 7H **35**
IP22: Thel 6H **31**
IP23: Occ 5B **72**
IP23: Thw 3K **69**
IP23: Yax 7E **36**
IP24: Barnh 6H **27**
IP28: B Mil 2G **25**
IP28: Frec 6C **24**
IP28: W Row 6A **22**
IP28: W'ton 2A **24**
(not continuous)
IP29: Harg 1F **51**
IP30: C'field 7G **81**
IP31: Nort 5J **57**
IP31: Tros 1D **28**
NR32: Cort 4H **7**
NR32: Oul 6B **8**
NR32: Oul B 6A **8**
NR33: Car C 7A **10**
NR34: Fros 3A **44**
Church La. Cl. IP28: B Mil 2G **25**
Churchman Cl. IP12: Melt 2J **121**
Church Mdw. IP14: Finn 6H **67**
IP22: Rick 6G **35**
IP23: Gisli 1K **67**
IP28: B Mil 2G **25**
Church Mdws. IP6: Henl 6J **115**
IP12: Wald 6C **140**
Church Pk. CO10: Stoke C 7J **99**
Church Path IP14: Finn 6H **67**
IP17: Fris 6D **92**
IP30: Rat 4K **83**
Church Ri. NR32: Oul B 7B **8**
Church Rd. CB8: Mou 6D **48**
CB9: L Thu 5C **96**
CO10: Gt Cor 6F **127**
CO10: L Wal 5C **108**
CO10: Newt 2C **128**
IP6: Cod 2G **115**
IP6: Otl 1K **117**
IP6: Play 1B **134**
IP7: Bild 6H **109**
IP9: Bent 6H **147**
IP9: Chelm 2G **151**
IP9: Stut 6C **150**
IP9: Tatt 7F **149**
IP10: Nac 6A **152**
IP11: Felix 2H **155**
IP12: Blax 3F **123**
IP12: But 6C **124**
IP13: Hask 3C **120**
IP13: Ket 5J **89**
IP13: W'orth 6J **73**
IP14: Bac 6A **68**
IP14: Batt 6E **110**
IP14: Comb, Stowm 7F **85**
IP14: Cott 6E **68**
IP14: Gt Fin 6J **83**
IP14: Mendl 2K **71**
IP14: Old N 5B **70**
IP14: Petta 2C **88**
IP14: Stowu 2K **85**
IP16: Leis 3G **93**
IP16: Thor 6D **94**
IP17: Fris 5D **92**
IP17: Snap . . . . .2C **94** & 7A **92**
IP19: Blyth 6J **43**
IP19: Hev 3B **74**
IP21: Wey 2C **40**
IP21: Wing 2J **39**
IP22: M Wes 3H **31**
IP22: Wort 1J **35**
IP27: B'don 4E **18**
IP28: W Row 6B **22**
IP29: Barr 4A **50**
IP29: Chev 2K **51**
IP29: Stann 4F **81**

Church Rd. IP30: B Geo 2B 82
IP30: Bey 3C 62
IP30: E'well 2C 64
IP30: Fels 6C 82
IP30: Roug 4H 61
IP30: Tost 2G 63
IP31: Bard 2C 32
IP31: Barni 2D 30
IP31: Gt Bar 3E 54
IP31: Honi 2H 29
IP31: Thur 6B 56
NR32: Blun 2H 7
NR32: Low 5H 9
NR33: Gisle 1F 17
NR33: Kess 4H 17
NR34: Ell 7J 13
NR34: Hens 6C 16
NR34: Mut 2A 16
NR35: Ears 4A 14
Church Row IP14: Fram 6E 88
IP33: Bury E 3H 157 (7G 53)
Church Sq. CO8: Bure 5B 142
Church St. CB8: Exn 1C 46
CB9: With 2B 98
CO6: Stoke N 2J 143
CO10: Boxf 7C 128
CO10: Clar 5C 102
CO10: Hund 2H 99
CO10: Lave 7B 106
CO10: S'bury 5C 126
IP7: Hadl 4H 129
IP12: Orf 7J 125
IP12: Wood 5H 121
IP13: F'ham 6D 90
IP13: W'orth 5K 73
IP14: W'den 4H 65
IP14: W'sett 4J 69
IP17: Pea 3J 77
IP17: Saxm 6J 91
IP18: Sou 4K 45
IP21: Fress 6C 40
IP21: Stradb 6H 39
IP23: Eye 7C 38
IP23: Occ 5A 72
NR34: Wang 6C 44
Church Ter. *CO8: Bure 5B 142*
(off Nayland Rd.)
IP13: Wick M 6B 118
IP19: Hunt 1C 74
IP19: Wen 2J 43
Church Vw. IP14: Haug 2B 70
IP14: Wyve 1D 68
IP16: Leis 3G 93
IP19: Holt 4E 42
IP31: Stowl 1H 57
Church Vw. Cl. IP12: Melt 3K 121
Church Wlk. CB9: Ked 6C 98
CB9: Stur 7J 101
CO10: L Mel 1J 105
CO10: S'bury 4D 126
IP7: Hadl 3H 129
IP9: Shot 3A 156
IP13: Laxf 6C 74
IP14: Stowm 4F 85
(off Station Rd. W.)
IP14: W'den 4H 65
IP15: Aldeb 5J 95
IP28: Mide 7H 23
Church Walks IP33: Bury E 6H 157
Churchway IP22: Redg 3D 34
Church Wood IP19: Holt 4E 42
Churchyard IP28: Mide 7H 23
IP33: Bury E 5J 157 (1H 59)
Cineworld Cinema
Bury St Edmunds 4F 157 (1F 59)
Haverhill 4G 101
Ipswich 5D 4 (1A 138)
Cinnabar Cl. IP8: Ips 6G 137
CITY, THE 6A 12
City Cotts. NR34: Bars 6A 12
Civic Dr. IP1: Ips 3C 4 (7K 131)
Civic Ind. Est. CB9: Have 6E 100
Clapgate La. IP3: Ips 3E 138
(not continuous)
Clapham Rd. Central NR32: Low 7J 9
Clapham Rd. Nth. NR32: Low 6J 9
Clapham Rd. Sth. NR32: Low 7J 9
Clappers Path IP13: Uff 5H 119
CLARE 5C 102 (2B 162)
Clare Ancient House Mus. *5C 102*
(off Church La.)
Clare Av. IP12: Wood 6F 121
Clare Castle Country Pk. 5D 102
Clare Cl. IP14: Stowm 7G 85
IP28: Mide 6K 23
IP33: Bury E 2D 58
Claremont Rd. NR33: Low 3H 11
Clarence Rd. CO10: Clar 3C 102
CO10: S'bury 3D 126
IP3: Ips 5F 139
NR32: Low 5J 9
Clarendale Est. CB8: Gt Bra 2A 96
Clarendon Rd. CB9: Have 5E 100
Clare Pk. Lake Golf Course 6B 102
Clare Pl. CB8: Newm 7H 47
Clare Rd. CO10: Clar 1A 102
CO10: Hund 3J 99
CO10: L Mel 7D 104
CO10: Posl 2C 102
IP4: Ips 5D 132
NR33: Kess 4K 17
Clarice House Day Spa 4E 130
Clarice House Health Spa Resort
4D 58
Clarke Cl. IP22: Pal 2C 36
Clarkes Cl. IP6: C Mary 7A 86
Clarkes La. NR33: Car C 3B 10
NR34: Ilk A 1H 15
Clarks Hill IP21: Wey 1C 40
Clarkson Ct. IP12: Wood 6G 121
Clarkson Rd. NR32: Oul B 7B 8
Clarkson St. IP1: Ips 2A 4 (7J 131)
Clark Wlk. IP32: Bury E 6D 52
Claude St. IP1: Ips 2D 4 (7A 132)
Claudian Cl. CB9: Have 4J 101
Claverton Way IP4: Rush A 1H 139
CLAY COMMON 2C 167
CLAYDON 4D 114 (1B 164)
Claydon Bus. Pk. IP6: Gt Bla 2B 114
Claydon Dr. NR32: Oul B 5E 8
Claydon Ind. Pk. IP6: Gt Bla 3B 114
Clay Drift IP31: Forn M 2A 54
Clay Field IP30: E'well 3E 64
Clayhall La. CO10: Act 4J 107
Clayhall Pl. CO10: Act 4H 107
Clay Hill IP8: Hint 3A 144
IP19: Ubb 4A 74
Clay Hill La. IP7: W'ham 2J 109
Clay Hills IP13: Denn, F'ham 7C 76
IP17: Kel 4J 91
IP19: H'orth 5A 42
Clayhive Dr. CB9: Have 4E 100
Clay La. CO10: Lave 6D 106
IP14: Bac 5B 68
IP22: Hep 7E 30
IP31: Ixw 5F 29
IP31: Sap 2K 29
CLAYPITS 7A 20
Claypits Av. CO8: Bure 6C 142
Clay Rd. IP32: Bury E 4D 52
Clay St. IP31: Wals W 6J 33
Clayton Ct. IP12: Wood 7E 120
Clearview NR34: Barnb 6C 6
Clearwing Cl. IP8: Ips 6G 137
Clematis Cl. IP17: Westl 5G 79
IP28: Red L 6H 25
Clemence St. NR32: Low 1H 11
Clementine Gdns. IP4: Ips 1E 138
Clement Rd. NR33: Low 3G 11
Clements Cl. CB9: Have 4E 100
IP21: Scole 1K 37
Clements Dr. CB9: Have 4E 100
Clements La. CB9: Have 4E 100
Clement Sq. NR33: Low 3G 11
Clements Rd. IP12: Melt 7F 119
Clement's Way IP28: B Row 2F 23
Clench Cl. IP4: Ips 3G 5 (7B 132)
Clench Rd. IP9: Holb 1D 150
Clerk's Piece NR34: Becc 4G 13
Clermont Av. CO10: S'bury 1C 126
Cleveland Rd. NR33: Low 2H 11
Cleves Rd. CB9: Have 4C 100
Cley Ct. CB9: Have 2B 100
Clibbon Ct. CO10: Gt Cor 5G 127
Clicket Hill CO8: Bure 6D 142
Clickett Hill Rd. IP11: Felix 4B 154
Cliff Ct. IP11: Felix 2J 155
Cliff Estate Seaview, The
NR33: Kess 4K 17
Cliff Farm La. NR33: Kess 2J 17
Cliff La. IP3: Ips 3C 138
Clifford Dr. NR33: Oul B 4D 10
Clifford Finch Way IP7: Hadl 1K 129
Clifford Rd. IP4: Ips 4K 5 (1D 138)
Clifford Road Air Raid Shelter Mus.
4K 5 (1D 138)
Cliff Quay IP3: Ips 4B 138
Cliff Rd. IP3: Ips 7H 5 (3C 138)
IP11: Felix 3J 155
IP12: Wald 6C 140
NR33: Low 3H 11
Cliffs, The NR33: Low 7G 11
Cliffside *NR34: Becc 3E 12*
(off Ballygate)
Clifton M. CB8: Kent 2C 48
Clifton Rd. NR33: Low 2H 11
Cliftonville NR33: Low 7G 11
Cliftonville Rd. NR33: Low 6G 11
Clifton Way IP2: Ips 4F 137
Clifton Wood IP9: Holb 2D 150
Clink, The IP19: Wal 2H 75
Clint Hill IP31: Sap 1K 29
Clint Rd. IP23: Thorn 1B 72
Clive Av. IP1: Ips 3K 131
Cloak La. CB8: W'rook 3G 97
Clockhall La. CO10: Hund 3H 99
Clocktower M. *CB8: Newm 5G 47*
(off Exeter Rd.)
Cloisters, The CO10: S'bury 2G 127
Cloncurry Gdns. IP11: Felix 5C 154
CLOPTON CORNER 1C 165
Clopton Dr. CO10: L Mel 5H 105
Clopton Gdns. IP7: Hadl 4H 129
CLOPTON GREEN
Bury St Edmunds 1K 83
Newmarket 3K 97 (1B 162)
Clopton Pk. CB8: W'rook 3K 97
Clopton Rd. IP6: Swil, Tud 6D 116
Close, The CO10: S'bury 3E 126
IP9: Tatt 6H 149
IP12: Sud 1H 125
IP14: Haug 5J 65
IP21: Hox 3D 38
NR32: Cort 6J 7
Cloutings Cl. IP17: Kel 3H 91
Clovelly Cl. IP4: Rush A 2K 139
Clovelly Ri. NR32: Low 5G 9
Clover Cl. IP2: Ips 2H 137
IP6: Nee M 5G 111
Clover Ct. CO10: Gt Cor 5H 127
IP14: Deb 3H 87
Clover Fld. CB9: Have 3C 100
Cloverfields IP31: Thur 6A 56
Clovers Ct. IP14: Stowm 4E 84
Clover Way IP28: Red L 5J 25
NR32: Low 3H 9
Clowes Ct. NR34: Becc 3E 12
Clubhouse, The IP12: Melt 7F 119
Clubs La. CO10: Boxf 6D 128
Clump Fld. IP2: Ips 4H 137
Clunch Cl. IP27: Lake 5A 20
Clyffe, The *NR33: Low 3H 11*
(off Kirkley Cliff)
Coachmans Ct. IP4: Ips 4E 4
Coachmans Paddock IP9: Holb 2D 150
Coastal Cotts. NR33: Kess 5K 17
Coastguard Ct. *IP15: Aldeb 6J 95*
(off High St.)
Coastguard La. NR33: Kess 5K 17
Coast Guards, The IP16: Thor 6D 94
Coast Rd. NR32: Cort 4H 7
Cobb Cl. IP32: Bury E 7B 54
Cobbler's Cnr. IP8: Hint 3A 144
Cobblers Ct. IP28: Mide 7J 23
Cobbold Cl. IP14: L Fin 6A 110
IP22: Wort 2K 35
Cobbold M. IP4: Ips 2G 5 (7B 132)
Cobbold Rd. IP11: Felix 4F 155
IP12: Wood 3F 121
Cobbold St. IP4: Ips 2F 5 (7B 132)
Cobden Pl. IP4: Ips 3F 5 (7B 132)
Cobham Rd. IP3: Ips 3G 139
Coblers Way CO10: Act 4G 107
Cock & Bell La. CO10: L Mel 3H 105
Cock Cnr. IP14: Haug 2B 70
COCKFIELD 7H 81 (1D 163)
Cockfield Hall La.
IP6: Weste, Witn 5A 116
Cockfield Rd. IP30: Fels 7A 82
Cock Hill CB9: Ked 7C 98
Cock Rd. IP14: Cott 6D 68
Cocks Grn. La. IP30: Gt Whe 1G 81
COCK STREET 3D 142
CODDENHAM 1G 115 (1B 164)
Coddenham Community & Sports Hall
1G 115
CODDENHAM GREEN 1B 164
Coddenham Rd.
IP6: C Mary, Nee M 4H 111
(not continuous)
Coddington Way IP31: Ixw 5J 29
Codling Rd. IP32: Bury E 6A 54
Codlins La. NR34: Becc, Worl 4G 13
Cody Rd. IP3: Ips 5G 139
Colbeck Rd. CB9: Have 1D 100
Colbourne Ct. *IP11: Felix 4F 155*
(off Ranelagh Rd.)
COLCHESTER 3A 164
COLCHESTER GREEN 6K 81
Colchester Rd.
CO8: Bure, M Bur 6B 142
IP4: Ips 4D 132
Coldfair Cl. IP17: Knod 6G 93
COLDFAIR GREEN 7G 93 (1A 166)
Coldhall La. IP13: F'ham 6E 90
Coldham La. IP23: Gisli 1K 67
Cold Store Rd. IP11: Felix 7B 154
Cole Dr. CO10: Gt Cor 6H 127
COLEGATE END 1B 160
Coleman Cl. IP22: Pal 2D 36
Cole Ness Rd. IP3: Ips 6E 138
Coleridge Rd. IP1: Ips 2H 131
Coles Cft. IP19: Wen 2H 43
Coles Hill IP19: Wen 2H 43
Coles Path IP31: Con W 1B 30
Coles Vw. IP19: Wen 2H 43
Colethorpe La. IP29: Barr 4A 50
College Cl. IP29: Horr 6A 58
College Grn. IP11: Felix 3H 155
College Heath Rd. IP28: Mide 5J 23
College La.
IP33: Bury E 6H 157 (2G 59)
NR34: Ell, Worl 6J 13
College Mdws. NR32: Low 5F 9
College Rd. IP13: F'ham 5C 90
IP14: Wyve 2B 68
NR33: Low 3H 11
College Sq.
IP33: Bury E 6H 157 (2G 59)
College St. IP4: Ips 5E 4 (1A 138)
IP33: Bury E 5H 157 (2G 59)
Collett's Wlk. IP12: Wood 5E 120
(not continuous)
Collimer Cl. IP9: Chelm 2G 151
Collimer Ct. IP11: Felix 2D 154
Collings Pl. CB8: Newm 4E 46
Collingwood Av. IP3: Ips 4F 139
Collingwood Flds. CO7: E Ber 2A 146
Collingwood Rd. IP12: Wood 3G 121
Collins Av. IP31: Stant 7E 32
Collins Cl. IP17: Saxm 5G 91
Collinson's IP2: Ips 1F 137
Colman Rd. NR32: Cort 5J 7
COLNE ENGAINE 3C 163
Colneis Rd. IP11: Felix 2F 155
Colne Rd. CO8: Bure 7A 142
Colne Valley Rd. CB9: Have 4F 101
Colneys Cl. CO10: S'bury 2C 126
Colonial Ct. IP16: Leis 3H 93
Colsterdale NR33: Car C 6C 10
Coltishall IP27: RAF L 4H 21
COLTON 3A 54
Colton's Ride IP31: Gt Bar 3A 54
Coltsfoot Cl. CB8: W'rook 2G 97
IP31: Ixw 5J 29
NR33: Low 6E 10
Coltsfoot Cres. IP32: Bury E 1B 60
COLTSFOOT GREEN 2G 97
Coltsfoot Rd. IP2: Ips 2G 137
Columbia Cl. IP5: Kesg 6A 134
Columbine Cl. NR33: Car C 4B 10
Columbine Gdns. IP2: Ips 1G 137
Columbines, The CO10: Cave 5J 103
Columbine Way IP23: Gisli 1K 67
Columbyne Cl. IP14: Stowu 1K 85
Colville Rd. NR33: Oul B 3D 10
Colville Rd. Works NR33: Oul B 2E 10
Colville Way NR33: Car C 6B 10
Combers, The IP5: Kesg 6E 134
COMBS 1E 110 (1A 164)
Combs Ct. IP14: Stowm 6F 85
COMBS FORD 6G 85 (1A 164)
Combs Grn. IP14: Comb 3C 110
Combs La. IP14: Gt Fin, Stowm 5B 84
Combs Wood Dr. IP14: Stowm 7F 85
Combs Wood Nature Reserve 7G 85
Comet Way IP28: Mide 6G 23
COMMERCIAL END 3A 158
Commercial Rd.
IP1: Ips 6C 4 (2K 137)
NR32: Low 1H 11
Commister La. IP31: Ixw 5H 29
Commodore Rd. NR32: Oul B 1D 10
COMMON, THE
Beccles 2F 13
Ipswich 6A 114
Lowestoft 2C 6
Southwold 4K 45
Common, The CO10: Lave 6C 106
IP20: Metf 6H 41
IP23: Melli 5A 36
Common Hill IP22: Pal 1D 36
Common La. IP12: B'well 3A 124
IP27: Eris 3F 21
IP31: Tros 1E 28
NR34: Becc 3F 13
Common La. Nth. NR34: Becc 2E 12
Common La. Nth. Ind. Est.
NR34: Becc 2F 13
Common Rd. IP22: Bote 7K 35
IP22: Hop 1J 31
Common St. CO10: Clar 4C 102
Compair Cres. IP2: Ips 5A 4 (1J 137)
Compass Cl. IP27: Lake 7C 20
Compass St. NR32: Low 6K 9
Compiegne Way
IP31: Bury E, Gt Bar 5H 53
IP32: Bury E 5H 53
IP33: Bury E 1J 157 (6H 53)
Conach Rd. IP12: Wood 5F 121
Coney Hill NR34: Becc 5G 13
Coney Wlk. IP31: Stant 6D 32
CONEY WESTON 1B 30 (2D 159)
Coney Weston Rd. IP31: Barni 1B 30
IP31: Sap 1J 29
Congreve Rd. IP1: Ips 2J 131
Conifer Cl. IP28: Mide 5K 23
NR34: Nor C 7B 6

Coningsbury IP27: RAF L 5H 21
Coniston Cl. IP11: Felix 1K 155
Coniston Rd. IP3: Ips 4F 139
Coniston Sq. E. IP3: Ips 4F 139
Coniston Sq. W. IP3: Ips 4F 139
Coniston Wlk. NR32: Low 4F 9
Connaught Rd. CB9: Have 4D 100
IP1: Ips 3F 131
Conrad Cl. NR33: Oul B 3C 10
Conrad Rd. NR33: Oul B 3C 10
Consent La. IP7: Bild 5H 109
Constable Cl. IP19: H'orth 6A 42
NR32: Oul B 7E 8
Constable Ct. IP13: Ket 6J 89
Constable Ho. *NR34: Becc 5F 13*
(off Banham Rd.)
Constable M. CO7: Ded 7K 145
Constable Rd. CB9: Have 2C 100
CO10: S'bury 3D 126
IP4: Ips 1G 5 (6B 132)
IP11: Felix 4G 155
IP33: Bury E 2E 58
Constable Way IP14: Stowm 3E 84
Constantine Rd.
IP1: Ips 5B 4 (1K 137)
Constitution Hill CO10: S'bury . . .3E 126
IP1: Ips 5K 131
IP6: Nee M 3G 111
IP18: Sou 5K 45
Convalescent Hill IP11: Felix 5F 155
Conway Cl. CB9: Have 3C 100
IP2: Ips 4K 137
IP11: Felix 1H 155
Conway Rd. IP32: Bury E 4F 53
CONYER'S GREEN 1D 54 (3C 159)
Conyers Way IP31: Gt Bar 1D 54
Cooke Cl. NR33: Low 7E 10
Cooke Rd. NR33: Low 7E 10
COOKLEY .2D 161
Cookley Rd. IP19: Cook, Wal 1F 75
COOKLEY STREET 1F 75
Cooks Cl. IP5: Kesg 5E 134
Cooks Rd. IP30: E'well 2E 64
Coombers IP9: Cap M 2G 147
Cooper Cl. IP17: Saxm 5H 91
Cooper La. IP29: Now 7J 59
Cooper Rd. IP6: Cod, Gos 2H 115
Coopers Cl. IP6: Witn 1B 116
Coopers Dr. NR33: Kess 5K 17
Coopersfield IP14: Deb 2H 87
Coopers La. NR33: Kess 6H 17
Coopers Rd. IP5: Martl H 6H 135
IP6: Barh 6F 115
Coopers Way IP6: Barh 3C 114
COPDOCK 7B 136 (2B 164)
Copdock Interchange
IP8: Ips 4D 136
COPDOCK MILL INTERCHANGE
. . . . .6D 136
Copellis Cl. CB9: Have 1F 101
Copland Way
NR34: Ell . . . . .7K 13 & 7A 6
Copleston Cen. 1G 139
Copleston Rd. IP4: Ips 1F 139
Coplow Dale NR33: Car C 7C 10
Copper Beech Dr.
NR33: Car C 5C 10
Copperfield Rd. IP2: Ips 1G 137
Copperfield Ter. NR32: Blun 3K 7
Copper Gro. IP8: Ips 6G 137
Coppers Cl.
IP33: Bury E 7K 157 (2H 59)
Copperwheat Av. IP18: Rey 1H 45
Coppice, The IP31: Gt Bar 2D 54
Coppice Cl. IP12: Melt 4H 121
Coppice Ct. NR33: Oul B 3F 11
Copplestone Cl. NR34: Worl 4K 13
Coppy Mdw. IP29: Hart 1H 103
Coprolite St. IP3: Ips 5H 5 (2C 138)
Copse Cl. IP5: Martl H 5J 135
IP33: Bury E 5H 59
Copse Wlk. *NR33: Car C 5B 10*
(off Hollow Gro. Way)
Copswood Cl. IP5: Kesg 6F 135
Copy Hill CB9: Hel B 7D 100
Coral Dr. IP1: Ips 4F 131
Coram St. IP7: Hadl 3F 129
Cordell Cl. CO10: L Mel 3J 105
Cordell Pl. CO10: L Mel 3J 105
Cordell Rd. CO10: L Mel 3H 105
Corder Rd. IP4: Ips 5B 132
Cordwainer Cl. CB9: Ked 5B 98
Cordwinders CO7: E Ber 5D 146
Cordy's La. IP11: T Mary 2A 154
Cordy's Mdw. IP13: W'orth 5G 73
Corks La. IP7: Hadl 3G 129
Cormorant Dr. IP14: Stowm 5H 85
(not continuous)
Cornard Rd.
CO10: S'bury 4E 126
CORNARD TYE 4K 127
Cornerth Cres. CO10: Gt Cor 5G 127
Corn Exchange
Ipswich 3D 4 (7A 132)
Cornfield Av. IP27: Lake 4B 20
Cornfield Cres. NR32: Cort 6J 7
Cornfield Rd. IP33: Bury E 7F 53
Cornflower Cl. IP2: Ips 2G 137
IP28: W Row 6C 22
Corn Hatches La. IP7: E'sett 7F 113
Corn Hill IP19: Wen 2H 43
Cornhill IP1: Ips 3D 4
IP33: Bury E 4G 157 (1G 59)
Cornhill Wlk. IP33: Bury E 4H 157
CORNISH HALL END 3A 162
Cornish Wlk. IP32: Bury E 5E 52
Cornith Cl. IP28: W Row 5A 22
Cornmill Grn. IP30: Wool 5B 64
Cornwallis Ct.
IP33: Bury E 6F 157 (2F 59)
(not continuous)
Cornwallis Rd. CB9: Have 5E 100
Cornwallis Ter. IP4: Ips 7D 132
Cornwall Rd. IP11: Felix 3D 154
Corona Ct. CO10: Act 4G 107
Coronation Dr. IP11: Felix 5C 154
Coronation Pl. IP27: B'don 5E 18
Coronation Ri. CO10: Gt Wal 6K 107
Coronation Rd. IP4: Ips 1F 139
Coronation Row IP17: Benh 3C 92
Coronation Ter. *NR33: Low 5G 11*
(off Pakefield St.)
Corporal Lillie Cl.
CO10: S'bury 5D 126
Corporation Av. IP2: Ips 6J 137
Corsbie Cl.
IP33: Bury E 7G 157 (2G 59)
Corsican Pine Cl. CB8: Newm 4F 47
CORTON 6J 7 (1D 167)
Corton Beach Holiday Village
NR32: Cort 5J 7
Corton Long La. NR32: Cort, Low . . .7G 7
Corton Rd. IP3: Ips 5F 139
NR32: Low 7K 7
Cotman Cl. NR32: Low 2G 9
Cotman Rd. IP3: Ips 5E 138
Cotmer Rd. NR33: Oul B 2C 10
Cotswold Av. IP1: Ips 4K 131
Cotswold Dr. CO10: L Mel 5H 105
Cotswold Way NR32: Oul 6D 8
Cottage Gdns. IP27: Lake 5B 20
Cottage Homes IP24: Elv 3J 27
Cottage Pl. IP1: Ips 2C 4 (7K 131)
Cottesford Cl. IP7: Hadl 4J 129
Cottingham Rd. IP8: Ips 4D 136
COTTON 6E 68 (3A 160)
Cotton End Rd. CB8: Exn 1C 46
Cotton La. IP14: Cott . . . .7G 67 & 4D 68
IP33: Bury E 2J 157 (7H 53)
Cotton La. Flats
IP33: Bury E 3J 157 (7H 53)
Coucy Cl. IP13: F'ham 5C 90
Coulson La. IP27: B'don 3F 19
COUNTESS CROSS 3C 163
County Court
Bury St Edmunds . . .3G 157 (7G 53)
Ipswich 3D 4 (7A 132)
Coupals Cl. CB9: Have 5H 101
Coupals Ct. CB9: Have 5H 101
Coupals Rd. CB9: Have 5H 101
Courier Cl. IP28: Mide 6H 23
Courtenay Cl. CO10: S'bury 1C 126
Courts, The IP6: Play 1B 134
IP11: Felix 4G 155
Court St. CO6: Nay 6J 143
Courtyard, The IP1: Ips . . .1B 4 (6K 131)
IP12: Sud 4F 125
IP14: Stowm 3D 84
IP17: Snap 4C 94
Cove Dam NR34: Nor C 4A 6
Covehite Ct. CB9: Have 5D 100
COVEHITHE 2D 167
Covell Cl. IP33: Bury E 2C 58
Coverdale NR33: Car C 6D 10
Covert Cl. CB9: Have 2F 101
Covert Rd. IP18: Rey 1J 45
Covey Way IP27: Lake 5C 20
Cow and Sheep Drove
IP28: W Row 2A 22
Cowell St. IP2: Ips 3A 138
Cow Fair IP30: Wool 5A 64
Cowfen La. IP22: Hind 3A 34
Cow La. IP9: Shot 3B 156
Cowley Rd. IP11: Felix 4F 155
COWLINGE 1B 162
Cowper St. IP4: Ips 7F 133
Cowslip Cl. IP2: Ips 2H 137
IP32: Bury E 1B 60
Cowslip Cres. NR33: Car C 4B 10
Cowslip Way IP6: Nee M 5G 111
Cox Cl. IP5: Kesg 7B 134
COX COMMON 2C 167
Coxhall Rd. IP9: Tatt 4J 149
Cox Hill CO10: Boxf 6D 128
Cox La. IP4: Ips 3F 5 (7B 132)
(not continuous)
IP31: Gt Bar 2E 54
Coxs Cl. CB9: Have 4B 100
NR34: Becc 5F 13
Cox's La. IP18: Rey 1J 45
Coytes Gdns. IP1: Ips 4D 4 (1A 138)
Crabbe St. IP4: Ips 7E 132
IP15: Aldeb 5K 95
Crabtree Cl. IP19: H'orth 5B 42
Crabtree Mdw. IP30: E'well 2E 64
Cracks La. IP12: Eyk 1E 124
Craftman's Way NR32: Oul B 1D 10
Crag Farm Rd. IP12: Sud 3K 125
Crag Path IP15: Aldeb 6K 95
Craig Cl. IP11: T Mart 5H 153
Cramswell Cl. CB9: Have 5D 100
Cranberry Sq. IP3: Ips 7G 139
Cranborne Chase IP4: Ips 4E 132
Cranbrook La. CO10: L Mel 7E 104
Crane Cl. IP12: Wood 7E 120
Crane Hill IP2: Ips 1G 137
Cranesbill Dr. IP32: Bury E 1B 60
Cranesbill Rd. NR33: Low 6E 10
Cranfield Cl. NR33: Low 6E 10
Cranfield Ct. IP4: Ips 4C 132
Cranfield Towers IP4: Ips 5E 4
Cranleigh Rd. NR33: Low 6E 10
CRANLEY 2B 160
Cranley Grn. Rd. IP23: Eye 7D 38
Cranmer Cliff Gdns. IP11: Felix . . .3J 155
CRANMER GREEN 6K 33 (2A 160)
Cranmoregreen La.
CO10: L Mel 7E 104
CRANMORE HILL 1F 105
CRANSFORD 3D 161
Cranwell Cres. IP3: Ips 5G 139
Cranwell Gro. IP5: Kesg 6C 134
Cranworth Cl. IP13: Gru 5H 117
Cranworth Gdns. NR32: Oul B 4E 8
Cranworth Rd. IP7: Hadl 5J 129
CRATFIELD 2D 161
Cratfield La. IP13: Laxf 4D 74
Cratfield Rd. IP19: Hunt 1A 74
IP21: Fress 5C 40
IP32: Bury E 2B 60
Craven Way CB8: Newm 3E 46
Crawford Av. IP14: Haug 3C 70
Crawford Cl. IP14: W'den 4H 65
Crawford La. IP5: Kesg 6C 134
Crayford Rd. CO10: S'bury 1C 126
Creed Wlk. IP32: Bury E 6D 52
Creeting Bottoms IP6: C Mary 5D 86
Creeting Hills IP6: C Mary 1J 111
Creeting Ri. IP14: Stowu 4J 85
Creeting Rd. E.
IP14: Stowm, Stowu 4H 85
Creeting Rd. W. IP14: Stowm 4G 85
CREETING ST MARY 7A 86 (1A 164)
CREETING ST PETER 1A 164
Crepping Hall Dr. IP9: Stut 6B 150
Crescent, The IP6: Barh 1B 114
IP13: Wick M 6A 118
IP14: Stowm 6G 85
IP31: Thur 6J 55
Crescent Rd. IP1: Ips 2B 4 (7K 131)
IP11: Felix 4F 155
IP15: Aldeb 5J 95
Crescents, The IP18: Rey 1H 45
Cresmedow Way IP30: E'well 3E 64
Crespigny Rd. IP15: Aldeb 6J 95
Crestview Dr. NR32: Low 4F 9
CRETINGHAM 2F 89 (3C 161)
Cretingham Golf Course 1G 89
Crick Ct. IP18: Sou 3J 45
Cricketers Cl. *CO10: S'bury 5D 126*
(off Priory Wlk.)
Cricket Fld. Rd. CB8: Newm 7H 47
Cricket Hill Rd. IP11: Felix 3C 154
Cricket Mdw. CB8: Stradi 7G 97
Crick's Rd. IP28: W Row 6B 22
Crisp Cl. NR32: Low 4G 9
Crispin Cl. CB9: Have 4C 100
Crockatt Rd. IP7: Hadl 1J 129
Crockfords Rd. CB8: Newm 7G 47
Crocus Cl. IP2: Ips 2H 137
IP28: Red L 6J 25
Croft, The CO8: Bure 5B 142
CO10: Glem 5A 104
CO10: S'bury 3D 126
IP30: Tost 2G 63
IP31: Bard 2D 32
NR32: Low 7H 9
Croft Cl. CB8: W'rook 1F 97
NR34: Worl 4H 13
Croft Ct. CO10: S'bury 4D 126
Croft La. CB9: Have 5G 101
Croft Lea CO10: L Wal 5C 108
Crofton Cl. IP4: Ips 6F 133
Crofton Rd. IP4: Ips 6F 133
Croft Pl. IP28: Mide 7J 23
Croft Ri. IP33: Bury E 5H 59
Croft Rd. CB8: Newm 4F 47
CO10: S'bury 3D 126
Croftside CO8: Bure 5B 142
Croft St. IP2: Ips 7E 4 (3A 138)
Cromarty Rd. IP4: Ips 5F 133
Cromer Rd. IP1: Ips 5H 131
Crome Wlk. NR32: Low 2G 9
Crompton Rd. IP2: Ips 6H 131
NR33: Oul B 2D 10
Cromwell Av. NR34: Becc 5E 12
Cromwell Cl. NR34: Becc 5E 12
Cromwell Ct. IP1: Ips 5D 4 (1A 138)
NR33: Car C 7C 10
Cromwell Rd.
NR34: Becc, R'field 7D 12
Cromwell Sq. IP1: Ips 4D 4 (1A 138)
Crooked Creek Rd. IP12: Rend . . .6D 122
Cropley Cl. IP32: Bury E 2A 60
Cross, The IP13: W'orth 6H 73
IP23: Eye 7C 38
(off Cross St.)
Cross Cl. CB9: Have 2F 101
CROSS END 3C 163
Crossfields CO6: Stoke N 2H 143
Crossgate Fld. IP11: Felix 3D 154
CROSS GREEN
Bradfield Combust 1D 163
Bury St Edmunds, IP29 . . . .1H 103
Bury St Edmunds, IP30
. . . . .5F 81 (1C 163)
Cross Grn. IP14: Deb 2J 87
IP14: Old N 5B 70
IP22: Thel 6F 31
Crossing Rd. IP22: Pal 2D 36
Cross Keys NR32: Low 6J 9
Cross La. Cl. IP27: Lake 5B 20
Crossley Gdns. IP1: Ips 3E 130
Cross Maltings IP7: Hadl 4H 129
Cross Roads IP24: Elv 4G 27
Crossroads, The IP23: Brom 5G 37
CROSS STREET 3D 38 (2B 160)
Cross St. CO10: S'bury 5C 126
IP11: Felix 2D 154
IP16: Leis 4H 93
IP21: Hox 3C 38
IP23: Eye 7C 38
IP30: Drin G 1G 83
IP30: E'well 3D 64
NR35: Bung 2B 14
Crosswell Drove IP27: Lake 3D 20
Crotchets Cl. IP9: Cap M 1H 147
Croutel Rd. IP11: Felix 3G 155
Crowe St. IP14: Stowm 4F 85
CROWFIELD 1B 164
Crowfield Rd. IP14: Ston A 6H 87
Crowfoot Gdns. NR34: Becc 3E 12
Crow Hall La. IP9: Stut 6C 150
Crowhurst Cl. NR33: Car C 5C 10
CROWLAND 2A 160
Crowland Cl. IP2: Ips 4J 137
Crowland Rd. CB9: Have 4E 100
Crow La. IP14: Stowm 5F 85
Crowley Rd. IP6: Nee M 4G 111
Crown & Anchor La.
IP13: F'ham 6D 90
Crown & Anchor M. IP1: Ips 2D 4
Crown Cl. IP12: Martl 3H 135
CROWN CORNER 2C 161
Crown Court
Bury St Edmunds . . .6K 157 (2H 59)
Ipswich 5B 4 (1K 137)
Crown Ct. NR34: Becc 3E 12
Crown Cres. IP31: Ixw 6H 29
Crownfield Rd. CO10: Glem 3A 104
Crownfields IP13: Uff 5H 119
Crown Ho. IP1: Ips 2D 4 (7A 132)
Crownland Rd. IP31: Wals W 7G 33
Crown La. IP12: Orf 7J 125
IP13: Wick M 6B 118
IP31: Con W 1B 30
IP31: Ixw 5H 29
(not continuous)
Crown Mdw. Ct. NR32: Low 6J 9
Crown Mdw. Wlk. NR32: Low 6H 9
Crown M. *IP31: Ixw 5H 29*
(off Thetford Rd.)
Crown Mill IP30: E'well 2E 64
Crown Pas. CB9: Have 3F 101
Crown Pl. IP12: Wood 6H 121
Crown Pools Swimming Complex
. . . . .2E 4 (7A 132)
Crown Score NR32: Low 6K 9
Crown St. IP1: Ips 2D 4 (7A 132)
IP6: Nee M 3G 111
IP11: Felix 3D 154
IP14: Stowm 3F 85
IP16: Leis 3J 93
IP27: B'don 4D 18
IP33: Bury E 5J 157 (1H 59)
Crown St. E. NR32: Low 6K 9
Crown St. W. NR32: Low 6J 9
Crown Wlk. CB8: Newm 5G 47

Crow St. IP31: Con W 2A 30
Crowswell Ct. IP11: T Mart 5H 153
CROXTON 1C 159
Croxton Cl. IP10: Kirt 2J 153
Crozier M. IP4: Ips 7F 133
Crunch Cft. CB9: Stur 6K 101
Cryspen Ct.
IP33: Bury E 3H 157 (7G 53)
Cuckfield Av. IP3: Ips 3J 139
CUCKOLD'S GREEN 1A 44
Cuckoo Hill CO8: Bure 5B 142
Cuckoo La. IP20: W'well 1F 41
Cucumber La.
NR34: Becc, Westo 6F 13
CULFORD 6A 28 (3C 159)
Culford Pl. IP3: Ips 2D 138
Culford Rd. IP28: Forn M 1F 53
IP31: Ing 5D 28
Culford Sports & Tennis Cen. 6A 28
Culford Ter. IP33: Bury E 6F 157
Culford Wlk. IP11: Felix 5B 154
Cullcott Cl. IP17: Yox 7J 77
Cullingham Rd. IP1: Ips 3A 4 (7J 131)
Cullum Rd.
IP33: Bury E 7H 157 (2G 59)
Culvers Mdw. IP31: Stant 6D 32
Culzean Gdns. NR32: Low 4F 9
Cumberland Av. IP32: Bury E 4E 52
Cumberland Cl. IP11: Felix 2J 155
IP18: Sou 4K 45
Cumberland M. IP12: Wood 6H 121
Cumberland Pl. NR32: Low 6K 9
Cumberland Rd. IP18: Sou 4K 45
Cumberland St. IP1: Ips 1B 4 (6K 131)
IP12: Wood 6G 121
Cumberland Towers IP1: Ips 1A 4
Cundle Grn. La. IP17: Snap 1B 94
Cundys Marsh IP15: Aldeb 4J 95
Cunningham Cl. IP27: B'don 6D 18
Cunningham Way NR33: Low 6G 11
Curlew Cl. IP14: Stowm 3H 85
IP27: Lake 6B 20
Curlew Ct. *IP17: Saxm 6G 91*
(off Brook Farm Rd.)
CURLEW GREEN 2H 91
Curlew Grn. NR32: Oul B 7B 8
Curlew Rd. IP2: Ips 3F 137
Curlews, The IP33: Bury E 5J 59
Curriers La. IP1: Ips 3D 4 (1A 138)
Curtis Cl. IP8: Ips 5E 136
Curtis Rd. IP32: Bury E 4E 52
Curtis Way IP5: Kesg 7D 134
Curwen Rd. IP14: Stowm 4E 84
Curzon Rd. CO10: S'bury 3G 127
Cut, The NR32: Cort 5J 7
Cutler Cl. NR32: Oul 6C 8
Cutler Rd. NR32: Oul 6C 8
CUTLERS GREEN 3A 162
Cutlers La. CO7: E Ber 1C 146
Cutler St. IP1: Ips 5D 4 (1A 138)
Cutters Cl. IP28: B Row 1D 22
Cutter's La. IP31: Pake 7G 29
Cuttings Cl. IP14: Mendl 2J 71
Cygnets, The IP15: Aldeb 4G 95
Cypress Cl. IP28: Mide 5K 23
Cypress Way NR33: Oul B 2E 10

D

Daffodil Cl. IP2: Ips 3G 137
Daffodil Wlk. NR33: Car C 4B 10
Dagworth La. IP14: Haug 4D 70
Daidy Hill IP21: Fress 6E 40
Daimler Rd. IP1: Ips 3E 130
Daines La. IP12: Melt 3K 121
Dains Pl. IP11: T Mary 1B 154
Dairy Cl. IP28: B Row 1D 22
Dairy Dr. IP28: Forn S 1D 52
Dairy Hill IP19: H'orth 4B 42
Dairy La. IP31: Ing 7D 28
NR34: Mut 7D 6
Dairy Rd. IP7: Sem 5A 112
Daisy Av. IP32: Bury E 1B 60
Daisy Ct. IP28: Red L 5K 25
Daisy Grn. La. IP23: Wick S 2F 69
Daking Av. CO10: Boxf 6B 128
Daking's Drift IP19: H'orth 5A 42
Dakota Rd. IP28: RAF M 1C 22
Dale End NR33: Car C 7D 10
Dale Hall La. IP1: Ips 3K 131
Dale Haven NR33: Car C 6C 10
Dale Rd. IP31: Stant 4C 32
Dales Rd. IP1: Ips 4H 131
Dales Vw. IP8: Wash 6A 136
Dales Vw. Rd. IP1: Ips 5J 131
Dale Tree Rd. IP29: Barr 6C 50
DALHAM 7H 49 (3B 158)
Dalham Pl. CB9: Have 3F 101
Dalham Rd.
CB8: Dalh, Mou 7D 48
DALLINGHOO 1C 165
Dallinghoo Rd.
IP13: Wick M 1F 119 & 6A 118
Dalton Rd. IP1: Ips 3B 4 (7K 131)
Damask Cl. NR33: Car C 5D 10
Damerson Went NR33: Kess 4K 17
DAM GREEN 1A 160
Dam La. IP22: B'gate 4K 35
NR33: Gisle 5F 17
Damselfly Rd. IP3: Ips 6G 139
Damson Cl. IP28: Red L 5J 25
Dandalan Cl. IP1: Ips 5G 131
Dane Cl. CB9: Ked 6B 98
Dane Common CB9: Ked 6B 98
Danes Cl. IP14: Stowm 5E 84
Danes Ct. CO10: Gt Cor 7G 127
Danescourt Av. IP14: Stowm 5E 84
Daneum Holt CO10: Clar 6B 102
Daneway Gdns. IP16: Leis 5H 93
Danforth Cl. IP13: F'ham 5B 90
Danforth Dr. IP13: F'ham 5B 90
Dangerous La. IP6: Barh 5F 115
Daniel Gdns. IP23: Eye 6C 38
Daniels Cl. CO10: Act 4G 107
Daphne Rd. IP12: Orf 7J 125
Darby Cl. IP32: Bury E 7B 54
Darby Rd. NR34: Becc 6E 12
Darby's Ct. IP33: Bury E 3H 157
Darcy Cl. IP32: Bury E 2A 60
Darkings La. IP30: Fels 7A 82
DARMSDEN 7J 111 (1A 164)
Darnford Gdns. IP3: Ips 1H 139
Darrell Rd. IP11: Felix 7C 154
DARROW GREEN 1C 161
DARSHAM 3D 78 (1A 166)
Darsham Cl. IP11: Felix 4C 154
Darsham Rd. IP17: Westl 5G 79
Darsham Station (Rail) 5K 77
Darsham Va. NR32: Oul B 4E 8
Darter Cl. IP3: Ips 6G 139
Darwin Cl. IP28: Mide 5J 23
Darwin Pl. CB8: Newm 7H 47
Darwin Rd. IP4: Ips 1D 138
Dash End CB9: Ked 6C 98
Dash End La. CB9: Ked 6C 98
Dashwood Cl. IP8: Ips 5F 137
Daundy Cl. IP2: Ips 1F 137
Davey Cl. IP3: Ips 5D 138
NR35: Bung 2E 14
Davey La. IP13: Char 1C 118
Davey's La. IP31: Bard 2E 32
David Lloyd Leisure
Ipswich 7J 139
Davidson Cl. CO10: Gt Cor 7H 127
Davoren Wlk. IP32: Bury E 6E 52
Dawes Cl. IP9: Cap M 1G 147
Dawnbrook Cl. IP2: Ips 5G 137
Dawn Pointon Pl. NR32: Low 5J 9
Dawson Drift IP5: Kesg 6C 134
Dawson Dr. IP11: T Mary 7J 153
Dawson M. NR32: Low 2F 9
Dawson's La. IP9: Hark 7K 151
Days Grn. IP9: Cap M 2F 147
Day's La. IP31: Barni 2B 30
Days Rd. IP9: Cap M 1G 147
Dazeley's La. CO7: E Ber 5E 146
Deacon Ct. IP11: Felix 2J 155
Deacon's Cl. CO10: Lave 5C 106
Dead La. CO7: Strat M, E Ber 5K 145
Deadman's La.
IP14: Batt, Comb 5E 110
IP17: Benh 7F 91
IP23: Stoke A 3A 72
IP30: Drin 5K 63
Deanery Cl. CO10: S'bury 1C 126
Deanery Tower 4G 129
Deans Cl. CB9: Have 2E 100
DEBACH 1C 165
DEBDEN 3A 162
DEBDEN GREEN 3A 162
Deben Av. IP5: Martl H 4F 135
Deben Ct. IP13: Wick M 6B 118
Deben Dr. CO10: S'bury 3F 127
DEBENHAM 2H 87 (3B 160)
Debenham Leisure Cen. 2G 87
Debenham Rd.
IP14: Petta, Wins G 2C 88
Debenham Way IP14: Petta 2C 88
Deben La. IP12: Sutt 2B 140
IP12: Wald 6D 140
Deben Mill Bus. Cen.
IP12: Wood 4J 121
Deben Ri. IP14: Deb 3H 87
Deben Rd. CB9: Have 3G 101
IP1: Ips 4H 131
IP12: Wood 5J 121
IP17: Saxm 5H 91
Debenside, The IP12: Melt 3K 121
Deben Swimming Pool 6H 121
Deben Valley Dr. IP5: Kesg 6C 134
Deben Vw. IP12: Wood 6H 121
Deben Way IP11: Felix 5D 154
IP12: Melt 3K 121
De Brink on the Green
IP5: Martl H 6G 135
(off Valiant Rd.)
Debtrac Cen. IP6: Nee M 6J 111
De Bures Wlk. CO10: Act 4G 107
De Burgh Pl. CO10: Clar 3C 102
Deck Wlk. IP32: Bury E 6E 52
DEDHAM 7K 145 (3A 164)
Dedham Dr. NR32: Oul B 5E 8
DEDHAM HEATH 3A 164
Dedham Mill CO7: Ded 7K 145
Dedham Pl. IP4: Ips 4F 5
Dedham Rd. CO7: Strat M, Ded 5J 145
Deepdale NR33: Car C 6D 10
Defoe Rd. IP1: Ips 1H 131
Degas Gdns. NR32: Low 2G 9
De Greys Cl. CO10: Gt Cor 6H 127
De Havilland Ct. IP28: Mide 6H 23
Delf Cl. IP7: Hadl 2J 129
Delius Cl. IP14: Stowm 3E 84
NR33: Oul B 3F 11
Dell, The CO10: S'bury 5F 127
IP24: Elv 4K 27
Dell Ct. NR33: Oul B 2D 10
Dell Rd. NR33: Oul B 2D 10
Dell Rd. E. NR33: Oul B 2E 10
DELL, THE 1C 167
Dellview NR33: Oul B 3C 10
Dellwood Av. IP11: Felix 3F 155
Delph Rd. IP27: Lake 4B 20
Delta Ter. IP3: Ips 5J 139
DELVIN END 3B 162
Demesne Gdns. IP5: Martl H 5G 135
Demoiselle Cres. IP3: Ips 6G 139
Dencora Bus. Cen. IP1: Ips 2F 131
Dencora Ho. IP1: Ips 2F 131
Dene Rd. NR32: Low 4J 9
Denes High School Community
Sports Centre, The 4H 9
DENHAM
Barrow 3B 158
Hoxne 2B 160
Denham Cl. IP33: Bury E 1D 58
Denham Ct. IP5: Martl H 7G 135
DENHAM END 7B 50
Denham La. IP29: Barr 7B 50
Denham Rd. CB8: Dalh 7H 49
IP21: Hox 4D 38
IP29: Barr 7B 50
DENHAM STREET 2B 160
Denmark Ct. IP22: Pal 1C 36
Denmark Gdns. IP9: Holb 2D 150
Denmark Hill IP22: Pal 1C 36
Denmark Rd. NR32: Low 1G 11
NR34: Becc 2E 12
DENNINGTON 6C 76 (3C 161)
Dennington Rd.
IP13: F'ham 7C 76 & 4B 90
IP13: Laxf 7B 74
Denny Av. IP14: Haug 3C 70
Denny's Hill IP20: Mendh 1H 41
Dennys La. IP17: Kel 2J 91
DENSTON 7K 97 (1B 162)
DENTON 1C 161
Denton Cl. IP2: Ips 4F 137
Denton Dr. NR33: Oul B 4E 10
Denysse Wlk. IP33: Bury E 1C 58
DEPDEN 7J 51 (1B 162)
DEPDEN GREEN 7H 51 (1B 162)
Depden La. IP29: Chev 5H 51
Depot Rd. CB8: Newm 3E 46
Derby Cl. IP4: Ips 1E 138
Derby Pl. IP31: Gt Bar 3C 54
Derby Rd. IP3: Ips 2E 138
Derby Road Station (Rail) 2E 138
Derby Way CB8: Newm 4D 46
Dereham Av. IP3: Ips 3D 138
Derrick Hill IP8: Will 1G 113
Derwent Gdns. NR32: Low 4F 9
Derwent Rd. IP3: Ips 3D 138
IP32: Bury E 4E 52
De Saumarez Dr. IP6: Barh 1B 114
Desmond Cl. NR32: Oul B 6C 8
Dettingen Way IP33: Bury E 7D 52
Devereaux Ct.
IP4: Ips 2F 5 (7B 132)
De Vere Cl. IP13: F'ham 6C 90
Devil's La. IP17: Westl 2E 78
Devlin Rd. IP8: Ips 5D 136
Devon Cl. IP32: Bury E 5E 52
Devon Rd. IP11: Felix 3E 154
IP14: Stowu 2J 85
Devonshire Rd. IP3: Ips 5K 5 (1D 138)
Dewar La. IP5: Kesg 6C 134
Dhobi Pl. IP1: Ips 6H 131
Dial La. IP1: Ips 3E 4 (7A 132)
IP15: Aldeb 5K 95
Diamond Cl. IP1: Ips 4F 131
Dickens Ct. NR32: Blun 2H 7
Dickens Rd. IP2: Ips 7G 131
Dickinson Ter. IP5: Kesg 6D 134
DICKLEBURGH 1B 160
Dick Perryman Ct.
CB8: Newm 6H 47
Didsbury Cl. IP2: Ips 4F 137
Digby Cl. IP5: Martl H 7G 135
Digby Rd. IP4: Ips 6G 133
Dillestone Ct. CB9: Stur 6K 101
Dillwyn St. IP1: Ips 3A 4 (7J 131)
Dillwyn St. W.
IP1: Ips 3A 4 (7J 131)
Dingle Marshes 1K 79
Dinsdale Ct. IP11: Felix 5E 154
Dinsdale Rd. IP16: Leis 3H 93
Diomed Dr. IP31: Gt Bar 3C 54
Dip, The CB8: Newm 7K 47
Dip Farm Golf Course 1H 9
Diprose Dr. NR32: Low 2F 9
Discovery Av. IP2: Ips 7F 5 (3B 138)
Discovery Dr. IP4: Ips 1J 5 (6C 132)
DISS 2B 160
Diss Golf Course 1G 37
Diss Rd. IP22: W'field 2H 33
IP31: Stant 6E 32
DITCHINGHAM 1D 161
DITCHINGHAM DAM 1B 14
Ditchingham Dam NR35: Dit 1B 14
Ditchingham Gro.
IP5: Rush A 7K 133
Ditton Cl. CB8: Newm 7G 47
DITTON GREEN 1A 162
Ditton Way IP3: Ips 2F 139
Dixon Dr. NR33: Oul B 2D 10
Dobbs Drift IP5: Kesg 6F 135
Dobbs La. IP5: Kesg 5F 135
IP10: Foxh 7E 134
Dobson Way NR34: Becc 3F 13
Dock Basin IP11: Felix 7B 154
Docking Drove IP27: Lake 1C 20
Dock La. IP12: Melt 3K 121
Dock Rd. IP11: Felix 7C 154
Docks, The IP11: Felix 6A 154
Dock St. IP2: Ips 6E 4 (2A 138)
Doctor's Drift IP12: Orf 6K 125
Doctors La. IP12: Orf 6J 125
IP21: Stradb 6H 39
Doctor Watson's La. IP5: Kesg 4A 134
Dodmans IP9: Cap M 2H 147
Dodson Va. IP5: Kesg 6C 134
Does Fld. IP14: Ston A 6H 87
Dog La. IP13: Tan 1A 90
Dogs Head St. IP4: Ips 4E 4 (1A 138)
Dogwood Cl. IP3: Pur F 4H 139
Dogwood Wlk. IP27: RAF L 4G 21
Dolphin Cl. IP16: Thor 6D 94
NR33: Low 5G 11
Dolvers Vw. IP28: Holy R 2H 23
Dombey Rd. IP2: Ips 1G 137
Dome Leisure Centre
Mildenhall 7K 23
Donegal Pk. IP28: B Row 1C 22
Donegal Rd. IP1: Ips 3F 131
Donkey La. CO7: Strat M 6K 145
IP6: Tud 1H 133 & 7E 116
IP17: Fris 6D 92
IP29: Laws 7E 80
IP29: Stann 4F 81
Dooley Rd. IP11: Felix 5B 154
Dorchester Rd. IP3: Ips 3H 139
IP33: Bury E 3D 58
Doric Pl. IP12: Wood 6H 121
Doris St. CB8: Newm 6F 47
DORKING TYE 3D 163
Dorley Dale NR33: Car C 7D 10
DORLEYS CORNER 1H 91
Dorothy Hodgkin Ct. NR34: Becc 6E 12
Dorset Cl. IP4: Ips 4D 132
Dotterel Way IP14: Stowm 4H 85
Double St. IP13: F'ham 6D 90
Douglas Cl. IP19: H'orth 3C 42
NR33: Car C 6C 10
Doug Smith Cl. CB8: Newm 3F 47
Dove Cl. IP9: Cap M 1G 147
IP14: Deb 2H 87
IP17: Saxm 5H 91
Dovedale IP11: Felix 5C 154
NR33: Car C 6E 10
Dovedale Cl. IP31: B Ash 3D 66
Dovedale Wlk. IP32: Bury E 4F 53
Dove Gdns. IP14: Stowm 4J 85
Dovehouse Hill IP29: Shim 1A 106
Dove Ho. Mdw. CO10: Gt Cor 6F 127
Dove Ho. Rd. CB9: Have 2F 101
Dove La. IP23: Eye 7D 38
DOVERCOURT 3C 165
Dove Rd. IP18: Rey 2H 45
Dover Rd. IP3: Ips 2F 139
Dover Ter. IP31: Ixw 6H 29
Dove St. IP4: Ips 4H 5 (1C 138)
NR32: Low 6J 9
Dowes Hill Cl. NR34: Becc 6E 12
DOWN FIELD 2A 158
Downham Blvd. IP3: Ips 7G 139
Downham Way IP27: B'don 3H 19

Downing Cl. CB8: Newm 7H 47
IP2: Ips 4H 137
IP12: Wood 6F 121
IP28: Mide 6K 23
IP32: Bury E 7A 54
Downing Dr. IP31: Gt Bar 2D 54
(not continuous)
Downlands IP7: E'sett 7H 113
Downs, The IP11: Felix 3C 154
IP30: Blac 3G 61
Downs Cres. CB9: Have 3E 100
Downside IP14: Stowm 4D 84
Downside Cl. IP2: Ips 6H 137
Downs Pl. *CB9: Have* *3E 100*
(off Downs Cres.)
Downton Dr. CB9: Have 3D 100
Dowson Dr. NR33: Kess 4H 17
Dragonfly Wlk. *IP3: Ips* *6G 139*
(off Emperor Cir.)
Drake Av. IP3: Ips 4F 139
Drake Cl. IP14: Stowm 4D 84
Drake Rd. CO10: S'bury 2F 127
Drake's Heath NR32: Low 6G 9
Drake Sq. Nth. IP3: Ips 4F 139
Drake Sq. Sth. IP3: Ips 4F 139
Drapers Cl. IP7: Hadl 3J 129
Drapers Hill IP21: Stradb 5H 39
Drapery Comn. CO10: Glem 5A 104
Drapery Row CB8: Newm 6G 47
Draycott Ri. IP22: Pal 2C 36
Drayman Sq. IP18: Sou 4K 45
Draymans Way IP3: Ips 3C 138
Drays, The CO10: L Mel 6G 105
Drift, The CB8: Exn 1A 46
CO7: E Ber 3B 148
CO10: Gt Cor 5H 127
IP3: Ips 5G 139
IP4: Ips 7E 132
IP5: Martl H 6G 135
IP6: Bark, Nee M 5F 111
IP6: Cod 1F 115
IP6: Henl 6J 115
IP9: Stut 6E 150
IP10: Levi 7D 152
IP11: T Mary *1B 154*
(off Black Barns)
IP13: Wick M 5C 118
IP22: Bote 4J 35
IP28: Cul 6A 28
IP30: Tost 2H 63
IP31: Forn M 3G 53
IP31: Sap 1J 29
IP31: Thur 7B 56
Drift Ct. IP6: Nee M 4G 111
Drift Rd. IP27: Lake 3A 20
Driftway, The IP4: Ips 7F 133
IP13: Gru 7J 117
IP28: Frec 5B 24
DRINKSTONE 6H 63 (3D 159)
DRINKSTONE GREEN . . .1F 83 (3D 159)
Drinkstone Pk. IP30: Drin 6F 63
Drinkstone Rd. IP30: Bey, Drin 3D 62
IP30: Ged 5B 82
Drinkwater Cl. CB8: Newm 5E 46
Drive, The IP5: Martl H 5J 135
IP18: Rey 2H 45
IP30: Rushb 7E 60
NR32: Oul B 6E 8
Dross La. IP21: Oak 1A 38
Drout's La. IP31: Barni 4D 30
Drove, The IP27: B'don 5C 18
Drove La. IP14: W'den 1H 65
Drovers Av. IP32: Bury E 1B 60
Drovers Ct. IP11: T Mary 7H 153
Drovers Yd. *IP16: Leis* *4J 93*
(off High St.)
Druids Cl. IP28: B Row 1G 23
Drum Fld. CO7: Strat M 6H 145
Drummond Ct.
IP33: Bury E 6F 157 (2F 59)
Drunkards' La. IP10: Falk, Kirt . . .1K 153
Drury Cl. IP30: Blac 4G 61
NR33: Kess 5K 17
Drury Dr. CO10: S'bury 1E 126
Drury Pk. IP17: Snap 2D 94
Drury Rd. IP6: Clay 4D 114
DRYBRIDGE HILL 6F 121
Drybridge Hill IP12: Wood 5F 121
Dryden Rd. IP1: Ips 2J 131
DUBLIN 7D 72
Dublin Rd. IP23: Dub, Occ 6C 72
Duchess Dr. CB8: Newm 7J 47
Duckamere IP8: B'ford 4C 130
Duck Corner IP12: Holl 1G 141
DUCK END 3A 162
Ducksen Rd. IP14: Mendl 2J 71
Ducks La. CB8: Exn 2C 46
Duddery, The CB8: W'rook 2H 97
Duddery Hill CB9: Have 5E 100
Duddery Rd. CB9: Have 4F 101
Dudleys Cl. IP22: Redg 2C 34
Dudley St. IP27: RAF L 3H 21
Duffs Hill CO10: Glem 2A 104
Dukes Cl. IP11: Felix 2J 155
Duke's Dr. IP19: H'orth 6A 42
Dukes Head St. NR32: Low 6K 9
Dukes Mdw. IP12: Wood 7E 120
IP30: C'field 4K 81
NR34: Becc 4F 13
Dukes Pk. IP12: Wood 7E 120
Duke's Rd. NR35: Bung 4C 14
Duke St. IP3: Ips 6H 5 (2C 138)
IP7: Bild 6J 109
IP7: Hadl 4H 129
IP8: Hint 3A 144
IP14: Haug 2B 70
IP31: Stant 6C 32
(not continuous)
NR34: Becc 5G 13
DULLINGHAM 1A 162
DULLINGHAM LEY 1A 162
Dullingham Rd. CB8: Newm 7F 47
Dumbarton Rd. IP4: Ips 5F 133
Dumfries Rd. IP4: Ips 4G 133
Dumpling Bri. La. IP27: Lake 5A 20
DUNBURGH 1A 12
Dunburgh Rd. NR34: Geld 1A 12
Dunche's La. IP6: C Mary 5B 86
Dundee Ho. IP4: Ips 5F 133
Dunes, The *IP16: Thor* *6D 94*
(off The Haven)
Dunhill La. IP22: Hep 4E 30
Dunlin Rd. IP2: Ips 4G 137
Dunlop Rd. IP2: Ips 7H 131
Dunn Cl. IP7: Hadl 4J 129
Dunnock Cl. IP14: Stowm 5J 85
Dunsey Wood Cl. CB9: Have 2D 100
DUNSTALL GREEN 3B 158
Dunster Dr. CB9: Have 3D 100
Dunston Dr. NR32: Oul 4D 8
Dunton Gro. IP7: Hadl 5J 129
DUNWICH 1K 79 (3C 167)
Dunwich Cliffs Est. Caravan Pk.
IP17: Dun 4K 79
Dunwich Cl. IP3: Ips 7G 139
Dunwich Ct. CB9: Have 3B 100
IP1: Ips 5G 131
Dunwich Heath 1A 166
Dunwich Mus. 1K 79
Dunwich Pl. IP31: Gt Bar 3D 54
Dunwich Rd. IP17: Dun, Westl 5H 79
IP18: Sou 4K 45
IP19: Blyth 6J 43
Dunwich Underwater
Exploration Exhibition 6J 125
Dunwich Way NR32: Oul B 4E 8
Durban Cl. IP19: H'orth 6B 42
Durban Rd. NR33: Low 2G 11
Durbar Ter. IP33: Bury E 7F 53
Durham Cl. IP32: Bury E 4E 52
Durham Rd. IP27: RAF L 3H 21
Durham Way CB8: Newm 4E 46
Durilda Grn. IP10: Kirt 2H 153
Durrant Rd. IP7: Hadl 2H 129
Durrant's Cl. NR33: Kess 4K 17
Durrant Vw. IP5: Kesg 6E 134
Dutchman Ct. NR33: Oul B 2C 10
DUTON HILL 3A 162
Dyehouse Mdw. CO10: L Mel 4G 105
Dyer Ct. IP7: Hadl 4K 129
Dyer Ter. NR34: Wrent 1D 44
Dyke Rd. IP11: Felix 6A 154
Dykes St. IP1: Ips 2D 4 (6A 132)

E

Eade's Wlk. *NR33: Car C* *4B 10*
(off Harebell Way)
Eagle Cl. IP14: Stowm 4H 85
Eagle Ct. NR34: Wrent 1D 44
Eagle Dr. IP15: Aldeb 3G 95
Eagle Pl. IP28: B Row 2F 23
Eagles Cl. IP11: Felix 4E 154
Eagle St. IP4: Ips 4F 5 (1B 138)
Eagle Wlk. IP32: Bury E 5E 52
Eagle Way IP5: Martl H 7G 135
Earlsbrook IP14: Bac 2E 68
Earls Cl. IP11: Felix 2J 155
IP19: H'orth 6A 42
EARLS COLNE 3C 163
Earlsfield IP27: RAF L 4G 21
Earlsford Rd. IP23: Melli 6A 36
EARL'S GREEN 3C 68 (3A 160)
Earls Grn. CB9: Have 3B 100
Earls Grn. Rd. IP14: Bac 3D 68
EARL SOHAM 3C 161
Earl Soham La. IP13: F'ham 5A 90
EARL STONHAM 3C 86 (1B 164)
EARSHAM 1D 161
Earsham Dam NR35: Ears 2A 14
EARSHAM STREET 1K 39 (2C 161)
Earsham St. NR35: Bung 2A 14
Easdale NR33: Car C 7D 10
Easlea Rd. IP32: Bury E 2A 60
East Anglia Transport Mus. 6A 10
EAST BARTON 6G 55
E. Barton Rd. IP31: Gt Bar 3E 54
EAST BERGHOLT 3B 146 (3A 164)
East Bergholt Place Garden 5E 146
East Bergholt Sports Cen. 2C 146
EAST BRIDGE 1A 166
Eastbury Ct. IP32: Bury E 2C 60
East Cliff IP18: Sou 4K 45
Eastcliff IP11: Felix 1K 155
East Cl. IP33: Bury E 7J 53
East Coast Cinema
Lowestoft 1J 11
EAST END
Colchester 3B 148 (3B 164)
Stowmarket 5K 87
East End La. CO7: E Ber 3B 148
East End Rd. IP14: Ston A 6H 87
Eastern Av. CB9: Have 3D 100
Eastern Cl. IP4: Rush A 2K 139
Eastern Way IP30: E'well 3E 64
IP32: Bury E 2K 157 (7J 53)
NR32: Low 7G 9
Eastfield Gdns. NR33: Car C 5D 10
Eastgate Ho. IP33: Bury E 4K 157
Eastgate St.
IP33: Bury E 4K 157 (1H 59)
EAST GREEN 1E 96 (1A 162)
East Grn. IP18: Sou 4K 45
EAST HARLING 1D 159
Eastland Ct. IP11: T Mary 1C 154
Eastlands IP21: Stradb 6H 39
Eastlands Ind. Est. IP16: Leis 3K 93
Eastlands La. IP14: Finn 5K 67
Eastlands Rd. IP16: Leis 3K 93
East La. IP13: Uff 5K 119
East Lawn IP4: Ips 5G 133
Eastlowhill Rd. IP30: Roug 7F 61
East Mill Grn. IP9: Bent 6H 147
EASTON 1C 165
Easton Farm Pk. 1C 165
Easton La. IP18: Rey 1K 45
Easton Rd. IP12: Sutt 2B 140
East Point Academy Sports Cen.
. . . . .2F 11
East Row IP9: Holb 2D 150
East St. CO10: S'bury 4E 126
IP18: Sou 4K 45
East Vw. IP5: Kesg 5E 134
IP17: Kel 3J 91
IP19: Wen 3J 43
IP28: Frec 5C 24
Eastview Terraces IP9: Shot G . . .6D 156
Eastward Ho IP16: Leis 4J 93
Eastward Pl. IP14: Stowm 3E 84
Eastway Ent. Cen. IP1: Ips 5F 131
Eastwood Av. NR33: Oul B 3E 10
EAST WRETHAM 1D 159
Eaton Cl. IP11: T Mary 1B 154
Eaton Gdns. IP11: Felix 6D 154
ECCLES ROAD 1A 160
Eccles Rd. IP2: Ips 4F 137
Economy Rd. NR33: Low 2H 11
Eddies, The NR33: Oul B 5D 10
Eddowes Rd. IP6: Barh 3D 114
Edelweiss Cl. NR33: Car C 5B 10
Edendale NR32: Oul B 6C 8
Eden Rd. CB9: Have 4F 101
IP4: Ips 1F 139
Edes Paddock IP31: Gt Bar 2D 54
Edgar Av. IP14: Stowm 6F 85
Edgeborough Cl. CB8: Kent 3A 48
Edgecomb Rd. IP14: Stowm 7F 85
Edge Health & Fitness Club, The
. . . . .4H 47
Edgerton Rd. NR33: Oul B 3E 10
Edgeworth Rd. IP2: Ips 4G 137
Edgworth Rd. CO10: S'bury 4D 126
Edies La. CO6: Leav 3B 142
Edinburgh Cl. IP14: Stowm 4G 85
IP24: Barnh 6J 27
Edinburgh Gdns. IP6: Clay 3D 114
Edinburgh Rd. CB8: Newm 5E 46
NR32: Low 5J 9
Edison Cl. IP3: Ips 6K 139
Edmonton Cl. IP5: Kesg 6A 134
Edmonton Rd. IP5: Kesg 5A 134
Edmund Cl. CB9: Have 3E 100
Edmund Rd. IP27: B'don 5C 18
Edward Cl. IP1: Ips 5H 131
Edward Fitzgerald Ct.
IP12: Wood 4F 121
Edwards La. IP19: B'field 7G 75
EDWARDSTONE 2D 163
Edwin Av. IP12: Wood 3G 121
Edwin Panks Rd. IP7: Hadl 3J 129
Edwin Ter. IP12: Wood 4G 121
Egerton Rd. IP1: Ips 2E 130
Egglestone Cl. IP2: Ips 5H 137
Eglantine Way CO6: Leav 3A 142
Egremont St. CO10: Glem 6A 104
Ehringshausen Way CB9: Have . . .4G 101
Eider Cl. IP14: Stowm 3H 85
Eileen Crisp Ct. *NR34: Becc* *4E 12*
(off Peddars La.)
El Alamein Rd. NR32: Low 4G 9
Elderberry Rd. IP3: Ips 7G 139
IP28: Red L 5J 25
Elder Cres. IP7: Gt Bri 1A 112
Elders, The IP27: Lake 6C 20
ELDER STREET 3A 162
Elderstub La. IP30: Blac, Roug 3E 60
Eldo Gdns. IP28: W Row 6B 22
Eldon Drove IP27: Lake 6A 20
Eldon La. IP28: Holy R 2J 23
Eldo Rd. IP28: W Row 6B 22
Eldred Cl. IP1: Ips 5F 131
IP32: Bury E 2A 60
Eldred Dr. CO10: Gt Cor 7H 127
Eleanor Pl. IP31: Gt Bar 2C 54
Elevenways IP28: W'ton 3A 24
Elgar Cl. NR33: Oul B 3F 11
Eliot Way IP14: Stowm 2D 84
Elizabeth Av. CB8: Newm 4E 46
Elizabeth Bonhote Cl.
NR35: Bung 4C 14
Elizabeth Cl. NR32: Low 5F 9
Elizabeth Ct. CO10: S'bury 3E 126
IP3: Ips 5K 5
IP23: Eye 5C 38
NR33: Low 3H 11
Elizabeth Dr. IP29: Chedb 5K 51
Elizabeth Pde. *CB8: Newm* *4E 46*
(off Elizabeth Av.)
Elizabeth Rd. IP27: B'don 4F 19
Elizabeth Way CO10: Ball 6B 126
IP11: Felix 5C 154
IP14: Stowm 4G 85
IP23: Eye 6C 38
Ellenbrook Cl. IP2: Ips 5F 137
Ellenbrook Grn. IP2: Ips 5F 137
Ellenbrook Rd. IP2: Ips 5F 137
IP8: Ips 5F 137
ELLINGHAM 1D 161
Ellington Rd. IP24: Barnh 6J 27
Elliott Av. IP18: Rey 1J 45
Elliott Cl. CB8: Newm 4G 47
Elliott St. IP1: Ips 2A 4 (7J 131)
Ellisons Cres. IP4: Ips 1H 5
Ellis St. CO10: Boxf 6C 128
Elliston Cl. IP30: E'well 2E 64
ELLOUGH 2C 167
ELLOUGH AIRFIELD 7K 13
ELLOUGH HILL 5H 13
Ellough Ind. Est. NR34: Ell 6K 13
Ellough Pk. Raceway 7K 13
Ellough Rd.
NR34: Becc, Ell, Worl 4G 13
Ellwood Cl. NR34: Becc 1E 12
Elm Cl. CB9: Have 3E 100
CO11: Brant 4C 148
IP12: Rend 6D 122
IP27: B'don 4H 19
IP27: Lake 4A 20
NR33: Car C 6B 10
Elm Coppice NR33: Car C 5D 10
Elm Ct. CB9: Stur 6K 101
IP1: Ips 3D 4
Elmcroft NR33: Oul B 5D 10
Elmcroft Cl. IP28: B Row 1F 23
Elmcroft La. IP11: Felix 1H 155
(not continuous)
Elmcroft Rd. IP1: Ips 3J 131
Elmdale Dr. NR33: Car C 5C 10
Elmdon Pl. CB9: Have 3G 101
Elm Dr. IP30: Hess 6D 62
IP31: Wals W 6H 33
Elmers La. IP5: Kesg 6D 134
Elm Est. CO7: E Ber 3B 146
Elm Gdns. IP11: T Mary 1B 154
Elm Gro. CO6: Nay 6H 143
CO10: Glem 5A 104
Elm Ho. IP11: Felix 3D 154
Elmhurst Av. NR32: Oul B 7D 8
Elmhurst Cl. CB9: Have 4G 101
Elmhurst Ct. IP12: Wood 5J 121
Elmhurst Dr. IP3: Ips 3D 138
Elmhurst Wlk. IP12: Wood 5J 121
Elm La. IP8: Cop 6A 136
IP9: Cap M 2H 147
Elm Lodge Rd. IP13: Laxf 6C 74
Elmore Gdns. NR32: Low 5G 9
Elm Rd. CO7: E Ber 3A 146
CO10: S'bury 4F 127
IP5: Rush A 6K 133
IP13: Wick M 6A 118
IP14: Stowm 4E 84
Elms, The IP13: F'ham 5C 90
IP29: Horr 6B 58
Elms Cl. IP31: Gt Bar 2E 54
ELMSETT 6H 113 (2A 164)
Elmsett Cl. IP14: Stowm 7H 85
Elmsett Rd. IP8: Off, S'ham 3G 113

Elms La. NR34: Wang 6C 44
Elmsley Way IP17: Yox 6G 77
Elms Rd. IP28: Frec . . . . .6C 24 & 4F 25
(not continuous)
IP28: Red L 5H 25
Elm St. IP1: Ips 3C 4 (7K 131)
ELMSWELL 2D 64 (3D 159)
Elmswell Rd. IP14: W'den 4H 65
IP30: Wool 4B 64
IP31: Gt Ash 5E 66
Elmswell Station (Rail) 2D 64
Elmtree Bus. Pk. IP30: E'well 1E 64
Elm Tree Cl. IP14: Old N 5A 70
Elm Tree La. CO6: Leav 3A 142
Elm Tree Rd. NR33: Oul B 3D 10
Elm Tree Rd. W. NR33: Oul B 4D 10
Elm Wlk. IP27: RAF L 4G 21
Elm Way IP14: Bac 6B 68
Elseys Yd.
IP33: Bury E 3G 157 (7G 53)
Elsmere Rd. IP1: Ips 5A 132
Elton Pk. IP2: Ips 7F 131
Elton Pk. Bus. Cen. IP2: Ips 7G 131
Elton Pk. Ind. Est. IP2: Ips 7G 131
ELVEDEN 3J 27 (2C 159)
Elveden Forest Holiday Village . . .2F 27
Elveden Rd. IP24: Barnh 6F 27
IP24: Elv 2K 27
Elveden Way CB9: Have 2A 100
Elvedon Cl. IP3: Ips 7F 139
Elvedon Way CB8: Newm 4E 46
ELY .2A 158
Ely Cl. IP33: Bury E 3H 59
Ely Ct. IP28: Mide 7J 23
Ely Rd. IP4: Ips 4D 132
IP6: Barh, Clay 3E 114
Emerald Cl. IP5: Kesg 5C 134
Emerald Wlk. *IP3: Ips 6G 139*
(off Demoiselle Cres.)
Emily Bray Ho. IP4: Ips 1K 5
Emily Frost Cl. CB8: W'rook 1F 97
Emlen St. IP1: Ips 3A 4 (7J 131)
Emmanuel Cl. IP2: Ips 4H 137
IP28: Mide 6K 23
Emmerson Way IP7: Hadl 2H 129
Emperor Circ. IP3: Ips 6G 139
Emsal Ct. IP2: Ips 7G 131
Emsworth Cl. IP32: Bury E 7K 53
Endgate Cl. NR34: Becc 5G 13
Engelhard Rd. CB8: Newm 5F 47
Ennerdale Cl. IP11: Felix 2J 155
Enstone Rd. NR33: Low 3G 11
Enterprise Ct. CB8: Newm 2E 46
Enterprise Dr. IP2: Ips 6A 4 (2J 137)
Enterprise Pk.
IP33: Bury E 1H 157 (6G 53)
Entry, The IP23: Wick S 1G 69
Epsilon Ter. IP3: Ips 5J 139
Epsom Dr. IP1: Ips 1J 131
Erbury Pl. CO10: Clar 4C 102
ERISWELL 7G 21 (2B 158)
Eriswell Dr. IP27: Lake 6B 20
Eriswell Rd. CB9: Have 3G 101
IP27: Eris 6F 21
IP27: Lake 6B 20
IP28: Holy R . . . . .1J 23 & 6F 21
Ernest Nunn Rd. IP14: Stowm 7J 85
Ernleigh Rd. IP4: Ips 7F 133
Errington Way IP30: Tost 2G 63
ERWARTON 5A 156 (3C 165)
Erwarton Wlk. IP9: Erw, Shot 4A 156
Eskdale Way NR32: Low 4F 9
Esplanade NR33: Low 2J 11
Essex Av. CO10: S'bury 1E 126
Essex Rd. NR32: Low 7G 9
Essex Way IP3: Pur F 5J 139
Estuary Cres. IP9: Shot G 7E 156
Estuary Dr. IP11: Felix 1J 155
Estuary Rd. IP9: Shot G 7D 156
Ethel Mann Rd. NR35: Bung 4C 14
Ethel Rd. NR32: Low 7H 9
Etna Rd. IP33: Bury E . . .1H 157 (6H 53)
Europa Rd. NR32: Low 4H 9
Europa Way IP1: Ips 5E 130
Euro Retail Pk. IP3: Ips 5J 139
Euroscope 6K 9
Eustace Rd. IP1: Ips 5G 131
EUSTON 2C 159
Euston Av. IP4: Rush A 7K 133
Euston Cl. IP33: Bury E . . .6F 157 (2F 59)
Euston Ct. IP11: Felix 4B 154
Euston Hall 2C 159
Evabrook Cl. IP2: Ips 5G 137
Evans Cl. IP18: Rey 2J 45
Evans Drift IP5: Kesg 6E 134
Evans Dr. NR32: Low 5F 9
Eve Balfour Way IP14: Haug 3C 70
Evelyn Cl. IP21: Hox 3C 38
Everard Cl. IP32: Bury E 5E 52
Evergreen Ct. IP28: Mide 5J 23
Evergreen La. CB8: Gt Bra 1A 96
Evergreen Rd. NR32: Low 6G 9
Evergreen Way IP28: Mide 5K 23
Everitt Ct. NR32: Oul B 1C 10
Everitt Rd. NR33: Oul B 1C 10
Eversley Rd. *IP18: Sou 4K 45*
(off Blackmill Rd.)
Everton Cres. IP1: Ips 4H 131
Evesham Cl. IP2: Ips 4J 137
Eves Orchard CO8: Bure 5B 142
Exchange Sq. NR34: Becc 3E 12
Exeter Ct. CB9: Have 5D 100
Exeter Cres. IP27: RAF L 4H 21
Exeter Rd. CB8: Newm 5G 47
(not continuous)
IP3: Ips 2F 139
IP6: Clay 3E 114
IP11: Felix 3E 154
Exmoor Rd. IP11: Felix 2E 154
EXNING 1C 46 (3A 158)
Exning Rd. CB8: Newm 2D 46
EYE 7C 38 (2B 160)
Eye Castle 7D 38
Eye Rd. IP21: Hox 4A 38
IP23: Brom 4H 37
IP23: Yax 6E 36
EYKE 1D 124 (1D 165)
Eyke Rd. IP12: B'well 4B 124
IP13: Cam A 3B 122
Eyre Cl. IP33: Bury E 7G 157 (2G 59)

F

Factory La. CO11: Brant, Catt 6B 148
IP29: Chev 4J 51
Factory St. NR32: Low 6J 9
Fagbury Rd. IP11: Felix 4A 154
Faiers Cl. *IP33: Bury E 4H 59*
(off Heron Rd.)
Fairbairn Av. IP5: Kesg 6D 134
Fair Cl. NR34: Becc 3E 12
Fairey Fox Dr. IP28: Mide 6G 23
Fairfax Ct. NR34: Becc 5E 12
Fairfax Gdns. IP6: Nee M 4H 111
Fairfield Av. IP11: Felix 3F 155
Fairfield Ct. IP13: F'ham 6D 90
Fairfield Cres. IP13: F'ham 6D 90
Fairfield Dr. IP17: Saxm 6H 91
NR33: Oul B 3C 10
Fairfield Hill IP14: Stowm 4F 85
Fairfield Ho. Gdns. IP17: Saxm . . .6H 91
Fairfield M. IP15: Aldeb 4H 95
Fairfield Pl. IP17: Saxm 6J 91
Fairfield Rd. IP3: Ips 4E 138
IP13: F'ham 7D 90
IP15: Aldeb 4H 95
IP17: Saxm 6H 91
IP18: Rey 1J 45
NR33: Oul B 3C 10
NR35: Bung 4C 14
Fairfields IP17: Dars 2D 78
Fair Grn. CO10: Glem 4A 104
Fairhaven Way CB8: Newm 4E 46
Fairhead Loke NR33: Car C 7A 10
Fairlawns CB8: Newm 7F 47
Fairlawns Rd. CB8: Newm 7F 47
Fairlight Cl. IP4: Ips 4E 132
Fairmead IP30: E'well 1E 64
Fairmile Cl. NR34: Worl 4J 13
Fairstead, The IP22: Bote 4J 35
Fairview Rd. IP19: H'orth 2C 42
Fairway, The IP15: Aldeb 3G 95
NR33: Oul B 4D 10
Fairways IP21: Stus 1G 37
Fairways, The IP4: Rush A 1J 139
Fakenham Hill IP31: Honi 2H 29
FAKENHAM MAGNA 2D 159
Falcon Cl. CB9: Have 3H 101
Falcon Dr. IP27: B'don 4J 19
Falconer Av. IP14: Old N 5A 70
Falconer Rd. CB9: Have 6H 101
Falcon Gro. IP14: Stowm 3J 85
Falcon La. NR35: Dit 2B 14
Falcon Res. Trailer Pk.
IP5: Martl H 5J 135
Falcon St. IP1: Ips 4E 4 (1A 138)
IP11: Felix 2D 154
Falcon Way IP28: B Row 1C 22
FALKENHAM 3K 153 (3C 165)
Falkenham Rd. IP10: Falk, Kirt . . .1H 153
Falklands Rd. CB9: Have 1F 101
Fallowfield IP30: Bey 3C 62
Fallowfield Ct. CB9: Have 4D 100
Fallowfields NR32: Oul 3E 8
Fallowfield Wlk. IP33: Bury E 5H 59
Falmouth Av. CB8: Newm 6F 47
Falmouth Cl. IP5: Kesg 7B 134
Falmouth Gdns. CB8: Newm 3G 47
Falmouth St. CB8: Newm 6F 47
Famona Rd. NR33: Car C 7A 10
Faraday Rd. IP4: Ips 1D 138
Farford Fld. CO10: Gt Cor 5H 127
Farina Cl. IP1: Ips 6H 131
FARLEY GREEN 1B 162
Farlingayes IP12: Wood 3G 121
Farm Cl. IP30: Drin G 1G 83
IP33: Bury E 5H 59
NR33: Car C 5C 10
NR35: Bung 3D 14
Farmerie Rd. CO10: Hund 2J 99
Farmland Cl. IP18: Rey 1H 45
Farm Mdw. IP30: E'well 2D 64
Farm Rd. IP17: Saxm 5H 91
FARNHAM 3D 161
Farnham Cl. NR32: Oul B 4E 8
Farnham Rd. IP12: Blax 1F 123
IP17: Snap 7A 92
Farnish Ho. IP22: Bote 5J 35
Farriers Cl. IP5: Martl H 5G 135
IP21: Stradb 6H 39
Farrier's Rd. IP14: Stowm 7E 84
Farriers Went IP11: T Mary 1C 154
Farrow Cl. IP16: Leis 3G 93
Farrows Cl. IP29: Chev 2K 51
Farthing Rd. IP1: Ips 6E 130
Farthing Rd. Ind. Est.
IP1: Ips 6E 130
Farthings, The IP28: Ick 3C 26
Farthings Went IP9: Cap M 2J 147
Fastnet Cl. CB9: Have 3J 101
Fastolf Cl. NR32: Low 5F 9
Faulkeners Way
IP11: T Mary 7H 153
Faversham Ct. NR33: Low 5F 11
Fawcett Rd. IP15: Aldeb 5J 95
Fawley Cl. IP4: Ips 6G 133
Fayrefield Rd. IP12: Melt 3K 121
Featherbroom Gdns.
IP13: Wick M 7B 118
Feathers Fld. IP11: Felix 3C 154
Feaveryears Yd. IP21: Fress 6D 40
Felaw St. IP2: Ips 7F 5 (2B 138)
Felbridge Ct. IP12: Wood 5G 121
Felix Cl. IP5: Kesg 6B 134
Felix Rd. IP3: Ips 5F 139
IP11: Felix 4G 155
IP14: Stowu 2J 85
FELIXSTOWE 5F 155 (3C 165)
Felixstowe Beach Holiday Pk.
IP11: Felix 6D 154
Felixstowe Driving Range 1E 154
FELIXSTOWE FERRY 3D 165
Felixstowe Ferry Golf Course . . .1K 155
Felixstowe Leisure Cen. 5E 154
Felixstowe Palace, The 4F 155
Felixstowe Rd. IP3: Ips . . .7K 5 (2D 138)
IP12: Martl 5H 135
Felixstowe Snooker & Pool Club
. . . . .6E 154
Felixstowe Station (Rail) 3F 155
Fellbrigg Av. IP5: Rush A 7K 133
Fellowship Grn. NR33: Kess 4K 17
Felnor Wlk. IP11: Felix 4F 155
FELSHAM 6C 82 (1D 163)
Felsham Ct. IP14: Stowm 7H 85
Felsham Ri. IP17: Saxm 5H 91
Felsham Rd.
IP30: B Geo, Ged . . . .3C 82 & 4A 82
IP30: C'field 5K 81
IP30: Rat 4J 83
Felton Wlk. IP32: Bury E 6D 52
FELTWELL 1B 158
Feltwell Pl. CB9: Have 3G 101
Fen Alder Carr Nature Reserve
. . . . .1G 111
Fen Bight Circ. IP3: Ips 7G 139
Fen Bight Wlk. IP3: Ips 7F 139
Fenbridge La. CO7: E Ber 6A 146
Fen Ct. NR33: Oul B 3F 11
Fen Field Units CB9: Have 5E 100
FENGATE 1E 18
Fengate Drove IP27: Weet 1E 18
Fen Grn. Cl. NR32: Oul 4D 8
Fenlands Cres. NR33: Oul B 3E 10
Fen La.
IP6: C Mary, C Pet
. . . . .1G 111 & 6A 86
IP7: Hit 3H 109
IP14: Forw G 5A 86
IP22: Bote 5J 35
IP22: Thel 5G 31
IP28: Holy R 1H 23
NR34: Becc 1E 12
Fen Mdw. IP11: T Mary 7J 153
Fen Meadow Wlk. IP12: Wood 6G 121
Fenn Cl. IP14: Stowm 7F 85
IP19: H'orth 3A 42
Fennel Dr. IP28: Red L 6J 25
Fennels Cl. CB9: Have 4F 101
Fenn Row IP12: But 4A 124
Fenns Mdw. IP14: Comb 3B 110
FENN STREET 4K 87
Fen Rd. IP22: B Nor 4H 31
IP22: Hind 6J 31
IP31: Pake 2C 56
FEN STREET
Diss 2G 31
Old Buckenham 1A 160
Fen St. CO6: Nay 6K 143
CO10: Boxf 6D 128
IP22: Redg 1C 34
Fenstreet Rd. IP17: Westl 7F 79
Fenton Rd. CB9: Have 3G 101
Fentons Way IP5: Kesg 6C 134
Fen Vw. IP8: Wash 6A 136
IP23: Thorn 2C 72
Fen Wlk. IP12: Wood 6G 121
Fen Way IP33: Bury E 1F 157 (6F 53)
Ferguson Way IP5: Kesg 6B 134
Ferini Art Gallery 5G 11
Fern Av. NR32: Oul B 6C 8
Ferndale Av. NR32: Low 5G 9
Ferndale Cl. CB8: Newm 3H 47
Ferndown Rd. IP11: Felix 2H 155
Ferneley Cres. CB8: Newm 5G 47
Fern Gro. CB9: Have 3D 100
Fernhayes Cl. IP2: Ips 4J 137
Fern Hill CO10: Glem 2A 104
Fernhill Cl. IP12: Wood 3H 121
Fern Ter. IP12: Bawd 7J 141
Fern Way IP28: Red L 6H 25
Ferriers La. CO8: Bure 6A 142
Ferry La. IP11: Felix 5A 154
(not continuous)
IP28: W Row, W'ton 7A 22
Ferry Quay IP12: Wood 6H 121
Ferry Rd. IP11: Felix 2H 155
IP12: Orf, Sud . . . . .6J 125 & 4K 125
IP18: Sou, Walb 7H 45
(not continuous)
FERSFIELD 1A 160
Festival Cl. IP17: Benh 3C 92
Fiddlers La. CO7: E Ber 3B 146
Field Cl. IP20: Metf 6G 41
IP30: Bey 3C 62
Field Ct. IP31: Stant 7D 32
Fielden Way CB8: Newm 4E 46
Fieldfare Cl. IP14: Stowm 4H 85
IP32: Bury E 7A 54
Field Farm Fisheries 2B 44
Field Grange NR32: Oul 3E 8
Field La. NR33: Kess 4J 17
Fld. Maple Cl. IP28: Red L 7J 25
Field Rd. IP27: B'don 5C 18
IP28: Holy R, Mide 6J 23
Fields, The IP12: Tun 6F 123
Field Stile Rd. IP18: Sou 4K 45
Fields Vw. CO10: S'bury 3E 126
Field Ter. Rd. CB8: Newm 4F 47
Field Vw. CB9: Have 2B 100
IP10: Buck 3B 152
IP31: Thur 6A 56
Fieldview Cl. IP18: Rey 1H 45
Fieldview Dr. NR32: Low 7F 9
Field Vw. Gdns. NR34: Becc 5G 13
Field Wlk. IP28: Mide 6J 23
Field Way IP14: Deb 3H 87
IP31: Stant 7D 32
Fife Rd. IP4: Ips 4F 133
Fillisters M. NR32: Low 7G 9
Finbars Wlk. IP4: Ips 4J 5 (1C 138)
Finborough Cl. IP4: Rush A 7K 133
Finborough Ct. IP14: Gt Fin 7J 83
Finborough Rd.
IP14: Gt Fin, One, Stowm 6J 83
Fincham Rd. IP28: Mide 6H 23
Finch Cl. IP14: Stowm 5K 85
FINCHINGFIELD 3A 162
Finchley Av. IP28: Mide 5H 23
Finchley Rd. IP4: Ips 2H 5 (7C 132)
Findley Cl. IP9: Stut 6B 150
FINGAL STREET 2C 161
Fingal St. IP13: W'orth 4F 73
Finley Way
IP33: Bury E 7F 157 (3F 59)
Finney's Drift IP10: Nac 5B 152
FINNINGHAM 6H 67 (3A 160)
Finningham La.
IP14: Bac, W'orpe . . . .5A 68 & 7F 67
Finningham Rd. IP14: Old N 5B 70
IP14: W'orpe 7F 67
IP22: Rick 7H 35
IP23: Gisli 4J 67
IP31: Wals W 6H 33
Finsbury Pl.
IP33: Bury E 6H 157 (2G 59)
Finsbury Sq. IP33: Bury E 6H 157
Fir Cl. IP13: Wick M 5B 118
NR34: Barnb 6D 6
Fircroft Rd. IP1: Ips 2K 131
Firebrass La. IP12: Sutt 3C 140
Firebronds Rd. IP9: Holb 3D 150
Firecrest Dr. IP14: Stowm 3H 85
Firefly Way IP3: Ips 6F 139
Firfield Cl. NR34: Becc 5E 12
Fir La. NR32: Low 6F 9
Firmin Cl. IP1: Ips 3A 4 (7J 131)

Firs, The IP18: Rey 1H **45**
IP27: Lake 5C **20**
NR33: Car C 6B **10**
NR34: Worl 4J **13**
Firs Mobile Home Park, The
IP33: Bury E 3K **59**
First Av. CO10: Glem 4B **104**
CO10: S'bury 2F **127**
First Drove IP27: Lake 5A **20**
Firs Way IP27: B'don 5F **19**
Fir Tree Cl. IP21: Wey 3D **40**
Firtree Cl. IP32: Bury E 6D **52**
Fir Tree Ct. IP28: Mide 6K **23**
Fir Tree Hill IP9: Holb 3E **150**
Fir Tree La. IP6: Clay 4D **114**
Fir Tree Ri. IP8: Ips 4E **136**
Fir Wlk. IP27: RAF L 5G **21**
Fishbane Cl. IP3: Ips 6E **138**
Fisher Cl. CB9: Have 3J **101**
IP17: Saxm 7H **91**
Fisherman's Way NR33: Kess 4K **17**
Fisher Row NR32: Oul 1A **10**
Fishers, The IP5: Kesg 6C **134**
Fisher's La. CO7: E Ber 2B **148**
Fisher Theatre 2B **14**
Fish Farm Ind. Est.
IP28: Forn S 3D **52**
Fish Pond Hill IP9: Hark 5J **151**
Fishpond La. IP31: Wals W 4G **33**
Fishpond Rd. IP12: Wald 6C **140**
Fishponds La. IP9: Holb 3E **150**
Fishponds Way IP14: Haug 2B **70**
Fiske Cl. IP32: Bury E 1A **60**
Fiske Gdns. NR32: Oul B 4E **8**
Fisk's La. IP1: Ips 2F **131**
Fitches, The IP17: Knod 7F **93**
Fitche's La. IP16: Aldr 7H **93**
IP17: Knod 7F **93**
Fitzgerald Ct. IP4: Ips 1E **138**
Fitzgerald Mdw. CO10: Boxf 6D **128**
Fitzgerald M. *IP17: Saxm* *5G* ***91***
(off Brook Farm Rd.)
Fitzgerald Rd. IP8: B'ford 4C **130**
IP12: Wood 4H **121**
Fitzgerald Wlk. IP33: Bury E 7C **52**
Fitzmaurice Rd. IP3: Ips 3F **139**
Fitzroy St. CB8: Newm 6F **47**
IP1: Ips 2E **4** (7A **132**)
Fitzwilliam Cl. IP2: Ips 4H **137**
IP12: Wood 6F **121**
Five Acres IP9: Holb 3D **150**
FIVEWAYS 1J **25**
Fiveways IP28: B Mil 1J **25**
Flaggy Pond Vw. CO6: Pols 5C **144**
Flat, The IP30: Rushb 7E **60**
Flatford Bridge Cottage 7C **146**
Flatford Cl. IP14: Stowm 7G **85**
Flatford La. CO7: E Ber 6C **146**
Flatford Mill 7C **146**
Flatford Rd. CB9: Have 3B **100**
CO7: E Ber 5A **146**
Flatts La. IP30: Tost 2H **63**
Flavian Cl. CB9: Have 4J **101**
Flax La. CO10: Glem 5A **104**
Fleetdyke Dr. NR33: Oul B 4D **10**
Fleetwood Av. IP11: Felix 3G **155**
Fleetwood Cl. IP6: C Mary 7A **86**
Fleetwood Rd. IP11: Felix 3G **155**
Fleming Av. IP28: Mide 6J **23**
Flemington Cl. IP28: Mide 5H **23**
FLEMPTON 3C **159**
Flempton Rd. IP28: Ris 1C **50**
Flemyng Rd. IP33: Bury E 1C **58**
Flensburgh St. NR32: Low 1J **11**
Fletcher Cl. IP6: Barh 3C **114**
Fletcher Rd. IP3: Ips 6D **138**
Fletchers La. IP5: Kesg 5E **134**
IP17: Midd 5D **78**
Flindell Dr. IP8: B'ford 3C **130**
Flint Cl. IP2: Ips 4K **137**
FLIXTON
Bungay 1D **161**
Lowestoft 2C **8**
Flixton Marsh La. NR32: Blun 2A **8**
Flixton Rd.
NR32: Blun, Flix, Lou, Oul 1G **7**
NR35: Bung 5A **14**
(not continuous)
Flixton Vw. NR32: Oul 3D **8**
Floral Loke NR32: S'ton 2C **6**
Flora Rd. NR33: Low 6F **11**
Flordon Rd. IP6: C Mary 2H **111**
Florence Rd. NR33: Low 6G **11**
Florence Ter. NR33: Low 2H **11**
FLOWTON 2A **164**
Flowton Rd. IP7: E'sett 6J **113**
IP8: S'ham 4K **113**
Floyd Rd. IP32: Bury E 5D **52**
Foden Av. IP1: Ips 3E **130**
Folly, The IP14: Haug 3A **70**
NR35: Bung 3B **14**
Folly End IP15: Aldeb 4H **95**
Folly Rd. CO10: Clar 1A **102**
CO10: Gt Wal 7J **107**
IP28: Mide 4G **23**
Fonnereau Rd. IP1: Ips 1D **4** (6A **132**)
Forbes Dr. NR34: Becc 5E **12**
Ford Cl. IP14: Stowm 6G **85**
IP28: W Row 4A **22**
FORDHAM
Isleham 2A **158**
West Bergholt 3D **163**
FORDHAM HEATH 3D **163**
Fordham Pl. IP4: Rush A 1K **139**
IP31: Ixw 5H **29**
Fordham Rd. CB8: Newm 1E **46**
IP28: Frec 6A **24**
Fordhams Cl. IP31: Stant 7C **32**
Ford La. IP13: B'ton 6F **89**
Fordley Rd. IP17: Midd 7A **78**
Fordson Way NR33: Car C 6B **10**
FORD STREET 3D **163**
Ford Vw. Rd. IP14: Stowm 6G **85**
Fore Hamlet IP3: Ips 5H **5** (1C **138**)
Forest Cl. IP27: B'don 5F **19**
Forest Ct. IP4: Ips 6E **132**
IP12: Rend 6C **122**
Forester Cl. IP8: Ips 6G **137**
Foresters Wlk. IP6: Barh 3C **114**
Forest Gdns. IP12: Rend 6C **122**
Forest Glade CB9: Have 1E **100**
Forest La. IP5: Martl H 7G **135**
Fore St. IP4: Ips 4F **5** (1B **138**)
IP13: F'ham 6C **90**
Fore Street Swimming Pool 5G **5**
Forest Rd. IP14: One 2A **84**
Forest Way IP28: Mide 7K **23**
Forfar Cl. IP4: Ips 4F **133**
Forge Bus. Cen. IP22: Pal 1D **36**
Forge Cl. IP10: Buck 2B **152**
IP17: Benh 2C **92**
(not continuous)
IP22: Pal 1D **36**
Forge End IP28: Forn S 1D **52**
Forge Ter. NR32: Oul B 1D **10**
Formula Dr. CB8: Newm 3E **46**
FORNCETT END 1B **160**
FORNCETT ST MARY 1B **160**
FORNCETT ST PETER 1B **160**
FORNHAM ALL SAINTS
1D **52** (3C **159**)
Fornham Ho. Cl. IP31: Forn M 2G **53**
Fornham Ho's. IP4: Ips 7F **133**
Fornham La. IP33: W'ley 7A **52**
Fornham Pk. IP28: Forn G 1F **53**
Fornham Rd. IP31: Gt Bar 3C **54**
IP32: Bury E, Forn M
1H **157** (5G **53**)
FORNHAM ST GENEVIEVE 1F **53**
FORNHAM ST MARTIN
3G **53** (3C **159**)
FORT GREEN 7J **95**
Forties Cl. CB9: Have 3J **101**
Fortress Flds. CO10: Gt Wal 6K **107**
Fortress Rd. NR33: Car C 6D **10**
Forum Ct.
IP32: Bury E 1H **157** (6G **53**)
FORWARD GREEN 1B **86** (1A **164**)
Foster Cl. IP18: Sou 3K **45**
Foundation St. IP4: Ips 5F **5** (1B **138**)
Foundry, The IP4: Ips 5E **4**
Foundry La. IP4: Ips 5E **4** (1A **138**)
Fountain Rd. IP12: Rend 7B **122**
Fountain's La. NR34: Nor C 7B **6**
Fountains Rd. IP2: Ips 5H **137**
IP33: Bury E 4D **58**
Fountain Way IP18: Rey 1J **45**
FOUR ASHES 7G **33** (2A **160**)
FOUR SISTERS INTERCHANGE
1A **146**
Fourth Av. CO10: Glem 4A **104**
Four Wheel Dr. IP30: Roug 2F **61**
Fowler's Cres. NR32: Cort 5J **7**
Fox & Hounds Cl. *IP31: Thur* *6K* ***55***
(off Station Hill)
Fox and Pin La. IP29: Now 6J **59**
Foxberry Gdns. IP3: Ips 2H **139**
Foxborough Rd. NR32: Low 3F **9**
(not continuous)
Foxburrow Cl. CB9: Have 2E **100**
Foxburrow Farm 1J **121**
Foxburrow Rd. IP3: Pur F 5K **139**
Foxburrow Wood 2G **9**
Fox Ct. IP14: Stowm 4G **85**
FOXEARTH 2C **163**
Foxearth Fisheries 7B **104**
Foxes La. IP20: Mendh 2H **41** & 4F **41**
Foxes Wlk. NR32: Low 2F **9**
Foxglade NR32: Oul B 6C **8**
Foxglove Av. IP6: Nee M 5G **111**
Foxglove Cl. IP28: Red L 7J **25**
NR33: Low 7F **11**
NR34: Worl 5H **13**
Foxglove Cres. IP3: Pur F 5J **139**
Fox Grn. CB8: Gt Bra 1A **96**
Foxgrove IP11: Felix 3H **155**
Foxgrove Gdns. IP11: Felix 3H **155**
Foxgrove La. IP11: Felix 3H **155**
Foxhall Cl. CO7: E Ber 2B **146**
Foxhall Flds. CO7: E Ber 3B **146**
Foxhall Heath Stadium 7A **134**
Foxhall Rd. IP3: Ips 5K **5** (1D **138**)
IP4: Ips, Rush A 2H **139**
Fox Hill IP12: Holl 3G **141**
Fox La. IP17: Dars 2B **78**
Fox Lea IP5: Kesg 5E **134**
Foxley Cl. IP3: Ips 2H **139**
FOX STREET 3A **164**
Foxtail Rd. IP3: Ips 6H **139**
Foxwood Cres. IP4: Rush A 1K **139**
Fox Yd. *IP18: Sou* *4K* ***45***
(off Gardner Rd.)
Framfield Rd. NR33: Car C 5B **10**
FRAMLINGHAM 6C **90** (3C **161**)
Framlingham Castle 5D **90**
Framlingham Cl. IP12: Sutt 2B **140**
Framlingham College Sports Cen.
4B **90**
Framlingham Ct. IP1: Ips 5J **131**
Framlingham Rd. IP13: Laxf 7A **74**
Framlingham Sports Cen. 4A **90**
Frampton Cl. CB8: Newm 4G **47**
Frampton Rd. IP3: Ips 6E **138**
FRAMSDEN 6E **88** (1B **164**)
Framsden Rd. IP13: Cret 2F **89**
IP14: Petta 2D **88**
Franciscan Way
IP1: Ips 4D **4** (1A **138**)
Francis Cl. CB9: Have 3E **100**
IP5: Kesg 5E **134**
Francis Rd. CO10: S'bury 4D **126**
NR33: Kess 4J **17**
Franklin Cl. IP15: Aldeb 4H **95**
Franklin Rd. IP3: Ips 4F **139**
IP15: Aldeb 4G **95**
Fraser Rd. IP1: Ips 6H **131**
IP8: B'ford 2C **130**
FRECKENHAM 5B **24** (2A **158**)
Freckenham Rd.
IP28: W'ton 4E **24** & 3A **24**
Fred Archer Way CB8: Newm 5G **47**
Fred Castle Way IP30: Roug 1E **60**
Fred Dannatt Rd. IP28: Mide 5G **23**
Fredericks Cl. IP9: Tatt 7F **149**
Frederick's Rd. NR34: Becc 4E **12**
Fred Winter Ho. *CB8: Newm* *4G* ***47***
(off Bill Rickaby Dr.)
Freehold Cl. IP6: Nee M 2G **111**
Freehold Rd. IP4: Ips 7E **132**
IP6: Nee M 2F **111**
Freelands IP14: Mendl 2K **71**
Freeman Av. IP6: Henl 6J **115**
Freeman Cl. IP7: Hadl 2H **129**
Freemantle Rd. NR33: Low 2H **11**
Freewood St. IP30: B Geo 3C **82**
Frenesi Cres. IP32: Bury E 1C **60**
FRENZE 1B **160**
Freshfields CB8: Newm 5F **47**
Freshwater Way NR32: Oul B 1D **10**
FRESSINGFIELD 6C **40** (2C **161**)
Fressingfield Rd. IP20: Metf 7G **41**
FRESTON 4K **149** (3B **164**)
Freston Hill IP9: Frest 2K **149**
Freston Rd. IP3: Ips 7G **139**
Friar Cl. CB9: Have 2E **100**
Friars IP9: Cap M 3J **147**
Friars Bri. Rd. IP1: Ips 4C **4** (1K **137**)
Friars Cl. IP11: Felix 2J **155**
Friars Ct. IP12: Melt 3K **121**
Friars Courtyard IP1: Ips 4D **4**
Friar's La.
IP33: Bury E 7H **157** (2G **59**)
Friars Mdw. IP21: Wey 2C **40**
Friars Rd. IP7: Hadl 3G **129**
Friars St. CO10: S'bury 4D **126**
IP1: Ips 4D **4** (1A **138**)
Friars Way IP30: Gt Whe 7D **60**
Friary Mdw. IP32: Bury E 4G **53**
Friday's Orchard IP16: Leis 4H **93**
FRIDAY STREET 3J **89**
Friday St. IP28: W Row 5A **22**
Friends Fld. CO8: Bure 5B **142**
Friends Wlk. IP5: Kesg 5D **134**
FRISTON 6D **92** (1A **166**)
Friston Bus. Cen. IP17: Fris 7D **92**
Friston Rd. IP12: Sutt 3C **140**
Fritillary Cl. IP8: Ips 6G **137**
FRITTON
Belton 1C **167**
Topcroft 1C **161**
Fritton Cl. IP2: Ips 5J **137**
NR32: Oul B 4E **8**
Fritton Ct. CB9: Have 5D **100**
Frobisher Rd. IP3: Ips 5C **138**
Frog Hall La. IP7: Hadl 3J **129**
Frogmore CB8: Exn 2C **46**
Frogs All. IP9: Shot 2C **156**
Frogs Hall Rd.
CO10: Lave 5C **106**
Frogs Hole NR32: Herr 1B **6**
Front Rd. IP3: Ips 6H **139**
Front St. IP12: Orf 6J **125**
IP14: Mendl 2J **71**
FROSTENDEN 4A **44**
Frostenden Cres.
NR32: Low 4G **9**
Fryth Cl. CB9: Have 2F **101**
Fuchsia La. IP4: Ips 1E **138**
Fulcher Cl. IP33: Bury E 4J **59**
Fulchers Fld. IP13: F'ham 5B **90**
Fulford Cl. IP28: Forn M 1F **53**
Fulham Way IP1: Ips 6H **131**
Fullers Cl. IP7: Hadl 3J **129**
Fullers Fld. IP6: Weste 1C **132**
Fullers Teasle NR33: Car C 6A **10**
Fulmar Way NR33: Oul B 4B **10**
Furness Cl. IP2: Ips 6H **137**
Furthest Drove IP27: Lake 7A **20**
Furze Cl. IP31: Thur 6J **55**
Fuzz Nature Reserve, The 5K **129**
Fynn La. IP6: Tud 7D **116** & 1H **133**
Fynn Rd. IP12: Wood 7E **120**
Fynn Valley Golf Course 6B **116**

G

Gables, The CB9: Stur 6K **101**
IP16: Leis 3G **93**
Gaell Cres. IP7: Hadl 4H **129**
Gage Cl. IP32: Bury E 6F **53**
GAINSBOROUGH 4F **139** (2B **164**)
Gainsborough Dr. IP19: H'orth 5A **42**
NR32: Low 2G **9**
Gainsborough Gymnastics Cen.
6F **139**
Gainsborough La. IP3: Ips 6D **138**
Gainsborough Rd. CB9: Have 2C **100**
CO10: S'bury 3D **126**
IP4: Ips 5B **132**
IP11: Felix 4F **155**
IP14: Stowm 4D **84**
IP33: Bury E 1D **58**
Gainsborough's House (Mus.) 4D **126**
Gainsborough Sports & Community Cen.
6F **139**
Gainsborough St.
CO10: S'bury 4D **126**
GAINSFORD END 3B **162**
Gala Bingo
Ipswich 1H **137**
Gallery, The CB8: Newm 5G **47**
Galley Cl. NR33: Car C 5A **10**
Galley La. CO10: Hund 2H **99**
Galley Rd. CO10: Hund 2H **99**
Gallops, The CB8: Newm 6H **47**
Gallows Hill IP7: Hadl 2G **129**
IP22: Redg 1C **34**
Gallows Hill Rd. IP7: Hadl 2F **129**
Galway Av. IP1: Ips 4G **131**
Game Cl. CO10: Gt Cor 7G **127**
Gamma Ter. IP3: Ips 5J **139**
Gandish Cl. CO7: E Ber 5C **146**
Gandish Rd. CO7: E Ber 5C **146**
Ganges Rd. IP9: Shot G 7D **156**
Gannet Cl. CB9: Have 3H **101**
Gannet Rd. IP2: Ips 3G **137**
Ganwick Cl. CB9: Have 1E **100**
Ganymede Cl. IP1: Ips 6F **131**
Gaol La. CO10: S'bury 4D **126**
NR34: Becc 3E **12**
Gap, The NR33: Oul B 3E **10**
GARBOLDISHAM 1A **160**
Garden Cl. IP9: Shot 4B **156**
IP31: Gt Bar 2D **54**
NR32: Low 6G **9**
NR35: Bung 3C **14**
Garden Ct. CB8: Newm 5F **47**
Gardeners Cl. IP7: Lay 7J **129**
Gardeners Rd. IP14: Deb 2H **87**
Gardeners Wlk. IP30: E'well 2D **64**
Garden Fld. IP11: Felix 3D **154**
Garden Flds. IP31: Tros 1D **28**
Garden Ho. La. IP22: Rick 6H **35**
IP30: Drin G 2G **83**
Gardenia Cl. IP12: Rend 5C **122**
Garden La. IP33: W'ley 1A **58**
NR34: Worl 4J **13**
Garden Mdw. Vw. IP14: Cott 6D **68**
Garden Pl. CO10: S'bury 4C **126**
Gardens, The IP14: Old N 5B **70**
IP30: Bey 3C **62**
IP31: Nort 4H **57**
NR33: Car C 7B **10**
Garden Sq. IP12: Rend 5C **122**
Garden Vw. IP28: B Row 1D **22**
Garden Vs. NR32: Low 5J **9**
Gardiner Cl. IP33: Bury E 2C **58**

Gardner Rd. IP18: Sou .4K 45
Garfield Cl. IP11: Felix .5E 154
Garfield Rd. IP11: Felix .5E 154
Garlands Cl. CB9: Have .3B 100
Garland St.
IP33: Bury E .3H 157 (7G 53)
Garrard Pl. IP31: Ixw .5H 29
Garrards, The IP5: Kesg .7B 134
Garrards Rd. IP7: E'sett .7H 113
Garrett Cl. IP17: Snap .2D 94
Garrett Cres. IP16: Leis .4J 93
Garrick Way IP1: Ips .2J 131
GARRISON, THE .7K 107
Garrison La. CO10: Gt Wal .7J 107
IP11: Felix .5E 154
Garrod App. IP12: Melt .7F 119
Garrods IP9: Cap M .2J 147
Garrods End IP29: Chev .4J 51
Gascoigne Dr. IP6: Henl .6J 115
Gas House Drove
IP27: B'don .3G 19
Gaskell Pl. IP2: Ips .5A 4 (1J 137)
GASTHORPE .1D 159
Gaston End CO7: E Ber .3B 146
Gaston St. CO7: E Ber .4B 146
Gas Works Rd. NR32: Low .6K 9
Gatacre Rd. IP1: Ips .1A 4 (6J 131)
Gate Farm Rd. IP9: Shot G .6E 156
Gatekeeper Cl. IP8: Ips .6G 137
Gaye Cres. IP23: Eye .6C 38
Gaye St. IP1: Ips .2B 4 (7K 131)
Gayfer Av. IP5: Kesg .5F 135
Gayford Ct. IP7: Hadl .4H 129
Gaymers La. IP11: T Mary .7H 153
GAZELEY .2G 49 (3B 158)
Gazeley Rd. CB8: Dalh .4G 49
CB8: Gaz, Kent .2B 48 & 1G 49
CB8: Mou .5D 48
GEDDING .4C 82 (1D 163)
Gedding Hill IP30: Ged .5D 82
Gedding Rd.
IP30: Drin, Drin G .1F 83 & 7H 63
Gedge Cl. IP33: Bury E .2C 58
Gedgrave Rd. IP12: Orf .7G 125
GELDESTON .1D 161
General Castle Way IP30: Roug .2F 61
Generals M. IP11: Felix .3C 154
Genesta Dr. IP31: Thur .6J 55
Geneva Av. IP5: Martl H .5J 135
Geneva Rd. IP1: Ips .2C 4 (7K 131)
Genevyll Cl. CO10: Cave .5H 103
Gentle Ct. IP27: B'don .3F 19
Gents La. IP29: Shim .1D 106
George Baldry Way NR35: Bung .4C 14
George Brown Way NR34: Becc .5F 13
George Cl. NR32: Oul B .7D 8
George Frost Cl. IP4: Ips .6B 132
George Gibson Cl. CB8: Exn .1C 46
George Hill IP31: Stant .5C 32
George Hill Units IP31: Stant .5D 32
George Lambton Av.
CB8: Newm .3F 47
George La. CO10: Glem .6A 104
IP13: Wick M .6B 118
IP31: Stant .5D 32
George St. IP7: Hadl .3H 129
IP8: Hint .1C 144
IP27: B'don .4G 19
George Westwood Way
NR34: Becc .1F 13
Georgian Ct. IP11: Felix .2E 154
Geralds Av. IP4: Ips .1E 138
GESTINGTHORPE .3C 163
Gibbon Cl. IP32: Bury E .1A 60
Gibbons St. IP1: Ips .3A 4 (7J 131)
GIBRALTAR .3H 117 (1B 164)
Gibraltar Cl. IP33: Bury E .7C 52
Gibraltar Rd. IP6: Otl .3H 117
Gibson Cl. IP3: Ips .4G 139
Gifford Cl. IP9: Holb .2D 150
Giffords Cl. IP5: Kesg .5E 134
Giffords La. CB8: W'rook .3K 97
Giffords Pl. IP4: Rush A .7K 133
Gilbert Cl. IP6: Nee M .3F 111
Gilbert Rd. CO10: Clar .3C 102
Giles Ct. IP6: Clay .4D 114
Giles Way IP6: Witn .4B 116
IP28: Ris .2E 50
Gilletts Rd. IP19: Wal .1K 75
GILLINGHAM .1C 12 (1C 167)
Gillingham Dam NR34: Gill .1C 12
Gilpin Rd. NR32: Oul B .7C 8
Gilstrap Rd. IP31: Forn M .4H 53
Gin La. IP13: Laxf .7D 74
Gippeswyk Av. IP2: Ips .7A 4 (2J 137)
Gippeswyk Rd. IP2: Ips .7B 4 (2K 137)
GIPPING .4E 70 (3A 160)
Gipping Cl. CB9: Have .5D 100
Gipping Ct. IP1: Ips .6C 4 (2K 137)
Gipping Pl. IP14: Stowm .2F 85
Gipping Rd. IP6: Gt Bla .3B 114
IP14: Stowu .1K 85
Gippingstone Rd. IP8: B'ford .4C 130
Gipping Way IP8: B'ford .3D 130
IP8: Spro .7D 130
IP14: Stowm .4F 85
Gipsies La. IP31: Thur .5E 56
Gipsy La. IP6: Nee M .2F 111
IP6: Otl .1H 117
IP12: Wood .3H 121
IP16: Aldr .7J 93
Girling St. CO10: S'bury .3D 126
Girton Cl. CB8: Newm .7H 47
IP12: Wood .6E 120
IP28: Mide .5J 23
Girton Rd. CB9: Have .4G 101
Girton Way IP2: Ips .5H 137
GISLEHAM .1F 17 (2D 167)
Gisleham Rd. NR33: Gisle .1F 17
GISLINGHAM .1K 67 (2A 160)
Gislingham Rd. IP14: Finn .6H 67
GISSING .1B 160
Glades, The NR32: Oul B .6C 8
Gladstone Rd. IP3: Ips .5K 5 (1D 138)
IP12: Wood .5H 121
NR32: Cort .5H 7
Gladstone Ter. NR34: Becc .4E 12
Glamis Cl. CB9: Have .3C 100
Glamorgan Rd. IP2: Ips .5K 137
Glanely Gdns. CB8: Exn .1C 46
Glanfield Wlk. IP33: Bury E .2C 58
Glanville Pl. IP5: Kesg .7B 134
Glanville Rd. IP7: Hadl .5J 129
Glassfield Rd. IP31: Stant .3E 32
Glastonbury Cl. IP2: Ips .5H 137
Glastonbury Rd. IP33: Bury E .2C 58
Glebe, The CB9: Have .2F 101
CO10: B Ele .1A 108
CO10: Lave .7B 106
IP29: Laws .6B 80
Glebe Cl. IP8: Spro .7D 130
IP9: Tatt .6G 149
IP29: Horr .7B 58
IP31: Ing .5D 28
NR32: Low .3H 9
Glebe End IP9: Cap M .1J 147
Glebe Rd. E. NR33: Kess .5K 17
Glebe Rd. W. NR33: Kess .5J 17
Glebes, The IP17: Snap .2D 94
Glebe Vw. NR34: Becc .5F 13
Glebe Way IP6: Barh .2D 114
IP14: Mendl .3J 71
Glemham Dr. IP4: Rush A .2K 139
GLEMSFORD .4A 104 (2C 163)
Glemsford Cl. IP11: Felix .5C 154
Glemsford Ct. *IP11: Felix .5C 154*
(off Glemsford Cl.)
Glemsford Pl. CB9: Have .3G 101
Glemsford Rd. CO10: Foxe .7B 104
IP14: Stowm .6G 85
NR32: Oul B .4E 8
Glenavon Rd. IP4: Ips .6H 133
Glenbourne Wlk. NR33: Car C .6B 10
Glencoe Rd. IP4: Ips .4G 133
Gleneagles Cl. IP11: Felix .2H 155
IP28: Forn M .1F 53
Gleneagles Dr. IP4: Ips .1H 139
Glenfield Av. IP11: Felix .2F 155
Glenhurst Av. IP4: Ips .5F 133
Glenside CO10: Gt Cor .5F 127
Glenwood NR33: Low .3H 11
Glenwood Ct. *CB8: Newm .6F 47*
(off High St.)
Glenwood Dr. NR34: Worl .4H 13
Glevering Mill Golf Course .4A 118
Global Ct. IP18: Rey .1K 45
Globe Cl. IP28: Mide .6J 23
Globe Yd. *CO10: S'bury .3D 126*
(off Inkerman Row)
Gloster Rd. IP5: Martl H .6H 135
Gloucester Av. NR32: Oul B .5E 8
Gloucester Ho. *IP11: Felix .3D 154*
(off The Walk)
Gloucester Pl. CO10: Clar .3C 102
Gloucester Rd. CB9: Have .5E 100
IP3: Ips .4E 138
IP32: Bury E .5E 52
Gloucester Way CO10: S'bury .1C 126
Goals Soccer Cen.
Ipswich .4G 5 (1B 138)
Gobbetts La. IP22: Hind .5C 34
Gobbitts Yd. *IP12: Wood .5H 121*
(off Thoroughfare)
Godbold Cl. IP5: Kesg .6D 134
Goddard Rd. IP1: Ips .2E 130
Goddard Rd. E. IP1: Ips .2F 131
GODDARD'S CORNER .3C 161
Godetia Ct. NR32: Low .4G 9
Godfrey's Cl. IP29: Horr .7A 58
Godfrey's Ct. *NR32: Low .6J 9*
(off Arnold St.)
Godfrey's Wood IP12: Wood .4H 121
Godolphin Cl. IP33: Bury E .3C 58
Godspeed Gdns. IP2: Ips .3B 138
Godyll Rd. IP18: Sou .4J 45
GOLDBROOK .2C 38
Goldcrest Ct. IP2: Ips .3F 137
Goldcrest Rd. IP2: Ips .3E 136
Golden La. IP29: Laws .5A 80
Goldenlond CO6: Stoke N .2H 143
Golden Miller Cl. CB8: Newm .2D 46
Golden Sq. La. NR34: Wrent .4D 44
Goldfinch Cl. IP14: Stowm .3H 85
Goldings Cl. CB9: Have .1F 101
Golding's La. IP16: Leis .5H 93
Golding Way CO10: Glem .5A 104
Goldsmith Cl. IP32: Bury E .6E 52
Goldsmith Rd. IP1: Ips .1G 131
Golf La. IP15: Aldeb .3G 95
Golf Links Rd.
IP28: B Mil, W'ton .3C 24
Golf Rd. IP11: Felix .3J 155
Gondree NR33: Car C .6D 10
Gonville Cl. IP12: Wood .6F 121
IP28: Mide .5K 23
Goodall Ter. IP5: Kesg .5E 134
Goodman Gro. IP5: Kesg .6E 134
Goodrich Cl. IP14: Cott .6E 68
Goodwin Bus. Pk. CB8: Newm .3E 46
Goodwood Cl. IP1: Ips .1K 131
Goosander Rd. IP14: Stowm .4H 85
Goose Grn. E. NR34: Becc .3F 13
Goose Grn. W. NR34: Becc .3F 13
Gorams Mill La. IP13: Laxf .5B 74
Gordon Richards Cl. CB8: Newm .3F 47
Gordon Rd. IP4: Ips .6E 132
NR32: Low .7J 9
Goring Rd. IP4: Ips .7F 133
GORLESTON-ON-SEA .1D 167
Gorleston Rd. NR32: Cort .6F 7
NR32: Oul, Oul B .7D 8
Gorse Cl. IP27: Lake .7C 20
IP28: Red L .6J 25
Gorse Grn. NR32: Low .5G 9
Gorsehayes IP2: Ips .3K 137
Gorselands IP12: Holl .2G 141
Gorse La. IP12: Sud .1H 125
IP18: Rey .2H 45
Gorse Rd. IP3: Ips .4F 139
IP18: Rey .3J 45
Gorse Vw. IP17: Westl .4J 79
Gorst Cl. IP32: Bury E .5E 52
GOSBECK .1B 164
GOSFIELD .3B 162
Gosford Cl. CO10: Clar .4C 102
Gosford Rd. NR34: Becc .3F 13
Gosford Way IP11: Felix .2H 155
Gosnold St.
IP33: Bury E .4G 157 (1G 59)
Gostling Pl. IP5: Kesg .5E 134
Gotsfield Cl. CO10: Act .3G 107
Gough Pl. IP31: Ixw .5H 29
Goulds Cl. IP22: Pal .1D 36
Governors M. IP33: Bury E .3J 59
Gowers Cl. IP5: Kesg .6E 134
Gowers End CO10: Glem .4B 104
Gower St. IP2: Ips .6E 4 (2A 138)
Gowle Rd. IP14: Stowm .2E 84
Goyfield Av. IP11: Felix .4E 154
Gracechurch St. IP14: Deb .2G 87
Grafton Cl. IP33: Bury E .1D 58
Grafton Way IP1: Ips .5C 4 (1K 137)
Graham Av. IP1: Ips .5K 131
Graham Cl. CB8: Newm .6F 47
Graham Rd. IP1: Ips .6J 131
IP11: Felix .3E 154
Grainger Cl. IP32: Bury E .1B 60
Grainge Way IP14: Haug .2B 70
Grammar School Pl.
CO10: S'bury .4D 126
Grampian Way NR32: Oul .6C 8
Granaries, The IP6: Tud .7D 116
Granary, The *CO8: Bure .5B 142*
(off High St.)
CO10: Clar .6C 102
IP7: Hadl .4J 129
(off Wilson Rd.)
IP12: Orf .7J 125
IP30: E'well .2D 64
Granary Cotts. IP17: Dars .6K 77
Granary Rd. CB8: Newm .7H 47
Granby Gdns. CB8: Newm .6H 47
Granby St. CB8: Newm .6H 47
Grand Av. NR33: Low .6G 11
Grange, The IP27: Lake .6B 20
Grange Bus. Cen. IP5: Kesg .6E 134
Grange Caravan Park, The
CO7: E Ber .2A 148
Grange Cl. IP5: Kesg .5F 135
IP11: Felix .3D 154
Grange Ct. IP12: Melt .4J 121
GRANGE FARM .6C 134
Grange Farm Av. IP11: Felix .4C 154
Grange La. IP5: Kesg .5F 135
IP28: B Mil .3F 25
Grange Mdws. IP30: E'well .2E 64
Grange Mill IP29: Chev .2J 51
Grange Pk. Dr. IP12: Wood .4H 121
Grange Rd. IP4: Ips .4J 5 (7C 132)
IP11: Felix .5C 154
IP23: Wick S .3G 69
NR32: Oul B .6C 8
NR34: Becc .4D 12
Grange Vw. IP17: Westl .6G 79
Grange Wlk. *IP33: Bury E .4H 59*
(off Heron Rd.)
Grannary, The IP4: Ips .5E 4
Grantchester Pl. IP5: Kesg .6A 134
Grantham Av. CO10: Gt Cor .7G 127
Grantham Cres. IP2: Ips .7A 4 (2J 137)
Grant Ri. IP12: Wood .4H 121
Granville Ct. IP6: Hemi .2K 115
Granville Gdns. IP28: Mide .7H 23
Granville Rd. IP11: Felix .5E 154
NR32: Low .7J 9
Granvilles Gdn. IP15: Aldeb .5J 95
Granville St. IP1: Ips .2B 4 (7K 131)
Grapes Farm Yd. IP14: Bac .6A 68
Grasmere Av. IP11: Felix .2J 155
Grasmere Cl. IP3: Ips .6F 139
Grasmere Dr. NR32: Low .4F 9
Gratton Dale NR33: Car C .7D 10
Gravel Dam NR32: Oul .6A 8
Gravel Drove IP28: W Row .6A 22
Gravel Pit La. CO11: Brant .3C 148
Gravel St. CO6: Nay .5J 143
Grayling Rd. IP8: Ips .6G 137
Graylings, The NR33: Car C .5C 10
Grays, The IP20: Mendh .1H 41
Grays Cl. IP7: Hadl .2K 129
IP23: Gisli .2J 67
Grays La. IP17: Benh .2B 92
Grayson Av. NR33: Low .6F 11
Grayson Dr. NR33: Low .7F 11
Gray's Orchard IP10: Kirt .2J 153
GREAT ASHFIELD .5E 66 (3D 159)
Gt. Back La. IP14: Deb .1H 87
GREAT BARDFIELD .3A 162
GREAT BARTON .3E 54 (3C 159)
GREAT BEALINGS .6A 120 (2C 165)
GREAT BLAKENHAM .2A 114 (1B 164)
GREAT BRADLEY .1A 96 (1A 162)
GREAT BRICETT .3A 112 (1A 164)
GREAT BROMLEY .3A 164
Gt. Colman St. IP4: Ips .3F 5 (7B 132)
Gt. Common Rd. NR34: Ilk A .2F 15
GREAT CORNARD .6G 127 (2C 163)
Great Cornard Country Pk. .7H 127
Great Cornard Sports Cen. .7G 127
Gt. Eastern Rd. CO10: S'bury .4E 126
Gt. Eastern Sq. IP11: Felix .3F 155
Great Fld. IP11: T Mary .7J 153
GREAT FINBOROUGH .6J 83 (1A 164)
Gt. Gipping St. IP1: Ips .4C 4 (1K 137)
GREAT GLEMHAM .3D 161
GREAT GREEN
Bury St Edmunds, IP30
.5K 81 (1D 163)
Bury St Edmunds, IP31 .5D 56
Hoxne .2B 160
Topcroft Street .1C 161
Great Harlings IP9: Shot G .6D 156
GREAT HENNY .3C 163
GREAT HOCKHAM .1D 159
GREAT HORKESLEY .3D 163
GREAT LIVERMERE .3B 28 (2C 159)
GREAT MAPLESTEAD .3C 163
GREAT MOULTON .1B 160
GREAT OAKLEY .3B 164
GREAT SAMPFORD .3A 162
GREAT SAXHAM .3B 158
GREAT THURLOW .7C 96 (1A 162)
Great Tufts IP9: Cap M .2J 147
GREAT WALDINGFIELD
.6J 107 (2D 163)
GREAT WENHAM .3A 164
GREAT WHELNETHAM .1C 163
Gt. Whip St. IP2: Ips .6E 4 (2B 138)
GREAT WILBRAHAM .1A 162
GREAT WRATTING .2A 162
GREAT YELDHAM .3B 162
Grebe Cl. IP2: Ips .4G 137
IP14: Stowm .4C 84
IP28: Mide .1G 25
GREEN, THE .7H 45
Green, The CO6: Leav .3A 142
CO6: Pols .5C 144
IP6: A'ing .4F 117
IP7: Gt Bri .3A 112
IP7: Hadl .3J 129
IP13: Gru .6H 117
IP13: Sax G .4C 90
IP14: Men G .7H 71
IP14: Petta .3C 88
IP14: Stowu .1K 85
IP22: Pal .1D 36
IP22: Redg .3D 34
IP23: Wick S .1F 69

Green, The
IP28: Forn S, Forn M, Forn G
. . . 2D 52
IP28: Ris . . . 1C 50
IP28: Tud . . . 5C 26
IP28: W Row . . . 4A 22
IP28: W'ton . . . 3A 24
IP29: Chedb . . . 6K 51
IP29: Dep . . . 7G 51
IP29: Hart . . . 1H 103
IP29: Horr . . . 5B 58
IP30: Bey . . . 3C 62
IP30: Hess . . . 7D 62
IP30: Tost . . . 2G 63
IP31: Bard . . . 2D 32
NR32: S'ton . . . 2C 6
NR33: Oul B . . . 3E 10
NR34: Barnb . . . 5D 6
Green Acre CO10: Gt Wal . . . 7J 107
Greenacre Cres. NR32: Low . . . 6F 9
Greenacres IP14: Old N . . . 6B 70
Greenbank IP19: H'orth . . . 3C 42
Green Cl. IP30: Drin G . . . 1F 83
Green Cres. IP10: Buck . . . 3B 152
Green Dr. NR33: Low . . . 5F 11
Greene King Brewery Mus.
. . . 6J 157 (2H 59)
Greene Rd. IP33: Bury E . . . 7C 52
Green Farm La. IP29: Barr . . . 7B 50
Green Farm Loke NR32: S'ton . . . 1F 7
Greenfield Rd. NR33: Oul B . . . 4E 10
Greenfields CB8: Newm . . . 6J 47
Greenfields Way CB9: Have . . . 4D 100
Greenfinch Av. IP2: Ips . . . 3F 137
Greenfinch Cl. IP14: Stowm . . . 3H 85
Green Fleet Dr. NR32: Oul . . . 4D 8
Greenford Way IP1: Ips . . . 6H 131
Greenham Comn. IP27: RAF L . . . 4H 21
Green Hill IP6: Cod . . . 1H 115
Green La. CB8: Kenn . . . 7H 25
CO7: Strat M, High . . . 4G 145
CO10: Hund . . . 3H 99
IP6: Tud . . . 1G 133 & 7D 116
IP9: Tatt . . . 6H 149
IP12: Martl . . . 3H 135
IP13: Petti, Wick M . . . 1K 119
IP14: E Sto . . . 4E 86
IP14: Finn . . . 7G 67
IP17: Sib . . . 4K 77
IP18: Rey . . . 1H 45
IP20: Harl, Rede . . . 1F 41
IP28: Red L . . . 7G 25
IP30: C'field . . . 5K 81
IP31: Barni . . . 1E 30
IP31: Gt Bar . . . 5D 54
IP31: Honi . . . 4F 29
NR32: S'ton . . . 1F 7
NR33: Kess . . . 5K 17
NR34: Barnb . . . 7C 6
Green La. Cl. IP18: Rey . . . 1H 45
Green Man Pl. IP12: Tun . . . 6F 123
Green Man Way IP12: Melt . . . 4J 121
Green Oak Glade IP8: Ips . . . 6F 137
Green Rd. CB8: Newm . . . 7G 47
CB9: Have . . . 3H 101
IP14: Haug . . . 2B 70
IP27: B'don . . . 5G 19
IP30: Wool . . . 5A 64
Greens, The IP4: Rush A . . . 2K 139
IP15: Aldeb . . . 3G 95
Greens Cotts. IP22: Redg . . . 3D 34
Greenspire Gro. IP8: Ips . . . 5D 136
GREENSTEAD GREEN . . . 3C 163
GREEN STREET . . . 1D 38 (2B 160)
Green St. IP21: Hox . . . 1C 38
GREENSTREET GREEN . . . 2A 164
Greenview IP29: Hart . . . 1J 103
Greenway IP31: Gt Bar . . . 3D 54
Greenway, The NR34: Becc . . . 4E 12
Greenways IP12: Sutt . . . 3C 140
Greenways Cl. IP1: Ips . . . 5K 131
Greenways Cres. IP32: Bury E . . . 7K 53
GREENWICH . . . 4C 138
Greenwich Bus. Pk. IP3: Ips . . . 4C 138
Greenwich Cl. IP3: Ips . . . 4C 138
Greenwich Rd. IP3: Ips . . . 4B 138
Greenwood Cl. CB9: Have . . . 4D 100
Greenwood Ct. IP32: Bury E . . . 1C 60
Greenwoods, The IP31: Pake . . . 2A 56
Greenwood Way NR32: Low . . . 1F 9
Gregory Rd. IP28: Mide . . . 5G 23
Gregory St. CO10: S'bury . . . 4D 126
Grenadier Rd. CB9: Have . . . 3B 100
Grenville Rd. CO10: S'bury . . . 1E 126
Gresham Av. NR32: Oul B . . . 6E 8
Gresham Cl. NR32: Oul B . . . 6E 8
Gresham Ct. IP1: Ips . . . 5K 131
Gresham Rd. NR34: Becc . . . 2E 12
Gresley Gdns. IP2: Ips . . . 3A 138
Gressland Ct. *IP5: Kesg* . . . *6C 134*
(off Mead Dr.)
Gresswell Ct. IP5: Martl H . . . 7H 135
Gretna Gdns. IP4: Ips . . . 4F 133
Greville Starkey Av. CB8: Newm . . . 4F 47
Greyfriars IP1: Ips . . . 4D 4
IP12: Wood . . . 7E 120
Greyfriars Priory (remains of) . . . 2K 79
Grey Friars Rd. IP1: Ips . . . 5D 4 (1A 138)
Greyfriars Rd. IP32: Bury E . . . 2A 60
Greyhound Cnr. IP6: Clay . . . 4D 114
Greyhound La. IP22: Hop . . . 3G 31
Greyhound Rd. CO10: Glem . . . 6A 104
Greys Cl. CO10: Cave . . . 6G 103
Grice Cl. NR33: Kess . . . 4K 17
Griffin Ct. IP2: Ips . . . 7F 5
Griffin La. IP14: Broc S . . . 4G 69
Griffith Cl. NR33: Kess . . . 4K 17
Grime Drove IP27: Lake . . . 2A 20
Grimsey Rd. IP16: Leis . . . 4J 93
Grimsey's La. IP16: Leis, Size . . . 5K 93
GRIMSTONE END . . . 7K 29 (3D 159)
Grimston La. IP11: T Mart . . . 7F 153
(not continuous)
Grimwade Cl. CO11: Brant . . . 6C 148
Grimwade St. IP4: Ips . . . 5G 5 (1B 138)
Grindle, The IP8: B'ford . . . 6B 130
Grindle Gdns. IP33: Bury E . . . 3H 59
Grinstead Gdns. IP6: Nee M . . . 5H 111
GRINSTEAD HILL . . . 5H 111
Grinstead Hill IP6: Nee M . . . 5H 111
GROMFORD . . . 1B 94 (1D 165)
Gromford La. IP17: Snap . . . 1B 94
Grosvenor Cl. IP4: Ips . . . 5C 132
Grosvenor Ct. IP3: Ips . . . 5F 139
Grosvenor Gdns. IP33: Bury E . . . 3F 59
Grosvenor Ho. Ct. IP28: Mide . . . 6H 23
Grosvenor Rd. CO10: S'bury . . . 1C 126
NR33: Low . . . 2H 11
Grosvenor Yd. CB8: Newm . . . 6G 47
GROTON . . . 4B 128 (2D 163)
Groton St. CO10: Gro . . . 4B 128
Grove, The IP1: Ips . . . 3A 132
IP5: Martl H . . . 5G 135
IP12: Wood . . . 5J 121
IP14: Stowm . . . 5G 85
IP28: B Row . . . 1B 22
NR35: Bung . . . 3D 14
Grove Av. CO10: L Wal . . . 5C 108
Grove Gdns. IP12: Wood . . . 4F 121
NR33: Car C . . . 5B 10
Grove Hill IP8: Bels, Ips . . . 7E 136
Grove Ho. IP8: Ips . . . 5F 137
Grove La. IP4: Ips . . . 4J 5 (1C 138)
IP9: Chelm . . . 4G 151
IP12: Orf . . . 5H 125
IP21: Stus . . . 3F 37
IP30: E'well . . . 1G 65
IP31: Stant . . . 7E 32
Grove M. IP11: Felix . . . 3E 154
Grove Pk. IP31: Wals W . . . 6H 33
IP33: Bury E . . . 7F 53
Grove Rd. CO11: Brant . . . 5C 148
IP9: Bent . . . 6H 147
IP11: Felix . . . 2F 155
IP12: Wood . . . 4F 121
IP13: Petti . . . 1G 119
IP17: Fris, Knod . . . 6D 92
IP31: Wals W . . . 6G 33
IP33: Bury E . . . 7F 53
NR32: Low . . . 1J 11
NR33: Car C . . . 5B 10
NR34: Becc . . . 3F 13
Grove Rd. Nth. NR33: Car C . . . 4C 10
Grovesbury End NR33: Car C . . . 5B 10
Groveside IP17: Yox . . . 6H 77
Grove Wlk. IP8: Ips . . . 6F 137
GRUNDISBURGH . . . 6H 117 (1C 165)
Grundisburgh Rd. IP6: Tud . . . 7D 116
IP12: Wood . . . 5F 121
IP13: Burg . . . 4J 117
IP13: Hask . . . 3A 120
Grundle Cl. IP31: Stant . . . 6D 32
Guildhall
Hadleigh . . . 4H 129
Guildhall La. NR34: Wrent . . . 3B 44
Guildhall Rd. NR34: Worl . . . 4K 13
Guildhall St.
IP33: Bury E . . . 5G 157 (1G 59)
Guilding's La. IP17: Snap . . . 1D 94
Guillemot Cl. IP14: Stowm . . . 4H 85
Guineas, The CB8: Newm . . . 5G 47
Guineas Cl. CB8: Newm . . . 3E 46
Gules Grn. La. IP21: Fress . . . 6D 40
Gull, The IP13: Dall, Dall . . . 4E 118
Gull Corner IP13: Gru . . . 5F 117
GULLING GREEN . . . 1C 163
Gull La. IP13: Gru . . . 5F 117
Gull Rd. IP17: Saxm . . . 6G 91
Gull St. IP21: Fress . . . 6C 40
Gulpher Bus. Pk. IP11: Felix . . . 1E 154
Gulpher Rd.
IP11: Felix . . . 2D 154 & 1G 155
Gunary Cl. CO10: Boxf . . . 6B 128
Gun Cotton Way IP14: Stowm . . . 4H 85
Gun Hill . . . 5K 45
Gun Hill CO7: Ded, Lang . . . 7F 145
Gun La. IP11: T Mart . . . 7G 153
NR32: Low . . . 6K 9
GUNTON . . . 4H 9
Gunton Av. NR32: Low . . . 1F 9
Gunton Church La. NR32: Low . . . 3H 9
Gunton Cliff NR32: Low . . . 3J 9
Gunton Dr. NR32: Low . . . 2J 9
Gunton Hall Resort NR32: Low . . . 1G 9
Gunton St Peter's Av. NR32: Low . . . 3H 9
Gurdon Rd. IP13: Gru . . . 5J 117
Gurlings Cl. CB9: Have . . . 1F 101
Guscott Cl. NR32: Low . . . 2F 9
Guston Gdns. IP10: Kirt . . . 2J 153
Guthrum Rd. IP7: Hadl . . . 3H 129
Guthrums Mdw. IP15: Aldeb . . . 3G 95
Guy Cook Cl. CO10: Gt Cor . . . 6H 127
Gwendoline Cl. IP4: Rush A . . . 2J 139
Gwendoline Rd. IP4: Rush A . . . 2J 139
Gwydyr Rd. IP2: Ips . . . 2G 137
Gymnasium St. IP1: Ips . . . 2B 4 (6K 131)
Gypsy La. CO10: Ball . . . 4A 126

H

HACHESTON . . . 1D 165
Hackney Rd. IP12: Melt . . . 4J 121
IP17: Pea . . . 3H 77
Hackney's Cnr. IP6: Gt Bla . . . 2A 114
Hackney Ter. IP12: Melt . . . 4J 121
HADDISCOE . . . 1C 167
Haddon App. IP12: Sutt . . . 7K 121
Hadenham Rd. NR33: Low . . . 7E 10
HADLEIGH . . . 3H 129 (2A 164)
Hadleigh Dr. NR32: Oul B . . . 5E 8
Hadleigh Ent. Pk. IP7: Hadl . . . 1J 129
Hadleigh Hall IP7: Hadl . . . 3G 129
HADLEIGH HEATH . . . 2D 163
Hadleigh High Leisure Cen. . . . 4K 129
Hadleigh Railway Walk
Local Nature Reserve . . . 6K 129
Hadleigh Rd.
CO7: E Ber, H Mar, Strat M . . . 1A 146
CO10: Boxf . . . 7D 128
IP2: Ips . . . 1F 137
IP7: Aldh, E'sett . . . 7G 113
IP7: Ned . . . 7J 109
IP7: Ray . . . 4F 145
IP8: Spro, Ips . . . 2C 136
(not continuous)
Hadleigh Rd. Ind. Est. IP2: Ips . . . 7H 131
Hadleigh Swimming Pool & Health Suite
. . . 3H 129
Hadrian Cl. CB9: Have . . . 4J 101
HADSTOCK . . . 2A 162
Haggar La. IP23: Thorn . . . 2B 72
Haggars Mead IP14: Forw G . . . 1A 86
Hague Cl. NR33: Car C . . . 4B 10
Hailes Mdw. IP14: Haug . . . 3C 70
Hailey's Ct. *NR33: Low* . . . *3H 11*
(off London Rd. Sth.)
Halcyon Cres. NR32: Low . . . 7H 9
Hale Cl. IP2: Ips . . . 4F 137
Hales Barn Rd. CB9: Have . . . 1D 100
Hales Barn Workshops
IP21: Stradb . . . 6F 39
Halesowen Cl. IP2: Ips . . . 6H 137
HALESWORTH . . . 4B 42 (2D 161)
Halesworth Airfield Mus. . . . 2E 42
Halesworth Gallery . . . 5B 42
Halesworth Golf Course . . . 7D 42
Halesworth Mus. . . . 4B 42
Halesworth Outdoor Swimming Pool
. . . 4C 42
Halesworth Rd. IP17: Sib . . . 1J 77
IP18: Rey . . . 2F 45
IP19: B'field . . . 4H 75
IP19: Cook, Wal . . . 1J 75
IP19: Hev . . . 3C 74
IP19: Wal . . . 2H 75
NR34: Bramp . . . 7G 15
NR34: Ugg . . . 7K 15
Halesworth Station (Rail) . . . 4B 42
Halfields IP27: Lake . . . 4A 20
Half Moon Cl. IP22: Hep . . . 7D 30
Half Moon La. IP13: Gru . . . 6J 117
IP22: Redg . . . 3D 34
Halfmoon La. IP27: Lake . . . 4A 20
Half Moon St. IP30: Rat . . . 4K 83
Halford Ct. IP8: Ips . . . 4E 136
Halifax Rd. IP2: Ips . . . 4K 137
IP28: RAF M . . . 2C 22
Halifax St. IP27: RAF L . . . 3H 21
Halifax Way CB8: Newm . . . 4E 46
Hall Cl. IP27: B'don . . . 3F 19
IP29: Dep . . . 7G 51
Hall Close, The IP28: Ick . . . 2C 26
Hall Dr. IP27: Lake . . . 4A 20
NR32: Oul B . . . 7B 8
Hall Farm Cl. IP12: Melt . . . 2J 121
Hall Farm La. IP15: Aldeb . . . 4H 95
IP33: W'ley . . . 7A 52
NR34: Hens . . . 6C 16
Hall Farm Rd. IP12: Melt . . . 2J 121
IP13: Gt Bea . . . 6A 120
Hall Fld. IP11: Felix . . . 3C 154
HALL GREEN . . . 1B 160
Hallifax Pl. IP29: Shim . . . 1E 106
Halliwell Rd. IP4: Ips . . . 7F 133
Hall La. CO7: L Wen . . . 1F 147
IP6: Witn . . . 4B 116
IP8: S'ham . . . 3J 113
IP9: Cap M . . . 1F 147
IP14: W'sett . . . 7J 69
IP22: Redg . . . 3D 34
IP23: Yax . . . 7D 36
IP28: Ris . . . 1C 50
NR32: Blun . . . 2J 7
NR32: Oul . . . 4B 8
Hallmark Cl. IP27: Lake . . . 6B 20
Hall Pond Way IP11: Felix . . . 3C 154
Hall Ri. CO10: Ball . . . 6B 126
Hall Rd. CB9: Ked . . . 5C 98
CO10: B Ele . . . 1A 108
CO10: Borl . . . 1A 126
CO10: Hund . . . 1J 99
CO10: Lave . . . 6B 106
IP5: Kesg . . . 3E 134
IP10: Foxh . . . 1A 152
IP13: Char . . . 3A 118
IP13: Kesg, L Bea . . . 3E 134
IP14: Stowm . . . 2D 84
IP19: Wen . . . 3J 43
IP23: Thorn . . . 4D 72
NR32: Blun . . . 3H 7
NR32: Oul B . . . 7B 8
NR33: Car C, Gisle, Rushm
. . . 7A 10
NR33: Kess . . . 4K 17
NR34: Bars, Ilk A . . . 5A 12
Halls Drift IP5: Kesg . . . 7B 134
Hall's La. IP31: Nort . . . 3H 57
Hall St. CO10: L Mel . . . 3H 105
Hall Wlk. IP8: B'ford . . . 3B 130
Hallwyck Gdns. CB8: Newm . . . 7F 47
HALSTEAD . . . 3C 163
Halton Cres. IP3: Ips . . . 5G 139
Hamblin Rd. IP12: Wood . . . 6J 121
Hamblin Wlk. IP12: Wood . . . 5J 121
Hambrook Cl. IP30: Gt Whe . . . 7C 60
Hambros, The IP31: Thur . . . 6J 55
Hamilton Ct. CB8: Newm . . . 7E 46
Hamilton Gdns. IP11: Felix . . . 5F 155
Hamilton Ho. IP4: Ips . . . 6E 132
Hamilton Rd. CB8: Newm . . . 4D 46
CO10: S'bury . . . 4D 126
IP3: Ips . . . 3F 139
IP11: Felix . . . 4F 155
NR32: Low . . . 7K 9
Hamiltons, The CB8: Newm . . . 7F 47
Hamilton St. IP11: Felix . . . 3D 154
Hamilton Way IP14: Stowm . . . 3F 85
Hamlet Ct. CO8: Bure . . . 6A 142
Hamlet Grn. CB9: Have . . . 5G 101
Hamlet Pk. CB9: Have . . . 5G 101
Hamlet Rd. CB9: Have . . . 4F 101
Hammer's La. IP31: Tros . . . 1D 28
Hammersmith Way IP1: Ips . . . 6G 131
Hammond Cl. CB8: Newm . . . 3E 46
Hammonds Wlk. IP19: Wen . . . 3J 43
HAMPERDEN END . . . 3A 162
Hampstead Av. IP28: Mide . . . 5H 23
Hampton Rd. IP1: Ips . . . 6H 131
Hanbury Cl. IP19: H'orth . . . 6A 42
Hanbury Paddocks IP28: Ris . . . 2D 50
Hanchet Sq.
IP33: Bury E . . . 5G 157 (1G 59)
Hanchett End CB9: Have . . . 2A 100
HANCHETT VILLAGE . . . 3B 100
Hancocks Cl. IP16: Leis . . . 4J 93
Handford Cut IP1: Ips . . . 3A 4 (7J 131)
Handford Rd. IP1: Ips . . . 3A 4 (7J 131)
Hanmer Av. IP28: Mide . . . 6J 23
Hanmer Wlk. IP33: Bury E . . . 1C 58
HANNINGFIELDS GREEN . . . 7E 80
Hanover Cl. CB8: Newm . . . 1E 46
IP32: Bury E . . . 5F 53
NR33: Oul B . . . 4E 10
Hanover Ct. CO10: S'bury . . . 5C 126
IP4: Ips . . . 2J 5 (7C 132)
IP30: E'well . . . 2D 64
Ha'penny Dr. IP9: Holb . . . 3D 150
Ha'penny Fld. IP9: Holb . . . 3D 150
Harbourage, The NR34: Becc . . . 4F 13
Harbour Rd. NR32: Oul B . . . 7D 8
Harbour Rd. Ind. Est.
NR32: Oul B . . . 1D 10
Harding's La. IP31: Nort . . . 7C 66
Hardpiece La. IP17: Westl . . . 6J 79
HARDWICK . . . 1C 161
Hardwick Cl. IP4: Rush A . . . 1J 139
Hardwick La. IP33: Bury E . . . 4F 59

Hardwick Pk. Gdns.
IP33: Bury E 5G **59**
Hardwick Rd. CB9: Have 3G **101**
Hardwick Shop. Cen.
IP33: Bury E 4H **59**
Hardy Cl. CO11: Brant 6B **148**
NR33: Oul B 2F **11**
Hardy Ct. CO10: S'bury 1E **126**
Hardy Cres. IP1: Ips 1H **131**
Harebell Rd. IP2: Ips 2H **137**
IP28: Red L 5J **25**
Harebell Way NR33: Car C 4B **10**
Harefield CO10: L Mel 1J **105**
Harepark Cl. IP19: H'orth 5A **42**
Hares Cl. IP5: Kesg 7C **134**
Hares Wlk. CO10: S'bury 2E **126**
Harewood Ter. CB9: Have 4E **100**
HARGATE 1B **160**
HARGRAVE 2G **51** (1B **162**)
Hargrave Av. IP6: Nee M 5G **111**
Hargrave Rd. IP29: Chev 2H **51**
HARKSTEAD 6H **151** (3B **164**)
Harkstead Rd. IP9: Holb 4F **151**
Harland St. IP2: Ips 3A **138**
HARLESTON
Starston 1C **161**
Stowmarket 3A **160**
Harleston Hill IP21: Fress 4C **40**
Harleston Rd. IP20: Metf 5F **41**
IP21: Fress 6C **40**
IP21: Wey 1D **40**
Harling Drove IP27: Weet 1G **19**
HARLING ROAD 1D **159**
Harling Way IP16: Leis 3G **93**
Harmer Pl. IP22: W'field 3H **33**
Harold Rd. NR33: Low 3H **11**
Harp Cl. Rd. CO10: S'bury 3E **126**
Harper's Est. CO6: Nay 6H **143**
Harper's Hill CO6: Nay 5G **143**
Harpers La. IP17: Saxm 6H **91**
Harp's Cl. Rd. NR32: Low 5G **9**
Harpur's Rd. CO10: Glem 5A **104**
Harrier Cl. IP3: Ips 5F **139**
Harrier Dr. NR33: Oul B 4D **10**
Harrier Way IP14: Stowm 4J **85**
IP28: B Row 1C **22**
Harrington Av. NR32: Low 2H **9**
Harrington Cl.
IP33: Bury E 7K **157** (2H **59**)
Harris Av. NR32: Low 4H **9**
Harris Ct. IP14: Deb 2H **87**
Harrison Grn. IP18: Rey 1J **45**
Harrison Gro. IP5: Kesg 5C **134**
Harrison Rd. NR32: Oul B 7D **8**
NR33: Low 7F **11**
Harrisons La. IP19: H'orth 3C **42**
Harris Way NR34: Becc 4F **13**
Harrod Cl. NR33: Low 2H **11**
Harrop Dale NR33: Car C 6D **10**
Harrow Cl. IP4: Ips 1E **138**
HARROW GREEN 6B **80**
Harrow Grn. IP29: Laws 6B **80**
Harrow La. IP16: Leis 1F **93**
IP17: Benh 4A **92**
Harrow Rd. CB9: Have 4D **100**
Harrow St. CO6: Leav 1B **142**
Harry Chamberlain Ct.
NR32: Low 4G **9**
Hart Cl. CB9: Have 2E **100**
HARTEST 1H **103** (1C **163**)
HARTEST HILL 1J **103**
Hartest La. IP29: Laws 6A **80**
Hartest Way CO10: Gt Cor 5G **127**
IP14: Stowm 7H **85**
Hartington Rd. IP15: Aldeb 6J **95**
Hartismere Ho. IP13: Laxf 6B **74**
Hartismere Sports Cen. 6B **38**
Hartley St. IP2: Ips 7E **4**
Hartree Way IP5: Kesg 6E **134**
HART'S GREEN 5E **80**
Hartshall La. IP31: Wals W 7K **33**
Harts La. IP22: Wort 2J **35**
Harvest Cl. IP14: Haug 2C **70**
Harvest Ct. IP11: Felix 4G **155**
NR33: Low 7E **10**
Harvest Dr. NR33: Low 7E **10**
Harvester La. IP28: B Row 1D **22**
Harvesters Way
IP5: Martl H 7F **135**
Harvest Ho. IP11: Felix 4G **155**
Harveys Cl. IP22: Rick 6H **35**
Harvey's La. IP6: Barh 5F **115**
Harvey Way IP12: Rend 6B **122**
HARWICH 3C **165**
Harwood Ter. *CB8: Newm 6G 47*
(off Mill Hill)
Haselmere Cl. IP32: Bury E 7K **53**
HASKETON 2C **120** (1C **165**)
Hasketon Rd. IP12: Wood 4F **121**
IP13: Burg 5K **117**
Haskins Wlk. IP5: Kesg 6E **134**
Haslemere Dr. IP4: Ips 2J **5** (7C **132**)
Hassell's Courtyard
CO10: L Mel 1H **105**
Hasted Cl. IP33: Bury E 2C **58**
Hatchley Cl. IP12: Sutt 2C **140**
Hatfield Rd. IP3: Ips 2E **138**
Hatter St. IP33: Bury E 5H **157** (1G **59**)
Hatton Ct. IP1: Ips 3E **4**
Haughgate Cl. IP12: Wood 4G **121**
Haugh La. IP12: Wood 3G **121**
IP14: Old N 1E **70**
IP31: Gt Ash 7E **66**
HAUGHLEY 2B **70** (3A **160**)
Haughley Dr. IP4: Rush A 7K **133**
HAUGHLEY GREEN 3A **160**
HAUGHLEY NEW STREET 5J **65**
Haughley Pk. 5G **65**
Haughley Rd. IP14: Harl 7K **65**
Hauliers Rd. IP11: Felix 6C **154**
Haven, The IP16: Thor 6D **94**
Haven, The (Local Nature Reserve)
7D **94**
Haven Av. NR32: Low 5G **9**
Havenbeach Marshes Caravan Pk.
IP18: Sou 6J **45**
Haven Cl. IP11: Felix 4C **154**
IP33: Bury E 3J **59**
Haven Ct. *NR32: Low 6K 9*
(off Crown St. E.)
Haven Exchange IP11: Felix 6C **154**
Haven Exchange Sth.
IP11: Felix 6C **154**
Haven Rd. IP16: Leis 4J **93**
Havens, The IP3: Ips 7J **139**
Havergate Rd. IP3: Ips 6H **139**
HAVERHILL 4F **101** (2A **162**)
Haverhill Arts Cen. 4F **101**
Haverhill Golf Course 5K **101**
Haverhill Indoor Bowls Club 4G **101**
Haverhill Rd. CB9: Ked, L Wrat 5A **98**
CB9: L Wrat 1G **101**
Haverhill Snooker & Bowl 5H **101**
Haverhill Sports Cen. 3G **101**
Haward St. NR32: Low 7H **9**
Hawbridge IP9: Cap M 1H **147**
Hawe's La. IP31: Nort 4G **57**
Hawes St. IP2: Ips 7F **5** (3B **138**)
Hawk Cl. IP28: B Row 1C **22**
HAWKEDON 1B **162**
HAWK END 1D **64**
Hawk End La. IP30: E'well 1D **64**
Hawker Dr. IP5: Martl H 5H **135**
Hawke Rd. IP3: Ips 5C **138**
Hawkes La. IP11: Felix 2C **154**
Hawkins Ct. CO10: S'bury 1E **126**
Hawkins Rd. CO10: S'bury 1F **127**
Hawks Mill St. IP6: Nee M 3G **111**
HAWSTEAD 1C **163**
Hawstead La. IP30: S'mere 6C **60**
Hawthorn Av. NR33: Oul B 3E **10**
Hawthorn Bus. Cen.
CO10: Boxf 7E **128**
Hawthorn Cl. IP14: Stowu 2J **85**
IP17: Knod 7G **93**
IP28: Red L 6J **25**
IP32: Bury E 5D **52**
NR34: Worl 4H **13**
Hawthorn Dr. IP2: Ips 4E **136**
IP29: Horr 6B **58**
Hawthorn La. IP27: RAF L 5G **21**
Hawthorn Pl. IP12: Wood 4F **121**
Hawthorn Rd. CB9: Have 2C **100**
CO10: Gt Cor 4G **127**
IP17: Midd 7C **78**
Hawthorns, The CO10: S'bury 1F **127**
IP31: Thur 6J **55**
Hawthorn Wlk. IP28: B Row 1E **22**
Hawthorn Way CO6: Leav 2A **142**
Hay Barn Mdw. IP30: Wool 4A **64**
Haycocks Rd. CB9: Have 2B **100**
Haygate IP23: Eye 6C **38**
Hayhill Rd. IP4: Ips 1H **5** (6C **132**)
Haylings Gro. IP16: Leis 5H **93**
Haylings Rd. IP16: Leis 5H **93**
Hayman Rd. IP3: Ips 5D **138**
Haynings Mill IP13: F'ham 5D **90**
Haysborder Rd. IP29: Barr 4A **50**
Hayward Cl. IP23: Eye 7D **38**
Haywards Flds. IP5: Kesg 5D **134**
Haywards M. IP17: Saxm 6J **91**
Hazel Cl. CB9: Have 4D **100**
IP12: Rend 5D **122**
IP28: Mide 7K **23**
Hazelcroft Rd. IP1: Ips 3J **131**
Hazel Dr. IP3: Pur F 5J **139**
IP29: Horr 7B **58**
Hazell Ct. *CO10: S'bury 3E 126*
(off Acton La.)
Hazelnut Cl. IP5: Rush A 4J **133**
Hazel Ri. IP6: Clay 4D **114**
Hazel Rd. IP32: Bury E 7C **54**
Hazel Shrub IP9: Bent 7G **147**
Hazel Wlk. IP28: Red L 5K **25**
Hazelwood IP7: E'sett 6H **113**
Hazelwood Cl. IP31: Thur 6K **55**
Hazlitt Rd. IP1: Ips 2J **131**
Headingham Cl. IP2: Ips 4J **137**
Headland Av. CB9: Have 4D **100**
Headlands, The *IP16: Thor 6D 94*
(off Admirals Wlk.)
Head La. CO10: Gt Cor 7F **127**
Head Way CO10: S'bury 1C **126**
Healey Cl. NR32: Low 2F **9**
Heasman Cl. CB8: Newm 4F **47**
HEATH, THE 7F **149** (3B **164**)
Heath, The IP30: B Grn, Wool 7D **64**
Heathbell Rd. CB8: Newm 6J **47**
Heath Cl. CO7: E Ber 3C **146**
IP30: Hess 7C **62**
Heathcote Pl. CB8: Newm 6H **47**
Heath Ct. IP11: T Mart 5H **153**
IP28: B Row 1F **23**
IP31: Thur 6K **55**
Heather Av. IP3: Ips 3G **139**
Heather Cl. IP5: Martl H 7F **135**
IP31: Thur 5J **55**
Heather Ct. IP28: B Row 1F **23**
Heathercroft Rd. IP1: Ips 2J **131**
Heatherhayes IP2: Ips 3J **137**
Heather Rd. NR32: Low 4J **9**
Heatherset Way IP28: Red L 6H **25**
Heather Way IP27: B'don 4H **19**
NR34: Worl 5J **13**
Heath Est. CO10: Gt Wal 6K **107**
Heath Farm Bus. Cen.
IP28: Forn S 5B **52**
Heath Farm Rd. IP28: Red L 6G **25**
Heathfield IP5: Martl H 7F **135**
Heathfield M. IP5: Martl H 7F **135**
Heathfield Rd. IP9: Holb 3D **150**
Heathfields IP11: T Mart 4G **153**
Heathgate Piece IP11: T Mary 7J **153**
Heathland Beach Caravan Pk.
NR33: Kess 2K **17**
Heathland Retreat Caravan Pk.
IP4: Rush A 2J **139**
Heathlands CO6: Leav 2A **142**
IP18: Rey 3G **45**
IP28: B Row 1G **23**
Heathlands Pk. IP4: Rush A 2J **139**
Heathland Way IP28: Mide 6K **23**
Heath La. IP4: Ips 1G **139**
IP31: Gt Bar 7F **29**
NR32: Blun 1H **7**
Heath Rd. CB8: Exn 6A **46**
CB8: Newm 6J **47**
CB25: Burw 6A **46**
CO6: Pols 5C **144**
CO7: E Ber 3C **146**
IP4: Ips 6G **133**
IP19: Wen 1G **43**
IP27: B'don 4G **19**
IP28: Mide 6K **23**
IP30: Hess 7B **62**
IP30: Wool 5B **64**
IP31: Nort 5G **57**
IP31: Sap 1K **29**
IP31: Thur 6J **55**
IP31: Tros 1C **28**
NR33: Oul B 1E **10**
Heath Vw. IP5: Kesg 7A **134**
IP16: Leis 4K **93**
IP17: Westl 4J **79**
Heath Wlk. IP12: Blax 2H **123**
Heathway CO10: Gt Wal 6J **107**
HECKFIELD GREEN 4D **38** (2B **160**)
HEDENHAM 1D **161**
Hedgerows, The NR32: Blun 1H **7**
Hedley La. NR33: Car C 6A **10**
Heigham Dr. NR33: Oul B 4E **10**
Heighams IP29: Barr 7B **50**
Heighams La. IP22: Hind 6B **34**
Heights, The NR34: Becc 4F **13**
Heldhaw Rd. IP32: Bury E 1A **60**
Helena Rd. IP3: Ips 7H **5** (2C **138**)
Helens Cl. IP22: Redg 3C **34**
HELIONS BUMPSTEAD 2A **162**
Helions Bumpstead Rd.
CB9: Have 7E **100**
Helions Pk. Av. CB9: Have 4F **101**
Helions Pk. Gdns. CB9: Have 4F **101**
Helions Pk. Gro. CB9: Have 4F **101**
Helions Service Rd.
CB9: Have 4F **101**
Helions Wlk. CB9: Have 4F **101**
Hellesdon Ct. IP27: B'don 3F **19**
HELMINGHAM 1B **164**
Helmingham Hall Gdns. 1B **164**
Helmingham Rd. IP6: A'ing 2G **117**
IP6: Otl 1K **117**
Helston Cl. IP5: Kesg 7B **134**
Hembling Ter. IP13: Cam A 3A **122**
HEMINGSTONE 3K **115** (1B **164**)
HEMLEY 2C **165**
Hemplands, The NR32: Low 5K **9**
HEMPNALL GREEN 1C **161**
HEMP'S GREEN 3D **163**
HEMPSTEAD 3A **162**
Hempstead Rd. CB9: Have 2B **100**
Hencote La. IP29: Bury E 6F **59**
Henderson Cl. CB9: Have 2B **100**
IP8: B'ford 4C **130**
HENGRAVE 3C **159**
Hengrave Cl. IP2: Ips 4J **137**
Hengrave Rd. IP28: Forn S 1C **52**
HENHAM 3A **162**
Henham Rd. NR32: Low 3F **9**
Hening Av. IP3: Ips 6H **139**
HENLEY 6J **115** (1B **164**)
Henley Av. IP1: Ips 2K **131**
Henley Cl. IP17: Saxm 6H **91**
Henley Ct. IP1: Ips 5A **132**
Henley Rd. IP1: Ips 1D **4** (1K **131**)
IP6: Aken, Henl 6J **115**
Henniker Rd. IP1: Ips 5E **130**
IP14: Deb 2H **87**
HENNY STREET 3C **163**
Henry Cl. CB9: Have 5C **100**
Henry Rd. IP3: Ips 5F **139**
Henry St. IP14: Deb 2G **87**
Henry Watson's Potteries 1J **33**
Henslow Rd. IP4: Ips 1F **139**
HENSTEAD 6C **16** (2C **167**)
Henstead Gdns. IP3: Ips 4E **138**
HEPWORTH 7D **30** (2D **159**)
Hepworth Av. IP33: Bury E 1E **58**
Hepworth Rd. IP22: Hep 4B **30**
IP31: Barni 3D **30**
IP31: Stant 7D **32**
Herbert Cl. CO10: S'bury 1F **127**
Herbert Rd. IP5: Kesg 5E **134**
Hercules Rd. IP12: Rend 6D **122**
Hereford Dr. IP6: Clay 3E **114**
Hereward Av. IP28: Mide 7J **23**
Heritage Cl. NR33: Kess 4H **17**
Heritage Grn. NR33: Kess 4H **17**
Heritage Workshop Cen.
NR32: Low 6K 9
(off Cumberland Pl.)
Herivan Cl. NR32: Oul 4D **8**
Herivan Gdns. NR32: Oul 4D **8**
Hermitage Ct. CO10: Clar 3D **102**
IP13: F'ham 6B **90**
Hermitage Mdw.
CO10: Clar 3D **102**
Heron Av. IP27: B'don 4H **19**
Heron Cl. IP14: Stowm 4C **84**
IP28: B Row 1C **22**
Heron Rd. IP2: Ips 3G **137**
IP17: Saxm 6G **91**
IP33: Bury E 4H **59**
Herons Cl. NR32: Oul B 6C **8**
Herons Way IP17: Benh 3C **92**
Herring Fishery Score
NR32: Low 7K **9**
HERRINGFLEET 1C **6** (1C **167**)
Herringfleet Windpump 1C **167**
HERRINGSWELL 3B **158**
Herringswell Rd. CB8: Kent 1B **48**
Hertford Cl. IP32: Bury E 4E **52**
Hertford Pl. IP15: Aldeb 6J **95**
Hertford Rd. CO10: Clar 3C **102**
Hervey Cl. IP9: Shot G 6D **156**
Hervey Rd. IP33: Bury E 3E **58**
Hervey St. IP4: Ips 1G **5** (6B **132**)
NR32: Low 7H **9**
Hervey Ter. IP9: Shot G 6D **156**
HESSETT 6D **62** (3D **159**)
Hessett Cl. IP14: Stowm 7H **85**
Hessett Rd. IP30: B Geo 1D **82**
Hethersett Cl. CB8: Newm 1E **46**
HEVENINGHAM 3B **74** (2D **161**)
Heveningham Long La.
IP17: Pea 1F **77**
Hexham Cl. IP2: Ips 4J **137**
Heycroft Way CO6: Nay 6H **143**
Heyford Ct. IP28: Mide 6H **23**
Heywood Cl. IP2: Ips 5G **137**
Hibbard Rd. IP8: B'ford 3E **130**
Hickford Hill CO10: Bel P 6E **102**
Hickling Dr. IP33: Bury E 5H **59**
Hicks Way CB9: Stur 6K **101**
Higgins Pl. *IP5: Martl H 6G 135*
(off The Drift)
HIGHAM
Barrow 3B **158**
Stratford St Mary 3A **164**
Higham Hill IP7: Ray, Ray 3F **145**
Higham Rd. CB8: Gaz 2H **49**
CO7: High, Strat M 4G **145**
IP28: High 1J **49**
IP28: Tud 6C **26**
Highbank CO10: Glem 4A **104**
High Baxter St.
IP33: Bury E 4H **157** (1G **59**)
High Beach IP11: Felix 4H **155**
High Beech NR32: Low 6G **9**

Highbridge Gravel Drove IP27: Lake 4A 20
Highbury Cotts. IP16: Leis 3F 93
Highbury Cres. IP33: Bury E 1E 58
Highbury Rd. IP27: B'don 5D 18
IP33: Bury E 1E 58
Highbury Way CO10: Gt Cor 5G 127
Highclere Cl. CB8: Newm 1D 46
Higher Dr. NR32: Oul B 5E 8
Highfield CO10: Clar 5D 102
IP19: Blyth 6J 43
IP23: Eye 6C 38
Highfield App. IP1: Ips 4H 131
Highfield Dr. IP6: Clay 3E 114
Highfield Rd. CO10: S'bury 2F 127
IP1: Ips 3G 131
IP11: Felix 4F 155
IP14: Stowu 2J 85
IP19: H'orth 6B 42
Highfields IP9: Bent 6H 147
IP27: Lake 5C 20
Highfields Dr. IP27: Lake 5B 20
HIGH GARRETT 3B 162
High Green *IP16: Leis* *3H 93*
(off Main St.)
Highgrove Cl. NR32: Low 5F 9
High Hall Cl. IP11: T Mart 5G 153
High Ho. Farm Rd. IP12: Sud 2K 125
Highland Dr. NR34: Worl 4H 13
Highlands IP27: Lake 6C 20
IP32: Bury E 6F 53
Highlands, The CB8: Exn 1D 46
Highlands Cl. IP6: Nee M 3F 111
Highlands La. IP12: Wood 4H 121
Highlands Rd. IP7: Hadl 4H 129
IP7: M Ele 1E 108
Highland Way NR33: Oul B 2E 10
High Leas NR34: Becc 5F 13
High Leas Cl. NR34: Becc 5F 13
High Lodge Forest Cen. 1C 159
High Path NR33: Kess 6K 17
High Rd. CO6: Leav 2A 142
IP6: Swil 4H 117
IP6: Witn 1B 116
IP11: T Mart, T Mary 4F 153
IP13: B'ham 4C 76
IP14: Gt Fin 7J 83
High Rd. E. IP11: Felix 3G 155
High Rd. W. IP11: Felix 3E 154
HIGH ROUGHAM 5A 62
High Row Fld. IP11: Felix 3H 155
HIGH STREET
Rumburgh 1D 161
Saxmundham 2A 166
Sudbourne 1B 78 (3C 167)
High St. CB8: Newm 6F 47
CB9: Have 4F 101
CO6: Nay 6K 143
CO8: Bure 5B 142
CO10: Act 4G 107
CO10: Cave 6H 103
CO10: Clar 5C 102
CO10: L Mel 1J 105
CO10: Lave 6C 106
IP1: Ips 3D 4 (7A 132)
IP6: Cod 2G 115
IP6: Nee M 3G 111
IP6: Tud 7C 116
IP7: Bild 5J 109
IP7: Hadl 3H 129
IP8: Spro 7C 130
IP11: Felix 1C 154
IP12: Orf 7J 125
IP13: Laxf 6B 74
IP13: Uff 5H 119
IP13: Wick M 5B 118
(Border Cot La.)
IP13: Wick M 7B 118
(Main Rd.)
IP14: Deb 2H 87
IP15: Aldeb 6J 95
IP16: Leis 3H 93
IP17: Dun 2J 79
IP17: Saxm 6J 91
IP17: Yox 6H 77
IP18: Sou 4K 45
IP22: Hop 2H 31
IP22: Thel 5A 34
IP23: Gisli 2J 67
IP23: Thorn 2D 72
IP27: B'don 2F 19
IP27: Lake 4A 20
IP28: Mide 7J 23
IP28: Tud 5B 26
IP30: Rat 4K 83
IP31: Ixw 6H 29
NR32: Low 5K 9
NR33: Kess 4H 17
NR34: Wang 6B 44
NR34: Wrent 1D 44
HIGHSTREET GREEN 3B 162
HIGH STREET GREEN 1A 164
High St. Mews IP7: Hadl 3H 129
HIGHTOWN GREEN 1D 163
Highview Cl. CO10: S'bury 1D 126
High Vw. Rd. IP1: Ips 4F 131
Highwood Ct. CB8: Gaz 3G 49
Highwood Cres. CB8: Gaz 3G 49
Highwood Rd. CB8: Gaz 3G 49
Hildabrook Cl. IP2: Ips 5G 137
HILDERSHAM 2A 162
Hildesley Ct. NR33: Low 5G 11
Hill, The CB9: Gt Thu 7C 96
CO10: Stans 3D 104
IP6: Tud 7D 116
IP17: Westl 5H 79
IP19: B'field 6H 75
IP27: B'don 5D 18
NR34: Barnb 7B 6
Hillary Cl. IP4: Ips 1E 138
Hill Cl. CB8: Newm 6E 46
CO10: L Mel 3J 105
Hill Cres. CB9: Have 2F 101
Hillcrest IP17: Fris 6D 92
IP17: Knod 6F 93
IP23: Gisli 1J 67
Hillcrest App. IP8: B'ford 3D 130
Hillcrest Cl. NR34: Worl 5H 13
Hillcrest Dr. NR32: Low 4G 9
Hillcrest Gdns. NR32: Low 5G 9
Hillcrest Rd. CO10: S'bury 1D 126
NR34: Becc 5E 12
Hill Farm Bus. Pk. IP6: Witn 2B 116
Hill Farm La. IP9: Chelm 2H 151
IP30: Drin 7J 63
Hill Farm Rd. IP6: Play 1B 134
IP13: Gru 4G 117
IP19: H'orth 5C 42
Hillfield Ct. IP18: Rey 2J 45
Hill Ho. Gdns. NR34: Wrent 2D 44
Hillhouse Gdns. NR33: Low 4G 11
Hill Ho. La. IP6: Nee M 2F 111
Hill Ho. Rd. IP3: Ips 5J 5 (1C 138)
Hill La. CB9: Stur 7K 101
Hill Ri. IP14: Stowm 7F 85
NR34: Bramp 5F 15
Hillrise Cl. NR34: Worl 5H 13
Hill Rd. IP18: Rey 2J 45
IP33: W'ley 7A 52
NR32: Low 7H 9
NR34: Wang 7C 44
Hillside CB8: Newm 6J 47
IP14: Stowm 7F 85
IP27: B'don 6C 18
Hillside Av. NR34: Worl 4H 13
Hillside Bus. Pk. IP32: Bury E 2B 60
Hillside Ct. NR35: Bung 4C 14
Hillside Cres. IP3: Ips 3F 139
Hillside Rd. CO10: S'bury 4F 127
IP18: Rey 2J 45
IP32: Bury E 2B 60
Hillside Rd. E. NR35: Bung 3C 14
Hillside Rd. W. NR35: Bung 4B 14
Hillside Way IP19: H'orth 3B 42
Hill Ter. CO10: Clar 4D 102
Hill Top IP31: Stant 5C 32
Hilltop Grn. NR32: Low 4G 9
Hilltop Ri. NR34: Worl 5H 13
Hilltop Way IP31: Stant 5C 32
Hill Vw. Bus. Pk. IP6: Clay 6E 114
Hill Vw. Ter. IP12: Wood 5H 121
Hilly Cl. IP31: Sap 2J 29
Hilly Flds. IP12: Wood 6F 121
Hilton Rd. IP3: Ips 4G 139
IP5: Martl H 5H 135
HINDERCLAY 6D 34 (2A 160)
Hinderclay Rd. IP22: Redg 2A 34
IP22: Rick 4F 35
IP22: W'field 1J 33
Hines Rd. IP3: Ips 2E 138
HINTLESHAM 1C 144 (2A 164)
Hintlesham Cl. IP4: Rush A 1K 139
IP14: Stowm 7G 85
Hintlesham Dr. IP11: Felix 3C 154
Hintlesham Golf Course 1C 144
Histon Cl. IP5: Kesg 6K 133
HITCHAM 1H 109 (1D 163)
Hitcham Rd. IP14: Deb 1H 87
Hitchcock Pl. CO10: S'bury 2D 126
HMP & YOI Warren Hill
IP12: Holl 1K 141
HMP Blundeston NR32: Blun 3H 7
HMP Hollesley Bay IP12: Holl 2K 141
Hobart Cl. NR32: Oul 5D 8
Hobart Way NR32: Oul 5D 8
Hobbies La. IP14: Mendl 2H 71
HOBBLES GREEN 1B 162
Hobbs La. CO10: Glem 6C 104
Hocket Cres. IP12: Tun 6F 123
(not continuous)
Hockey Hill IP14: W'sett 6J 69
Hockley Hole La. CO10: Boxf 7C 128
Hockney Gdns. IP3: Ips 6E 138
HOCKWOLD CUM WILTON 1B 158
Hockwold Rd. IP27: Weet 1E 18
Hodgkinson Rd. IP11: Felix 5B 154
Hodson Cl. IP32: Bury E 5E 52
Hoe La. CO10: Pent 7K 103
Hogarth Rd. IP3: Ips 5D 138
Hogarth Sq. IP3: Ips 5E 138
Hogarth Wlk. NR32: Low 2G 9
HOGGARD'S GREEN 4H 81 (1C 163)
Hoggars Rd. IP14: Mendl 3F 71
Hog La. IP19: Wen 4J 43
Hog's La. CO7: E Ber 6D 146
Holbecks La. IP7: Hadl 4G 129
Holbein Way NR32: Low 2G 9
Holborn Av. IP28: Mide 5H 23
HOLBROOK 3D 150 (3B 164)
Holbrook Barn Rd. CO10: Boxf 6D 128
Holbrook Cl. CO10: Gt Wal 7J 107
Holbrook Cres. IP11: Felix 4C 154
Holbrook Rd. CB9: Have 5D 100
IP3: Ips 5C 138
IP9: Hark, Holb 6G 151
IP9: Stut 6C 150
NR32: Oul B 4E 8
Holcombe Cres. IP2: Ips 4F 137
Holden Cl. IP2: Ips 7F 5 (3B 138)
NR32: Oul B 7B 8
Holderness Rd. IP32: Bury E 6J 53
HOLDER'S GREEN 3A 162
Holdsworth Cl. CO10: Glem 6A 104
Holfen Cl. IP12: Martl 3J 135
Holkham Cl. IP4: Rush A 1K 139
Holland Ri. IP19: Hunt 1D 74
Holland Rd. IP4: Ips 7D 132
IP11: Felix 5E 154
Hollands Rd. CB9: Have 4F 101
HOLLESLEY 2G 141 (2D 165)
Hollesley Av. CB9: Have 3B 100
HOLLESLEY HEATH 1H 141
Hollesley Rd. IP12: Alder 5H 141
IP12: Rend 7B 122
Holliday Cl. IP32: Bury E 7B 54
Hollies, The *NR32: Low* *7J 9*
(off Stanley St.)
Hollingsworth Rd. IP14: Stowm 5G 85
NR32: Low 5H 9
Hollowell Cl. NR32: Oul 4D 8
Hollow Gro. Way NR33: Car C 5B 10
Hollow Hill CB9: With 2A 98
Hollow La. IP6: C Mary 7A 86
IP9: Chelm 2H 151
IP13: B'ham 3E 76
IP13: Saxt 2A 90
IP22: M Wes 1E 30
IP31: Thur 1C 62
NR33: Car C 5B 10
(not continuous)
Hollow Rd. IP8: Wash 6A 136
IP31: Bury E 7J 53
IP32: Bury E 7J 53
Holly Blue Cl. IP8: Ips 6G 137
HOLLYBUSH CORNER 3C 82
Hollybush Dr. IP11: Felix 1J 155
Hollybush La. IP30: B Geo 2D 82
Holly Cl. IP3: Pur F 5K 139
IP13: L Bea 1D 134
IP28: Holy R 2H 23
IP28: Red L 6H 25
IP29: Horr 6B 58
NR34: Worl 5H 13
Hollycroft Cl. IP1: Ips 2J 131
Hollydene Cl. NR32: Oul 6C 8
Holly End IP5: Martl H 7F 135
Holly Grange Rd. NR33: Kess 6K 17
Holly Gro. NR34: Becc 4F 13
Holly Hill NR32: Oul 5B 8
Hollyhock Ct. IP28: Red L 5J 25
Hollyhock Wlk. *IP28: Red L* *5J 25*
(off Juniper Rd.)
Holly La. IP5: Rush A 3J 133
IP8: Bels 7E 136
IP9: Stut 5A 150
IP12: Melt 2H 121
IP13: L Bea 1D 134
IP27: Lake 6B 20
NR34: Mut 2C 16
Holly Rd. IP1: Ips 1C 4 (6K 131)
IP5: Kesg 5K 133
IP7: Gt Bri 1A 112
IP8: Off 1F 113
IP8: Will 4E 112
NR32: Oul B 7D 8
Holly Tree Cl. IP16: Leis 4G 93
Holly Wlk. IP28: B Row 1E 22
Holman Ct. IP2: Ips 5A 4 (1J 137)
Holm Cl. NR34: Worl 4K 13
Holm Ct. IP5: Kesg 5D 134
Holme Cl. IP22: Hop 3J 31
Holme Ct. NR32: Oul 6B 8
Holme Oaks Ct. IP3: Ips 3D 138
Holmere Dr. IP19: H'orth 5A 42
Holmes Hill IP17: Pea 1H 77
Holm Oak IP9: Holb 2D 150
Holmsey Grn. IP28: B Row 1E 22
Holmsey Grn. Gdns.
IP28: B Row 1E 22
Holst Cl. NR33: Oul B 3F 11
Holst Mead IP14: Stowm 2E 84
HOLTON 4E 42 (2D 161)
Holton Av. NR32: Oul B 4E 8
Holton Hall Pk. (Caravan Pk.)
IP19: Holt 3E 42
Holton Rd. IP19: H'orth 4C 42
HOLTON ST MARY 3A 164
Holt's La. IP6: C Mary 2J 111
Holyhouse Drift IP31: Gt Bar 1D 54
Holyrood Cl. IP2: Ips 5H 137
Holystone Way NR33: Car C 5B 10
Holy Trinity Hospital Almshouses
CO10: L Mel 1J 105
Holywell Cl. IP33: Bury E 3G 59
Holywell Farm IP28: Holy R 2J 23
HOLYWELL ROW 2H 23 (2B 158)
Holywells Cl. IP3: Ips 7J 5 (2C 138)
Holywells Ct. IP3: Ips 5F 139
Holywells Rd. IP3: Ips 7H 5 (3C 138)
Home Farm La. IP33: Bury E 5G 59
Homefield CO10: Boxf 6C 128
IP9: Cap M 2J 147
Homefield Av. NR33: Oul B 3E 10
NR34: Becc 3E 12
Homefield Paddock NR34: Becc 3E 12
Homefield Rd. CB9: Have 6D 100
Homefield Rd. Units
CB9: Have 6E 100
Home Mdw. IP13: Laxf 6B 74
IP30: C'field 6F 81
Homeorr Ho. IP11: Felix 4G 155
Homeport NR32: Low 5K 9
Homer Cl. IP1: Ips 1H 131
HOMERSFIELD 1C 161
Homestall Cres. CB9: With 2A 98
Homestead, The NR33: Car C 6C 10
Homestead Dr. IP28: B Row 1F 23
Homey Bri. Rd. CO6: Pols 6A 144
Honey Hill
IP33: Bury E 6J 157 (2H 59)
Honey La. CO6: Leav 4C 142
Honeymeade Cl. IP31: Stant 7D 32
Honeypot La. IP22: W'field 4J 33
Honeypot Mdw. NR35: Bung 3B 14
Honeysuckle Cl. CB9: Have 2D 100
IP28: Red L 7J 25
NR33: Low 6F 11
Honeysuckle Gdns. IP2: Ips 2G 137
Honeysuckle Way IP32: Bury E 7A 54
HONEY TYE 4C 142 (3D 163)
HONINGTON 2H 29 (2D 159)
Honington Ri. IP31: Honi 3F 29
HOO 1C 165
Hood Dr. IP6: Gt Bla 2A 114
Hood Rd. IP3: Ips 5C 138
Hood's La. NR34: Stov 6J 15
Hook La. IP7: Hadl 5J 129
Hooper Sq. IP33: Bury E 7C 52
Hoo Rd. IP13: Char 2D 118
Hope Cotts. IP17: Yox 6H 77
Hope Ct. IP3: Ips 6H 5 (2C 138)
Hope Cres. IP12: Melt 4H 121
Hopelyn Cl. NR32: Low 4G 9
Hop Mdw. CO7: E Ber 4A 146
HOPTON 3H 31 (2D 159)
HOPTON COMMON 1J 31
HOPTON ON SEA 1D 167
Hopton Ri. CB9: Have 2A 100
Hopton Rd. IP22: Gar 1K 31
IP22: Thel 3K 31 & 6F 31
IP31: Barni 3D 30
Hopyard La. IP14: Haug 4J 65
Horace Eves Cl. CB9: Have 2E 100
HORHAM 1H 73 (2C 161)
Horham Rd. IP21: Ath 4G 73
IP21: Horh 1F 73
HORKESLEY HEATH 3D 163
Horkesley Hill CO6: Nay 6H 143
HORKESLEY PARK 7K 143
Horkesley Rd. CO6: Nay 7J 143
Hornbeam Av. IP28: Red L 7J 25
Hornbeam Cl. NR33: Oul B 5E 10
NR34: Worl 4H 13
Hornbeam Dr. IP29: Horr 7B 58
Hornbeam Rd. IP14: Stowu 2J 85
IP28: Mide 6K 23
HORNER'S GREEN 4C 128
Horn Hill NR33: Low 2H 11
Hornings Pk. IP29: Horr 5B 58
HORRINGER 6B 58 (3C 159)
Horringer Rd. IP33: Bury E 4D 58
Horse & Groom La. *NR34: Becc* *3E 12*
(off Hungate La.)
Horsecroft Rd.
IP29: Bury E, Haws 6E 58
IP33: Bury E 6E 58
Horsefair IP30: Wool 4A 64
Horsefair Cl. IP14: Mendl 2J 71

HORSEHEATH 2A 162
Horseheath Rd. CB9: With 2A 98
Horseman Ct. IP5: Martl H 6H 135
Horse Pond Cl. CO10: Gt Cor 7H 127
Horseshoe Dr. IP28: Red L 5J 25
Horseshoe La. CB9: Have 4D 100
Horseshoe Ri. IP31: Stant 6D 32
Horseshoes, The IP31: Nort 5K 57
Horsham Av. IP3: Ips 3H 139
Horsham Cl. CB9: Have 2B 100
HORSLEY CROSS 3B 164
HORSLEYCROSS STREET 3B 164
Hospital Rd.
IP33: Bury E 7F 157 (2E 58)
Hossack Rd. IP3: Ips 6E 138
Hotson Rd. IP18: Sou 3K 45
Houghton Dr. NR32: Oul 4D 8
Houghton Pl. IP4: Rush A 1K 139
Houldsworth Ter. *CB8: Newm 6F 47*
(off Black Bear La.)
House Martins, The *IP11: Felix . . .2E 154*
(off Cage La.)
Howard Cl. CB9: Have 4C 100
IP13: F'ham 6C 90
Howard De Walden Way
CB8: Newm 5G 47
Howard Ho. IP2: Ips 7A 4
Howard Rd. NR35: Bung 3D 14
Howards Cl. IP22: Wort 3K 35
IP23: Gisli 2J 67
Howard St. IP4: Ips 6F 133
Howards Wlk. IP17: Saxm 6J 91
Howards Way IP5: Kesg 5E 134
Howe Av. IP3: Ips 3G 139
Howe La. IP30: C'field 7H 81
Howe Rd. CB9: Have 2D 100
Howes Av. IP31: Thur 6K 55
HOWE STREET 3A 162
Howe Way CO10: Act 4G 107
Howlets Ter. IP9: Chelm 2G 151
Howlett Cl. IP5: Kesg 6E 134
HOWLETT END 3A 162
Howlett Way IP11: T Mart 6H 153
Howley Gdns. NR32: Low 2F 9
HOXNE 1C 38 (2B 160)
Hoxne Cl. IP14: Stowm 7G 85
Hoxne Rd. IP21: Syle 1F 39
IP23: Eye 7D 38
Hoxter Way CO10: S'bury 1D 126
Hoylake Cl. IP28: Forn M 1F 53
Hubbard's Av. NR32: Low 2H 9
Hubbards Cl. IP17: Saxm 5G 91
Hubbard's Hill IP17: Pea 1G 77
Hubbard's La. IP30: Hess 7D 62
Hubbard's Loke NR32: Low 2H 9
Huckleberry Cres. IP3: Ips 7G 139
Hudson Cl. CB9: Have 5H 101
Hudson Way IP29: Barr 7B 50
Hugh Ager Cl. IP14: Stowm 7F 85
Hughes Rd. CO7: E Ber 2A 146
Hull St. IP27: RAF L 3H 21
Hulver Ct. IP3: Ips 4F 139
Hulver La. IP17: Snap 1B 94
Hulver Rd. NR34: Mut 2A 16
HULVER STREET 2C 167
Humber Doucy La. IP4: Ips 2E 132
Hummingbird Cl. IP32: Bury E 7C 54
Humphry Rd. CO10: S'bury 3D 126
HUNDON 2J 99 (2B 162)
Hundon Pl. CB9: Have 3G 101
Hundon Rd. CB9: Ked 6C 98
CO10: Hund 6C 98
Hundred Acre Way
IP28: H'well, Red L 7J 25
Hungarian Cl. IP13: Petti 3F 119
Hungate NR34: Becc 3E 12
Hungate Ct. NR34: Becc 3E 12
Hungate La. NR34: Becc 3E 12
HUNSTON 4A 66 (3D 159)
HUNSTON GREEN 7A 66
Hunston Rd. IP31: B Ash 3C 66
Hunt Cl. IP14: Stowm 7F 85
Hunter Dr. IP31: Thur 6K 55
Hunter Rd. IP3: Ips 6G 139
IP31: Honi 4F 29
IP32: Bury E 5D 52
Hunters End IP11: T Mary 1B 154
Hunters La. IP20: Metf 7F 41
Hunters Ride IP5: Martl H 6H 135
Huntingdon Cl. NR33: Low 6F 11
HUNTINGFIELD 1D 74 (2D 161)
Huntingfield Rd. IP16: Leis 4H 93
IP33: Bury E 2C 58
Huntley Ct. IP19: H'orth 3C 42
HUNT'S CORNER 1A 160
Hunts Hill CO10: Glem 5A 104
Hurdle Drove IP28: W Row 1A 22
Hurdle Makers Hill IP8: Spro 2A 136
Hurn Crag Rd. IP18: Rey 2J 45
Hurricane Pl. IP3: Ips 5F 139
Hurstfen Drove
IP28: Holy R, Mide 2K 23
Hurstlea Ct. IP6: Nee M 3G 111
Hurstlea Rd. IP6: Nee M 3F 111
Hutland Rd. IP4: Ips 1K 5 (6D 132)
Hutton Cl. IP33: Bury E 7D 52
Hutton Ct. IP23: Eye 6D 38
Hyams La. IP9: Holb 3C 150
IP9: Stut 7B 150
Hyde Pk. Cnr. IP1: Ips 2C 4
IP12: Sud 1H 125
Hyde Pk. Ho. IP1: Ips 2D 4
Hyde Rd. CO10: S'bury 4D 126
Hyem's La. IP11: Felix 1G 155
Hyntle Cl. IP2: Ips 1G 137
Hyperion Ct. IP1: Ips 5F 131
Hyperion Way CB8: Newm 1E 46

I

Icanho Cen.
Stowmarket 3C 84
Ice Ho. Quay NR32: Oul B 1D 10
Iceni Way CB8: Exn 1B 46
CB9: Have 6G 101
Icepits Cl. IP31: Gt Bar 2G 55
Icewell Hill CB8: Newm 5G 47
Ickleton Pl. CB9: Have 3G 101
ICKLINGHAM 2B 26 (2B 158)
Icklingham Rd. IP28: Tud 5C 26
Icknield Way CB8: Kent 2E 48
Ickworth Ct. IP11: Felix 5B 154
Ickworth Cres. IP4: Rush A 1K 139
Ickworth Dr. IP33: Bury E 2F 59
Ickworth Pk. 3C 159
IKEN 2A 166
Ilex Cl. IP33: Bury E 3G 59
Iliffe Way IP14: Stowm 4F 85
ILKETSHALL ST ANDREW
. . . . .2H 15 (1D 161)
ILKETSHALL ST LAWRENCE 1D 161
ILKETSHALL ST MARGARET 1D 161
ILLINGTON 1D 159
Industrial Cen.
IP2: Ips 6E 4 (2A 138)
Infirmary La. IP13: F'ham 6D 90
Ingate NR34: Becc 4F 13
Ingelow Gdns. IP4: Ips 7F 133
INGHAM 5E 28 (2C 159)
Ingham Rd. CB9: Have 3G 101
IP31: Ing 5E 28
Ingram's Well Rd.
CO10: S'bury 4E 126
Inkerman Cl. IP7: Hadl 3H 129
Inkerman Row CO10: S'bury 3D 126
Inkerman Ter. IP7: Hadl 3H 129
Innes End IP8: Ips 4E 136
Innocence La. IP10: Kirt 2F 153
Inverness Rd. IP4: Ips 3E 132
Ion Rd. IP32: Bury E 5E 52
IP Central IP4: Ips 4G 5
IPSWICH 4E 4 (2B 164)
Ipswich Ancient House 3E 4
Ipswich & District Indoor Bowling Club
. . . . .6F 133
Ipswich Av. IP12: Sutt 2B 140
Ipswich Cl. IP12: Sutt 2B 140
Ipswich Ct.
IP33: Bury E 2H 157 (7G 53)
Ipswich Crematorium IP4: Ips 5D 132
Ipswich Eastern By-Pass
IP5: Brigh, Foxh, Martl H 4G 135
IP10: Brigh, Foxh 3A 152
Ipswich Film Theatre *3D 4*
(within Corn Exchange)
Ipswich Golf Range 7K 137
Ipswich Hockey Club 3D 132
Ipswich Mus. 2D 4 (7A 132)
Ipswich (Purdis Heath) Golf Course
. . . . .4K 139
Ipswich Rd. CO7: Ded, Strat M . . .7G 145
CO11: Brant 4C 148
CO11: Catt 7A 148
IP6: Nee M 4H 111
IP6: Otl 2H 117
IP6: Witn 5B 116
IP7: E'sett 6H 113
IP7: Hadl 1K 129
IP8: Off 1G 113
IP9: Hark 6H 151
IP9: Holb 1D 150
IP10: Nac 7J 139
IP12: Orf 5H 125
IP12: Wald 6A 140
IP12: Wood 1K 135
IP13: Char 4C 118
IP13: Gru 7H 117
IP14: Deb 3J 87
IP14: Stowm 6G 85
IP21: Thran 7F 37
IP23: Yax 7D 36
IP30: Roug 2E 60
NR32: Low 5J 9
Ipswich Southern By-Pass
IP3: Ips 7G 139
IP8: Bels, Ips . . . . .6D 136 & 1F 149
IP9: Wher 1F 149
IP10: Buck, Foxh, Nac 7H 139
Ipswich Sports Club 4A 132
Ipswich Station (Rail) 6B 4 (2K 137)
Ipswich St. IP14: Stowm 4F 85
IP27: RAF L 3H 21
IP33: Bury E 2H 157 (7G 53)
Ipswich Town FC 4B 4 (1K 137)
Ipswich Transport Mus. 4G 139
Ipswich Way IP14: Petta 4B 88
Ipswich Western By-Pass
IP8: Ips, Wash, Spro, B'ford
. . . . .5C 136
Ireland Rd. IP3: Ips 5D 138
Irex Rd. NR33: Low 6G 11
Iris Cl. IP2: Ips 1H 137
Iris Ct. IP28: Red L 5K 25
Irlam Rd. IP2: Ips 4F 137
Iron Foundry Rd. IP14: Stowm 4G 85
Isham Pl. IP3: Ips 6H 5 (2C 138)
Isinglass Cl. CB8: Newm 7K 47
ISLEHAM 2A 158
Isleham Rd. IP28: W'ton 2A 24
Ivry Lodge IP1: Ips 1C 4 (6K 131)
Ivry St. IP1: Ips 1B 4 (6K 131)
Ivy Cl. IP13: W'orth 5J 73
Ivy Ct. IP28: Red L 6J 25
Ivy Gdns. IP14: Finn 6H 67
Ivy La. NR33: Oul B 2B 10
Ivy Lodge Rd.
IP13: Cam A . . . . . .3C 122 & 4E 122
Ixer La. IP30: B Com 1J 81
IXWORTH 6H 29 (2D 159)
Ixworth Rd. CB9: Have 5D 100
IP31: Gt Bar . . . . .2F 55 & 7F 29
IP31: Honi 2H 29
IP31: Nort, Stowl 1G 57
IP31: Thur 5K 55
IP31: Tros 1D 28
IP31: Wals W 6F 33
IXWORTH THORPE 2D 159

J

Jackdaw Cl. IP14: Stowm 3H 85
Jack Jarvis Cl. CB8: Newm 6G 47
Jack's Grn. Rd. IP6: C Mary 1G 111
Jack's La. IP14: Comb 1A 110
Jacksnipe Cl. IP14: Stowm 4H 85
Jackson Cl. IP5: Kesg 6F 135
Jackson Ct. IP5: Martl H 6G 135
Jackson Pl. IP6: Barh 1C 114
Jackson Way IP6: Nee M 4G 111
Jacobs Cl. CO10: Gt Cor 6G 127
IP31: Stant 6C 32
Jacob's Ct. NR32: Low 6J 9
Jacobs Mdw. IP30: Rat 4K 83
Jacob's St. NR32: Low 6J 9
Jacobs Way IP12: Wood 5H 121
Jacqueline Cl. IP13: Gru 6J 117
IP33: Bury E 6F 157 (2F 59)
Jaguar Cl. IP1: Ips 4E 130
James Boden Cl. IP11: Felix 3D 154
James Carter Rd. IP28: Mide 5G 23
James Hatfield Ho. IP2: Ips 7F 5
Jameson Pl. CO10: S'bury 3D 126
James Stiff Cotts. IP30: Roug 5H 61
Jamestown Blvd. IP2: Ips 3B 138
Janebrook Rd. IP2: Ips 4G 137
Janet Hadenham Cl.
NR34: Worl 4K 13
Jankyn's Pl.
IP33: Bury E 5F 157 (1F 59)
Janus Cl. CB9: Have 5J 101
Jaques Cl. CO10: Glem 4B 104
Jarman Cl. IP33: Bury E 3J 59
Jarman's La. IP28: W Row 4B 22
Jarrold Cl. IP31: Barni 3E 30
Jarvis Way CB8: Newm 4E 46
Jasmine Cl. IP2: Ips 3H 137
IP11: T Mart 5H 153
Jasmine Ct. IP27: B'don 5D 18
Jasmine Grn. NR32: Low 6H 9
Jasmine Rd. IP28: Red L 6J 25
JASPER'S GREEN 3B 162
Java Lodge Rd. IP13: Petti 2H 119
Jay Cl. CB9: Have 4H 101
Jays Cft. Rd. IP12: Rend 5C 122
Jaywick Rd. CB9: Have 3F 101
Jeaffresons Well IP13: F'ham 5D 90
Jeannie Mann Ct. NR32: Low 4G 9
Jeavons La. IP5: Kesg 6E 134
Jeddah Way CB8: Kenn 3A 48
Jefferies Rd. IP4: Ips 3H 5 (7C 132)
Jellicoe Av. NR33: Oul B 3C 10
Jenkins Grn. NR32: Low 3F 9
Jennens Way CO10: Act 4G 107
Jenner Cl. NR35: Bung 4C 14
Jenners Cl. IP12: Melt 4J 121
Jennings Drift IP5: Kesg 6D 134
Jermyn Av. IP32: Bury E 7B 54
Jermyns Cl. IP9: Cap M 1J 147
Jermyns Rd. IP18: Rey 1H 45
Jermyn Way IP19: H'orth 6A 42
Jersey Ct. IP28: B Row 1E 22
Jervis Cl. IP9: Holb 3D 150
Jerwood Dancehouse 5E 4
Jetty La. IP12: Wood 7H 121
Jewell Vw. IP5: Kesg 6D 134
Jew's La. IP12: Melt 7G 119
Jim Joel Ct. *CB8: Newm 5G 47*
(off Howard De Walden Way)
Jim Mollison Ct. IP28: Mide 6H 23
Jimmy's La. CO11: Brant 3E 148
Job's La. IP22: Pal 2C 36
Jocelyn Cl. IP32: Bury E 4E 52
Jockey's La. IP14: Comb 4B 110
IP14: Fram 4C 88
Joes Rd. CO10: Gt Cor 4K 127
John Childs Way NR35: Bung 4C 14
John Lang Ct. NR33: Oul B 2C 10
John Lawrence Cl. NR34: Becc 6E 12
John Oaksey Ho. *CB8: Newm 4G 47*
(off Bill Rickaby Dr.)
John Shepherd Rd. IP21: Fress 6C 40
Johnson Cl. IP2: Ips 3A 138
Johnson Rd. IP29: Barr 7B 50
Johnson Way NR32: Low 2F 9
John St. IP3: Ips 7H 5 (2C 138)
IP16: Leis 4H 93
NR33: Low 2H 11
John Swain Cl. IP6: Nee M 3F 111
Jolly's Way IP31: Wals W 7H 33
Jordan Cl. IP6: C Mary 1H 111
Jordayn Ri. IP7: Hadl 3J 129
Joseph Cl. IP7: Hadl 3J 129
Josselyns, The IP11: T Mary 7J 153
Jovian Way IP1: Ips 6F 131
Joyce Rd. NR35: Bung 3D 14
Jubilee Av. IP14: Stowm 7F 85
Jubilee Cl. IP6: Clay 3D 114
IP11: T Mart 5H 153
IP12: Blax 2H 123
IP13: Laxf 6B 74
Jubilee Ct. IP14: Stowu 1K 85
IP19: H'orth 6B 42
Jubilee Cres. IP14: Stowu 1K 85
Jubilee Rd. CO10: S'bury 3E 126
IP27: Lake 3A 20
NR33: Low 7F 11
NR35: Bung 4B 14
Jubilee Ter. IP30: E'well 3E 64
Jubilee Wlk. CB9: Have 4F 101
Jubilee Way CO10: Act 4G 107
IP28: Mide 7J 23
NR32: Low 6K 9
Jubys Hill IP6: Witn 2B 116
Judas La. IP23: Yax 6C 36
JUDE'S FERRY 7B 22
Judith Av. IP17: Knod 7F 93
Julian Cl. CB9: Have 4J 101
July Ct. CB8: Newm 3F 47
Junction Rd. IP28: Mide 6H 23
June Av. IP1: Ips 3K 131
NR32: Low 5G 9
Juniper Cl. IP28: Mide 6K 23
Juniper Rd. IP28: Red L 5J 25
IP32: Bury E 7C 54
Jupiter Cl. CB9: Have 5H 101
Jupiter Rd. IP4: Ips 6F 133
Justinian Cl. CB9: Have 5J 101

K

Kalen Ct. NR33: Gisle 7D 10
Karen Cl. IP1: Ips 4K 131
Kate's La. IP14: W'den 4H 65
Katwijk Way NR32: Low 1J 11
Kays Cl. IP5: Kesg 6C 134
Keats Cl. IP17: Saxm 5G 91
Keats Cres. IP1: Ips 2H 131
Kebbles CO10: Glem 3A 104
KEDINGTON 6C 98 (2B 162)
Kedington Cl. IP30: Blac 3G 61
Kedington Ct. CO10: Act 4G 107
Keel Cl. NR33: Car C 5A 10
Keens La. IP18: Rey 2G 45
Keep, The CB9: Have 4D 100
Keeper's La. CO6: Leav 2E 142
IP11: T Mary 1A 154
Keep Ri. NR35: Bung 2B 14
Keiffer Cl. CO10: Gt Wal 6K 107
Keightley Way IP6: Tud 7C 116
Kelly-Pain Ct. NR32: Low 5H 9
Kelly Rd. IP2: Ips 1G 137
KELSALE 3J 91 (3D 161)
Kelsale Cl. NR32: Oul B 4E 8
Kelso Pl. IP29: Laws 6B 80
Kelso Rd. IP33: Bury E 3D 58

Kelvedon Dr. IP4: Rush A 1K 139
Kelvin Rd. IP1: Ips 4H 131
Kemball St. IP4: Ips 1E 138
Kembold Cl. IP32: Bury E 1A 60
Kempshorne Cl. NR32: Oul 4D 8
Kemps La. NR34: Becc 5E 12
Kempson Dr. CO10: Gt Cor 6H 127
Kempson Way IP32: Bury E 1B 60
Kempsters, The IP11: T Mary 1C 154
Kempton Cl. IP1: Ips 2K 131
Kempton Cross NR34: Worl 4H 13
Kempton Rd. IP1: Ips 2J 131
Kemsley Rd. IP11: Felix 3E 154
Kendal Grn. IP11: Felix 1J 155
Kendall Cl. IP32: Bury E 1B 60
Kendall Ct. IP28: Tud 5C 26
Kendal Rd. NR33: Low 4G 11
Kennedy Av. IP19: H'orth 7A 42
Kennedy Cl. IP4: Ips 7E 132
IP19: H'orth 7B 42
Kennedy St. IP27: RAF L 3H 21
Kennels, The IP12: Rend 6A 122
Kennels La. IP13: Hask 1D 120
Kennels Rd. IP10: Foxh 1A 152
KENNETT 3B 158
KENNETT END 2A 48
Kennett Pk. Cl. CB8: Kenn 3A 48
Kennett Rd. CB8: Mou 5D 48
IP28: H'well 7K 25
Kennett Station (Rail) 1A 48
KENNINGHALL 1A 160
KENNYHILL 2A 158
Kensington Ct. IP14: Stowm 5F 85
NR33: Low 4H 11
Kensington Rd. IP1: Ips 5J 131
IP14: Stowm 5F 85
NR33: Low 4H 11
KENTFORD 2B 48 (3B 158)
Kentford Paddocks CB8: Kent 2B 48
Kentford Rd. IP11: Felix 4B 154
Kent Ho. IP11: Felix 2D 154
KENTON 3B 160
Kenton Rd. IP14: Deb 3J 87
Kent Rd. IP14: Stowm 3E 84
NR32: Low 7G 9
Kents La. NR35: Bung 3D 14
Kentwell 2C 163
Kentwell Cl. IP4: Rush A 2K 139
Kenyon Cl. CO7: Strat M 6H 145
Kenyon Dr. CO10: Gt Wal 7K 107
Kenyon St. IP2: Ips 7E 4 (2A 138)
Kerrison Cotts. IP23: Thorn 1B 72
Kerrison Rd. NR35: Bung 4D 14
Kerry Av. IP1: Ips 3F 131
KERSEY 2A 164
Kersey Av. CO10: Gt Cor 5G 127
Kersey Cl. IP14: Stowm 7G 85
Kersey Rd. IP11: Felix 4C 154
Kersley Hall La.
IP21: Stradb . . . . .1K 73 & 7H 39
KESGRAVE 7C 134 (2C 165)
Kesgrave Dr. NR32: Oul B 5E 8
KESSINGLAND 4H 17 (2D 167)
KESSINGLAND BEACH . . .6K 17 (2D 167)
Kessingland Beach Holiday Village
NR33: Kess 7K 17
Kessingland Cotts. NR33: Kess 4K 17
Kesteven Rd. IP2: Ips 7A 4 (2K 137)
Kestrel Cl. IP28: B Row 1C 22
Kestrel Dr. IP14: Stowm 5J 85
IP27: B'don 4J 19
Kestrel Grn. NR33: Oul B 3B 10
Kestrel Rd. CB9: Have 4H 101
IP2: Ips 3F 137
IP33: Bury E 4H 59
Keswick Cl. IP11: Felix 2H 155
KETTLEBASTON 1D 163
Kettlebaston Way IP4: Ips 4B 132
Kettleborrow Cl. IP31: Ixw 6J 29
KETTLEBURGH 6J 89 (3C 161)
Kettleburgh Rd. IP13: F'ham 7C 90
Kettle La. IP6: C Mary 4K 111
Kettle Way CO11: Brant 5C 148
Kevington Dr. NR32: Oul B 6B 8
Key St. IP4: Ips 5F 5 (1B 138)
Keytes Way IP6: Gt Bla 2A 114
Khartoum Rd. IP4: Ips 1K 5 (6D 132)
Kilbourn Rd. NR33: Low 7F 11
Kilbrack NR34: Becc 4F 13
Kilbrack Gdns. NR34: Becc 3F 13
Kildare Av. IP1: Ips 3F 131
Killick Cres. NR33: Car C 5B 10
Kiln Bottom IP7: Hadl 1J 129
Kiln Cotts. IP14: Stowm 5E 84
Kiln Dr. CO10: Gt Cor 5G 127
Kiln Farm La. IP22: Rick 7G 35
Kiln Fld. IP11: Felix 3C 154
Kiln La. IP12: Alder 7H 141
IP13: Gt Bea 6A 120
IP17: Benh 1C 92
IP17: Ster 5A 92
IP30: E'well 3B 64
Kiln Ri. IP22: Rick 6J 35
Kiln Rd. NR34: Wang 4D 44
Kiln Row IP30: Wool 4C 64
Kimberley Rd. NR33: Low 2F 11
Kingbird Rd. IP32: Bury E 7C 54
King Edward VII Dr.
IP9: Shot G 7E 156
King Edward VII Rd. CB8: Newm . . .4E 46
King Edward Av. IP13: Wick M . . .5B 118
King Edward Rd. IP3: Ips 3F 139
IP16: Leis 3H 93
Kingfisher Av. IP2: Ips 3F 137
Kingfisher Cl. CB9: Have 3H 101
Kingfisher Ct. NR33: Oul B 4B 10
Kingfisher Cres. IP18: Rey 2G 45
Kingfisher Dr. IP6: Gt Bla 2A 114
IP27: B'don 4H 19
Kingfisher Leisure Cen. 5E 126
Kingfisher Ri. IP17: Saxm 5H 91
Kingfisher Rd. IP32: Bury E 7B 54
Kingfishers CO10: S'bury 5C 126
Kingfisher Way IP14: Stowm 5K 85
IP28: Mide 7K 23
King George V Memorial Homes
IP3: Ips 3D 138
King George Av. CB8: Exn 1B 46
King George's Av. IP16: Leis 3J 93
Kingpin Bowling Cen. 6H 135
Kings Av. IP4: Ips 4H 5 (1C 138)
IP13: F'ham 4B 90
Kingsbury Rd. IP11: T Mary 1B 154
Kingsbury Wlk. *CO10: Gt Cor 6H 127*
(off Kempson Dr.)
Kings Cl. CO10: Act 4G 107
IP12: Wood 6F 121
IP28: Mide 6K 23
IP30: Roug 6K 61
Kings Ct. CB8: Exn 1B 46
CB8: Newm 2F 47
King's Dam NR34: Gill 1B 12
Kings Dr. CB8: Newm 7H 47
Kingsfield Av. IP1: Ips 5A 132
Kingsfleet Golf Course 1K 155
Kings Fleet Rd. IP11: Felix 5D 154
Kingsgate Dr. IP4: Ips 5D 132
KINGSHALL GREEN 1D 82
KINGSHALL STREET 7K 61 (3D 159)
Kingshall St.
IP30: B Geo, Roug . . .6K 61 & 1D 82
Kings Hill CB9: Ked 7B 98
CO10: Gt Cor 5F 127
Kingsland IP9: Shot 5B 156
Kingsland La. CO6: Leav 3A 142
King's La. CO10: New G 4K 105
Kingsley Cl. IP1: Ips 2J 131
Kingsmead Cl. IP14: Stowm 3E 84
Kings Mdw. CB9: Ked 7B 98
CO10: Gt Cor 5F 127
Kingsmead Rd. IP14: Stowm 3E 84
Kings M. IP33: Bury E . . .5G 157 (1G 59)
Kings Pde. IP28: Red L 4K 25
Kings Rd. CO10: Glem 4A 104
IP16: Leis 4H 93
IP33: Bury E 5F 157 (1F 59)
NR35: Bung 4C 14
Kings Theatre
Newmarket 6F 47
Kingston Cl. NR33: Low 6F 11
Kingston Ct. NR34: Becc 3G 13
Kingston Dr. NR34: Becc 3F 13
Kingston Farm Rd.
IP12: Wood 7G 121
Kingston Pas. CB8: Newm 6G 47
Kingston Rd. IP1: Ips 5H 131
IP12: Wood 6H 121
King St. CO10: S'bury 4D 126
IP1: Ips 3D 4 (7A 132)
IP11: Felix 3D 154
IP15: Aldeb 6K 95
IP21: Wey 2C 40
IP28: Mide 7J 23
Kings Warren Bus. Pk.
IP28: Red L 4J 25
King's Way IP3: Ips 4F 139
Kingsway CB8: Newm 5F 47
IP12: Wood 5J 121
IP28: Mide 7J 23
Kingswood Av. NR33: Car C 5C 10
Kingsworth Rd. IP32: Bury E 7K 53
King William St. IP6: Nee M 3G 111
Kinross Rd. IP4: Ips 4F 133
Kinsey Vw. IP5: Kesg 7B 134
Kipling Cl. NR33: Kess 4K 17
Kipling Rd. IP1: Ips 2H 131
Kipling Way IP14: Stowm 2D 84
KIRBY CANE 1D 161
Kirby Cane Wlk. NR32: Oul B 5F 9
Kirby Cl. IP4: Ips 6E 132
Kirby Ri. IP6: Barh 3D 114
Kirby St. IP4: Ips 6E 132
Kirkdale Ct. NR33: Low 5G 11
Kirkham Cl. IP2: Ips 4J 137
KIRKLEY 3G 11 (1D 167)
Kirkley Cliff NR33: Low 3H 11
Kirkley Cliff Rd. NR33: Low 4H 11
Kirkley Ct. CB9: Have 3B 100
Kirkley Gdns. NR33: Low 3G 11
Kirkley Pk. Rd. NR33: Low 3G 11
Kirkley Ri. NR33: Low 2H 11
Kirkley Run NR33: Low 2F 11
Kirkley St. NR33: Low 3G 11
Kirkstead Rd. IP33: Bury E 3D 58
Kirkstone Way NR32: Low 4F 9
Kirkton Cl. IP9: Shot G 6D 156
Kirkwood Dr. NR33: Car C 6B 10
KIRTLING 1A 162
KIRTLING GREEN 1A 162
Kirtling Pl. CB9: Have 3G 101
KIRTON 1H 153 (3C 165)
Kirton Rd. IP11: T Mart 3H 153
Kitchen Cl. IP23: Wick S 1G 69
Kitchener Cl. IP27: Lake 4A 20
Kitchener Rd. IP1: Ips 5H 131
IP16: Leis 3H 93
Kitchener Way IP9: Shot G 7D 156
Kitchen Hill
CO10: Bulm, S'bury 4A 126
Kite Cres. IP14: Stowm 3H 85
Kitson Mdws. IP33: W'ley 1A 58
Kitten Cl. CB9: Have 3H 101
Kittiwake Cl. IP2: Ips 3G 137
NR33: Oul B 4C 10
Kittiwake Ct. IP14: Stowm 4H 85
KITTLE'S CORNER 4F 89
Klick Fitness
Ipswich 5B 4 (1K 137)
Klondyke IP32: Bury E 5F 53
Knappers Way IP27: B'don 4G 19
Knapton Ct. IP4: Ips 4E 4
Knettishall Heath Country Pk. . . .1D 159
Knevetts Cl. IP21: Stradb 6G 39
Knight Rd. IP12: Rend 6C 122
Knights Cl. IP11: Felix 2J 155
IP14: Deb 2H 87
IP14: Old N 5A 70
Knights Ct. CB9: Have 4D 100
NR32: Low 7H 9
Knightsdale Rd. IP1: Ips 4J 131
Knights La. IP5: Kesg 6D 134
Knightswood NR32: Low 3G 9
Knights Yd. NR34: Becc 2E 12
KNODISHALL 6F 93 (1A 166)
Knoll, The IP12: Alder 5H 141
IP13: F'ham 6D 90
IP17: Pea 2J 77
Knoll Cl. IP22: Redg 3C 34
Knowle, The IP31: Stant 7D 32
KNOWLES GREEN 5G 51
Knox La. IP31: Bard 3D 32
Knutsford Cl. IP8: Ips 5E 136
Kylborne Cl. IP33: Bury E 1C 58
Kyson Hill 7G 121
Kytson Rd. IP31: Forn M 4G 53

L

Laburnham Cl. IP13: W'orth 6H 73
Laburnham Dr. IP14: Batt 7A 110
Laburnum Av. IP28: Mide 6K 23
Laburnum Cl. IP3: Pur F 4J 139
IP8: Ips 4E 136
IP28: Red L 6H 25
Laburnum Gdns. IP5: Rush A 4J 133
IP12: Martl 4G 135
Laburnum Rd. NR35: Bung 3B 14
Laburnum Wlk. IP27: B'don 5H 19
Laburnum Way CO6: Nay 5H 143
Lacewing Cl. IP8: Ips 6G 137
Lacey's La. CB8: Exn 2B 46
Lacey St. IP4: Ips 3H 5 (7C 132)
Lachlan Grn. *IP12: Wood 3G 121*
(off Cobbold Rd.)
LACKFORD 2B 158
Lackford La. IP28: Ris 1B 50
Lackford Pl. IP3: Ips 6G 139
Lacon Rd. IP8: B'ford 3C 130
Lacy Ct. IP33: Bury E 3F 157
Ladbrook Cl. IP7: E'sett 6F 113
Ladyfield IP14: Haug 3C 70
Ladygate CB9: Have 5D 100
Lady La. IP1: Ips 3C 4
IP7: Hadl 2J 129
Lady La. Ind. Est. IP7: Hadl 2J 129
Lady Margaret Gdns.
IP12: Wood 6E 120
Lady Miriam Way IP32: Bury E 7C 54
Lady Row IP9: Shot 4B 156
Lady's Mdw. NR34: Becc 2E 12
Lady St. CO10: Lave 6C 106
Ladywell Rd. IP14: W'orpe 7F 67
Ladywood Rd. IP4: Ips 6G 133
LA Fitness
Bury St Edmunds 2B 60
Lagonda Dr. IP1: Ips 4E 130
La Grange Pl. CB8: Exn 1B 46
Lake Av. IP32: Bury E 4E 52
Lakeland Dr. NR32: Oul B 7E 8
LAKENHEATH 5A 20 (1B 158)
Lake Side IP14: Stowm 4E 84
Lakeside Av. IP16: Thor 6C 94
Lakeside Cl. IP2: Ips 4G 137
IP18: Rey 2H 45
Lakeside Pk. Dr. IP18: Rey 3H 45
Lakeside Ri. NR32: Blun 3H 7
Lakeside Rd. IP2: Ips 4G 137
Lake Vw. Rd. NR33: Oul B 1D 10
Lakforth CO10: L Mel 3J 105
LAMARSH 3C 163
Lamarsh Hill CO8: Bure 5A 142
Lamarsh Hill Bungs.
CO8: Bure 6A 142
LAMB CORNER 3A 164
Lamb Ct. IP28: B Mil 2G 25
Lambert Cl. IP7: Hadl 2H 129
IP13: F'ham 6C 90
IP19: H'orth 5B 42
Lambert Dr. CO10: Act 4H 107
Lamberts La. IP5: Rush A 3G 133
IP14: Mendl 5F 71
Lambeth Cl. IP1: Ips 5J 131
Lambeth Way IP14: L Sto 1D 86
Lamble Cl. IP28: B Row 2F 23
Lambourne Cl. IP32: Bury E 7A 54
Lambourne Rd. IP1: Ips 1K 131
Lambsale Mdw. IP17: Saxm 5J 91
Lambseth St. IP23: Eye 6C 38
Lambs La. IP29: Laws 6A 80
Lamdin Rd. IP32: Bury E 3F 53
Lammas Cl. IP31: Bard 2D 32
Lampitt Way IP31: Sap 2J 29
Lanark Rd. IP4: Ips 4F 133
Lancaster Av. IP32: Bury E 5F 53
Lancaster Cl. IP29: Chedb 6K 51
Lancaster Dr. IP5: Martl H 7H 135
Lancaster Ho. *IP11: Felix 3D 154*
(off The Walk)
Lancaster Ipswich Athletics
Track & Stadium 4D 132
Lancaster Rd. CO10: S'bury 1C 126
IP4: Ips 3H 5 (7C 132)
IP28: RAF M 2C 22
Lancaster Way IP6: Clay 3D 114
Lancers, The IP12: Wood 7E 120
Lancewood Wlk. IP27: RAF L 5G 21
Lancing Av. IP4: Ips 5E 132
Landguard Caravan Pk.
IP11: Felix 7C 154
Landguard Ct. IP11: Felix 7D 154
Landguard Fort 3C 165
Landguard Rd. IP11: Felix 7D 154
Landsdown Rd.
CO10: S'bury 2F 127
Landseer Cl. IP3: Ips 5E 138
Landseer Ct. CB9: Have 5E 100
Landseer Rd. IP3: Ips 3C 138
Landspring La. NR33: Oul B 3D 10
Lane, The IP17: Yox 5G 77
NR34: Wrent 1D 44
Lane End CB9: Have 2A 100
Lanercost Way IP2: Ips 4J 137
Langdale Cl. IP11: Felix 2J 155
Langdale Pk. NR32: Low 4F 9
Langer Pk. Ind. Est.
IP11: Felix 5D 154
Langer Rd. IP11: Felix 7D 154
Langford Cl. IP14: Stowm 2D 84
LANGHAM
Bury St Edmunds . . .1A 66 (3D 159)
Colchester 3A 164
Langham Rd. IP12: Blax 1J 123
IP17: Farn 1J 123
IP31: B Ash 2C 66
Langham Way CB9: Have 2A 100
Langlaagte Ter. *IP17: Knod 6G 93*
(off St Andrew's Rd.)
Langley Av. IP11: Felix 3D 154
Langley Cl. IP11: Felix 3D 154
Langley Gdns. NR33: Oul B 4E 10
Langridge, The IP31: Ixw 4G 29
Langstons IP11: T Mary 7K 153
LANGTON GREEN 5D 38
Langton Gro. IP23: Eye 5C 38
Langton Pk. IP23: Eye 7J 37
Langton Pl.
IP33: Bury E 5H 157 (1G 59)
Langton Rd. IP33: Bury E 2D 58
Languidic Cl. CO10: Gt Cor 5H 127
Lansbury Rd. IP19: H'orth 5B 42
Lansdowne Rd. IP4: Ips 1E 138
IP11: Felix 2G 155
NR33: Low 6E 10
Lanwades Bus. Pk. CB8: Kenn 3A 48
Lanwades Pk. CB8: Kenn 3A 48
Lanyard Pl. IP12: Wood 5H 121
Lapwing Cl. IP31: Thur 6K 55

Lapwing Ct. IP28: Mide 7K 23
Lapwing Gro. IP14: Stowm 4H 85
Lapwing Rd. IP2: Ips 3F 137
Larch Cl. IP27: Lake 4B 20
Larchcroft Cl. IP1: Ips 3K 131
Larchcroft Rd. IP1: Ips 3J 131
Larches, The NR34: Wrent 1D 44
Larch Gro. CO6: Nay 6H 143
Larch Ho. IP11: Felix 4D 154
Larch Rd. NR32: Low 5G 9
Larch Way IP28: Red L 7J 25
Larchwood Cl. IP2: Ips 1E 136
Larcoms Lawne IP13: B'ton 1K 89
Largent Gro. IP5: Kesg 5E 134
Lark Cl. IP14: Stowm 5J 85
IP27: B'don 4J 19
IP28: W'ton 2C 24
Lark Hill CB8: Mou 6C 48
Larkhill Ri. IP4: Rush A 1J 139
Larkhill Way IP11: Felix 3C 154
Lark Ri. CO10: Ball 6C 126
IP5: Martl H 6G 135
Lark Rd. IP28: Mide 7K 23
Larks Cl. CB9: Have 4H 101
Larksfield Rd. IP9: Stut 5C 150
Larks Ga. IP28: Forn S 1E 52
Larkspur Cl. IP28: Red L 5H 25
NR32: Low 7H 7
Larkspur Rd. IP2: Ips 3H 137
Larks Ri. IP19: H'orth 5C 42
Larksway IP11: Felix 5C 154
Lark Valley Ct. IP28: Forn M 2F 53
Lark Valley Dr. IP28: Forn M 2F 53
Lark Valley Trade Park, The
IP32: Bury E 3F 53
LARLING 1D 159
La Salle Cl. IP2: Ips 3K 137
Lathbury Ct.
IP33: Bury E 3H 157 (7G 53)
Latimer Cl. IP3: Ips 6K 139
Lattens Sq. NR32: Low 6H 9
Lattice Av. IP4: Ips 7G 133
Latymere Cl. NR33: Gisle 4F 17
Laud M. IP3: Ips 4E 138
Laud's Cl. IP11: T Mary 7H 153
Laundry La. IP19: Hunt 1D 74
IP33: Bury E 3H 59
Laureate Gdns. CB8: Newm 3E 46
Laureate Paddocks CB8: Newm 3E 46
Laureate Paddocks Ind. Est.
CB8: Newm 3E 46
Laureate School Rd.
CB8: Newm 3E 46
Laurel Av. IP5: Kesg 6A 134
Laurel Cl. CB9: Have 1C 100
IP28: Holy R 2H 23
IP28: Red L 6J 25
IP31: Thur 6K 55
Laurel Ct. IP30: E'well 3E 64
Laurel Dr. CO10: L Mel 4H 105
IP6: Gt Bla 2B 114
Laurelhayes IP2: Ips 3J 137
Laurel Rd. NR33: Low 3G 11
Laurels, The IP21: Fress 6B 40
NR34: Worl 5J 13
Laurels End NR34: Becc 4F 13
Laurel Way IP6: Clay 4D 114
Lavender Cl. IP27: B'don 5D 18
IP28: Red L 6H 25
NR33: Oul B 2E 10
Lavender Fld. CB9: Have 3C 100
Lavender Hill IP2: Ips 2H 137
LAVENHAM 6C 106 (2D 163)
Lavenham Guildhall 6C 106
Lavenham-Long Melford Railway Walk
2D 163
Lavenham Rd. CO10: Act 1F 107
CO10: Gt Wal 7J 107
IP2: Ips 1G 137
Lavenham Way IP14: Stowm 6G 85
NR32: Oul B 5E 8
LAWFORD 3A 164
Lawford Pl. *IP4: Rush A 1K 139*
(off Seckford Cl.)
Lawn Gro. NR32: Oul 3E 8
Lawns, The IP4: Ips 5G 133
Lawn Way IP11: Felix 3D 154
Lawrence Dr. NR32: Low 2G 9
Law's Drift IP10: Kirt 1F 153
LAWSHALL 7C 80 (1C 163)
Lawshall Rd. IP29: Hart 1J 103
Lawshall Row IP29: Laws 6B 80
Lawson Ct. NR33: Low 3H 11
Lawson Pl. IP32: Bury E 1A 60
Lawson Rd. NR33: Low 2H 11
LAXFIELD 6C 74 (2C 161)
Laxfield & District Mus. 6C 74
Laxfield Rd. IP13: B'ham 1C 76
IP13: Denn 5C 76
IP21: Fress 6C 40
IP21: Stradb 5J 39
Laxfield Way NR33: Low 5E 10
Layer Rd. CB9: Have 4D 100
Layham Dr. IP32: Bury E 5G 53
Layham Gdns. IP14: Stowm 7H 85
Layham Rd. IP7: Hadl 5H 129
Layhill Cl. IP32: Bury E 2K 59
Laywood Cl. IP32: Bury E 7K 53
Layzell Cft. CO10: Gt Cor 6H 127
Lea, The IP18: Walb 7H 45
Leabrook Cl. IP32: Bury E 7A 54
Leader's Way CB8: Newm 4E 46
Leamans La. IP14: Cott 7G 67
Leamon Ct. IP27: B'don 3G 19
Leas, The NR32: Oul 3E 8
Lea's Drift NR33: Car C 4B 10
Leather La. CB9: Have 4D 100
Leathes Cl. NR32: Oul B 7E 8
LEAVENHEATH 3A 142 (3D 163)
Lee Brook Cl. IP28: Frec 6C 24
Leech Wlk. IP32: Bury E 5E 52
Lee Cl. CB9: Have 1E 100
Lee Gdns. NR34: Worl 4J 13
Leeks Cl. IP7: Hadl 2H 129
Leeks Hill IP12: Melt 3J 121
Lee Rd. IP3: Ips 3D 138
IP15: Aldeb 5J 95
Lees Ct. CO10: Glem 5A 104
Leeward Ct. IP11: Felix 3F 155
Leggatt Dr. IP8: B'ford 3C 130
Leggett Wlk. NR34: Becc 4G 13
Le Grice Wlk. IP32: Bury E 6E 52
Leicester Cl. IP2: Ips 5H 137
Leighton Rd. IP3: Ips 6E 138
Leighton Sq. IP3: Ips 6E 138
LEISTON 4J 93 (1A 166)
Leiston Abbey (remains of) 1J 93
Leiston Ct. *IP16: Leis 4J 93*
(off High St.)
Leiston Film Theatre 4J 93
Leiston Leisure Cen. 4K 93
Leiston Rd. CB9: Have 4D 100
IP15: Aldeb 1G 95
IP16: Theb 7E 78
IP17: Knod 7F 93
IP17: Midd 6C 78
NR32: Low 7J 9
Leisure Way NR32: Low 2G 9
Lely Rd. IP3: Ips 6D 138
Lemons Hill IP9: Tatt 6H 149
Lentins, The IP14: Petta 2C 88
Leona Cres. NR33: Car C 7B 10
Leonard Dr. NR32: Low 2F 9
Leopold Gdns. IP4: Ips 5F 133
Leopold Rd. IP4: Ips 5E 132
IP11: Felix 4F 155
Leslie Rd. IP3: Ips 5G 139
Lester Piggott Way CB8: Newm 3F 47
LETHERINGHAM 1C 165
Letton Cl. IP9: Cap M 2H 147
Leverett's La. IP18: Walb 7G 45
LEVINGTON 7D 152 (3C 165)
Levington Ct. *NR33: Low 1J 11*
(off London Rd. Sth.)
Levington La. IP10: Buck 4B 152
Levington Rd. IP3: Ips 2E 138
IP10: Nac 6A 152
IP11: Felix 7D 154
Lewes Cl. IP3: Ips 3J 139
Lewis Cl. IP22: Hop 2J 31
Lewis La. IP9: Stut 6A 150
Leyland Ct. NR32: Low 7G 9
Ley Rd. IP29: Barr 6B 50
Leys, The IP30: Tost 3G 63
Leys La. IP21: Yax 4D 36
IP23: Yax 4D 36
Leys Rd. IP30: Tost 3G 63
Leyton Av. IP28: Mide 5H 23
Liberator Cl. CO10: Gt Wal 7K 107
Liberty Cl. IP32: Bury E 7B 54
Library M. IP12: Rend 6C 122
LIDGATE 1B 162
Lidgate Ct. IP11: Felix 4B 154
Lidgate Rd. CB8: Dalh 7H 49
Lifeboat Station
Aldeburgh 5K 95
Lowestoft 1J 11
Southwold 7J 45
Lighthouse Score NR32: Low 5K 9
Lilac Cl. IP27: B'don 5C 18
Lilac Dr. IP27: Lake 5B 20
NR32: Low 5G 9
Lilac Wlk. IP6: Nee M 5G 111
Lilley Cl. IP33: Bury E 3C 58
Lily Cl. IP28: Red L 6G 25
Lily Way NR33: Car C 4B 10
Lime Av. NR32: Oul 6C 8
Lime Cl. IP13: Uff 6H 119
IP13: Wick M 6B 118
IP27: Lake 6B 20
IP28: Mide 6K 23
IP28: Red L 5H 25
Limecroft Cl. IP1: Ips 2J 131
Lime Gro. CO10: Ball 6B 126
Lime Gro. Est. CB9: Have 6H 101
Limekiln Cl. IP6: Clay 4D 114
Limekiln Quay IP12: Wood 5J 121
Lime Kiln Quay Rd.
IP12: Wood 5J 121
Limerick Cl. IP1: Ips 3G 131
Limes, The CO10: L Mel 4H 105
IP5: Rush A 4H 133
IP13: F'ham 5B 90
IP14: One 2A 84
IP17: Saxm 5H 91
IP19: H'orth 6A 42
IP29: Horr 6B 58
Limes Av. IP8: B'ford 3E 130
Limes Cl. IP22: Pal 2D 36
Lime Tree Av. IP16: Leis 4H 93
Lime Tree Cl. IP22: W'field 1J 33
IP30: Hess 6D 62
Limetree Cl. IP6: Nee M 4H 111
Limetree Dr. IP3: Pur F 4H 139
Lime Tree Pl. IP1: Ips 6G 131
IP14: Stowm 5G 85
Lime Wlk. CO10: Act 4G 107
IP30: Fels 7B 82
IP32: Bury E 7C 54
Lincoln Av. IP17: Saxm 7G 91
Lincoln Cl. IP1: Ips 2K 131
Lincoln Ct. NR33: Kess 4J 17
Lincoln Gdns. IP6: Clay 3D 114
Lincoln Grn. IP33: Bury E 4G 59
Lincoln Rd. IP28: RAF M 2C 22
Lincoln Ter. IP11: Felix 5E 154
Linda Cl. NR32: Cort 6J 7
Lindbergh Rd. IP3: Ips 5G 139
Linden Cl. IP15: Aldeb 3H 95
Linden Ct. IP23: Eye 7D 38
Linden Rd. IP15: Aldeb 3G 95
Linden Wlk. IP28: B Row 1D 22
Lindisfarne Cl. IP2: Ips 5J 137
Lindisfarne Rd.
IP33: Bury E 4D 58
LINDSELL 3A 162
LINDSEY 2D 163
Lindsey Av. CO10: Gt Cor 5G 127
Lindsey Ct. CO10: Gt Cor 5G 127
Lindsey Rd. IP4: Ips 6G 133
LINDSEY TYE 2D 163
Lindsey Way IP14: Stowm 7G 85
Lingfield Rd. IP1: Ips 1K 131
Lingheath Rd. IP27: B'don 4H 19
Ling Rd. IP22: Pal, Wort 1B 36
Lings Field IP13: Ket 6H 89
Lingside IP5: Martl H 7G 135
Ling's La.
IP9: Hark, Chelm 4J 151 & 4F 151
Link, The IP9: Bent 6G 147
IP13: Laxf 6B 74
Link La. IP9: Bent 6G 147
Link Rd. IP9: Cap M 2H 147
IP9: Shot G 6D 156
Links Av. IP11: Felix 2F 155
Links Cl. CO10: Glem 4B 104
IP28: W'ton 3C 24
IP33: Bury E 5H 59
NR33: Oul B 4E 10
Linksfield IP5: Rush A 6J 133
Linksfield Gdns.
IP5: Rush A 6K 133
Links Rd. NR32: Low 3J 9
Links Vw. CO10: Newt 2C 128
Linkwood Equestrian Cen. 1A 82
Linkwood Rd. IP30: Rushb 7F 61
Linnet Cres. IP27: B'don 4H 19
Linnet Dr. IP14: Stowm 5J 85
Linnet Pl. IP33: Bury E 7K 157
Linnet Rd. IP2: Ips 2F 137
IP33: Bury E 2E 58
LINSTEAD PARVA 2D 161
LINTON 2A 162
Linton Cl. CB8: Newm 4F 47
Linton Gdns. IP33: Bury E 3E 58
Linton Pl. CB9: Have 3G 101
Lion Barn Ind. Est.
IP6: Nee M 5H 111
Lionel Hurst Cl.
CO10: Gt Cor 6H 127
Lion Grn. IP29: Barr 7C 50
Lion La. IP6: Nee M 5H 111
Lion Rd. CO10: Glem 4A 104
IP22: Pal 3A 36
Lion St. IP1: Ips 3D 4 (7A 132)
Lisburn Rd. CB8: Newm 6H 47
Lister Rd. IP1: Ips 4H 131
IP7: Hadl 4K 129
LISTON 5F 105 (2C 163)
Liston La. CO10: Lis, L Mel 5F 105
Lithgo Paddock IP31: Gt Bar 2D 54
Lit. Back La. IP14: Deb 2H 87
LITTLE BARDFIELD 3A 162
LITTLE BEALINGS 1D 134 (2C 165)
LITTLE BLAKENHAM 2B 164
LITTLE BRADLEY 4D 96 (1A 162)
Lit. Bramford La.
IP1: Ips 1A 4 (6J 131)
LITTLE BROMLEY 3A 164
LITTLE CHADACRE 1C 106
Little Chad Cl. IP29: Shim 1C 106
LITTLE CORNARD 3C 163
Lit. Croft St. IP2: Ips 7E 4 (3A 138)
LITTLE DITTON 1A 162
Lit. Gipping St. IP1: Ips 3C 4 (7K 131)
LITTLE GLEMHAM 1D 165
LITTLE GREEN 1H 67 (2A 160)
Little Green IP30: E'well 2D 64
Lit. Green Cl. IP23: Gisli 1H 67
Little Gro. IP9: Cap M 2H 147
Little Gulls IP9: Cap M 2G 147
Little Hall 6C 106
Little Hill IP7: Gt Bri 3B 112
LITTLE HORKESLEY 3D 163
Lit. Horsey Pk. IP13: Cam A 3A 122
Little La. IP13: Wick M 5A 118
LITTLE LONDON 3G 65
Little London IP27: Eris 7G 21
Lit. London Hill IP14: Deb 1G 87
Little Lumpkid IP7: Hadl 1J 129
LITTLE MAPLESTEAD 3C 163
Lit. Meadows Dr. IP6: Otl 1K 117
Lit. Mill La. IP29: Barr 5C 50
Littlemoor Rd. IP17: Midd 6A 78
(not continuous)
LITTLE OAKLEY 3C 165
Little Orchard IP9: Holb 3D 150
LITTLE OUSE 1A 158
LITTLEPORT 1A 158
Little St John's St.
IP12: Wood 5H 121
Little St Mary's CO10: L Mel 5H 105
LITTLE SAMPFORD 3A 162
LITTLE SAXHAM 3B 158
Little's Cres. IP2: Ips 7E 4 (2A 138)
LITTLE STONHAM 1E 86 (3B 160)
Little St. IP17: Yox 5G 77
LITTLE THURLOW 6C 96 (1A 162)
LITTLE THURLOW GREEN 5E 96
Little Tufts IP9: Cap M 2J 147
LITTLE WALDEN 2A 162
LITTLE WALDINGFIELD
5C 108 (2D 163)
LITTLE WENHAM 1F 147 (3A 164)
LITTLE WHELNETHAM 1C 163
Lit. Whelnetham Rd.
IP30: S'mere 7C 60
Lit. Whip St. IP2: Ips 6E 4 (2A 138)
LITTLE WHITTINGHAM GREEN 2C 161
LITTLE WILBRAHAM 1A 162
LITTLE WRATTING 2A 162
LITTLE YELDHAM 3B 162
Livermere Cl. IP31: Gt Bar 1D 54
Livermere Drift IP31: Forn M 1J 53
Livermere Rd. IP31: Gt Bar 3C 54
IP31: Gt Liv, Tros 3B 28
Llewellyn Drift IP5: Kesg 6C 134
Lloyd Rd. IP9: Shot G 7D 156
Lloyds, The IP5: Kesg 6C 134
Lloyds Av. IP1: Ips 3D 4 (7A 132)
NR33: Kess 4J 17
Loam Pit La. IP19: H'orth 4C 42
Locarno Rd. IP3: Ips 3F 139
Loch Rannoch Cl. IP30: E'well 2D 64
Lock Cl. IP14: Deb 2H 87
Lockington Cl. IP14: Stowm 5G 85
Lockington Cres. IP14: Stowm 5F 85
Lockington Rd. IP14: Stowm 5F 85
Lockington Wlk. IP14: Stowm 5F 85
Locks La. CO6: Leav 3A 142
IP28: B Row 1E 22
NR34: Wrent 1D 44
Lockwood Cl. IP12: Wood 5G 121
Loddon Rd. NR34: Gill 1C 12
Lode St. IP27: B'don 3F 19
Lodge Cl. IP14: Old N 5A 70
IP31: Gt Bar 2E 54
IP31: Thur 6A 56
Lodge Farm Dr. IP11: Felix 3H 155
Lodge Farm La. IP12: Melt 1K 121
NR34: Bars 5A 12
Lodge Farm Rd. CO10: Glem 6B 104
Lodge La. IP6: Gt Bla 4B 114
IP19: Blyth 7J 43
Lodge Rd.
IP13: Gt Bea, L Bea
1E 134 & 7A 120
IP13: Uff 5H 119
IP18: Walb 7F 45
IP19: Holt 4E 42
Lofft Cl. IP31: Stant 6D 32
Loftus Av. IP18: Rey 2J 45
Loganberry Rd. IP3: Ips 7G 139
Loggers La. IP22: Thel 6H 31
Loke, The NR32: Blun 1J 7
Lombard Ct. IP4: Ips 6D 132
Lombardy Rd. CO10: S'bury 1C 126
London La. IP14: Harl 7K 65

London Rd. IP1: Ips 3A 4 (7J 131)
IP2: Ips 2G 137
IP8: Cop, Ips, Wash 7A 136
IP9: Cap M 3J 147
(not continuous)
IP17: Dars 1B 78
IP19: Blyth 7G 43
IP19: H'orth 6A 42
IP24: Elv 4G 27
IP27: B'don 5D 18
NR33: Kess, Low . . . . .3J 17 & 7F 11
NR34: Becc, Westo 4E 12
NR34: Bramp 6G 15
NR34: Fros, Wrent 4A 44
London Road, Ipswich (Park & Ride) .4C 136
London Rd. Nth. NR32: Low 1J 11
(not continuous)
London Rd. Sth. NR33: Low 5G 11
Lone Barn Ct. IP1: Ips 5F 131
Long Acre IP18: Rey 2H 45
NR33: Low 6G 11
Longacre IP17: Westl 4H 79
Longacre Gdns. IP33: Bury E 3E 58
Long Av. IP17: Saxm 5G 91
Longbeach Dr. NR33: Car C 6C 10
Long Bessels IP7: Hadl 3H 129
Long Brackland
IP33: Bury E 2H 157 (7G 53)
Longbrook Cl. NR33: Car C 5D 10
Longcroft IP11: Felix 2D 154
Longden Av. NR32: Oul B 6E 8
Long Fld. IP11: Felix 2C 154
Longfield Rd. IP9: Cap M 1H 147
Long Flds. Path NR32: Oul 4C 8
Longfield Way NR32: Oul B 6C 8
LONG GARDENS 3C 163
Long Grn. IP22: Wort 1F 35
(not continuous)
Long La. CO10: L Mel 1G 105
Long Marsh Cl. IP18: Rey 2J 45
Long Meadow CO10: Lave 7B 106
Longmeadow IP33: Bury E 3E 58
Long Meadow Wlk. NR33: Car C . . .4C 10
LONG MELFORD 4H 105 (2C 163)
Long Melford By-Pass
CO10: L Mel 1K 105
Long Pastures CO10: Glem 6A 104
Long Perry IP9: Cap M 2J 147
Long Rd. NR33: Car C, Oul B 6D 10
Long Row IP12: Sud 2H 125
IP16: Leis 3J 93
IP33: Bury E 6K 157
Long Shop Museum, The 3H 93
LONG STRATTON 1B 160
Long St. IP4: Ips 5H 5 (1C 138)
LONG THURLOW 3A 160
Long Thurlow Rd. IP31: Gt Ash 4E 66
Lonsdale Cl. IP4: Ips 1K 5 (6D 132)
Looe Rd. IP11: Felix 3H 155
Looms La.
IP33: Bury E 4H 157 (1G 59)
Lophams Cl. CB9: Have 1E 100
Loraine Way IP8: B'ford, Spro 1B 130
Lordscroft La. CB9: Have 3F 101
Lord's Highway, The IP14: E Sto . . .5B 86
Lord's Wlk. IP27: RAF L 4G 21
Lorne Pk. Rd. NR33: Low 3H 11
Lorne Rd. IP18: Sou 4K 45
NR33: Low 3H 11
Lothingland Cl. NR32: Oul 3E 8
Lothing St. NR32: Oul B 7E 8
Lotus Cl. IP1: Ips 4E 130
Loudham Hall Rd.
IP13: Cam A, Petti 1K 119
Loudham La. IP13: Uff 6J 119
LOUND .1D 167
Lound Rd. NR32: Blun 1G 7
Love La. IP6: Cod 2G 115
IP7: Lay 5F 129
IP12: Melt 4J 121
IP13: F'ham 6C 90
IP17: Westl 6H 79
IP17: Yox 7J 77
IP23: Thorn 2B 72
NR33: Low 5E 10
NR35: Bung 5B 14
Love Rd. NR32: Low 7H 9
Lover's La. IP16: Leis 1J 93
Lovetofts Dr. IP1: Ips 4F 131
(not continuous)
Lovewell Rd. NR33: Low 3H 11
Lwr. Barn Rd. IP8: Chat 3D 144
Lwr. Baxter St.
IP33: Bury E 4H 157 (1G 59)
Lwr. Brook M. IP4: Ips 4E 4
Lwr. Brook St. IP4: Ips 4E 4 (1A 138)
Lwr. Broom Rd. IP30: Wool 4K 63
Lower Byfield IP7: M Ele 2D 108
Lower Cres. IP6: Barh 1B 114
Lwr. Dales Vw. Rd. IP1: Ips 5J 131
Lwr. Downs Slade CB9: Have 3F 101
Lwr. Farm Rd. IP14: R'hall 1B 112
Lower Gorse IP30: Blac 3E 60
Lower Grn. CB8: Dens 7K 97
CO10: Stoke C 6J 99
IP30: Fels 6C 82
LOWER HACHESTON 4D 118
Lower Harlings IP9: Shot G 7D 156
Lwr. Haugh La. IP12: Wood 4G 121
LOWER HOLBROOK 5F 151 (3B 164)
Lwr. Houses Rd. IP9: Hark 5K 151
LOWER LAYHAM 7J 129 (2A 164)
Lwr. North St. CO10: Hund 2J 99
Lwr. Olland St. NR35: Bung 2B 14
Lwr. Orwell St. IP4: Ips . . .5F 5 (1B 138)
Lwr. Park Wlk. IP19: Holt 4E 42
LOWER RAYDON 3G 145 (3A 164)
Lower Reeve CO10: Gt Cor 7G 127
Lower Rd.
CO10: Borl . . . . . . .7G 105 & 1A 126
CO10: Glem . . . . . .5K 103 & 7A 104
CO10: Hund 2H 99
CO10: Lave 5C 106
IP6: Aken, Weste 1A 132
IP6: Cod 1G 115
IP6: Hemi 2K 115
IP8: S'ham 3K 113
IP13: Gru 7J 117
IP13: Uff 7J 119
IP14: One 4A 84
IP30: Rat 4K 83
Lwr. Rose La. IP22: Pal 1E 36
Lwr. Stoke Rd. CO10: Ashe 7K 99
LOWER STREET 6C 150
Lower St. CO7: Ded, Strat M 7G 145
CO10: Cave 6H 103
CO10: Stans 3C 104
IP6: Bay, Nee M 5J 111
IP8: Spro 6C 130
IP9: Stut 6C 150
IP13: Gt Bea 6A 120
IP13: Uff 6J 119
LOWER THURLTON 1C 167
Lwr. Ufford Rd.
IP13: Petti, Uff 4K 119
Lowes Hill IP17: Kel 2K 91
LOWESTOFT 6K 9 (1D 167)
Lowestoft Arts Cen. *NR32: Low 6K 9*
(off St Peter's St.)
Lowestoft Ent. Pk. NR33: Oul B 1E 10
Lowestoft Haven Marina
NR33: Oul B 1E 10
Lowestoft Maritime Mus. 5K 9
Lowestoft Mus. 1C 10
Lowestoft Railway Indoor Bowls Club 3G 11
Lowestoft Rd. IP18: Rey 2J 45
NR32: Blun 2J 7
NR33: Car C 6C 10
NR34: Becc, Nor C, Worl .4F 13 & 7A 6
(not continuous)
Lowestoft Station (Rail) 1J 11
Lowestoft Town FC
Crown Meadow 6J 9
Low Farm Dr. NR33: Car C 6B 10
Lowgate St. IP23: Eye 7D 38
Low Green IP29: Now 7K 59
IP30: Rushb 7K 59
Lowlands Cl. NR33: Kess 5K 17
Low La. IP6: C Mary 7A 114
Low Rd. IP12: Eyk 1D 124
IP13: Hask 2C 120
IP13: Laxf 6E 74
IP14: Deb 4G 87
IP17: Dars 4C 78
IP17: Fris 7D 92
IP17: Kel 3J 91
IP19: B'field 6J 75
IP19: Ubb 4A 74
IP19: Wen 1G 43
NR34: Bramp 6F 15
NR35: Mett 2E 14
Lowry Cl. CB9: Have 2C 100
Lowry Gdns. IP3: Ips 6E 138
Lowry Way IP14: Stowm 3D 84
NR32: Low 3H 9
Low's La. IP22: Pal 1D 36
Low St. CO10: Glem 4B 104
IP13: B'ham 1A 76
IP13: B'ton, Ket 1K 89
IP21: Hox 1B 38
IP31: Bard 3D 32
Lowther St. CB8: Newm 6F 47
Loxley Rd. NR33: Oul B 3D 10
Lucas Rd. CO10: S'bury 4E 126
Lucena Ct. IP14: Stowm 4E 84
Lucerne Cl. IP28: Red L 6H 25
NR33: Car C 4B 10
Ludbrook Cl. IP6: Nee M 3F 111
Ludgate C'way. IP23: Eye 7E 38
Ludham IP27: RAF L 4H 21
Ludlow Cl. IP1: Ips 1K 131
Luff Mdw. IP6: Nee M 3G 111
Lugano Av. IP5: Martl H 5J 135
Lulworth Av. IP3: Ips 3H 139
Lulworth Dr. CB9: Have 3D 100
Lulworth Pk. NR32: Low 4F 9
Lummis Va. IP5: Kesg 6C 134
Lundy Cl. CB9: Have 4J 101
LUNDY GREEN 1C 161
Lupin Cl. IP18: Rey 3H 45
Lupin Rd. IP2: Ips 2G 137
Lupin Way IP6: Nee M 5G 111
Luther Rd. IP2: Ips 7C 4 (2K 137)
Lutus Cl. CO10: Clar 6B 102
Lydgate Cl. IP32: Bury E 4E 52
Lydgate Ct. IP33: Bury E 3H 59
Lydgate Rd. IP14: Stowm 3E 84
Lyle Cl. IP5: Kesg 6E 134
Lyminster Cl. IP32: Bury E 7K 53
Lymm Rd. NR32: Low 3G 9
Lyncroft Rd. NR33: Low 6G 11
Lyndhurst Av. IP4: Ips 1G 139
Lyndhurst Rd. NR32: Low 4J 9
Lyngate Av. NR33: Oul B 4E 10
Lynnbrook Cl. IP2: Ips 5G 137
Lynn's Hall Cl. CO10: Gt Wal 7K 107
Lynton Gdns. NR32: Low 5H 9
Lynwood Av. IP11: Felix 3G 155
Lyon Cl. *IP5: Kesg 5E 134*
(off Howards Way)
IP23: Yax 7E 36
Lysander Dr. IP3: Ips 6G 139
Lytham Rd. IP3: Ips 7K 139

M

Macaulay Rd. IP1: Ips 1H 131
McCalmont Way CB8: Newm 7K 47
Macdonald-Buchanan Ho.
CB8: Newm 5G 47
(off Howard De Walden Way)
Machonochie Way NR33: Low 2H 11
McIntyre Wlk. IP32: Bury E 6E 52
Mackenzie Dr. IP5: Kesg 5B 134
Mackintosh Cl. IP3: Ips 1F 139
McLaren Ct. NR34: Becc 5F 13
McLean Dr. NR33: Kess 4J 17
Macmillan Way IP33: Bury E 5F 59
Macpherson Robertson Way
IP28: Mide 6G 23
Mafeking Pl. IP16: Leis 3J 93
Magdalen Cl. NR32: Low 5F 9
Magdalen Ct. IP23: Eye 7C 38
Magdalen Dr. IP12: Wood 7E 120
Magdalene Cl. IP2: Ips 4H 137
Magdalen Rd. IP7: Hadl 3H 129
Magdalen St. IP23: Eye 7C 38
Magingley Cres.
IP5: Rush A 7K 133
Magistrates' Court
Bury St Edmunds . . .6K 157 (2H 59)
Ipswich 3C 4 (1K 137)
Lowestoft 7K 9
Magna Ho.
IP33: Bury E 3K 157 (7H 53)
Magnolia Cl. IP28: B Row 1D 22
IP28: Red L 6H 25
Magnolia Ct. NR32: Low 6G 9
Magnolia Dr. IP12: Rend 6C 122
IP27: Lake 6B 20
Magpie Cl. IP8: Ips 4E 136
MAGPIE GREEN 2A 160
Maidenhair Way
IP28: Red L 5H 25
MAIDENHALL 4K 137
Maidenhall App.
IP2: Ips 7D 4 (4K 137)
Maidenhall Grn. IP2: Ips 4K 137
Maidenhall Sports Cen. 4A 138
MAIDENSGRAVE 7F 121
Maiden Way IP7: Hadl 3H 129
Maid Marion Ct. IP33: Bury E 3F 59
Maids Cross Hill IP27: Lake 5C 20
Maids Cross Way IP27: Lake 4B 20
Maidstone Rd. IP11: Felix 3D 154
IP12: Sutt 2D 140
NR32: Low 7H 9
Main Rd. IP5: Kesg, Martl 5K 133
IP6: Hemi 3K 115
IP6: Henl 4J 115
IP6: Tud . . . . .2E 132 & 7D 116
IP6: Weste 2C 132
IP8: S'ham 3J 113
IP9: Chelm 2F 151
(not continuous)
IP9: Shot, Shot G 4C 156
IP10: Buck 2B 152
IP12: Martl 4G 135
IP13: Hach, L Hac 4C 118
IP13: Petti 2J 119
IP17: Benh 2C 92
IP17: Carl, Kel, Saxm 1H 91
Main Rd. IP17: Dars 5K 77
IP17: Yox 7H 77
IP31: Gt Ash 5E 66
Main St. IP16: Leis 3H 93
Mais Ct. IP2: Ips 4H 137
Maisie's Mdw. IP13: W'orth 5G 73
Maitland Rd. IP6: Nee M 5H 111
Major's Cl. IP29: Chedb 6K 51
Major's Cnr. IP4: Ips 3F 5 (7B 132)
Malcolm Way CB8: Newm 4H 47
Maldon Ct. CO10: Gt Cor 4G 127
(not continuous)
Malin Cl. CB9: Have 4J 101
Mallard Ct. IP2: Ips 3H 137
Mallard Ho. Bus. Cen.
IP13: L Bea 2D 134
Mallard Rd. IP17: Saxm 6G 91
IP18: Rey 2H 45
Mallards, The IP27: Lake 6B 20
Mallard Way CO10: Gt Cor 6H 127
IP2: Ips 4G 137
IP12: Holl 2G 141
IP14: Stowm 4C 84
IP27: B'don 5H 19
Mallets La. IP12: Orf 7J 125
Mallowhayes Cl. IP2: Ips 3K 137
Mallow Wlk. CB9: Have 3B 100
Mallow Way NR33: Car C 5B 10
Malmesbury Cl. IP2: Ips 5J 137
Malt Cl. CB8: Newm 6H 47
IP13: Laxf 6B 74
Malt Cotts. IP19: Hunt 1C 74
Malthouse, The CO10: L Mel 6G 105
Malthouse La.
IP32: Bury E 1G 157 (6G 53)
Malthouse Project, The 3G 157
Malting Cotts. CB9: Stur 7K 101
MALTING END 4G 97
Malting Fld. IP30: E'well 3D 64
Malting La. CO10: Clar 5C 102
IP13: Gru 6H 117
Malting Row IP31: Honi 2H 29
Maltings, The IP10: Kirt 2H 153
IP27: B'don 3F 19
IP31: Wals W 6G 33
NR34: Becc 1E 12
NR35: Bung 2C 14
Maltings Cl. CB8: Mou 6C 48
CO8: Bure 5A 142
IP19: H'orth 4B 42
IP29: Chev 2K 51
Maltings Cotts. IP17: Snap 4C 94
Maltings Gth. IP31: Thur 6J 55
Maltings La. IP31: Ing 5E 28
Maltings M. IP7: Hadl 4H 129
Maltings Way
IP32: Bury E 1G 157 (6G 53)
Malting Ter. IP2: Ips 7F 5 (2B 138)
IP19: B'field 7J 75
Maltsters Score *NR32: Low 6K 9*
(off Spurgeon Score)
Maltsters Wlk. IP14: Stowm 7E 84
Maltsters' Way NR32: Oul B 1C 10
Maltward Av. IP33: Bury E 1C 58
Malvern Cl. CB8: Newm 7H 47
IP3: Ips 3F 139
IP5: Rush A 6K 133
Malvern Ri. NR32: Low 5G 9
Malvern Rd. IP33: Bury E 3D 58
Malyon Rd. IP7: Hadl 1J 129
Manchester Rd. IP2: Ips 4F 137
Manderston Rd. CB8: Newm 5E 46
Manderville Rd. IP33: Bury E 2D 58
Mandy Cl. IP4: Ips 7E 132
Mannall Wlk. IP5: Kesg 5E 134
Manners Rd. IP31: Forn M 4H 53
Manning Rd. IP11: Felix 6E 154
IP32: Bury E 7B 54
Mannings Family Fun Cen. 7E 154
Manning's La. IP22: W'field 2J 33
Mannington Cl. IP4: Rush A 1K 139
MANNINGTREE 3B 164
Manningtree Rd. CO7: Ded 7A 146
CO7: E Ber . . . . . . .5E 146 & 5A 148
IP9: Stut 6A 150
Manningtree Station (Rail) 7A 148
Manns Ct. IP30: E'well 3E 64
Manor Ash Dr. IP32: Bury E 7A 54
Manor Cl. CO10: Cave 5G 103
IP18: Walb 7G 45
NR34: Worl 5J 13
Manor Ct. *IP28: Mide 7J 23*
(off High St.)
NR32: Low 6K 9
(off Gun La.)
Mnr. Farm Cl. CB9: Have 5G 101
IP18: Sou 4K 45
Mnr. Farm Dr. IP30: Bey 3D 62
Mnr. Farm Gro. IP8: Hint 3A 144
Mnr. Farm Rd. IP28: W Row 5A 22
Manor Gdns. IP17: Saxm 7K 91
Manor Gth. IP31: Pake 2A 56

Manor Ho. Cl. *IP27: B'don* 4E 18
(off St Peter's App.)
Manor Ho. Estate, The
IP12: Bawd 7G 141
Manor Ho. La. NR34: Becc 2E 12
Manor La. IP9: Stut 6A 150
IP29: Horr 6B 58
Manor Pk. IP21: Horh 1H 73
Manor Pk. Rd. IP18: Sou 4K 45
NR32: Cort 6H 7
Manor Rd. CB9: Have 4G 101
CO10: S'bury 2D 126
IP4: Ips 5B 132
IP5: Martl H 5G 135
IP7: Bild 6J 109
IP7: E'sett 4F 113
IP11: Felix 7D 154
IP11: T Mary 1A 154
IP13: Hask 4D 120
IP27: B'don 4D 18
IP28: Mide 7H 23
IP30: Hess 7C 62
NR35: Bung 4B 14
Manor Ter. IP11: Felix 7D 154
Manor Vw. IP28: B Mil 2G 25
IP31: Nort 7A 66
Manor Wlk. NR33: Kess 5J 17
Manor Wood IP28: Red L 4J 25
Mansbrook Blvd. IP3: Ips 6G 139
Mansbrook Vs. IP3: Ips 7J 139
Mansfield Av. IP1: Ips 3H 131
Manson Ct.
IP33: Bury E 3J 157 (7H 53)
Manston IP27: RAF L 5J 21
Manthorp Cl. IP12: Melt 2J 121
Manwick Rd. IP11: Felix 6E 154
Maple Cl. IP2: Ips 3J 137
IP7: Gt Bri 2A 112
IP12: Rend 6C 122
IP23: Yax 6C 36
IP27: RAF L 4G 21
IP33: Bury E 3F 59
Maple Covert NR32: Oul 2E 8
Maple Grn. IP31: Gt Bar 2D 54
Maple Gro. IP6: Barh 1C 114
Maple Ho. IP11: Felix 4D 154
Maple Pk. CB9: Have 6H 101
Maple Rd. CO10: Gt Cor 6G 127
IP14: Stowu 2J 85
NR33: Oul B 2E 10
Maples, The IP4: Rush A 5J 133
Maple Way CO6: Leav 3B 142
IP23: Eye 6D 38
NR34: Becc 3F 13
Marbella Grn. NR33: Car C 5D 10
Marbled White Dr. IP8: Ips 6G 137
March Pl. CO10: Clar 3C 102
Marcus Cl. CB9: Have 4J 101
Marcus Rd. IP11: Felix 3J 155
Mardle, The NR33: Car C 7B 10
Mardle Rd. NR34: Wang 7D 44
Mare Hill CO10: Hund 4J 99
Margaret Rd. IP14: Stowm 2E 84
Margaret St. IP11: Felix 3D 154
Margate Rd. IP3: Ips 3F 139
Margery Girling Ho.
IP11: Felix 2H 155
Marham Rd. NR32: Low 6H 9
Marigold Av. IP2: Ips 3G 137
Marigold Dr. IP28: Red L 7H 25
Marina NR32: Low 7J 9
Marina Gdns. IP11: Felix 6D 154
Marina Theatre 7J 9
Marine Pde. NR33: Low 2J 11
Mariners Ct. IP15: Aldeb 4H 95
Mariners Score NR32: Low 6K 9
Mariners St. NR32: Low 6K 9
Mariners Way IP15: Aldeb 4H 95
Marion Cl. NR34: Becc 5F 13
Maritime Ct. IP4: Ips 5F 5 (1B 138)
Markant Cl. IP32: Bury E 7A 54
Market Bri. IP14: Deb 2H 87
Market Cross IP33: Bury E 4H 157
Market Cross Pl. IP15: Aldeb 5K 95
Market Hill CB9: Have 3F 101
CO10: Clar 5C 102
CO10: S'bury 4D 126
IP12: Orf 7J 125
IP12: Wood 5H 121
IP13: F'ham 6C 90
IP27: B'don 3F 19
Market La. CO10: Lave 6C 106
NR32: Ashb, S'ton 1D 6
NR32: Blun 2J 7 & 4F 7
Market M.
IP33: Bury E 4G 157 (1G 59)
Market Pl. CO10: Lave 6C 106
IP7: Bild 6J 109
IP7: Hadl 4H 129
IP14: Stowm 4F 85
IP17: Saxm 6J 91
IP18: Sou 4K 45
Market Pl. IP19: H'orth 5B 42
IP28: Mide 7J 23
NR33: Kess 4H 17
NR35: Bung 2B 14
Market Row NR34: Becc 3E 12
Market St. CB8: Newm 6G 47
IP13: Laxf 6C 74
IP28: Mide 7J 23
NR34: Becc 3E 12
Market Thoroughfare
IP33: Bury E 4G 157
MARKET WESTON 2D 159
Market Weston Rd. IP22: Hep 5C 30
Markhams Cl. CB9: Have 2E 100
Mark Jennings La.
IP33: Bury E 2J 157 (7H 53)
Marlborough Ct. CB9: Have 4D 100
NR32: Oul B 7E 8
Marlborough Dr. CO10: S'bury 3E 126
Marlborough Rd. IP4: Ips 1D 138
IP13: Saxt, Sax G 2A 90
IP18: Sou 3K 45
NR32: Oul B 7E 8
MARLESFORD 1D 165
Marlesford Rd.
IP13: Cam A, Marl 1B 122
Marley Cl. IP31: Thur 5J 55
Marlow Rd. IP1: Ips 4F 131
Marram Grn. NR33: Kess 4J 17
Marriott's Wlk. IP14: Stowm 5F 85
Marsden Cl. NR33: Low 6F 11
Marsh, The IP22: Wort 2K 35
Marshall Cl. IP5: Kesg 5C 134
Marshalls Mdw. IP14: Stowu 2J 85
Marsham's Piece NR33: Car C 4B 10
Marsh La. IP9: Shot G 6E 156
IP11: Felix 1J 155
IP22: Wort 2K 35
NR32: Herr 1B 6
NR32: S'ton 2B 6
NR33: Car C 5A 10
NR33: Kess 7J 17
NR34: Gill 1B 12
NR34: Hens 4A 16
NR34: Nor C 5A 6
NR34: Worl 3K 13
Marsh Rd. CO10: Boxf 6D 128
NR33: Oul B 2C 10
Marsh Vw. NR34: Becc 3F 13
Marsh Wlk. CO10: Act 4G 107
Marsh Way
IP33: Bury E 1F 157 (6F 53)
Martello La. IP11: Felix 3J 155
Martello Pl. IP11: Felix 3J 155
Martello Rd. NR32: Low 4G 9
Martello Tower (L)
Shotley Gate 7E 156
Marten's La. CO6: Pols 6C 144
Martin Cl. IP27: B'don 4H 19
IP28: Mide 1G 25
NR33: Car C 6C 10
Martinet Grn. IP3: Ips 5G 139
Martin Rd. IP2: Ips 7D 4 (2A 138)
Martin's Av. NR33: Low 3G 11
Martins Mdw. IP23: Gisli 1J 67
Martins M. CB9: Have 2B 100
Martins Rd. CO10: S'bury 2G 127
Martin's Score NR32: Low 6K 9
Martinsyde IP5: Martl H 5H 135
MARTLESHAM 4G 135 (2C 165)
Martlesham (Park & Ride) 4G 135
Martlesham By-Pass
IP12: L Bea, Martl 1H 135
Martlesham Creek Ind. Est.
IP12: Martl 2J 135
MARTLESHAM HEATH
6G 135 (2C 165)
Martlesham Heath Control Tower Mus.
5F 135
Martlesham Leisure Health &
Fitness Cen. 6H 135
Martlesham Rd. IP13: L Bea 2E 134
Martyns Ri. CO10: L Mel 6H 105
Marvens, The IP8: Wash 5C 136
Mary Day Cl. IP6: Cod 1G 115
Mary La. CO10: Hund 2H 99
Maryon Rd. IP3: Ips 6F 139
Masefield Rd. IP14: Stowm 2D 84
Mason Cl. CB9: Have 1E 100
Mason Ct. IP6: Barh 3C 114
IP14: Mendl 1J 71
Mason Gdns. IP28: W Row 5B 22
Masons Cl. IP4: Ips 7D 132
Mason's La. IP30: Wool 4A 64
Mast Cl. NR33: Car C 5A 10
Masterlord Ind. Est.
IP16: Leis 3H 93
Masterson Gro. IP5: Kesg 7C 134
Mather Way IP2: Ips 7F 5 (2B 138)
Matlock Cl. IP2: Ips 4E 136
Matlock Dale NR33: Car C 6D 10
Matson Rd. IP1: Ips 5H 131
Matt Dawson Cl. CB8: Newm 3F 47
Matthews Cl. CO7: Strat M 6G 145
Matthews La. CB8: Gt Bra 2A 96
Maude St. IP3: Ips 7H 5
Maudslay Rd. IP1: Ips 3E 130
Mauldens Mill IP13: F'ham 5C 90
Maulkin Cl. IP32: Bury E 7B 54
Maundy Cl.
IP33: Bury E 7F 157 (2F 59)
Mautby Way NR33: Oul B 4E 10
Maybury Rd. IP3: Ips 5F 139
Maybush La. IP11: Felix 3H 155
Maycroft Cl. IP1: Ips 1J 131
Mayes Mdw. CB8: Mou 6C 48
Mayfair Rd. NR35: Bung 3C 14
Mayfield CO6: Leav 3B 142
Mayfield Av. NR33: Kess 4K 17
Mayfield La. IP5: Martl H 7G 135
Mayfield Rd. IP4: Ips 6G 133
IP33: Bury E 4H 59
NR33: Car C 5B 10
Mayfields IP5: Martl H 7G 135
IP27: Lake 4A 20
Mayfield Way IP14: Mendl 1J 71
Mayflower Av. IP17: Saxm 7G 91
Mayflower Way
CO10: S'bury 1E 126
Mayfly Cl. IP8: Ips 6G 137
Mayhew Rd. IP12: Rend 6C 122
Maynewater La.
IP33: Bury E 7J 157 (2H 59)
Maynewater Sq.
IP33: Bury E 7J 157 (2H 59)
Mayo Ct. IP1: Ips 3G 131
Mayors Av. IP1: Ips 5A 132
Mayor's Field Caravan Park, The
IP15: Aldeb 3J 95
Mayors' Walk, The
IP1: Ips 1E 4 (6A 132)
MAYPOLE GREEN
Bury St Edmunds 3D 82 (1D 163)
Haddiscoe 1C 167
Woodbridge 5A 76
Maypole Mdw. IP22: Rick 5J 35
Maypole Ter. CB9: Have 4F 101
May Rd. IP3: Ips 4G 139
NR32: Low 7H 9
Mays Ct. IP11: Felix 5E 154
Mead, The CO10: Gt Cor 7G 127
Mead Dr. IP5: Kesg 6C 134
Meadow Cl. CO10: Lave 7B 106
IP9: Chelm 2H 151
IP11: T Mart 5H 153
IP14: Stowm 4D 84
IP30: Fels 6C 82
IP33: Bury E 3E 58
Meadow Ct. IP30: E'well 1D 64
IP31: Stant 7D 32
Meadow Cres. IP3: Pur F 5K 139
Meadow Cft. IP11: Felix 5C 154
Meadow Dr. IP27: Lake 4B 20
IP29: Horr 6B 58
Meadow Gdns. NR34: Becc 5D 12
Meadowlands IP10: Kirt 1H 153
IP12: Sud 1H 125
IP30: Wool 4A 64
NR32: Blun 1H 7
NR34: Wrent 1D 44
Meadowlands Cl. IP17: Yox 6G 77
Meadow La. CB8: Newm 7K 47
CO10: S'bury 5D 126
IP31: Thur 4A 56
Meadow Pl. CO10: S'bury 5D 126
Meadow Rise IP16: Aldr 7J 93
Meadow Rd. CO10: S'bury 4D 126
NR32: Oul 4E 8
NR35: Bung 3D 14
Meadows, The IP14: Cott 7H 67
IP28: W'ton 3B 24
IP30: Drin G 1F 83
(not continuous)
Meadow Shop. Centre, The
IP14: Stowm 4F 85
Meadowside IP13: Wick M 5B 118
Meadowside Gdns.
IP4: Rush A 5J 133
Meadows Pl. *IP7: Hadl* 3H 129
(off Meadows Way)
Meadows Way IP7: Hadl 3H 129
Meadowsweet Cl.
CB9: Have 2D 100
NR33: Car C 4C 10
Meadow Va. IP14: E Sto 2E 86
Meadowvale Cl. IP4: Ips 6D 132
NR34: Becc 6E 12
Meadow Valley IP7: Gt Bri 3A 112
Meadow Vw. IP6: Nee M 3F 111
IP10: Buck 2B 152
IP30: Wool 7C 64
NR35: Bung 1B 14
Meadow Vw. Rd. CO10: Ball 5C 126
Meadow Wlk. IP17: Benh 3C 92
Meadow Way CB8: Gaz 3G 49
IP21: Stradb 6G 39
IP29: Barr 6B 50
NR33: Car C 7B 10
Mead Rd. IP32: Bury E 1C 60
Meads, The NR32: Low 4J 9
Mead Way IP14: Mendl 1J 71
Mear Cl. IP12: Sutt 3D 140
Meare, The 6C 94
Mecca Bingo
Ipswich 3E 4 (7A 132)
Mechanical Music Mus. 5C 68
Meddler Gdn. CB8: Kent 2B 48
Medite Ho. IP3: Ips 7J 139
Medway Rd. IP3: Ips 4D 138
Meekings Rd. CO10: S'bury 3G 127
Meeting Fld. CO10: L Mel 4H 105
MEETING GREEN 1G 97 (1B 162)
Meeting La. IP13: Gru 6H 117
Meeting Wlk. CB9: Have 4G 101
Melbourne Dr. IP28: Mide 6H 23
Melbourne Rd. IP4: Ips 6H 133
NR32: Low 5J 9
Melford Cl. IP4: Rush A 1K 139
Melford Ct. CO10: L Mel 4H 105
IP3: Ips 7J 139
MELFORD GREEN 2J 105
Melford Hall 2J 105
Melford Rd. CO10: Act 2F 107
CO10: Cave 6J 103
CO10: Lave 7B 106
CO10: S'bury 1B 126
IP14: Stowm 6G 85
IP29: Laws 7A 80 & 1B 106
Melford Way IP11: Felix 5B 154
MELLIS 5A 36 (2A 160)
Mellis Cl. CB9: Have 2A 100
Mellis Ct. IP11: Felix 3C 154
Mellis Rd. IP22: B'gate, Wort 2J 35
IP23: Gisli 1K 67
IP23: Melli, Yax 5A 36
Mells Rd. IP19: Wal 1K 75
Melplash Cl. IP3: Ips 2J 139
Melplash Rd. IP3: Ips 2J 139
Melrose Cl. NR32: Oul 3E 8
Melrose Gdns. CB8: Newm 5E 46
IP4: Ips 5F 133
Melso Cl. CO10: Gt Cor 6F 127
MELTON 3K 121 (1C 165)
Melton Cl. CB8: Newm 7H 47
Melton Grange Rd. IP12: Melt 4H 121
Melton Hill IP12: Wood 5J 121
Melton Mdw. Rd. IP12: Melt 4J 121
MELTON PARK 7F 119
Melton Rd. IP12: Holl 1H 141
IP12: Melt 4J 121
Melton Station (Rail) 3K 121
Melville Rd. IP4: Ips 4K 5 (1D 138)
Menai Ct. IP1: Ips 1B 4 (6K 131)
MENDHAM 2H 41 (1C 161)
Mendham Low Rd.
IP20: Rede, W'well 3F 41
Mendip Dr. IP5: Rush A 7K 133
Mendip Rd. NR32: Oul 6D 8
MENDLESHAM 2J 71 (3B 160)
MENDLESHAM GREEN
7H 71 (3A 160)
Mendlesham Rd. IP14: Cott 7E 68
IP14: Mendl 1F 71
Mercers Rd. IP32: Bury E 6K 53
Merchants Ct. IP4: Ips 5E 4
Mere, The 5D 90
Mere Cl. IP31: Gt Bar 2H 55
Meredith Rd. IP1: Ips 3G 131
Mere Farm Cotts. IP31: Gt Bar 2H 55
(not continuous)
Mere Gdns. IP4: Rush A 2K 139
Mere La. IP28: Forn S, Ris 2A 52
Mere Vw. IP31: Gt Liv 3B 28
Meridian Gdns. CB8: Newm 4J 47
Meridian Ri. IP4: Ips 1H 5 (6C 132)
Meriton Ri. IP7: Hadl 5K 129
Merlin Ct. IP2: Ips 6B 4
Merlin Rd. IP2: Ips 3E 136
Mermaid Cl. IP32: Bury E 5G 53
Merriam Cl. CO11: Brant 5C 148
Merrifield Rd. NR33: Low 6E 10
Merrill Hgts. IP2: Ips 3A 138
Merrion Cl. IP2: Ips 4E 136
Merrylees NR34: Becc 4F 13
Mersey Rd. IP3: Ips 4D 138
Merville NR33: Car C 6D 10
Messenger Cl. NR35: Bung 4B 14
METFIELD 6G 41 (1C 161)
Metfield Rd. IP20: Metf 6H 41
(Christmas La.)
IP20: Metf 5F 41
(Sandpit Hill)
Metis Pl. IP1: Ips 6F 131
METTINGHAM 1D 161
Mews, The IP11: Felix 4G 155
Meynell Gdns. CB8: Newm 3G 47

Micawber M. NR32: Blun 1J 7
Michaelhouse Way
IP31: Stant 6C 32
Michael's Mt. IP13: L Bea 1D 134
Michigan Cl. IP5: Kesg 6B 134
MICKFIELD 3B 160
Mickfield M. IP11: Felix 3C 154
Micklefields IP31: Stant 6D 32
Micklegate Rd. IP11: Felix 6D 154
Micklesmere Dr. IP31: Ixw 6J 29
MICKLEY GREEN 3E 80 (1C 163)
Middlefield Dr. IP14: Gt Fin 6J 83
MIDDLE GREEN 5K 15
MIDDLE HARLING 1D 159
MIDDLETON
Saxmundham 5D 78 (1A 166)
Sudbury 7D 126 (3C 163)
Middleton Cl. IP2: Ips 4F 137
IP28: B Row 2G 23
Middleton Hall Cotts.
CO10: Midd 6D 126
MIDDLETON MOOR 5A 78
Middleton Rd.
CO10: Ball, Midd 5B 126
IP6: Barh 3D 114
IP17: Yox 7J 77
Middle Way CO10: L Mel 3J 105
NR32: Low 3H 9
MIDDLEWOOD GREEN 3A 160
Middlewood Way IP14: Forw G 1A 86
Midhurst Cl. IP32: Bury E 7K 53
Midmeadow NR34: Becc 3E 12
Mid Suffolk Bus. Pk. IP23: Eye 7H 37
Mid Suffolk Leisure Cen. 3D 84
Mid Suffolk Light Railway Mus. . . . 7J 69
Mights Rd. IP18: Rey, Sou 3J 45
Milano Av. IP5: Martl H 5J 135
Milburn Drove CB8: Mou 6C 48
MILDEN 2D 163
Milden Cl. IP14: Stowm 7G 85
Milden Ct. IP28: Mide 7J 23
MILDENHALL 7J 23 (2B 158)
Mildenhall
Dome Leisure Cen. 7K 23
Mildenhall Drove
IP28: B Row, Ken H 1B 22
Mildenhall Ind. Est.
IP28: Mide 5H 23
Mildenhall Mus. 7J 23
Mildenhall Pl. CB9: Have 3G 101
Mildenhall Rd. CB7: Ford 7A 24
IP28: B Mil 2F 25
IP28: B Mil, Ick 1J 25
IP28: Frec 5C 24
IP28: Holy R 2J 23
IP28: Ick 1A 26
IP28: W Row 4B 22
IP28: W'ton 2C 24
IP32: Bury E 3F 53
Mildenhall Swimming Pool 7J 23
Milden Rd. CO10: B Ele 3A 108
IP2: Ips 1G 137
Mildmay Rd. IP3: Ips 5E 138
MILE END
Bury St Edmunds 1G 103
Colchester 3D 163
Prickwillow 1A 158
Mile End IP27: B'don 6C 18
Miles Hawk Way IP28: Mide 6G 23
Miles Paddock IP14: Cott 6D 68
Mill, The IP4: Ips 5E 4 (1A 138)
Millars Cl. IP31: Wals W 6H 33
Mill Bank NR32: Oul 6E 8
Millbank CB8: Newm 5F 47
Mill B'way. IP12: Orf 5H 125
Mill Cl. CB8: Exn 1B 46
IP9: Cap M 2F 147
IP11: Felix 5C 154
IP11: T Mart 5G 153
IP12: Orf 6H 125
IP22: Wort 3J 35
IP30: Wool 5B 64
IP31: Wals W 5G 33
MILL COMMON 2C 167
Mill Comn. IP12: Blax 2J 123
Milldown IP19: Holt 5E 42
MILL END 1A 162
Millennium Grandstand, The
Newmarket Racecourse 7C 46
Millennium Way IP5: Kesg 7E 134
NR32: Low 3F 9
Miller Cl. IP30: E'well 2E 64
NR33: Low 4G 11
Millers Cl. IP7: Hadl 3J 129
IP14: Stowm 7E 84
NR35: Bung 3C 14
Millers Ct. IP6: Barh 3C 114
Millers La. IP27: B'don 5D 18
Millers Ri. IP27: Lake 4B 20
Millers Vw. IP1: Ips 6H 131
Millers Way IP13: F'ham 5B 90
IP22: W'field 2J 33
Mill Farm Pl. IP8: Bels 7E 136
Mill Fld. IP8: B'ford 3D 130
IP14: Petta 2C 88
IP15: Aldeb 4J 95
Millfield IP6: A'ing 2G 117
IP23: Eye 6B 38
Millfield Av. IP14: Stowm 5E 84
Millfield Cl. IP17: Saxm 7H 91
Millfield Dr. IP14: Bux 6F 83
Millfield Gdns. IP4: Ips 7E 132
Millfield Rd. IP18: Walb 7H 45
IP31: Barni 3E 30
Millfields IP14: Haug 2C 70
IP17: Pea 3G 77
NR34: Wang 6C 44
Millfields Way CB9: Have 3F 101
Mill Gallery (Pottery) 4G 117
Mill Gdns. IP30: E'well 3E 64
MILL GREEN
Boxford 2D 163
Dickleburgh 1B 160
Stowmarket 6F 83
MILL HILL 3B 106
Mill Hill CB8: Newm 5G 47
CB9: Have 4F 101
CO10: S'bury 4C 126
IP9: Cap M 1F 147
IP13: Burg 5J 117
IP14: Cott 6D 68
IP16: Aldr 7H 93
IP17: Pea 2H 77
IP27: B'don 4H 19
IP30: Rat 3J 83
Mill Hill Dr. IP19: H'orth 4A 42
Mill Hill Est. IP16: Aldr 7H 93
MILL HILLS 5H 121
MILL HOLE 6H 91
Mill Hoo IP12: Alder 5J 141
Mill Ho. IP4: Ips 5F 5
Mill La. CB8: Exn 1B 46
(not continuous)
CO6: Pols 6B 144
CO7: Ded 7K 145
CO10: Cave 7F 103
CO10: Hund 2J 99
CO10: S'bury 4C 126
IP6: Barh, Henl 5G 115
IP6: C Mary 2A 86
IP6: C Mary, C Pet 1G 111
IP6: C Pet 5K 85
IP6: Cod 2G 115
IP6: Gt Bla 2A 114
IP6: Nee M 5H 111
IP6: Witn 4B 116
IP7: E'sett 6F 113
IP7: Gt Bri 4A 112
IP7: Lay 7J 129
IP8: B'ford 3D 130
IP8: Cop, Wash 5B 136
(not continuous)
IP8: S'ham 3K 113
IP9: Chelm 2G 151
IP11: Felix 4C 154
IP11: T Mart 5G 153
IP12: Alder 5H 141
IP12: But 5C 124
IP12: Martl 4H 135
IP12: Tun 7J 123
IP12: Wood 5H 121
IP13: B'ton 1K 89
IP13: Cam A 6E 118
IP13: Denn 6B 76
IP13: Hask 2A 120
IP13: Ket 7H 89
IP13: Wick M 6B 118
IP14: Comb 4C 110
IP14: Forw G 2A 86
IP14: Stowm 5K 85
IP16: Aldr 7H 93
IP17: Benh 3C 92
IP18: Sou 4K 45
IP20: Metf 5G 41
IP20: Nee 1A 40
IP21: Stradb 5J 39
IP21: Wey 2D 40
IP22: Hop 1J 31
IP22: Redg 1C 34
IP22: Rick 6G 35
IP23: Stoke A 1K 69
IP23: Thorn 2C 72
IP24: Barnh 7G 27
IP29: Barr 6C 50
IP30: Wool 5A 64
IP31: Thur 5J 55
NR32: Cort 6J 7
NR34: Barnb 6C 6
(not continuous)
NR34: Ilk A 2F 15
NR34: Wrent 1D 44
Mill Mdw. IP21: Fress 6B 40
Mill M. CB8: Newm 5G 47
Mill Pk. Gdns. IP28: Mide 1E 24
Mill Piece IP10: Nac 4A 152
Mill Pouch IP11: T Mary 7H 153
Mill Reef CB8: Newm 3G 47
Mill Reef Cl. CB8: Newm 1D 46
Mill Ri. IP9: Holb 3D 150
IP17: Saxm 7H 91
Mill Rd. CB8: Gaz 1G 49
CB9: Have 4F 101
CB9: Ked 6B 98
CO7: E Ber 3D 146
CO10: Clar 5D 102
CO10: Hund 1H 99
IP12: Wald 7C 140
IP13: B'ham 2B 76
IP13: Laxf 6B 74
IP13: W'orth 5F 73
IP14: Batt 7A 110
IP14: Bux 6F 83
IP14: Cott 5D 68
IP14: Mendl 2H 71
IP14: Wyve 2B 68
IP17: Fris 7C 92
IP17: Knod 6F 93
IP17: Pea 2F 77
IP17: Saxm 6H 91
IP17: Westl 6H 79
IP19: Holt 5E 42
IP19: Wiss 4A 42
IP22: Bote 5J 35
IP22: Thel 5G 31
IP23: Occ 5B 72
IP27: Lake 5B 20
IP29: Chev 3J 51
IP31: Barni 3D 30
IP31: Gt Bar 1C 54
IP31: Honi 2H 29
IP31: Pake 7H 29
IP33: Bury E 5F 157 (1F 59)
NR33: Low 2H 11
NR34: Becc 6F 13
NR34: Mut 2A 16
Mill Rd. Dr. IP3: Pur F 5K 139
Mill Rd. Sth. IP22: Bote 5K 35
IP33: Bury E 6F 157 (2F 59)
Mills, The IP4: Rush A 5J 133
IP13: F'ham 6C 90
Mills Dr. NR32: Cort 6J 7
Millside IP23: Yax 7E 36
Mills La. CO10: L Mel 7H 105
Mills Mdw. IP13: F'ham 6D 90
Mills Rd. CO10: S'bury 3F 127
MILL STREET 7B 144
Mill St. CO6: Nay 6J 143
CO6: Pols 7B 144
IP14: Stowu 3K 85
IP17: Midd 6C 78
IP17: Westl 6H 79
IP23: Gisli 1G 67
IP28: Mide 1E 24
Mill Ter. IP14: Men G 7H 71
Mill Tye CO10: Gt Cor 7F 127
Mill Vw. CB8: Gaz 2G 49
Mill Vw. Cl. IP12: Wood 5F 121
Millway NR34: Barnb 6C 6
Millway La. IP22: Pal, Wort 1A 36
Milner Rd. CO10: S'bury 3G 127
Milner St. IP4: Ips 4H 5 (1C 138)
Milnes Way NR33: Car C 6A 10
Milnrow IP2: Ips 4E 136
Milton Cl. IP17: Saxm 5G 91
Milton Rd. E. NR32: Low 7J 9
Milton Rd. Nth. IP14: Stowm 4G 85
Milton Rd. Sth. IP14: Stowm 5G 85
Milton Rd. W. NR32: Low 7J 9
Milton St. IP4: Ips 6F 133
Mimosa Wlk. NR32: Low 6G 9
Minden Cl.
IP33: Bury E 4K 157 (1H 59)
Minden Dr. IP16: Leis 4J 93
IP33: Bury E 1D 58
Minden Rd. CO10: S'bury 4E 126
NR32: Low 6H 9
Minerva Cl. CB9: Have 5J 101
Minos Rd. NR32: Low 4H 9
Minos Way IP1: Ips 5F 131
Minsmere Ri. IP17: Midd 5D 78
Minsmere Rd. IP3: Ips 6H 139
IP17: Dun 3H 79
Minsmere Way CO10: Gt Cor 5H 127
Minster Rd. CB9: Have 2F 101
Minton Ent. Pk. CB8: Newm 2E 46
Mirbeck's Cl. NR34: Worl 4K 13
Mission La. CO7: E Ber 2A 148
Mistletoe Cl. IP28: Red L 7J 25
MISTLEY 3B 164
MISTLEY HEATH 3B 164
Mistley Way IP12: Wood 4G 121
Mitchell Av. IP32: Bury E 3F 53
Mitford Cl. IP1: Ips 1J 131
Mitford Rd. IP17: Benh 3A 92
Mitre Cl. IP30: Wool 5K 63
Mitre Way IP3: Ips 6J 5
Moat Farm Cl. IP4: Ips 5D 132
Moat Gro. IP14: Petta 3B 88
Moat La. IP30: Roug 6J 61
MOATS TYE 4E 110 (1A 164)
Moat Wlk. CB9: Have 3D 100
Mobbs Way NR32: Oul 5D 8
Model Farm IP14: Comb 1E 110
Moffat Av. IP4: Ips 4F 133
Mole Hill CB8: W'rook 3F 97
Moll's La. NR34: Bramp 6F 15
Monarch Cl. CB9: Have 3B 100
Monarch Way IP8: Ips 6F 137
NR33: Car C 6A 10
Monastery Ct. IP7: Hadl 2J 129
Monastery Hill IP17: Dun 2K 79
Monckton Av. NR32: Oul B 6E 8
Monckton Cres. NR32: Oul B 6E 8
Monet Sq. NR32: Low 3G 9
MONEWDEN 1C 165
Monewden Rd. IP13: Char 2B 118
Moneypiece Cl. CB9: Have 2E 100
Moneypot Hill IP22: Redg 1D 34
Monks Cl. IP11: Felix 2J 155
MONKS ELEIGH 2E 108 (2D 163)
Monks Ga. IP8: Spro 7C 130
Monkshood Cl. NR33: Low 7F 11
MONK SOHAM 3C 161
MONK SOHAM GREEN 3C 161
MONK STREET 3A 162
Monmouth Cl. IP2: Ips 5K 137
Montague Rd. IP11: Felix 4G 155
Montana Pl. NR32: Low 7G 9
Montana Rd. IP5: Kesg 6A 134
Montfort Ct. CB9: Have 4E 100
Montgomery Av. NR32: Low 4G 9
Montgomery Rd. IP2: Ips 4K 137
Monton Ri. IP2: Ips 4F 137
Montrose Ct. IP3: Ips 6K 5 (2D 138)
Moonhall Bus. Pk. CB9: Have 6F 101
Moon Hall La. CB9: Have 6E 100
Moorbridge La. IP14: Harl 6J 65
Moor Bus. Pk. NR34: Ell 7J 13
Mooreland Dr. IP31: Gt Bar 2G 55
Moore Rd. IP1: Ips 2H 131
IP30: Roug 2F 61
Moore's Cl. IP14: Deb 2H 87
Moorfield Cl. IP5: Kesg 5C 134
Moorfield Rd. IP12: Wood 5F 121
Moor Grn. Cl. CB8: W'rook 1G 97
Moorhall C'way. IP23: Eye 7C 38
Moorlands IP12: Holl 1G 141
Moor Rd. IP17: Midd 5B 78
Moorsfield CO10: Gt Cor 7G 127
Moorside IP18: Walb 7G 45
Moor's Way IP12: Wood 5F 121
Morecambe Ct. IP4: Ips 6E 132
Moreton Hall Employment Area
IP32: Bury E 2B 60
Moreton Hall Health Club 1K 59
Morgan Ct. IP6: Clay 4D 114
Morgan Dr. IP1: Ips 4E 130
Morgan Mdw. IP14: Comb 1E 110
Morland Rd. IP3: Ips 6D 138
Morley Av. IP12: Wood 6G 121
Morley Cl. IP28: B Row 1F 23
Morleys La. IP23: Gisli 3J 67
MORNINGTHORPE 1C 161
Mornington Av. IP1: Ips 4H 131
MORRIS GREEN 3B 162
Morris Way IP6: Nee M 4G 111
Mors End CO7: Strat M 5H 145
Mortimer La. IP28: Frec 4B 24
Mortimer Pl. CO10: Clar 3C 102
Mortimer Rd. IP14: Stowm 3H 85
IP32: Bury E 1C 60
Mortlocks CO10: Lave 5C 106
Morton Peto Cl. NR32: S'ton 3C 6
Morton Rd. NR33: Low 5G 11
Moss La. IP6: Weste 1D 132
Mottram Cl. IP2: Ips 4E 136
MOULTON 6D 48 (3A 158)
Moulton Av. CB8: Kent 2A 48
Moulton Cl. CO10: S'bury 3E 126
Moulton Rd. CB8: Gaz 2F 49
CB8: Kenn, Kent 4A 48
CB8: Mou 7D 48
CB8: Mou, Newm . . . . 5H 47 & 7A 48
Mountbatten Cl. CO10: S'bury 1E 126
Mountbatten Ct. IP1: Ips 1A 4
Mountbatten Rd. CO10: S'bury . . . 1E 126
NR32: Low 4G 9
NR35: Bung 4B 14
MOUNT BURES 3D 163
Mount Cl. IP30: Hess 7C 62
Mount Dr. IP3: Pur F 5K 139
MOUNT PLEASANT 4J 99
Mt. Pleasant IP7: Ray, Ray 1G 145
IP13: F'ham 5B 90
IP17: Pea 3H 77
IP18: Rey 1J 45
IP19: H'orth 3B 42
NR32: Low 5H 9

Mount Rd. CB9: Have 4F **101**
IP27: B'don 5G **19**
IP31: Bury E, Roug 7C **54**
IP32: Bury E 7J **53**
Mounts, The IP17: Pea 2H **77**
Mounts Pit La. IP27: B'don 4G **19**
Mouse La. IP30: Blac 3G **61**
Moverley Way IP15: Aldeb 4J **95**
Mowbrays, The IP13: F'ham 6D **90**
Mow Hill IP6: Witn 3B **116**
Mowlands IP9: Cap M 2J **147**
Mowness Hall La. IP14: L Sto 1E **86**
Moyes Rd. NR32: Oul B 7C **8**
Moyse Av. IP18: Rey 1J **45**
Moyse's Hall Mus. . . . . .4H **157 (1G 59)**
Mudds Yd.
IP33: Bury E . . . . . . .3H **157 (7G 53)**
Mulberry Cl. IP28: Mide 7K **23**
NR33: Oul B 3C **10**
NR34: Becc 3F **13**
Mulberry Gdns. IP6: Gt Bla 2B **114**
Mulberry Rd. IP3: Ips 7G **139**
Mumford Rd. IP1: Ips 5G **131**
Munday's La. IP12: Orf 6H **125**
MUNDFORD 1C **159**
Mundford Rd. IP27: Weet 2F **19**
Mundy's La. IP20: Mendh 2H **41**
Munnings Cl. CB8: Newm 5G **47**
CB9: Have 2C **100**
IP3: Ips 6F **139**
NR33: Car C 6B **10**
Muriel Cl. IP7: Hadl 3J **129**
Muriel King Cl. IP30: Hess 6D **62**
Murillo Dr. NR32: Low 2H **9**
Murray Pk. CB8: Newm 7F **47**
Murray Rd. IP3: Ips 3E **138**
Murrills Rd. IP3: Pur F 5J **139**
Murton Slade CB9: Have 3F **101**
Mus. of East Anglian Life 5F **85**
Museum St. IP1: Ips . . . . .3D **4 (7A 132)**
Mussiden Pl. IP12: Wood 5G **121**
Mustards Gapp CB9: Have 4H **101**
Mustow St.
IP33: Bury E . . . . . . .4J **157 (1H 59)**
MUTFORD . . . . .2B **16 (2C 167)**
Mutford Cl. NR32: Oul B 7E **8**
Mutford Grn. IP27: Lake 4A **20**
Mutford Wood
NR33: Car C, Mut . . . . .7E **6** & 1B **16**
Mutfordwood La.
NR33: Car C . . . . .1B **16** & 7A **10**
NR34: Mut 1B **16**
Mutton La. IP13: B'ton 1K **89**
Mutton Mdw. IP14: Old N 6B **70**
Mylford Cl. IP32: Bury E 2K **59**
Mylodon Rd. NR32: Low 4H **9**
Myrtle Cl. IP27: RAF L 5G **21**
IP33: Bury E . . . . .2F **157 (7F 53)**
NR32: Low 6G **9**
Myrtle Rd. IP3: Ips . . . . . . .7J **5 (2C 138)**

N

NACTON . . . . .5B **152 (2C 165)**
Nacton Cl. IP12: Sutt 2B **140**
Nacton Cres. IP3: Ips 4F **139**
Nacton La. IP31: Gt Bar 2C **54**
Nacton Rd. IP3: Ips . . . . . .7K **5 (2D 138)**
(not continuous)
IP10: Buck 3A **152**
IP11: Felix 7D **154**
Namco Funscape
Ipswich 6F **131**
Nansen Rd. IP3: Ips 4F **139**
Narrow Way IP19: Wen 3J **43**
Nash Gdns. IP3: Ips 6F **139**
Nat Flatman St. CB8: Newm 6H **47**
National Horseracing Mus. 6G **47**
Nato Pl. IP27: RAF L 3H **21**
NAUGHTON 2A **164**
Naughton Gdns. IP14: Stowm 7G **85**
Naughton Rd. IP7: What 5E **112**
Naunton Rd. IP12: Wood 5F **121**
Navarre St. IP1: Ips . . . . . . .2E **4 (7A 132)**
Naverne Mdws. IP12: Wood 5H **121**
Navigation App. IP14: Stowm 4G **85**
NAYLAND . . . . .6J **143 (3D 163)**
Nayland Rd. CB9: Have 5D **100**
CO8: Bure 6B **142**
IP11: Felix 5B **154**
Naylor Ct. IP14: Stowm 3D **84**
Neale Cl. IP16: Leis 3G **93**
Neale St. IP1: Ips . . . . .2E **4 (7A 132)**
Neath Dr. IP2: Ips 5J **137**
Neave Cl. IP19: Wal 3H **75**
Neaves La. IP21: Stradb 7H **39**
NEDGING . . . . .7K **109 (2A 164)**
Nedging Rd. IP7: Ned 7K **109**
NEDGING TYE 2A **164**
Neeches Yd. *NR34: Becc 1E 12*
(off Fen La.)
NEEDHAM 1C **161**
Needham Lake Nature Reserve
. . . . .4H **111**
NEEDHAM MARKET . . .3G **111 (1A 164)**
Needham Market Station (Rail)
. . . . .4H **111**
Needham Rd. IP6: Cod 2F **115**
IP14: Stowm 6G **85**
Needham Rd. (East) Ind. Est.
IP14: Stowm 7J **85**
NEEDHAM STREET . . . . .4E **48 (3B 158)**
Needham St. CB8: Gaz . . .2E **48** & 1G **49**
NEEDLE CORNER 7K **151**
Nelson Cl. IP6: A'ing 4F **117**
Nelson Ct. NR32: Low 7K **9**
Nelson Rd. CO10: S'bury 2F **127**
IP4: Ips 6E **132**
IP33: Bury E . . . . .4F **157 (1F 59)**
NR33: Low 6F **11**
Nelson Way IP12: Wood 3G **121**
NR34: Becc 4D **12**
Nelson Wharf NR33: Oul B 2E **10**
Nene Dr. IP3: Ips 7H **139**
Neptune All. IP15: Aldeb 6J **95**
Neptune Quay IP3: Ips . . . .6H **5 (2C 138)**
Neptune Sq. IP4: Ips 5G **5**
Neptune St. NR32: Low 1H **11**
Nethergate St. CO10: Clar 5C **102**
IP22: Hop 2G **31**
NR35: Bung 1A **14**
Nether Hall Cl. CO10: Gt Wal 7K **107**
Netherhall Cl. IP14: Old N 5D **70**
Nether Rd. CO10: Cave 5G **103**
Nether St. IP30: Roug 6A **62**
Netherwood Ct. IP5: Martl H 7G **135**
Netley Cl. IP2: Ips 6H **137**
Netley Rd. IP33: Bury E 3D **58**
Neve Gdns. IP28: W Row 6C **22**
Neville's Cl. IP33: Bury E 1F **59**
Newall Rd. IP24: Barnh 6J **27**
Newark Cl. IP2: Ips 5H **137**
Newark Rd. NR33: Low 3G **11**
Newberry Rd. IP7: Bild 6J **109**
NEWBOURNE 2C **165**
Newbourne Gdns. IP11: Felix 5C **154**
Newbourne Rd.
IP12: Martl, Wald
. . . . .4K **135** & 4A **140**
NEW BUCKENHAM 1A **160**
Newbury Ho. IP4: Ips 7F **133**
Newbury Rd. IP4: Ips 7F **133**
Newby Cl. IP19: H'orth 5A **42**
Newby Dr. IP4: Rush A 1K **139**
New Cardinal St.
IP1: Ips . . . . .5C **4 (1K 137)**
New Cheveley Rd. CB8: Newm 7H **47**
Newcombe Rd. NR32: Low 7K **9**
Newcome Ct. NR32: Oul 6C **8**
New Ct. IP27: B'don 6D **18**
New Cut *CB8: Newm 6G 47*
(off Wellington St.)
CO8: Bure 6A **142**
CO10: Glem 6A **104**
IP7: Hadl 3J **129**
IP17: Saxm 6J **91**
IP19: H'orth 4B **42**
New Cut E. IP3: Ips . . . . . . .6E **4 (2A 138)**
New Cut W. IP2: Ips . . . . . .7F **5 (2B 138)**
Newell Ct. IP7: Hadl 4H **129**
Newell Ri. IP6: Clay 4D **114**
NEW ENGLAND 2B **162**
Newgate NR34: Becc 2E **12**
New Grn. Av. IP31: Thur 6K **55**
Newhaven Way IP7: Hadl 2J **129**
Newland Av. NR34: Worl 4H **13**
Newlands IP7: E'sett 6H **113**
Newlands Cl. IP31: Stant 7D **32**
NR33: Low 6E **10**
Newlands La. CO6: Nay 6K **143**
New Lea IP13: B'ham 2B **76**
Newman Dr. IP5: Kesg 6E **134**
NEWMAN'S GREEN . . . .6F **107 (2C 163)**
Newman's Rd. CO10: S'bury 3D **126**
NEWMARKET . . . . .6G **47 (3A 158)**
New Market NR34: Becc 3E **12**
Newmarket (Park & Ride) 2F **47**
Newmarket Bus. Pk.
CB8: Newm 2E **46**
Newmarket Lawn Tennis Club 6F **47**
Newmarket Leisure Cen. 4F **47**
Newmarket Racecourse 7A **46**
Newmarket Rd.
CB8: Kenn . . . . .7F **25** & 2A **48**
CB8: Mou 6C **48**
CB8: Snail 1H **47**
IP28: B Mil 4F **25**
(not continuous)
IP28: L Sax, Ris 2A **50**
(not continuous)
IP28: Red L 5H **25**
IP28: W'ton 2C **24**
IP33: Bury E 6B **52**
Newmarket Station (Rail) 7G **47**
NEW MISTLEY 3B **164**
Newnham Av. IP12: Wood 6E **120**
Newnham Cl. IP28: Mide 6K **23**
Newnham Ct. IP2: Ips 5G **137**
New Place Ho. IP2: Ips 7A **4**
Newquay Cl. IP5: Kesg 7K **133**
New Quay Ct. IP12: Wood 5J **121**
New Quay La. IP12: Wood 4J **121**
New Quay Ter. *IP12: Wood 4J 121*
(off New Quay La.)
New Queens Rd. CO10: S'bury . . .2D **126**
New River Grn. CB8: Exn 1B **46**
New Rd. CB8: Exn 1B **46**
CO10: L Mel 4G **105**
IP11: T Mary 1B **154**
IP12: Melt 1H **121**
IP13: B'ham 1E **76**
IP13: F'ham 5C **90**
IP13: W'orth 4K **73**
IP14: Helm 2E **88**
IP21: Thran 3D **36**
IP28: Ken H, W Row 1A **22**
IP29: Barr 4B **50**
IP29: Chev 1K **51**
IP30: E'well 3D **64**
IP30: Roug 7K **55**
IP30: Tost 2H **63**
IP31: Honi 4F **29**
IP31: Ixw 6J **29**
IP31: Tros 1C **28**
NR33: Kess 5J **17**
NR34: Barnb 6D **6**
NR34: Becc 1E **12**
Newry Av. IP11: Felix 4E **154**
Newson Av. NR34: Mut 2A **16**
Newson's Mdw. NR32: Low 6H **9**
Newson St. IP1: Ips . . . . . .1C **4 (6K 131)**
New St. CO10: Glem 4A **104**
CO10: S'bury 3D **126**
IP4: Ips . . . . .5G **5 (1B 138)**
IP12: Wood 5H **121**
IP13: F'ham 4A **90**
IP21: Fress 6A **40**
IP21: Stradb 6G **39**
IP28: Mide 7J **23**
New St. Cl. IP21: Stradb 6G **39**
Newthorpe IP30: Blac 4G **61**
NEWTON . . . . .2C **128 (2D 163)**
Newton B'way. IP12: Orf 6H **125**
Newton Cft. CO10: S'bury 4F **127**
Newton Green Golf Course 2B **128**
Newton Pl. CB9: Have 3G **101**
Newton Rd.
CO10: Gt Cor, S'bury 4E **126**
IP3: Ips 2E **138**
IP14: Stowm, Stowu 1F **85**
Newton St. IP4: Ips . . . . .3G **5 (7B 132)**
NEW TOWN 5G **73**
New Village CO11: Brant 6B **148**
New Way IP2: Ips 7H **131**
Nicholas Dr. IP18: Rey 2J **45**
Nicholas Everitt Pk. 1C **10**
Nicholas Rd. IP11: Felix 4B **154**
Nicholls Cl. IP13: Uff 6H **119**
Nicholson Dr. NR34: Becc 6F **13**
Nicholsons Ct. CO10: Newt 2C **128**
Nicholson Sq. NR32: Low 6H **9**
Nick's La. IP23: Brom 6H **37**
Nidderdale NR33: Car C 6D **10**
Nightingale Av. IP18: Rey 2H **45**
Nightingale Cl. IP14: Stowm 5J **85**
IP18: Walb 7F **45**
IP19: H'orth 7B **42**
IP28: Mide 7K **23**
IP33: Bury E 2F **59**
Nightingale Piece IP12: Orf 6J **125**
Nightingale Rd. IP3: Ips 6E **138**
IP27: B'don 4J **19**
NR33: Low 6G **11**
Nightingale Sq. IP3: Ips 6E **138**
Nimbus Way CB8: Newm 1E **46**
Nine Acres IP2: Ips 7F **131**
Ninfield Cl. NR33: Car C 5C **10**
Nirvana Fitness 7D **10**
Noah's Ark La. CO10: S'bury 4C **126**
Noahs Dr. NR33: Kess 4H **17**
Noaks Rd. IP7: Ray 3J **145**
Nock Gdns. IP5: Kesg 7B **134**
Noel Murless Dr. CB8: Newm 3F **47**
Noel Rd. NR32: Oul B 7B **8**
Noel's Wlk. NR34: Becc 2E **12**
Nonsuch Mdw. CO10: S'bury 5D **126**
Norbury Rd. IP4: Ips 5F **133**
Nordalls, The NR33: Kess 5J **17**
Norfolk & Suffolk Aviation Mus.
. . . . .1D **161**
Norfolk Av. CB8: Newm 4E **46**
Norfolk Cres. IP13: F'ham 5C **90**
Norfolk Rd. IP4: Ips . . . . . .2G **5 (7B 132)**
IP32: Bury E 5F **53**
NR34: Wang 6C **44**
Norfolk St. NR32: Low 7G **9**
Norman Cl. IP11: Felix 2J **155**
IP12: Melt 4H **121**
Norman Cres. IP3: Ips 4E **138**
Normandie Way CO8: Bure 6A **142**
Normandy Cl. IP14: Stowm 7F **85**
Normandy Rd. NR32: Low 4G **9**
Normanhurst Cl. NR32: Low 6F **9**
Norman Rd. IP32: Bury E 4F **53**
Normans CO10: Lave 5C **106**
NORMANSTON 6G **9**
Normanston Dr.
NR32: Low, Oul B 7E **8**
(not continuous)
Norman Way CO10: Lave 5C **106**
Norny Cl. CB9: Have 1E **100**
Norse Av. IP29: Stann 3G **81**
Northacre NR33: Kess 4J **17**
North Av. CB9: Have 3D **100**
North Cliff NR33: Kess 4K **17**
Northcliffe Ct. *IP11: Felix 3J 155*
(off Maybush La.)
North Cl. IP4: Ips 5C **132**
IP14: Bac 6B **68**
IP31: Stant 6D **32**
NORTH COMMON 6B **30**
NORTH COVE . . . . .7A **6 (2C 167)**
Northcroft CO10: S'bury 4D **126**
North Dr. IP22: Hep 6C **30**
North East Suffolk Bus. Cen.
NR33: Low 7D **10**
NORTH END
East Harling 1D **159**
Great Yeldham 3B **162**
North End Av. IP16: Thor 6D **94**
North End Rd. CB8: Exn 1B **46**
North Entrance IP17: Saxm 6J **91**
Northern Rd. CO10: S'bury 2F **127**
Northern Rose Cl. IP32: Bury E 7B **54**
Northern Way IP32: Bury E 3E **52**
Northfen Drove IP27: Lake 2E **20**
Northfield Cl. NR32: Oul 3E **8**
Northfield Ct. IP15: Aldeb 4J **95**
Northfield La. IP15: Aldeb 4J **95**
Northfield Rd. IP14: One 2A **84**
Northgate NR32: Low 6G **9**
NR34: Becc 2E **12**
Northgate Arts Cen. 4D **132**
Northgate Av. IP32: Bury E 5F **53**
Northgate Lodge IP33: Bury E 2H **157**
Northgate Sports Cen. 4D **132**
Northgate St. IP1: Ips . . . . .2E **4 (7A 132)**
IP33: Bury E . . . . . . .2H **157 (7G 53)**
Northgate St. Bus. Pk.
IP33: Bury E . . . . . . .3J **157 (7H 53)**
NORTH GREEN
Alburgh 1C **161**
Cratfield 2D **161**
Framlingham 3D **161**
Saxmundham 3D **161**
North Grn. IP18: Sou 3K **45**
North Hill IP12: Wood 4G **121**
North Hill Gdns.
IP4: Ips . . . . .2J **5 (7C 132)**
North Hill Rd. IP4: Ips . . . .2J **5 (7C 132)**
North Hill Wlk. IP4: Ips . . .2J **5 (7C 132)**
Northlands La. IP23: Gisli 1G **67**
North Lawn IP4: Ips 5F **133**
NORTH LOPHAM 1A **160**
North Pde. IP18: Sou 4K **45**
NR32: Low 4J **9**
North Pde. Gdns. IP18: Sou 3K **45**
North Pl. IP28: Mide 7J **23**
North Quay Retail Pk.
NR32: Low 7G **9**
North Ri. CO10: Gt Cor 5F **127**
North Rd. IP18: Sou 3K **45**
IP27: Lake 7C **20**
North St. CO10: Hund 1J **99**
CO10: S'bury 3D **126**
IP28: Frec 5C **24**
North St. Pde. *CO10: S'bury 4D 126*
(off North St.)
North St. Pas. *CO10: S'bury 4D 126*
(off North St.)
North Ter. IP28: Mide 6J **23**
Northumberland Av.
IP32: Bury E 4E **52**
North Warren 7A **94**
North Warren IP15: Aldeb 1G **95**
Northwood Cl. NR33: Oul B 3E **10**
NORTON . . . . .5H **57 (3D 159)**
NORTON LITTLE GREEN
. . . . .7A **66 (3D 159)**
Norton Rd. CB9: Have 5D **100**
IP30: Tost 3G **63**
IP31: Gt Ash 7C **66**
IP31: Nort 3G **63**
IP31: Thur 6K **55**
NORTON SUBCOURSE 1C **167**
Norton Way IP13: F'ham 4B **90**
Norwich Ct. IP1: Ips . . . . . .1A **4 (6J 131)**

Norwich Rd. CB8: Newm ... 3K **47**
IP1: Ips ... 1A **4** (2G **131**)
IP6: Barh, Clay ... 1C **114**
IP6: C Mary ... 7D **86**
IP14: Broc G, Broc S ... 5G **69**
IP14: E Sto ... 7D **86**
IP19: H'orth ... 4B **42**
IP23: Brom ... 5G **37**
IP27: RAF L ... 3H **21**
NR32: Low ... 7G **9**
NR34: Becc, Gill, Worl ... 1C **12**
NR35: Dit ... 1B **14**
Norwich Rd. Ind. Est.
NR32: Low ... 7G **9**
Norwood Rd. IP27: B'don ... 6D **18**
Nosterfield End CB21: Cas C ... 6A **100**
Notcutts CO7: E Ber ... 5D **146**
Notley Dr. CB9: Have ... 2A **100**
Notley Rd. NR33: Low ... 2F **11**
Nottidge Rd. IP4: Ips ... 3J **5** (7C **132**)
Nowton Ct. IP29: Now ... 6K **59**
Nowton Rd. IP29: Now ... 5J **59**
IP33: Bury E, Now ... 3J **59**
Noyes Av. IP13: Laxf ... 6B **74**
Nunn Cl. IP12: Martl ... 3H **135**
Nunnery Grn. CB8: W'rook ... 2F **97**
Nunn's La. IP20: Metf ... 6J **41**
Nunn Sq. IP32: Bury E ... 5D **52**
Nursery Cl. IP28: Mide ... 7K **23**
NR35: Bung ... 2B **14**
Nursery Gdns. IP14: Broc S ... 4G **69**
Nursery Rd. CO10: Gt Cor ... 7G **127**
Nursery Wlk. IP11: Felix ... 3E **154**
Nuthatch Cl. IP14: Stowm ... 4H **85**
Nuttery Va. IP21: Hox ... 4B **38**

O

Oak Av. NR34: Worl ... 3J **13**
Oak Cl. IP4: Rush A ... 6J **133**
IP11: Felix ... 4D **154**
IP14: Gt Fin ... 6J **83**
IP28: Forn M ... 1F **53**
Oak Cnr. IP13: Cret ... 2F **89**
Oak Cres. IP23: Eye ... 6C **38**
Oakdene IP10: Kirt ... 2H **153**
Oakdene Gdns. IP28: B Row ... 2F **23**
Oak Dr. IP28: B Row ... 1F **23**
Oak Eggar Chase IP8: Ips ... 6F **137**
Oakes Cl. IP32: Bury E ... 6E **52**
Oakes Rd. IP32: Bury E ... 6D **52**
Oakey Fld. Rd. IP31: Thur ... 6A **56**
Oakey Ley IP30: B Geo ... 3C **82**
Oak Farm La. IP14: Mendl ... 3K **71**
IP23: Wick S ... 3F **69**
Oakfield Cl. IP14: Bac ... 6B **68**
Oakfield Pl. CB8: Newm ... 6H **47**
Oakfield Rd. IP8: Cop ... 7C **136**
IP14: Bac ... 6C **68**
Oak Grn. IP19: H'orth ... 6B **42**
Oak Gro. IP8: Spro ... 7C **130**
IP31: Forn M ... 4H **53**
OAK HILL ... **1K 141**
Oak Hill Cl. NR34: Wrent ... 1D **44**
Oak Hill La. IP2: Ips ... 7B **4** (3K **137**)
(not continuous)
Oak Ho. IP2: Ips ... 4F **137**
IP6: Clay ... 4D 114
(off Alasdair Pl.)
Oaklands CO6: Leav ... 1C **142**
IP18: Rey ... 2J **45**
IP30: Wool ... 5B **64**
Oaklands Dr. IP27: B'don ... 6C **18**
Oaklands Pk. IP33: Bury E ... 3K **59**
Oaklands Ter. NR33: Kess ... 2J **17**
Oak La. IP1: Ips ... 3E **4**
IP12: Wood ... 5H **121**
IP27: RAF L ... 4G **21**
IP30: E'well ... 1E **64**
IP30: Roug ... 6J **61**
IP30: Wool ... 7D **64**
NR34: Becc ... 6G **13**
Oak La. Ct. *IP12: Wood ... 5H 121*
(off New St.)
Oaklee IP2: Ips ... 5J **137**
OAKLEY ... **2B 160**
Oakley Sq. IP15: Aldeb ... 5K **95**
Oak Mdw. Cl. IP19: Wen ... 2J **43**
Oak M. NR35: Bung ... 3B **14**
Oak Rd. CO10: Gt Cor ... 5G **127**
IP14: Stowu ... 2J **85**
IP31: Thur ... 6D **56**
Oaks, The IP5: Martl H ... 7F **135**
IP22: W'field ... 2H **33**
IP29: Horr ... 6B **58**
IP30: B Grn ... 7E **64**
Oaks Bus. Park, The
CB8: Newm ... 2F **47**
Oaks Dr. CB8: Newm ... 2F **47**
Oaksmere Bus. Pk. IP23: Eye ... 5A **38**
Oaksmere Gdns. IP2: Ips ... 4J **137**
Oakstead Cl. IP4: Ips ... 7E **132**
Oak Tree Cl. IP12: Holl ... 2G **141**
Oaktree Dr. IP12: Eyk ... 1D **124**
Oak Vw. *IP6: Tud ... 7C 116*
(off Westerfield La.)
IP17: Pea ... 3H **77**
Oak Way IP19: H'orth ... 7A **42**
Oakwood Ho. IP5: Kesg ... 6B **134**
Oakwood Pk. IP17: Yox ... 7J **77**
Oakwood Rd. NR33: Oul B ... 4E **10**
Oast Ct. IP33: Bury E ... 7K **157**
Oatfields IP21: Fress ... 6B **40**
Oatlands Cl. NR33: Car C ... 5D **10**
Oban St. IP1: Ips ... 1B **4** (6K **131**)
Observation Ct. IP1: Ips ... 4C **4** (1K **137**)
OCCOLD ... **5B 72** (**2B 160**)
Occold Rd. IP23: Occ ... 4E **72**
O'Feld Ter. IP11: Felix ... 2H **155**
Offord Cl. IP5: Kesg ... 7D **134**
OFFTON ... **1F 113** (**2A 164**)
Offton Rd. IP7: E'sett ... 5J **113**
IP14: R'hall ... 2D **112**
Ogden Gro. IP5: Kesg ... 7B **134**
Ogilvie Almshouses, The
IP16: Aldr ... 7K **93**
Ogilvie Homes IP16: Aldr ... 5J **93**
Ohio Cl. NR33: Car C ... 6D **10**
Old Angel La. IP19: Blyth ... 6J **43**
Old Bakery Row *IP14: Deb ... 2H 87*
(off Gracechurch St.)
Old Bank M. NR34: Wrent ... 1D **44**
Old Barningham Rd. IP31: Stant ... 6C **32**
Old Barrack Rd. IP12: Wood ... 7E **120**
Old Bredfield Rd. IP13: Uff ... 6G **119**
Old Brewery Yd. IP19: H'orth ... 5A **42**
OLD BUCKENHAM ... **1A 160**
Old Bury Rd. IP21: Stus ... 3E **36**
(not continuous)
IP22: Pal ... 4A **36**
(not continuous)
IP31: Stant ... 6C **32**
Old Cattle Mkt. IP1: Ips ... 4E **4**
Old Church La. IP33: W'ley ... 7A **52**
Old Church Rd.
IP12: Melt ... 1K **121** & 7H **119**
IP13: Melt ... 7H **119**
Old Clements La. CB9: Have ... 4E **100**
Old College Cl. NR34: Becc ... 3E **12**
Old Convent Orchard
IP33: Bury E ... 6G **157** (2G **59**)
Old Ct. CO10: L Mel ... 3J **105**
Old Dairy Bus. Pk. IP31: Gt Bar ... 3E **54**
Old Dairy Ct. IP28: Mide ... 1E **24**
Old Farm Rd. NR33: Car C ... 4C **10**
NR34: Becc ... 3F **13**
OLD FELIXSTOWE ... **2H 155** (**3D 165**)
Oldfield Rd. IP8: Ips ... 5D **136**
Old Forge Cl. IP22: Wort ... 2H **35**
Old Forge Ct. IP27: B'don ... 4F **19**
Old Forge M. *IP12: Melt ... 2K 121*
(off Yarmouth Rd.)
Old Foundry Pl. IP16: Leis ... 3H **93**
Old Foundry Rd.
IP4: Ips ... 2F **5** (7B **132**)
Old Fox Yd. *IP14: Stowm ... 4F 85*
(off Ipswich St.)
Old Grammar La. NR35: Bung ... 3B **14**
Old Gravel Way IP27: Lake ... 7A **20**
Old Hall Cl. IP6: Henl ... 6J **115**
IP11: Felix ... 3H **155**
OLDHALL GREEN ... **4K 81**
Old Hall La. IP17: Westl ... 5G **79**
IP30: C'field ... 5F **81**
IP31: Forn M ... 3G **53**
Old Hall Mdw. IP30: Rat ... 3K **83**
Old Hall Rd. IP9: Shot ... 3C **156**
Old Haverhill Rd. CB9: L Wrat ... 4A **98**
Old High Rd. IP17: Yox ... 7H **77**
Old Homes Rd. IP16: Thor ... 6D **94**
Olding Rd. IP33: Bury E ... 7D **52**
Old Ipswich Rd. IP6: Clay ... 4D **114**
IP23: Yax ... 7D **36**
Old Kirton Rd. IP11: T Mart ... 5G **153**
Old La. IP29: Stann ... 4F **81**
NR32: Low ... 7H **7**
Old London Rd. IP9: Cap M ... 4H **147**
Old Maids' La. IP13: B'ton ... 2K **89**
Old Main Rd. IP13: Petti ... 3J **119**
Old Malting Ct. IP12: Wood ... 5J **121**
Old Maltings, The *IP6: Nee M ... 3G 111*
(off Crown St.)
Old Maltings App. IP12: Wood ... 4J **121**
Old Market NR34: Becc ... 2E **12**
Old Market Ct. *CO10: S'bury ... 4D 126*
(off Burkitts La.)
Old Market Pl. CO10: S'bury ... 4D **126**
Old Market Plain NR32: Low ... 6K **9**
Old Market St. IP14: Mendl ... 2J **71**
NR32: Low ... 6K **9**
Old Mill Ct. IP31: Bard ... 2D **32**
Old Mill La. IP28: B Mil ... 2J **25**
NR34: Becc ... 4E **12**
Old Mill Ter. NR34: Becc ... 1E **12**
Old Nelson St. NR32: Low ... 7K **9**
OLD NEWTON ... **5A 70** (**3A 160**)
Old Norton Rd. IP31: Thur ... 6K **55**
Old Norwich Rd. IP1: Ips ... 6E **114**
IP23: Yax ... 6E **36**
Old Orchard IP7: Lay ... 7K **129**
IP14: Mendl ... 2J **71**
Old Orchard Cl. IP19: H'orth ... 6A **42**
Old Paper Mill La. IP6: Clay ... 4D **114**
Old Post Office La. IP12: Blax ... 2H **123**
IP31: Thur ... 7B **56**
Old Post Office Rd. IP29: Chev ... 3J **51**
Old Priory Gdns. NR34: Wang ... 6C **44**
Old Railway Rd.
NR35: Bung, Ears ... 2A **14**
Old Rectory Cl. IP6: Barh ... 2D **114**
Old Rectory Gdns. IP23: Occ ... 5B **72**
IP31: Stant ... 7C **32**
Old Rectory La. IP29: Shim ... 4C **106**
Old Rectory Rd. IP13: B'ham ... 2B **76**
Old Rectory Wlk. IP9: Cap M ... 2G **147**
Old Road, The CO6: Leav ... 1B **142**
Old Rope Wlk. CB9: Have ... 4D **100**
Old School Cl. IP16: Leis ... 3H **93**
NR34: Bramp ... 5H **15**
Old School Ct. IP14: Stowm ... 4F **85**
Old School Dr. IP18: Rey ... 1G **45**
Old School Ho. IP9: Shot G ... 7E **156**
Old School M. IP14: Stowm ... 4F **85**
Old School Rd. IP29: Whep ... 1B **80**
Old Schools Ct. IP30: E'well ... 2C **64**
Old Station Rd. CB8: Newm ... 5H **47**
IP14: Mendl ... 3J **71**
IP19: H'orth ... 3A **42**
(not continuous)
Old Stores Cl. IP13: W'orth ... 6H **73**
Old Stowmarket Rd. IP30: Wool ... 5B **64**
Old St. IP14: Haug ... 2B **70**
Old Street, The IP9: Cap M ... 2J **147**
Old Suffolk Rd. CB8: Dalh ... 7G **49**
Old Tannery Sq. IP14: Stowm ... 4F **85**
Old Town La. IP33: Bury E ... 5J **59**
Old Vicarage Dr. IP31: B Ash ... 3C **66**
Olive Cl. IP27: RAF L ... 4G **21**
Olive Ct. NR32: Low ... 5G **9**
Oliver Cl. NR33: Car C ... 7C **10**
Oliver Rd. IP33: Bury E ... 7C **52**
Olivers Cl. CO10: L Mel ... 4J **105**
Olive Way IP28: Red L ... 5H **25**
Olland Ct. NR35: Bung ... 3B **14**
Olle Cl. IP33: Bury E ... 5J **59**
OLMSTEAD GREEN ... **2A 162**
Olympus Cl. IP1: Ips ... 3E **130**
One Eyed La. IP21: Wey ... 1C **40**
ONEHOUSE ... **2A 84** (**1A 164**)
Onehouse La. IP1: Ips ... 4K **131**
Onehouse Rd. IP14: Stowm ... 4C **84**
Ontario Rd. NR33: Low ... 2H **11**
Opal Av. IP1: Ips ... 4F **131**
Orchard, The IP14: W'den ... 3H **65**
IP27: B'don ... 4F **19**
IP30: Fels ... 6B **82**
Orchard Av. NR33: Oul B ... 2D **10**
Orchard Cl. CB9: Have ... 4E **100**
IP12: Wood ... 3H **121**
IP23: Eye ... 7C **38**
IP23: Gisli ... 2J **67**
IP28: Ris ... 2C **50**
IP30: Bey ... 4C **62**
IP30: E'well ... 1E **64**
IP30: Roug ... 6K **61**
IP31: Gt Liv ... 3B **28**
NR32: Blun ... 1J **7**
Orchard Cft. NR33: Car C ... 5D **10**
Orchard End IP13: Gru ... 6J **117**
Orchard Farm Barns
IP29: Barr ... 6B **50**
Orchard Gdn. NR33: Oul B ... 2D **10**
Orchard Ga. IP2: Ips ... 1E **136**
IP6: Nee M ... 3F **111**
Orchard Grn. NR34: Becc ... 4F **13**
Orchard Gro. IP5: Kesg ... 6A **134**
IP6: Clay ... 5D **114**
Orchard La. IP13: Gt Bea ... 7A **120**
IP31: Thur ... 4B **56**
NR32: Blun ... 1J **7**
Orchard Pl. CB8: Kent ... 2B **48**
IP13: Wick M ... 6A **118**
Orchard Ri. IP13: B'ham ... 2B **76**
NR34: Worl ... 4J **13**
Orchard Rd. IP8: B'ford ... 3C **130**
IP16: Leis ... 4H **93**
Orchard Row *IP11: Felix ... 3D 154*
(off Grange Rd.)
Orchards, The IP13: Laxf ... 6B **74**
Orchard St. IP4: Ips ... 3G **5** (7B **132**)
IP33: Bury E ... 3H **157** (7G **53**)
Orchard Ter. *NR33: Low ... 2H 11*
(off Clifton Rd.)
Orchard Valley IP19: Holt ... 4D **42**
Orchard Vw. CO6: Leav ... 3B **142**
Orchard Way CO10: Glem ... 6A **104**
IP29: Barr ... 6C **50**
IP29: Horr ... 6B **58**
IP31: B Ash ... 3D **66**
Orchid Cl. IP2: Ips ... 2G **137**
IP14: Deb ... 2G **87**
IP19: H'orth ... 4B **42**
Orchid Dr. IP28: Red L ... 6J **25**
Orchids Cl. NR35: Bung ... 3D **14**
Orchids Way IP6: Nee M ... 5G **111**
Ord Rd. IP31: Forn M ... 4H **53**
Oregon Rd. IP5: Kesg ... 6A **134**
ORFORD ... **7J 125** (**3A 166**)
Orford Castle & Museum ... **7H 125**
Orford Dr. NR32: Oul B ... 5E **8**
Orford Rd. CB9: Have ... 5E **100**
IP11: Felix ... 7D **154**
IP12: But ... 5C **124**
IP12: B'well ... 4C **124**
IP12: Sud ... 2F **125**
Orford St. IP1: Ips ... 2B **4** (6K **131**)
Oriel Cl. CO10: Gt Cor ... 5G **127**
Orion Av. IP6: Gt Bla ... 4A **114**
Orion Ct. IP6: Gt Bla ... 4A **114**
Orkney Cl. CB9: Have ... 4J **101**
Orkney Rd. IP4: Ips ... 4E **132**
Orttewell Rd.
IP32: Bury E ... 6A **54**
Orvis La. CO7: E Ber ... 5D **146**
Orwell Av. IP17: Saxm ... 5H **91**
Orwell Bus. Cen. IP3: Ips ... 4C **138**
Orwell Country Pk. ... **6D 138**
Orwell Ct. IP12: Wood ... 7F **121**
IP18: Sou ... 4J 45
(off York Rd.)
Orwell Dr. NR32: Oul B ... 5E **8**
Orwell Gdns. IP2: Ips ... 3J **137**
Orwell Hgts. IP2: Ips ... 4G **137**
Orwell Ho. IP11: Felix ... 4B **154**
Orwell Meadows Caravan Site
IP10: Nac ... 7G **139**
Orwell Pl. IP4: Ips ... 4F **5** (1B **138**)
Orwell Retail Pk.
IP2: Ips ... 1J **137**
Orwell Ri. IP9: Chelm ... 1H **151**
Orwell Rd. IP3: Ips ... 2E **138**
IP11: Felix ... 5E **154**
IP14: Stowm ... 6F **85**
Orwell Vw. Rd. IP9: Shot ... 4C **156**
Osborne Rd. IP3: Ips ... 2E **138**
Osborne St. NR32: Low ... 5K **9**
Osier Cl. IP12: Melt ... 4J **121**
Osier Rd. IP33: Bury E ... 2G **157** (7G **53**)
Osiers, The IP14: Stowm ... 3F **85**
Osiers Driving Range ... **1J 37**
Osmund Wlk. *IP33: Bury E ... 2C 58*
(off Flemyng Rd.)
Osprey Cl. IP32: Bury E ... 7C **54**
Osprey Dr. IP14: Stowm ... 4J **85**
Osprey Grn. NR33: Oul B ... 3B **10**
Osprey Rd. CB9: Have ... 4H **101**
Oswyn Cl. IP32: Bury E ... 2K **59**
OTLEY ... **1K 117** (**1C 165**)
OTLEY BOTTOM ... **3K 117**
Otley Ct. IP11: Felix ... 3C **154**
Otley Hall ... **1C 165**
Otley Rd. IP12: Sutt ... 3C **140**
Otter Cl. IP14: Stowm ... 6G **85**
OULTON ... **4D 8** (**1D 167**)
OULTON BROAD ... **3E 10** (**1D 167**)
Oulton Broad North Station (Rail)
... **7E 8**
Oulton Broad South Station (Rail)
... **2C 10**
Oulton Ct. NR32: Oul ... 4D **8**
Oulton Ind. Est. NR32: Oul ... 5D **8**
Oulton Rd. IP3: Ips ... 3C **138**
NR32: Cort ... 7F **7**
NR32: Low, Oul B ... 4F **9**
Oulton Rd. Nth. NR32: Oul ... 3E **8**
Oulton St. NR32: Oul ... 4E **8**
Oulton Works NR33: Oul B ... 1E **10**
OUSDEN ... **1B 162**
Ousden Rd. IP29: Harg ... 3F **51**
Outney Comn. NR35: Bung ... 2A **14**
Outney Meadow Caravan Pk.
NR35: Bung ... 1A **14**
Outney Rd. NR35: Bung ... 2A **14**
Out Northgate
IP33: Bury E ... 1H **157** (6G **53**)
Out Risbygate IP33: Bury E ... 1E **58**
Out Westgate
IP33: Bury E ... 7F **157** (2F **59**)
Overchurch Cl. CB9: Have ... 4E **100**
Overing Av. CO10: Gt Wal ... 6K **107**
OVINGTON ... **2B 162**
Ovington Pl. CB9: Have ... 3G **101**
Owell, The IP31: Pake ... 2B **56**
OXEN END ... **3A 162**
Oxer Cl. IP30: E'well ... 2E **64**
Oxford Cl. CO10: Gt Cor ... 5F **127**
IP28: Mide ... 6G **23**

Oxford Dr. IP7: Hadl 1H 129
IP12: Wood 7E 120
Oxford Rd. IP4: Ips 4H 5 (1C 138)
IP5: Kesg 6A 134
IP12: Tun 6G 123
NR32: Low 5J 9
Oxford St. CB8: Exn 1B 46
Oxlip Ho. IP32: Bury E 7C 54
Oysterbed Rd. IP11: Felix 5A 154

P

Packard Av. IP3: Ips 4F 139
Packard Pl. IP8: B'ford 3D 130
Packway La. IP31: Thur 4E 56
Padbrook Ct. IP3: Ips 5K 5
Paddock, The IP31: Ixw 6H 29
Paddock Cl. IP33: Bury E 1C 58
Paddock Farm IP31: Con W 1B 30
Paddock Hill NR33: Oul B 2D 10
Paddocks, The CO8: Bure 6A 142
IP5: Martl H 5G 135
IP6: Tud 7C 116
IP19: H'orth 4C 42
IP21: Stradb 4G 39
IP27: B'don 3H 19
IP27: Lake 6B 20
IP28: B Row 1G 23
IP28: W'ton 2C 24
IP31: B Ash 3D 66
NR33: Kess 4K 17
Paddocks Dr. CB8: Newm 7G 47
Paddocks Grn. NR34: Worl 4J 13
Paddocks Way IP7: Bild 6J 109
Paddock Way IP29: Chedb 6K 51
IP31: Tros 1D 28
Paddock Wood Cl.
NR33: Car C 5B 10
Padstow Rd. IP5: Kesg 7A 134
Padua Ho. IP4: Ips 2K 5 (7D 132)
Pageant Pl. IP13: F'ham 6E 90
Page Gdns. IP5: Kesg 5E 134
Page's Cl. IP14: Stowm 4E 84
Pages Hill Rd. IP29: Whep 1C 80
Paget Cl. IP6: Nee M 3F 111
Paget Pl. CB8: Newm 3G 47
Paget Rd. IP1: Ips 1B 4 (6K 131)
Page Wlk. IP3: Ips 6H 5 (2C 138)
Paigle Cl. IP30: E'well 3D 64
Pains Cl. NR34: Worl 4K 13
Pains Hill IP14: L Sto 2E 86
PAKEFIELD 5G 11 (1D 167)
Pakefield NR33: Low 6F 11
Pakefield Rd. NR33: Low 4H 11
Pakefield St. NR33: Low 5G 11
PAKENHAM 2C 56 (3D 159)
Pakenham Fen 1C 56
Pakenham Pl. CB9: Have 4G 101
Pakenham Rd.
IP31: Gt Bar, Pake 2H 55
IP31: Thur 5B 56
Pakenham Watermill 7J 29
Pakenham Windmill 7H 29
Palace St. CB8: Newm 6G 47
Palfrey Hgts. CO11: Brant 5C 148
PALGRAVE 2D 36 (2B 160)
Palmcroft Cl. IP1: Ips 2J 131
Palmcroft Rd. IP1: Ips 2J 131
Palmer Cl. NR32: Low 2G 9
Palmer Dr. IP27: Lake 4A 20
Palmers La. IP18: Walb 7G 45
NR34: Wrent 1D 44
Palmerston Ct. IP4: Ips 3H 5
Palmerston Rd. IP4: Ips . . .3H 5 (7C 132)
Palmer St. IP31: Wals W 7G 33
Palmerswent Cl.
CO10: L Mel 3J 105
Pamment's La. IP28: W Row 6A 22
Pannels Cl. CO10: Glem 5A 104
Pannington Hall La.
IP9: Wher 2F 149
Papeley Mdw. IP29: Barr 6D 50
Paper Mill La. IP6: Clay 5C 114
IP8: B'ford 7C 114
Parade, The CB9: Ked 6C 98
IP33: Bury E 7C 52
Parade Rd. IP4: Ips 1K 5 (6D 132)
Parade Rd. Sth. NR33: Low 2J 11
Paradise Pl. IP16: Leis 4H 93
Pardoe Pl. IP4: Rush A 1J 139
PARHAM 3D 161
Parham Airfield Mus. 3D 161
Park, The IP31: Gt Bar 2C 54
Park & Ride
London Road, Ipswich 4C 136
Martlesham 4G 135
Newmarket 2F 47
Park Av. CB8: Newm 6H 47
IP11: Felix 3G 155
IP17: Saxm 6H 91
IP28: Forn M 1F 53
Park Cl. CB8: Mou 6D 48
CO10: S'bury 3F 127
IP5: Martl H 5G 135
IP12: Rend 6B 122
NR33: Car C 5C 10
Park Cotts. CB8: Newm 6H 47
Park Ct. IP11: Felix 6D 154
Park Dr. NR34: Worl 4H 13
Park End IP17: Saxm 6H 91
Parker Av. IP11: Felix 5A 154
Parker Pl. CO10: S'bury 1C 126
Parker's Drove IP28: W Row 5A 22
Parkers Pl. IP5: Martl H 5G 135
Parker's Rd. IP14: Cott 7C 68
Parkers Wlk. CB8: Newm 1E 46
Parker's Way CO6: Nay 6J 143
PARKESTON 3C 165
Parkeston Rd. IP11: Felix 4C 154
Park Farm Bus. Cen.
IP28: Forn G 1G 53
Park Farm Dr. IP28: H'well 4K 25
IP31: Stant 7D 32
Park Gdn. IP28: W Row 5A 22
Park Hill IP16: Leis 3H 93
Parkhill NR32: Oul 3E 8
Parkington Wlk. IP32: Bury E 6D 52
(not continuous)
Parkington Way IP22: W'field 1J 33
Parkins, The IP9: Cap M 1J 147
Parklands IP13: Uff 6H 119
Parklands, The NR33: Car C 5C 10
Parklands Cl. CO10: Glem 4B 104
Parklands Grn. IP28: Forn G 1F 53
Park La. CB8: Newm 6G 47
CO10: Glem 4B 104
IP10: Kirt 1H 153
IP13: Char 3E 118
IP15: Aldeb 5J 95
IP18: Sou 5K 45
IP29: Now 7F 59
IP31: Gt Bar 2E 54
Park Mdws. NR32: Oul 2E 8
Park Nth. IP4: Ips 5B 132
Park Pl. IP17: Yox 7H 77
Park Rd. CB9: Have 2C 100
CO6: Boxt, Nay 7J 143
CO6: Stoke N 2K 143
CO7: E Ber 2A 148
CO10: Lave 5A 106
CO10: S'bury 3F 127
IP1: Ips 5A 132
IP6: Nee M 3G 111
IP13: Gru 7H 117
IP14: Comb 2D 110
IP14: W'den 5H 65
IP15: Aldeb 5H 95
IP17: Benh 4A 92
IP19: H'orth 3A 42
IP30: Drin, Drin G . . . .5G 63 & 1F 83
IP33: Bury E 2D 58
NR32: Low 6J 9
Parkside CB9: Have 5E 100
IP28: B Row 1G 23
IP31: Stant 6C 32
Parkside Av. IP4: Ips 1F 5 (6B 132)
Parkside Dr. NR32: Low 6F 9
Park St. CO6: Stoke N 2J 143
Park Ter. CO10: L Mel 4H 105
IP12: Melt 7F 119
Park Vw. CB9: With 2B 98
IP11: T Mary 7H 153
IP13: W'orth 6H 73
IP14: W'den 4H 65
IP22: Bote 4K 35
IP27: B'don 5E 18
Parkview IP28: B Row 2G 23
Park Vw. Rd. IP1: Ips 4J 131
Park Wlk. IP19: Holt 3E 42
Parkway IP13: Wick M 5B 118
IP33: Bury E 3F 157 (2F 59)
Parkway Ho.
IP33: Bury E 3F 157 (7F 53)
Parkwood IP1: Ips 1D 4 (6A 132)
Parkwood Dr. CO10: S'bury 1D 126
Parliament Rd. IP4: Ips 1F 139
Parmenter Dr. CO10: Gt Cor 6H 127
Parnell Cl. IP1: Ips 2H 131
Parnell La. IP30: E'well 1C 64
Parnell Rd. IP1: Ips 2H 131
Parnham Pl. IP4: Rush A 1K 139
Parr Rd. CB9: Have 5C 100
Parry Cl. IP19: H'orth 3B 42
Parsley Cl. IP28: Red L 5K 25
Parsonage Cl. IP11: Felix 4C 154
Parsonage Gdns. *CB9: Have* *4D 100*
(off Baron's Ct.)
Parsonage Grn. IP30: C'field 6J 81
Parsonage Gro. CO8: Bure 6A 142
Parsonage Hill CO8: Bure 6A 142
Parsons Cl. IP27: B'don 5E 18
Parsons Ct. IP33: W'ley 7A 52
Parsons Fld. IP15: Aldeb 4J 95
Parsons Hill IP12: Holl 2G 141
Partridge Cl. CO10: Boxf 6C 128
IP14: Stowm 4H 85
IP31: Thur 6K 55
Partridge Ct. *IP14: Stowm* *4F 85*
(off Violet Hill Rd.)
Partridge Rd. IP2: Ips 3F 137
Partridge Wlk. IP27: B'don 4J 19
Pashford Cl. IP27: Lake 5C 20
Pashford Pl. IP3: Ips 6G 139
Pashlers All. *CO10: Clar* *5C 102*
(off Market Hill)
Paske Av. CB9: Have 4E 100
Pastures, The IP4: Rush A 1K 139
NR32: Oul 2E 8
Pates Cnr. IP29: Laws 6B 80
Patricia Cl. NR32: Oul B 6C 8
Patterdale Gdns. NR32: Low 4F 9
Pattern Bush Cl. CO11: Brant 5C 148
Patteson Rd. IP3: Ips 7H 5 (2C 138)
Patticroft CO10: Glem 3A 104
Pauline St. IP2: Ips 7E 4 (2A 138)
Paul Mellon Ho. CB8: Newm 5G 47
Paul's Rd. IP2: Ips 1H 137
Pavilion Ct. CB9: Have 4G 101
Paxton Chadwick Cl.
IP16: Leis 4J 93
Paynesfield IP14: Fram 6D 88
Payne St. NR33: Low 2H 11
Peace Ct. *IP16: Thor* *6D 94*
(off Old Homes Rd.)
Peace Pl. *IP16: Thor* *6D 94*
(off Old Holmes Rd.)
Peacock Cl. IP8: Ips 4E 136
NR33: Car C 7B 10
Peacock Ri. IP31: Ixw 6H 29
Peacocks Cl. CO10: Cave 5G 103
Peacock's Pyghtle IP12: Orf 6J 125
Peacocks Rd. CO10: Cave 4G 103
Peacock St. IP5: Kesg 6E 134
Peak Dale NR33: Car C 6D 10
Peakhall La. CO10: Act 2J 107
Pearce Rd. IP3: Ips 1E 138
Pear Cl. IP23: Gisli 1K 67
Pearcroft Rd. IP1: Ips 2K 131
Pearl Cl. IP6: Otl 1K 117
Pearl Rd. IP1: Ips 5F 131
Pearmain Wlk. CB9: Have 3B 100
Pearse Way IP3: Pur F 5J 139
Pearson Rd. IP3: Ips 1G 139
Pearsons Cl. CO10: Glem 5A 104
Pearsons Pl. IP6: Henl 5K 115
Pearsons Way IP8: Wash 5B 136
Peart Gro. IP5: Kesg 7D 134
Pear Tree Cl. IP17: Carl 3H 91
Pear Tree Pl. IP14: Gt Fin 7J 83
Peasecroft Rd. IP31: Ixw 5H 29
PEASENHALL 3J 77 (3D 161)
Peasenhall Cl. IP12: Sutt 2A 140
Peasenhall Rd. IP19: Wal 4H 75
Peasey Gdns. IP5: Kesg 7C 134
PEATS CORNER 3B 160
Pebble Cl. NR32: Low 5F 9
PEBMARSH 3C 163
Peckham St.
IP33: Bury E 2G 157 (7G 53)
Pecockes Cl. CO10: Gt Cor 6H 127
Peddars Cl. IP31: Ixw 5H 29
Peddars Ct. CO10: L Mel 4H 105
NR32: Low 4G 9
Peddars La. NR34: Becc 4E 12
Peddars Way NR32: Low 4G 9
Pedler's La. NR33: Kess 6H 17
Peel St. IP1: Ips 2D 4 (7A 132)
Peel Yd. IP5: Martl H 5G 135
Peewit Caravan Pk.
IP11: Felix 6D 154
Peewit Ct. IP11: Felix 5C 154
Peewit Hill IP11: Felix 5C 154
Peewit Rd. IP2: Ips 3E 136
Pegasus M. NR32: Oul B 7C 8
Pelican Cl. IP2: Ips 3G 137
Pemberton Wlk. *IP33: Bury E* *4J 59*
(off Raven Rd.)
Pembroke Av. IP12: Wood 6F 121
Pembroke Cl. CB8: Newm 7H 47
IP2: Ips 3K 137
IP28: Mide 6J 23
Pembroke Pl. CO10: S'bury 1C 126
Pembroke Rd. IP13: F'ham 4B 90
IP33: Bury E 3D 58
Pembrooke Way NR32: Low 4F 9
Penbry Gdns. IP31: B Ash 2D 66
Pendleton Rd. IP2: Ips 5F 137
Penfold Rd. IP11: Felix 4F 155
Peninsula Sports Cen. 2D 150
Penn Cl. IP9: Cap M 1J 147
Pennine Way NR32: Oul 6D 8
Pennings, The (Local Nature Reserve)
. . . . .7E 38
Pennyfields NR35: Bung 4B 14
Pennygate Dr. NR33: Oul B 3D 10
Penny La. IP3: Pur F 5K 139
NR32: Oul 6D 8
Penny Mdw. IP9: Cap M 1H 147
Pennyroyal Gdns. IP2: Ips 2G 137
Penryn Rd. IP5: Kesg 6K 133
Penshurst Rd. IP3: Ips 2H 139
Pentland Wlk. NR32: Low 4F 9
PENTLOW 6J 103 (2C 163)
Pentlow Dr. CO10: Cave 6J 103
Pentlow Hawke Cl. CB9: Have 4G 101
Pentlow La. CO10: Cave, Pent 6J 103
PENTLOW STREET 7K 103
Penzance Rd. IP5: Kesg 7K 133
Peppercorn Way
IP2: Ips 7F 5 (3A 138)
Pepper La. IP31: Thur 1B 62
Pepper Pl. IP5: Kesg 7D 134
Peppers Cl. IP27: Weet 1E 18
Peppers La. IP9: Wher 1G 149
Pepys Av. NR34: Worl 4K 13
Percy Ruse Cl. CO10: S'bury 4G 127
Peregrine Dr. IP14: Stowm 3H 85
Peregrine Way NR33: Kess 5K 17
Perfect U Health Club 2E 46
Periman Cl. CB8: Newm 4G 47
Periwinkle Cl. NR33: Car C 4B 10
Perkins Rd. IP30: Roug 2E 60
Perkins Way IP3: Ips 5D 138
IP30: Tost 1G 63
Permain La. IP4: Ips 1J 5 (6C 132)
Perrydown La. IP30: C'field 7H 81
Perryfields CO10: Gt Cor 7G 127
Persimmon Wlk. CB8: Newm 1E 46
(not continuous)
Pesthouse La. IP6: Barh 1B 114
Petch Cl. IP33: Bury E . . .2H 157 (7G 53)
Peterfen Drove IP27: Lake 3F 21
Peterhouse Cl. IP2: Ips 4H 137
IP28: Mide 7K 23
Peterhouse Cres. IP12: Wood 6E 120
Peterhouse Dr. CB8: Newm 7G 47
Peter's Gro. IP9: Cap M 1H 147
Petingo Cl. CB8: Newm 2D 46
Petit Couronne Way NR34: Becc . . .5G 13
Peto Way NR32: Low 6F 9
PETTAUGH 2C 88 (1B 164)
Pettaugh Rd.
IP14: Petta, Ston A 6H 87
Petticoat La. IP29: Barr 6C 50
IP33: Bury E 2F 59
PETTISTREE 1J 119 (1C 165)
Pettiward Cl. IP14: Gt Fin 6J 83
Pettwood Gdns. IP9: Holb 2D 150
Petunia Way IP27: B'don 5D 18
Phalaris Way CB8: Newm 6G 47
Pheasant Cl. IP31: Thur 6K 55
Pheasant Ri. IP8: Wash 6B 136
Pheasant Rd. IP2: Ips 3G 137
Pheasant Way IP27: B'don 3J 19
Pheonix Cl. CO10: S'bury 3D 126
Philip Av. IP11: Felix 5C 154
Philipps Cl. CB8: Newm 5D 46
Philip Rd. IP2: Ips 7D 4 (2A 138)
IP32: Bury E 4F 53
Phillipps Rd. IP6: Barh 3D 114
Phillips Cres. IP6: Nee M 4H 111
Phillips Fld. Rd. CO10: Gt Cor . . .6F 127
Phoenix Rd. IP4: Ips 6E 132
Phoenix Way IP14: Stowm 4H 85
PICCADILLY CORNER 1C 161
Picketts Rd. IP11: Felix 3H 155
Pickwick Cres.
IP33: Bury E 3J 157 (1H 59)
Pickwick Dr. NR32: Blun 1J 7
Pickwick Rd. IP2: Ips 1G 137
Picton Av. IP1: Ips 4B 132
Pier Av. IP18: Sou 3K 45
Pier Rd. IP11: Felix 7B 154
Pier Ter. NR33: Low 1J 11
Pigeon La. IP28: Forn S 1D 52
Pigeons La. IP8: Wash 4A 136
IP17: Yox 6J 77
Pightle, The *CB8: Newm* *6G 47*
(off Church La.)
CB9: Have 3F 101
IP6: Nee M 3G 111
IP9: Cap M 1J 147
NR34: Nor C 7B 6
Pightle Cl. IP30: E'well 2D 64
Pig La. *NR34: Becc* *2E 12*
(off Queen's Rd.)
Pilbroughs Wlk. IP5: Kesg 6D 134
(Fairbairn Av.)
IP5: Kesg 6B 134
(Twelve Acre App.)
Pilgrim Ct. CB8: Kenn 2A 48
Pilgrims Ct. *CO8: Bure* *5B 142*
(off Cuckoo Hill)
Pilgrims Grn. IP21: Fress 6C 40
Pilgrims Way IP14: Gt Fin 7J 83
IP16: Thor 6D 94
NR35: Bung 3C 14

Pilots Way IP12: Wood 5G 121
(Seckford Ter.)
IP12: Wood 6F 121
(Warren Hill Rd., not continuous)
Pimpernel Rd. IP2: Ips 3G 137
Pinbush Cl. NR33: Low 7E 10
Pinbush Rd. NR33: Low 7E 10
Pine Av. IP1: Ips 4K 131
Pine Bank IP5: Martl H 7F 135
Pine Cl. CO11: Brant 5C 148
IP12: Rend 6C 122
IP23: Eye 6D 38
IP27: RAF L 4G 21
Pinecroft Ri. CO10: Ball 6B 126
Pinecroft Rd. IP1: Ips 3J 131
Pinecroft Way IP6: Nee M 4H 111
Pine Dr. IP3: Pur F 5K 139
(not continuous)
Pine Gro. IP13: Gru 7J 117
Pine Ho. IP11: Felix 4D 154
Pine Leys IP32: Bury E 5F 53
Pine Ridge IP28: B Row 1F 23
Pines, The CO10: S'bury 2F 127
IP6: Clay 4D 114
IP11: Felix 2K 155
IP28: Holy R 2H 23
Pine Sq. IP7: Gt Bri 1A 112
Pine Tree Cl. NR34: Worl 4J 13
Pinetree Cl. IP5: Kesg 6K 133
Pine Tree Ct. IP22: Hop 2H 31
Pine Trees Av. IP28: Mide 7K 23
Pine Vw. IP14: Bac 6C 68
Pineview Cl. IP14: Stowm 5F 85
Pine Vw. Rd. IP1: Ips 4J 131
Pinewood IP12: Wood 7F 121
Pinewood Av. NR33: Oul B 3E 10
Pinewood Dr. IP27: B'don 4F 19
Pinewood Gdns.
NR34: Nor C 7B 6
PINFORD END 1C 163
Pinhoe Dr. CB9: Have 3A 100
Pinkney's La. IP18: Sou 4K 45
PINMILL 1H 151 (3C 165)
Pin Mill Cl. IP2: Ips 5E 136
Pin Mill Rd. IP9: Chelm 2H 151
Pinners La. IP13: Hask 4C 120
Pinners Way IP33: Bury E 2E 58
Pintail Cl. IP2: Ips 4G 137
IP27: Lake 6B 20
Pintail Rd. IP14: Stowm 4J 85
Pinza Cl. CB8: Newm 1E 46
(off Parkers Wlk.)
Piperell Way CB9: Have 6F 101
Pipers Cl. CB9: Have 5H 101
Pipers Mdw. IP13: W'orth 6H 73
Pipers Va. Cl. IP3: Ips 5C 138
Pipers Vale Local Nature Reserve
. . . . .6D 138
Pipes Cl. IP13: Gru 6J 117
Pippin Cl. IP32: Bury E 7A 54
Pippin Ct. IP28: Red L 5J 25
Pippins, The CO10: Glem 5B 104
IP3: Ips 2F 139
IP14: Stowu 2K 85
NR32: Blun 1J 7
Pipp's La. IP6: Weste 7A 116
Pirnhow St. NR35: Dit 1C 14
Pit, The IP13: Cam A 2C 122
Pitcairn Rd. IP1: Ips 5G 131
Pitches Vw. IP18: Rey 1G 45
Pitman's Gro. IP19: B'field 7J 75
Pitts End CO7: E Ber 3C 146
PIXEY GREEN 2C 161
Place Farm Cl. IP7: Hadl 2J 129
Plaisir Pl. NR32: Low 6J 9
(off Thurston Rd.)
Plampin Cl. CO10: Newt 2C 128
Planche, The IP31: Thur 1B 62
Plantation, The IP15: Aldeb 4H 95
Plantation Way IP14: Batt 6A 110
IP28: Red L 6J 25
Planters Gro. NR33: Oul B 2E 10
Plashwood Rd.
IP14: Haug, W'den 4J 65
Platers Wlk. IP16: Leis 3H 93
Platten Cl. IP6: Nee M 3F 111
Platters Cl. IP3: Ips 7F 139
Platters Rd. IP11: Felix 6D 154
Playfield Rd. IP9: Cap M 2J 147
PLAYFORD 1B 134 (2C 165)
Playford Ct. CO10: S'bury 3D 126
(off Inkerman Row)
Playford La. IP5: Rush A 4J 133
Playford Rd. IP4: Ips 6H 133
IP5: Rush A 3B 134
IP13: L Bea 3B 134
Pleasant Pl. NR34: Becc 5E 12
Pleasant Row IP4: Ips 5F 5 (1B 138)
IP33: Bury E 6F 157
Pleasurewood Cl. NR32: Low 3G 9
Pleasurewood Hills 7J 7
PLEDGDON GREEN 3A 162
Plough La. CO6: Leav 3B 142
CO10: S'bury 4C 126
Plough Rd. IP9: Cap M 2G 147
IP30: Wool 5A 64
Plough St. IP3: Ips 6J 5 (2C 138)
Plover Cl. IP14: Stowm 4J 85
IP28: B Row 1C 22
Plover Rd. IP2: Ips 4G 137
Plovers Ct. IP27: B'don 4J 19
Plovers Way IP33: Bury E 5J 59
NR33: Oul B 4C 10
Plumbers Arms Cl.
IP31: Nort 5H 57
Plummer Cl. IP31: Ixw 6J 29
Plummers Dell IP6: Gt Bla 2B 114
Plumpton Av. IP28: Mide 6J 23
Plumptons Ct.
IP33: Bury E 6G 157 (1G 59)
Plum Tree Ri. IP7: Gt Bri 1A 112
Plumtrees NR32: Oul B 6C 8
Plymouth Rd. IP11: Felix 2E 154
Pochard Cl. IP14: Stowm 3J 85
Pokeriage Gdns. IP31: Thur 7A 56
Policeman's Loke NR32: S'ton 2C 6
Police Sta. Rd. NR32: Low 7J 9
Police Sta. Sq. IP28: Mide 7J 23
(off King St.)
Pollard Ct. IP2: Ips 4F 137
Pollard Piece NR33: Car C 4B 10
Pollards La. IP28: W Row 4B 22
Polls La. NR34: R'field 7D 12
POLSTEAD 5C 144 (3D 163)
Polstead Cl. IP14: Stowm 6H 85
POLSTEAD HEATH 2D 163
Polstead Hill CO6: Pols 5C 144
Polstead Rd. CO10: Boxf 7E 128
Polstead St. CO6: Stoke N 1J 143
Pond Cl. IP11: Felix 3C 154
Pond End IP6: Henl 5K 115
Pond Farm IP23: Thorn 2C 72
Pondgrove Cl. IP32: Bury E 7A 54
Pond Hall Rd. IP7: Hadl 4K 129
IP8: Hint 3A 144
Pond La. IP19: U Hol 1C 42
IP27: B'don 5D 18
Pond Piece IP13: B'ton 1K 89
Pontins Wlk. IP5: Kesg 7C 134
Poole Cl. IP3: Ips 3H 139
Poole St. CO10: Cave 6G 103
Pooley's Yd. IP2: Ips 6B 4 (2K 137)
POOL STREET 3B 162
Popes Ct. CB9: Stur 6K 101
Poplar Cl. CB9: Have 2C 100
IP6: Clay 4D 114
IP28: Mide 5J 23
IP29: Barr 6C 50
Poplar Ct. CO10: Gt Cor 4G 127
Poplar Est. IP28: B Row 1G 23
Poplar Farm La. IP31: Thur 4D 56
Poplar Hill IP14: Stowm 1E 110
Poplar La. IP8: Wash 3D 136
Poplar Mdw. IP30: Rushb 7E 60
Poplar Rd. CO10: Gt Cor 4G 127
NR33: Car C 6C 10
Poplars, The CO11: Brant 3C 148
IP6: Cod 1G 115
IP28: B Row 1G 23
Poplar Ter. NR33: Kess 5K 17
Poplar Vw. CB9: L Brad 4D 96
Poppy Cl. IP2: Ips 2H 137
IP28: Red L 5K 25
IP32: Bury E 1A 60
NR34: Worl 5J 13
Popson St. NR35: Bung 2A 14
Portal Av. IP5: Martl H 4G 135
Portal Cl. IP24: Barnh 6J 27
Porter Rd. IP3: Pur F 5K 139
Porthole Cl. NR33: Car C 5A 10
Portland Cres. IP12: Wood 6F 121
Portland Grn. CB8: Newm 6E 46
Portland Rd. CB8: Newm 6E 46
Portman Road 4B 4 (1K 137)
Portman Rd. IP1: Ips 3C 4 (7K 131)
Portman's Wlk. IP1: Ips . . .4A 4 (1J 137)
PORT OF FELIXSTOWE, THE 5B 154
Port of Felixstowe Rd.
IP11: Felix 4B 154
Portsch Cl. NR33: Car C 6D 10
POSLINGFORD 2B 162
Poslingford Cnr. CO10: Posl 3C 102
Posting Ho. Ct. IP23: Eye 7D 38
(off Buckshorn La.)
Post Mill Cl. IP4: Ips 2K 5 (7D 132)
IP13: Gru 7H 117
Post Mill Cres. IP13: Gru 7H 117
Post Mill Gdns. IP13: Gru 7H 117
Postmill Gdns. IP31: Wals W 5G 33
Post Mill La. IP21: Fress 6B 40
Post Mill Orchard IP13: Gru 7H 117
Post Office Cnr. IP9: Stut 6C 150
Post Office Cotts. IP21: Wey 3D 40
Post Office Hill CB8: W'rook 3G 97
Post Office La. CO10: Glem 4A 104
IP12: Martl 2J 135
Post Office Rd. IP17: Knod 6F 93
Post Office Row CO10: Act 4G 107
POTASH 4H 147
Potash La. IP9: Bent 4H 147
IP14: Wyve 1B 68
IP23: Eye 6G 37
Pot Kiln Rd. CO10: Gt Cor 6G 127
Pot Kilns, The CO10: Gt Cor 5H 127
Potkins La. IP12: Orf 6H 125
Potland La. CO10: Lave 6B 106
POTTERGATE STREET 1B 160
Potters App. IP5: Kesg 7B 134
Potters Brook IP13: F'ham 6B 90
Pottersfield CO10: Gt Cor 7G 127
Potter's La. IP22: Rick 7K 35
IP31: Stant 7D 32
Potters Va. IP22: Hind 6D 34
Pottery Hill IP22: W'field 1J 33
Pott Hall Rd. IP28: W Row 6C 22
Pound, The IP29: Now 7K 59
Pound Cl. IP19: H'orth 5B 42
IP31: Wals W 7H 33
Pound Corner IP13: Gru 7H 117
IP31: Barni 2D 30
NR34: Wang 6C 44
Pound Farm Dr. NR32: Oul B 4E 8
POUND GREEN 5C 96 (1B 162)
Pound Grn. Rd. IP13: B'ham 1E 76
Pound Hill IP7: Gt Bri 3A 112
IP14: Bac 6B 68
Pound Hill Cl. IP14: Bac 6B 68
Pound La. IP7: Hadl 3H 129
IP8: B'ford 3C 130
(Acton Rd.)
IP8: B'ford 6A 114
(Loraine Way)
IP8: Cop 7B 136
IP9: Cap M 2G 147
IP14: Stowm 3F 85
IP21: Horh 1H 73
IP22: W'field 3K 33
NR32: Blun 2H 7
Pound Mdw. IP28: Forn S 1D 52
Pound Mdw. Ct. IP28: Mide 7J 23
Pound Pl. NR34: Becc 2E 12
Pound Rd. NR34: Becc 2E 12
Pound Wlk. NR34: Becc 2E 12
Pouy St. IP17: Sib 1J 77
Powling Rd. IP3: Ips 4E 138
Pownall Rd. IP3: Ips 6H 5 (2C 138)
POYSTREET GREEN 1D 163
Prentice Rd. IP14: Stowm 4G 85
Prentices La. IP12: Wood 4E 120
Prentice St. CO10: Lave 6C 106
Prentice Way IP3: Ips 2F 139
Prescott Dr. IP30: E'well 3E 64
Presidents, The IP28: B Row 1E 22
Presland Ct. IP27: Lake 4A 20
Presmere Rd. IP13: Petti 2H 119
PRESTON 1D 163
Preston Dr. IP1: Ips 3H 131
Preston Rd. CO10: Lave 5C 106
Prestwick Av. IP11: Felix 2H 155
Pretyman Av. IP14: Bac 6B 68
Pretyman Rd. IP3: Ips 3F 139
IP11: Felix 7D 154
Prevetts Way IP15: Aldeb 4J 95
PRICKWILLOW 1A 158
Priestley Rd. IP6: Nee M 4F 111
Priestly Cl. IP14: Stowm 2D 84
Prigg Wlk. IP32: Bury E 6E 52
Primack Rd. IP32: Bury E 1C 60
Primrose All. IP18: Sou 5K 45
Primrose Cl. NR33: Low 7E 10
Primrose Dr. IP27: B'don 5D 18
Primrose Hill CB9: Have 4E 100
IP2: Ips 2H 137
Primrose La.
NR33: Gisle . . . . .4E 16 & 3F 17
NR34: Becc 6D 12
Primrose Ri. NR34: Worl 5H 13
Primrose Way IP6: Nee M 5G 111
Prince Charles Av. IP32: Bury E . . .4E 52
Prince Charles Cl.
CO10: S'bury 3E 126
Prince Cl. CB8: Exn 1B 46
Princedale Cl. IP1: Ips 4J 131
Prince of Wales Cl.
IP33: Bury E 1E 58
Prince of Wales Dr. IP2: Ips 4J 137
Princes Cl. IP27: B'don 5D 18
Princes Gdns. IP8: S'ham 3K 113
IP11: Felix 4E 154
Princes Grn. IP19: H'orth 6A 42
Princes Rd. IP11: Felix 5E 154
NR32: Low 6H 9
NR35: Bung 4B 14
Princess Rd. IP18: Rey 1J 45
Princes St. IP1: Ips 6B 4 (2K 137)
IP33: Bury E 1F 59
Princess Way CB8: Newm 5E 46
CB9: Have 3D 100
Prince St. CO10: S'bury 3D 126
Princes Wlk. NR32: Low 6F 9
Princethorpe Rd. IP3: Ips 2G 139
Prior's Av. IP33: Bury E 2E 58
Priors Cl. IP30: Roug 6K 61
NR32: Low 3H 9
Prior's Footpath IP33: Bury E 1E 58
Priors' Hill Rd. IP15: Aldeb 5J 95
Priors Way IP15: Aldeb 5J 95
Priory Av. CB9: Have 4E 100
Priory Cl. IP21: Stradb 6H 39
IP22: Pal 2D 36
IP31: Ing 5D 28
Priory Cres. IP21: Fress 6B 40
Priory Gdns. CO10: S'bury 5D 126
PRIORY HEATH 5G 139
Priory La. IP14: Deb 2J 87
IP17: Dars 2C 78
NR35: Bung 2B 14
Priory Rd. CO10: S'bury 2C 126
IP11: Felix 3H 155
IP17: Snap . . . . .2D 94 & 7B 92
IP19: Blyth 6J 43
IP21: Fress 7B 40
IP22: Pal 2C 36
NR34: Becc 4E 12
NR34: Wrent 1C 44
Priory Wlk. CO10: S'bury 5D 126
PRISTOW GREEN 1B 160
Prittlewell Cl. IP2: Ips 5H 137
Private Rd. IP12: Martl 3H 135
NR33: Oul B 2D 10
Privet Grn. NR33: Oul B 2F 11
Privet Way IP28: Red L 7J 25
Progress Way IP23: Eye 7H 37
Promenade IP16: Leis 5H 93
Prospect Hill
CO10: Gt Cor, L Cor 7J 127
Prospect Pl. IP12: Melt 4J 121
IP16: Leis 3J 93
NR33: Low 6G 11
Prospect Rd. IP1: Ips 2A 4 (7J 131)
IP31: Nort 5K 57
NR32: Oul B 7A 8
Prospect Row
IP33: Bury E 4G 157 (1G 59)
Prospect St. IP1: Ips 2A 4 (7J 131)
Prospect Ter. CB9: Ked 6C 98
(off Rectory Rd.)
Provan Ct. IP3: Ips 2F 139
Providence La. IP1: Ips . . .1A 4 (6J 131)
Providence Pl. NR34: Becc 2E 12
Providence St. IP1: Ips . . .3D 4 (7A 132)
Prussia La.
IP33: Bury E 6K 157 (2H 59)
Puddingmoor NR34: Becc 3D 12
PUDDLEDOCK 1A 160
Puddle Duck La. NR34: Worl 5J 13
Puffin Ct. IP14: Stowm 4J 85
PULHAM MARKET 1B 160
PULHAM ST MARY 1C 161
Pump Ct. CO10: Lave 6C 106
Pump Ho. La. IP17: Sib 3K 77
Pump La. IP27: B'don 4H 19
IP33: Bury E 4H 157 (1G 59)
Pump St. IP6: Nee M 4H 111
IP12: Orf 7J 125
Punchard Way IP11: T Mary 7J 153
Purcell Rd. IP14: Stowm 2D 84
Purdis Av. IP3: Pur F 5K 139
PURDIS FARM 4K 139
Purdis Farm La.
IP3: Foxh, Pur F 4J 139
Purplett Ho. IP2: Ips 7F 5
Purplett St. IP2: Ips 7F 5 (2B 138)
Pursehouse Cl. IP23: Gisli 1J 67
Put Hawk's La. IP6: Bark 7F 111
Putney Cl. IP1: Ips 5H 131
IP27: B'don 6D 18
Putticks La. CO7: E Ber 3D 146
PUTTOCK END 2C 163
Pyes Mdw. IP30: E'well 2E 64
Pykenham's Gatehouse 3E 4
Pykenham Way IP7: Hadl 3H 129
Pytches Cl. IP12: Melt 4H 121
Pytches Rd. IP12: Wood 4H 121

Q

QM Ind. Pk. IP3: Ips 5G 139
Q Tower 5E 154
(off South Hill)
Quadling St. IP1: Ips 5D 4 (1A 138)
Quadrangle Centre, The
IP3: Ips 5G 139
Quail Cl. IP14: Stowm 3H 85
Quaker La.
IP30: Bey, Hess, Roug 4A 62
IP31: Bard 2D 32

Quaker's La. CB9: Have 4F 101
Quakers Way IP16: Leis 4J 93
Quantock Cl. IP5: Rush A 6K 133
Quantrill Ter. IP5: Kesg 7D 134
Quantum Bus. Pk. IP1: Ips 2F 131
Quaves La. NR35: Bung 2B 14
Quay, The IP12: Wald 6D 140
NR34: Becc 1E 12
Quay La. CO10: S'bury 5D 126
IP18: Rey 1F 45
Quay Point *IP12: Wood 6H 121*
(off Station Rd.)
Quays Barns IP28: Ris 2D 50
Quay Side IP12: Wood 6H 121
Quayside IP4: Ips 5F 5
Quayside Bus. Cen.
NR33: Oul B 1E 10
Quayside Ct. IP27: Lake 4A 20
Quayside Pl. IP12: Wood 6J 121
Quay's Rd. IP28: Ris 2D 50
Quay St. IP12: Orf 7J 125
IP12: Wood 6H 121
IP19: H'orth 4B 42
Quay Theatre, The 5D 126
Quay View Business Pk.
NR32: Low 7F 9
Quebec Dr. IP5: Kesg 5B 134
Queech, The *IP9: Cap M 1J 147*
(off Thorney Rd.)
Queech Pl. IP6: Barh 1C 114
Queech Wood Cl. IP6: Barh 1C 114
QUEEN ADELAIDE 1A 158
Queen Elizabeth Cl. IP16: Leis 5H 93
Queen Elizabeth Dr. NR34: Becc 6G 13
Queens Av. IP12: Wood 6F 121
Queensberry Rd. CB8: Newm 6F 47
IP3: Ips 5E 138
Queenscliffe Rd.
IP2: Ips 7A 4 (3J 137)
Queens Cl. CB9: Have 3D 100
CO10: Gt Cor 6G 127
CO10: S'bury 3D 126
IP14: Comb 3C 110
(not continuous)
IP17: Saxm 6H 91
IP19: H'orth 6A 42
IP33: Bury E 1E 58
Queensdale Cl. IP1: Ips 4K 131
Queens Dr. IP19: H'orth 6A 42
IP28: Mide 7H 23
Queensgate Dr. IP4: Ips 5D 132
Queen's Head All. IP13: F'ham 6C 90
Queen's Head La. IP12: Wood 5G 121
Queen's Highway NR32: Oul 5B 8
Queensland IP9: Shot 5B 156
Queens La. IP29: Chedb 6K 51
Queens Rd. CO10: S'bury 2D 126
IP11: Felix 5F 155
IP18: Rey 1J 45
IP18: Sou 5K 45
IP27: B'don 5D 18
IP33: Bury E 1E 58
NR32: Low 5J 9
NR34: Becc 2E 12
NR35: Bung 4B 14
Queens Row IP7: Hadl 4H 129
Queens Sq. *CB9: Have 3F 101*
(off Queen St.)
IP3: Ips 4F 139
Queen St. CB8: Newm 6H 47
CB9: Have 3F 101
CB9: With 2B 98
IP1: Ips 4D 4 (1A 138)
IP7: Hadl 3H 129
IP11: Felix 3D 154
IP18: Sou 4K 45
IP21: Stradb 4H 39
Queens Vw. CB8: Exn 1A 46
Queens Way IP3: Ips 4F 139
NR32: Blun 3K 7
Queensway CB8: Exn 1B 46
CB9: Have 3D 100
CO10: Act 4G 107
CO10: Gt Cor 6G 127
IP28: Mide 7H 23
Queen Victoria Dr. IP9: Shot G 7D 156
Quendon Pl. CB9: Have 3G 101
(not continuous)
Quentin Cl. IP1: Ips 5G 131
QUIDENHAM 1A 160
Quilter Dr. IP8: Ips 6E 136
Quilter Rd. IP11: Felix 4G 155
Quince Cl. CO11: Brant 4C 148
Quinnell Way NR32: Low 2F 9
Quinton Rd. IP6: Nee M 4F 111
Quintons Cnr. CO7: E Ber 2C 146
Quinton's La. IP11: Felix 3H 155
(Carol Cl.)
IP11: Felix 2G 155
(Rosemary Av., not continuous)
Quintons Rd. CO7: E Ber 3B 146
Quoits Fld. IP6: Clay 4D 114
Quoits Mdw. IP14: Ston A 6G 87
Qwysson Av.
IP33: Bury E 2J 157 (7H 53)

R

RACECOURSE 3G 139
Rachel Ct. IP4: Ips 2G 5 (7C 132)
Rackham's Cnr. NR32: Cort 5F 7
Radcliffe Dr. IP2: Ips 4E 136
Radcliffe Rd. IP27: RAF L 4H 21
Radiator Rd. CO10: Gt Cor 6F 127
Radnor Cl. IP32: Bury E 7A 54
RADWINTER 3A 162
Raeburn Rd. IP3: Ips 5D 138
Raeburn Rd. Sth. IP3: Ips 6C 138
Raedwald Dr. IP32: Bury E 1K 59
Raedwald Way IP14: Deb 3H 87
Raes Yd. IP33: Bury E 3G 157
RAF LAKENHEATH 4H 21
RAF MILDENHALL 1D 22
Raglan Rd. NR32: Low 7J 9
Raglan St. NR32: Low 6J 9
(not continuous)
Rag's La. IP30: Wool 5A 64
Raile Wlk. CO10: L Mel 3J 105
Railway App. IP11: Felix 3F 155
Railway Ter. CB9: Ked 7B 98
IP27: Weet 2F 19
Raine Av. CB9: Have 3C 100
Raingate St.
IP33: Bury E 6K 157 (2H 59)
Raleigh Cl. CO10: S'bury 1F 127
Raleigh Rd. CO10: S'bury 1F 127
Ram Meadow 3J 157 (7H 53)
Ramplin Cl. IP33: Bury E 1J 157
Rampling Cl. IP7: Hadl 2H 129
RAMSEY 3C 165
Ramsey Cl. IP2: Ips 5J 137
Ramsey Rd. IP7: Hadl 2K 129
Ramsgate Dr. IP3: Ips 3F 139
Ramsholt Rd. IP12: Alder 5F 141
Randall Cl. IP5: Kesg 6E 134
Randolph Cl. IP4: Ips 1F 139
Rands Rd. IP7: Lay 7F 129
Rands Way IP3: Ips 4F 139
Randwell Cl. IP4: Ips 1F 139
Ranelagh Rd. IP2: Ips 6A 4 (1H 137)
IP11: Felix 4F 155
Ranger, The IP4: Ips 5F 5
Ransome Cl. IP8: Spro 7C 130
Ransome Cres. IP3: Ips 4F 139
Ransome Rd. IP3: Ips 4F 139
Ransomes Europark IP3: Ips 6J 139
(not continuous)
Ransomes Sports & Social Club
5E 132
Ransomes Way IP3: Ips 6H 139
Ransom Rd. IP12: Wood 4F 121
Ranson Rd. IP6: Nee M 4F 111
Rant Score NR32: Low 6K 9
Ranulph Cl. IP5: Kesg 7B 134
Ranville NR33: Car C 6D 10
Ranworth Av. NR33: Oul B 3D 10
Raphael Wlk. *NR32: Low 2G 9*
(off Gainsborough Dr.)
Rapier St. IP2: Ips 3B 138
Rapsy Tapsy La. IP23: Eye 6A 38
Rattler's Rd. IP27: B'don 4F 19
RATTLESDEN 4K 83 (1D 163)
Rattlesden Cl. IP14: Stowm 7F 85
Rattlesden Rd. IP14: Bux 6F 83
IP30: Drin G 1F 83
Raven Cl. IP14: Stowm 3H 85
IP28: Mide 1G 25
Raven Rd. IP33: Bury E 5J 59
Ravensfield Rd. IP1: Ips 4G 131
Ravens La. IP8: B'ford 3C 130
Ravensmere NR34: Becc 1E 12
Ravensmere E. NR34: Becc 2E 12
Ravens Way IP12: Martl 3H 135
Ravenswood Av. IP3: Ips 6F 139
Ravenswood Way IP3: Ips 6F 139
Raven Way IP7: Hadl 5H 129
Ravenwood M. NR33: Oul B 4F 11
Ravine, The NR32: Low 5J 9
RAYDON 1J 145 (3A 164)
Raydon Cft. IP14: Stowm 7H 85
Raydon La. IP12: Orf 6K 125
Raydon Rd. CO7: H Mar 3J 145
Raydon Way CO10: Gt Cor 5H 127
Rayes La. CB8: Newm 5G 47
Rayleigh Rd. IP1: Ips 4G 131
Rayment Drift IP5: Kesg 6C 134
Raymond Ct. CB9: Have 5F 101
Raynham Rd. IP32: Bury E 5F 53
Raynsford Rd. IP30: Gt Whe 7C 60
REACH 3A 158
Reade Rd. IP9: Holb 2D 150
READING GREEN 2B 160
Reading Rd. IP4: Ips 6F 133
Reavell Pl. IP2: Ips 5A 4 (1J 137)
Reckford Rd. IP17: Westl 7G 79
Recreation Cl. IP11: Felix 2E 154
Recreation La. IP11: Felix 2E 154
Recreation Rd. CB9: Have 4E 100
IP14: Stowm 4E 84
Recreation Wlk. CO10: Gt Cor 6G 127
Recreation Way IP3: Ips 4G 139
IP28: Mide 7J 23
Rectory Cl. CO10: Glem 4A 104
IP7: Ray 2K 145
NR34: Worl 4J 13
Rectory Cnr. IP29: Laws 6A 80
Rectory Fld. IP9: Chelm 2G 151
Rectory Gdns. CO10: L Mel 1H 105
IP7: Ray 2K 145
IP27: Weet 1E 18
IP30: Bey 4C 62
IP31: Thur 6B 56
Rectory Grn. IP19: H'orth 4A 42
IP22: Redg 3D 34
Rectory Gro. IP29: Whep 2C 80
Rectory Hill CO6: Pols 7B 144
CO7: E Ber 5B 146
IP22: Rick 6G 35
(not continuous)
Rectory La. CO11: Brant 4D 148
IP8: Hint 1C 144
IP10: Kirt 1H 153
IP19: H'orth 5A 42
IP21: Stus 2G 37
IP27: Weet 1E 18
IP30: Wool 5A 64
NR34: Worl 4K 13
Rectory Mdw. IP28: Forn S 2D 52
IP30: Rat 3K 83
Rectory Pk. CO10: Boxf 7C 128
Rectory Pl. IP29: Denh 7B 50
Rectory Rd. CB9: Ked 6C 98
CO10: Gt Wal 7K 107 & 7A 108
CO10: Midd 7D 126
CO10: Newt 2C 128
IP2: Ips 7D 4 (3A 138)
IP6: Hemi 4H 115
IP7: What 7B 112
IP9: Hark 5J 151
IP12: Blax 2F 123
IP12: Holl 2G 141
IP12: Orf 6J 125
IP14: Bac 4D 68
IP14: Wyve 1B 68
IP17: Midd 5E 78
IP23: Brom 5H 37
IP23: Melli 6A 36
IP29: Whep 3C 80
NR33: Car C 6B 10
NR33: Low 3H 11
Rectory St. IP19: H'orth 4B 42
Redan St. IP1: Ips 1B 4
Red Barn Dr. CO6: Leav 3A 142
Redbarn La. IP17: Ster 5A 92
Red Barn Piece IP13: Gru 7J 117
Redberry Way IP28: Red L 6G 25
Redbrick Cotts. IP27: Weet 2G 19
Reddells Cl. CO10: S'bury 3E 126
REDE 1C 163
Rede La. IP6: Barh, Clay, Henl 7G 115
REDENHALL 1C 161
Rede Rd. IP29: Whep 4A 80
Rede Way CO10: Gt Cor 5H 127
Rede Wood (Local Nature Reserve)
7H 115
Redgate La. IP9: Wher 2H 149
REDGRAVE 3D 34 (2A 160)
Redgrave Bus. Cen. IP22: Redg 1C 34
Red Hall Ct. IP11: Felix 4H 155
Redhill Cl. IP1: Ips 5H 131
Red Hill Rd. IP7: Aldh, Hadl 1J 129
(not continuous)
Red Ho. Cl. IP11: T Mart 5G 153
NR32: Oul 3E 8
Red Ho. La. CO10: Gt Cor 7F 127
CO10: S'bury 4D 126
IP16: Leis 5J 93
Redhouse La. IP12: Bawd 7J 141
Redhouse Rd. IP13: B'ham 1C 76
Red Ho. Wlk. IP10: Levi 6D 152
REDISHAM 2C 167
Redisham Cl. NR32: Low 3F 9
Red La. IP9: Cap M 3H 147
IP17: Ster 3D 92
REDLINGFIELD 2B 160
Redlingfield Rd. IP21: Horh 2F 73
IP23: Occ 5B 72
Red Lion Cl. IP21: Hox 3C 38
RED LODGE 6J 25 (2A 158)
Red Rose Cl. IP12: Alder 5J 141
Redshank Cl. CB9: Have 4H 101
Red Sleeve IP9: Cap M 2G 147
Redstone M. *IP12: Wood 5H 121*
(off New St.)
Redwald Rd. IP12: Rend 5D 122
Red Willows Trad. Est.
IP14: One 4B 84
Redwing Cl. IP2: Ips 3F 137
Redwing Dr. IP14: Stowm 3J 85
Redwing Rd. IP33: Bury E 5J 59
Redwold Cl. IP12: Martl 2J 135
Redwood Gdns.
IP33: Bury E 4J 157 (1H 59)
Redwood La. IP27: RAF L 5G 21
Redwood Terraces IP13: Uff 6H 119
REEDHAM 1C 167
Reedland Way IP11: Felix 3C 154
Reed Pl. IP30: Roug 6K 61
Reed's Bldgs. IP33: Bury E 2J 157
Reeds La. CB9: Have 3F 101
Reeds Way IP14: Stowu 1K 85
Reeve Cl. IP28: Tud 5B 26
IP31: Ixw 5H 29
IP32: Bury E 4F 53
Reeve Gdns. IP5: Kesg 5C 134
Reeve Lodge IP11: T Mart 6G 153
Reeve's Cl. NR35: Bung 3C 14
Reeve St. NR32: Low 6J 9
Regal Theatre
Stowmarket 5G 85
Regan Cl. NR32: Low 3F 9
Regatta Quay IP4: Ips 5F 5 (1B 138)
Regent Ct. *CB8: Newm 5G 47*
(off Rowley Dr.)
Regent Rd. NR32: Low 7J 9
Regent St. IP4: Ips 3H 5 (1C 138)
IP14: Stowm 3F 85
Regent Theatre
Ipswich 3F 5
Regina Cl. IP4: Ips 1F 139
Reigate Cl. IP3: Ips 3F 139
Releet Cl. IP7: Gt Bri 2A 112
Rembrandt Cl. NR32: Low 2H 9
Rembrandt Gdns.
IP33: Bury E 7F 157 (3F 59)
Rembrandt Way
IP33: Bury E 7F 157 (3F 59)
Rembrow Rd. IP9: Cap M 2G 147
Remembrance Rd. IP16: Thor 7D 94
Rendall La. IP14: Old N, Stowu 7E 70
RENDHAM 3D 161
Rendham Hill IP17: Pea 3J 77
Rendham Rd. IP17: Carl 3F 91
IP17: Saxm 5F 91
RENDLESHAM 6C 122 (1D 165)
Rendlesham Ct. IP1: Ips 1A 4
Rendlesham M. IP12: Rend 7B 122
Rendlesham Rd.
IP1: Ips 2A 4 (6J 131)
(not continuous)
IP11: Felix 3C 154
Renfrew Rd. IP4: Ips 5F 133
Renoir Pl. NR32: Low 3G 9
Renson Cl. IP30: Hess 7C 62
REYDON 2J 45 (3D 167)
Reydon Bus. Pk. IP18: Rey 1J 45
Reydon Cl. CB9: Have 3B 100
Reydon Ho. IP3: Ips 4E 138
Reydon M. NR32: Low 2F 9
Reydon Wood Wildlife Nature Reserve
7D 44
Reynolds Av. IP3: Ips 6E 138
Reynolds Cl. CB9: Have 2C 100
IP3: Ips 5E 138
Reynolds Ct. IP11: Felix 3C 154
Reynolds Rd. IP3: Ips 5E 138
Reynolds Wlk. IP33: Bury E 7C 52
NR32: Low 2G 9
(off Gainsborough Dr.)
Reynolds Way CO10: S'bury 1F 127
Ribblesdale NR33: Car C 6D 10
Riby Rd. IP11: Felix 5E 154
Richard Burn Way
CO10: S'bury 1D 126
Richard Crampton Rd.
NR34: Becc 5E 12
Richards Cl. NR33: Oul B 3D 10
Richards Dr. IP13: L Bea 1D 134
Richardsons La. IP9: Chelm 2F 151
Richardsons Rd. CO7: E Ber 3C 146
Richard Walker Cl. IP32: Bury E 6B 54
Richer Cl. IP31: B Ash 3C 66
Richer Rd. IP31: B Ash 3D 66
Richmond Ho. IP4: Ips 4G 5
Richmond Pl. NR33: Low 3H 11
Richmond Rd. IP1: Ips 6H 131
IP27: B'don 6D 18
NR33: Low 3H 11
RICKINGHALL 5J 35 (2A 160)
Rickinghall Rd. IP22: Hind 6D 34
IP31: Wals W 6K 33
Rider Haggard La.
NR33: Kess 4K 17
Ridgeville NR33: Car C 6E 10
Ridgeway IP14: Stowm 4D 84
Ridgeways, The NR33: Car C 4C 10
RIDGEWELL 2B 162

Ridings, The CO6: Leav ... 1B 142
NR34: Worl ... 4J 13
Ridley Rd. IP33: Bury E ... 7C 52
Rigbourne Hill NR34: Becc ... 5F 13
Rigbourne Hill La. NR34: Becc ... 5F 13
Riggle St. IP13: B'ton ... 1J 89
Riley Cl. IP1: Ips ... 4E 130
Rimmer Cl. CO10: S'bury ... 1F 127
Ringham Rd. IP4: Ips ... 7E 132
RINGSFIELD ... 7A 12 (2C 167)
RINGSFIELD CORNER ... 2C 167
Ringsfield Rd. NR32: Low ... 5F 9
NR34: Becc, R'field ... 7B 12
NR34: Ilk A ... 3H 15 & 4K 15
RINGSHALL ... 1A 164
RINGSHALL STOCKS ... 2C 112 (1A 164)
Rio Cl. NR33: Car C ... 4B 10
Ripon Rd. IP12: Sutt ... 2D 140
Risbridge Dr. CB9: Ked ... 6B 98
RISBY ... 2C 50 (3B 158)
Risby Bus. Pk. IP28: Ris ... 2B 50
Risby Cl. IP4: Ips ... 7F 133
Risbygate Sports Club ... 1E 58
Risbygate St.
IP33: Bury E ... 4F 157 (1F 59)
Riseway Cl. IP33: Bury E ... 5H 59
RISHANGLES ... 3B 160
Rishangles Rd. IP23: Thorn ... 2D 72
Rishton Rd. NR32: Low ... 7J 9
Rising Sun Hill IP30: Rat ... 4K 83
Rissemere La. E. IP18: Rey ... 1J 45
Ritabrook Rd. IP2: Ips ... 5G 137
Rivendale NR33: Car C ... 6C 10
Riverbank Cl. CO10: Clar ... 5D 102
River Cl. IP31: Pake ... 2B 56
River Gdns. IP14: Stowm ... 6G 85
River Hill IP8: B'ford ... 4E 130
River La. IP19: H'orth ... 5B 42
IP33: Bury E ... 3K 59
Riverside IP13: F'ham ... 6C 90
IP13: Hask ... 3B 120
Riverside Bus. Cen. NR33: Low ... 2G 11
Riverside Bus. Pk. NR33: Low ... 1G 11
Riverside Cl. IP28: Mide ... 7H 23
Riverside Cotts. IP17: Yox ... 6H 77
Riverside Ct. IP32: Bury E ... 5G 53
Riverside Ind. Est.
IP13: Wick M ... 5B 118
Riverside Ind. Pk. IP2: Ips ... 3B 138
Riverside Pl. *IP8: B'ford ... 3D 130*
(off Mill La.)
Riverside Rd. IP1: Ips ... 6G 131
NR33: Low ... 1G 11
Riverside Theatre
Woodbridge ... 6H 121
Riverside Vw. IP13: Wick M ... 5B 118
Riverside Wlk. CB8: Mou ... 5D 48
Riverside Way IP27: B'don ... 2F 19
Rivers St. IP4: Ips ... 1K 5 (6D 132)
River Vw. NR34: Gill ... 1D 12
Riverview IP12: Melt ... 3K 121
River Vw. Rd. IP9: Hark ... 6H 151
River Wall IP12: Wood ... 6H 121
Rivett Cl. IP10: Kirt ... 1H 153
Rivetts Loke NR34: Becc ... 4E 12
Rivish La. CO10: L Mel ... 4H 105
Rixon Cres. IP12: Melt ... 7F 119
Roamwood Grn. La. IP14: Deb ... 1F 87
Roanoke Wlk. IP2: Ips ... 3B 138
Robeck Rd. IP3: Ips ... 5C 138
Robert Boby Way
IP33: Bury E ... 5F 157 (1G 59)
Robert Linge Cres. IP27: B'don ... 4G 19
Robertsbridge Wlk.
NR33: Car C ... 5C 10
Roberts Cl. IP5: Kesg ... 6D 134
Roberts Rd. IP16: Leis ... 3J 93
Robin Cl. CB9: Have ... 4H 101
IP14: Stowm ... 5J 85
IP28: Mide ... 7K 23
IP31: Thur ... 6K 55
Robin Dr. IP2: Ips ... 3F 137
Robin Hatch CB8: Newm ... 7G 47
Robin Hill NR32: Low ... 6F 9
Robin Hood Ct.
IP33: Bury E ... 7F 157 (3F 59)
ROBINHOOD END ... 3B 162
Robin Rd. IP33: Bury E ... 5J 59
Robinson Cl. IP33: Bury E ... 7D 52
Robinson Rd. IP21: Scole ... 1K 37
Robinsons Cl. IP23: Melli ... 5A 36
Robinsons Mill IP23: Melli ... 5A 36
Robinson Wlk.
IP32: Bury E ... 6E 52
Robin Wlk. IP27: B'don ... 4J 19
Robin Way CO10: Ball ... 6B 126
Rochdale NR33: Car C ... 6E 10
Rochester Rd. NR33: Low ... 5G 11
Rochester Way CO10: S'bury ... 1C 126
Rochfort Av. CB8: Newm ... 4E 46
Rockall Cl. CB9: Have ... 4J 101
Rockalls Rd. CO6: Pols ... 5C 144
Rock Barracks Woodbridge Airfield
... 1D 140
Rockingham Rd.
IP33: Bury E ... 7K 157 (3H 59)
Rock Rd. NR32: Oul B ... 7C 8
Rockstone La. IP19: Cook ... 1J 75
Rodber Way NR32: Low ... 2F 9
Rodbridge Cnr. CO10: L Mel ... 7G 105
Rodbridge Hill CO10: L Mel ... 7G 105
Rodney Ct. IP12: Wood ... 3G 121
Roebuck, The IP27: Eris ... 3G 21
Roebuck Dr. IP27: Lake ... 7C 20
Rogeron Cl. CO10: Hund ... 2H 99
Rogers Cl. IP11: Felix ... 2E 154
Roger's La. IP29: Hart ... 2F 103
Rogue's La. IP13: Petti ... 7A 118
Rokewood Pl. IP29: Stann ... 3G 81
Rolfe Cl. IP28: W Row ... 4A 22
Roma Av. IP5: Martl H ... 5J 135
Roman Flds. IP30: Wool ... 5B 64
ROMAN HILL ... 7H 9
Roman Rd. IP7: Gt Bri ... 2A 112
NR32: Low ... 7H 9
Roman Way CB9: Have ... 5J 101
CO10: L Mel ... 5H 105
IP11: Felix ... 2J 155
IP19: H'orth ... 5A 42
Romany La. NR33: Kess ... 1J 17
Romany Rd. NR32: Oul B ... 1B 10
Romney Pl. NR32: Low ... 2G 9
Romney Rd. IP3: Ips ... 6E 138
Romsey Rd. IP33: Bury E ... 3D 58
Ronald La. IP17: Carl ... 4J 91
Ronden Cl. NR34: Becc ... 6E 12
Rookery, The IP23: Eye ... 7D 38
IP27: B'don ... 4C 18
Rookery Cl. NR33: Oul B ... 2E 10
Rookery Drove IP28: B Row ... 1D 22
Rookery Grn. *IP28: B Row ... 1D 22*
(off Rookery Drove)
Rookery La. IP31: Wals W ... 6H 33
Rookery Park Golf Course ... 4A 10
Rookery Wlk. IP27: Lake ... 4A 20
Rookery Way IP14: Old N ... 5B 70
ROOKSEY GREEN ... 1D 163
Rook's La. NR34: Becc ... 2E 12
Rookwood Way CB9: Have ... 5F 101
Roosevelt Wlk. NR33: Car C ... 4B 10
Roper Ct. IP3: Ips ... 1G 139
Roper's Ct. CO10: Lave ... 6B 106
Ropers Gdns. IP30: E'well ... 1E 64
Ropers La. CO10: L Mel ... 6G 105
Ropes Dr. IP5: Kesg ... 5B 134
Rope Wlk. IP4: Ips ... 4G 5 (1B 138)
IP18: Sou ... 3J 45
NR33: Car C ... 5A 10
Rosbrook Cl. IP33: Bury E ... 2D 58
Rosebery Ct. IP11: Felix ... 6E 154
Rosebery Rd. IP4: Ips ... 4K 5 (1D 138)
IP11: Felix ... 4G 155
Rosebery Way CB8: Newm ... 4E 46
Rose Ct. IP9: Shot ... 4C 156
IP28: Red L ... 5K 25
NR32: Low ... 6G 9
Rosecroft Rd. IP1: Ips ... 3J 131
Rosedale Cl. NR33: Car C ... 5D 10
Rosedale Gdns. NR33: Car C ... 5D 10
Rose Farm Caravan Site
IP9: Shot G ... 6C 156
Rosefinch Cl. CB9: Have ... 4H 101
Rose Gardens, The IP31: Thur ... 7A 56
ROSE GREEN
Kersey ... 2D 163
Wakes Colne ... 3D 163
Rose Grn. La. IP28: B Row ... 1F 23
Rose Hall Gdns. NR35: Bung ... 3B 14
ROSE HILL ... 2E 138
Rose Hill CB9: With ... 1C 98
IP6: Witn ... 6A 116
IP13: Gru ... 6H 117
Rosehill Cres. IP3: Ips ... 6K 5 (2D 138)
Rosehill Rd. IP3: Ips ... 6K 5 (2D 138)
Rosehip Av. IP28: Red L ... 6G 25
Rose La. IP1: Ips ... 4E 4 (1A 138)
IP22: Pal ... 2D 36
IP23: Wick S ... 1F 69
IP30: E'well ... 2D 64
NR35: Bung ... 3B 14
Rose La. Cl. IP22: Pal ... 1D 36
Rosemary Av. IP11: Felix ... 2G 155
Rosemary Cl. IP28: Red L ... 6J 25
Rosemary Gdns. CO10: S'bury ... 1E 126
Rosemary La. IP4: Ips ... 4E 4 (1A 138)
IP17: Carl, Kel ... 3G 91
IP21: Wing ... 1K 39
NR34: Becc ... 2E 12
Rosemary Rd. IP32: Bury E ... 4F 53
Rosery La. IP13: Gt Bea ... 6A 120
Rose Wlk. IP6: Nee M ... 5G 111
Rosewood NR33: Oul B ... 1D 10
Rosewood Cl. IP27: RAF L ... 5G 21
Ross Cl. CB9: Have ... 4J 101
Ross Rd. IP4: Ips ... 4F 133
Rotheram Rd. IP7: Bild ... 6J 109
ROTTEN END ... 3D 161
Rotten Row CO10: Newt ... 4B 128
Rotterdam Rd. NR32: Low ... 7G 9
ROUGHAM ... 6K 61 (3D 159)
ROUGHAM GREEN ... 6H 61
Rougham Hill IP33: Bury E ... 3K 59
Rougham Ind. Est. IP30: Roug ... 2E 60
Rougham Rd. IP30: B Geo ... 1C 82
IP33: Bury E ... 3J 59
(not continuous)
Roughlands IP27: Lake ... 5B 20
Rought Av. IP27: B'don ... 5G 19
Rounce's La. NR33: Car C ... 6B 10
ROUND MAPLE ... 2D 163
Roundridge Rd. IP9: Cap M ... 1J 147
Roundwood Rd. IP4: Ips ... 6E 132
Rousies Cl. IP7: Hadl ... 3J 129
Rous Memorial Ct. CB8: Newm ... 6H 47
Rous Rd. CB8: Newm ... 6H 47
Routh Av. IP3: Pur F ... 5K 139
Row, The CO7: Strat M ... 5G 145
IP8: B'ford ... 2C 130
IP29: Boxt ... 3G 103
IP29: Hart ... 1H 103
Rowan Cl. CB9: Have ... 2D 100
IP3: Pur F ... 4H 139
IP6: Clay ... 4E 114
Rowan Dr. IP27: B'don ... 4F 19
IP32: Bury E ... 7B 54
Rowan Grn. IP30: E'well ... 2E 64
Rowanhayes Cl. IP2: Ips ... 3K 137
Rowan Pl. *IP28: Red L ... 7J 25*
(off Aspen Way)
Rowans Way CO6: Leav ... 3A 142
Rowan Wlk. IP28: Mide ... 6K 23
Rowan Way IP31: Thur ... 5J 55
NR33: Oul B ... 3C 10
NR34: Worl ... 5H 13
Rowarth Av. IP5: Kesg ... 6C 134
Rowell Cl. CB9: Have ... 1F 101
Rowe's Hill IP13: Laxf ... 7D 74
Rowland Ho. *IP11: Felix ... 3C 154*
(off Winston Cl.)
Rowley Cl. CO11: Brant ... 5C 148
Rowley Ct. CB8: Newm ... 6E 46
CB9: Stur ... 6K 101
Rowley Dr. CB8: Newm ... 6E 46
Rowley Hill CB9: Stur ... 6J 101
Rowntree Cl. NR32: Low ... 2F 9
Rows, The CB8: Newm ... 6E 46
Roxburgh Rd. IP4: Ips ... 4F 133
Royal Av. NR32: Low ... 5J 9
Royal Hospital School ... 5E 150
Royalls, The IP5: Kesg ... 5E 134
Royal Naval Patrol Service Mus.
... 5K 9
Royal Norfolk & Suffolk Yacht Club
... 1J 11
Royal Palace Cl. CB8: Newm ... 2D 46
Royal Plain NR33: Low ... 1J 11
Royal Ter. NR33: Low ... 1J 11
Royal Thoroughfare NR33: Low ... 1J 11
Royal Worlington &
Newmarket Golf Course ... 3C 24
Roy Av. IP3: Ips ... 1F 139
Roy Cl. IP5: Kesg ... 6B 134
ROYDON ... 1A 160
Roydon Drift CO10: Act ... 1K 105
Roydon Way NR32: Oul B ... 4E 8
Roylands La. CO10: Boxf ... 7D 128
Royston Dr. IP2: Ips ... 4F 137
IP31: Thur ... 7K 55
Rozel Ct. IP28: B Row ... 1G 23
Rozlyne Cl. NR33: Car C ... 5D 10
Rubens Rd. IP3: Ips ... 5E 138
Rubens Wlk. CO10: S'bury ... 1F 127
NR32: Low ... 2H 9
(off Spencer Dr.)
Ruby Cl. NR32: Cort ... 6J 7
Rudlands IP8: Ips ... 5E 136
Ruffles Rd. CB9: Have ... 4H 101
Rugby Rd. CO10: Gt Cor ... 7G 127
Rules Yd. CO10: Boxf ... 6C 128
RUMBURGH ... 1D 161
Rumburgh Rd. NR32: Low ... 3G 9
Run Mdw. NR33: Car C ... 3B 10
Runnacles Way IP11: Felix ... 3C 154
Runnymede Ct. *NR32: Low ... 6J 9*
(off Alexandra Rd.)
Runnymede Grn. IP33: Bury E ... 3G 59
RUSHALL ... 1B 160
RUSHBROOKE ... 6E 60 (3C 159)
Rushbrooke La. IP33: Bury E ... 3K 59
Rushbury Cl. IP4: Ips ... 5F 133
Rush Cl. IP4: Rush A ... 2J 139
Rush Ct. *IP5: Kesg ... 5E 134*
(off Howards Way)
RUSHFORD ... 1D 159
Rushford Rd. IP31: Con W ... 1A 30
Rushlake Way NR33: Car C ... 5C 10
Rushmeadow Way IP11: Felix ... 1J 155
RUSHMERE ... 4C 16 (2C 167)
Rushmere Golf Course ... 7H 133
Rushmere Pl. CB9: Have ... 3G 101
(not continuous)
Rushmere Rd. IP4: Ips ... 6E 132
NR33: Car C, Gisle, Rushm
... 2D 16 & 7A 10
NR34: Hens ... 6B 16
RUSHMERE ST ANDREW
... 5J 133 (2B 164)
Rushmere Sports Club ... 4J 133
RUSHMERE STREET ... 4J 133
Rushton Dr. NR33: Car C ... 6A 10
Ruskin Cl. CB9: Have ... 2C 100
IP14: Stowm ... 2D 84
Ruskin Rd. IP4: Ips ... 5K 5 (1D 138)
Russell Baron Rd. IP31: Forn M ... 4G 53
Russell Cl. IP12: Wood ... 4F 121
IP17: Pea ... 3H 77
Russell Ct. IP11: Felix ... 7D 154
Russell Rd. IP1: Ips ... 5B 4 (1K 137)
IP11: Felix ... 6E 154
RUSSEL'S GREEN ... 2C 161
Russet Cl. IP14: Finn ... 6G 67
IP32: Bury E ... 7A 54
NR34: Becc ... 5F 13
Russet Dr. IP28: Red L ... 5J 25
Russet Rd. IP4: Ips ... 1J 5 (6C 132)
Russett Cl. CB9: Have ... 3B 100
Rutland Ct. CB9: Have ... 4D 100
Rutland Hill CB8: Newm ... 6H 47
Rutland Sq. IP33: Bury E ... 6K 157
Rydal Av. IP11: Felix ... 1J 155
Rydal Cl. IP14: Stowm ... 4D 84
Rydal Wlk. IP3: Ips ... 4G 139
Ryders Way IP22: Rick ... 6J 35
Ryeburn Cl. NR33: Kess ... 4H 17
Rye Cl. IP3: Ips ... 2H 139
NR33: Car C ... 5C 10
Rye Ct. CB9: Have ... 4E 100
Ryedale NR33: Car C ... 6E 10
Ryefields IP31: Thur ... 6A 56
Rye Hill CO10: S'bury ... 4G 127
Rylands IP9: Cap M ... 1H 147
Rylands Cl. IP31: Thur ... 5A 56

S

SACKERS GREEN ... 4A 128
Sackville St. CB8: Newm ... 5H 47
Sackvylle St. IP14: Deb ... 2G 87
Saddlemakers La. IP12: Melt ... 1J 121
Saddlers Mdw. IP13: Gru ... 5J 117
Saddlers Pl. IP5: Martl H ... 6G 135
Saddlers Yd. IP31: Ixw ... 6H 29
Saffron Cl. IP27: B'don ... 5E 18
Saffrons Cl. IP30: Wool ... 5B 64
Saffron Sq. NR33: Low ... 7F 11
Sage Ct. IP28: Red L ... 5K 25
Sagehayes Cl. IP2: Ips ... 3K 137
St Agnes Way IP5: Kesg ... 7K 133
St Albans CB8: Newm ... 3G 47
St Andrew *CB8: Newm ... 5G 47*
(off Icewell Hill)
St Andrew's Church Cl.
IP5: Rush A ... 4H 133
St Andrews Cl. IP4: Ips ... 1H 139
IP12: Melt ... 2K 121
IP14: Gt Fin ... 6J 83
IP23: Wick S ... 2G 69
IP31: Barni ... 3D 30
St Andrews Ct. IP33: Bury E ... 5G 157
St Andrews Dr. IP9: Chelm ... 2G 151
IP28: Forn M ... 1F 53
St Andrew's Pl. IP12: Melt ... 2K 121
St Andrews Rd. CO10: Gt Cor ... 5F 127
IP11: Felix ... 3F 155
IP17: Knod ... 7G 93
NR34: Becc ... 6F 13
St Andrew's St. IP28: Mide ... 7J 23
St Andrew's St. Nth.
IP33: Bury E ... 2G 157 (7G 53)
St Andrew's St. Sth.
IP33: Bury E ... 4G 157 (1G 59)
St Andrews Wlk. IP4: Rush A ... 7K 133
St Annes Cl. IP12: Wood ... 7E 120
NR34: Becc ... 4F 13
St Anne's Dr. IP28: Mide ... 6H 23
St Anne's Rd. NR34: Becc ... 4F 13
St Anthony *CB8: Newm ... 5G 47*
(off Icewell Hill)
St Anthonys Cres.
IP4: Ips ... 2K 5 (7D 132)
St Anthony's Way IP27: B'don ... 3H 19
St Aubyns Ct. *NR33: Low ... 3H 11*
(off London Rd. Sth.)
St Aubyns Rd. IP4: Ips ... 1E 138
NR33: Low ... 3H 11
St Audrys IP12: Melt ... 7F 119
St Audrys Golf Course ... 7G 119

St Audrys La. IP12: Melt 1K 121
St Audrys Pk. Rd. IP12: Melt 7F 119
St Audrys Rd. IP12: Melt 1K 121
St Augustine Rd. IP3: Ips 2H 139
St Augustine's Gdns. IP3: Ips 3G 139
St Austell Cl. IP5: Kesg 7A 134
St Bartholomews La.
CO10: S'bury 2C 126
St Benedicts Cl. CO10: S'bury . . .1C 126
St Benedicts Rd. IP27: B'don 4G 19
NR34: Becc 2E 12
St Benet's Dr. NR34: Becc 5F 13
St Botolph's Ct. IP33: Bury E 7K 157
St Botolph's La.
IP33: Bury E 7K 157 (2J 59)
St Botolph's Pl. CB9: Have 4E 100
St Botolph's Way CB9: Have 3E 100
St Brelades Cl. IP23: Yax 6E 36
St Catherine's Cl. IP28: Mide 5K 23
NR33: Oul B 5E 10
St Catherine's Ct. IP2: Ips 5G 137
St Catherine's Rd.
CO10: L Mel 4H 105
St Clements Chu. La.
IP4: Ips 5G 5 (1B 138)
St Crispins Cl. IP5: Kesg 6E 134
ST CROSS SOUTH ELMHAM 1C 161
St David CB8: Newm 5G 47
(off Icewell Hill)
St Davids Cl. IP27: B'don 4G 19
NR34: Becc 6F 13
St Davids La. IP12: Holl 1J 141
St David's Rd. IP3: Ips 3F 139
St Denys CB8: Newm 5G 47
(off Mill Hill)
St Dominic's Dr. IP27: B'don 3H 19
St Edmund Cl. IP31: Ixw 5J 29
St Edmunds Abbey (Remains of)
. . . . .5J 157 (1H 59)
St Edmundsbury Cathedral
. . . . .5J 157 (1H 59)
St Edmundsbury Ho.
IP4: Ips 3K 5 (7D 132)
St Edmundsbury M.
IP33: Bury E 6H 157 (2G 59)
St Edmundsbury Retail Pk.
IP32: Bury E 2A 60
St Edmunds Cl. IP12: B'well 3A 124
IP12: Wood 6F 121
IP14: Stowm 2E 84
NR34: Becc 6F 13
St Edmunds Ct. IP18: Sou 4K 45
(off North Grn.)
NR34: Becc 4F 13
(off St Anne's Rd.)
St Edmunds Cres. NR33: Kess 4K 17
St Edmund's Dr. IP30: E'well 1D 64
St Edmunds Ho. IP21: Hox 3D 38
St Edmund's La. CO8: Bure 5B 142
St Edmunds Pl. IP1: Ips 5A 132
IP33: Bury E 2H 157
St Edmunds Rd. IP1: Ips 5K 131
IP11: Felix 6D 154
IP14: Stowm 3E 84
IP18: Sou 3K 45
St Etienne IP14: Fram 6D 88
St Fabians Cl. CB8: Newm 4F 47
St Francis Cl. IP27: B'don 3H 19
St Francis Ho. IP1: Ips 4D 4
St George CB8: Newm 5G 47
(off Icewell Hill)
St George's Cl. NR34: Becc 4E 12
St George's Ct. IP1: Ips 2D 4
IP32: Bury E 4F 53
St George's Dr. IP22: Rick 5J 35
St George's La. IP18: Rey 3G 45
St George's Rd. IP11: Felix 2H 155
IP31: Stowl 1H 57
NR33: Low 5G 11
NR34: Becc 4E 12
St Georges Sq. IP18: Rey 2G 45
St George's St. IP1: Ips 2D 4 (7A 132)
St George's Ter. IP11: Felix 2H 155
St Gotthards Av. IP5: Martl H 5J 135
St Gregorys Cl. IP12: Rend 5D 122
St Gregorys Ct. CO10: S'bury 3C 126
St Helena Wlk. IP28: Mide 5J 23
St Helen's Chu. La.
IP4: Ips 3H 5 (7C 132)
St Helen's St. IP4: Ips 3F 5 (7B 132)
St Isidores IP5: Kesg 6E 134
St Ives Cl. IP5: Kesg 7A 134
St James CB8: Newm 5G 47
(off Mill Hill)
St James Ct. CB9: Have 3D 100
IP33: Bury E 5K 157
St James' Grn. IP18: Sou 4K 45
St James La. IP33: Bury E 1F 59
ST JAMES SOUTH ELMHAM 1D 161
St James's St. IP17: Dun 1K 79
St John's Av. CB8: Newm 7H 47
St John's Cl. IP28: Mide 5K 23
St John's Ct. IP4: Ips 7F 133
IP11: Felix 4E 154
St Johns Hill IP12: Wood 5H 121
NR35: Bung 4C 14
St Johns Mdw. IP20: Metf 6G 41
St John's Pl.
IP33: Bury E 3G 157 (7G 53)
St John's Rd. IP4: Ips 7D 132
IP17: Saxm 6H 91
NR33: Low 2J 11
NR35: Bung, Ilk J 3B 14
(not continuous)
St John's Row IP14: Fram, Helm . . .7C 88
St John's St. IP12: Wood 5H 121
IP28: B Row 2F 23
IP33: Bury E 4G 157 (1G 59)
St John's Ter. IP12: Wood 5H 121
St Lawrence Cl. NR34: Becc 6F 13
St Lawrence Grn. IP5: Kesg 5B 134
St Lawrence St. IP1: Ips . . .3E 4 (7A 132)
St Lawrence Way IP5: Kesg 5B 134
St Leger Dr. CB8: Newm 2E 46
St Leonard's Rd. IP3: Ips 3F 139
NR33: Low 3H 11
St Margaret's Ct. IP18: Rey 1H 45
St Margaret's Cres. IP16: Leis 3G 93
St Margaret's Dr. IP27: B'don 5D 18
St Margaret's Grn.
IP4: Ips 2F 5 (7B 132)
ST MARGARET SOUTH ELMHAM
. . . . .1D 161
St Margaret's Pl. CB8: Stradi 7G 97
St Margaret's Plain
IP4: Ips 2F 5 (7B 132)
NR32: Low 6J 9
St Margaret's Rd. NR32: Low 5H 9
NR35: Bung 4B 14
St Margaret's St.
IP4: Ips 3F 5 (7B 132)
St Martin's Cl. CB8: Exn 2C 46
St Martins Ct. IP5: Kesg 6E 134
St Martins Grn. IP11: T Mart 5H 153
St Martin's La. IP24: Barnh 6G 27
(not continuous)
St Martin's Mdw. IP24: Barnh 6G 27
St Martin's St.
IP33: Bury E 2H 157 (7G 53)
St Mary Elms Chu. Path IP1: Ips . . .3D 4
St Mary's Av. IP14: Haug 2B 70
St Mary's Church 6J 157 (2H 59)
St Marys Cl. CO10: S'bury 1G 127
IP8: B'ford 4D 130
IP8: Off 1F 113
IP11: T Mary 7H 153
IP14: Bac 6B 68
IP21: Horh 1H 73
IP23: Gisli 1K 67
IP28: Mide 1F 25
St Marys Ct. IP1: Ips 3D 4
IP16: Thor 6D 94
(off Church Rd.)
IP33: Bury E 6F 157 (2F 59)
St Mary's Cres. IP11: Felix 2D 154
IP31: B Ash 3C 66
St Marys Dr. IP6: Play 1B 134
St Marys Gdns. IP6: C Mary 2H 111
IP14: Mendl 2J 71
St Mary's M. IP27: Lake 5A 20
St Marys Pk. IP10: Buck 3B 152
St Mary's Rd. IP4: Ips 1K 5 (6D 132)
IP6: C Mary 3G 111
IP14: Stowm 3D 84
NR34: Becc 3D 12
St Mary's Sq. CB8: Newm 6G 47
IP33: Bury E 6J 157 (2H 59)
St Mary's St. NR35: Bung 2B 14
St Marys Vw. IP31: Pake 2B 56
St Marys Way IP6: Weste 1D 132
St Matthew's Av. NR34: Becc 6F 13
St Matthew's Chu. La. IP1: Ips 2C 4
St Matthew's Ho. IP1: Ips 2C 4
St Matthew's St.
IP1: Ips 2C 4 (7K 131)
St Michael's Cl. IP5: Kesg 7A 134
IP13: F'ham 5D 90
IP33: Bury E 3H 157
NR32: Oul B 7B 8
NR34: Becc 6F 13
ST MICHAEL SOUTH ELMHAM . . .1D 161
St Michael's Way IP19: Wen 3J 43
St Nicholas Cl. IP30: Rat 4K 83
IP32: Bury E 7J 53
St Nicholas Ct. IP1: Ips 4D 4
ST NICHOLAS SOUTH ELMHAM
. . . . .1D 161
St Nicholas St. IP1: Ips . . .4D 4 (1A 138)
St Nicholas Wlk. IP27: B'don 3H 19
ST OLAVES 1C 167
St Olaves Pct. IP32: Bury E 5E 52
St Olaves Rd. IP5: Kesg 5C 134
IP32: Bury E 5E 52
NR32: Herr 1A 6
St Osyth Cl. IP2: Ips 6H 137
St Patrick CB8: Newm 5G 47
(off Mill Hill)
St Pauls Cl. IP15: Aldeb 4J 95
NR34: Becc 6F 13
St Peter's IP7: M Ele 2E 108
St Peter's App. IP27: B'don 4E 18
St Peters Av. CB8: Mou 7D 48
IP6: Clay 4C 114
St Peter's Brewery 1D 161
St Peters Cl. CB8: Mou 6D 48
IP6: Clay 3C 114
IP6: Henl 6J 115
IP12: Wood 6E 120
IP13: Char 3C 118
IP14: Stowm 4D 84
St Peters Ct. CO10: S'bury 4D 126
(off Christopher La.)
IP1: Ips 5E 4
IP6: Clay 3D 114
IP33: Bury E 6G 157
NR32: Low 6J 9
(off Chapel St.)
St Peter's Cft. CO10: Clar 5C 102
St Peter's Path IP19: Holt 3E 42
(off Lodge Rd.)
St Peter's Pl. IP27: B'don 5E 18
St Peters Rd. IP14: Stowm 4D 84
IP15: Aldeb 4J 95
NR33: Car C 6B 10
NR33: Low 3H 11
St Peter's St. IP1: Ips 4E 4 (1A 138)
NR32: Low 6H 9
St Peters Ter. IP33: Bury E 7G 157
St Peters Way IP31: Thur 6B 56
St Philips Rd. CB8: Newm 5E 46
St Quinton's Ct. NR33: Low 4G 11
St Raphael Ct. IP1: Ips 4H 131
St Stephen's Chapel 5D 142
St Stephen's Chu. La. IP1: Ips 4E 4
St Stephens Cl. IP33: Bury E 7J 53
St Stephen's Cres. IP27: B'don 3H 19
St Stephens La. IP1: Ips . . .3E 4 (7A 132)
St Thomas Cl. IP27: B'don 3H 19
St Thomas's Way IP30: Gt Whe . . .7D 60
St Wendred's Way CB8: Exn 2B 46
St William Ct. IP5: Kesg 5D 134
Salehurst Rd. IP3: Ips 3J 139
Salisbury Ct. CB9: Have 4E 100
Salisbury Grn. IP33: Bury E 4H 59
Salisbury Rd. IP3: Ips 2E 138
IP18: Sou 4K 45
NR33: Low 2H 11
Salisbury Ter. CO10: S'bury 3D 126
(off Gainsborough Rd.)
Sallows Cl. IP1: Ips 6H 131
Sally Wood's La. IP6: C Mary 2J 111
Salmet Cl. IP2: Ips 3J 137
Salmond Dr. IP24: Barnh 6J 27
Salmon Wlk. IP32: Bury E 6E 52
Salter Cl. IP32: Bury E 2A 60
Salter Hall M. CO10: S'bury 4C 126
(off Plough La.)
Salters Gdns. IP13: Gru 6H 117
Salters La. IP19: Wal 1J 75
Saltgate NR34: Becc 2E 12
Salthouse St. IP4: Ips 5G 5 (1B 138)
Saltwater Way NR33: Oul B 1D 10
Sam Alper Ct. CB8: Newm 3F 47
Samford Cl. IP9: Holb 1D 150
Samford Ct. IP9: Tatt 6H 149
NR34: Worl 4J 13
Samford Pl. IP8: Spro 7D 130
Sampson Dr. CO10: L Mel 3J 105
Samson Cl. IP32: Bury E 4E 52
Samuel Ct. IP4: Ips 2G 5 (7B 132)
Samuel St. Wlk.IP33: Bury E 4H 59
Samuel Vince Rd. IP21: Fress 6B 40
Sancroft Wlk. IP33: Bury E 7C 52
Sancroft Way IP21: Fress 6B 40
Sanctuary, The IP16: Thor 6D 94
Sanctuary Cl. NR33: Kess 4H 17
Sanctuary Ct. IP16: Thor 6D 94
(off The Sanctuary)
Sanctuary Gdns. NR32: Oul 3E 8
Sand Acre Cl. IP28: Mide 6K 23
Sandbank Rd. NR33: Oul B 5D 10
Sandbanks Ct. IP17: Saxm 6H 91
Sanderling Cl. IP28: Mide 7K 23
Sanderling Way IP14: Stowm 3J 85
Sanders Cl. NR32: Oul B 4E 8
Sandford Rd. IP14: Old N 6D 70
Sandgalls, The IP27: B'don 4E 18
Sandgalls Dr. IP27: Lake 5C 20
Sandgalls Rd. IP27: Lake 5B 20
SANDHILL 1A 158
Sand Hill CO10: Boxf 7D 128
Sandholme Cl. IP33: Bury E 4H 59
Sandhurst Av. IP3: Ips 6K 5 (2D 138)
Sandling Cres. IP4: Rush A 1J 139
Sandlings, The IP3: Ips 5H 139
IP15: Aldeb 3G 95
Sandown Cl. IP1: Ips 2J 131
Sandown Rd. IP1: Ips 2J 131
Sandpath IP21: Fress 6C 40
Sandpiper Cl. CB9: Have 3G 101
Sandpiper Rd. IP2: Ips 4G 137
IP14: Stowm 3H 85
IP33: Bury E 4J 59
Sandpit Cl. IP4: Rush A 1K 139
Sandpit Dr. IP31: Thur 6A 56
Sandpit Hill IP20: Metf 5F 41
Sandpit La. IP31: Thur 6A 56
NR34: Ell, Worl 5K 13
Sandringham Cl. IP2: Ips 4H 137
Sandringham Ct. CO10: S'bury . . .4F 127
NR32: Low 7H 9
Sandringham Rd. NR32: Low 7H 9
Sands La. NR32: Oul, Oul B 6B 8
Sandy Cl. IP11: T Mart 5H 153
Sandy Drove IP27: B'don 3C 18
IP27: Lake 5D 20
IP28: Tud 4C 26
Sandy Hill IP6: Cod 3G 115
Sandy Hill La. IP3: Ips 4C 138
Sandy La. CO10: Ball, Bulm 6A 126
CO11: Brant 4B 148
IP6: Barh 1C 114
IP6: C Mary 2H 111
IP6: Weste 1B 132
IP12: Martl, Wood 2J 135
IP12: Wald 5D 140
IP13: L Bea 1D 134
IP13: Wick M 7C 118
IP14: Batt 7D 110
IP17: Carl 4G 91
IP17: Dun 2H 79
IP17: Ster 4D 92
IP19: Holt 4E 42
IP30: Blac, Rushb 4C 60
IP31: Barni 2D 30
(not continuous)
IP32: Bury E 5F 53
NR33: Gisle 4F 17
NR34: Bramp 7F 15
Sanfoin Cl. IP28: Red L 6J 25
San Francisco Wlk.
NR33: Car C 4B 10
SANTON DOWNHAM 1C 159
SAPISTON 2J 29 (2D 159)
Sapiston Rd. IP31: Honi 2H 29
Sapling Cl. IP12: Rend 6D 122
Sapling Pl. IP4: Rush A 1J 139
Sapphire Cl. IP1: Ips 5F 131
Sarah Ct. CB9: Have 5F 101
Sarsen Cl. IP19: H'orth 4C 42
Sassoon Cl. CB8: Newm 5G 47
Saturn Cl. NR32: Low 4J 9
Saturn Rd. IP1: Ips 5F 131
Saunders La. IP31: Nort 4J 57
Saunders M. IP2: Ips 7F 5
Sawmill Cl. IP17: Saxm 6J 91
Sawmill La. IP10: Nac 4A 152
Sawston Cl. IP2: Ips 4J 137
Sawyers IP7: E'sett 7G 113
Sawyers Cl. IP9: Cap M 2H 147
Saxham Bus. Pk. IP28: L Sax 4D 50
Saxham Ct. CB9: Have 2A 100
SAXHAM STREET 3A 160
SAXMUNDHAM 6J 91 (3D 161)
Saxmundham Mus. 6J 91
Saxmundham Rd. IP13: F'ham 6D 90
IP15: Aldeb 3F 95
IP16: Leis 3F 93
IP17: Fris 5B 92
Saxmundham Station (Rail) 6J 91
Saxon Cl. CB8: Exn 1D 46
IP11: Felix 2J 155
IP14: Deb 3H 87
Saxonfields IP17: Snap 1D 94
Saxon Ga. IP28: Holy R 2H 23
Saxon Mdws. IP31: Huns 4A 66
Saxon Pl. IP27: Lake 5A 20
NR35: Bung 2B 14
Saxon Ri. IP33: Bury E 3E 58
Saxon Rd. IP17: Saxm 6H 91
NR33: Low 6G 11
SAXON STREET 1A 162
Saxons Way IP19: H'orth 5B 42
Saxon Way IP12: Melt 3H 121
SAXTEAD 1C 90 (3C 161)
SAXTEAD GREEN 4B 90 (3C 161)
Saxtead Green Mill 4B 90
SAXTEAD LITTLE GREEN 1A 90
Saxtead Rd. IP13: Denn 7A 76
IP13: F'ham, Sax G
. . . . .4D 90 & 4A 90
Scalesbrook La. IP19: U Hol 2E 42
Scales St. NR35: Bung 2A 14
Scaltback Cl. CB8: Newm 3E 46
Scampton IP27: RAF L 5H 21
Scarlin Rd. IP33: Bury E 3C 58
Schneider Cl. IP11: Felix 7C 154
School Av. IP30: E'well 2D 64

School Cl. IP9: Cap M 2H 147
IP27: Lake 5B 20
IP28: W Row 4A 22
IP31: Nort 5H 57
IP31: Stant 7D 32
NR34: Barnb 6C 6
School Corner IP14: Deb 1H 87
School Cotts. IP29: Harg 2G 51
School Cres. CB9: Ked 6B 98
Schoolfield CO10: Glem 4A 104
School Gdns. IP31: Gt Liv 2B 28
SCHOOL GREEN 3B 162
School Grn. CO10: Stoke C 6J 99
Schoolhall La.
IP33: Bury E 3H 157 (7G 53)
Schoolhall St.
IP33: Bury E 6K 157 (2H 59)
School Hill CO10: Boxf 7C 128
IP8: Wash 6B 136
IP10: Nac 6A 152
IP12: Blax 2H 123
IP13: Ket 5J 89
School Ho's. IP13: Gru 5H 117
School La. CB9: Have 4C 100
CO7: E Ber 3A 146
CO7: Strat M 5H 145
CO10: L Mel 2H 105
CO11: Brant 4C 148
IP6: Cod 1H 115
IP12: B'well 3A 124
IP12: Holl 3G 141
IP12: Martl 2J 135
IP12: Wald 7C 140
IP13: Uff 5H 119
IP14: Forw G 1B 86
IP17: Benh 3C 92
IP18: Rey 1G 45
IP19: H'orth 4A 42
IP20: Metf 6G 41
IP22: Thel 6H 31
IP27: B'don 4F 19
IP31: Bard 2D 32
IP31: Forn M 2G 53
IP31: Gt Bar 2E 54
IP31: Thur 6B 56
NR34: Becc 6E 12
School Mdw. IP14: Stowm 7G 85
IP14: W'den 4H 65
IP30: Drin 6H 63
NR34: Barnb 6C 6
School Rd. CB8: Mou 5D 48
CB9: Ked 6B 98
IP6: Cod 2G 115
IP6: Henl 5K 115
IP9: Shot G 7E 156
IP9: Tatt 4H 149
IP12: Blax 3H 123
IP12: Holl 3G 141
IP12: Sud 1H 125
IP12: Tun 6F 123
IP12: Wald 6C 140
IP14: Helm 7C 88
IP14: Old N 6D 70
IP17: Knod 6F 93
IP22: Hind 6D 34 & 4F 35
IP28: Ris 2C 50
IP30: E'well 2C 64
IP31: Gt Ash 6E 66
IP31: Gt Bar 2E 54
IP31: Thur 6A 56
NR33: Oul B 1E 10
NR34: Ilk A 3G 15
NR34: R'field 4K 15
Schools Cl. IP14: Mendl 2J 71
School St. CO6: Stoke N 2J 143
CO10: S'bury 4D 126
IP6: Nee M 4G 111
School Ter. CB9: With 2B 98
School Wlk. *NR34: Becc 4E 12*
(off Peddars La.)
School Yd.
IP33: Bury E 4G 157 (1G 59)
Schoorl Cl. IP7: Hadl 4J 129
Schreiber Rd. IP4: Ips 6F 133
Scofield Ct. CO10: Gt Cor 5F 127
SCOLE 1K 37 (2B 160)
Sconch Beck Rd. IP20: Mendh 1J 41
Scopes Rd. IP5: Kesg 5C 134
Score, The NR34: Becc 2E 12
Scossels CO10: Glem 3A 104
Scotland St.
CO6: Stoke N 2J 143 & 7D 144
Scots Pine Ct. IP28: Red L 5J 25
Scott Av. IP28: Mide 6J 23
Scott La. IP12: Melt 7F 119
Scott Rd. IP3: Ips 5F 139
IP31: Ixw 5J 29
Scotts Cl. NR33: Kess 4J 17
Scott's Hill IP14: Ston A 5F 87
Scotts Yd. IP14: Comb 1D 110
Scrivener Dr. IP2: Ips 4D 136
IP8: Ips 4D 136
Scroby Ct. NR32: Oul 6B 8
Scuffin's La. IP14: Cott 6D 68
Sculthorpe IP27: RAF L 4H 21
Seabreeze Rd. IP14: Stowm 5E 84
Seabrook Cl. CO10: Hund 1H 99
Seabrooks, The CO10: Glem 6A 104
Seago St. NR32: Low 7J 9
Seagull Theatre 5G 11
Sea Lake Rd. NR32: Oul B 1D 10
Seaman Av. IP17: Saxm 6G 91
Sea Rd. IP11: Felix 7D 154
Seaton Rd. IP11: Felix 3D 154
Seavert Cl. NR33: Car C 6D 10
Seaview Rd. IP18: Rey 2J 45
Sea Vw. Wlk. NR33: Low 5G 11
Seaward Av. IP16: Leis 4J 93
Sebert Rd. IP32: Bury E 1A 60
Seckford Almshouses
IP12: Wood 5G 121
Seckford Cl. IP4: Rush A 1K 139
Seckford Foundation
IP12: Wood 5F 121
Seckford Golf Course 7D 120
Seckford Hall Rd. IP12: Wood 7E 120
IP13: Gt Bea 7C 120
Seckford St. IP12: Wood 5G 121
Seckford Ter. IP12: Wood 5G 121
Second Av. CO10: Glem 4B 104
CO10: S'bury 2E 126
IP11: T Mary 1A 154
Sedan Wlk. IP1: Ips 5C 4
Sedge Fen Rd. IP27: Lake 4A 20
Sedge Way
IP33: Bury E 2F 157 (7F 53)
Sedlescombe Rd. NR33: Car C 4C 10
Sefton Way CB8: Newm 4D 46
Segger Vw. IP5: Kesg 7C 134
Segmore La. IP17: Pea 2F 77
Selby St. NR32: Low 7H 9
Selkirk Rd. IP4: Ips 5F 133
Selvale Way IP11: Felix 4D 154
Selway Dr. IP32: Bury E 1C 60
Selwyn Cl. CB8: Newm 7G 47
IP2: Ips 7D 4 (2A 138)
IP28: Mide 5K 23
SEMER 2A 164
Semer Cl. IP14: Stowm 7G 85
Semer Rd. IP7: What 5B 112
Sergeants Wlk. IP33: Bury E 3G 157
Serpentine Rd. IP3: Ips 4F 139
Servite Ho. IP4: Ips 2K 5 (7D 132)
Seven Acres NR33: Low 7F 11
Seven Acres Bus. Pk.
IP12: Wald 5A 140
Seven Acres La. IP18: Walb 7F 45
Seven Cotts. IP5: Rush A 4G 133
Seven Cotts. La. IP5: Rush A 4G 133
Sevengardens Rd. IP13: Burg 5K 117
Seven Tree Rd. IP28: Ick 1C 26
Severalls La. IP13: Denn 5A 76
Several Rd. IP13: Saxt, Sax G 4B 90
Severals, The CB8: Newm 4H 47
Severn Rd. IP3: Ips 3D 138
IP32: Bury E 4E 52
SEWARDS END 3A 162
Sewells IP7: Hit 1H 109
Sewells, The *IP33: Bury E 4H 59*
(off Kestrel Rd.)
Sewell Wontner Cl. IP5: Kesg 5C 134
Sextons Mdws.
IP33: Bury E 7K 157 (3H 59)
Seymour Av. IP27: B'don 5C 18
Seymour Cl. CB8: Newm 6J 47
Seymour Dr. CB9: Have 4C 100
Seymour Rd. IP2: Ips 7D 4 (2A 138)
Shackleton Rd. IP3: Ips 3F 139
Shackleton Sq. IP3: Ips 3F 139
Shaddick Rd. IP18: Rey 1H 45
SHADINGFIELD 2C 167
Shadingfield Cl. NR32: Low 3F 9
Shadowbush Cl. CB9: Have 2E 100
SHADWELL 1D 159
Shadwell Cl. IP27: Weet 1E 18
Shadwell Wlk. IP33: Bury E 7C 52
Shaftesbury Ct. CB9: Have 4D 100
NR33: Low 4H 11
Shaftesbury Sq.
IP4: Ips 4G 5 (1B 138)
Shafto Rd. IP1: Ips 5G 131
Shaker's La. IP32: Bury E 7J 53
IP33: Bury E 7J 53
(not continuous)
Shakespeare Rd. IP1: Ips 1G 131
IP14: Stowm 2D 84
SHALFORD 3B 162
SHALFORD GREEN 3B 162
Shamrock, The *IP4: Ips 5F 5*
(off Key St.)
Shamrock Av. IP2: Ips 2G 137
Shamrock Ho. IP1: Ips 3F 131
Shannon Cl. CB9: Have 4J 101
Shannon Hgts. IP12: Holl 3G 141
Shannon Rd. IP3: Ips 6E 138
Shardlow Cl. CB9: Have 2B 100
Sharon Dr. NR32: Low 5G 9
Sharon Rd. IP33: Bury E 1D 58
Sharpes Cnr. IP27: Lake 3A 20
(not continuous)
Sharpes Ct. IP28: Mide 7H 23
Sharpe's Hill IP29: Barr 6D 50
Sharpe's Row IP30: Wool 6C 64
Sharp Rd. IP33: Bury E 4F 59
Sharp's Grn. IP29: Horr 7B 58
Sharp's La. IP29: Horr 7B 58
Sharpstone St. IP6: Barh 1B 114
Shaw Av. NR33: Car C 6C 10
Shawlands Av. CO10: Gt Cor 4G 127
Shaw Rd. CO10: L Mel 3J 105
Shaw Valley Rd. IP12: Martl 3H 135
Shearman Ct. CB9: Have 4E 100
Shearman Rd. IP7: Hadl 4K 129
Shearwater Way IP14: Stowm 4J 85
IP18: Rey 2H 45
Sheepcote La. IP14: Stowm 4J 85
Sheepcote Pl. IP14: Stowm 4J 85
Sheepdrift Rd. IP12: B'well 2C 124
Sheepgate NR34: Becc 3E 12
Sheepgate La. CO10: Clar 4C 102
Sheep La. IP31: Thur 3K 55
Sheepshead Hill CO10: Gt Cor 5H 127
Sheerwater Cl. IP32: Bury E 7B 54
Shelbourne Cl. IP5: Kesg 6D 134
Sheldrake Dr. IP2: Ips 5F 137
Sheldrick Way IP28: Mide 7G 23
SHELFANGER 1B 160
SHELLEY 1F 145 (3A 164)
Shelley Av. CO10: Gt Cor 5G 127
Shelley Cl. IP14: Stowm 7H 85
Shelley M. *IP17: Saxm 5G 91*
(off Brook Farm Rd.)
Shelley Rd. IP7: Ray, Shel 1F 145
IP32: Bury E 4F 53
Shelley St. IP2: Ips 7E 4
Shelley Way IP14: Bac 3D 68
SHELTON 1C 161
SHELTON GREEN 1C 161
Shelton Hill IP21: Stradb 5H 39
Shelton Pl. NR34: Becc 5F 13
Shelton Rd. NR33: Low 6E 10
Shenley Rd. IP3: Ips 5F 139
Shenstone Dr. IP1: Ips 2J 131
Shepherd Dr. IP8: Ips 4E 136
Shepherds Ct. CB9: Have 4D 100
Shepherds Dr. IP29: Laws 6B 80
Shepherds Fold IP12: Holl 2G 141
Shepherds La. CO10: Glem 3A 104
IP9: Holb 3D 150
IP14: Stowm 2C 84
IP18: Rey 3G 45
IP22: B'gate 3H 35
Sheppards Way IP5: Kesg 6D 134
Sherborne Av. IP4: Ips 3E 132
Sherborne Rd. IP33: Bury E 3D 58
Sherbourne St. CO10: Edw 4A 128
Sheridan Cl. IP14: Stowm 2C 84
Sheridan Wlk. NR34: Worl 4H 13
Sheringham Ct. IP14: Stowm 5G 85
Sherrington Rd. IP1: Ips 5J 131
Sherwood Flds. IP5: Kesg 6C 134
Shetland Cl. IP4: Ips 4E 132
Shetland Rd. CB9: Have 4J 101
Shetlands IP31: Stant 6C 32
Shickle Pl. IP22: Hop 2J 31
Shilling St. CO10: Lave 6C 106
Shillitoe Cl. IP33: Bury E 1F 59
SHIMPLING
Bury St Edmunds
4C 106 (1C 163)
Dickleburgh 1B 160
Shimpling Cl. IP14: Stowm 7G 85
Shimpling Rd. IP29: Hart 1J 103
SHIMPLING STREET 1D 106 (1C 163)
SHINGLE STREET 2D 165
Shinham Bri. IP31: Gt Bar 3F 55
Ship Gdns. IP28: Mide 1E 24
Ship La. IP8: B'ford 4D 130
Ship Launch Rd.
IP3: Ips 7G 5 (3C 138)
SHIPMEADOW 1D 161
Ship Mdw. Wlk. IP12: Wood 5H 121
Shippea Hill Rd. IP28: B Row 1C 22
Ship Rd. NR33: Low 6E 10
Shire Ct. CB9: Have 4D 100
Shirehall Way
IP33: Bury E 6K 157 (2H 59)
Shire Hall Yd. IP4: Ips 5F 5 (1B 138)
Shires, The NR32: Low 7H 7
Shirley Cl. IP1: Ips 2J 131
Shoals, The *NR32: Low 5K 9*
(off Whapload Rd.)
Shoals Wlk. NR33: Oul B 3D 10
Shop Cl. IP29: Denh 7B 50
Shop Drove IP28: W Row 4A 22
Shop Grn. IP14: Bac 3E 68
Shop Hill CB8: W'rook 2G 97
Shop St. IP13: W'orth 5F 73
Shore La. IP9: Hark 6G 151
IP10: Nac 7A 152
Shores Cl. IP28: Frec 5B 24
Short Brackland
IP33: Bury E 4H 157 (7G 53)
Shorter's End IP14: W'orpe 7G 67
SHORT GREEN 1A 160
Shortgrove La. IP22: Hop 3H 31
Shortlands IP8: Ips 5F 137
Short La. IP18: Walb 7F 45
NR33: Car C 7B 10
Short Rd. NR32: Blun 2J 7
Short St. NR33: Low 5G 11
Short Wlk. IP12: But 6C 124
SHOTLEY 4B 156 (3C 165)
Shotley Cl. IP2: Ips 4E 136
IP11: Felix 4C 154
SHOTLEY GATE 7E 156 (3C 165)
Shotley M. CB9: Have 3A 100
IP12: Sutt 2B 140
Shotley Rd. IP9: Chelm 2H 151
SHOTTISHAM 2D 165
Shottisham Rd. IP12: Alder 4H 141
SHROPHAM 1D 159
Shrubberies, The CB8: Newm 7K 47
Shrubbery Cl. IP11: Felix 4E 154
IP30: Hess 7D 62
Shrubbery Rd. IP13: Hask 3C 120
Shrub Ho. Cl. IP28: B Row 1E 22
Shrubland Av. IP1: Ips 4G 131
Shrubland Cl. IP6: Barh 1B 114
Shrubland Dr. IP4: Rush A 1K 139
Shrublands IP28: Mide 7J 23
SHUDY CAMPS 2A 162
Siam Pl. CO10: S'bury 4D 126
SIBLE HEDINGHAM 3B 162
SIBTON 3K 77 (3D 161)
Sibton Abbey 2J 77
Sibton Rd. IP17: Pea 2J 77
SICKLESMERE 7C 60 (3C 159)
Sicklesmere Rd. IP30: Rushb 3J 59
IP33: Bury E 3J 59
Sidecentre Gate *IP5: Martl H 6G 135*
(off The Chase)
Sidegate Av. IP4: Ips 5E 132
Sidegate La. IP4: Ips 4E 132
Sidegate La. W. IP4: Ips 4D 132
Siding Rd. NR34: Barnb 5C 6
Sidings, The IP12: Melt 3K 121
Silent St. IP1: Ips 4E 4 (1A 138)
Silk Factory Row CO10: Glem 3A 104
Silk Mill Cl. IP7: Hadl 4H 129
Silk St. IP4: Ips 3G 5 (7B 132)
Siloam Pl. IP3: Ips 6H 5 (2C 138)
Silverdale Av. IP14: Stowm 3E 84
Silverdale Cl. IP1: Ips 4J 131
Silver Dr. IP15: Aldeb 3G 95
SILVER GREEN 1C 161
Silver Hill IP8: Hint 1D 144
Silver Leys IP9: Bent 6H 147
SILVERLEY'S GREEN 2C 161
Silver St. CB9: Ked 6C 98
IP14: Old N 4A 70
Silver Way IP32: Bury E 4J 53
Silverwood Cl. NR33: Low 5F 11
Simm's La. CB9: Ked, Hund 7D 98
Simon Ho. IP4: Ips 2K 5 (7D 132)
Simon's Cross IP13: Wick M 5A 118
Simons Rd. IP12: Wood 3H 121
Simpson Cl. IP3: Ips 5D 138
Sinclair Dr. IP2: Ips 3A 138
Singleton Ct. CO10: Gt Cor 6F 127
Sir Alf Ramsey Way IP1: Ips 4A 4
Sirdar Rd. IP1: Ips 2A 4 (7J 131)
Sir John Leman Rd.
NR34: Becc 5G 13
Sir John Mills Theatre 1A 4 (6J 131)
Siskin Grn. NR33: Oul B 4C 10
Siskin St. IP14: Stowm 4H 85
Sisters Ct. IP7: Hadl 2H 129
Sitwell Gdns. IP13: F'ham 6C 90
SIX MILE BOTTOM 1A 162
SIZEWELL 1A 166
Sizewell Rd. IP16: Leis 4J 93
Sizewell Sports & Social Club 4K 93
Skamacre Cres. NR32: Low 6G 9
Skate's Hill CO10: Glem 6A 104
Skeaping Cl. CB8: Newm 5G 47
SKEET'S GREEN 4F 115
Skelton's Drove IP28: B Row 1D 22
Skilmans Hill IP18: Sou 5K 45
Skinners Cl. IP20: Metf 6G 41
Skinners La. IP20: Metf 6G 41
IP31: Bard 2D 32
Skinner St.
IP33: Bury E 4H 157 (1G 59)
Skipper Rd. IP8: Ips 6G 137
Skipper's La. CB9: With 1A 98
Skoulding Cl. NR33: Oul B 2E 10
Skoulding Pl. IP19: H'orth 4B 42

Skylark Cl. IP32: Bury E 6C **54**
Skylark La. IP8: Ips 4E **136**
Skylark Way IP14: Stowm 4H **85**
Skyliner Way IP32: Bury E 1B **60**
Slade, The IP6: Barh, Clay 2E **114**
Slades Cl. CO10: Glem 4B **104**
Slade St. IP4: Ips 5F **5** (1B **138**)
Slaters Dr. CB9: Have 1D **100**
SLAUGHDEN **7J 95**
Slaughden Rd. IP15: Aldeb 7J **95**
Slaughden Sailing Club **7J 95**
Sleaford Cl. IP2: Ips 7A **4** (3J **137**)
Slip Ponds IP10: Buck 3B **152**
Sloeberry Rd. IP3: Ips 7G **139**
Sloe La. IP17: Knod 7F **93**
IP17: Snap 7A **92**
Slough Hill IP29: Shim 1C **106**
Slough La. CO10: Act 2H **107**
IP29: Horr 4A **58**
Slough Rd. CO7: E Ber 3B **148**
CO11: Brant 3B **148**
IP22: Bote 7K **35**
Slugs La. NR32: S'ton 2B **6**
Slushy La. IP9: Hark 5H **151**
Smaley La. CO10: L Mel 3H **105**
Smallfen La. IP27: B'don 3D **18**
Smallgate NR34: Becc 2E **12**
SMALLWORTH **1A 160**
Smart St. IP4: Ips 5F **5** (1B **138**)
Smeeth Drove IP27: Lake 1F **21**
Smith Cres. NR33: Kess 4J **17**
Smithers Cl. IP9: Cap M 2H **147**
Smithfield IP12: Melt 4J **121**
Smiths Cl. IP13: W'orth 6H **73**
Smiths Pl. IP5: Kesg 6D **134**
Smiths Row Art Gallery **4H 157**
Smith's Wlk. NR33: Oul B 3B **10**
Smith Wlk. IP33: Bury E 4J **59**
SMITHWOOD GREEN **1D 163**
Smithy Cl. IP29: Stann 4H **81**
IP30: Roug 6J **61**
(not continuous)
Smock Mdw. IP7: Bild 6J **109**
Smyth Cl. IP17: Pea 3J **77**
Smyth Ct. *IP16: Leis 4J 93*
(off High St.)
Snab Hill NR33: Gisle 4G **17**
SNAILWELL **3A 158**
Snailwell Rd. CB8: Newm 4G **47**
Snailwell Short Rd. CB8: Snail 1E **46**
Snakes & Ladders (Children's Play Cen.)
Ipswich **5J 5**
SNAPE . . . .**2D 94 (1D 165)**
Snape Dr. NR32: Oul B 4E **8**
Snape Hill
IP22: Rick, W'field . . .1K **33** & 6F **35**
Snape Maltings Concert Hall **4C 94**
Snape Maltings Gallery **3C 94**
Snape Rd. IP12: Sud 1G **125**
IP12: Tun 6G **123**
IP17: Knod 7F **93**
Snapes La. CO10: B Ele 2A **108**
Snells La. IP11: Felix 1F **155**
SNETTERTON **1D 159**
Snowcroft IP9: Cap M 2H **147**
Snowdens Yd. IP18: Sou 4K **45**
Snowdon Ct. CB9: Have 5D **100**
Snowdon Hill IP13: Wick M 6B **118**
Snowdon Rd. IP2: Ips 4K **137**
Snowdrop Cl. IP32: Bury E 1B **60**
NR33: Car C 4B **10**
Snowdrop Way IP28: Red L 6G **25**
Snow Hill CO10: Clar 2A **102**
Snow Hill Steps *IP11: Felix 5E 154*
(off Undercliff Rd. W.)
SNOW STREET **1A 160**
Snows Way CO11: Brant 5C **148**
Soames Cl. IP14: Stowm 3E **84**
Soane St. IP4: Ips 2F **5** (7B **132**)
Soers Cl. IP23: Thorn 2C **72**
SOHAM **2A 158**
SOHAM COTES **2A 158**
Solace Cl. NR35: Bung 3D **14**
Sole Bay Bowls Club **2H 45**
Solomon Rd. NR33: Kess 4K **17**
SOMERLEYTON . . . .**2C 6 (1C 167)**
Somerleyton Hall **1E 6**
Somerleyton Rd. NR32: Blun 3G **7**
NR32: Oul 4E **8**
Somerleyton Station (Rail) **3B 6**
Somerset Ct. *CB9: Have 4D 100*
(off York Rd.)
Somerset Rd. IP4: Ips 5D **132**
SOMERSHAM . . . .**3K 113 (2A 164)**
Somersham Rd. IP8: B'ford 1A **130**
SOMERTON **1C 163**
Somerton Av. NR32: Low 5H **9**
Somerton Rd. IP29: Hart 1G **103**
Somerville Lea IP15: Aldeb 4J **95**
Song Thrush Cl. IP14: Stowm 4H **85**
Sorrel Cl. IP2: Ips 3H **137**
IP6: Barh 1B **114**
Sorrel Ct. IP28: Red L 6J **25**
Sorrel Horse M. IP4: Ips 5G **5**
Sorrell Grn. IP14: Wyve 1B **68**
Sorrell Wlk. IP5: Martl H 6F **135**
Sorrel Wlk. CB9: Have 2C **100**
SOTTERLEY **2C 167**
Sotterley Cl. NR32: Low 2F **9**
Sotterley Rd. NR32: Oul B 4E **8**
Sound, The NR33: Oul B 4D **10**
Sounds, The CB8: Dalh 7H **49**
South Cl. IP4: Ips 5C **132**
IP12: Melt 7F **119**
IP16: Leis 4J **93**
IP33: Bury E 2F **59**
NR34: Becc 5D **12**
SOUTH COVE **2C 167**
South Dr. CB8: Newm 5F **47**
IP22: Hep 7C **30**
Sth. Elmham Ter. NR33: Oul B 1D **10**
Southend Rd. NR35: Bung 3B **14**
Southend Rd. Ind. Est.
NR35: Bung 3B **14**
South Entrance IP17: Saxm 7J **91**
Southern Belle Cl. IP32: Bury E . . .7B **54**
Southern La. IP22: Redg 2A **34**
SOUTHEY GREEN **3B 162**
Southfield Dr. IP16: Leis 4H **93**
Southfield Gdns. NR33: Oul B 3E **10**
Southfields Cl. CB8: Newm 5E **46**
Southgate Av. IP28: Mide 4H **23**
Southgate Gdns. CO10: L Mel 5H **105**
IP33: Bury E 3J **59**
Southgate Grn. IP33: Bury E 3J **59**
Southgate Rd. IP8: Ips 5D **136**
Southgate St. CO10: L Mel 5H **105**
IP33: Bury E 6K **157** (2H **59**)
South Grn. IP18: Sou 5K **45**
South Hill IP11: Felix 5E **154**
South Leet Cl. NR32: Oul 4D **8**
Sth. Lodge Dr. IP28: Forn G 1F **53**
SOUTH LOPHAM **1A 160**
Sth. Lowestoft Ind. Est.
NR33: Low 7E **10**
SOUTHOLT **3B 160**
Southolt Rd. IP13: Bed 7G **73**
IP21: Ath 4J **73**
South Pde. IP32: Bury E 4F **53**
South Rd. IP27: Lake 1G **21**
NR34: Becc 5D **12**
South Strand CO11: Lawf 7B **148**
South St. IP1: Ips 1B **4** (6K **131**)
IP28: Ris 3C **50**
Sth. Suffolk Bus. Cen.
CO10: S'bury 4F **127**
South Vw. IP13: Char 3D **118**
IP20: Mendh 1H **41**
South Vw. Cl. NR32: Low 6G **9**
South Vw. Grn. IP9: Bent 6H **147**
Southwell Rd. NR33: Low 2G **11**
SOUTHWOLD . . . .**4K 45 (3D 167)**
Southwold Bus. Cen. IP18: Sou . . .3K **45**
Southwold Golf Course **4H 45**
Southwold Lighthouse **4K 45**
Southwold Mus. **4K 45**
Southwold Pier **3K 45**
Southwold Rd. IP19: Bly, Bulc 1K **43**
IP19: Holt 5E **42**
NR34: Bramp 5H **15**
NR34: Wrent 1D **44**
Southwold Sailing Club **5H 45**
Southwold Sailors Reading Room
. . . .**4K 45**
Southwood Cl. IP17: Saxm 7J **91**
(not continuous)
Sovereign Ct. CB8: Newm 7H **47**
SOWLEY GREEN **1B 162**
Spalding La. IP5: Kesg 7B **134**
Spanbies Rd. CO7: Strat M 6H **145**
Spa Pavilion Theatre, The
Felixstowe **5G 155**
Sparhawk St.
IP33: Bury E 6J **157** (2H **59**)
Sparrow Ct. IP14: Deb 2H **87**
Sparrowhawk Rd. IP19: H'orth 1C **42**
Sparrow Rd. CO10: Gt Cor 5G **127**
Sparrows Cft. Rd. IP12: Rend 5C **122**
Sparrows Ri. IP6: Nee M 3H **111**
Sparrows Yd. *IP6: Nee M 3H 111*
(off Crown St.)
Spartan Cl. CB9: Have 3B **100**
Spashett Rd. NR32: Low 4F **9**
Spearmint Way IP28: Red L 6G **25**
Spears Hill IP22: Wort 1F **35**
Speckled Wood Cl. IP8: Ips 6F **137**
Speedwell Cl. NR33: Low 6F **11**
Speedwell Rd. IP2: Ips 2H **137**
Spencer Dr. NR32: Low 2G **9**
Spencer Rd. IP12: Rend 5D **122**
Spencers Piece IP30: Rat 3K **83**
Spencer Way IP14: Stowm 3D **84**
Spenser Rd. IP1: Ips 2G **131**
Sperling Dr. CB9: Have 1D **100**
SPEXHALL **1D 161**
Spexhall Way NR32: Low 3G **9**
Spicers La. CO10: L Mel 3H **105**
Spicer Way CO10: Gt Cor 7G **127**
Spike's La. IP14: Stowm 1E **84**
Spilsby IP27: RAF L 4H **21**
Spindler Cl. IP5: Kesg 6D **134**
Spindle Rd. CB9: Have 2C **100**
Spinner Cl. IP1: Ips 5F **131**
Spinners La. IP18: Sou 4J **45**
Spinney, The CO10: L Mel 4H **105**
IP4: Rush A 2K **139**
IP17: Saxm 5J **91**
NR34: Becc 4G **13**
Spinney Cl. IP17: Kel 4J **91**
IP27: B'don 5F **19**
NR34: Nor C 7B **6**
Spinney Gdns. NR33: Car C 5B **10**
Spinney Hill IP8: Flow 6K **113**
Spire Chase CO10: S'bury 1F **127**
Spitfire Cl. IP3: Ips 5F **139**
Splash La. IP10: Kirt 1F **153**
Spong, The IP20: Metf 6H **41**
Spong La. IP30: E'well 3D **64**
Spooners La. IP7: Hadl 3H **129**
Spoonmans La. IP14: Stowm 3J **85**
Sprats Water La. NR33: Car C 3A **10**
Spring Cl. CB9: Have 3B **100**
CO10: Lave 5C **106**
IP12: Rend 7B **122**
IP23: Gisli 1K **67**
Spring Ct. IP4: Ips 3K **5** (7D **132**)
Springfield IP18: Rey 2G **45**
Springfield Av. IP11: Felix 3F **155**
IP33: Bury E 2F **157** (7F **53**)
Springfield Dr. IP27: Lake 5B **20**
Springfield Gdns. NR33: Oul B 4E **10**
Springfield La. IP1: Ips 5H **131**
Springfield Rd. CO10: S'bury 2D **126**
IP8: S'ham 4K **113**
IP15: Aldeb 4G **95**
IP33: Bury E 3F **157** (7F **53**)
Springfields IP23: Gisli 1K **67**
Spring Gdns. CO10: L Mel 3H **105**
Springhurst Cl. IP4: Ips . . .3K **5** (7D **132**)
Springland Cl. IP4: Ips 7E **132**
Springlands Way CO10: S'bury . . .1D **126**
Spring La. CO10: Lave 5C **106**
IP6: Cod 1H **115**
IP13: Uff 4J **119**
IP13: Wick M 5C **118**
IP33: Bury E 2F **157** (7F **53**)
Spring Mdw. CO10: Glem 3A **104**
IP6: Play 1B **134**
Spring Ri. CB9: Have 5H **101**
Spring Rd. IP4: Ips 3J **5** (7C **132**)
IP8: Wash 4A **136**
IP31: Bard 1D **32**
Spring Row IP14: Stowm 3F **85**
Spring St. CO10: Lave 6C **106**
Springtail Rd. IP8: Ips 6G **137**
Springwood Dr. IP17: Pea 2H **77**
Spring Wood Nature Reserve . . .**7G 137**
Sprites End IP11: T Mary 1C **154**
Spriteshall La. IP11: T Mary 1C **154**
Sprites La. IP2: Ips 3E **136**
IP8: Ips 5E **136**
SPROUGHTON . . . .**7D 130 (2B 164)**
Sproughton Bus. Pk. IP1: Ips 5E **130**
Sproughton Ct. IP8: Spro 7C **130**
Sproughton Rd. IP1: Ips 6F **131**
IP8: Spro 6D **130**
Spruce Cl. IP27: RAF L 4H **21**
Spruce Ct. NR32: Low 5H **9**
Spruce Dr. IP27: B'don 4G **19**
Spur End IP12: Melt 3K **121**
Spurgeon Score NR32: Low 6K **9**
Square, The IP5: Martl H 6G **135**
IP7: Hadl 2J **129**
IP13: Denn 5C **76**
IP14: Stowm 6G **85**
Squire's Ct. CB9: Have 4D **100**
Squires La. IP5: Martl H 5G **135**
Squires Wlk. NR32: Low 3H **9**
Squirrells, The IP9: Cap M 1H **147**
Squirrells Mill Rd. IP7: Bild 5J **109**
Stable Ct. IP5: Martl H 5G **135**
Stable Flats IP24: Elv 3J **27**
Stafford Ct. NR32: Oul 4D **8**
Staithe, The NR33: Oul B 3D **10**
Staithe Cl. NR35: Bung 2B **14**
Staithe Ct. *NR34: Becc 2E 12*
(off Ravensmere)
Staithe Rd. NR35: Bung 2B **14**
Staith La. NR32: S'ton 2B **6**
STAMBOURNE **3B 162**
Stamford Cl. IP2: Ips 6H **137**
Stamford Ct. *IP33: Bury E 3F 59*
(off Vinery Rd.)
Stamford St. CB8: Newm 7H **47**
Stammers Pl. IP5: Kesg 5E **134**
Stanford St. NR32: Low 7H **9**
Stanhope Cl. IP17: Snap 2D **94**
Stanley Av. IP3: Ips 2E **138**
Stanley Cotts. IP11: Felix 3D **154**
Stanley Rd. CB8: Newm 6J **47**
CO10: S'bury 3D **126**
IP11: Felix 5F **155**
NR33: Oul B 2D **10**
Stanley St. NR32: Low 7J **9**
Stanley Wood Av.
CO10: S'bury 2E **126**
Stannard Way CO10: Gt Cor 5F **127**
STANNINGFIELD . . . .**3G 81 (1C 163)**
Stanningfield Rd.
IP30: Gt Whe . . . . . . .7C **60** & 1F **81**
STANSFIELD **1B 162**
Stansfield Cl. NR33: Oul B 3D **10**
STANSTEAD . . . .**2D 104 (2C 163)**
STANTON . . . .**7D 32 (2D 159)**
STANTON CHARE . . . . . .**5B 32 (2D 159)**
Stanton Cl. NR32: Low 3H **9**
NR34: Becc 5F **13**
Stanton Pl. CB9: Have 3G **101**
Stanton Rd. IP31: Bard 2E **32**
IP31: Barni . . . . .5A **30** & 4D **30**
IP31: Ixw, Stant 6J **29**
STANTON STREET . . . . .**3H 57 (3D 159)**
Stanton Windmill **2D 159**
Stanway Cl. CO10: Glem 4B **104**
STANWELL GREEN . . . . .**2B 72 (2B 160)**
Stanwell Grn. IP23: Thorn 2B **72**
Staple Cl. IP31: Wals W 7H **33**
Staplehurst Cl. NR33: Car C 5B **10**
Starfield Cl. IP4: Ips 7F **133**
Starhouse La. IP14: One 4B **84**
Star La. IP4: Ips 5E **4** (1A **138**)
Starling Way IP14: Stowm 3H **85**
Starre Rd. IP33: Bury E 1C **58**
STARSTON **1C 161**
Station App. CB8: Newm 7G **47**
IP17: Saxm 6J **91**
Station Hill CO8: Bure 6A **142**
IP31: Thur 6K **55**
IP32: Bury E 2H **157** (6G **53**)
Station Rd. CB8: Kenn 1A **48**
CB9: Have 3F **101**
CO10: Clar 5D **102**
CO10: L Mel 6H **105**
CO10: S'bury 4D **126**
IP6: Clay 4C **114**
IP7: Hadl 4H **129**
IP9: Bent, Tatt 6H **147**
IP11: T Mary 1B **154**
IP12: Blax . . . . .2E **122** & 3F **123**
IP12: Melt 2K **121**
IP12: Wood 6H **121**
IP13: Cam A 2D **122**
IP13: F'ham 6C **90**
IP13: Laxf 5A **74**
IP14: Bac, Cott, Finn
. . . . .5C **68** & 7G **67**
IP14: Haug, Old N 2B **70**
IP14: W'sett 7J **69**
IP16: Leis 3H **93**
IP17: Yox 6J **77**
IP18: Sou 3J **45**
IP19: Blyth 5J **43**
IP19: H'orth 4B **42**
IP24: Barnh 6F **27**
IP27: Lake 4A **20**
IP28: B Mil, Mide 1E **24**
IP28: L Sax 4D **50**
IP30: E'well 2D **64**
NR32: Cort 6J **7**
NR32: Low 4J **9**
NR32: S'ton 3B **6**
NR34: Becc 3E **12**
NR34: Bramp 5F **15**
Station Rd. E. IP14: Stowm 4G **85**
Station Rd. Ind. Est.
IP30: E'well 1D **64**
Station Rd. W. IP14: Stowm 4F **85**
Station Sq. NR32: Low 1J **11**
Station St. IP2: Ips 7E **4** (3A **138**)
Station Ter. IP13: F'ham 7C **90**
Station Way IP27: B'don 2F **19**
Station Yd. IP2: Ips 6B **4** (2K **137**)
IP6: Nee M 4H **111**
IP7: Hadl 4J **129**
IP17: Dars 5K **77**
IP28: Mide 1E **24**
Staverton Cl. IP12: Eyk 1D **124**
Stayngate Wlk. NR32: Oul 4D **8**
Stearn Dr. IP14: One 3A **84**
Stearn's La. IP14: Forw G 2A **86**
Stebbings Cl. IP12: Holl 2G **141**
Stebbings La. IP12: Holl 2F **141**
Stedman Ter. IP18: Rey 1J **45**
Steeds Mdw. CO10: L Mel 3H **105**
Steeles Cl. IP30: Wool 5A **64**
Steeles Rd. IP30: Wool 5B **64**
STEEPLE BUMPSTEAD **2A 162**
Steeplechase CO10: Hund 1G **99**

Steeple End IP19: H'orth 5B 42
Steeple Vw. IP14: Stowu 1K 85
NR32: Low 5G 9
Steggall Cl. IP6: Nee M 2F 111
Stella Maris IP2: Ips 1F 137
Stennetts Cl. IP11: T Mary 7H 153
Stephen Cl. CB9: Have 3E 100
CO10: L Mel 6G 105
Stephen Ct. IP4: Ips 7F 133
Stephen Rd. IP5: Kesg 5E 134
Stephensons Pl. IP32: Bury E 6F 53
Stephensons Wlk. NR32: Low 4J 9
Stepping Hill NR34: Becc 3D 12
STERNFIELD 3E 92 (3D 161)
Sternfield Rd. IP17: Ster 2D 92
STETCHWORTH 1A 162
Stevenson App. CO10: Gt Cor 6G 127
Stevenson Rd. IP1: Ips 3B 4 (7K 131)
Stevens St. NR32: Low 7H 9
STEVENTON END 2A 162
Steward Rd. IP33: Bury E 4J 59
Stewart Fld. IP14: Cott 7G 67
Stewart Young Gro. IP5: Kesg 6D 134
Stimpson Cl. NR32: Low 2F 9
Stirling Cl. IP28: W Row 6B 22
NR32: Oul 4E 8
Stirling Dr. CB9: Have 3D 100
Stirling Gdns. CB8: Newm 5E 46
Stirrups La. NR32: Cort 5F 7
Stobart Cl. NR34: Becc 5G 13
STOCK CORNER 1B 22
STOCKHOLD GREEN 7C 56
STOCKING GREEN 3A 162
Stockley Cl. CB9: Have 4H 101
Stockmers End IP9: Cap M 2H 147
Stocks Hill IP8: S'ham 3K 113
Stocks La. IP18: Walb 7G 45
Stockton Cl. IP7: Hadl 5K 129
STOKE 2A 138
STOKE ASH 2B 160
Stokebridge Maltings
IP2: Ips 6E 4 (2A 138)
STOKE BY CLARE 6J 99 (2B 162)
STOKE-BY-NAYLAND 2J 143 (3D 163)
Stoke by Nayland Golf Course 1E 142
Stoke Farm Dr. IP14: Batt 6B 110
Stoke Hall Rd. IP2: Ips 6D 4 (2A 138)
STOKE PARK 5J 137
Stoke Pk. Dr. IP2: Ips 6H 137
Stoke Pk. Gdns. IP2: Ips 5J 137
Stoke Quay IP2: Ips 6F 5
Stoke Rd. CO6: Leav 1B 142
CO6: Nay 6K 143
CO10: Clar 6A 102
IP23: Thorn 1B 72
Stoke St. IP2: Ips 6D 4 (2A 138)
STOKE TYE 6A 144
Stollery Cl. IP5: Kesg 6C 134
Stonalls IP30: Wool 4K 63
Stone All. NR35: Bung 1B 14
Stonebridge Av. IP33: Bury E 3F 59
Stonebridge La. IP14: Old N 7D 70
Stonechat Rd. IP2: Ips 4E 136
STONE COMMON 2F 123
Stonecroft Gdns. IP2: Ips 3H 137
STONECROSS GREEN 3A 80
Stonegrove Rd. IP11: Felix 7C 154
Stoneham Aspal Rd.
IP14: Petta 3B 88
Stonehouse Rd. IP7: Hadl 3J 129
Stonelands Ho. *IP11: Felix 2C 154*
(off Runnacles Way)
Stone Lodge La.
IP2: Ips 7B 4 (3J 137)
Stone Lodge La. W. IP2: Ips 3H 137
Stone Lodge Wlk.
IP2: Ips 7B 4 (3J 137)
Stone Pl. IP12: Wood 5H 121
STONES GREEN 3B 164
STONE STREET
Rumburgh 1D 161
Sudbury 7C 128 (3D 163)
Stone St. CO10: Boxf 7C 128
IP7: Hadl 1F 129
IP19: H'orth 1C 42
Stone St. Rd. CO10: Boxf 7C 128
Stoney La. IP29: Barr 5D 50
IP31: Thur 6B 56
Stoney Rd. IP13: Gru 4F 117
STONHAM ASPAL 6G 87 (1B 164)
Stonham Barns IP14: Ston A 6H 87
Stonham Barns Golf Cen. 7J 87
Stonham Rd. IP6: Crow 7H 87
IP14: Cott 7E 68
Stony La. IP16: Thor 6D 94
Stopford Ct. IP1: Ips 1A 4 (6J 131)
Stores Hill CB8: Dalh 7G 49
Stores St. IP27: B'don 4F 19
Stour Av. IP11: Felix 5D 154
Stour Cl. CO10: Glem 7B 104
IP17: Saxm 5H 91
Stour Gdns. CO10: Gt Cor 7G 127
Stour Grn. CO10: Clar 6C 102
Stourmead Cl. CB9: Ked 6B 98
Stourside IP9: Shot G 7D 156
Stour St. CO10: Cave 7F 103
CO10: S'bury 4D 126
Stour Va. CO10: Clar 6B 102
Stour Valley Path CO7: E Ber 6A 148
Stour Valley Rd. CB9: Have 4G 101
Stour Vw. CO7: Ded 7K 145
STOVEN 6K 15 (2C 167)
Stoven Cl. NR32: Low 3G 9
Stowe Lodge IP14: One 3C 84
Stow La. IP31: Pake, Stowl 1G 57
STOWLANGTOFT 1H 57 (3D 159)
Stow Lodge Cen.
Stowmarket 3C 84
STOWMARKET 4F 85 (1A 164)
Stowmarket Bus. Pk.
IP14: Stowm 7J 85
Stowmarket Golf Course 5J 83
Stowmarket Meadlands Recreation Club 6H 85
Stowmarket Rd.
IP6: Badl, Nee M 7K 85 & 2F 111
IP6: Gt Bla 1A 114
IP14: Haug, W'den 4H 65
IP14: Old N 1F 85 & 7A 70
IP14: Ston A 2E 86 & 5F 87
IP14: Stowu 3H 85
IP30: Rat 3K 83
IP30: Wool 5A 64
Stowmarket Station (Rail) 4G 85
Stow Rd. IP31: Ixw, Pake, Stowl 6H 29
STOWUPLAND 1K 85 (1A 164)
Stowupland Rd. IP14: Stowm 3G 85
Stowupland Sports Cen. 1K 85
Stowupland St. IP14: Stowm 4G 85
STRADBROKE 6H 39 (2C 161)
Stradbroke Ct. IP33: Bury E 5J 59
NR33: Low 5F 11
Stradbroke Rd. IP4: Ips 6E 132
IP18: Sou 4K 45
IP21: Fress 7B 40
IP21: Horh 1H 73
NR33: Low 6E 10
Stradbroke Swim & Fitness Cen. 6G 39
STRADISHALL 7G 97 (1B 162)
Straight Rd.
CO7: E Ber 4E 146 & 2A 148
IP14: Batt 6B 110
IP29: Whep 4E 80
Strand, The IP2: Wher 6A 138
Strasbourg Sq. CB9: Have 3G 101
Stratford Ct. IP1: Ips 2H 131
Stratford Rd. CO7: Ded 7G 145
IP1: Ips 3G 131
STRATFORD ST ANDREW 3D 161
STRATFORD ST MARY 6H 145 (3A 164)
STRATFORD ST MARY INTERCHANGE 5J 145
Strattonhall Drift IP10: Levi 7E 152
STRATTON ST MICHAEL 1C 161
Strawberry Flds. CB9: Have 4C 100
Strawberry Hill IP6: Witn 2A 116
Straw La. CO10: S'bury 4D 126
Street, The CB8: Dalh 7H 49
CB8: Gaz 2G 49
CB8: Gt Bra 1A 96
CB8: Mou 6D 48
CB8: Stradi 7G 97
CB9: Gt Thu, L Thu 5C 96
CB9: Stur 6K 101
CO7: E Ber 4A 146
CO7: Strat M 6G 145
CO10: Gt Wal 7A 108
CO10: L Wal 5C 108
CO10: Midd 7D 126
CO10: Pent 7K 103
CO10: Stoke C 7H 99
IP5: Rush A 5H 133
IP6: Tud 7D 116
IP6: Witn 4B 116
IP7: E'sett 6H 113
IP7: Gt Bri 2A 112
IP7: Hit 2G 109
IP7: Lay 7J 129
IP7: M Ele 2E 108
IP7: Ray 1J 145
IP7: What 6D 112
IP8: B'ford 2B 130
IP8: Chat 4B 144
IP8: Wash 6B 136
IP9: Cap M 2G 147
IP9: Hark 6H 151
IP9: Holb 1C 150
IP9: Shot 4B 156
IP9: Wher 1F 149
IP10: Nac 5A 152
IP12: Alder, Bawd 5H 141
Street, The IP12: But 5C 124
IP12: Eyk 2C 124
IP12: Holl 2G 141
IP12: Martl 2J 135
IP12: Melt 3K 121
IP13: B'ton 1K 89
IP13: Char 3C 118
IP13: Cret 1F 89
IP13: Denn 5C 76
IP13: Gru 6H 117
IP13: Ket 6H 89
IP13: L Bea 1D 134
IP13: Petti 1J 119
IP14: Bac 3E 68
IP14: Broc G, Broc S 4G 69
IP14: Fram 6C 88
IP14: Ston A 5F 87
IP17: Dars 2B 78
IP17: Midd 5D 78
IP17: Pea 3J 77
IP17: Ster 3E 92
IP17: Westl 5H 79
IP18: Walb 7F 45
IP19: B'field 6H 75
IP19: Blyth 6J 43
IP19: Hev 3B 74
IP19: Holt 5D 42
IP19: Hunt 1C 74
IP19: Wen 2H 43
IP19: Wiss 2A 42
IP20: Mendh, W'well 2G 41
IP20: Metf 6G 41
IP21: Horh 1F 73
IP21: Wey 2D 40
IP22: Bote, Rick 6H 35
IP22: Hep 5C 30
IP22: Hind 6C 34
IP22: Redg 1B 34
(not continuous)
IP22: W'field 3H 33
IP23: Brom 4K 37
IP23: Occ 5B 72
IP23: Stoke A 1K 69
IP23: Thorn 2B 72
IP23: Yax 6E 36
IP24: Barnh 6G 27
IP27: B'don 4D 18
IP27: Eris 6G 21
IP28: B Mil 2G 25
IP28: B Row 1E 22
IP28: Cul 6A 28
IP28: Frec 5C 24
IP28: Holy R 2H 23
IP28: Ick 2B 26
IP28: W'ton 2B 24
IP29: Barr 6B 50
IP29: Boxt 3G 103
IP29: Chedb 6K 51
IP29: Horr 7B 58
IP29: Laws 7C 80
IP29: Shim 1D 106
IP30: B Com 1J 81
IP30: Drin 6H 63
IP30: Hess 6D 62
IP30: Wool 4A 64
IP31: B Ash 2D 66
IP31: Con W 1A 30
IP31: Forn M 2G 53
IP31: Gt Bar 3E 54
IP31: Gt Liv 2B 28
IP31: Huns 3A 66
IP31: Ing 6D 28
IP31: Nort 5H 57
IP31: Pake 2A 56
IP31: Stant 7D 32
IP31: Stowl 1G 57
IP31: Tros 1C 28
IP31: Wals W 6F 33
NR32: Blun 1H 7
NR32: Cort 5J 7
NR32: S'ton 2B 6
NR33: Car C 7B 10
NR33: Rushm 5C 16
NR34: Barnb 7C 6
NR34: Bramp 6F 15
NR34: Nor C 7B 6
Street Farm Cl. IP10: Buck 3B 152
IP28: Holy R 2H 23
Street Farm Ct. IP20: Mendh 2H 41
Street Farm Gdns. IP23: Gisli 1J 67
Street Farm La. IP31: Ixw 5H 29
Street Farm Rd. IP17: Saxm 6J 91
Streetfield Cl. IP29: Shim 1E 106
STREETLY END 2A 162
Stretton Av. CB8: Newm 7H 47
Strickland Mnr. Hill IP17: Yox 6F 77
Strickland Pl. IP18: Sou 4K 45
Stricklands Rd. IP14: Stowm 5G 85
Strickmere CO7: Strat M 6G 145
Strikes
Sudbury 2F 127
Strowger's Way NR33: Kess 4K 17
Struggler's La. IP6: Witn 5B 116
Struston Mead IP10: Kirt 1H 153
Stuart Cl. IP4: Ips 1K 5 (6D 132)
IP11: Felix 1J 155
IP27: B'don 4F 19
Stuart Dr. NR34: Becc 4F 13
Stuarts Dr. CO10: S'bury 4F 127
Stubbins La. CB8: Gaz 2G 49
CO7: H Mar 1A 146
IP14: W'den 2G 65
Stubbs Cl. CB9: Have 2C 100
IP3: Ips 5E 138
Stubbs Wood NR32: Low 2H 9
Studio Cl. IP17: Westl 5H 79
Studlands Bus. Cen.
CB8: Newm 3D 46
STUDLANDS PARK 1E 46
Studlands Pk. Av. CB8: Newm 3D 46
(not continuous)
Studlands Pk. Ind. Est.
CB8: Newm 2D 46
Stump St. IP13: Petti 2H 119
STUNTNEY 2A 158
Sturdee Av. IP3: Ips 3F 139
Sturgeon Way IP31: Stant 7C 32
STURMER 6K 101 (2A 162)
Sturmer End Ind. Est.
CB9: Have 5H 101
Sturmer Rd. CB9: Have 5G 101
CB9: Ked 7B 98
STUSTON 1G 37 (2B 160)
STUSTON COMMON 1G 37
Stuston La. IP21: Stus 1G 37
Stuston Rd. IP21: Stus 1G 37
STUTTON 6B 150 (3B 164)
Stutton Cl. IP9: Stut 6C 150
Sub-Station Rd. IP11: Felix 6C 154
SUDBOURNE 1H 125 (2A 166)
Sudbourne Rd. IP11: Felix 3C 154
IP12: Orf 4H 125
SUDBURY 4D 126 (2C 163)
Sudbury Retail Pk.
CO10: S'bury 3G 127
Sudbury Rd. CO6: Stoke N 1H 143
CO8: Bure 4B 142
CO10: Act 4G 107
CO10: L Mel 7G 105 & 1B 126
CO10: Lave 7B 106
CO10: Newt 1A 128
IP11: Felix 4B 154
IP30: Gt Whe, S'mere 7C 60
Sudbury Sports Cen. 2E 126
Sudbury Station (Rail) 4E 126
Suffolk Apple Juice & Cider Place 1D 161
Suffolk Bus. Cen. IP32: Bury E 2C 60
Suffolk Ct. IP27: B'don 3F 19
Suffolk Dr. IP12: Rend 6B 122
Suffolk Golf Course, The 1E 52
Suffolk Horse Mus. 5H 121
Suffolk New College
(University of East Anglia) 4H 5 (1C 138)
Suffolk Owl Sanctuary 6H 87
Suffolk Pl. IP12: Wood 5J 121
Suffolk Punch Trust, The 1J 141
Suffolk Regiment Mus. 7E 52
Suffolk Retail Pk.
IP1: Ips 2A 4 (7J 131)
Suffolk Rd. CO10: S'bury 3D 126
IP4: Ips 1G 5 (6B 132)
IP32: Bury E 4E 52
NR32: Low 1J 11
Suffolk Sands Holiday Pk.
IP11: Felix 7C 154
Suffolk Showground 5K 139
Suffolk Ski Cen. 7K 137
Suffolk Sq. CO10: S'bury 3D 126
Suffolk Villa Gallery Art Cen. 3H 11
Suffolk Water Pk. 7B 114
Suffolk Way CB8: Newm 4E 46
Suffolk Wildlife Cen. 2A 10
Sulleys Hill IP7: Ray, Ray 3G 145
Sullivan Pl. IP12: Wald 6C 140
Summerfield IP27: Lake 5B 20
Summerfield Cl. IP4: Ips 5H 133
Summerfield Ct. IP4: Ips 5H 133
Summerfield Gdns. NR33: Oul B 3F 11
Summer La. IP12: B'well 3A 124
IP22: Rick 7G 35
Summer Rd. IP31: Wals W 4F 33
NR32: Low 7J 9
Summers Rd. IP32: Bury E 4D 52
Summit Bus. Pk. IP11: Felix 7D 154
Sunbeam Cl. NR33: Car C 6A 10
Suncrest Ri. IP14: Stowu 4J 85
Sunderland Rd. IP11: Felix 7C 154
Sunfield Cl. IP4: Ips 7F 133
Sunhaven Ind. Est. *NR32: Low 6K 9*
(off Cumberland Pl.)
Sun La. CB8: Newm 6G 47
IP12: Wood 5H 121

Sunningdale Av. IP4: Ips 1H 139
IP28: Mide 7H 23
NR33: Low 5G 11
Sunningdale Dr. IP11: Felix 2G 155
Sunnybrook Cl. IP23: Gisli 1H 67
Sunnyfields NR33: Oul B 2F 11
Sunnyhill IP12: Wald 6C 140
Sunnyside *CB8: Newm* 6G 47
(off Park La.)
Sunray Av. IP11: Felix 2G 155
Surbiton Rd. IP1: Ips 5H 131
Surrey Cl. IP13: F'ham 6C 90
Surrey Rd. IP1: Ips 3A 4 (7J 131)
IP11: Felix 4E 154
Surrey St. NR32: Low 7J 9
Sussex Croft IP12: Sutt 2B 140
Sussex Rd. IP32: Bury E 4D 52
NR32: Low 5J 9
Sutherland Dr. NR32: Low 2G 9
SUTTON 2D 165
Sutton Cl. IP12: Wood 5J 121
IP32: Bury E 1A 60
SUTTON COMMON 2B 140
Sutton Grn. IP9: Stut 7E 150
Sutton Hgts. *IP12: Wood* 4J 121
(off Old Maltings App.)
Sutton Hoo 2C 165
Suttons Rd. NR34: Worl 4K 13
Suvla Cotts. *IP8: B'ford* 3C 130
(off Ravens La.)
SWAFFHAM BULBECK 3A 158
SWAFFHAM PRIOR 3A 158
Swain Ct. NR33: Low 5F 11
Swainston Way IP13: Denn 6B 76
Swallow Cl. IP11: Felix 1H 155
Swallow Dr. IP14: Stowm 5J 85
IP27: B'don 4H 19
Swallowfields NR33: Car C 6C 10
Swallow Rd. IP2: Ips 3E 136
Swallowtail Cl. IP8: Ips 6G 137
Swan Cl. IP5: Martl H 6H 135
IP14: Stowm 4D 84
IP19: H'orth 5B 42
Swan Farm M. IP8: Wash 5C 136
Swanfield CO10: L Mel 4H 105
IP29: Laws 7D 80
Swan Gro. CB8: Exn 1B 46
Swan Hill IP8: Wash 5B 136
Swan La. CB8: Exn 1B 46
CB9: Have 3F 101
CO10: L Mel 4H 105
IP6: Weste 1C 132
IP13: Cret 1F 89
IP19: H'orth 5B 42
(not continuous)
IP31: Con W 1A 30
IP33: Bury E 6K 157 (2H 59)
NR34: Barnb 6C 6
Swan Mdw. CO7: Strat M 6G 145
Swan Rd. IP13: W'orth 6H 73
Swansea Av. IP2: Ips 5K 137
SWAN STREET 3C 163
Swan St. CO10: Boxf 6B 128
Swatchway Cl. IP3: Ips 7F 139
Swaynes CO7: Strat M 5G 145
Sweden Pl. IP27: B'don 5E 18
Sweet Briar Cl. CO6: Leav 3A 142
Sweetbriar La. NR34: Fros 4B 44
SWEFLING 3D 161
Swift Cl. NR33: Car C 6C 10
Swift Dr. IP14: Stowm 4J 85
SWILLAND 1B 164
Swilland Rd. IP6: Otl 4H 117
Swill Tub La. IP14: Bac 7C 68
Swinburne Rd. IP1: Ips 2G 131
Swine's Grn. NR34: Becc 4F 13
SWINGLETON GREEN 3D 108 (2D 163)
Swingleton Hill IP7: M Ele 3D 108
Swinton Cl. IP2: Ips 5F 137
Swonnell's Ct. NR32: Oul B 1C 10
Swonnell's Wlk. NR32: Oul B 7C 8
Sycamore Av. NR33: Oul B 2D 10
Sycamore Cl. IP7: Gt Bri 2A 112
IP8: Ips 5E 136
IP16: Leis 4H 93
IP22: Pal 2C 36
NR34: Worl 5H 13
Sycamore Dr. IP12: Rend 5C 122
IP28: B Row 1D 22
IP32: Bury E 7C 54
Sycamore Rd. CO10: Gt Cor 4G 127
IP14: Stowu 2J 85
Sycamores, The *IP19: H'orth* 4B 42
(off Bridge St.)
Sycamore Wlk. IP27: RAF L 4G 21
Sycamore Way CO11: Brant 4C 148
Sydney Brown Ct. *IP7: Hadl* 4H 129
(off Magdalen Rd.)
SYLEHAM 1F 39 (2C 161)
Syleham Rd. IP21: Hox 1E 38
IP21: Wing 1G 39
Sylvester Rd. IP16: Leis 4J 93
Symonds Rd. IP32: Bury E 1K 59

T

Tacket St. IP4: Ips 4F 5 (1B 138)
Tacon Cl. IP23: Eye 7C 38
Tacon Rd. IP11: Felix 7D 154
Tailors Grn. IP14: Bac 6A 68
Takers La. IP14: Stowm 6G 85
Talbot Rd. CO10: S'bury 1E 126
Talbots Mdw. IP21: Stus 1G 37
Tallboys Cl. IP5: Kesg 5C 134
Tallou Ct. IP32: Bury E 1A 60
Tally Ho Cnr. CO7: Strat M 6H 145
Talmash Gdns.
IP2: Ips 7A 4 (2J 137)
Tamage Rd. CO10: Act 4G 107
Tan Ho. *NR34: Becc* 2E 12
(off St Benedict's Rd.)
Tannersfield Way
CB8: Newm 5F 47
Tanners Vw. IP1: Ips 6H 131
Tannery Dr.
IP33: Bury E 7J 157 (3H 59)
Tannery Rd. IP14: Comb 3E 110
TANNINGTON 3C 161
Tannington Rd. IP13: Bed 7G 73
TAN OFFICE 7K 71
TAN OFFICE GREEN 4J 51 (1B 162)
Tan Office La. IP14: Men G 7J 71
IP29: Chev 4J 51
Tansy Cl. NR33: Low 6E 10
Tansy Mdw. IP21: Fress 6B 40
Tanyard Ct. IP12: Wood 6H 121
IP13: F'ham 5C 90
Target Hill IP20: Home 1K 41
Tarn Hows Cl. IP11: Felix 2J 155
Tarragon Wlk. IP28: Red L 7G 25
Tasmania Rd. IP4: Ips 7H 133
Tasman Rd. CB9: Have 4H 101
Tassel Rd. IP32: Bury E 7A 54
Tattersalls Cres. *CB8: Newm* 7G 47
(off The Avenue)
TATTINGSTONE 6H 149 (3B 164)
TATTINGSTONE WHITE HORSE 3B 164
Taunton Cl. IP1: Ips 1K 131
Taunton Rd. IP11: Felix 2E 154
Tavern Ct. IP14: Stowm 4F 85
Tavern La.
IP33: Bury E 4G 157 (7G 53)
Tavern St. IP1: Ips 3E 4 (7A 132)
IP14: Stowm 4F 85
Tawney Cl. IP9: Cap M 2H 147
Tawney's Ride CO8: Bure 5C 142
Tayberry Cl. IP28: Red L 5K 25
Tayberry Pl. IP3: Ips 7G 139
Tayfen Rd.
IP32: Bury E 2G 157 (7G 53)
IP33: Bury E 2G 157 (7G 53)
Tayfen Ter.
IP32: Bury E 1H 157 (6G 53)
Tayler Cl. IP7: Hadl 4H 129
Tayler Rd. IP7: Hadl 4H 129
Taylors Farm IP14: Batt 6B 110
Taylors Farm Rd. CB9: Ked 5C 98
Teal Cl. IP2: Ips 3F 137
IP18: Rey 2H 45
Teal Dr. IP14: Stowm 4J 85
Teal Wlk. IP27: B'don 3J 19
Teasel Cl. CB9: Have 2C 100
IP28: Red L 7G 25
Tedder Cl. IP24: Barnh 6J 27
Tedder Rd. NR32: Low 4G 9
Teesdale NR33: Car C 6D 10
Telegraph Rd. IP28: Ick 3D 26
Telesia Ct. NR32: Low 4G 9
Temperance Pl. NR34: Becc 3E 12
Templar's Ct. CB9: Have 4D 100
TEMPLE BAR 3A 14
Temple Cl. IP28: Ick 2B 26
Temple End CB9: L Thu 6A 96
Temple Pattle CO11: Brant 6B 148
Temple Rd. IP3: Ips 2G 139
IP14: Stowm 5F 85
Tenby Rd. IP2: Ips 5K 137
Tennis Fld. IP29: Chev 2J 51
Tennyson Cl. IP12: Wood 4F 121
Tennyson Rd.
IP4: Ips 4K 5 (1D 138)
IP17: Saxm 5G 91
IP32: Bury E 4E 52
NR32: Low 7J 9
Tenterden Cl. NR33: Car C 4C 10
Tenter Fld. CO7: Strat M 6H 145
Tenter Piece CO10: Lave 6B 106
Tentree Rd. CO10: Gt Wal 5J 107
Tern Cl. CB9: Have 4H 101
Tern Rd. IP2: Ips 4G 137
IP14: Stowm 4H 85
Terrace, The CB8: Newm 6F 47
IP15: Aldeb 5J 95
IP17: Snap 2D 94
IP18: Walb 7H 45
Terra Cotta Pl. CO10: Stans 1D 104
Terry Gdns. IP5: Kesg 6E 134
Tetley Cl. IP13: F'ham 5B 90
Tewkesbury Pl. IP31: Gt Bar 3C 54
Thackeray Gro. IP14: Stowm 3D 84
Thackeray Rd. IP1: Ips 2G 131
Thanet Rd. IP4: Ips 7F 133
Thatchers Wlk. IP14: Stowm 7F 85
THAXTED 3A 162
The ....
Names prefixed with 'The' for example 'The Acorns' are indexed under the main name such as 'Acorns, The'
Theatre Royal
Bury St Edmunds 7J 157 (2H 59)
Theatre St. IP12: Wood 5G 121
Thebe Cl. IP1: Ips 5F 131
THEBERTON 1A 166
Theberton Rd. IP3: Ips 5F 139
Thedwastre Cl. IP30: E'well 2E 64
Thedwastre Rd. IP31: Thur 7A 56
Thellusson Rd. IP12: Rend 5D 122
THELNETHAM 6H 31 (2A 160)
Thelnetham Rd. IP22: B Nor 4G 31
IP22: Hop 3H 31
THELVETON 1B 160
Theobald Cl. IP6: Nee M 3G 111
Theobalds Cl. CO10: L Mel 6G 105
THETFORD 1C 159
Thetford Forest Pk. 7F 19 (1C 159)
Thetford Rd. IP1: Ips 6J 131
IP24: Barnh 4F 27
IP24: F Mag 1G 29
IP27: B'don, San D 3G 19
IP28: Mide 7K 23
IP31: Con W 1A 30
(not continuous)
IP31: F Mag 1G 29
IP31: Forn M 3G 53
IP31: Ixw 4G 29
Thieves La. IP31: Pake 7H 29
Thingoe Hill
IP32: Bury E 1G 157 (6G 53)
Third Av. CO10: Glem 4A 104
Thirling Ct. IP5: Martl H 7G 135
Thirlmere Ct. IP11: Felix 2J 155
Thirlmere Dr. IP14: Stowm 4D 84
Thirlmere Wlk. NR32: Low 4F 9
Thistle Cl. IP2: Ips 2H 137
Thistledown NR33: Car C 5C 10
Thistledown Dr. IP31: Ixw 4J 29
Thistle Way IP28: Red L 5J 25
THISTLEY GREEN 4A 22 (2A 158)
Thixendale NR33: Car C 7D 10
Thomas Arne Cl. IP14: Stowm 2E 84
Thomas Av. IP11: T Mary 7J 153
Thomas Bardwell Dr.
NR35: Bung 4C 14
Thomas Chyd. Cl. IP12: Melt 7G 119
Thomas Cl. IP31: Ixw 6J 29
Thomas Cres. IP5: Kesg 7D 134
Thomas La.
IP33: Bury E 6G 157 (2G 59)
Thomas Walls Cl. IP13: Gru 6J 117
Thomas Young Cl. IP14: Stowm 7F 85
Thompson Cl. IP13: Gru 6H 117
IP14: Haug 2C 70
Thompson Dr. IP12: Rend 6E 122
Thompson Rd. IP1: Ips 5H 131
Thompson Wlk. IP32: Bury E 6E 52
Thomsons La. IP6: A'ing 1G 117
Thong Hall Rd.
IP13: Petti, Wick M 6A 118
THORINGTON 3C 167
Thorington Rd. IP19: B'field 7K 75
THORINGTON STREET 3A 164
Thornbush La. IP8: B'ford 5B 130
IP14: E Sto 3E 86
THORNDON 2C 72 (3B 160)
THORNEY GREEN 2J 85
Thorney Grn. Rd. IP14: Stowu 2J 85
Thorney Hall Cl. IP14: Stowm 4G 85
Thorney Rd. IP9: Cap M 2G 147
Thornham Cl. NR33: Low 5E 10
THORNHAM MAGNA 2B 160
THORNHAM PARVA 2B 160
Thornham Rd. IP23: Gisli 1K 67
Thornham Walled Garden 2B 160
Thornhayes Cl. IP2: Ips 3J 137
Thornhill Rd. IP6: Barh, Clay 2D 114
Thornley Dr. IP4: Ips 5G 133
Thornley Rd. IP11: Felix 4H 155
THORNS 2F 97 (1B 162)
Thorns Cl. CB8: W'rook 2F 97
Thorns Cnr. CB8: W'rook 2F 97
Thorns Mdw. CB8: W'rook 2F 97
Thornton Rd. IP33: Bury E 4E 58
Thorn Wlk. IP12: Sutt 3C 140
Thorn Way IP11: Felix 4D 154
Thornycroft Gdns. NR33: Car C 6A 10
Thoroughfare IP1: Ips 3E 4
IP12: Wood 5H 121
IP19: H'orth 4B 42
THORPE 1C 167
THORPE ABBOTTS 2B 160
THORPE COMMON 5F 153 (3C 165)
THORPE GREEN 1D 163
Thorpe La. IP11: T Mart 5F 153
IP14: Deb 3J 87
THORPE MORIEUX 1D 163
THORPENESS 6D 94 (1A 166)
Thorpeness Golf Course 6C 94
Thorpe Rd. IP15: Aldeb 4K 95
IP16: Thor 2K 95
THORPE STREE 5C 34
THRANDESTON 2B 160
Thrandeston Rd. IP23: Brom 5G 37
IP23: Melli 5A 36
Threadneedle St. IP7: Hadl 3H 129
THREE CROSSWAYS, THE 6H 87
Three Marsh La. IP18: Rey 2H 45
Three Stiles La. IP12: Martl 3J 135
Threshers Yd. IP28: Mide 7H 23
Throckmorton Rd. NR35: Bung 3D 14
Through Duncans IP12: Wood 6F 121
Through Jollys IP5: Kesg 5D 134
Thunderbird Way IP27: RAF L 3H 21
Thurleston La.
IP1: Ips 1H 131 & 1J 131
Thurlow Cl. IP17: Saxm 6G 91
Thurlow Ct. IP14: Stowm 4F 85
Thurlow Pl. CB9: Have 3G 101
Thurlow Rd. CB8: Gt Bra 2B 96
CB9: With 2C 98
THURLTON 1C 167
Thurmans La.
IP11: T Mart, T Mary 7H 153
(not continuous)
Thurne Rd. NR33: Oul B 4E 10
THURSTON 6K 55 (3D 159)
Thurston Ct. IP11: Felix 5B 154
THURSTON END 1B 162
THURSTON PLANCHE 1C 62
Thurston Rd. IP30: Bey 2C 62
IP30: Roug 7H 55
IP31: Gt Bar 2G 55
IP31: Pake 2A 56 & 7G 29
NR32: Low 6J 9
Thurston Station (Rail) 6K 55
THWAITE 3K 69 (3B 160)
Thwaite Rd. IP23: Thorn 4A 72
IP23: Thw, Wick S 3G 69
Thyme Cl. IP28: Red L 5J 25
Tibbenham's Score NR32: Cort 6J 7
Tibbys Way IP18: Sou 4K 45
TIBENHAM 1B 160
Tiberius Cl. CB9: Have 4J 101
Tide Mill
Woodbridge 6J 121
Tide Mill Way IP12: Wood 6J 121
Tideway NR32: Oul B 1D 10
Tidy Rd. IP12: Rend 5C 122
Tiggins La. IP17: Kel 2J 91
TILBURY GREEN 2B 162
TILBURY JUXTA CLARE 2B 162
Tilia Ct. NR34: Ell 7K 13
Till Rd. NR32: Low 7J 9
Timbers, The IP31: Honi 2H 29
Timperley Cl. IP7: Hadl 2H 129
Timperley Rd. IP7: Hadl 2J 129
Timperleys IP8: Hint 1C 144
TIMWORTH GREEN 7E 28 (3C 159)
Tinabrook Cl. IP2: Ips 5G 137
Tinkers End IP16: Thor 6D 94
Tinkers La. IP7: Hadl 4H 129
NR34: Hens 5A 16
Tin River Cl. NR35: Bung 3D 14
Tintern Cl. IP2: Ips 4J 137
Tippett Av. IP14: Stowm 2E 84
Titan Ct. IP1: Ips 5F 131
Titchwell Dr. IP3: Ips 6H 139
Tithe Av. IP28: B Row 2E 22
Tithe Cl. CB8: Gaz 2H 49
(not continuous)
Title Rd. IP17: Midd 6D 78
TIVETSHALL ST MARGARET 1B 160
TIVETSHALL ST MARY 1B 160
Toad Row NR34: Hens 7D 16
Todd Way IP32: Bury E 1C 60
TOFT MONKS 1C 167
Tokio Rd. IP4: Ips 7E 132
Toller Cl. IP12: Orf 6J 125
Toller Rd. IP3: Ips 3C 138
Tolley Cobbold St. IP28: B Row 1D 22
Tollgate Bus. Cen. IP31: Forn M 4G 53
Tollgate Ct. IP6: Barh 3D 114
Tollgate La. IP32: Bury E 5E 52
Toll Ga. Rd. IP9: Cap M 2H 147
Tolworth Rd. IP4: Ips 7E 132

Tom Crisp Way NR33: Low 5E 10
Tom Jennings Cl. CB8: Newm 4F 47
Tomline Ct. IP10: Nac 5A 152
Tomline Rd. IP3: Ips 1E 138
IP11: Felix 5F 155
Tomline Wlk. IP33: Bury E 7C 52
Tommy Flowers Dr. IP5: Kesg 6E 134
Tomo Bus. Pk. IP14: Stowm 5H 85
Tomo Ind. Est. IP14: Stowm 4G 85
Tomo Rd. IP14: Stowm 4H 85
Tomtit's La. IP14: W'den 3J 65
Tonning St. NR32: Low 1J 11
Tooks Comn. NR34: Ilk A 2H 15
Tooks Comn. La. NR34: Ilk A 1H 15
Tooley's Ct. IP4: Ips 4F 5
TOPCROFT 1C 161
TOPCROFT STREET 1C 161
Toper La. IP33: Bury E . . . 7K 157 (2H 59)
Top Green CB8: Dens 7K 97
TOPPESFIELD 3B 162
Toppesfield Cl. IP7: Hadl 4H 129
Toppesfield Gdns. IP7: Hadl 4G 129
Top Rd. IP13: Hask 2C 120
IP21: Fress 6A 40
IP21: Wing 4K 39
NR34: Ilk A, Ilk L 4F 15
Topsfield CO10: Gt Cor 7G 127
Top St. IP12: Martl 1J 135
Tortoiseshell Cl. IP8: Ips 6G 137
TOSTOCK 2G 63 (3D 159)
Tostock Rd. IP30: Bey 3D 62
Tot Hill IP14: Haug 4B 70
Touchey's La. CO7: E Ber 5E 146
Tourist Info. Cen.
Aldeburgh 5K 95
Brandon 3F 19
Bury St Edmunds . . . 5H 157 (1G 59)
Felixstowe 5F 155
Ipswich 4E 4 (1A 138)
Lavenham 6C 106
Lowestoft 1J 11
Mid Suffolk 5F 85
Mildenhall 7J 23
Newmarket 6G 47
Southwold 4K 45
Sudbury 4D 126
Woodbridge 6H 121
Tovells IP13: Uff 5H 119
Tovell's Rd. IP4: Ips 7D 132
Tower Chu. Yd. IP1: Ips 3E 4
Tower Cl. IP27: B'don 4E 18
Tower Cotts. IP24: Barnh 6G 27
Tower Ct. CB9: Have 4D 100
Tower Fld. Rd. IP12: Rend 7B 122
Tower Hill NR34: Becc 5F 13
Tower Hill Rd. IP12: Holl 2G 141
Tower La. IP15: Aldeb 5J 95
Tower Mill La. IP7: Hadl 3J 129
Tower Mill Rd. IP1: Ips 6H 131
NR35: Bung 3B 14
Tower Ramparts
IP1: Ips 2D 4 (7A 132)
(not continuous)
Tower Ramparts Shop. Cen.
IP1: Ips 3E 4 (7A 132)
Tower Rd. IP11: Felix 4E 154
NR33: Low 7F 11
Tower St. IP1: Ips 3E 4 (7A 132)
Towlers Ct. IP27: B'don 4F 19
Town End Cl. CB9: Have 2E 100
Town Farm Cl. IP20: Metf 6G 41
Town Farm Est. IP12: Orf 6H 125
Town Grn. IP14: Stowm 4E 84
Town Hall Galleries 3D 4
(off Princes St.)
Townhouse La. IP22: W'field 1K 33
Townhouse Rd. IP31: Wals W 6H 33
Townlands Dr. NR34: Becc 5E 12
Town La. IP13: Gru 5J 117
Townlane Rd. IP33: Bury E 5H 59
Townsend Way NR32: Low 2F 9
Townsfield Cotts. IP13: Denn 5C 76
Town Steps IP15: Aldeb 5J 95
TOWN STREET 5D 18 (1B 158)
Trafalgar Cl. IP4: Ips 2K 5 (7D 132)
Trafalgar Rd. CO10: S'bury 2F 127
Trafalgar St. NR32: Low 1H 11
Trafford Cl. IP14: Old N 5A 70
Tranmere Gro. IP1: Ips 3H 131
Traverse, The
IP33: Bury E 4H 157 (1G 59)
Treetops IP11: Felix 1D 154
Treeview IP14: Stowm 4C 84
Trefoil Cl. IP2: Ips 2H 137
Trefoil Ct. CB9: Have 4E 100
Trelawny Ho. IP11: Felix 7C 154
Tremlett La. IP5: Kesg 6F 135
Trent Rd. IP3: Ips 4D 138
IP32: Bury E 3F 53
Trevethan Cl. IP32: Bury E 6E 52
Trevose IP11: Felix 4G 155
Triangle Yd. NR32: Low 6K 9
TRIMLEY LOWER STREET
. . . . 7F 153 (3C 165)
Trimley Rd. IP10: Kirt 2H 153
TRIMLEY ST MARTIN
. . . . 5H 153 (3C 165)
TRIMLEY ST MARY 1B 154 (3C 165)
Trimley Sports Club 5G 153
Trimley Station (Rail) 1B 154
Trinity Av. IP11: Felix 5A 154
IP28: Mide 6J 23
Trinity Cl. IP5: Kesg 6K 133
IP12: Wood 7E 120
IP18: Sou 4K 45
Trinity Dr. CB8: Newm 7H 47
Trinity Gdns. NR35: Bung 2B 14
Trinity Gild CO10: Lave 6C 106
Trinity Ind. Est. IP11: Felix 6B 154
Trinity Link CB9: Have 2F 101
Trinity M. IP33: Bury E . . . 3F 157 (7F 53)
Trinity Rd. NR32: Low 7K 9
Trinity St. IP3: Ips 7J 5 (2C 138)
IP18: Sou 4K 45
NR35: Bung 2B 14
Trinity Terminal 6A 154
Trinity Wlk. IP14: Stowu 1K 85
Troon Ct. IP28: Forn M 1F 53
Troon Gdns. IP4: Ips 4F 133
Trossachs, The NR32: Oul 6C 8
TROSTON 1D 28 (2C 159)
Troston Rd. IP31: Honi 4F 29
Truman Lodge IP16: Thor 6D 94
(off The Benthills)
Trundley Cl. CB9: Have 1E 100
Truro Cres. IP5: Kesg 7A 134
Trustram's Drift IP29: Shim 3E 106
Truswell Ter. CO11: Brant 6C 148
Tubby Wlk. NR32: Oul 3E 8
TUDDENHAM 5C 26 (2B 158)
Tuddenham Av. IP4: Ips . . . 1H 5 (6C 132)
Tuddenham La. IP5: Rush A 3F 133
IP6: Tud 3F 133
IP6: Witn 4C 116
Tuddenham Rd. IP4: Ips . . . 1F 5 (6B 132)
IP28: B Mil 2J 25
Tuddenham Rd. Bus. Cen.
IP4: Ips 2E 132
TUDDENHAM ST MARTIN
. . . . 7C 116 (2B 164)
Tudor Cl. CB9: Have 4G 101
CO10: S'bury 2D 126
IP9: Shot G 6D 156
IP13: F'ham 6C 90
IP21: Hox 3D 38
IP29: Chedb 5K 51
Tudor Ct. IP23: Occ 5A 72
Tudor Grn. CO10: S'bury 1D 126
Tudor Pl. IP4: Ips 3G 5 (7B 132)
Tudor Rd. CO10: S'bury 1D 126
Tudor Wlk. NR33: Car C 5D 10
Tuffen La. IP22: Hind 7H 31
Tuffs Rd. IP23: Eye 5D 38
Tulyar Wlk. CB8: Newm 1E 46
Tuns Fld. IP30: C'field 7J 81
Tuns La. IP33: Bury E 6J 157 (2H 59)
TUNSTALL 6G 123 (1D 165)
Tunstall Dr. NR32: Oul B 4E 8
Tunstall Grn. IP12: Tun 6F 123
Tunstall Rd. IP13: Cam A 2C 122
Tupman Wlk. IP33: Bury E 3J 157
Turban, The IP12: Wood 5H 121
Turing Ct. IP5: Kesg 6E 134
Turino Av. IP5: Martl H 6J 135
Turin St. IP2: Ips 7E 4 (2A 138)
Turkentine Cl. CO10: Gt Cor 6J 127
Turkeyhall La. IP14: Bac 5B 68
Turnberry Cl. NR33: Oul B 5E 10
Turnberry Dr. IP28: Forn M 2F 53
Turnbull Cl. IP5: Kesg 6E 134
Turner Cl. CB9: Have 2C 100
CO10: S'bury 1F 127
NR32: Low 2H 9
Turner Gdns. IP12: Wood 7E 120
Turner Gro. IP5: Kesg 5D 134
Turner La. IP14: Haug 2B 70
Turner Rd. IP3: Ips 6E 138
IP14: Stowm 3D 84
Turn La. IP12: Wood 6H 121
Turnpike IP14: L Sto 1E 86
Turnpike Hill CB9: With 2B 98
Turnpike La. IP12: Melt 4J 121
IP28: Red L 7G 25
Turnpike Rd. CB8: Kenn 7G 25
IP28: Red L 7G 25
Turnstile La. NR35: Bung 2B 14
(off Lwr. Olland St.)
Turnstone Cl. IP28: Mide 7J 23
Turnstone Dr. IP32: Bury E 7C 54
Turrell Dr. NR33: Kess 4J 17
Turret Grn. Ct. IP1: Ips 4E 4 (1A 138)
Turret La. IP4: Ips 4E 4 (1A 138)
Tutelina Ri. IP30: Gt Whe 7C 60
Tutelina Rd. IP30: Gt Whe 7C 60
Tut Hill IP28: Forn S 5B 52
Tweed Cl. CB8: Mou 5D 48
Twelve Acre App. IP5: Kesg 6B 134
Twickenham Av. IP27: B'don 6E 18
Twinnings, The IP14: Stowm 7E 84
Twin Oak Dr. IP13: B'ham 1C 76
TWINSTEAD 3C 163
TWINSTEAD GREEN 3C 163
Two Acres IP9: Cap M 1J 147
Two Counties Est. CB9: Have 6H 101
Two Ho. Cl. IP13: Wick M 5B 118
Tydeman Cl. IP4: Ips 1J 5 (6C 132)
Tydemans Ct. IP14: Stowm 4F 85
TYE GREEN 3A 162
Tye Grn. CO10: Glem 4A 104
Tye Grn. Paddock CO10: Glem . . . 4A 104
Tye La. IP8: B'ford 2A 130
Tye Rd. IP3: Ips 6H 5 (2C 138)
Tyes Cnr. IP13: Bed 7G 73
Tylers Grn. IP11: T Mary 1B 154
Tyler St. IP2: Ips 7F 5 (2B 138)
Tylers Way IP14: Stowm 7F 85
Tymmes Pl. IP13: Hask 2D 120
Tyndale Gdns. IP11: Felix 3H 155
Tyrell Oak IP14: Gipp 4E 70
Tyrone Cl. IP1: Ips 3F 131

U

UBBESTON GREEN 2D 161
Ubbeston Way NR33: Low 5E 10
UFFORD 5H 119 (1C 165)
Ufford Pk. Golf Course 7H 119
Ufford Pl. CB9: Have 3G 101
IP13: Uff 6J 119
Ufford Rd. IP12: B'well, Eyk 7K 119
UGGESHALL 2C 167
Uggeshall Cl. NR32: Low 3F 9
Ullswater NR33: Car C 7C 10
Ullswater Av. IP11: Felix 1J 155
Ullswater Rd. IP13: Cam A 3A 122
Ulster Av. IP1: Ips 4F 131
Undercliff IP11: Felix 5F 155
Undercliff Rd. E. IP11: Felix 4H 155
Undercliff Rd. W. IP11: Felix 5E 154
Underhill IP14: Stowm 5E 84
Underwood Cl. NR32: Low 2F 9
UNDLEY 1A 158
Undley Rd. IP27: Lake 7A 20
Unicorn Pl. IP33: Bury E 7J 53
Union Hill IP7: Sem 7A 112
Union La. NR32: Oul 3D 8
Union Pl. NR33: Low 2H 11
Union Rd. IP14: One 3B 84
NR32: Low 7H 9
Union St. IP4: Ips 3F 5 (7B 132)
Union St. E. IP14: Stowm 4F 85
Union St. W. IP14: Stowm 4F 85
(not continuous)
Unitarian Meeting House
Ipswich 4D 4
Unity Rd. IP14: Stowm 5F 85
Unity St. IP3: Ips 6J 5 (2C 138)
University Av. IP3: Ips 6H 5 (2B 138)
University of East Anglia
Suffolk New College
. . . . 4H 5 (1C 138)
UPEND 1B 162
UPGATE STREET 1A 160
Upland Rd. IP4: Ips 7E 132
Uplands, The IP16: Thor 6C 94
NR34: Becc 4G 13
Uplands Cl. NR33: Car C 5B 10
Uplands Cres. CO10: S'bury 2D 126
Uplands Rd. CO10: S'bury 2D 126
IP16: Thor 6C 94
Uplands Rd. Nth. NR33: Car C 4C 10
Uplands Rd. Sth. NR33: Car C 6B 10
Uplands Way IP19: H'orth 3B 42
Upper Av. IP19: H'orth 3B 42
Up. Barclay St. IP4: Ips . . . 3F 5 (1B 138)
Up. Brook St. IP4: Ips 4E 4 (7A 132)
Up. Cavendish St. IP3: Ips 1E 138
UPPER DOVERCOURT 3C 165
Up. East St. CO10: S'bury 3E 126
Upperfield Dr. IP11: Felix 2G 155
Up. Grange Rd. NR34: Becc 4D 12
Upper Grn. CO10: Stoke C 6J 99
IP30: Fels 6C 82
Up. Heyford IP27: RAF L 5H 21
Up. High St. IP1: Ips 1D 4 (7A 132)
UPPER LAYHAM 7J 129 (2A 164)
Upper Mdw. IP31: Wals W 6H 33
Up. Melton Ter. IP12: Melt 7G 119
Up. Moorfield Rd. IP12: Wood . . . 4G 121
Upper Nth. St. CO10: Hund 1J 99
Up. Olland St. NR35: Bung 2B 14
Up. Orwell Courts IP4: Ips 4F 5
Up. Orwell St. IP4: Ips 4F 5 (1B 138)
Upper Reeve CO10: Gt Cor 7G 127
Up. Rose La. IP22: Pal 1D 36
UPPER STREET 6A 150 (3B 164)
Upper St. CO7: Strat M 6G 145
CO10: Stans 1D 104
IP6: Witn 1B 116
IP7: Lay 7K 129
Up. Street La. IP22: W'field 2G 33
UPPER TOWN
Bury St Edmunds 1A 56
Stowmarket 1J 65
Upper Tye CO10: Gt Cor 6H 127
UPPER WEYBREAD 3A 40
UPSHER GREEN 7B 108
Upsons Way IP5: Kesg 5E 134
Up Street IP31: Bard 2D 32
UPTHORPE 2D 159
Upthorpe Rd. IP31: Stant 7D 32
Upton Cl. IP4: Ips 3J 5 (7C 132)
Upton Pl. IP16: Leis 4H 93
Upwood IP27: RAF L 4H 21
Urban Rd. IP16: Leis 3J 93
Uvedale Ct. IP6: Nee M 4H 111
Uvedale Gdns. IP6: Nee M 4H 111
Uxbridge Cres. IP3: Ips 5G 139

V

Vale La. IP33: Bury E 3J 59
Valentine Way IP30: Hess 7D 62
Vale Ter. CO8: Bure 6B 142
Valiant Rd. IP5: Martl H 6G 135
Valiant St. IP28: B Row 1D 22
Valley Cl. CO11: Brant 4C 148
IP1: Ips 4A 132
IP12: Wood 5H 121
IP19: Holt 4E 42
Valley Ct. IP16: Leis 3H 93
Valley Farm Dr. IP8: Spro 2A 136
Valley Farm La. IP12: Melt 2H 121
Valley Farm Rd. IP12: Melt 2H 121
Valley La. IP9: Wher 3F 149
IP14: Bux 7F 83
IP14: Gt Fin . . . . 6J 83 & 2A 110
Valley Rd.
CO10: Gt Wal, Newt
. . . . 1K 127 & 1A 128
IP1: Ips 6J 131
IP4: Ips 6J 131
IP7: Gt Bri 1A 112
IP14: Batt 7E 110
IP16: Leis 3J 93
Valley Ter. IP16: Leis 3J 93
Valley Vw. CO10: Stans 2D 104
Valleyview Dr. IP4: Rush A 2K 139
Valley Vw. Ri. IP12: Martl 2J 135
Valley Wlk. IP11: Felix 3E 154
Valley Wash CO10: Hund 1G 99
Valley Way CB8: Newm 5E 46
Vallibus Cl. NR32: Oul 4D 8
Valsheda, The IP4: Ips 5F 5
Van Dyck Cl. NR32: Low 2G 9
Vandyck Rd. IP3: Ips 6E 138
Vange Pl. CB9: Have 3G 101
Vanners Rd. CB9: Have 4F 101
Vaughan St. IP2: Ips 7E 4 (2A 138)
Velda Cl. NR33: Oul B 5E 10
Venlaw, The NR33: Low 4G 11
Ventris Cl. IP2: Ips 1F 137
Verdure Cl. NR32: Oul 3E 8
Vere Gdns. IP1: Ips 3A 132
Vermeer Cl. NR32: Low 2G 9
Vermont Cl. IP4: Ips 6C 132
Vermont Cres. IP4: Ips 1G 5 (6B 132)
Vermont Rd. IP4: Ips 1G 5 (6B 132)
Verneuil Av. IP14: Stowm 7E 84
Vernon St. IP2: Ips 6E 4 (2A 138)
Vetch Wlk. CB9: Have 2C 100
Veyses End CO7: Strat M 5H 145
Viburnum Grn. NR32: Low 6H 9
Vicarage Cl. IP8: B'ford 4D 130
Vicarage Farm La. IP31: Gt Bar . . . 1D 54
Vicarage Fld. CO10: Gt Cor 6G 127
Vicarage Gdns. IP14: Deb 2H 87
IP28: Mide 7H 23
Vicarage Hill IP12: Wood 5H 121
Vicarage La. CO10: Act 4G 107
CO10: New G 6F 107
IP8: B'ford 4D 130
IP9: Wher 2G 149
NR35: Mett 3E 14
Vicarage Rd. CB8: Newm 6H 47
IP11: Felix 4C 154
IP13: Laxf 6C 74
IP14: Wins 4K 87
IP21: Wing 2G 39
Victoria Av. IP27: B'don 4E 18
Victoria Cl. IP31: Thur 6A 56
Victoria Cotts. CB8: Newm 6H 47
Victoria Ct. NR33: Low 3H 11
Victoria Gdns.
IP22: W'field 2J 33
Victoria Hill IP23: Eye 6C 38

Victoria Ho. IP1: Ips 2A 4
IP33: Bury E 3F 157
(off Springfield Rd.)
Victoria Mill Rd. IP13: F'ham 7A 90
Victoria Rd. CB9: Have 4B 100
IP11: Felix 5E 154
IP12: Wood 5H 121
IP14: Stowm 3G 85
IP15: Aldeb 5H 95
NR33: Oul B 2D 10
Victoria Row IP27: Eris 7G 21
Victoria St. IP1: Ips 2A 4 (7J 131)
IP11: Felix 4F 155
IP18: Sou 4K 45
IP33: Bury E 1F 59
Victoria Ter. IP21: Fress 6C 40
IP30: E'well 1E 64
NR33: Low 2J 11
Victoria Way CB8: Newm 2E 46
Victor Rd. IP31: Honi 4F 29
Victory Cl. IP33: Bury E 4J 59
Victory Ct. IP14: Stowm 6G 85
Victory Rd. IP4: Ips 6E 132
IP16: Leis 4H 93
View Point Rd. IP11: Felix 7C 154
Viking Cl. IP12: Martl 3J 135
IP23: Gisli 1G 67
Viking Hgts. IP12: Martl 3J 135
Viking Rd. IP14: Stowm 5E 84
Vikings Cl. IP29: Stann 3G 81
Village Way IP12: Wald 6C 140
NR32: Low 3G 9
Vincent Cl. CB8: Newm 2E 46
IP1: Ips 5G 131
Vincent Drift IP5: Kesg 6F 135
Vine Cl. IP31: Con W 1B 30
Vinefields, The
IP33: Bury E 4K 157 (1H 59)
Vine Rd. IP6: Otl 1K 117
Vinery Cl. IP13: Wick M 6B 118
Vinery Rd.
IP33: Bury E 7F 157 (3F 59)
Vines, The IP17: Kel 2J 91
Vine Wlk. IP9: Cap M 2H 147
Vinnicombe Ct. IP2: Ips 5G 137
Violet Cl. IP2: Ips 2H 137
IP32: Bury E 1B 60
Violet Hill Rd. IP14: Stowm 3E 84
Virginia Rd. IP28: RAF M 2C 22
Virginia St. IP2: Ips 3B 138
Visdelou Ter. IP9: Shot G 6E 156
Vista Ct. IP2: Ips 6B 4
Vyces Rd. IP13: F'ham 6B 90

W

Wacker Fld. Rd. IP12: Rend 6D 122
WACTON 1B 160
Wadd La. IP17: Snap . . . .1A 94 & 7A 92
Waddlegoose La. IP14: Deb 1K 87
Waddling La.
NR32: Blun, S'ton . . . . . .3C 6 & 1A 8
Wade Cres. CO10: L Wal 5C 108
Wade Hall La. NR34: Nor C 5B 6
Wadehall New Dam NR34: Nor C . . .5C 6
Wadehall Old Dam NR34: Nor C 5C 6
Wades Gro. IP5: Kesg 6E 134
Wade's La. IP7: Ray 1G 145
IP9: Shot 1A 156
Wades Wood IP30: Wool 4A 64
Wadgate Rd. IP11: Felix 4D 154
Wadhurst Rd. IP3: Ips 3H 139
Waggoners Ct. IP12: Wood 5G 121
Wagtail Dr. IP14: Stowm 3H 85
IP32: Bury E 7B 54
WAINFORD 1D 14
Wainford Cl. NR34: Worl 4J 13
Wainford Rd. NR35: Bung 1E 14
Wainwright Cl. NR32: Low 2F 9
Wainwright Gdns. IP6: Gt Bla 2A 114
Wainwright Way IP5: Kesg 5D 134
Wake Av. IP28: Mide 7J 23
WAKES COLNE 3C 163
WALBERSWICK 7G 45 (3C 167)
Walberswick Way NR32: Oul B 5F 9
WALCOT GREEN 1B 160
Walcott Wlk. NR33: Low 4G 11
Waldegraves, The CO8: Bure 6B 142
Waldingfield Rd. CO10: Act 4H 107
CO10: S'bury 3E 126
WALDRINGFIELD 6C 140 (2C 165)
Waldringfield Golf Course 5A 140
WALDRINGFIELD HEATH 6A 140
Waldringfield Rd.
IP12: Martl . . . . . . .3K 135 & 4B 140
Walk, The IP1: Ips 3E 4 (7A 132)
IP5: Kesg 5B 134
IP11: Felix 2D 154
(not continuous)
IP14: Bac 3C 68
NR34: Becc 3E 12
Walkbarn La. IP11: T Mart 4F 153
Walker Chase IP5: Kesg 7C 134
Walker Cl. IP3: Ips 1G 139
Walker Gdns. NR34: Wrent 1D 44
Walkers Way NR35: Bung 3B 14
Wallace Rd. IP1: Ips 5G 131
Wallers Gro. IP2: Ips 2H 137
Wallis Ct. IP28: Mide 5G 23
Wall St. IP5: Kesg 6F 135
Walmer Cl. NR33: Low 4F 11
Walmer Rd. NR33: Low 4F 11
Walnut Cl. CO10: Act 3G 107
IP11: Felix 1J 155
IP22: Hop 3H 31
IP27: B'don 5H 19
IP27: RAF L 4G 21
Walnut Gro. IP28: W'ton 2A 24
Walnut Mdw. IP10: Kirt 1H 153
Walnuts, The IP13: Uff 5H 119
NR34: Worl 4H 13
Walnuts La.
IP13: Petti, Wick M 1J 119
Walnut Tree Av. IP12: Rend 6C 122
Walnut Tree Cl. IP8: B'ford 3C 130
IP14: Stowu 2K 85
Walnut Tree La. CO10: S'bury 4C 126
IP9: Hark 6H 151
Walnut Tree Mdw. IP14: Ston A . . .6G 87
Walnut Tree Wlk. IP14: Stowm 4E 84
WALPOLE 3H 75 (2D 161)
Walpole La. IP19: Wal 3H 75
Walpole Rd. IP19: B'field 7F 75
IP19: Cook 1J 75
IP19: H'orth 7A 42
(not continuous)
WALSHAM LE WILLOWS
. . . . .6G 33 (2A 160)
Walsham Rd. IP14: Finn 3F 67
IP22: W'field 3H 33
IP31: Ixw, Stant, Stowl 5J 29
(not continuous)
Walsingham Cl. CO10: Gt Cor . . .6H 127
Walsingham Ct. IP2: Ips 6H 137
Walsingham M. IP22: Rick 6H 35
Walsingham Rd. IP33: Bury E 3D 58
Waltham Cl. IP2: Ips 4J 137
WALTHAM'S CROSS 3A 162
WALTON 2D 154 (3C 165)
Walton Av. IP11: Felix 6C 154
Walton Cl. IP14: Stowm 2D 84
Walton Ho. IP1: Ips 3A 4
Walton Rd. IP11: Felix 5A 154
NR32: Low 7H 9
Walton Way IP27: B'don 5F 19
Wamil Rd. IP28: Mide 7F 23
Wamil Wlk. IP28: Mide 1D 24
Wamil Way IP28: Mide 7H 23
WANGFORD
Beccles 6C 44 (3C 167)
Lakenheath 1B 158
Wangford Rd. IP18: Rey 1F 45
IP27: Lake 2D 20
NR34: Ugg . . . . .7K 15 & 4B 44
NR34: Wang 7C 44
Wannock Cl. NR33: Car C 5C 10
Wantisden Cnr. IP12: But 5C 124
Warbler Way IP14: Stowm 4H 85
Ward Cl. IP7: Hadl 1H 129
WARD GREEN 3A 160
Wardlaw Ct. IP14: Deb 2H 87
Wardley Cl. IP2: Ips 5F 137
Ward Rd. IP8: Ips 5D 136
Wards Vw. IP5: Kesg 5E 134
Wareham Av. IP3: Ips 3H 139
Warene Cl. IP13: F'ham 6C 90
War Memorial Mus. 5K 9
Warner Way CO10: S'bury 3F 127
WARREN, THE 1K 45
Warren Av. IP17: Saxm 6J 91
Warren Chase IP5: Kesg 6E 134
Warren Cl. IP27: B'don 4G 19
IP27: Lake 6B 20
IP30: E'well 3D 64
IP31: B Ash 2D 66
Warren Ct. CB9: Have 4D 100
Warrener's Reach IP27: Lake 7C 20
WARREN HEATH 5K 139
Warren Heath Av. IP3: Ips 4H 139
Warren Heath Rd. IP3: Ips 4H 139
Warren Hill La. IP15: Aldeb 2H 95
Warren Hill Rd. IP12: Wood 6F 121
WARREN HILLS 2J 37
Warren La. IP5: Martl H 6G 135
IP9: Erw 4A 156
IP14: W'den 4E 64
IP30: E'well 3D 64
IP30: Wool 6D 64
Warren Rd. CB8: Kenn 5J 25
IP28: Red L 5J 25
NR32: Low 4J 9
Warrens La. IP22: Bote 5J 35
Warrington Rd. IP1: Ips . . .1C 4 (6K 131)
Warrington St. CB8: Newm 7G 47
Warwick Av. IP12: Wood 4G 121
IP19: H'orth 3C 42
Warwick Ct. CB9: Have 3D 100
Warwick Dr. IP32: Bury E 4E 52
Warwick Rd. IP4: Ips 2J 5 (7C 132)
Wash, The IP17: Midd 7D 78
WASHBROOK 5B 136 (2B 164)
WASHBROOK STREET 3A 136
Washington St. IP28: B Row 1D 22
Wash La. CB8: W'rook 4G 97
CO10: Boxf 7E 128
IP6: Witn 2B 116
IP13: Denn 5D 76
IP14: Gt Fin, One 4C 84
IP14: Mendl 4J 71
IP17: Midd 7C 78
IP17: Westl 5G 79
IP19: Mells 7E 42
IP19: Spex, Wiss 1A 42
IP19: Wen 2G 43
IP22: Hind 7K 31
IP22: Wort 1F 35
IP30: Drin . . . . .7K 63 & 1H 83
NR33: Kess 5K 17
NR34: Becc, R'field 7D 12
(not continuous)
NR34: Ugg 4B 44
Wash La. Cnr. IP14: Gt Fin 4B 84
Watch Ho. Hill NR35: Mett 2E 14
Waterbeach Rd. IP12: Sutt 2E 140
Watercourse, The CB8: Newm 5G 47
WATER END 2A 162
Water Farm Dr. IP7: Ray 1J 145
Waterford Rd. IP1: Ips 3F 131
Waterfront Building
Ipswich 5G 5 (1C 138)
Waterhead La. IP12: Melt 2K 121
Watering Cl. IP8: S'ham 3J 113
Water La. CB8: Dens, Stradi 6H 97
CB8: Gt Bra 1A 96
CB9: Stur 6K 101
CO6: Nay 7H 143
CO6: Pols 5C 144
CO8: Bure 5A 142
CO10: Cave 5H 103
CO10: L Mel 5H 105
IP7: Lay 7J 129
IP13: Wick M 6D 118
IP13: W'orth 4F 73
IP14: Deb 2H 87
IP21: Wey 1D 40
IP22: Rick 7G 35
IP22: Thel 5G 31
IP24: Barnh 6G 27
NR32: Low 5H 9
Waterlane Leisure Cen. 5H 9
Waterloo Av. IP16: Leis 3G 93
Waterloo Cl. CB8: Newm 1D 46
Waterloo M. IP16: Leis 3H 93
Waterloo Pk. IP16: Leis 3H 93
Waterloo Rd. IP1: Ips 1A 4 (6J 131)
NR33: Low 2J 11
Watermill Cl. IP7: Lay 7J 129
Water Mill La. IP21: Hox 1C 38
Waters Av. NR33: Car C 6B 10
WATERSIDE 2A 158
Water St. CO10: Lave 6C 106
Water Vole Cl. IP14: Stowm 6G 85
Waterworks Rd. IP28: RAF M 2C 22
Waterworks St. IP4: Ips . . .4G 5 (1B 138)
Watery La. IP13: Hask 2B 120
Watson Cl. IP33: Bury E 4H 59
Watson Way IP12: Alder 5H 141
Watt Cl. IP12: Alder 5J 141
WATTISFIELD 2H 33 (2A 160)
Wattisfield Rd. IP22: Hind 6B 34
IP31: Wals W 6G 33
WATTISHAM 1A 164
Wattisham Airfield 1A 112
Wattisham Rd. IP7: Bild 5J 109
WATTISHAM STONE 2K 109
Watts Ct. IP4: Ips 4F 5 (1B 138)
Waveney & Oulton Broad Yacht Club
. . . . .1C 10
Waveney Cl. IP17: Saxm 5H 91
Waveney Cres. NR33: Low 2F 11
Waveney Dr. NR33: Low 2F 11
Waveney Gymnastics Club 2G 11
Waveney Hill NR32: Oul B 1A 10
Waveney Mkt. Nth. NR32: Low 7K 9
Waveney Residential Pk.
NR34: Becc 2E 12
Waveney Rd. IP1: Ips 5G 131
IP11: Felix 5D 154
IP32: Bury E 4F 53
NR32: Low 1J 11
NR34: Becc 4E 12
NR35: Bung 4D 14
Waveney Ter. CB9: Have 4F 101
Waveney Valley Bus. Pk.
NR35: Dit 2C 14
Waymil Ct. IP28: Mide 7H 23
Wayne Cl. NR32: Low 3G 9
Wayside Cl. IP14: Stowm 7F 85
Weald, The NR32: Oul 6D 8
Weatherby Cres. CB8: Newm 4G 47
Weaver Cl. IP1: Ips 5F 131
Weavers Cl. CO10: Lave 5C 106
IP7: Hadl 3H 129
IP14: Stowm 7E 84
Weaver's Ct. CO10: S'bury 4D 126
Weavers Dr. CO10: Glem 5A 104
Weaver's La. CO10: S'bury 4D 126
Weavers Ter. CO10: S'bury 4D 126
(off Weavers La.)
Weavers Way IP6: Barh 3C 114
Webb Rd. IP14: Stowm 7F 85
Webb's Cl. IP14: Comb 2E 110
Webbs Ct. IP5: Kesg 6C 134
Webb's Row IP27: B'don 3G 19
Webb St. IP2: Ips 7E 4 (3A 138)
Webster St. NR35: Bung 2A 14
Weddell Rd. CB9: Have 5H 101
WEETING 1B 158
Weir Pl. IP10: Kirt 1H 153
Welbeck Cl. IP11: T Mary 1C 154
NR34: Barnb 6C 6
Welbourne Way NR34: Barnb 6C 6
Welburn Cl. IP12: Rend 6C 122
Welch Cl. NR34: Mut 2B 16
Welham La. IP28: Ris 2B 50
Welhams Way CO11: Brant 5C 148
Well Belt CB8: Newm 7J 47
Well Bottom CB8: Newm 3K 47
Well Cl. Sq. IP13: F'ham 6C 90
Wellesley Rd. IP4: Ips 5K 5 (1D 138)
Well Fld. IP6: Henl 6J 115
Wellington Cl. IP7: Hadl 2H 129
IP27: B'don 4G 19
IP28: W Row 6C 22
Wellington Cotts. NR32: Low 6J 9
(off Clapham Rd. Nth.)
Wellington Ct. IP1: Ips 1A 4
Wellington Esplanade
NR33: Low 3H 11
Wellington Rd. IP23: Eye 6D 38
IP28: RAF M 2C 22
NR33: Low 6F 11
Wellington St. CB8: Newm 6G 47
IP1: Ips 1A 4 (6J 131)
Wellington Ter. CB9: Have 4D 100
Well La. CO10: Clar 5C 102
Wells Cl. IP4: Ips 3G 5 (7C 132)
Wells Ct. IP28: Mide 6H 23
Wells Hall Rd. CO10: Gt Cor 6G 127
Well St. IP33: Bury E 3H 157 (1G 59)
Wells Way IP14: Deb 3G 87
Wellum Cl. CB9: Have 4D 100
(off York Rd.)
Wembley Av. NR34: Becc 4E 12
Wendling IP27: RAF L 4H 21
Wendy Cl. IP9: Chelm 2H 151
Wenham La. CO7: Strat M 1C 146
Wenham Rd. IP8: Cop 7A 136
WENHASTON 2H 43 (3C 167)
Wenhaston La. IP19: Blyth 7F 43
Wenhaston Rd. IP19: Wen 5K 75
Wenhaston Way NR32: Oul B 5E 8
Wensleydale NR33: Car C 6D 10
Wensum Gdns. NR32: Low 5H 9
Wentford Ct. CB9: Have 3B 100
Wentford Vw. CO10: Clar 2C 102
Wentworth Cl. IP7: Hadl 4K 129
IP8: Nett 2K 113
IP28: Forn M 2F 53
Wentworth Dr. IP8: Ips 4E 136
IP11: Felix 2H 155
IP28: Mide 6H 23
Wentworth Rd. IP3: Ips 6K 139
IP15: Aldeb 5K 95
Wentworth Ter. CB9: Have 3D 100
Wentworth Way NR33: Oul B 5E 10
Wesel Av. IP11: Felix 4C 154
Wesleyan Chapel La. NR32: Low . . .6K 9
(off High St.)
Wesley Cl. NR34: Becc 6E 12
Wesley Ho. NR32: Low 6K 9
(off High St.)
Wesley St. NR32: Low 6J 9
Wesley Way IP1: Ips 5H 131
W. Bank Terminal IP2: Ips 4A 138
Westbar IP16: Thor 6D 94
(off The Sanctuary)
WEST BERGHOLT 3D 163
WESTBOURNE 5H 131
Westbourne Ct. CB9: Have 3F 101
Westbourne Rd. IP1: Ips 4H 131
Westbury Av. IP33: Bury E 1D 58
Westbury Rd. IP4: Ips 5F 133
West Dr. IP27: B'don 5D 18
IP28: Mide 7H 23
Westend La. CB9: Ked 6C 98
West End Rd. IP1: Ips 4A 4 (1J 137)

WESTERFIELD 1C 132 (2B 164)
Westerfield Bus. Cen.
IP6: Weste 2C 132
Westerfield Ct. IP4: Ips 6B 132
Westerfield La.
IP6: Tud . . . . .1E 132 & 7C 116
Westerfield Rd. IP4: Ips . . .1F 5 (6B 132)
IP6: Weste . . . . . .1C 132 & 7A 116
Westerfield Station (Rail) 2C 132
Westerings, The CO6: Nay 5H 143
Western Av. CB9: Have 2D 100
IP11: Felix 2J 155
Western Cl. IP4: Rush A 2K 139
Western's End CO11: Brant 5C 148
Western Way IP33: Bury E 7D 52
Westfield CO10: Clar 6B 102
Westgarth Gdns. IP33: Bury E 2E 58
Westgate IP16: Thor 6D 94
Westgate St. CO10: L Mel 1H 105
IP1: Ips 3D 4 (7A 132)
IP33: Bury E 6H 157 (2G 59)
West Gro. NR33: Low 6F 11
WESTHALL 2C 167
Westhall Gro. End IP21: Stradb . . .5H 39
Westhall Rd. NR32: Low 3G 9
W. Herne La. IP22: Redg 1A 34
West Hill IP16: Aldr 7H 93
Westholme Cl. IP12: Wood 6G 121
Westholme Rd. IP1: Ips 4J 131
WESTHORPE 3A 160
Westhorpe Rd. IP14: Finn 6G 67
IP14: Wyve 1D 68
Westland IP5: Martl H 6G 135
Westland Rd. NR33: Oul B 3D 10
West La. IP15: Aldeb 6J 95
West Lawn IP4: Ips 5F 133
WESTLETON 5H 79 (1A 166)
Westleton Heath Nature Reserve
. . . . .3F 79
Westleton Rd.
IP17: Dars, Yox . . . . .6K 77 & 4A 78
IP17: Dun 3J 79
Westleton Way IP11: Felix 3C 154
WESTLEY 7A 52 (3C 159)
Westley La. IP29: Horr 1A 58
(not continuous)
IP33: Horr, W'ley 1A 58
Westley Rd. IP33: Bury E 1C 58
WESTLEY WATERLESS 1A 162
Westley Way IP31: B Ash 3C 66
West Lodge IP6: Nee M 2G 111
West Mdws. IP1: Ips 1E 130
West Mill Grn. IP9: Bent 6G 147
Westminster Cl. IP4: Ips 1F 139
Westminster Dr. IP33: Bury E 3D 58
Westmorland Rd. IP11: Felix 1J 155
WESTON 2C 167
Weston Bury La. IP22: Hep 6A 30
WESTON COLVILLE 1A 162
Weston Ct. IP14: Stowm 5F 85
WESTON DITCH 2A 22 (2A 158)
WESTON GREEN 1A 162
Weston Rd. NR32: Low 3G 9
Weston Way CB8: Newm 3F 47
West Rd. IP3: Ips 6J 139
IP33: Bury E 1E 58
Westropps CO10: L Mel 6H 105
WEST ROW 6A 22 (2A 158)
West Row Indoor Bowls Club 5A 22
West Row Rd.
IP28: Mide, W Row 5D 22
West Side Cl. NR32: Low 3H 9
WEST STOW 2C 159
West Stow Anglo-Saxon Village
. . . . .2B 158
West Stow Country Pk. 2C 159
West St. IP28: Ick 2B 26
West Suffolk Athletics Arena 7E 52
West Suffolk Crematorium
IP28: Ris 5A 52
West Suffolk Golf Course 1A 22
WEST TOFTS 1C 159
West Vw. IP14: Bac 6B 68
IP14: Stowm 4D 84
IP17: Kel 3J 91
IP23: Occ 5B 72
West Vw. Abbey Oaks
IP8: Spro 7B 130
West Vw. Gdns. IP23: Gisli 1K 67
Westward Deals CB9: Ked 6C 98
Westward Ho IP16: Leis 2G 93
WEST WICKHAM 2A 162
West Wood IP31: Gt Bar 3C 54
Westwood Av. IP1: Ips 5J 131
NR33: Oul B 3D 10
Westwood Ct. IP1: Ips 1A 4 (6J 131)
WEST WRATTING 1A 162
Wetherby Cl. IP1: Ips 1K 131
WETHERDEN 4H 65 (3A 160)
Wetherden Rd.
IP14: Haug, W'den 2K 65
IP30: E'well 3E 64
WETHERINGSETT 6J 69 (3B 160)
WETHERSFIELD 3B 162
WETHERUP STREET 3B 160
Wexford Rd. IP1: Ips 3F 131
WEYBREAD 1C 40 (1C 161)
Weybread Rd. IP21: Syle 1G 39
WEYBREAD STREET 3E 40
Weyland Rd. IP6: Witn 1B 116
Weylands Cl. IP14: Forw G 1A 86
Weymouth Rd. IP4: Ips 7D 132
Whapload Rd. NR32: Low 5K 9
Wharfedale NR33: Car C 6E 10
Wharfedale Rd. IP1: Ips 4J 131
Wharf La. CO8: Bure 6B 142
Wharfside IP4: Ips 6E 4
Wharton St. NR35: Bung 2B 14
WHATFIELD 6D 112 (2A 164)
Whatfield Rd. IP7: Aldh, What . . .6D 112
IP7: E'sett 6F 113
Whatfield Way IP14: Stowm 7G 85
Whatley Cl. IP30: E'well 3E 64
WHEATACRE 1C 167
Wheatacre Dr. NR32: Cort 6H 7
Wheatfield Rd. NR33: Car C 5C 10
Wheatfields IP7: What 6D 112
IP22: Rick 6H 35
IP31: Thur 6A 56
Wheat Sheaf Vs. IP28: B Row 1E 22
Wheelers Yd. CO7: E Ber 3D 146
Wheelwright Cl. *IP30: Blac 3G 61*
(off Mouse La.)
Wheelwrights, The
IP11: T Mary 7J 153
Wheelwrights Cl. IP9: Stut 6C 150
WHEPSTEAD 2C 80 (1C 163)
Whepstead Rd. IP29: Horr 7D 58
Wherry La. IP4: Ips 5G 5
Wherry Rd. NR35: Bung 3D 14
WHERSTEAD 1G 149 (2B 164)
Wherstead Rd. IP2: Ips . . .7E 4 (6A 138)
Whights Cnr. IP8: Cop, Wash 5C 136
Whinchat Cl. IP2: Ips 3F 137
Whincroft IP13: Wick M 7B 118
Whinfield IP5: Martl H 5F 135
Whinfield Ct. IP5: Martl H 5G 135
Whinlands IP17: Knod 6F 93
Whinlands, The IP16: Thor 6D 94
Whinland Wlk. *NR32: Low 5F 9*
(off Breckland Way)
Whin Marsh IP15: Aldeb 4J 95
Whinneys, The IP5: Kesg 5D 134
Whinyard Way IP11: Felix 1J 155
Whiskin Cl. NR32: Oul B 6C 8
Whitby Rd. IP4: Ips 5D 132
IP33: Bury E 3D 58
Whitearch Touring Caravan Pk.
IP17: Benh 3B 92
WHITEASH GREEN 3B 162
White Caville CB9: Have 3B 100
WHITE COLNE 3C 163
White Elm Rd. IP30: Wool 4K 63
White Elm St. IP3: Ips 6J 5 (2C 138)
White Fen Drove IP27: Lake 2B 20
White Foot La. IP13: Burg 4J 117
Whitegates CB8: Newm 6J 47
White Hall Cl. CO10: Gt Wal 7J 107
Whitehall Pl. *IP12: Wood 5H 121*
(off Thoroughfare)
Whitehall Rd. IP14: Old N 7A 70
White Hart La. IP27: B'don 3F 19
White Horse Cl. IP11: Felix 2H 155
White Horse Hill IP9: Tatt 4G 149
White Horse La. CB9: Ked 6B 98
IP30: B Geo 1C 82
White Horse Rd. CB9: Ked 6B 98
CO7: E Ber 5C 146
IP9: Cap M 2J 147
White Horse St. IP27: B'don 5D 18
NR32: Low 6K 9
WHITE HOUSE 3G 131
White Ho. Barns IP30: E'well 1E 64
White Ho. Beach Caravan Club Site
NR33: Kess 6K 17
White Ho. Gdns. NR34: Becc 4D 12
Whitehouse Ind. Est. IP1: Ips 2E 130
White Ho. Rd. IP1: Ips 2E 130
(not continuous)
White Lion Ct. *IP7: Hadl 4H 129*
(off High St.)
White Lodge CB8: Newm 4F 47
White Lodge Gdns. IP5: Kesg 5C 134
White Mullein Dr. IP28: Red L 7H 25
Whites Cl. IP21: Stradb 7H 39
Whites Fld. CO7: E Ber 3A 146
White's La. IP17: Westl 5H 79
NR33: Kess 4H 17
Whites Mdw. IP14: W'den 4H 65
WHITESTREET GREEN 3D 163
Whitethorn Rd. IP3: Pur F 5K 139
Whiteup's La. IP14: Mendl 5G 71
White Womans La. IP12: Eyk 1D 124
Whitewood Wlk. IP27: RAF L 4G 21
Whiting Rd. NR32: Oul 6B 8
Whiting St.
IP33: Bury E 5H 157 (1G 59)
Whitland Cl. IP2: Ips 6J 137
Whitlands CO10: Glem 4A 104
Whittle Rd. IP2: Ips 7H 131
WHITTON 2H 131
Whitton Chu. La. IP1: Ips 1G 131
Whitton Cl. NR33: Oul B 3D 10
Whitton Ct. NR33: Oul B 2F 11
Whitton La. IP1: Ips 1F 131
Whitton Leyer IP8: B'ford 3E 130
Whitton Pk. IP1: Ips 1H 131
Whitton Sports & Community Cen.
. . . . .1G 131
Whitworth Cl. IP2: Ips 4F 137
WICKEN 2A 158
WICKER STREET GREEN 2D 163
WICKHAMBROOK 2G 97 (1B 162)
Wickhambrook Ct. IP11: Felix 4B 154
Wickhambrook Rd.
CB8: Stradi 5G 97
IP29: Harg 4F 51
WICKHAM GREEN 1F 69 (3A 160)
Wickham La.
IP14: Cott . . . . .5D 68 & 7J 67
WICKHAM MARKET . . .6B 118 (1D 165)
Wickham Market Station (Rail)
. . . . .3B 122
Wickham Rd. IP14: Finn 6H 67
IP23: Thw 3K 69
WICKHAM ST PAUL 3C 163
WICKHAM SKEITH 1G 69 (3A 160)
WICKHAM STREET
Eye 1F 69 (3A 160)
Newmarket 4J 97
Wicklow Rd. IP1: Ips 3F 131
Wicks La. IP14: Forw G 1A 86
Widgeon Cl. IP2: Ips 3H 137
WIGGENS GREEN 2A 162
Wiggin Cl. IP28: B Mil 2G 25
Wiggs Acre NR34: Barnb 6C 6
Wigg's Way NR32: Cort 5J 7
Wigmore Cl. IP2: Ips 5H 137
Wigston Rd. IP33: Bury E 2C 58
Wilberforce St. IP1: Ips . . .2A 4 (6J 131)
WILBY
Banham 1A 160
Stradbroke 2C 161
Wilbye Cl. IP32: Bury E 2A 60
Wilby Rd. IP21: Stradb 6H 39
Wilderness Hill IP8: Hint 1B 144
Wilderness La. IP12: Wood 4H 121
WILDE STREET 2B 158
Wilde St. NR32: Low 6K 9
Wilding Ct. IP12: Wood 6F 121
Wilding Dr. IP5: Kesg 6D 134
Wilding Rd. IP8: Ips 5D 136
Wildmere La.
IP28: B Row, Holy R 1H 23
Wilford Bri. Rd. IP12: Melt 3K 121
Wilford Bri. Spur IP12: Melt 3K 121
Wilfred Hurry Cl. IP8: B'ford 4C 130
Wilfred Sherman Cl.
CB8: Newm 5G 47
Wilkes Ct. IP5: Kesg 6E 134
Wilkes Way IP14: Stowm 4F 85
Wilkinson Dr. IP5: Kesg 7C 134
Wilkinson Way IP12: Melt 4H 121
Wilks Rd. IP33: Bury E 4H 59
Willcox Av. IP33: Bury E 7C 52
Willets Pond CO7: E Ber 5C 146
William Armstrong Cl.
IP30: E'well 2E 64
William Barnaby Yd.
IP33: Bury E 6H 157 (2G 59)
William Blake Ct. CB9: Have 2D 100
William Booth Way IP11: Felix . . .3C 154
William Cl. IP12: Eyk 1D 124
William Ho. IP4: Ips 2G 5 (7B 132)
William Paul Tenements IP2: Ips . . .7D 4
Williamsport Way IP6: Nee M 5J 111
William St. IP1: Ips 2E 4 (7A 132)
Williams Way IP28: W Row 5B 22
William Tubby Ho. NR32: Oul B . . .1C 10
William Wood Ho.
CO10: S'bury 4D 126
(off School St.)
Willie Snaith Rd. CB8: Newm 2E 46
WILLINGHAM GREEN 1A 162
WILLISHAM TYE 1A 164
Willoughby Ri. IP12: Holl 2G 141
Willoughby Rd. IP2: Ips . . .6C 4 (2K 137)
Willoway Pk. IP28: Red L 6G 25
Willowbrook Cl. NR33: Car C 6A 10
Willow Cl. CB9: Have 2C 100
CO10: S'bury 5D 126
IP6: Clay 4D 114
IP14: Gt Fin 6J 83
IP21: Stradb 5H 39
IP27: B'don 5G 19
IP28: Holy R 2H 23
Willow Cl. IP31: B Ash 2D 66
IP31: Wals W 6H 33
NR34: Worl 5J 13
WILLOW CORNER 1J 35
Willow Cres. CB8: Newm 6H 47
Willowcroft Rd. IP1: Ips 3J 131
Willow Farm Mdw.
IP13: W'orth 6H 73
Willow Gdns. NR35: Bung 3B 14
Willow Grn. IP13: W'orth 6H 73
IP31: Honi 2H 29
Willow Gro. CO6: Nay 5H 143
Willow Ho's. IP14: W'den 4H 65
Willow La. IP14: Cott 6E 68
Willow Marsh La. IP17: Dars 1A 78
Willow Pk. *IP28: B Row 1C 22*
(off Rookery Drove)
Willow Rd. NR33: Low 7F 11
Willows, The IP5: Rush A 4J 133
IP28: Mide 1E 24
Willow Tree Cl.
IP13: Wick M 6A 118
Willowvale NR32: Oul 2E 8
Willow Wlk. IP6: Nee M 2G 111
Willow Way IP7: Gt Bri 2A 112
IP12: Rend 6C 122
IP33: Bury E 2F 157 (7F 53)
Will Rede Cl. NR34: Becc 5E 12
Wilmslow Av. IP12: Wood 5F 121
Wilmslow Dr. IP2: Ips 4E 136
WILNEY GREEN 1A 160
Wilson Rd. IP7: Hadl 4J 129
IP8: Ips 5D 136
NR33: Low 4H 11
WIMBISH 3A 162
WIMBISH GREEN 3A 162
Wimbledon Av. IP27: B'don 6D 18
Wimble La. IP14: Mendl 4F 71
Wimborne Av. IP3: Ips 2H 139
Wimpole Cl. IP5: Rush A 7K 133
Wincanton Cl. IP4: Ips 4E 132
Winchester Cl. IP14: Stowm 4D 84
Winchester Gdns. IP6: Barh 2E 114
Winchester Rd. IP33: Bury E 2D 58
Winchester Way IP2: Ips 6H 137
Windermere Cl. IP3: Ips 6F 139
Windermere Pk. NR32: Low 4F 9
Windermere Rd. CO10: S'bury . . .3F 127
IP11: Felix 1J 155
IP14: Stowm 4E 84
Windgap La. IP14: Haug 2C 70
Windham Rd. CO10: S'bury 3F 127
Windiate Ct. *IP5: Kesg 6D 134*
(off Ropes Dr.)
Winding Piece IP9: Cap M 2H 147
Windings Rd. IP7: E'sett 7H 113
Windmill Av. IP30: Wool 5K 63
Windmill Cl. CO10: Gt Cor 7G 127
IP8: S'ham 3K 113
IP27: Lake 6B 20
Windmill Grn. IP31: Stant 7D 32
Windmill Hill CB8: Exn 1C 46
CO10: L Mel 1F 105
IP9: Cap M 2F 147
Windmill La. IP21: Syle 1F 39
Windmill Pl. CO10: Stans 2D 104
Windmill Ri. CO10: Hund 1J 99
IP14: W'den 4H 65
IP33: Bury E 6F 157 (2F 59)
Windmill Row CO10: Glem 4B 104
Windrush Rd. IP5: Kesg 5C 134
Windsor Circ. IP27: RAF L 3H 21
Windsor Cl. IP24: Barnh 6J 27
IP29: Laws 5B 80
Windsor Gallery Art Cen. 2H 11
WINDSOR GREEN 7F 81 (1C 163)
Windsor Oaks IP30: Roug 7K 61
Windsor Pl. CO10: S'bury 4F 127
Windsor Rd. CB8: Newm 5E 46
IP1: Ips 6H 131
IP11: Felix 5D 154
IP18: Rey 1H 45
NR33: Low 2H 11
Windsor Ter. CB9: Have 3C 100
NR33: Kess 4K 17
Windward Way NR33: Oul B 4D 10
WINFARTHING 1B 160
Winfrith Rd. IP3: Ips 2H 139
Wingate Ho. IP1: Ips 1A 4
WINGFIELD 2J 39 (2C 161)
Wingfield Av. IP27: Lake 4B 20
Wingfield Barns 3K 39
Wingfield Cl. IP27: Lake 4B 20
WINGFIELD GREEN 2G 39
Wingfield Mdws. IP14: Ston A 6G 87
Wingfield Rd. IP21: Syle 1F 39
IP21: Wey 2A 40
IP27: Lake 4B 20
Wingfield St. IP4: Ips 4F 5 (1B 138)
NR35: Bung 3B 14
Wings Rd. IP27: Lake 5A 20
Wings Rd. Cl. IP27: Lake 5B 20

Winifred Fison Ho's.
IP12: Melt . . . 2K **121**
Winnipeg Rd. NR32: Low . . . 6J **9**
Winsford Rd. IP32: Bury E . . . 7A **54**
WINSTON . . . 3B **160**
Winston Av. IP4: Ips . . . 5G **133**
NR33: Oul B . . . 2D **10**
Winston Cl. IP11: Felix . . . 3C **154**
NR33: Kess . . . 4K **17**
Winston Head La. IP14: Ston A . . . 1A **88**
Winston Rd. IP14: Wins . . . 3J **87**
IP18: Rey . . . 2J **45**
Wintergreen Rd. IP28: Red L . . . 6G **25**
Winthrop Cl. CO10: S'bury . . . 2J **127**
Winthrop Rd. IP33: Bury E . . . 2C **58**
Winthrops, The CO10: Edw . . . 5A **128**
Wishing Well Cl. IP27: B'don . . . 3G **19**
WISSETT . . . 2D **161**
Wissett Cl. IP19: H'orth . . . 3A **42**
Wissett Rd. IP19: H'orth . . . 3A **42**
Wissett Way NR32: Low . . . 3G **9**
WISSINGTON . . . 7F **143**
Wiston Rd. CO6: Nay . . . 7F **143**
WITHERMARSH GREEN . . . 3A **164**
Withersdale Rd. IP20: Mendh . . . 2H **41**
IP21: Wey . . . 1E **40**
WITHERSDALE STREET . . . 1C **161**
WITHERSFIELD . . . 2B **98** (2A **162**)
Withersfield Rd. CB9: Gt Thu . . . 7B **96**
CB9: Gt Wra, With . . . 1C **98**
CB9: Have . . . 1D **100**
Withindale Cen. . . . 6G **105**
Withipoll St. IP4: Ips . . . 2F **5** (7B **132**)
WITNESHAM . . . 3B **116** (1B **164**)
Witnesham Chu. La. IP6: Witn . . . 3B **116**
Witnesham Rd.
IP6: Weste, Witn . . . 7A **116**
Witney Cl. IP3: Ips . . . 6G **139**
Witney Grn. NR33: Low . . . 6F **11**
Witney Rd. NR33: Low . . . 6F **11**
Wittons La. IP21: Hox . . . 3D **38**
WIX . . . 3B **164**
Wixfield Pk. IP7: Gt Bri . . . 2A **112**
WIXOE . . . 2B **162**
Wollaston Cl. IP32: Bury E . . . 5D **52**
Wollaston Rd. NR32: Low . . . 7J **9**
Wolsey Apartments, The IP4: Ips . . . 5E **4**
Wolsey Cotts. IP17: Yox . . . 7F **77**
Wolsey Gdns. IP11: Felix . . . 5F **155**
Wolsey Ho. NR34: Becc . . . 5G **13**
Wolsey Rd. IP14: Stowm . . . 3E **84**
Wolsey's Gateway . . . 5E **4**
Wolsey St. IP1: Ips . . . 5D **4** (1A **138**)
Wolsey Theatre, The
Ipswich . . . 3C **4** (7K **131**)
Wolton Rd. IP5: Kesg . . . 6C **134**
Wolves Farm La. IP7: Hadl . . . 1K **129**
WOODBRIDGE . . . 5J **121** (2C **165**)
Woodbridge IP27: RAF L . . . 4H **21**
Woodbridge Mus. . . . 5H **121**
Woodbridge Rd.
IP4: Ips . . . 3F **5** (7B **132**)
IP4: Rush A . . . 6H **133**
IP5: Rush A . . . 6H **133**
IP12: But . . . 7A **124**
IP12: Newb . . . 7B **140**
IP12: Tun . . . 4E **122** & 7F **123**
IP12: Wald . . . 5B **140**
IP13: F'ham . . . 7C **90**
IP13: Gru, Hask . . . 5J **117**
Woodbridge Rd. E. IP4: Ips . . . 6G **133**
Woodbridge Station (Rail) . . . 6H **121**
Woodbridge Wlk. IP12: Holl . . . 1H **141**
Woodchurch Av. NR33: Car C . . . 5B **10**
Wood Cl. IP12: Rend . . . 7B **122**
IP27: B'don . . . 5G **19**
IP30: Tost . . . 1G **63**
Woodcock Cl. CB9: Have . . . 4H **101**
Woodcock Ri. IP27: B'don . . . 3J **19**
Woodcock Rd. IP2: Ips . . . 4G **137**
Woodcote IP14: Stowm . . . 4D **84**
Wood Cotts. IP5: Rush A . . . 4G **133**
Woodcrest IP23: Eye . . . 6C **38**
Woodcutters Way IP27: Lake . . . 4B **20**
WOODDITTON . . . 1A **162**
Woodditton Rd. CB8: Newm . . . 7F **47**
WOODEND GREEN . . . 3A **162**
Wood Farm Bus. Cen.
IP6: Crow . . . 7H **87**
Wood Farm La. IP18: Rey . . . 6E **44**
Wood Farm Rd. IP13: Gru . . . 7F **117**
Woodfield Dr. IP14: Stowm . . . 5G **85**
Woodfield La. IP9: Stut . . . 5A **150**
IP14: Stowm . . . 5F **85**
Woodfields IP21: Stradb . . . 6G **39**
Woodford Gdns. IP32: Bury E . . . 5G **53**
Woodgates Rd. CO7: E Ber . . . 1C **146**
Woodhall Bus. Pk.
CO10: S'bury . . . 1E **126**
Woodhall Cl. CO10: S'bury . . . 2D **126**
Woodhall Rd. CO10: S'bury . . . 2D **126**
Woodhouse Sq.
IP4: Ips . . . 4G **5** (1B **138**)
Woodland Av. NR34: Worl . . . 4J **13**
Woodland Cl. IP14: One . . . 2A **84**
IP28: Ris . . . 1B **50**
IP31: Thur . . . 7B **56**
Woodland Dr. NR35: Bung . . . 5B **14**
Woodland Ho's. IP10: Nac . . . 6A **152**
Woodland Pl. IP31: Gt Bar . . . 2C **54**
Woodlands IP7: Hadl . . . 2F **129**
IP8: Ips . . . 5E **136**
IP9: Chelm . . . 2G **151**
IP16: Leis . . . 5H **93**
IP27: Lake . . . 3B **20**
Woodlands, The IP14: Finn . . . 5H **67**
NR32: Low . . . 7H **7**
Woodlands Av. NR33: Car C . . . 6B **10**
Woodlands Bus. Pk. IP30: Roug . . . 1F **61**
Woodlands Ri. IP27: B'don . . . 6C **18**
Woodlands Rd. IP7: Ray . . . 1K **145**
IP8: Hint . . . 4A **144**
IP9: Holb . . . 1C **150**
IP30: Roug . . . 1F **61**
Woodland Way IP1: Ips . . . 1E **130**
Wood La. IP22: Hep . . . 6C **30**
NR32: Flix, Oul . . . 4B **8**
NR34: Wang . . . 7E **44**
Woodlark Cl. IP2: Ips . . . 5G **137**
Woodlark Dr. IP14: Stowm . . . 3H **85**
Woodleys Yd. *IP18: Sou . . . 4K 45*
(off High St.)
Woodpecker Av. NR33: Oul B . . . 4C **10**
Woodpecker Cl. IP14: Stowm . . . 5J **85**
Woodpecker Rd. IP2: Ips . . . 3F **137**
Woodpeckers CO10: S'bury . . . 5D **126**
Wood Rd. IP13: B'ham . . . 4C **76**
IP30: B Grn . . . 6E **64**
Woodruff Cl. IP32: Bury E . . . 7K **53**
Woodrush Rd. IP3: Pur F . . . 4H **139**
Woods Cl. CB9: Stur . . . 6K **101**
Woodsdale Gro. IP31: Honi . . . 4F **29**
Woodside IP5: Martl H . . . 5J **135**
IP14: Stowm . . . 4D **84**
NR34: Becc . . . 5G **13**
NR34: Bramp . . . 5H **15**
Woodside Bus. Cen. IP31: Ing . . . 5E **28**
Woodside Cl. IP33: Bury E . . . 5H **59**
NR33: Car C . . . 6B **10**
Woods La. IP12: Melt, Wood . . . 3G **121**
Woods Loke E. NR32: Low . . . 5F **9**
Woods Loke W. NR32: Oul B . . . 5E **8**
Woodspring Cl. IP2: Ips . . . 4J **137**
Woodstone Av. IP1: Ips . . . 4A **132**
Woods Wlk. IP5: Kesg . . . 7D **134**
Woodthorpe Cl. IP7: Hadl . . . 4K **129**
Woodthorpe Rd. IP7: Hadl . . . 4J **129**
Wood Vw. IP17: Sib . . . 3K **77**
Woodville Rd. IP4: Ips . . . 4K **5** (1D **138**)
Woodward Av. IP14: Bac . . . 6B **68**
Woodward Cl. IP2: Ips . . . 1F **137**
Woolhall St.
IP33: Bury E . . . 5G **157** (1G **59**)
Woollards Cl. IP1: Ips . . . 3A **4** (7J **131**)
Woollards Gdns. CO10: L Mel . . . 3H **105**
Woolmers Cl. IP14: Stowm . . . 6F **85**
Woolner Cl. IP6: Barh . . . 3C **114**
IP7: Hadl . . . 3J **129**
Woolnough Rd. IP12: Wood . . . 4G **121**
Woolnoughs, The
IP5: Kesg . . . 6D **134**
WOOLPIT . . . 5B **64** (3D **159**)
Woolpit & District Mus. . . . 5A **64**
Woolpit Bus. Pk. IP30: Wool . . . 4K **63**
WOOLPIT GREEN . . . 7B **64**
WOOLPIT HEATH . . . 6C **64**
Woolpit Rd.
IP30: Rat, Wool . . . 7B **64** & 1K **83**
IP31: Nort . . . 5H **57**
WOOLVERSTONE . . . 3B **164**
Woolverstone Cl. IP2: Ips . . . 5E **136**
WOOTTEN GREEN . . . 7H **39**
Wootton Dr. IP1: Ips . . . 5A **132**
Worcester Cl. IP32: Bury E . . . 7A **54**
Worcester Rd. IP3: Ips . . . 6E **138**
Wordsworth Cl. IP17: Saxm . . . 5G **91**
Wordsworth Cres. IP1: Ips . . . 2G **131**
Wordsworth Rd. IP14: Stowm . . . 2D **84**
IP32: Bury E . . . 4F **53**
Worell Dr. NR34: Worl . . . 4H **13**
WORKHOUSE GREEN . . . 3D **163**
Workhouse Hill IP29: Hart . . . 1H **103**
Workshop La. IP10: Nac . . . 5B **152**
World's End Rd. IP13: Saxt . . . 1A **90**
WORLINGHAM . . . 4J **13** (1C **167**)
Worlingham Way NR32: Oul B . . . 4F **9**
WORLINGTON . . . 2B **24** (2A **158**)
Worlington Rd.
IP28: Mide, W'ton . . . 1D **24**
IP28: Tud . . . 5A **26**
WORLINGWORTH . . . 6H **73** (3C **161**)
Worlingworth Rd.
IP21: Ath, Horh, Wilb . . . 1H **73**
WORMINGFORD . . . 3D **163**
Worsdell Cl. IP2: Ips . . . 3A **138**
Worsley Cl. IP2: Ips . . . 4F **137**
WORTHAM . . . 2H **35** (2A **160**)
Wortham Pl. CB9: Have . . . 3F **101**
(not continuous)
Worthing Rd. NR32: Low . . . 5J **9**
WORTWELL . . . 1C **161**
WRABNESS . . . 3B **164**
Wragg Dr. CB8: Newm . . . 3G **47**
Wratting Rd. CB9: Gt Thu . . . 7C **96**
CB9: Have . . . 3F **101**
Wren Av. IP2: Ips . . . 3F **137**
Wren Cl. IP14: Stowm . . . 4J **85**
IP27: B'don . . . 4H **19**
IP28: Mide . . . 7K **23**
IP31: Thur . . . 6K **55**
IP32: Bury E . . . 6C **54**
NR33: Car C . . . 6C **10**
Wrens Pk. IP11: Felix . . . 1J **155**
WRENTHAM . . . 1D **44** (2C **167**)
Wright Cl. IP14: Stowm . . . 7F **85**
Wright La. IP5: Kesg . . . 5D **134**
Wright Rd. IP3: Ips . . . 4G **139**
Wrights Way CO6: Leav . . . 3A **142**
IP30: Wool . . . 4K **63**
Wroxham Rd. IP3: Ips . . . 3D **138**
Wyards La. IP31: Thur . . . 6E **56**
Wyatt Cl. IP30: E'well . . . 1E **64**
Wye Rd. IP3: Ips . . . 3E **138**
Wyken Hall Gdns. . . . 2D **159**
Wyken Rd. IP31: Stant . . . 3E **32** & 7D **32**
Wykes Bishop St.
IP3: Ips . . . 6H **5** (2C **138**)
Wymering Rd. IP18: Sou . . . 4K **45**
Wyndham Way CB8: Newm . . . 3G **47**
Wynterton Cl. IP3: Ips . . . 5F **139**
Wynton Ri. IP14: Stowm . . . 6G **85**
Wyseman Pl. CO11: Catt . . . 6B **148**
Wytchwoods, The IP14: Petta . . . 3B **88**
Wyvern Rd. IP3: Ips . . . 5G **139**
WYVERSTONE . . . 1D **68** (3A **160**)
WYVERSTONE GREEN . . . 2E **68**
Wyverstone Rd. IP14: Bac . . . 2E **68**
IP14: Wyve . . . 1A **68**
WYVERSTONE STREET
. . . 1B **68** (3A **160**)
Wy-Wurry Caravan Pk.
NR32: Cort . . . 5J **7**

Y

Yarmouth Pl. CB9: Have . . . 3F **101**
Yarmouth Rd. IP1: Ips . . . 7J **131**
IP12: Melt . . . 2K **121** & 7G **119**
IP13: Melt, Uff . . . 7G **119**
IP13: Uff . . . 4H **119**
NR32: Cort, Low . . . 5F **7**
NR35: Bung . . . 1A **14**
Yarrow Dr. NR33: Car C . . . 5B **10**
Yarrow Wlk. IP28: Red L . . . 7J **25**
YAXLEY . . . 6E **36** (2B **160**)
Yaxley Hall La. IP23: Yax . . . 7E **36**
Yaxley Rd. IP23: Eye . . . 7A **38**
Yeldham Pl. CB9: Have . . . 3F **101**
Yellowhammer Cl. IP14: Stowm . . . 3J **85**
Yeoman Cl. IP1: Ips . . . 7H **131**
Yeoman Cres. IP7: Hadl . . . 4J **129**
Yeoman Rd. IP11: Felix . . . 5C **154**
Yeomanry Yd.
IP33: Bury E . . . 5F **157** (1F **59**)
Yeoman's Cl. NR35: Bung . . . 3C **14**
Yeoman Way IP7: Hadl . . . 4J **129**
Yeovil Rd. NR32: Low . . . 6H **9**
Yetton Ward Ho. IP11: Felix . . . 3D **154**
Yew Cl. IP27: RAF L . . . 4G **21**
Yew Ct. IP2: Ips . . . 3J **137**
Yewdale NR33: Car C . . . 7C **10**
Yew Dr. IP27: B'don . . . 4G **19**
Yewlands IP30: Fels . . . 6C **82**
Yew Tree Cl. IP28: Mide . . . 5K **23**
Yew Tree Ct.
IP33: Bury E . . . 7F **157** (3F **59**)
Yew Tree Gdns.
IP28: W Row . . . 6B **22**
Yewtree Gro. IP5: Kesg . . . 6K **133**
Yew Tree Ri. IP13: Wick M . . . 5B **118**
Yewtree Ri. IP8: Ips . . . 5E **136**
York Cl. CO10: S'bury . . . 2D **126**
IP28: B Row . . . 1C **22**
IP33: Bury E . . . 1E **58**
York Cotts. CB8: Exn . . . 1B **46**
York Cres. IP6: Clay . . . 3D **114**
York Rd. CB9: Have . . . 4D **100**
CO10: S'bury . . . 3D **126**
IP3: Ips . . . 2E **138**
IP5: Martl H . . . 7G **135**
IP11: Felix . . . 4F **155**
IP18: Sou . . . 4J **45**
IP33: Bury E . . . 1E **58**
NR32: Low . . . 7H **9**
York Ter. IP33: Bury E . . . 1F **59**
YOXFORD . . . 6H **77** (3D **161**)
Yoxford M. IP12: Sutt . . . 2B **140**
Yoxford Rd. IP17: Midd . . . 4A **78**
IP17: Sib . . . 2K **77**
IP17: Westl . . . 6F **79**

Z

Zanetta Ct. NR32: Low . . . 7H **9**

HOSPITALS, HOSPICES and selected HEALTHCARE FACILITIES covered by this atlas.

N.B. Where Hospitals and Hospices are not named on the map, the reference given is for the road in which they are situated.

ALDEBURGH COMMUNITY HOSPITAL 5J **95**
Park Road
ALDEBURGH
IP15 5ES
Tel: 01728 451600

BECCLES & DISTRICT WAR MEMORIAL HOSPITAL 4E **12**
St Mary's Road
BECCLES
NR34 9NQ
Tel: 01502 719800

CARLTON COURT HOSPITAL 6B **10**
St Peters Road
Carlton Colville
LOWESTOFT
NR33 8AG
Tel: 01502 527900

FELIXSTOWE COMMUNITY HOSPITAL 4G **155**
Constable Road
FELIXSTOWE
IP11 7HJ
Tel: 01394 458820

IPSWICH HOSPITAL 7G **133**
Heath Road
IPSWICH
IP4 5PD
Tel: 01473 712233

LOWESTOFT HOSPITAL 7J **9**
Tennyson Road
LOWESTOFT
NR32 1PT
Tel: 01502 587311

NEWMARKET COMMUNITY HOSPITAL 4F **47**
Exning Road
NEWMARKET
CB8 7JG
Tel: 01638 564000

PATRICK STEAD HOSPITAL 3C **42**
Bungay Road
HALESWORTH
IP19 8HP
Tel: 01986 872124

ST CLEMENTS HOSPITAL 2G **139**
Foxhall Road
IPSWICH
IP3 8LS
Tel: 01473 329148

ST EDMUNDS BMI HOSPITAL 7K **157** (2H **59**)
St Marys Square
BURY ST EDMUNDS
IP33 2AA
Tel: 01284 701371

ST ELIZABETH HOSPICE 1G **139**
565 Foxhall Road
IPSWICH
IP3 8LX
Tel: 01473 727776

ST NICHOLAS' HOSPICE .5G **59**
Macmillan Way
Hardwick Lane
BURY ST EDMUNDS
IP33 2QY
Tel: 01284 766133

SOUTHWOLD & DISTRICT HOSPITAL 3K **45**
Field Stile Road
SOUTHWOLD
IP18 6LD
Tel: 01502 723333

TREEHOUSE HOSPICE 3G **139**
St Augustine Gardens
IPSWICH
IP3 8NS
Tel: 01473 271334

VIOLET HILL DAY HOSPITAL 3F **85**
Violet Hill Road
STOWMARKET
IP14 1NH
Tel: 01449 618100

WALNUTTREE HOSPITAL 4C **126**
Walnut Tree Lane
SUDBURY
CO10 1BE
Tel: 01787 884500

WEST SUFFOLK HOSPITAL 4G **59**
Hardwick Lane
BURY ST EDMUNDS
IP33 2QZ
Tel: 01284 713000

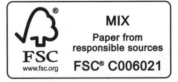

The representation on the maps of a road, track or footpath is no evidence of the existence of a right of way.

The Grid on this map is the National Grid taken from Ordnance Survey® mapping with the permission of the Controller of Her Majesty's Stationery Office.

SAFETY CAMERA INFORMATION

PocketGPSWorld.com's CamerAlert is a self-contained speed and red light camera warning system for SatNavs and Android or Apple iOS smartphones/tablets. Visit www.cameralert.co.uk to download.

Safety camera locations are publicised by the Safer Roads Partnership which operates them in order to encourage drivers to comply with speed limits at these sites. It is the driver's absolute responsibility to be aware of and to adhere to speed limits at all times.

By showing this safety camera information it is the intention of Geographers' A-Z Map Company Ltd., to encourage safe driving and greater awareness of speed limits and vehicle speed. Data accurate at time of printing.

Printed and bound in the United Kingdom by Polestar Wheatons Ltd., Exeter.